Step-By-Step

LEGAL

Forms and
Agreements
for Business & Personal Use

Step-By-Step

LEGAL

Forms and
Agreements
for Business & Personal Use

Charles B. Chernofsky

Griffith G. deNoyelles, Jr.

Round Lake Publishing

Round Lake Publishing Co.
31 Bailey Avenue
Ridgefield, CT 06877

Printed in the United States of America

0987654321

ISBN 0-13-847468-0

This publication is designed to provide helpful information in regard to the subject matter covered. It is sold with the understanding that the publisher is not engaged in rendering legal, accounting or other professional service. If legal advice or other expert assistance is required, the services of a competent professional person should be sought.

The publisher cannot in any way assure that the forms in this book will be used for the purposes intended and accordingly does not assume any responsibility for their use.

Acknowledgements

Our thanks to the legions of attorneys and judges who have preceded us and whose fine tuning of language have made many provisions of these and other legal forms standards for the profession.

Special thanks to attorney Paula Walter, Professor of Law at Baruch College in New York City, who rechecked our forms and instructions to ensure their accuracy.

Most of all, we want to express our appreciation to our "forms widows," Adrianne Chernofsky and Judith Levin, for their understanding and support when, in the toil of our labor on this book, we worked late, missed meals and sometimes whole weekends.

Contents

Chapter 3 BUYING AND SELLING GOODS

Chapter 4 BORROWING AND LENDING MONEY

Chapter 6 OPERATING A CORPORATION

Chapter 7 BUYING AND SELLING A BUSINESS

Chapter 8 GENERAL CONTRACT CLAUSES

Chapter 9 EMPLOYEES AND REPRESENTATIVES

Chapter 10 RELEASES, POWERS OF ATTORNEY AND NOTARY STATEMENTS

GLOSSARY & INDEXES

What This Book Can Do for You

This book is designed help you deal effectively with many situations you encounter in your personal and business life. It will help you write a will or a living will, rent a house or apartment (either as tenant or landlord), sell your car or borrow money. It will also help you start (or sell) a business, prepare an employee contract, appoint someone to act for you or write a consulting agreement. In fact, there are more than 160 forms covering a great many situations individuals and business people experience.

What makes the book so unique and helpful are the step-by-step instructions accompanying each form, explaining *exactly what to put in each blank*, in language that is concise and easy to follow.

While no book can be a substitute for an attorney, many of the forms in this book cover basic situations and may not necessarily require an attorney's involvement. Others, of a more complex nature, can be completed by you but should be reviewed by an attorney. Still others cover technical areas and are included primarily for informational purposes. In these cases, an attorney should prepare the forms, but you will have the advantage of knowing what should be included.

Be sure to read the next section, "How to Use this Book," before starting to use the forms. It contains helpful advice and information you should have to help you in their preparation.

How to Use This Book

The format

Each form in this book is introduced by a brief explanation of how to use it and when it is to be used. Any necessary warnings follow. *Pay particular attention to these warnings—they were designed to protect the user.*

The form is shown on the right side of the page, with step-by-step instructions on how to fill it in immediately to the left. When a form continues beyond one page, a notation appears below the form:

(*Document continued on next page*)

Be sure to read and use the entire form.

Filling in the blanks

Each blank in the form is numbered to correspond to an instruction. The numbers in the blanks are in brackets:

> EXAMPLE: I, _____[1]_____, residing at

In some forms, the legal language *of the form itself* contains numbers. These numbers are in parentheses:

> EXAMPLE: upon three (3) days' notice

When the blanks get filled in, the underlines and bracketed numbers are to be deleted. *The numbers in parentheses are NOT to be deleted since they are part of the form.*

Be sure to fill in all the blanks. If some blanks are not filled in, the form will be open to interpretation.

Deleting or changing sections

When the instructions call for a section of the form to be deleted or changed, that section appears in italics preceded by a bracketed number corresponding to the instruction:

EXAMPLE: *[6]The Creditor shall*

Delete or change the italicized text and remove the bracketed number.

Making choices

Sometimes the instructions ask the user to choose between two or more alternatives. When this occurs, the choices in the form are in italics, separated by **OR** so that they are easily seen:

EXAMPLE: The apartment *[8][is]* **OR** *[is not]* to be vacated

Choose only one of the alternatives and *delete the others* and the bracketed number. Of course, the word **OR** must also be deleted.

Signing the forms

If the person signing the form is an individual or the sole owner or proprietor of a business, he is acting for himself and should sign the form in his own name. The instructions state where individuals are to sign.

Any other form of business—such as a corporation, partnership or joint venture—is a "created" entity which cannot act by itself. It can only act through people such as officers, directors, managers or others authorized to act for the business. In those cases, the signer should *follow the instructions for signing by corporations.*

IMPORTANT NOTES

State and local laws

The forms in this book were designed to be usable in 49 states. The one exception is Louisiana, whose laws are based on French rather than English law. However, a number of the forms caution that local or state law must be checked, since that particular form's requirements vary by locale.

This is particularly true for the real estate forms; the reader should check his local and state housing authorities or a local attorney to be sure of meeting the necessary legal requirements.

The use of "he" and "him"
The use of the masculine gender throughout the instructions in this book is for the sake of clarity and simplicity.

If you don't understand a form
If you don't understand the purpose of a particular form or how to fill it in, *don't use it!* Instead, seek advice from an attorney.

Wills and Gifts 1

The forms in this chapter provide a method for voicing and preserving for posterity a person's wishes concerning his property and body, both during his lifetime and when he can no longer express those wishes himself.

Wills A Will protects the maker of the Will and his heirs by preserving the wishes of the maker regarding the orderly distribution of his property. Without a Will, the state decides the distribution, based on formulas that typically leave the property to relatives. The forms in this section provide simple Wills for the most common situations.

Living Wills The Living Will preserves the voice of the maker by addressing medical decisions to be made when he is unable to speak for himself as a result of medical incapacity. The Durable Power of Attorney provides for the appointment of another person to make decisions on behalf of the maker.

Gifts An Anatomical Gift establishes in writing a person's wish to donate his body parts or organs after his death. The Gift to a Minor contains the elements necessary to establish, primarily for tax purposes, a gift to a minor while the maker of the gift is still alive.

Personal Records This form organizes the detailed record of a person's assets and liabilities as well as important personal information. It can also be used as a checklist to ensure that a person's affairs are in order.

INTRODUCTION TO WILLS

The basic purpose of a Will is to speak for its maker (also known as the Testator) after his death and to provide for the distribution of the Testator's assets upon his death. In addition, a Will should clearly revoke any earlier Wills or Codicils (supplements to a Will). Typically, the Will provides for 1) the payment of debts, funeral expenses and estate taxes and 2) naming of an Executor (the person who will apply to the court for probate of the Will, and who will administer the estate) and Successor Executor. The Executor will be responsible for gathering the deceased's assets, paying the deceased's bills and the estate's bills and estate taxes, and distributing whatever remains in accordance with the Will. Since the Executor assumes personal liability, most jurisdictions provide that he or she is entitled to a statutorily determined commission or fee, payable out of the deceased's estate.

WARNINGS

As far as the wording of a Will is concerned, the only requirement is that the Will be clear as to the deceased's intention. However, one of the few absolutes in the law relates to the proper *signing* of Wills. Since a Will speaks for the deceased after he is no longer able, the courts must be absolutely satisfied that the document claiming to be the deceased's Will in fact is his Will. This is accomplished by having Witnesses to the signing of the Will who can later testify that the deceased had asked them to Witness the signing of his Will and that the deceased did, in fact, sign the Will in the presence of all of the Witnesses together; in short **THE WILL MUST BE SIGNED BY THE TESTATOR ONLY IN THE PRESENCE OF THE WITNESSES.** The Witnesses will then sign the Will as well.

While most states require that a Will be witnessed by only two people, the use of three is strongly recommended because it increases the odds that the Executor will be able to locate at least two. No state requires more than three Witnesses.

Anyone of majority age can act as a Witness to the signing of a Will, with one exception: most states prevent a beneficiary of a Will from serving as a Witness to the Will's execution. The person named as the Executor or Trustee can act as a Witness, unless that person is also a beneficiary.

It is also strongly urged that each page of the Will be signed by the Testator along the left margin or at least initialled on either the lower left or right corner.

A final caveat: some states require that if more than one Will is signed, all must be found and admitted to probate. The technology of photocopiers has become so good that it is frequently impossible to tell which document is an original and which is the copy. To avoid confusion, it is strongly recommended that *no* photocopies be made *after* signing.

The question of where to store a Will inevitably arises. A Will that has been lost or mistakenly destroyed is the same as no Will at all. It is strongly urged that the Will be maintained in a safe but accessible place with other important personal papers where it will be found by the Executor. The Will should NOT be stored in a safety deposit box because the box may be sealed upon the death of the Testator.

SIMPLE WILL—ALL TO SPOUSE (1-01)

This Will should be used when the desire of the Testator (the person making the Will) is to leave all assets remaining (after the payment of his debts, funeral expenses and expenses of administration of his estate and federal and state estate taxes) to one's spouse.

Many states mandate, by statute, that spouses shall not disinherit one another, and the states assign a percentage share of the estate to a surviving spouse (the percentage varies with each state) that must be left to that spouse. Most jurisdictions do not have laws preventing the Testator from disinheriting his surviving children.

SIMPLE WILL—ALL TO SPOUSE

LAST WILL AND TESTAMENT OF
_____[1]_____

1. The name of the Testator (the person making the Will.)

2. If the Testator is or has been known by any other name (or has assets in another form of his name such as the use of his middle name), insert this other name. If not, delete the words "also known as _____[2]_____."

3. The Testator's address.

4. The city in which the Testator resides.

5. The county in which the Testator resides.

6. The state in which the Testator resides.

_____[1]_____, *[also known as* _____[2]_____,*]* presently residing at _____[3]_____, in the City of ____[4]____, County of ____[5]____ and State of ____[6]____, being of sound and disposing mind and memory do hereby make, publish and declare this to be my Last Will and Testament.

FIRST: I hereby revoke all former Wills and Codicils heretofore made by me.

SECOND: I direct that my Executor pay and discharge all of my just debts, including the expenses of my last illness, funeral and administration expenses as soon as shall be practicable. I further direct that any and all federal, state, foreign or other estate, transfer, inheritance, succession, legacy and similar taxes, including interest and penalties thereon, if any, imposed upon or with respect to any property required to be included in my gross estate under the provisions of any such tax law, and whether passing hereunder or by any codicil hereto or otherwise, or upon or with respect to any person with respect to any such property, shall be paid out of my residuary estate as an expense of administration and shall not be equitably prorated or charged against the gifts provided herein.

THIRD: I give, devise and bequeath all of the rest, residue and remainder of my property, real, personal and mixed, of whatsoever kind and nature and wheresoever situated, of which I shall die seized or possessed, and all property over or with respect to which I shall have any

(Document continued on next page)

7. The name of the spouse.

8. The spouse's address.

9. The name of the Executor.

10. The Executor's address.

11. The name of the Successor Executor (who may act in the event of the death or refusal of the Executor to act).

12. The Successor Executor's address.

13. The date of signing the Will.

14. The Testator's name printed directly below the line, with the Testator to sign above the line.

15. The number of pages of the Will.

power of appointment, remaining after the payment of my debts, funeral and administration expenses and any taxes which may be payable, absolutely and forever to my spouse _____[7]_____, presently residing at _____[8]_____, irrespective of whether there are any children born of our marriage after the date of execution of this Will. I make no specific provision for any children born of our marriage since I am confident that my spouse will make provision for them.

FOURTH: I nominate, constitute and appoint _____[9]_____, presently residing at _____[10]_____, as the Executor of this Will. In the event of (his)(her) death or resignation or failure or refusal to act in said capacity, I nominate, constitute and appoint _____[11]_____, presently residing at _____[12]_____, as the Successor Executor of this Will.

FIFTH: I direct that no bond, security or other undertaking shall be imposed upon or required at any time or in any jurisdiction of any individual named herein for the faithful performance of his duties.

IN WITNESS WHEREOF, I have set my hand and seal this __[13]__ day of _____, 19__.

_____(L.S.)
[14]

The foregoing consisting of __[15]__ pages inclusive of this page, the original of which was signed or initialled by the above named Testator

(Document continued on next page)

16. The date of signing by the Witnesses (which should be the same date as in No. 13).

17. The name of each Witness printed directly below the line, with each Witness to sign above the line.

18. The address of each Witness.

prior to the execution thereof, was signed, published and declared by said Testator as and for his Last Will and Testament, in our presence and hearing and we thereupon, at his request, and in the presence of each other subscribed our names as witnesses this __[16]__ day of _____, 19__.

_____ residing at _____
     [17]   [18]
                              _____

_____ residing at _____
     [17]   [18]
                              _____

_____ residing at _____
     [17]   [18]
                              _____

SIMPLE WILL—ALL TO SURVIVING SPOUSE AND
ALTERNATIVE BEQUEST TO ADULT CHILD(REN) (1-02)

This Will should be used when the Testator (the person making the Will) has a spouse and one or more adult children. It provides that all assets remaining after the payment of the Testator's debts, funeral expenses and expenses of administration of the estate and federal and state estate taxes go to the surviving spouse. In the event that the spouse dies before the Testator, all assets remaining go to the Testator's adult child or children in equal share.

The term "per stirpes" at the end of paragraph 3 means that while all of the Testator's children will receive equal shares if they survive the Testator, if any of the Testator's children were to die before the Testator but have children of their own, the pre-deceased child's children would split only their parent's share. Suppose, for example, the Testator had 3 children and Child No. 1 had no children of his own, Child No. 2 had two children and Child No. 3 had three children. If Child No. 2 and Child No. 3 died before the Testator, upon the death of the Testator, Child No. 1 would inherit one-third, Child No. 2's children would split No. 2's one-third such that each would inherit one-half each of the one-third share of Child No. 2 (which is one-sixth of the total), and Child No. 3's children would split No. 3's one-third share such that each would inherit one-third each of the one-third of Child No. 3 (which is one-ninth of the total).

If, on the other hand, the term "per capita" is substituted for "per stirpes," using the same example, the Testator's Child No. 1 and the Testator's five grandchildren (two by Child No. 2 and three by Child No. 3) would all share equally such that each would receive one-sixth of the total.

If "per capita" is desired, change the last word at the end of the THIRD paragraph to "capita."

Note that this form assumes that if any of the Testator's children should die before the Testator, it would be the Testator's wish that any children of that child (the Testator's grandchildren) would inherit that parent's share. If this is not what the Testator wishes, the word "surviving" should be inserted in front of the word "issue" before blank #9 in the document, and the words "per stirpes" at the end of that paragraph should be deleted.

SIMPLE WILL—ALL TO SURVIVING SPOUSE AND
ALTERNATIVE BEQUEST TO ADULT CHILD(REN)

1. The name of the Testator (the person making the Will).

2. If the Testator is or has been known by any other name (or has assets in another form of his name such as the use of his middle name), insert this other name. If not, delete the words "also known as _____[2]_____."

3. The Testator's address.

LAST WILL AND TESTAMENT OF
_____[1]_____

_____[1]_____, *[also known as* _____[2]_____,*]* presently residing at _____[3]_____, in the City of

(Document continued on next page)

4. The city in which the Testator resides.

5. The county in which the Testator resides.

6. The state in which the Testator resides.

7. The name of the spouse.

8. The spouse's address.

9. The name of the person (a child, not necessarily a minor, of the Testator) who will inherit in the event that the spouse has died before the Testator.

10. The address of the child named in No. 9.

11. The name of the Testator's second child (Note: this form assumes that the Testator has a spouse and two children; if the Testator has only one child, delete "and __[11]__, presently residing at ___[12]___ in equal shares per stirpes."

12. The address of the child named in No. 11.

13. If the Testator has more than two children, add "and ___[11]___, presently residing at ___[12]___" for each additional child.

_____[4]_____, County of _____[5]_____ and State of _____[6]_____, being of sound and disposing mind and memory do hereby make, publish and declare this to be my Last Will and Testament.

FIRST: I hereby revoke all former Wills and Codicils heretofore made by me.

SECOND: I direct that my Executor pay and discharge all of my just debts, including the expenses of my last illness, funeral and administration expenses as soon as shall be practicable. I further direct that any and all federal, state, foreign or other estate, transfer, inheritance, succession, legacy and similar taxes, including interest and penalties thereon, if any, imposed upon or with respect to any property required to be included in my gross estate under the provisions of any such tax law, and whether passing hereunder or by any Codicil hereto or otherwise, or upon or with respect to any person with respect to any such property, shall be paid out of my residuary estate as an expense of administration and shall not be equitably prorated or charged against the gifts provided herein.

THIRD: I give, devise and bequeath all of the rest, residue and remainder of my property, real, personal and mixed, of whatsoever kind and nature and wheresoever situated, of which I shall die seized or possessed, and all property over or with respect to which I shall have any power of appointment, remaining after the payment of my debts, funeral and administration expenses and any taxes which may be payable, absolutely and forever to my spouse, _____[7]_____, presently residing at _____[8]_____. Should my spouse _____[7]_____ fail to survive me, I give, devise and bequeath all of my said property to my issue, _____[9]_____, presently residing at _____[10]_____, *and* _____[11]_____, *presently residing at* _____[12]_____, *[13] in equal shares per stirpes.*

FOURTH: In the event that any of the legatees under this Will shall die with me in a common accident or disaster, or under such circumstances as make it impossible or difficult to determine which of us died first or in the

(Document continued on next page)

14. The name of the Executor.

15. The Executor's address.

16. The name of the Successor Executor (who may act in the event of the death or refusal of the Executor to act.)

17. The Successor Executor's address.

18. The date of signing the Will.

19. The Testator's name printed directly below the line, with the Testator to sign above the line.

20. The number of pages of the Will.

21. The date of signing by the Witnesses, which should be the same date as No. 18.

22. The name of each Witness printed directly below the line, with each Witness to sign above the line.

23. The address of each Witness.

event that any such legatee shall die within sixty (60) days of my death, regardless of the circumstances, it shall be conclusively presumed that such legatee shall have predeceased me and deemed not to have survived me.

FIFTH: I nominate, constitute and appoint _____[14]_____, presently residing at _____[15]_____, as the Executor of this Will. In the event of (his)(her) death or resignation or failure or refusal to act in said capacity, I nominate, constitute and appoint _____[16]_____, presently residing at _____[17]_____ as the Successor Executor of this Will.

SIXTH: I direct that no bond, security or other undertaking shall be imposed upon or required at any time or in any jurisdiction of any individual named herein for the faithful performance of (his)(her) duties.

IN WITNESS WHEREOF, I have set my hand and seal this __[18]_ day of _____, 19__.

_____(L.S.)
[19]

The foregoing consisting of __[20]__ pages inclusive of this page, the original of which was signed or initialled by the above named Testator prior to the execution thereof, was signed, published and declared by said Testator as and for his Last Will and Testament, in our presence and hearing and we thereupon, at his request, and in the presence of each other subscribed our names as witnesses this __[21]__ day of _____, 19__.

_____ residing at _____
[22]   [23]

                                      _____

_____ residing at _____
[22]   [23]

                                      _____

_____ residing at _____
[22]   [23]

                                      _____

SIMPLE WILL—ALL TO SURVIVING SPOUSE AND ALTERNATIVE BEQUEST TO CHILD(REN) WITH SIMPLE TRUST IF ANY CHILD IS A MINOR (1-03)

This Will should be used when the Testator (the person making the Will) has a spouse and one or more children. It provides that all assets remaining after the payment of the Testator's debts, administration expenses of the estate and federal and state estate taxes go to the surviving spouse. In the event that the spouse dies before the Testator, all assets remaining go to the Testator's child or children in equal share.

This Will also provides that if, at the time of the Testator's death, any beneficiary is a minor, that beneficiary's share is not to be given outright to that beneficiary but is to be held in Trust. Many states define the age of majority as eighteen. However, some states provide that minority ends only on reaching the twenty first birthday.

Note that this form provides that any Trust shall terminate and the property then held in Trust shall be paid out when the beneficiary reaches the age of 21. The Testator may, if he so desires, provide that the Trust will not terminate until some later age. However, if the Trust is to terminate at some later age, the Testator should be aware that some states recognize the so-called "Rule Against Perpetuities" which, simply stated, prohibits holding property in Trust for a period longer than a "life in being plus 21 years" when measured from the date of the Testator's death (and *not* from the date of making the Will). This means that while the Testator is free to provide for any termination date he wishes for any minor beneficiary who is alive at the time of his death, the Trust for that beneficiary must terminate not later than the date upon which the Testator's grandchild (born after the death of the Testator) reaches 21. Suppose for example, that one of the Testator's children is, at the time of the Testator's death, only 17 years old—that child's share would go into Trust. Further suppose that this child married at 19, had a child of his or her own and died thereafter, but before reaching the age of 21 (and the termination of the Trust). That child's share would go to his child (the Testator's grandchild) but would be held in Trust for the grandchild since the grandchild is also a minor. The Rule Against Perpetuities holds that the Trust must terminate on the date that this grandchild reaches 21.

The term used here, "per stirpes," means that while all of the Testator's children would receive equal shares if they survive the Testator, if any of the Testator's children were to die before the Testator but have children of their own, the pre-deceased child's children would split only their parent's share. Suppose, for example, the Testator had 3 children and Child No. 1 had no children of his own, Child No. 2 had two children and Child No. 3 had three children. If Child No. 2 and Child No. 3 died before the Testator, upon the death of the Testator, Child No. 1 would inherit one-third, Child No. 2's children would split No. 2's one-third such that each would inherit one-half each of the one-third share of Child No. 2 (which is one-sixth of the total), and Child No. 3's children would split No. 3's one-third share such that each would inherit one-third each of the one-third of Child No. 3 (which is one-ninth of the total).

If on the other hand, the term "per capita" were substituted for "per stirpes," using the same example, the Testator's Child No. 1 and the Testator's five grandchildren (two by Child No. 2 and three by Child No. 3) would all share equally such that each would receive one-sixth of the total.

SIMPLE WILL—ALL TO SURVIVING SPOUSE AND
ALTERNATIVE BEQUEST TO CHILD(REN) WITH
SIMPLE TRUST IF ANY CHILD IS A MINOR *continued*

If "per capita" is desired, change the last word at the end of the THIRD paragraph to "capita."

This form assumes that if any of the Testator's children should die before the Testator, it would be the Testator's wish that any children of that child (the Testator's grandchildren) would inherit that parent's share. If this is not what the Testator wishes, the word "surviving" should be inserted in front of the word "issue" before blank #9 in the document, and the words "per stirpes" at end of that paragraph should be deleted.

SIMPLE WILL—ALL TO SURVIVING SPOUSE AND
ALTERNATIVE BEQUEST TO CHILD(REN) WITH
SIMPLE TRUST IF ANY CHILD IS A MINOR

LAST WILL AND TESTAMENT OF
_____[1]_____

1. The name of the Testator (the person making the Will).

2. If the Testator is or has been known by any other name (or has assets in another form of his name such as the use of his middle name), insert this other name. If not, delete the words "also known as _____[2]_____."

3. The Testator's address.

4. The city in which the Testator resides.

5. The county in which the Testator resides.

6. The state in which the Testator resides.

_____[1]_____, *also known as* _____[2]_____, presently residing at _____[3]_____, in the City of _____[4]_____, County of ____[5]____ and State of _____[6]_____, being of sound and disposing mind and memory do hereby make, publish and declare this to be my Last Will and Testament.

FIRST: I hereby revoke all former Wills and Codicils heretofore made by me.

SECOND: I direct that my Executor pay and discharge all of my just debts, including the expenses of my last illness, funeral and administration expenses as soon as shall be practicable. I further direct that any and all federal, state, foreign or other estate, transfer, inheritance, succession, legacy and similar taxes, including interest and penalties thereon, if any, imposed upon or with respect to any property required to be included in my gross estate under the provisions of any such tax law, and whether passing hereunder or by any Codicil hereto or otherwise, or upon or with respect to any person with respect to any such property, shall be paid out of my residuary estate as an expense of administration and shall not be equitably prorated or charged against the gifts provided herein.

THIRD: I give, devise and bequeath all of the rest, residue and remainder of my property, real, personal and

(Document continued on next page)

7. The name of the spouse.

8. The spouse's home address.

9. The name of the person (a child, not necessarily a minor, of the Testator) who will inherit in the event that the spouse has died before the Testator.

10. The address of the child named in No. 9.

11. The name of the Testator's second child (Note: this form assumes that the Testator has a spouse and two children; if the Testator has only one child, delete "and __[11]__, presently residing at __[12]__ in equal shares per stirpes."

12. The address of the child named in No. 10.

13. If the Testator has more than two children, add "and __[11]__, presently residing at __[12]__" for each additional child.

mixed, of whatsoever kind and nature and wheresoever situated, of which I shall die seized or possessed, and all property over or with respect to which I shall have any power of appointment, remaining after the payment of my debts, funeral and administration expenses and any taxes which may be payable, absolutely and forever to my spouse, _____[7]_____, presently residing at _____[8]_____. Should my spouse _____[7]_____ fail to survive me, I give, devise and bequeath all of my said property to my issue, _____[9]_____, presently residing at _____[10]_____, *and* _____[11]_____, *presently residing at* _____[12]_____, *[13] in equal shares per stirpes.*

FOURTH: Despite the foregoing, if any property becomes payable or distributable under this Will to a person who is then under the age of twenty-one (21) years, such property shall not vest in such person but shall be set apart and held by my Trustee, hereinafter named, in Trust, for the following uses and purposes:

(a) To hold, manage, invest and reinvest the said property, to collect and receive the income therefrom, and to pay the net income, in quarter-annual installments to such child until the termination of the Trust herein created.

(b) In addition to the said payment of net income from said Trust, my Trustee is authorized to pay from the principal of the Trust, at any time or from time to time, such portion or portions of the principal as my Trustee, in his sole and uncontrolled discretion may determine to be in the best interests of such child in order to provide for the health, education and general welfare of such child.

(c) When such child attains the age of twenty-one (21) years, one-half (1/2) of the then principal of the Trust shall be paid over and distributed absolutely and forever to such child, and when such child attains the age of twenty-five (25) years, the remaining principal of the Trust then held shall be paid over and distributed absolutely and forever to such child together with any and all undistributed income and the Trust herein created shall cease and terminate. In the event that such child shall die before the termination of the Trust as herein provided but shall leave issue surviving, my Trustee shall divide the remaining principal then held in Trust for such child together with any

(Document continued on next page)

14. The name of the Executor.

15. The Executor's address.

16. The name of the Successor Executor (who may act in the event of the death or refusal of the Executor to act.)

17. The Successor Executor's address.

18. The name of the Trustee of the Trust(s) created if any beneficiary is a minor at the time of the Testator's death. Note: DO NOT name the Testator's spouse as Trustee because under this form, the Testator's children inherit only if the spouse had died before the Testator. The Trustee and the Executor can be the same person.

19. The Trustee's address.

undistributed income into such number of equal shares as shall provide one share for each of such child's issue and shall thereupon be held in Trust by my said Trustee in accordance with the provisions of the Trust herein created, except that each such separate Trust shall cease and terminate upon the attaining of the age of twenty-one (21) years by each such issue of such child. In the event that such child shall die before the termination of the Trust as provided herein and shall leave no issue surviving, the Trust herein created shall cease and terminate on the date of such child's death and the remaining principal then held, together with any undistributed income, shall be paid absolutely and forever to those persons who would have been my heirs at law had I died intestate on the date of such child's death.

FIFTH: In the event that any of the legatees under this Will shall die with me in a common accident or disaster, or under such circumstances as make it impossible or difficult to determine which of us died first or in the event that any such legatee shall die within sixty (60) days of my death, regardless of the circumstances, it shall be conclusively presumed that such legatee shall have predeceased me and deemed not to have survived me.

SIXTH: I nominate, constitute and appoint _____[14]_____, presently residing at _____[15]_____, as the Executor of this Will. In the event of (his)(her) death or resignation or failure or refusal to act in said capacity, I nominate, constitute and appoint _____[16]_____, presently residing at _____[17]_____, as the Successor Executor of this Will. I nominate, constitute and appoint _____[18]_____, presently residing at _____[19]_____, as the Trustee of any Trust herein created.

SEVENTH: I direct that no bond, security or other undertaking shall be imposed upon or required at any time or in any jurisdiction of any individual named herein for the faithful performance of (his)(her) duties.

(Document continued on next page)

20. The date of signing the Will.

21. The Testator's name printed directly below the line, with the Testator to sign above the line.

22. The number of pages of the Will.

23. The date of signing by the Witnesses, which should be the same date as No. 20.

24. The name of each Witness printed directly below the line, with each Witness to sign above the line.

25. The address of each Witness.

IN WITNESS WHEREOF, I have set my hand and seal this __[20]__ day of _____, 19__.

_____(L.S.)
[21]

The foregoing consisting of __[22]__ pages inclusive of this page, the original of which was signed or initialled by the above named Testator prior to the execution thereof, was signed, published and declared by said Testator as and for his Last Will and Testament, in our presence and hearing and we thereupon, at his request, and in the presence of each other subscribed our names as witnesses this __[23]__ day of _____, 19__.

_____ residing at _____
[24]   [25]

_____

_____ residing at _____
[24]   [25]

_____

_____ residing at _____
[24]   [25]

_____

CODICIL TO WILL (1-04)

A Codicil is a written supplement, alteration or modification of a Will and is typically used when the proposed modifications are deemed to be minor and not of enough importance to justify rewriting the entire Will, or when time constraints prohibit rewriting the entire Will. A Codicil does not supersede a prior Will. Rather it alters, modifies or explains the prior Will. For this reason, it is regarded as part of the Will and the Will and the Codicil are read as one document. A Codicil is considered to ratify and republish those parts of the prior Will that are **not** specifically altered or modified by the Codicil. Because a Codicil does not supersede, revoke or modify the entire prior Will but only specific portions, care must be taken as to those portions of the Will that are to be modified and those that are to remain. The same is true of second or subsequent Codicils.

A Codicil must be signed and witnessed with the same formality as a Will. See "Introduction to Wills" at the beginning of this chapter.

WARNING

Despite the foregoing, the authors have found that any time savings achieved by preparing a Codicil versus a new Will are minimal. They believe that the wiser practice is to avoid the use of Codicils. The authors strongly recommend preparing a new Will even when changes are slight.

CODICIL TO WILL

1. Identify the Codicil as "First," "Second" and so forth.

2. The name of the Testator (the person making the Codicil).

3. If the Testator is or has been known by any other name (or has assets in another form of his name such as the use of his middle name), insert this other name. If not, delete the words "also known as _____[3]_____."

4. The Testator's address.

5. The city in which the Testator resides.

6. The county in which the Testator resides.

7. The state in which the Testator resides.

_____[1]_____ CODICIL TO LAST WILL
AND TESTAMENT
OF
_____[2]_____

_____[2]_____, *[also known as* _____[3]_____,*]* presently residing at _____[4]_____, in the City of _____[5]_____, County of _____[6]_____ and State of _____[7]_____,

(Document continued on next page)

8. The date of the Will being modified.

9. If this is the first Codicil to the Will, delete the words "and the ___[10]___ Codicil thereto dated ___[11]___" and skip to No. 12.

10. The number of the most recent Codicil to the Will.

11. The date of the most recent Codicil to the Will.

12. Use this paragraph for adding to a Will a bequest for a certain amount of money. Otherwise delete this paragraph, skip to No. 16, and renumber the remaining paragraphs.

13. The name of the person receiving the bequest.

14. The address of the person named in No. 13.

15. The amount of the bequest, in words and numbers.

16. Use this paragraph for a bequest of a specific asset such as shares of stock of a specific corporation, a painting, a piece of jewelry or the like. Otherwise delete this paragraph, skip to No. 20, and renumber the remaining paragraphs.

17. The name of the person receiving the specific asset.

18. The address of the person named in No. 17.

19. A specific description of the asset. (The more specific you are, the more likely you are to avoid a fight between the heirs.)

being of sound and disposing mind and memory do hereby make, publish and declare this to be the ____[1]____ Codicil to my Last Will and Testament dated _____[8]_____ *[9][and the ____[10]____ Codicil thereto dated _____[11]_____.*

    [12]FIRST: I give devise and bequeath absolutely and forever to _____[13]_____, presently residing at _____[14]_____, the sum of _____[15]_____ Dollars ($____[15]____).

    [16]SECOND: I give, devise and bequeath absolutely and forever to _____[17]_____, presently residing at _____[18]_____, my _____[19]_____.

(Document continued on next page)

20. Use this paragraph to modify, by either enlarging or reducing, the amount of a bequest in the Will. Otherwise delete this paragraph, skip to No. 25, and renumber the remaining paragraphs.

21. The name of the person whose prior bequest is being modified.

22. The address of the person named in No. 21.

23. The amount of the modified bequest, in words and numbers.

24. The specific number of the article or paragraph of the Will being modified.

25. Use this paragraph to revoke a prior bequest. Otherwise delete this paragraph, skip to No. 30, and renumber the remaining paragraph.

26. A description of the bequest being revoked.

27. The name of the person whose bequest is being revoked.

28. The address of the person named in No. 27.

29. The specific number of the article or paragraph of the Will being modified.

30. Use this paragraph for changing the Executor named in the Will. Otherwise delete this paragraph and skip to No. 34.

31. The name of the person now chosen to be the Executor.

32. The address of the person named in No. 31.

33. The name of the former Executor.

[20]THIRD: I give, devise and bequeath to _____[21]_____, presently residing at _____[22]_____, the sum of _____[23]_____ Dollars ($____[23]____) in lieu of and in place of and not in addition to the bequest made to him by Article __[24]__ of my Last Will and Testament dated _____[8]_____.

[25]FOURTH: I hereby revoke in all respects the legacy of _____[26]_____ given to _____[27]_____, presently residing at _____[28]_____ made to him by Article __[29]__ of my Last Will and Testament dated _____[8]_____.

[30]FIFTH: I nominate, constitute and appoint _____[31]_____, presently residing at _____[32]_____, as the Executor of my Last Will and Testament dated _____[8]_____ in place of _____[33]_____ and I hereby revoke the

(Document continued on next page)

CODICIL TO WILL *continued*

34. The date of signing the Codicil.

35. The Testator's name printed directly below the line, with the Testator to sign above the line.

36. The number of pages of the Codicil.

37. The date of signing by the Witnesses (which should be the same date as No. 34).

38. The name of each Witness printed directly below the line, with each Witness to sign directly above the line.

39. The address of each Witness.

nomination of _____[33]_____ as the Executor of my Last Will and Testament dated _____[8]_____.

      IN WITNESS WHEREOF, I have set my hand and seal this __[34]__ day of _____, 19__.

_____(L.S.)
                [35]

  The foregoing consisting of __[36]__ pages inclusive of this page, the original of which was signed or initialled by the above named testator prior to the execution thereof, was signed, published and declared by said Testator as and for the ____[1]____ Codicil to his Last Will and Testament dated _____[8]_____, in our presence and hearing and we thereupon, at his request, and in the presence of each other subscribed our names as witnesses this __[37]__ day of _____, 19__.

_____ residing at _____
      [38]   [39]

                                 _____

_____ residing at _____
      [38]   [39]

                                 _____

_____ residing at _____
      [38]   [39]

                                 _____

AFFIDAVIT OF DECEDENT'S DOMICILE (1-05)

An Affidavit of Decedent's Domicile (a person's legal address) is used by the representative of a deceased person in connection with a transfer of the deceased's property. The representative may be an Executor (who is acting under the authority of a Will) or an Administrator (someone appointed by a court when the deceased left no Will). Or it can be someone acting as a surviving tenant (the survivor of two or more people who own property jointly) with authority to act in a specific situation.

An Affidavit of Decedent's Domicile is usually provided by a bank or stock transfer agent; the instructions presented here can be used as a guide to filling it out.

This form must be signed before a Notary Public.

AFFIDAVIT OF DECEDENT'S DOMICILE

1. The state where the Affidavit is signed.

2. The county where the Affidavit is signed.

STATE OF _____[1]_____)
COUNTY OF _____[2]_____)   ss.:

3. The name of the person giving the Affidavit.

_____[3]_____ being duly sworn, deposes and says:

4. The residence address, including street address, city, state and zip code of the representative (the person whose name is given in No. 3).

My residence address is _____[4]_____.
I am the *[5][* _____*[6]*_____ *of* _____*[7]*_____, *a corporation duly organized under the laws of the State of* _____*[8]*_____,] *[9][Executor]* **OR** *[Administrator]* **OR** *[Surviving Tenant]* of the Estate of _____[10]_____

5. If the person making the Affidavit is not an officer or director of a corporation, bank or the like, delete the words "___[6]___ of ___[7]___, a corporation duly organized under the laws of the State of _____[8]_____."

6. The corporate title of the person named in No. 3, i.e. President, Secretary or the like.

7. The name of the corporation.

8. The state of incorporation of the corporation named in No. 7.

(Document continued on next page)

9. Choose one.

10. The name of the deceased person.

11. The place of death (the street address if available, and the city and state).

12. The date of death, including month, day and year.

13. Choose one.

14. The residence address (number and street) of the deceased person named in No. 10 on the date of death.

15. The county in which the deceased resided on the date of death.

16. The state in which the deceased resided on the date of death.

17. The number of years, in numbers, the deceased lived at the address given in No. 14.

18. If known, the day, month and year that the deceased began living at the address at which he lived on the date of death. Otherwise delete, beginning with "such residence" to the end of the line.

19. If known, the year in which the deceased last voted. Otherwise delete the paragraph and skip to No. 23.

20. If known, the street address at which deceased last voted. Otherwise delete "at _____" through the end of the paragraph and skip to No. 23.

21. The county in which No. 20. is located.

22. The state in which No. 20 is located.

23. Choose one.

who died at _____[11]_____ on _____[12]_____.

At the time of *[13][his]* **OR** *[her]* death, decedent's domicile (legal residence) was at _____[14]_____, in the County of _____[15]_____, State of _____[16]____. The decedent resided at such address for ____[17]_____ years, *such residence having commenced on* _____[18]_____.

Decedent last voted in the year __[19]__ at _____[20]_____, in the County of _____[21]_____, in the State of _____[22]____.

Decedent's principal place of business at the time of [23][his] **OR** *[her] death was at*

(Document continued on next page)

24. The address where the deceased worked on the date of death, or last place of business if not working at time of death. If not known, or if the deceased did not work, delete this paragraph and skip to No. 27.

25. The county in which No. 24 is located.

26. The state in which No. 24 is located.

27. Choose one.

28. The address of the deceased as stated on the deceased's most recently filed federal income tax return.

29. The county in which No. 28 is located.

30. The state in which No. 28 is located.

31. The name or names of such other states in which the deceased resided in the three years prior to his death, and the dates of residence in those states. If the deceased had no other residences within the three year period prior to his death, delete "except as follows."

32. The name of the person giving the Affidavit printed directly below the line, with that person to sign above the line.

33. A Notary Public fills in the date and signs and seals the form by affixing his stamp or seal.

_____*[24]*_____, *in the County of*
_____*[25]*____, *in the State of* _____*[26]*_____.

　　Decedent's most recent federal income tax return shows *[27][his]* **OR** *[her]* legal residence as _____*[28]*_____, *in the County of* _____*[29]*_____, *in the State of* _____*[30]*_____.

　　Within three years prior to death decedent was not a resident of any other state *[31][except as follows:]*
_____.

　　Any and all debts, taxes and claims against the estate have been paid or provided for; this affidavit is made for the purpose of securing the transfer or delivery of property owned by decedent at the time of decedent's death to a purchaser or the person or persons legally entitled thereto under the laws of decedent's domicile and that any apparent inequality in distribution has been satisfied or provided for out of other assets in the estate.

　　　　　　　　　　　_____
　　　　　　　　　　　　　　　　　　　　　[32]

Sworn to before me this

__[33]__ day of _____, 19__.

_____[33]_____
Notary Public

LIVING WILL (1-06)

A Living Will is used by an individual to express his desires regarding medical treatment in the event he becomes unable to participate in making such decisions. It is called a Living Will because it is to be given force and effect during that person's life (unlike a regular Will which has no effect until after death). Most states now recognize an individual's right to refuse medical treatment and to request the care that the individual desires. This form can and should be made to conform with the individual's personal wishes as suggested in the instructions below.

Copies of the Living Will should be given to all people likely to be involved in providing medical care or making decisions relating to such care. The form should note the location of the original Living Will. The original Living Will should be kept with other important papers; however, the authors recommend that the original Living Will be kept in a safe deposit box *only* if the person making the Living Will is not the sole person who has access to the box.

WARNINGS

The law regarding the validity of a Living Will varies from state to state. A particular state may have specific rules regarding the length of effectiveness, requirements for witnesses and the like. The reader is cautioned to verify with the state in which he lives what constitutes compliance with that state's requirements for a Living Will. The language provided here is general, setting forth the individual's directions and desires. However, even where a state has no legislation specifically recognizing a Living Will, this form still will be clear evidence of the individual's desires.

The Living Will only states the wishes of the person making the Living Will. It does not name any one person to be the "voice" of that person. The person making the Living Will should use the Durable Power of Attorney which follows to designate his "voice." Some states require (and the authors strongly urge) that the Living Will be used **only** in conjunction with a Durable Power of Attorney.

LIVING WILL
of
_____[1]_____

[Also Known As _____[2]_____]

1. The name of the person making the Living Will (the "Declarant").

2. If the Declarant has been known by any other name, insert this other name. If not, delete the words "also known as _____[2]_____."

TO MY FAMILY, MY PHYSICIAN, MY ATTORNEY AND ANY MEDICAL FACILITY IN WHOSE CARE I MAY COME OR HAPPEN TO BE AND ALL OTHERS WHO MAY BE RESPONSIBLE FOR MY HEALTH, WELFARE OR AFFAIRS:

If the time comes when I can no longer take part in decisions for my own future, let this statement stand as an expression of my wishes and direction while I am still of sound mind.

If I should be in an incurable or irreversible mental

(Document continued on next page)

3.   The language in this section can be changed to conform to the Declarant's wishes.

4.   If applicable, insert other instructions. Otherwise delete this text.

5.   The language in this paragraph can be changed to conform to the Declarant's wishes.

or physical condition so that there is no reasonable anticipation of my recovery from severe physical or mental incapacity, I direct that I be permitted to die and I do not want to be kept alive by medications, artificial means, or so-called "heroic measures." I request and direct that treatment, including medication, water and fluids be mercifully administered to me to alleviate pain and suffering so as to keep me comfortable even though this may shorten my remaining life.

These instructions are set forth after careful thought and are in accordance with my clear convictions and beliefs. I want the wishes and directions here expressed carried out to the extent permitted by law unless I have rescinded them in a new writing or by clearly indicating that I have changed my mind. Those concerned with my health and welfare are specifically asked to take whatever action necessary, including legal action, to realize my wishes and instructions. I hope that those to whom this document is directed will regard themselves as morally bound to abide by its contents if and to the extent that the provisions of this document are not legally enforceable.

[3][If at any time there is no reasonable expectation of my recovery from extreme physical or mental disability, I feel especially strong about, and specifically refuse the following measures of artificial life support:

(a) Electrical or mechanical resuscitation of my heart when it has stopped beating.

(b) Nasogastric tube feeding when I am paralyzed or unable to take nourishment by mouth.

(c) Mechanical respiration when I am no longer able to sustain my own breathing.]

[4][My other personal instructions are:]

[5][I would like to live out my last days at home rather than in a hospital if it does not jeopardize the chance of my recovery to a meaningful and sentient life and does not impose an undue burden on my family.]

(Document continued on next page)

6. The Declarant's name printed directly below the line, with the Declarant to sign above the line.

7. The date of signing the Living Will.

8. The name of the Witness printed directly below the line, with the Witness to sign above the line.

9. The date of signing by the Witness.

10. The Witness's complete address.

11. The Witness's telephone number.

12. The Notary Public completes this section and affixes his stamp or seal.

13. The specific location of the Living Will.

14. The address of the location of the Living Will.

Signed:_____   Date:_____[7]_____
         [6]

Witness: _____   Date:_____ [9]_____
       [8]
      Address:_____[10]_____
      Tel. No.:_____[11]_____

Witness: _____   Date:_____ [9]_____
       [8]
      Address:_____[10]_____
      Tel. No.:_____[11]_____

STATE OF ____[12]____, COUNTY OF____[12]____, ss:

    On _____[12]_____, 19__, before me personally came _____[12]_____ to me known, and known to me to be the individual described in and who executed the foregoing LIVING WILL, and duly acknowledged to me that (s)he executed the same.

                _____
                     Notary Public

The ORIGINAL Living Will is in the _____[13]_____, located at _____[14]_____.

(Document continued on next page)

15. The name of each person who has a copy of the Living Will.

16. The address of each person who has a copy of the Living Will.

COPIES of this Living Will have been distributed to:

_____[15]_____ residing at _____[16]_____

_____

_____[15]_____ residing at _____[16]_____

_____

_____[15]_____ residing at _____[16]_____

_____

DURABLE POWER OF ATTORNEY (1-07)

A Durable Power of Attorney is used by an individual (the Declarant) to express in writing, while he is capable of making decisions, his desires to appoint another person (the attorney-in-fact) to make health care or medical treatment decisions in the event he becomes unable to participate in the making of such decisions. The attorney-in-fact is empowered to make decisions based on the Declarant's wishes as well as specific instructions which have been conveyed.

Copies of the Durable Power of Attorney (together with the Living Will) should be given to all people likely to be involved in providing medical care or making decisions relating to such care. The form should note the location of the original of the Durable Power of Attorney (and the Living Will). The original Durable Power of Attorney (and the Living Will) should be kept with other important papers; however, the authors recommend that the original Durable Power of Attorney, like the Living Will, be kept in a safe deposit box *only* if the person making the Living Will is not the sole person who has access to the box.

WARNINGS

This form should be used in conjunction with the form immediately preceding, the Living Will.

As with the Living Will, the law regarding the validity of a Durable Power of Attorney varies from state to state. A particular state may have specific rules regarding the length of effectiveness, requirements for witnesses and the like. The reader is cautioned to verify with the state in which he lives what constitutes compliance with that state's requirements for a Durable Power of Attorney. The language provided here is general, setting forth the individual's designation of a person to act. However, even where a state has no legislation specifically recognizing a Durable Power of Attorney (and Living Will), this form will still be clear evidence of the individual's desires.

The Durable Power of Attorney only designates who the maker of the Durable Power wishes to act as his "voice." By itself it does not express any evidence of what that "voice" should say. That is the function of the Living Will. Some states require (and the authors strongly urge) that the Living Will be used **only** in conjunction with a Durable Power of Attorney.

DURABLE POWER OF ATTORNEY

1.   The name of the person making the appointment (the Declarant).

2.   If the Declarant has been known by any other name, insert this other name. If not, delete the words "also known as ____[2]___."

3.   The name of the person being appointed (the attorney-in-fact).

4.   The address of the person being appointed at the time of the signing of the Durable Power of Attorney.

I, _____[1]_____ [, *also known as* _____[2]_____,] hereby designate _____[3]_____, presently residing at _____[4]_____, to serve as my attorney-in-fact for the purpose of making health care and medical

(Document continued on next page)

5. This section can be changed to conform to the Declarant's wishes.

6. The Declarant's name printed directly below the line, with the Declarant to sign above the line.

7. The date of signing the Durable Power of Attorney.

8. The name of the Witness printed directly below the line, with the Witness to sign above the line.

9. The date of signing by the Witness.

10. The Witness's complete address.

11. The Witness's telephone number.

treatment decisions *[5][, including decisions to withhold or withdraw life-support,]* on my behalf. Unless I have rescinded this appointment in a new writing, this power of attorney shall remain effective in the event that I become incompetent or otherwise unable to make or communicate such decisions for myself.

Signed:_____ Date:_____[7]_____
[6]

Witness: _____ Date:_____ [9]_____
[8]
    Address:_____[10]_____
    Tel. No.:_____[11]_____

Witness: _____ Date:_____ [9]_____
[8]
    Address:_____[10]_____
    Tel. No.:_____[11]_____

(Document continued on next page)

12. The Notary Public completes this section and affixes his stamp or seal.

13. The specific location of the Durable Power of Attorney.

14. The address of the location of the Durable Power of Attorney.

15. The name of each person who has a copy of the Durable Power of Attorney.

16. The address of each person who has a copy of the Durable Power of Attorney.

STATE OF ____[12]____, COUNTY OF____[12]____, ss:

On _____[12]_____, 19__, before me personally came _____[12]_____ to me known, and known to me to be the individual described in and who executed the foregoing DURABLE POWER OF ATTORNEY, and duly acknowledged to me that (s)he executed the same.

_____
Notary Public

The ORIGINAL Durable Power of Attorney is in the _____[13]_____, located at _____[14]_____.

COPIES of this Durable Power of Attorney have been distributed to:

_____[15]_____ residing at _____[16]_____

_____

_____[15]_____ residing at _____[16]_____

_____

_____[15]_____ residing at _____[16]_____

_____

STATEMENT OF ANATOMICAL GIFT
MADE BY A LIVING DONOR (1-08)

This form is to be used by an individual to evidence an intent, made while living, to donate some or all of his organs or body parts upon his death. This form speaks for the individual, while he is still living, of a gift which does not take effect until his death. The gift can be revoked or modified at any time prior to death.

The intent to make a gift of organs or body parts can be included in a Will but this separate form is strongly recommended since the normal delays associated with locating a Will or the probate of a Will may be such that the value or usefulness of an organ will be lost and the intent of the person making the gift (the Donor) may be thwarted. If the Donor resides in a state which makes reference to organ donation on its driver's license, the organ donation portion of the license can be filled out to indicate the location of this form.

ANATOMICAL GIFT
by
_____[1]_____
[Also known as _____[2]_____]

1. The name of the person making the gift (the Donor).

2. If the Donor has been known by any other name, insert this other name. If not, delete the words "also known as ____[2]____."

3. Choose one.

4. If it is the Donor's intent to donate only certain organs or body parts, insert the names of those specific organs or body parts.

5. Choose one and fill in the specific name and address.

6. If it is the Donor's intent to donate specific organs or body parts to specific, but different, physicians or institutions, fill in this section, including the names and the addresses of the physicians or institutions. Otherwise delete this section.

I, _____[1]_____ *[, also known as _____[2]_____,]* state that I am over the age of eighteen (18) years and I am of sound and disposing mind.

I hereby make the following ANATOMICAL GIFT to take effect upon my death: *[3][any needed organs or part(s).]* **OR** *[ONLY the following organs or part(s):* _____[4]_____. *]*

The foregoing ANATOMICAL GIFT(S) are made to: *[5][the physician in attendance at the time of my death.]* **OR** *[the hospital where I am physically located at the time of my death.]* **OR** *[the following named physician:* _____.] **OR** *[the following named hospital/medical or teaching school/storage facility or other medical institution:_____.]*

[6][I hereby make the following ANATOMICAL GIFT(S) to the following to take effect upon my death:

Organ/Body Part	Recipient
_____	_____
_____	_____
_____	_____
	_____]

(Document continued on next page)

7. Choose one.

8. The Donor's name printed directly below the line, with the Donor to sign above the line.

9. The date of signing the Statement of Anatomical Gift.

10. The name of the Witness printed directly below the line, with the Witness to sign above the line.

11. The date of signing by the Witness.

12. The Witness's complete address.

13. The Witness's telephone number.

The foregoing ANATOMICAL GIFT(S) are made *[7][without limitation and for any purpose authorized by law.]* **OR** *[for transplantation.]* **OR** *[for medical research/ education.]*

It is my specific wish and desire that my relatives, friends and other interested physicians honor the foregoing ANATOMICAL GIFT(S) and not interfere with this purpose and intent.

Signed:_____ Date:_____[9]_____
                  [8]

Witness: _____ Date:_____ [11]_____
                  [10]
            Address:_____[12]_____
            Tel. No.:_____[13]_____

Witness: _____ Date:_____ [11]_____
                  [10]
            Address:_____[12]_____
            Tel. No.:_____[13]_____

(Document continued on next page)

14. The Notary Public completes this section and affixes his stamp or seal.

15. The specific location of the Statement of Anatomical Gift.

16. The address of the location of the Statement of Anatomical Gift.

17. The name of each person who has a copy of the Statement of Anatomical Gift.

18. The address of each person who has a copy of the Statement of Anatomical Gift.

STATE OF ____[14]____, COUNTY OF____[14]____, ss:

On _____[14]_____, 19__, before me personally came _____[14]_____ to me known, and known to me to be the individual described in and who executed the foregoing STATEMENT OF ANATOMICAL GIFT, and duly acknowledged to me that (s)he executed the same.

_____
Notary Public

The ORIGINAL Statement of Anatomical Gift is in the _____[15]_____, located at _____[16]_____.

COPIES of this Statement of Anatomical Gift have been distributed to:

_____[17]_____ residing at _____[18]_____

_____

_____[17]_____ residing at _____[18]_____

_____

_____[17]_____ residing at _____[18]_____

_____

GIFT TO A MINOR (1-09)

Lifetime gifts to minors may serve as an important element of a person's estate planning. Under the "Uniform Gifts to Minors Act" (which most states have adopted) an adult can make an irrevocable gift to a minor of money, securities (including stocks, bonds, notes and the like, either registered or unregistered), life insurance policies or annuity contracts. Gifts to minors may also be made in one's Will, a so-called testamentary disposition. The purpose of this form is only for a gift made during the lifetime of the person making the gift (the Donor). The person receiving the gift is called the Donee. In order for a gift to be effective, the law requires (a) donative intent—unequivocal evidence of the Donor's intent to make the gift, and (b) delivery of the gift to the person receiving the gift (the Donee) or in the case of a minor, to a custodian. This form provides written evidence of the donative intent by the maker of the gift (the Donor) and delivery of the gift by acknowledgement of receipt by the custodian.

WARNINGS

A gift to a minor under the "Uniform Gifts to Minors Act" is **irrevocable**. Once made (meaning upon delivery with donative intent), the gift cannot be undone or unmade, and the Donor can no longer exercise any ownership rights. Also, since the gift is irrevocable, when the minor Donee attains the age of majority, the Donee has the absolute right to claim physical control and ownership of the property in his own name. In states where 18 is the majority age, the Donor may wish to specify that full transfer of the property be deferred until the age of 21.

Your tax planner should be consulted regarding the subject of a gift, the age of majority in your state and the tax consequences to the minor as well as to the adult Donor.

GIFT TO A MINOR

1. The name of the adult making the gift (the Donor).

2. The name of the person who will be the custodian. In some cases the Donor may be the custodian and in other cases the custodian must be an adult other than the Donor, as when the gift is an unregistered security. The custodian also may be a bank.

3. The name of the minor to whom the gift is being made (the Donee).

4. The state where the gift is being made.

5. A thorough description of the property being delivered to the custodian.

I, _____[1]_____, hereby deliver to
_____[2]_____ as custodian for
_____[3]_____ under the _____[4]_____
Uniform Gifts to Minors Act, the following property:
_____[5]_____
_____.

(Document continued on next page)

6. The name of the Donor printed directly below the line, with the Donor to sign above the line.

7. The date of delivery of the gift.

8. The name of the custodian printed directly below the line, with the custodian to sign above the line.

Note: in addition to the use of this form, the simplification of gifts to minors under the Uniform Gifts to Minors Act permits making a gift by transferring ownership simply by delivering the property and registering it in the name of the custodian by use of the words "As custodian for ___(name of Minor)___ under the __(name of state)__ Uniform Gift to Minors Act." This is usable for a gift of money, an insurance policy, or a registered security provided that the requirements of the specific financial institution for the registration of ownership are followed.

_____
[6]

_____[2]_____ hereby acknowledges receipt of the above described as custodian for the above minor under the _____[4]_____ Uniform Gifts to Minor Act.

Dated: _____[7]_____

_____
[8]

RECORD OF PERSONAL AND BUSINESS INFORMATION (1-10)

     This form is a personal record of the diverse information that is a part of every person's life—but which most people do not have in one place. The purpose of this document is to help focus one's thinking in assembling this information so that it is complete and available if needed by someone in his absence. Once done, the form should be reviewed periodically and updated if necessary (because of moving, job change, birth of a child or the like).

     The form is self explanatory. Add or delete categories as appropriate.

RECORD OF PERSONAL
AND BUSINESS INFORMATION

Name _____ Date of Birth_____

Social Security Number_____ Passport No._____

Address: _____

Phone No. Home:_____ Business:_____

Occupation and Place of Business: _____
_____

Military History, if any _____

If Married:

Date _____ Place of Marriage _____

Spouse's Name _____ Date of Birth_____

Social Security Number_____ Passport No._____

Address _____

Phone No. Home:_____ Business:_____

Occupation and Place of Business: _____
_____

Military History, if any _____

If Divorced:

Name(s) of Former Spouse (s):
_____

Date(s) of Divorce _____

(Document continued on next page)

If any children:

Name of child	Date of Birth	Address
_____	_____	_____
_____	_____	_____
_____	_____	_____
_____	_____	_____

Other relations (parents, siblings, grandparents)

Name & Relationship	Date of Birth	Address
_____	_____	_____
_____	_____	_____
_____	_____	_____
_____	_____	_____
_____	_____	_____

ASSETS

A. BANKING:

    1. Checking Accounts:

Name and address of Bank	Account No.	Joint Owner
_____	_____	_____
_____	_____	_____
_____	_____	_____
_____	_____	_____

(Document continued on next page)

2. Savings Accounts (including IRA accounts):

Name and address of Bank	Account No.	Joint Owner
_____	_____	_____
_____	_____	_____
_____	_____	_____
_____	_____	_____

3. Certificates of Deposit (including IRA accounts):

Name and address of Bank	Account No.	Joint Owner
_____	_____	_____
_____	_____	_____
_____	_____	_____
_____	_____	_____

4. Mortgages, Loans, Notes:

Name of Lender	Amount of Loan	Monthly Payment	Maturity Date
_____	$_____	$_____	_____
_____	$_____	$_____	_____
_____	$_____	$_____	_____

5. Safe Deposit Box(es)

Location	Joint Owner
_____	_____
_____	_____

(Document continued on next page)

B. REAL ESTATE:

Owned:

Location	Estimated Value	Mortgage
_____	_____	$_____
_____	_____	$_____

Leased:

Location	Expiration Date	Annual Rental
_____	_____	_____
_____	_____	_____

C. STOCKS (exclusive of own business) AND BONDS

1. Brokerage Accounts:

Name and Address of Brokerage Firm	Account Number	Tel. Number
_____	_____	_____
_____	_____	_____

2. Stocks:

Name of Stock	No. of Shares	Date Purchased	Purchase Price
_____	_____	_____	$_____
_____	_____	_____	$_____
_____	_____	_____	$_____
_____	_____	_____	$_____

(Document continued on next page)

3. Bonds:

Description of Bond	Face Value	Date Purchased	Purchase Price
_____	_____	_____	$_____
_____	_____	_____	$_____
_____	_____	_____	$_____
_____	_____	_____	$_____

D. INSURANCE (Life and otherwise):

Company	Policy No.	Amount	Beneficiary

a) Owned by you
   on your life:

Company	Policy No.	Amount	Beneficiary
_____	_____	$_____	_____
_____	_____	$_____	_____

b) Owned by others
   on your life:

_____	_____	$_____	_____
_____	_____	$_____	_____

c) Owned by you
   on life of others:

_____	_____	$_____	_____
_____	_____	$_____	_____

d) Group Life Insurance (paid for by your company):

_____	_____	$_____	_____
_____	_____	$_____	_____

(Document continued on next page)

e) Property and
   Liability Insurance:

_____   _____ $_____   _____

_____   _____ $_____   _____

f) Accident &
   Health Insurance:

_____   _____ $_____   _____

_____   _____ $_____   _____

g) Disability Insurance:

_____   _____ $_____   _____

_____   _____ $_____   _____

E. MISCELLANEOUS PROPERTY

1. Personal Property (e.g. Autos, boats, jewelry, art collection, stamp collection, professional equipment, patents, trademarks or copyrights, contract rights)

Description Of Item	Location	Est. Value
_____	_____	$_____
_____	_____	$_____
_____	_____	$_____
_____	_____	$_____
_____	_____	$_____
_____	_____	$_____
_____	_____	$_____

(Document continued on next page)

2. Interests in Estates and Trusts

Will or Trust   Interest

_____   _____

_____   _____

3. Interests in Pension, profit sharing, stock bonus or other retirement plan(s):

Name and Address   Description   Beneficiary
of Plan

_____   _____   _____

_____   _____   _____

_____   _____   _____

F. MISCELLANEOUS BUSINESS INTERESTS

Description   Location

_____   _____

_____   _____

_____   _____

_____   _____

(Document continued on next page)

LIABILITIES

Debts, including mortgages, credit card obligations, loans against life insurance, obligations under divorce agreements:

Total Amount of Debt	Monthly Payment	Lender
$_____	$_____	_____
$_____	$_____	_____
$_____	$_____	_____
$_____	$_____	_____
$_____	$_____	_____
$_____	$_____	_____
$_____	$_____	_____

MISCELLANEOUS INFORMATION

Name and Address of Physician: _____

_____

Name and Address of Dentist: _____

_____

Name and Address of Attorney: _____

_____

Name and Address of Accountant: _____

_____

(Document continued on next page)

5. Credit Cards Held:

Credit Card	Account No.	Line of Credit
_____	_____	_____
_____	_____	_____
_____	_____	_____
_____	_____	_____
_____	_____	_____

6. Gifts and Transfers (over $10,000) During Lifetime:

Name of Recipient	Amount of Gift	Date of Gift
_____	$_____	_____
_____	$_____	_____
_____	$_____	_____
_____	$_____	_____
_____	$_____	_____
_____	$_____	_____

WILL

Names and addresses of Executors	Name and Address of Attorney
_____	_____
_____	_____
_____	

Special Instructions

_____

_____

Buying, Selling and Leasing Real Estate 2

Real estate is as old as the Earth itself and transactions relating to the land are almost as old. Real estate transactions are perhaps the most common of all transactions, since everyone has or will come in contact with real estate, whether as owner or renter.

Option to Purchase a Residence An Option is an agreement to sell real estate at some future time, at a price agreed upon in the present, if the buyer elects to do so by exercising the Option. These forms easily can be adapted for commercial transactions or even for unimproved land (land with no buildings on it).

Brokerage Agreements Every present and would-be home owner is likely to encounter a real estate broker and his brokerage agreement. These forms set forth the most commonly used types of agreements and explain the important distinctions between them.

Buying and Selling Real Estate The most significant financial transaction in most people's lives is the purchase or sale of a home. These forms provide a basic contract and a menu of common provisions that can be added to the basic contract and can serve as a checklist of issues to consider when buying or selling a home.

Mortgages A mortgage is security for a loan made by a lender to a borrower to enable the borrower to purchase real estate. The mortgage and associated forms will help the borrower or lender understand the provisions that are typically included in such documents.

Leases An alternative to owning real estate outright is to "borrow" the use of it for a period of time and for an agreed upon price—to lease. This section presents forms for both residential and commercial leases and for the transactions associated with leases, such as applications, renewals and sub-leases.

OPTION TO PURCHASE REAL ESTATE (2-01)

An Option to Purchase Real Estate is a contract in which the owner of real estate (the OPTIONOR) gives to another (the OPTIONEE) the exclusive right for a specified period of time to purchase the property on the terms agreed upon. In a Contract of Sale, both the seller and the buyer are bound. In an Option, the owner of the property (as proposed seller and OPTIONOR) cannot normally revoke the Option and is bound to sell the property as agreed. On the other hand, the holder of the Option (the OPTIONEE) can elect to purchase or not.

OPTION TO PURCHASE REAL ESTATE

1. The date of the Option.

OPTION to purchase granted _____[1]_____,19__, by _____[2]_____ (hereinafter, the "OPTIONOR") to _____[3]_____ (hereinafter, the "OPTIONEE").

2. The name of the owner of the property giving the Option (the OPTIONOR).

3. The name of the person purchasing the Option (the OPTIONEE).

1. THE PARTIES

1.1   OPTIONOR _____[4]_____.

4. If the OPTIONOR is an individual, identify by inserting the words "residing at _____" and fill in the address. If the OPTIONOR is a corporation, insert the words "a corporation formed and existing under the laws of the State of _____ and maintains its principal office at _____" and fill in the state in which incorporated and the address of the corporation.

(a) OPTIONOR is the owner of certain real property improved by a building located at _____[5]_____ (the "Property") and more particularly described in Schedule A attached.

(b)   OPTIONOR is desirous of granting to OPTIONEE an Option to purchase the Property.

5. A short description of the property such as the street address. In addition, it is recommended that on a separate sheet, headed "Schedule A," the so-called "metes and bounds" be set forth that describe the property by feet and compass direction—which is the best description of the property. This description is typically found in the property's original deed. The information should be copied from that deed EXACTLY.

(Document continued on next page)

6. If the OPTIONEE is an individual, insert the words "residing at _____" and fill in the address. If the OPTIONEE is a corporation, insert the words "a corporation formed and existing under the laws of the State of _____ and maintains its principal office at _____" and fill in the state in which incorporated and the address of the corporation.

7. The dollar amount, in words and in numbers, being paid for the Option. Note that this is for the purchase of the Option itself, not for the purchase of the property.

8. The time of day at which the Option expires, for example: 12 Noon, 5:00 P.M. or the like.

9. The date on which the Option expires.

10. Insert the method of exercising the Option. The example given is for exercise by mailing, which is the recommended method as it provides a means of getting a delivery receipt via Certified Mail—Return Receipt Requested.

11. The recommended procedure is for a complete proposed contract to be annexed to the Option with each page of the proposed contract initialled (but not signed) by the parties. If so, insert the words "as annexed." If the complete form cannot be attached, the terms of the purchase agreement should be stated as completely as possible.

1.2   OPTIONEE _____[6]_____.

(a)   OPTIONEE is desirous of purchasing from OPTIONOR an Option to purchase the Property.

2.   GRANT OF OPTION

2.1   OPTIONOR, in consideration of the payment of the sum of _____[7]_____ Dollars ($____[7]____) (the "Option Price"), the receipt of which is hereby acknowledged, grants to the OPTIONEE, the exclusive Option to purchase the Property.

3.   OPTION PERIOD AND EXERCISE OF OPTION

3.1   This Option, if not exercised in accordance with the terms and conditions, shall expire and terminate at ____[8]____ on _____[9]_____.

3.2   *[10][This Option may be exercised at any time during the option period and prior to the expiration of this Option only as follows: by giving written notice of exercise of the Option sent by certified or registered mail, return receipt requested, sent to OPTIONOR at the address set forth above (or such other address as OPTIONOR may have previously in writing designated).]*

4.   CONTRACT OF SALE/TERMS OF PURCHASE

4.1   The contract of sale to be entered into by the parties shall be _____[11]_____.

5.   FAILURE TO EXERCISE OPTION

5.1   If OPTIONEE shall fail to exercise this Option either in strict accord with the terms and conditions contained herein or within the time provided herein, the consideration paid for this Option shall be retained by OPTIONOR and neither party shall have any further rights or claims against the other by reason of this Option.

6.   BROKER

6.1   OPTIONOR and OPTIONEE each represent to the other that such party has not dealt with any broker or person or entity acting on behalf of any broker *other than*

(Document continued on next page)

12. The name of the real estate broker involved who brought the parties together or who assisted either party. If there is no broker involved, delete "other than" through the remainder of the sentence, delete all of paragraph 6.2, renumber paragraph 6.3 as 6.2, and skip to No. 14.

13. The party who will be paying the broker.

14. If the right to purchase the property may not be assigned by OPTIONEE to another, insert "not" and delete the space after "OPTIONEE."

15. If the OPTIONEE has only a limited right to assign, insert any limitations after "OP-TIONEE."

16. The name of the OPTIONOR if a corporation. Otherwise delete the line.

17. If the OPTIONOR is an individual, delete "BY" and print the OPTIONOR's name directly below the line, with the OPTIONOR to sign above the line. If the OPTIONOR is a corporation, print the name and title of the individual acting for the corporation directly below the line, with that person to sign above the line.

18. The name of the OPTIONEE if a corporation. Otherwise delete the line.

19. If the OPTIONEE is an individual, delete "BY" and print the OPTIONEE's name directly below the line, with the OPTIONEE to sign above the line. If the OPTIONEE is a corporation, print the name and title of the individual acting for the corporation directly below the line, with that person to sign above the line.

_____[12]_____ *in connection with this transaction.*

6.2 _____[13]_____ *shall pay the commission of such broker pursuant to a separate agreement. The broker shall not be deemed a third-party beneficiary of this provision.*

6.3   This Section 6 shall survive the closing.

7.   ASSIGNMENT

7.1   The Option granted herein may *[14]* be assigned by the OPTIONEE _____[15]_____.

IN WITNESS WHEREOF, the parties have signed this agreement as of the date first above written.

_____[16]_____

BY_____
[17]

_____[18]_____

BY_____
[19]

NOTICE OF EXERCISE OF OPTION
TO PURCHASE REAL ESTATE (2-02)

An Option Agreement will typically state the method for exercising the Option which must be followed exactly. The holder of the Option (the OPTIONEE) who ignores the specific terms of the Option does so at his peril since a possible result may be that the OPTIONOR will refuse to recognize the exercise of the Option. Even if not specifically required, it is recommended that Notice of Exercise of Option be in writing.

Note: this form assumes that the proposed Contract of Sale will have been attached to the Option Agreement and is complete in all of its terms. If so, it can and should be signed by the OPTIONEE and returned together with the Notice of Exercise.

NOTICE OF EXERCISE OF OPTION
TO PURCHASE REAL ESTATE

1. The name and address of the OPTIONOR (the owner of the property giving the Option).

_____ [1]_____
_____
_____

2. The date of the Option Agreement.

3. A brief description of the property such as the street address.

This will confirm that the undersigned, as OPTIONEE of the Option Agreement made by you as OPTIONOR dated _____[2]_____ for the purchase of the property located at _____[3]_____, hereby elects to exercise the Option to purchase.

4. Delete if the terms of the contract do not provide for the payment of a deposit (sometimes referred to as "earnest money") upon delivery of the contract to the OPTIONOR.

Two (2) copies of the form of Contract of Sale as signed by the OPTIONEE are enclosed *[4][together with a check in the form payable and in the amount specified in the Contract of Sale]*.

5. The time of day for the closing.

Please sign and return one (1) copy of the Contract of Sale to the undersigned.

6. The date for the closing.

7. The location for the closing.

Further, the undersigned designates __[5]__, on _____[6]_____ at _____[7]_____ for the closing of the purchase in accordance with the terms and conditions stated in the Option Agreement.

8. The date of signing the Notice of Exercise.

Dated: _____[8]_____

9. The name of the OPTIONEE if a corporation. Otherwise delete the line.

_____[9]_____

10. If the OPTIONEE is an individual, delete "BY" and print the OPTIONEE's name directly below the line, with the OPTIONEE to sign above the line. If the OPTIONEE is a corporation, print the name and title of the individual acting for the corporation directly below the line, with that person to sign above the line.

*BY*_____
[10]

EXTENSION OF OPTION TO PURCHASE REAL ESTATE (2-03)

An Extension of Option to Purchase Real Estate is a contract in which the owner (OPTIONOR) agrees with another (OPTIONEE) to extend a previously agreed upon right to purchase the property for an additional specified period of time.

EXTENSION OF OPTION TO PURCHASE REAL ESTATE

1. The date of the Extension.

2. The name of the owner of the property giving the Extension (the OPTIONOR).

3. The name of the person receiving the Extension (the OPTIONEE).

4. If the OPTIONOR is an individual, insert the words "residing at _____" and fill in the address. If the OPTIONOR is a corporation, insert the words "a corporation formed and existing under the laws of the State of _____ and maintains its principal office at _____" and fill in the state in which incorporated and the address of the corporation.

5. If the OPTIONEE is an individual, insert the words "residing at _____" and fill in the address. If the OPTIONEE is a corporation, insert the words "a corporation formed and existing under the laws of the State of _____ and maintains its principal office at _____" and fill in the state in which incorporated and the address of the corporation.

6. A short description of the property such as the street address.

7. The expiration date of the Option.

8. The dollar amount, in words and numbers, being paid for the Extension.

OPTION EXTENSION AGREEMENT made _____[1]_____, 19__, by _____[2]_____ (hereinafter, the "OPTIONOR") and _____[3]_____ (hereinafter, the "OPTIONEE").

1. THE PARTIES AND THE OPTION

    1.1   OPTIONOR _____[4]_____.

    1.2   OPTIONEE _____[5]_____.

    1.3   The parties acknowledge that OPTIONOR, as the owner of real property located at _____[6]_____ (the "Property"), for consideration the receipt of which is acknowledged, has given to OPTIONEE an Option to purchase the Property which expires on _____[7]_____.

2. EXTENSION OF OPTION

    2.1   In consideration of the payment to OPTIONOR by OPTIONEE of the sum of _____[8]_____ Dollars ($____[8]____) simultaneously with the signing of this Agreement, the receipt of which is acknowledged, the Option will be

(Document continued on next page)

9.   The time of day at which the extended Option will expire, for example: 12 Noon, 5:00 P.M. or the like.

10.   The date on which the extended Option will expire. Note: if the parties do not agree to additional extensions, paragraphs 2.2 and 2.3 should be deleted, and 2.4 and 2.5 should be renumbered 2.2 and 2.3 respectively, then skip to No. 21.

11.   The dollar amount, in words and numbers, being paid for any additional extension.

12.   The time of day at which the payment for any additional extension must be delivered.

13.   The date on which the payment for any additional extension must be delivered.

14.   The time of day at which the additional extended Option will expire.

15.   The date on which the additional extended Option will expire.

16.   The dollar amount, in words and numbers, being paid for any further additional extension.

17.   The time of day at which the payment for any further additional extension must be delivered.

18.   The date on which the payment for any further additional extension must be delivered.

19.   The time of day at which the further additional extended Option will expire.

20.   The date on which the further additional extended Option will expire.

extended and terminate and expire at __[9]__ on _____[10]_____.

     2.2   Upon payment to OPTIONOR by OPTIONEE of an additional sum of _____[11]_____ Dollars ($____[11]____) not later than __[12]__ on _____[13]_____, the Option will be further extended and then terminate and expire at __[14]__ on _____[15]_____.

     2.3   Upon payment to OPTIONOR by OPTIONEE of an additional sum of _____[16]_____ Dollars ($____[16]____) not later than __[17]__ on _____[18]_____, the Option will be further extended and then terminate and expire at __[19]__ on _____[20]_____.

     2.4   The Option shall terminate and expire at the time and date of the extension period for which OPTIONEE has made payment.

     2.5   Any extension of the Option upon payments as set forth in the paragraph shall be an extension of the expiration of the Option only and all other terms and conditions in the Option shall remain in force and effect.

(Document continued on next page)

21. If the OPTIONEE (pur-chaser) will be given a credit at the closing of the sale for the Option and extension pay-ments, delete both blanks. Otherwise insert "not" in both places.

22. The name of the OP-TIONOR if a corporation. Oth-erwise delete the line.

23. If the OPTIONOR is an individual, delete "BY" and print the OPTIONOR's name directly below the line, with the OP-TIONEE to sign above the line. If the OPTIONOR is a corpora-tion, print the name and title of the individual acting for the corporation directly below the line, with that person to sign above the line.

24. The name of the OP-TIONEE if a corporation. Oth-erwise delete the line.

25. If the OPTIONEE is an individual, delete "BY" and print the OPTIONEE's name directly below the line, with the OP-TIONEE to sign above the line. If the OPTIONEE is a corpora-tion, print the name and tile of the individual acting for the corporation directly below the line, with that person to sign above the line.

3.   PURCHASE PRICE

3.1   The payment for the Option and any payments for extension of the expiration of the Option shall _[21]_ be applied towards the purchase price of the Property and OPTIONEE shall _[21]_ receive a credit at the closing equal to the amount(s) paid for the Option and any extension.

IN WITNESS WHEREOF, the parties have signed this agreement as of the date first above written.

_____[22]_____

BY_____
                [23]

_____[24]_____

BY_____
                [25]

ASSIGNMENT OF OPTION TO PURCHASE REAL ESTATE (2-04)

An Assignment of an Option to Purchase Real Estate is a contract in which the holder of the Option (the OPTIONEE) agrees as ASSIGNOR with another (the ASSIGNEE) to assign his Option so that the ASSIGNEE would have the right to purchase the property on the same terms and conditions as the OPTIONEE. In short, the ASIGNEE would "stand in the shoes" of the OPTIONEE.

ASSIGNMENT OF OPTION TO PURCHASE REAL ESTATE

1. The date of signing the Assignment of the Option.

2. The name of the holder of the Option (referred to in the original Option agreement as OPTIONEE and now known as the ASSIGNOR) who is selling his rights to the Option.

3. The name of the person receiving the Assignment of the Option (the ASSIGNEE).

4. If the ASSIGNOR is an individual, insert the words "residing at _____" and fill in the address. If the ASSIGNOR is a corporation, insert the words "a corporation formed and existing under the laws of the State of _____ and maintains its principal office at _____" and fill in the state in which incorporated and the address of the corporation.

5. If the ASSIGNEE is an individual, insert the words "residing at _____" and fill in the address. If the ASSIGNEE is a corporation, insert the words "a corporation formed and existing under the laws of the State of _____ and maintains its principal office at _____" and fill in the state in which incorporated and the address of the corporation.

6. A short description of the property such as the street address.

ASSIGNMENT OF OPTION made _____[1]_____, 19__, by _____[2]_____ (the "ASSIGNOR") and _____[3]_____ (the "ASSIGNEE").

1.   THE PARTIES

1.1   ASSIGNOR _____[4]_____.

1.2   ASSIGNEE _____[5]_____.

1.3   The parties acknowledge that ASSIGNOR is the holder of an Option to purchase real property located at _____[6]_____ (the "Property") which

(Document continued on next page)

7. The time of day at which the Option will expire, for example: 12 Noon, 5:00 P.M. or the like.

8. The expiration date of the Option.

9. The dollar amount, in words and numbers, being paid for the Assignment of the Option.

10. The name of the AS-SIGNOR if a corporation. Otherwise delete the line.

11. If the ASSIGNOR is an individual, delete "BY" and print the ASSIGNOR's name directly below the line, with that person to sign above the line. If the ASSIGNOR is a corporation, print the name and title of the individual acting for the corporation directly below the line, with that person to sign above the line.

12. The name of the AS-SIGNEE if a corporation. Otherwise delete the line.

13. If the ASSIGNEE is an individual, delete "BY" and print the ASSIGNEE's name directly below the line, with that person to sign above the line. If the ASSIGNEE is a corporation, print the name and title of the individual acting for the corporation directly below the line, with that person to sign above the line.

expires at ___[7]___ on _____[8]_____ (the "Option"), a copy of which is annexed.

1.4   ASSIGNOR as OPTIONEE of the Option represents to ASSIGNEE that the Option has not expired and that it is assignable.

2.   ASSIGNMENT OF OPTION

2.1   In consideration of the sum of _____[9]_____ Dollars ($____[9]____) paid by ASSIGNEE to ASSIGNOR, the receipt of which is acknowledged, ASSIGNOR assigns to ASSIGNEE all of ASSIGNOR's right, title and interest in and to the Option.

IN WITNESS WHEREOF, the parties have signed this agreement as of the date first above written.

_____*[10]*_____

*BY*_____
[11]

_____*[12]*_____

*BY*_____
[13]

INTRODUCTION TO
REAL ESTATE BROKERAGE AGREEMENTS

An OWNER wishing to sell his real estate may try to sell the PROPERTY himself by placing a "for sale" sign on the PROPERTY or by placing his own advertisement in the newspaper. The more likely scenario is that the owner will use a real estate broker. The BROKER will probably ask that the OWNER sign a commission agreement. Three of the most common types of Brokerage Agreements follow.

WARNINGS

Every state requires that real estate brokers be licensed and that any person seeking a commission for procuring or obtaining a buyer must be a licensed real estate broker. **Any use of this or the following real estate brokerage forms for any purpose other than providing information may violate the laws of your state.** The purpose of these forms is solely to educate the OWNER as to the most common forms of Brokerage Agreements so the OWNER will understand what he is agreeing to by signing a Brokerage Agreement. Neither the authors nor the publisher nor any seller of this work will assume responsibility or be liable for any use of these forms for other than informational purposes.

Brokers may use other forms or different language from that which is supplied here. Brokerage Agreements are negotiable. Discuss the terms of any Agreement *before* signing any document and if your BROKER refuses to accept your terms, talk to another BROKER.

Generally, the law states that unless a written Agreement provides otherwise, the BROKER is entitled to a commission when the BROKER has produced a buyer who is "ready, willing and able" to meet the OWNER's terms—even if the PROPERTY is not actually sold. Therefore, an Agreement should provide that the commission will be earned only after the real estate transaction has closed.

An important point that should be agreed to in advance is whether the OWNER who sells the PROPERTY on his own will be required to pay the entire commission or a portion of it to the BROKER. Although under any Brokerage Agreement, other than the "Exclusive Right to Sell" type of Agreement, the OWNER is permitted to sell the PROPERTY on his own without paying the commission, most BROKERS are reluctant to forgo a significant portion of that commission since money has been spent for advertising and marketing the property. This issue should be negotiated carefully between the OWNER and the BROKER prior to signing the Brokerage Agreement.

Negotiate and enter into a written Brokerage Agreement *before* the BROKER brings any prospective buyers.

"OPEN LISTING" REAL ESTATE
BROKERAGE AGREEMENT (2-05)

The most common type of Brokerage Agreement is the so-called "Open Listing" whereby the OWNER as the seller agrees to pay a brokerage commission to the BROKER only if the BROKER can demonstrate that he produced the buyer. The listing is "Open" in that the OWNER is free to list the PROPERTY with other brokers or sell the PROPERTY himself. If the Agreement does not state or imply "Exclusive" it is probably an "Open Listing."

WARNING

Every state requires that real estate brokers be licensed and that any person seeking a commission for procuring or obtaining a buyer must be a licensed real estate broker. **Any use of this or the following real estate brokerage forms for any purpose other than providing information may violate the laws of your state.** The purpose of this and the following forms is solely to educate the OWNER as to the most common forms of Brokerage Agreements so the OWNER will have knowledge as to what he is agreeing to by signing a Brokerage Agreement. Neither the authors nor the publisher nor any seller of this work will assume responsibility or be liable for any use of these forms for other than informational purposes.

"OPEN LISTING" REAL ESTATE
BROKERAGE AGREEMENT

1. The date of signing the Agreement.

2. The name of the OWNER of the PROPERTY.

3. The OWNER's address.

4. The name of the licensed real estate broker (BROKER).

5. The address of the BRO-KER.

6. The address of the PROP-ERTY to be sold.

7. The period of time the BROKER will have to procure a buyer (usually between three and six months, but may be shorter or longer).

8. A short statement of the terms the OWNER will accept, especially the price, but also terms such as whether the OWNER will take a purchase money mortgage or the like. (A purchase money mortgage means that the seller is willing to furnish the mortgage for the PROPERTY he is selling.)

AGREEMENT made _____[1]_____, between _____[2]_____ of _____[3]_____ ("OWNER"), and _____[4]_____ of _____[5]_____ ("BROKER").

1.   OWNER REPRESENTATION. OWNER represents that he is the owner in fee simple of the property located at _____[6]_____ (the "PROP-ERTY") and agrees to convey THE PROPERTY if it is sold to a person procured by BROKER on the terms and conditions set forth.

2.   EMPLOYMENT. OWNER grants to BROKER a non-exclusive agency to sell the PROPERTY for a period of _____[7]_____ from the date of this agreement.

3.   TERMS OF SALE.
_____[8]_____
_____.

(Document continued on next page)

9. The commission that the OWNER agrees to pay and the BROKER agrees to accept—usually set forth as a percentage of the purchase price but may be stated as a dollar amount.

10. The name of the BROKER.

11. The name of the individual acting for the BROKER printed directly below the line, with that person to sign above the line.

12. The name of the OWNER printed directly below the line, with the OWNER to sign above the line.

4.   COMMISSION. BROKER shall be entitled to a commission of __[9]__ percent of the purchase price if BROKER procures a purchaser for THE PROPERTY upon the terms stated, which commission shall be earned, and payable out of the purchase price, when, as, and if and in the event title shall actually close.

IN WITNESS WHEREOF, the parties have signed this agreement as of the date first above written.

_____[10]_____

BY_____
                    [11]

_____
            [12]

"EXCLUSIVE AGENCY" REAL ESTATE
BROKERAGE AGREEMENT (2-06)

Under the "Exclusive Agency" type of Brokerage Agreement, the OWNER as seller agrees to pay a commission to a particular BROKER as the sole and exclusive agent of the OWNER. If the OWNER sells the PROPERTY, he must pay the agreed upon commission to this BROKER even if the buyer was procured by another BROKER. The only exception to this is if the OWNER sells the PROPERTY himself in which case the "Exclusive Agency" is terminated and the OWNER is not liable for the BROKER's commission.

The key language to look for in this type of Brokerage Agreement is "Exclusive Agency."

WARNING

Every state requires that real estate brokers be licensed and that any person seeking a commission for procuring or obtaining a buyer must be a licensed real estate broker. **Any use of this or the preceding or following forms for any purpose other than providing information may violate the laws of your state.** The purpose of these forms is solely to educate the OWNER as to the most common forms of Brokerage Agreements so the OWNER will have knowledge as to what he is agreeing to by signing a Brokerage Agreement. Neither the authors nor the publisher nor any seller of this work will assume responsibility or be liable for any use of these forms for other than informational purposes.

"EXCLUSIVE AGENCY" REAL ESTATE
BROKERAGE AGREEMENT

1. The date of the Agreement.

2. The name of the OWNER of the PROPERTY.

3. The OWNER's address.

4. The name of the licensed real estate broker (BROKER).

5. The address of the BROKER.

6. The address of the PROPERTY to be sold.

7. The period of time the BROKER will have to procure a buyer (usually between three and six months, but may be shorter or longer).

AGREEMENT made _____[1]_____, between _____[2]_____ of _____[3]_____ ("OWNER"), and _____[4]_____ of _____[5]_____ ("BROKER").

1.   OWNER REPRESENTATION. OWNER represents that he is the owner in fee simple of the property located at _____[6]_____ (the "PROPERTY") and agrees to convey the PROPERTY if it is sold to a person procured by BROKER on the terms and conditions set forth.

2.   EMPLOYMENT. OWNER grants to BROKER an exclusive agency to sell the PROPERTY for a period of _____[7]_____ from the date of this agreement.

(Document continued on next page)

8. A short statement of the terms the OWNER will accept, especially the price, but also terms such as whether the OWNER will take a purchase money mortgage or the like. (A purchase money mortgage means that the seller is willing to furnish the mortgage for the PROPERTY he is selling.)

9. The commission that the OWNER agrees to pay and the BROKER agrees to accept—usually set forth as a percentage of the purchase price but may be stated as a dollar amount.

10. The name of the BRO-KER.

11. The name of the individual acting for the BROKER printed directly below the line, with that person to sign above the line.

12. The name of the OWNER printed directly below the line, with the OWNER to sign above the line.

3.　　TERMS OF SALE.

_____[8]_____

_____.

4.　　COMMISSION. BROKER shall be entitled to a commission of __[9]__ percent of the purchase price if BROKER procures a purchaser for THE PROPERTY upon the terms stated, which commission shall be earned, and payable out of the purchase price, when, as, and if and in the event title shall actually close.

IN WITNESS WHEREOF, the parties have signed this agreement as of the date first above written.

_____[10]_____

BY_____
　　　　　[11]

_____
　　　　　[12]

"EXCLUSIVE RIGHT TO SELL" REAL ESTATE
BROKERAGE AGREEMENT (2-07)

Under the "Exclusive Right to Sell" type of Brokerage Agreement, the OWNER agrees to pay a commission to one particular BROKER if the PROPERTY is sold—regardless of who procured the buyer (even if the OWNER has sold the PROPERTY himself).

For this reason, the "Exclusive Right to Sell" Brokerage Agreement typically provides that the BROKER is entitled to a commission even if the PROPERTY is taken off the market during the term of the Agreement. This form of Agreement also typically provides that the BROKER is entitled to his commission even if the PROPERTY was sold after the expiration of the Agreement to a buyer the BROKER procured during the term of the Agreement. This effectively prohibits the OWNER from defeating the BROKER by taking the PROPERTY off the market or refusing other offers until after the expiration of the contract and then selling to another party, since the BROKER will still be entitled to his commission.

The key language to look for in this type of Brokerage Agreement is "Exclusive Right to Sell," "Sole Right to Sell" and references to a prohibition from removing the PROPERTY from the market.

WARNING

Every state requires that real estate brokers be licensed and that any person seeking a commission for procuring or obtaining a buyer must be a licensed real estate broker. **Any use of this or the preceding forms for any purpose other than providing information may violate the laws of your state.** The purpose of these forms is solely to educate the OWNER as to the most common forms of Brokerage Agreements so the OWNER will have knowledge as to what he is agreeing to by signing a Brokerage Agreement. Neither the authors nor the publisher nor any seller of this work will assume responsibility or be liable for any use of these forms for other than informational purposes.

"EXCLUSIVE RIGHT TO SELL" REAL ESTATE
BROKERAGE AGREEMENT

1. The date of the Agreement.

2. The name of the OWNER of the PROPERTY.

3. The OWNER's address.

4. The name of the licensed real estate broker (BROKER).

5. The address of the BROKER.

6. The address of the PROPERTY to be sold.

AGREEMENT made _____[1]_____, between _____[2]_____ of _____[3]_____ ("OWNER"), and _____[4]_____ of _____[5]_____ ("BROKER").

1.   OWNER REPRESENTATION. OWNER represents that he is the owner in fee simple of the property located at _____[6]_____ (the "PROPERTY").

2.   EMPLOYMENT. OWNER grants to BROKER the sole and exclusive right to offer for sale or

(Document continued on next page)

7. The period of time the BROKER will have to procure a buyer (usually between three and six months, but may be shorter or longer).

8. A short statement of the terms the OWNER will accept, especially the price, but also terms such as whether the OWNER will take a purchase money mortgage or the like. (A purchase money mortgage means that the seller is willing to furnish the mortgage for the PROPERTY he is selling.)

9. The commission that the OWNER agrees to pay and the BROKER agrees to accept— usually set forth as a percentage of the purchase price but may be stated as a dollar amount.

10. The name of the BROKER.

11. The name of the individual acting for the BROKER printed directly below the line, with that person to sign above the line.

12. The name of the OWNER printed directly below the line, with the OWNER to sign above the line.

sell the PROPERTY for a period of _____[7]_____ from the date of this agreement.

3.   TERMS OF SALE.
_____[8]_____
_____.

4.   COMMISSION. BROKER shall be entitled to a commission of __[9]__ percent of the purchase price if BROKER procures a purchaser for THE PROPERTY upon the terms stated, which commission shall be earned, and payable out of the purchase price, when, as, and if and in the event title shall actually close.

5.   WITHDRAWAL OF PROPERTY/SALE AFTER TERMINATION. If, during the term of the agreement, OWNER shall remove or withdraw the PROPERTY from the market or otherwise prevent or interfere with BROKER from selling the PROPERTY, BROKER shall nevertheless be entitled to the commission at the rate set forth herein. If, after termination of this agreement, the PROPERTY shall be sold to or on behalf of a buyer initially procured by BROKER, BROKER shall nevertheless be entitled to the commission at the rate set forth herein.

IN WITNESS WHEREOF, the parties have signed this agreement as of the date first above written.

_____[10]_____

BY_____
[11]

_____
[12]

OFFER TO PURCHASE REAL ESTATE (2-08)

An Offer to Purchase Real Estate is just that—an offer. It is not binding on either the buyer (PURCHASER) or the SELLER until signed by the SELLER. It may be revoked in writing by the PURCHASER at any time before the Seller signs the form. However, on signing an Offer to Purchase, the PURCHASER has immediately obligated himself to the terms of the Offer. The PURCHASER does not pay any money until the Offer is accepted.

WARNING

This form is recommended only for very simple real estate transactions in which all of the essential terms of the agreement can be spelled out. For more complex transactions, it is recommended that the "Offer" be made in the form of a full Contract of Sale, which follows, containing all terms and conditions.

OFFER TO PURCHASE REAL ESTATE

1. The name of the PUR-CHASER. If the PURCHASER is an individual, add the words "residing at _____" and fill in the address. If the PURCHASER is a corporation, add the words "a corporation formed and existing under the laws of the State of _____ and maintains its principal office at _____" and fill in the state in which incorporated and the address of the corporation.

2. The name of the SELLER. If the SELLER is an individual, add the words "residing at _____" and fill in the address. If the SELLER is a corporation, add the words "a corporation formed and existing under the laws of the State of _____ and maintains its principal office at _____" and fill in the state in which incorporated and the address of the corporation.

_____[1]_____ ("PURCHASER") offers to purchase from _____[2]_____ ("SELLER") the real

(Document continued on next page)

3. A short description of the property such as the street address. In addition, it is recommended that on a separate sheet, headed "Schedule A", the so-called "metes and bounds" be set forth that describe the property by feet and compass direction— which is the best description of the property. This description is typically found in the property's original deed. The information should be copied from that deed EXACTLY.

4. The dollar amount, in words and numbers, being offered for the property.

5. The dollar amount, in words and numbers, of the down payment.

6. The dollar amount, in words and numbers, representing the balance of the purchase price. (Note: make certain that the amount of the down payment and the amount of the balance equal the total amount being offered.)

property located at _____[3]_____ and which is more fully described in Schedule A attached, together with all rights, privileges, easements and all improvements, buildings and fixtures in their present condition as are now on or attached to the property (collectively, the "PROPERTY") on the following terms:

1. PURCHASE PRICE - PURCHASER agrees to pay to SELLER for the PROPERTY the sum of _____[4]_____ Dollars ($____[4]____) as follows:

    (a) down payment (earnest money) in the amount of _____[5]_____ Dollars ($____[5]____) to be paid in accordance with the terms of this offer and to be deposited in escrow to a special or trust account and

    (b) the balance of _____[6]_____ Dollars ($____[6]____) to be paid at the closing of title in cash, bank check or certified check to the order of the SELLER.

2. TITLE - SELLER shall give a warranty deed conveying such title as a reputable title insurance company would insure, free and clear of liens or encumbrances and with rights of dower, if any, released except:

    (a) Restrictions of record and easements, reservations, conditions and laws and governmental regulations affecting the use and maintenance of the PROPERTY, provided they are not violated by any improvements on or to the PROPERTY,

    (b) zoning ordinances, if any,

    (c) encroachments or projections, if any, of record,

    (d) taxes and assessments not yet due and payable.

3. APPORTIONMENTS - The following shall be apportioned as of midnight of the day before the closing: rents as and when collected; interest on existing mortgages; premiums on insurance policies if transferred; taxes, water charges and sewer rents, fuel oil or gas.

4. POSSESSION - SELLER shall deliver possession of the PROPERTY to the PURCHASER on the date of the closing. If the PROPERTY or any part is damaged or destroyed before the closing, PURCHASER shall have the

(Document continued on next page)

7. The name and address of the Escrow Agent.

8. The time of day of the closing, for example: 12 Noon, 5:00 P.M. or the like.

9. The date of the closing.

10. The address of the closing.

11. The time of day at which the Offer expires.

12. The date on which the Offer expires.

right either (a) to receive any insurance proceeds or (b) to cancel and revoke this Offer and to the return of all money previously paid or deposited.

5.   ESCROW AND CLOSING - The down payment shall be deposited with and held in escrow by _____[7]_____ within five (5) days of receipt of this Offer as accepted by SELLER. The closing will take place at ___[8]___ on _____[9]_____ at _____[10]_____ at which time PURCHASER shall pay the balance of the purchase price and SELLER shall present the deed in recordable form, all keys and any occupancy permits required by law.

6.   DEFAULT - The parties agree that if PURCHASER shall default in paying the balance due at the closing, SELLER shall be entitled to retain the down payment as liquidated damages and if SELLER shall default, PURCHASER shall be entitled to specific performance by SELLER.

6.   ACCEPTANCE - PURCHASER may IN WRITING revoke this Offer at any time prior to its acceptance. Unless an accepted copy of this Offer is delivered to PURCHASER on or before __[11]__ on _____[12]_____ this Offer will expire and neither party will have any obligation to the other. Upon acceptance and payment of the down payment by PURCHASER, this Offer will become a binding agreement containing all material terms and conditions necessary and

(Document continued on next page)

OFFER TO PURCHASE REAL ESTATE *continued*

13. The name of the PURCHASER if a corporation. Otherwise delete the line.

14. If the PURCHASER is an individual, delete "BY" and print the PURCHASER's name directly below the line, with the PURCHASER to sign above the line. If the PURCHASER is a corporation, print the name and title of the individual acting for the corporation directly below the line, with that person to sign above the line.

15. The PURCHASER's address and telephone number.

16. The name of the SELLER.

17. The name of the SELLER if a corporation. Otherwise delete the line.

18. If the SELLER is an individual, delete "BY" and print the SELLER's name directly below the line, with the SELLER to sign above the line. If the SELLER is a corporation, print the name and title of the individual acting for the corporation directly below the line, with that person to sign above the line.

there being no additional conditions, representations, warranties or the like, either written or oral.

_____[13]_____

BY_____
[14]

Address: _____[15]_____

_____[15]_____

Telephone Number: _____[15]_____

ACCEPTANCE OF OFFER

_____[16]_____ ("SELLER") acknowledges that he is the owner of the PROPERTY, consents to the deposit of the down payment in escrow with _____[7]_____ and accepts the Offer to purchase the PROPERTY on the terms and conditions of this Offer.

_____[17]_____

BY_____
[18]

CONTRACT FOR SALE OF RESIDENCE (2-09)

This form contains the basic terms of a Contract for Sale of Residence. It is complete as it exists; however it is suggested that you carefully examine each contract clause that follows in this chapter and include those that are appropriate to your transaction.

WARNINGS

The use of several methods of identifying the property to be sold is very important, even though it may seem redundant. It is vital that the property be identified precisely and without ambiguity or confusion so that the Seller is selling neither more nor less than he intends to sell and so that the Buyer knows exactly what he is buying. For this reason, the authors strongly urge the use of several methods of identifying the property as indicated in this form.

Further, the authors strongly urge that the Seller carefully examine his deed (the document the Seller received when he purchased the property) and use exactly the same property description as the deed contains.

The authors also strongly urge that the Seller give only the same type of deed as the Seller himself received (see Instruction No. 30 below).

CONTRACT FOR SALE OF RESIDENCE

1. The date of signing the agreement.

2. The name of the Seller.

3. The address of the Seller.

4. The name of the Buyer.

5. The address of the Buyer.

6. Delete if the sale is for land only.

7. The city in which the property is located.

8. The county in which the property is located.

9. The state in which the property is located.

Note: the information for Nos. 10 through 20 is typically found on the Seller's deed or the tax map of the property located in the office of the local tax authority.

10. Delete through No. 15 if your locale does not use a "block and lot" system of identifying property.

WARNING: NO REPRESENTATION IS MADE THAT THIS CONTRACT FOR THE SALE AND PURCHASE OF REAL PROPERTY COMPLIES WITH THE SO-CALLED "PLAIN ENGLISH" LAWS OF THIS STATE

CONTRACT OF SALE made _____[1]_____, between _____[2]_____, _____[3]_____ ("Seller"), and _____[4]_____, _____[5]_____ ("Buyer").

1. AGREEMENT - Seller agrees to sell and Buyer agrees to purchase the real property *[6][including all buildings and improvements on and to said property]* located in the City of _____[7]_____, County of _____[8]_____, State of _____[9]_____, *[10][identified on the Tax Map of*

(Document continued on next page)

11. The name of the town, county or district where the tax map referred to is filed.

12. Identify the specific tax map by the date it was filed.

13. The Section in which the property being sold is located.

14. The Block in which the property being sold is located.

15. The Lot(s) being sold.

16. The address of the property.

17. The title of the city, county, district or state office responsible for recording deeds.

18. Choose one (see No. 19 for explanations).

19. The number of the "Liber" (book) or "Reel" (microfilm) where the Seller's deed was actually recorded.

20. The page number of the Liber or Reel where the Seller's deed was actually recorded.

21. Choose one, and on either a separate page headed "Schedule A" or after the words "beginning at a point" insert the legal description (the so-called "metes and bounds") of the property. Note: this is the best description of the property. It is typically found in the property's original deed. The information should be copied from that deed EXACTLY.

22. The purchase price, in words.

23. The purchase price, in numbers.

_____[11]_____, dated _____[12]_____ as Section ___[13]___, Block ___[14]___, Lot(s) ___[15]___], known by the street address _____[16]_____ and intended to be the same property conveyed to Seller by Deed recorded in the Office of _____[17]_____ at *[18][Liber]* **OR** *[Reel]* __[19]__, Page __[20]__, (the "Premises") and more particularly described *[21][on Schedule A annexed to and made part of this Contract]* **OR** *[as follows: beginning at a point* _____ _____ *]*

2. STREET RIGHTS - This sales includes all the right, title and interest, if any, of the Seller in and to any land lying in the bed of any street, or highway opened or proposed, in front of or adjoining the Premises, to the center line thereof. It also includes any right of the Seller to any unpaid award by reason of any taking by condemnation and/or for any damage to the Premises by reason of change of grade of any street or highway. The Seller will deliver, at no additional cost to the Buyer, at the closing, or after the closing, on demand, any document which Buyer may require to collect the award and damages.

3. PURCHASE PRICE - The purchase price is _____[22]_____ Dollars ($_____[23]_____) payable as follows:

(Document continued on next page)

24. The amount of the deposit, in numbers, due on signing the contract (which is negotiable, and customarily, though not necessarily, 10% of the purchase price).

25. Delete through No. 26 if the Seller is not assigning his present mortgage to the Buyer. Note: even if the parties are willing, such an assignment will probably require the written approval of the lender holding the Seller's mortgage.

26. The amount, in numbers, of the Seller's present mortgage being assigned by the Seller and assumed by the Buyer.

27. Delete through No. 28 if this sale is "all cash to the Seller"—that is, if the Seller will receive the entire sale price in cash at the closing. Note: a sale is "all cash to the Seller" even if the Seller must use part of the proceeds of the sale to satisfy or pay off the Seller's existing mortgage.

28. The amount, in numbers, of the purchase money mortgage the Buyer will pay. (A purchase money mortgage is a loan given by the Seller, as opposed to one given by a bank, to the Buyer to enable the Buyer to purchase the property. The loan is secured by a mortgage.)

29. The balance, in numbers, due and payable at the closing. Note that regardless of how the transaction is structured, the amounts inserted at No's 24, 26, 28 and 29 *must* equal the total purchase price inserted at No. 22.

By check on the signing of this contract, subject to collection, to be held in escrow $_____[24]_____

[25][By allowance for and subject to Seller's existing mortgage in principal amount remaining $_____[26]_____*]*

[27][By a purchase money mortgage and note given by Buyer as Mortgagor to Seller as Mortgagee $_____[28]_____*]*

Balance due and payable at closing $_____[29]_____

All money payable for other than the purchase price shall be paid by cash or personal check of Buyer not to exceed $500.00. All money payable toward the purchase price shall be paid by cash not to exceed $500.00, certified check of Buyer, or official check of any bank, savings bank, trust company, or savings and loan association having a banking office in the State of _____[9]_____, payable to the order of the Seller, or the order of the Buyer duly endorsed to the order of the Seller in the presence of the Seller.

4. VIOLATIONS - Seller shall comply with all notices of violations of law or municipal ordinances, order, or requirements noted in or issued by any governmental department having authority as to lands, housing, buildings, fire, health and labor conditions affecting the premises as of the date of this Contract, and the Premises shall be conveyed free of them. This provision shall survive closing. The Seller shall furnish Buyer with such authorization necessary to make any searches.

5. LIEN OF BUYER - All money paid on account of this contract and the reasonable expense of examination of the title to the Premises and of any survey and survey inspection charges are by this contract made liens on the Premises and are collectable out of the Premises. Any such lien shall not continue after default in performance of this contract by the Buyer.

6. BUYER'S CREDIT - Seller shall have the option to credit the Buyer, as an adjustment to the purchase price, with the amount of any unpaid taxes, assessments, water charges and sewer rents, together with any interest and pen-

(Document continued on next page)

30. The type of deed being given by the Seller, for example: "Quit Claim," "Bargain and Sale Deed without Covenants," "Bargain and Sale Deed with Covenants." Note that the Seller should give only the exact same type or form of deed that the Seller himself received when he purchased the property.

alties, to the closing date, if any official bills, computed to that date, are produced at closing. If there is anything else affecting the sale which is the obligation of Seller to pay or discharge at closing, Seller may use any part of the balance of the purchase price in payment or discharge. If the title insurance company engaged by Buyer will nevertheless insure title free and clear of such matter or insure the Premises against enforcement of such matter against the Premises, Seller shall also have the option to deposit money with the title insurance company engaged by Buyer to assure such payment or discharge. Upon request made within a reasonable time before closing, Buyer agrees to provide separate certified checks as may be requested by Seller to assist in clearing these matters.

7. DEFAULTS - If the Seller shall be unable to convey title in accordance with the terms of this contract, the sole liability of the Seller will be to refund to Buyer any amounts paid on account of this contract, including amounts expended or charges incurred for examination of title, searches, survey and survey inspections and the like made under this contract. Upon such refund and payment this contract shall be deemed cancelled, and neither Seller nor Buyer shall have any further rights against the other by reason of this contract.

If Buyer shall willfully default in the performance of any of the terms and conditions of this contract imposed upon Buyer, Buyer shall forfeit and Seller shall have, without limitation or exclusion of any other rights, the right to retain the entire deposit previously paid by Buyer upon signing of this contract as liquidated damages.

8. DEED - The deed shall be the usual _____[30]_____ deed in proper statutory form for recording. The deed shall be duly signed and acknowledged in such form as to convey to Buyer the Premises in fee simple, free and clear of

(Document continued on next page)

31. The location where the closing will be held.

32. The time of day of the closing.

33. The day, month and year scheduled for the closing.

any encumbrances except as may be permitted by this contract.

9. CLOSING - As used in this contract, the term "closing" means the settlement of the obligations of Seller and Buyer to each other under this contract. Closing includes the payment of the purchase price to the Seller and the delivery to the Purchaser of the deed.

If Seller is a corporation, Seller will deliver to Buyer at closing a resolution of its Board of Directors authorizing the sale and delivery of the deed, and a certificate of the Secretary or other authorized officer of the Seller certifying the resolution and stating the facts showing that the transfer is in conformity with the requirements of the laws of the state of incorporation of such corporation. The deed will contain a recital sufficient to establish compliance with such state law.

The closing will take place at
_____[31]_____, at ___[32]___, on
_____[33]_____.

10. TRANSFER AND RECORDING TAXES - Seller will deliver a certified check at the closing payable to the order of the appropriate State, City or County officer in the amount of any applicable transfer tax, recording tax, or both, payable by reason of the sale of the Premises, the delivery or recording of the deed, together with any required tax return. Buyer agrees to duly complete the tax return and to cause the check and the tax return to be delivered to the appropriate officer promptly after closing.

11. ENTIRE AGREEMENT - All prior understandings and agreements between Buyer and Seller are merged in this contract, which alone fully and completely expresses their agreement. This contract is entered into after full investigation, neither party relying upon any statement or representation, not set forth in this contract, made by anyone else.

12. MODIFICATION OF CONTRACT - This contract may not be changed or terminated except in writing.

13. BINDING EFFECT/BENEFIT - This contract shall also bind and be for the benefit of the heirs, executors, administrators, successors, distributees, and assigns of the respective parties.

(Document continued on next page)

34. The name of the Buyer if a corporation. Otherwise delete the line.

35. The name of the Witness to the signing of the contract printed below the line, with the Witness to sign above the line.

36. If the Buyer is an individual, delete "BY" and print the Buyer's name directly below the line, with the Buyer to sign above the line. If the Buyer is a corporation, print the name and title of the individual acting for the corporation directly below the line, with that person to sign above the line.

37. The name of the Seller if a corporation. Otherwise delete the line.

38. If the Seller is an individual, delete "BY" and print the Seller's name directly below the line, with the Seller to sign above the line. If the Seller is a corporation, print the name and title of the individual acting for the corporation directly below the line, with that person to sign above the line.

14. CONSTRUCTION - Any singular word or term in this contract shall also be read as in the plural whenever the sense of this contract may require. Any masculine terms in this contract shall also be read as in the feminine whenever the sense of this contract may require.

IN WITNESS WHEREOF, this contract has been duly executed by the parties on the date first written above.

Witness:

_____
[34]

_____   BY_____
[35]   [36]

_____
[37]

BY_____
[38]

INTRODUCTION TO CONTRACT CLAUSES
TO BE USED WITH
CONTRACT FOR SALE OF RESIDENCE

All of the following clauses may be incorporated into the preceding "Contract for Sale of Residence." They may be placed in any order the writer wishes and numbered accordingly. This section is intended to act as a check-list of common contract provisions. Reference to this section during negotiation for the sale of a house will help the Seller prepare a contract that contains all the necessary provisions.

CONTRACT CLAUSE—
PURCHASE MONEY MORTGAGE (2-10)

This clause should be included in the Contract for Sale of Residence if any part of the purchase price is to be paid by a loan from the Seller to the Buyer that will be secured by a Mortgage (a Purchase Money Mortgage).

CONTRACT CLAUSE—
PURCHASE MONEY MORTGAGE

1.   The number of this clause when inserted into the Contract for Sale of Residence.

2.   The principal amount, in words and numbers.

3.   The amount, in numbers, of each monthly installment.

4.   The rate of interest, in words and numbers.

5.   The term of the loan in years or months, in words.

6.   Choose one.

7.   Delete if the Buyer will not be permitted to prepay the Note.

8.   Insert any remaining terms. Otherwise delete.

9.   Identify the party that will have the responsibility of preparing the Note and Mortgage, typically the Seller.

10.   Delete if the Buyer will not pay for the title insurance.

[1] PURCHASE MONEY MORTGAGE - As a portion of the purchase price, Buyer, as Mortgagor, shall deliver at the closing to Seller, as Mortgagee, and Seller shall accept a Note secured by a Purchase Money Mortgage in the principal amount of _____[2]_____ Dollars ($_____). The Note shall be payable in monthly installments of $_____[3]_____ with interest on the remaining principal balance due at the rate of ___[4]___ percent (___%) per annum. Buyer, as Mortgagor, shall pay to Seller, as Mortgagee, at the closing a payment of interest only at said interest rate calculated on the entire principal amount for the period from and including the date of the closing to and including the last day of the month in which the closing shall have occurred. Payments of principal and interest shall commence on the 1st day of the second full month after the date of the closing and shall continue monthly until the maturity date on which date all remaining unpaid principal and all accrued interest shall be due and payable. The term of the Note and Mortgage shall be _____[5]____ [6][years.] **OR** [months.] [7][The Note shall permit the prepayment by the Buyer, as Mortgagor, at any time and without penalty.] [8][Additionally, the Note and Mortgage shall contain the following terms:

_____

_____

_____.]

_____[9]_____ shall prepare the Note and Mortgage which shall be in recordable form. Buyer agrees to reimburse Seller for the cost of Seller's reasonable attorneys' fees in preparing or reviewing such Note and Mortgage.

Seller shall have the right to obtain such credit, judgment and lien searches and reports as he shall see fit and Buyer agrees to pay all costs of obtaining any searches or reports. Buyer also agrees to sign and deliver to Seller or others that Seller may designate, such forms of consent or authorization as may be required. Buyer agrees at the closing to pay all mortgage and mortgage recording taxes, fees and charges *[10][and the cost of mortgagee title insurance]*.

CONTRACT CLAUSE—
DEFERRED PAYMENTS
SECURED BY RENTAL PAYMENTS (2-11)

This clause should be inserted into the Contract for Sale of Residence if any portion of the purchase price is to be paid by or secured by rental payments by the Buyer. This arrangement differs from a purchase money mortgage in which the Seller furnishes the mortgage to the Buyer. With a purchase money mortgage, the buyer receives title at the closing and becomes the legal owner of the property, making mortgage payments to the Seller. In the Deferred Payments situation, the Buyer takes possession, but not title, at the closing and the deed is held in escrow by the Seller (and not recorded) until the Buyer has paid in full.

Deferred Payments may appear attractive to a Seller if a Buyer does not want to close for some extended period of time or if the only interested Buyer appears unlikely to qualify for a mortgage. This arrangement has very different tax consequences from an outright sale for both the Buyer and the Seller. For this reason, it should be considered very carefully and each party should consult with a knowledgeable accountant or tax preparer.

Note that the last paragraph of this form provides that a Buyer who defaults loses not only any rental payments made but also his deposit or down-payment and all other money already paid. This is a harsh provision that the parties may want to modify. The parties are free to negotiate any default penalties they wish.

CONTRACT CLAUSE—
DEFERRED PAYMENTS
SECURED BY RENTAL PAYMENTS

1. The number of this clause when inserted into the Contract for Sale of Residence.

2. The portion of the purchase price, in words and numbers, being paid over time in the form of rental payments.

3. The number of months of rental payments, in words and numbers.

4. The monthly rental, in words and numbers.

[1] DEFERRED PAYMENT SECURED BY RENTAL PAYMENTS - The parties agree that the sum of _____[2]_____ Dollars ($_____) of the purchase price shall be paid monthly commencing on the 1st day of the month immediately following the closing and the 1st day of each and every month thereafter for ____[3]____ (__) months as rental payments in the amount of _____[4]_____ Dollars ($_____) per month. All such payments are to be made by check, subject to collection, directly to Seller at the address designated by him.

Seller agrees that until the sum of _____[2]_____ Dollars ($_____) has been paid in full, all such monthly rental payments shall be equal to one-twelfth (1/12) of the annual charge and shall be applied as follows and in the following order, it being the understanding of the parties that such payments are to be applied so as to keep Seller "current" with each such obligation:

(Document continued on next page)

CONTRACT CLAUSE—
DEFERRED PAYMENTS
SECURED BY RENTAL PAYMENTS *continued*

5. Modify as appropriate. (For example, if the Seller's mortgage provides that a portion of the mortgage payments go towards taxes, no portion of the rent being paid by the Buyer should be allocated to taxes.)

6. The approximate amount of principal, in words and numbers, remaining due on the Seller's existing mortgage.

7. The name of the holder of the Seller's existing mortgage.

8. The monthly mortgage payment, in words and numbers, due on the Seller's existing mortgage.

Note: the information for Nos. 9 through 12 is typically found on the Seller's deed or the tax map of the property located in the office of the local tax authority.

9. The Tax Map date or other identifying feature.

10. The Tax Map Section in which the property is located.

11. The Tax Map Block in which the property is located.

12. The Lot(s) in which the property is located.

13. The present amount of the real estate taxes, in words and numbers.

14. The amount of insurance, in words and numbers.

[5] *(i) Seller's existing mortgage in the amount of _____[6]_____ Dollars ($_____) held by _____[7]_____, and in accordance with which, Seller is required to pay the sum of _____[8]_____ Dollars ($_____) per month, it being understood that if this amount may by its terms be increased or decreased, the amount of rent due to Seller shall be adjusted accordingly on Seller's written notification to Buyer which shall include a copy of such notice of adjustment by the holder;*

(ii) all real estate or real property taxes, assessments, levies, and the like charged against the real property and improvements identified on the Tax Map of ____[9]____ as Section __[10]__, Block __[11]__, Lot(s) __[12]__, in the amount of _____[13]_____ Dollars ($_____) per year, it being understood that if this amount, whether by change in the tax rate or by change in assessment be increased or decreased, the amount of rent due to Seller shall be adjusted accordingly on Seller's written notification to Buyer which shall include a copy of such tax bill;

(iii) the payment of all premiums to keep and maintain all of the buildings, improvements on and to the property and including all fixtures, equipment and personal property included in this sale (the Premises), insured against loss, damage or destruction by fire, hazard, vandalism, liability or other insurable casualty in the amount of not less than _____[14]_____ Dollars ($_____) per year, it being understood that if this amount be increased or decreased, the amount of rent due to Seller shall be adjusted accordingly on Seller's written notification to Buyer which shall include a copy of such increase or decrease as provided by the insurance company; and it being further specifically UNDERSTOOD AND AGREED that Seller shall have no obligation to insure the person, liability or personal property of the Buyer.

It is also understood and agreed that Seller will not be responsible for, nor will any portion of the rent paid by Buyer be applied to or applicable to, the payment of any

(Document continued on next page)

CONTRACT CLAUSE—
DEFERRED PAYMENTS
SECURED BY RENTAL PAYMENTS *continued*

15. The number of days, in words and numbers, during which the Buyer must fix any default of which the Seller has provided written notice (typically 10 or 15 days but may be longer or shorter as the parties might agree).

fuel, utility or telephone charges. Buyer agrees that he will contract separately and in his own name with the supplier(s) for fuel, utility or telephone, that he will pay all such costs when due and that he will not permit or take any act which may result in the creation of a lien against the Premises.

Buyer agrees not to remove or alter any portion of the real property, buildings or improvements, fixtures, equipment or personal property included in this sale (the Premises) without the express written consent of Seller and further agrees to neither commit nor permit any waste to the Premises. Buyer specifically agrees to maintain heat in and to the Premises so as to protect the Premises from the elements and agrees that Seller may use all or a portion of any amount previously paid for such purpose as Seller may deem necessary.

During the term of this agreement, and if Buyer is not in default of any of his obligations, Seller agrees that he will not further or in the future encumber or mortgage the Premises nor take any act which will result in an increase in the previously mentioned costs, nor will Seller undertake or perform any work on or to the Premises which may result in creation of a mechanic's lien against the Premises without the express written consent of Buyer. Buyer agrees that he will not further or in the future encumber or mortgage the Premises nor take any act which will result in an increase in the previously mentioned costs, nor will Buyer undertake or perform any work on or to the Premises which may result in creation of a mechanic's lien against the Premises without the express written consent of Seller.

Buyer shall be entitled to possession of the Premises upon Seller's signing of this agreement and may continue in possession while not in default of any of Buyer's obligations. If Buyer has not defaulted (or has after notice, timely cured any default) and has paid all sums required by this agreement, Seller shall deliver to Buyer the deed conveying title to the Premises.

IN THE EVENT OF DEFAULT BY BUYER WHICH SHALL REMAIN UNCURED FOR ___[15]___ (__) DAYS AFTER WRITTEN NOTICE TO BUYER, BUYER SHALL FORFEIT POSSESSION AND AS WELL SHALL FORFEIT ANY AND ALL MONIES PREVIOUSLY PAID ON ACCOUNT OF THIS AGREEMENT, WHETHER AS RENT OR AS A PORTION OF THE PURCHASE PRICE.

CONTRACT CLAUSE—
TITLE SUBJECT TO EXISTING MORTGAGE (2-12)

Most, but not all, mortgages contain a so-called "due on sale" provision requiring that the Mortgage must be paid off at the time the property is sold. This clause may be disregarded if the Seller's Mortgage contains such a provision.

This clause *should* be included in the Contract for Sale of Residence if the Seller's Mortgage is *not* to be satisfied and discharged (paid off) at or prior to the closing since a lien on the property will remain until the existing Mortgage is paid off.

CONTRACT CLAUSE—
TITLE SUBJECT TO EXISTING MORTGAGE

1. The number of this clause when inserted into the Contract for Sale of Residence.

2. Identify the Seller's existing Mortgage, for example: "First," "Second" or the like which will exist after the closing.

3. The name of the holder of the existing Mortgage.

4. The principal balance, in numbers, of the existing Mortgage remaining due at the closing.

5. The annual rate of interest, in numbers, of the existing Mortgage.

6. The amount of the monthly installments, in numbers, of the existing Mortgage.

7. Insert other components of the monthly installments such as real property taxes, water and sewer bills, insurance or the like.

8. The maturity date of the existing Mortgage.

[1] EXISTING MORTGAGE - The Premises will be sold to Buyer subject to the lien of existing mortgage(s) as follows: a __[2]__ mortgage held by _____[3]_____ now in the unpaid principal amount of approximately $_____[4]_____ with interest at the rate of __[5]__ percent per year payable in monthly installments of $____[6]____, which include principal, interest and _____[7]_____, and with the balance of principal and interest due and payable on _____[8]_____. If there is a mortgage escrow account held for the payment of taxes, insurance or other expenses, Seller agrees, if permitted by the holder, to assign same to Buyer, and Buyer agrees to pay the amount of the escrow account to the Seller at the closing.

The Seller agrees that: (a) only the payments required by the Existing Mortgage will be made; (b) no existing Mortgage contains any provision allowing the holder of the mortgage to require its immediate payment in full or to change any interest rate or other terms by reason of the transfer of title or closing, or Seller will pay, discharge and satisfy in full such existing mortgage at or before the closing; and (c) any existing mortgage will not be in default at the time of closing.

Mortgage Estoppel Certificate - Seller agrees to deliver to Buyer at closing, in such form as may be recorded, dated not more than 30 days before closing and signed by the holder of each existing mortgage, a certificate certifying the amount of the unpaid principal and interest, date of maturity, and rate of interest. Seller agrees to pay the fees for recording the certificate.

CONTRACT CLAUSE—
BUYER TO ASSUME EXISTING MORTGAGE (2-13)

This clause should be included in the Contract for Sale of Residence if the Seller's existing Mortgage is to be assumed by the Buyer so that after the closing the Buyer will make all payments. The terms of the Seller's existing Mortgage must be reviewed to determine if an assignment by the Seller of the existing Mortgage will be permitted by the holder of the Seller's Mortgage. The Seller must also determine whether an assumption of his existing Mortgage actually relieves him of any further obligation, or whether it merely gives the holder of the Mortgage the right to go after the Seller *and* the Buyer in the event of non-payment. If the Seller were to remain obligated, he might decide not to permit his Mortgage to be assigned.

CONTRACT CLAUSE—
BUYER TO ASSUME EXISTING MORTGAGE

1. The number of this clause when inserted into the Contract for Sale of Residence.

2. Identify the Seller's existing Mortgage, for example: "First," "Second" or the like that will exist after the closing.

3. The name of the holder of the existing Mortgage.

4. The principal balance, in numbers, remaining due on the existing Mortgage at the time of the closing.

5. The annual rate of interest, in numbers, of the existing Mortgage.

6. The amount of the monthly installments, in numbers, of the existing Mortgage.

7. A description of other items, such as real property taxes, water and sewer bills, insurance or the like, which are included in the monthly bill.

8. The maturity date of the existing Mortgage.

[1] BUYER TO ASSUME EXISTING MORTGAGE - As a portion of the purchase price, Seller agrees to assign and Buyer agrees to assume and, commencing with the date of the closing, to pay as required and save Seller harmless from the existing mortgage(s) as follows: a _____[2]_____ mortgage held by _____[3]_____ now in the unpaid principal amount of approximately $_____[4]_____ with interest at the rate of __[5]__ percent per year payable in monthly installments of $_____[6]_____, which include principal, interest, and _____[7]_____, and with the balance of principal and interest due and payable on _____[8]_____. If there is a mortgage escrow account held for the payment of taxes, insurance or other expenses, Seller agrees, if permitted by the holder, to assign same to Buyer, and Buyer agrees to pay the amount of the escrow account to the Seller at the closing.

The parties acknowledge that the assignment by Seller and the assumption by Buyer of the existing mortgage is subject to the written consent to the assignment and assumption by the holder of the existing mortgage. Buyer and Seller agree to execute such documents, consents, authorizations and the like as may be required by the holder of the existing mortgage. Buyer agrees to pay all costs, charges and fees associated with any credit, judgment and lien searches as may be required by the holder and also agrees to pay all recording fees, mortgage taxes and the like.

CONTRACT CLAUSE—
BUYER TO OBTAIN MORTGAGE COMMITMENT
(MORTGAGE CONTINGENCY) (2-14)

This clause should be included in the Contract for Sale of Residence if any portion of the purchase price will be paid by a loan to the Buyer from a bank or other lending institution and the sale will be abandoned if the Buyer cannot obtain such a loan. Typically, the bank will issue a document called a "commitment" by which it is committing to make a loan at the closing. This clause provides that the Buyer has a fixed period of time to apply to a bank and that he has an additional fixed period of time to receive the commitment and further, that if he does not receive the commitment *and* advises the Seller in writing, the deal is off and the deposit is refunded to the Buyer. If the Buyer does not notify the Seller in writing that he has not been able to obtain the commitment, this "bail-out" is considered waived and the Buyer will be obligated to close. If the Buyer cannot close, he will forfeit his deposit.

CONTRACT CLAUSE—
BUYER TO OBTAIN MORTGAGE COMMITMENT
(MORTGAGE CONTINGENCY)

1. The number of this clause when inserted into the Contract for Sale of Residence.

2. The state in which the property is located.

3. The amount of the loan sought by the Buyer, in words and numbers.

4. The county in which the property is located.

5. The period of time in which the Buyer will have to apply for the loan (typically five business days).

[1] MORTGAGE CONTINGENCY - This sale and the obligations of the Buyer are subject to and conditioned upon the Buyer obtaining a commitment for a loan secured by a mortgage on the Premises pursuant to which any commercial or savings bank, savings and loan association, insurance company, financing company or other lender licensed to transact business in the state of _____[2]_____ shall agree to lend not less than _____[3]_____ Dollars ($_____) at not more than the prevailing interest rate for such loans offered by such lenders within the County of _____[4]_____ to non-depositors, for a term of not more than thirty (30) years, the proceeds of which loan are to be applied towards the purchase price. Such mortgage shall be obtained by Buyer at his sole cost and expense.

Buyer shall apply for such mortgage and shall furnish to the lending institution within _____[5]_____ after receipt of this agreement as signed by Seller such complete financial information as may be required by the lending institution and at the same time pay such fee as may be required. Buyer shall advise Seller of the name(s) and address(es) of such lending institution(s) to which application has been made and the date(s) of making of such applications.

Buyer shall accept any commitment complying with the terms of this paragraph and agrees to pay all application, appraisal, commitment, origination and other fees as

(Document continued on next page)

CONTRACT CLAUSE—
BUYER TO OBTAIN MORTGAGE COMMITMENT
(MORTGAGE CONTINGENCY) *continued*

6. The date by which the Buyer must have obtained the loan commitment (typically 30 to 45 days from the date of the Buyer's receipt of the signed contract from the Seller).

may be required and to promptly comply with the requirements of the commitment.

Provided that Buyer shall have fulfilled all of Buyer's obligations as contained in this paragraph, if such commitment is not obtained by _____[6]_____, Buyer shall have the right to terminate this agreement on written notice given not more than five (5) days thereafter, and in such event, the deposit or down-payment paid by Buyer shall be refunded to Buyer without interest and this agreement shall terminate and neither party shall have any further obligation or liability to the other.

In the event, however, that Buyer shall fail to give such timely written notice of termination, this condition regarding the obtaining of a commitment shall be deemed waived.

CONTRACT CLAUSE—
FIXTURES AND OTHER PERSONAL PROPERTY
INCLUDED IN SALE (2-15)

This clause should be included in the Contract for Sale of Residence if there are any fixtures (such as equipment that may be an integral part of the operation of the residence or physically attached to the residence) or personal property, including furniture, that is made part of the sale. This clause should also be used to specifically *exclude* any fixtures or personal property that are *not* part of the sale. Experience has taught that this provision should list as much as possible (both included and excluded items) to avoid surprises at the closing.

CONTRACT CLAUSE—
FIXTURES AND OTHER PERSONAL PROPERTY
INCLUDED IN SALE

1. The number of this clause when inserted into the Contract for Sale of Residence.

2. Delete and add items as appropriate.

3. Delete and add items as appropriate.

[1] FIXTURES/PERSONAL PROPERTY - Included in this sale are all fixtures and articles of personal property attached to or used in connection with the Premises, unless specifically excluded. The Seller represents that the fixtures and personal property are paid for and owned by the Seller free and clear of any security interests or liens other than the existing mortgage(s).

Fixtures and personal property included in this sale are, but are not limited to: *[2]heating, air conditioning, plumbing, electrical and lighting fixtures, bathroom and kitchen fixtures and cabinets, storm windows and doors, screens, shades, venetian blinds, awnings, window boxes, mail boxes, wall-to-wall carpets, mantels, sump pumps, well pump, shrubbery, fences, exterior sheds, ranges, refrigerators, freezers, washing machines, clothes dryers, dishwashers, garbage disposal units, drapery and curtain hardware and rods,* _____

_____
_____.

Not included in this sale are the following: [3]furniture, household furnishings, _____

_____
_____.

CONTRACT CLAUSE—
SALE SUBJECT TO (STATEMENT OF
PERMITTED ENCUMBRANCES) (2-16)

This clause sets forth the permitted exceptions to giving clear title. It should be included in the Contract for Sale of Residence so that the Seller cannot be held to sell something that he cannot sell because he does not have "ownership" or control of it. An example would be a stoop which may extend past the Seller's property line and "encroach" on the next door neighbor's property but to which the neighbor has never objected. The insertion of this clause will allow the sale to go through even though the Seller cannot "sell" that portion of the land underneath the stoop that is his neighbor's property (and also will allow the Seller to avoid the expense of removal of the stoop and construction of a "legal" stoop). The Seller does not want the Buyer to be able to back out of the sale because the Seller cannot give clear title.

CONTRACT CLAUSE—
SALE SUBJECT TO (STATEMENT OF
PERMITTED ENCUMBRANCES)

1.   The number of this clause when inserted into the Contract for Sale of Residence.

2.   Insert such other matters that may "run with the land" and which the Seller must sell to the Buyer, such as utility or power company easements. These can be found in the Seller's deed. Otherwise delete this section and the preceding "; and."

[1] SALE SUBJECT TO/STATEMENT OF PERMITTED ENCUMBRANCES - The premises are sold and are to be transferred subject to:

(a)   laws and government regulations that affect the use and maintenance of the Premises, provided that they are not violated by the building and improvements existing on the Premises or by their current use;

(b)   the consent by the Seller or any former owner of the premises for the erection of any structure(s) on, under, or above any street or streets on which the Premises abuts;

(c)   encroachments of stoops, areas, cellar steps, trim, and cornices, if any, upon any street or highway;

(d)   any state of facts an accurate survey may show, provided same does not render title unmarketable; and

(e)   covenants and restrictions of record, if any, provided the existing use of the property does not violate such covenants or restrictions; and

[2] (f)_____

_____

_____

CONTRACT CLAUSE—
TITLE REPORT/MATTERS/OBJECTIONS (2-17)

This clause should be included in the Contract for Sale of Residence if the Buyer plans on obtaining a title inspection or report and title insurance. Even if the Buyer does not want title insurance, invariably the bank that is financing the purchase will insist on it (at least to the extent of the loan). This clause also gives the Seller an "out." If he chooses he may (but isn't required to) correct problems with the title, but may choose to terminate the contract instead.

CONTRACT CLAUSE—
TITLE REPORT/MATTERS/OBJECTIONS

1. The number of this clause when inserted into the Contract for Sale of Residence.

2. The county in which the property is located.

3. The party who will obtain the title report (typically the Buyer, since he will want to or be required to obtain title insurance).

4. The party who will be given a copy of the title report (typically the Seller).

5. The date by which the title report must be given to the party in No. 4.

[1] TITLE REPORT/MATTERS/OBJECTIONS - Seller will give and Buyer agrees to accept such title as any licensed title company with an office in the County of _____[2]_____ will be willing to approve and insure in accordance with the standard form of title policy issued by such company, subject only to those matters provided for in this agreement.

_____[3]_____ shall apply for and obtain and pay all costs and fees for and shall furnish to _____[4]_____, on or before _____[5]_____, a complete abstract of title to the Premises current and up to date through the date of signing the contract and certified as correct by such title company that Seller has good and marketable title to the Premises free and clear of all encumbrances except those specifically stated in this contract. Both the Buyer and the Seller will be allowed a reasonable time for examination of any title report after the date of receipt by that party, the attorney of that party's selection, or a title company of that party's selection.

If Seller shall be unable to deliver to Buyer good and marketable title in accordance with this Contract but subject to those matters set forth in this Contract, Seller shall not be required to bring any action or proceeding or otherwise incur any expense to make title marketable. If Buyer shall refuse such title as Seller can deliver, Seller may rescind this contract and refund to Buyer the deposit, without interest, and if incurred by Buyer, the charges and fees for the examination of title to the Premises and this agreement shall terminate and neither party shall have any obligation or liability to the other.

CONTRACT CLAUSE—
PROPERTY SOLD "AS IS" (2-18)

This clause should be included in the Contract for Sale of Residence as protection to the Seller since it puts the burden on the Buyer to inspect and evaluate the property, fixtures and personal property included in the sale. In effect, this provision tells the Buyer that "what you see is what you get" and nothing more.

Also, note that this clause contains the Seller's representation to the Buyer that the building and major systems are in working order. The Seller should resist giving such a representation but may have to if the Buyer refuses to sign the contract without it.

CONTRACT CLAUSE—
PROPERTY SOLD "AS IS"

1. The number of this clause when inserted into the Contract for Sale of Residence.

2. Choose one.

3. Delete if not required by the Buyer.

[1] PROPERTY SOLD "AS IS" - Buyer acknowledges that he has *[2][inspected]* **OR** *[had full opportunity to inspect]* the buildings and improvements and all personal property included in this sale and is fully acquainted with their condition. Buyer agrees to purchase the Premises, the buildings and improvements and all personal property strictly "AS IS" and in their present condition subject only to reasonable use, wear and tear and natural deterioration between now and date of closing.

[3][Seller represents that the plumbing, heating/air conditioning and electrical systems and any appliances included in this sale will be in working order on the date of the closing.]

Buyer shall have the right, upon reasonable notice to Seller, to inspect the Premises, the buildings and improvements and all personal property during the twenty-four (24) hour period before closing.

CONTRACT CLAUSE—
PEST/ENGINEER'S INSPECTION (2-19)

This clause should be included in the Contract for Sale of Residence if the Buyer insists upon either a termite inspection or engineer's inspection of the property. In the event that the Buyer insists upon one but not the other, delete the appropriate subparagraph.

CONTRACT CLAUSE—
PEST/ENGINEER'S INSPECTION

1. The number of this clause when inserted into the Contract for Sale of Residence.

[1] PEST/ENGINEER'S INSPECTION - Buyer shall have ten (10) days from the date of receipt of this contract as signed by the Seller to obtain at Buyer's sole cost and expense:

(a) Termite/pest/infestation inspection. If the termite, pest and infestation inspection report indicates the presence of such infestation, Seller shall have the option of: (i) eliminating the infestation at Seller's sole cost and expense; or (ii) cancelling this contract by return of the down payment made by Buyer. Written notice of the Seller's intent to exercise either option shall be served upon Buyer within ten (10) days of receipt of such report.

(b) A physical inspection of the Premises, buildings and improvements and all fixtures and personal property included in this sale by a qualified engineer, architect or the like. If the engineer's report indicates structural or mechanical deficiencies, Seller shall have the option of: (i) correcting all or some deficiencies at Seller's sole cost and expense prior to the closing (and closing may be adjourned for this purpose at Seller's option); (ii) allowing a credit against the purchase price to be paid by Buyer in an amount equal to the reasonable estimate obtained by Buyer to correct all or some of the deficiencies; (iii) a combination of either of the foregoing; or (iv) cancelling this contract. Written notice of the Seller's intent to exercise any option shall be served upon Buyer within ten (10) days of receipt of such report.

If Seller shall elect to terminate this Contract, the deposit previously paid by Buyer upon signing this Contract shall be refunded and neither party shall have any further obligation or liability to the other.

CONTRACT CLAUSE—
DUTY TO APPORTION TAXES, FUEL OIL, ETC. (2-20)

This clause should be included in the Contract for Sale of Residence if there are any charges or costs for the property for which payments will have been made prior to the closing but which cover a period subsequent to the closing. The classic example of such a charge is real estate tax, typically paid annually or semi-annually. The closing, of course, rarely takes place on the first day of the new tax period. Since the Seller will have moved out in the middle of the tax period, he will be entitled to a credit for the real estate taxes already paid for the period from the closing until the end of the period that his tax payment covers. This payment will be apportioned.

CONTRACT CLAUSE—
DUTY TO APPORTION TAXES, FUEL OIL, ETC.

1.   The number of this clause when inserted into the Contract for Sale of Residence.

2.   Insert any other charges that are to be apportioned. If there are none, delete this section and the preceding "; and."

[1] APPORTIONMENTS - Items to be apportioned. The following are to be apportioned as of midnight of the day before closing:

    (a)   rents as and when collected;

    (b)   interest on existing mortgage(s);

    (c)   premiums on existing transferable insurance policies or renewals of those expiring prior to the closing;

    (d)   taxes, water charges, and sewer rents, if any, on the basis of the fiscal year for which assessed;

    (e)   fuel, if any; and

    *[2] (f)*_____
_____
_____.

If the closing shall occur before a new tax rate is fixed, the apportionment of taxes shall be upon the basis of the old tax rate for the preceding period applied to the latest assessed valuation.

Any errors or omissions in computing apportionments of any of the above items at closing shall be corrected, and this provision shall survive closing.

CONTRACT CLAUSE—
PROPERTY TO BE INSURED AGAINST LOSS (2-21)

This clause should be included in the Contract for Sale of Residence to provide for insurance to cover any loss, damage or destruction to the property between the signing of the contract and the closing. This clause provides that the Seller will pay the cost of the insurance.

CONTRACT CLAUSE—
PROPERTY TO BE INSURED AGAINST LOSS

1. The number of this clause when inserted into the Contract for Sale of Residence.

2. The amount of insurance coverage to be maintained, in words and numbers. This amount should be at least as much as the sale price of the property, but full replacement coverage is the more prudent approach.

3. The state in which the property is located.

[1] PROPERTY INSURED AGAINST LOSS - Until the closing of title as provided in this agreement, Seller shall pay all premiums and costs necessary and shall keep and maintain all of the buildings and improvements on and to the property and including all fixtures, equipment and personal property included in this sale (the Premises), insured against loss, damage, destruction by fire, hazard, vandalism, liability and other insurable casualty in an amount of not less than _____[2]_____ Dollars ($_____) . The policy(s) of insurance shall be maintained with a reputable insurance company licensed to transact business in the state of _____[3]_____ and shall provide that in the event of a claim, the loss-payee who shall receive benefits shall be either or both Seller and Buyer to the extent of their respective interests in the Premises.

CONTRACT CLAUSE—
PROPERTY DAMAGED OR DESTROYED (2-22)

Neither a Seller nor a Buyer likes to think about what would happen if the property were damaged or destroyed between the signing of the contract and the closing. But both the Seller and the Buyer should. Many states have laws that provide for this situation. If a contract does not specifically deal with this potential problem, your state's law may. However, the parties to a contract are free to fashion their own remedies.

This clause sets forth one method for dealing with the problem of loss or damage to the property and should be included in the Contract for Sale of Residence if your state's law does not establish any method or if you wish to fashion your own.

CONTRACT CLAUSE—
PROPERTY DAMAGED OR DESTROYED

1. The number of this clause when inserted into the Contract for Sale of Residence.

2. The number of days (typically five), in words and numbers, that the Seller will have for giving notice of the loss or destruction to the Buyer.

3. The number of days, in words and numbers, that the Seller will have to complete the repair or replacement. The parties may agree on a shorter or longer period depending on the Seller's estimate of the time such repair/replacement is likely to take. However, 60 days is the typical period since at the time of signing the contract the parties do not know what kind or degree of repair or replacement would be required.

[1] RISK OF LOSS OR DAMAGE - The risk of loss or damage to the Premises, or to the fixtures, equipment and personal property included in this sale, by fire or other cause, until the time of the closing, is assumed by Seller, but without any obligation on the part of Seller, except at Seller's option, to repair or replace any such loss or damage. Seller shall have the option to elect to make either repair or replacement. Seller shall notify Buyer of the loss or damage within ___[2]___ (__) days after the occurrence or by the date of closing, whichever occurs first. Seller's notice to Buyer will also advise Buyer whether or not Seller will repair or replace the loss or damage and if Seller elects to do so, that he will complete the repair or replacement within ___[3]___ (__) days and the closing will be adjourned for this purpose and without cost or penalty to either Seller or Buyer. If Seller elects to make repair/ replacement, Seller's notice will also state the adjourned date for the closing.

If Seller does not elect to make repair/replacement, or if Seller elects to make repair/replacement but fails to complete same before the adjourned closing date, Buyer shall advise Seller of Buyer's option of either:

(i)   declaring this agreement cancelled in which event the deposit or down-payment paid by Buyer shall be refunded to Buyer without interest and neither party shall have any further obligation or liability to the other; or

(ii)   completing the purchase in accordance with this agreement without reduction in the purchase price except that if Seller's insurance covers the loss or damage, Seller shall turn over to Buyer at the closing the net proceeds (after legal and other expenses of collection) actually

(Document continued on next page)

4. The number of days, in words and numbers, that the Buyer will have to notify the Seller as to what the Buyer intends to do.

collected by Seller under the provisions of any insurance policies to the extent that they are attributable to the loss or damage to any property included in this sale and if Seller has not received such proceeds Seller shall assign (without recourse to Seller) Seller's insurance attributable to the loss or damage to any property included in this sale, less any sums expended by Seller.

Buyer's option, whether resulting from either: (i) Seller's election to not make repair/replacement, or (ii) Seller's failure, within the time provided, to make repair/replacement despite having elected to do so, shall be exercised within ___[4]___ (__) days of the earlier of: (i) Seller having advised Buyer of Seller's election to not make repair/replacement, or (ii) Seller's assignment of any insurance proceeds. Buyer's option resulting from Seller's failure to timely make repair/replacement shall be exercised within ___[4]___ (__) days of the adjourned closing date.

CONTRACT CLAUSE—
DEPOSIT TO BE HELD IN ESCROW (2-23)

This clause should be included in the Contract for Sale of Residence if the deposit or down-payment paid by the Buyer when he signs the contract will not be given outright to the Seller until the closing but is to be held in escrow until then. Any third party selected by both the Seller and the Buyer can hold the funds (act as Escrow Agent), for example: an attorney (even the Seller's attorney, but not the Buyer's attorney), a title or abstract company, or even a bank if the parties open an account which requires both of their signatures for any withdrawals. Neither of the parties themselves should act as the Escrow Agent since, in the event of a default, neither party would want the defaulting party to be holding the deposit.

Note that the Escrow Agent must consent to being appointed as Escrow Agent. This consent is indicated by the Escrow Agent signing the contract under the words "I hereby agree to act as Escrow Agent," typically on the same page as the parties' signatures appear.

CONTRACT CLAUSE—
DEPOSIT TO BE HELD IN ESCROW

1.   The number of this clause when inserted into the Contract for Sale of Residence.

2.   The amount, in words and numbers, of the deposit or down-payment that will be held in escrow. This amount should be the same as appears in the Contract for Sale of Residence (typically, but not necessarily, 10% of the purchase price).

3.   Delete if the escrow funds will not be held in an interest bearing account. This is a negotiable term between the parties and must also be agreed to by the Escrow Agent. It is usually dependent on the sum of money involved and the length of time between contract signing and closing.

4.   The name of the Escrow Agent.

5.   The address of the Escrow Agent.

6.   The state where the property is located.

7.   Delete if the Escrow Agent is not the Seller's attorney.

[1] DEPOSIT TO BE HELD IN ESCROW - The sum of _____[2]_____ Dollars ($_____) (the "Escrow Fund") paid by Buyer as a deposit and on account of the purchase price shall be held in escrow in an *[3][interest bearing]* account maintained by _____[4]_____, with office at _____[5]_____, (the "Escrow Agent"), until the closing or sooner termination of this agreement. In the event of a default by Buyer, the Escrow Fund shall be paid over to Seller as liquidated damages. In the event that this sale is not closed for any other reason, the Escrow Fund shall be refunded to Buyer. Interest, if any, earned by the Escrow Fund shall be paid to the party entitled to and who actually does receive the Escrow Fund. In the event that there shall be a dispute as to whether Seller or Buyer is entitled to all or part of the Escrow Funds, and the Escrow Agent shall have received written notice of the dispute, then the Escrow Agent may retain the Escrow Fund until the dispute is settled or may deposit the Escrow Fund into a court of competent jurisdiction in the state of ____[6]____ (which court the parties agree shall have jurisdiction) and the Escrow Agent shall be released thereby from any and all obligations and liability for the Escrow Funds. In no event shall the Escrow Agent incur any liability of any kind hereunder for any act done or step taken or omitted by him or for any mistake of fact or law, except for the Escrow Agent's own willful misconduct or malfeasance. *[7][The Escrow Agent shall have the right to represent Seller in any dispute with respect to the Escrow Fund or otherwise.]*

CONTRACT CLAUSE—
SELLER TO PAY BROKERAGE COMMISSION (2-24)

This clause should be included in the Contract for Sale of Residence even if there was no broker who brought about the sale since it protects both the Seller and the Buyer. Note that this clause provides that the Seller will pay the broker's commission since the law in most states is that the broker is the agent for the Seller and not the Buyer.

CONTRACT CLAUSE—
SELLER TO PAY BROKERAGE COMMISSION

1. The number of this clause when inserted into the Contract for Sale of Residence.

2. Delete to the end of this paragraph if no broker brought about the sale.

3. The name of the broker.

4. The address of the broker.

[1] REAL ESTATE BROKER - Buyer represents to Seller that Buyer has not dealt with any real estate broker in connection with this purchase *[2][other than _____[3]_____, located at _____[4]_____ and Seller agrees to pay the commission as earned by said broker as more fully stated in a separate brokerage commission agreement. Buyer agrees to indemnify and hold Seller harmless from and against any and all liability, cost and expense (including reasonable attorneys' fees and disbursements) which may be incurred by Seller as a result of a claim for brokerage commission or other compensation made by any other broker who has dealt with Buyer in connection with this transaction. The provisions of this paragraph shall survive the closing or earlier termination of this agreement].*

CONTRACT CLAUSE—
OPTION TO CANCEL (2-25)

A Seller does not want to give a real estate Buyer an option to cancel. However, a Buyer may insist on such right or refuse to sign the contract. This clause should be included in the Contract for Sale of Residence if the Buyer insists on such an option.

CONTRACT CLAUSE—
OPTION TO CANCEL

1. The number of this clause when inserted into the Contract for Sale of Residence.

2. The number of business days, in words and numbers, that the Buyer will have to exercise his right to cancel (typically 3). Note: the law in most states is that legal holidays (either federal or state) do not count as business days.

[1] OPTION TO CANCEL - Within ___[2]___ (__) business days of the later of the signing of this contract or the date of actual receipt of this contract by Buyer as signed by Seller, Buyer may by written notice, cancel this agreement for any reason. Written notice, postmarked not later than the last day of the cancellation period, shall be sent to Seller by registered or certified mail, return receipt requested. Seller shall immediately refund to Buyer the deposit or down-payment paid on signing the contract and upon such refund this agreement shall terminate and neither party will have any further obligation or liability to the other.

MORTGAGE NOTE (Fixed Rate) (2-26)

A Note documents a loan from a Lender to a Borrower. A Mortgage Note is a special type of Note in which the Borrower gives to the Lender security (collateral) in the form of an interest in the Borrower's real property. This interest is known as a Mortgage. The property owner who is borrowing the money and giving this security interest is called the Mortgagor. The Lender is called the Mortgagee.

This form provides for a loan to be repaid at a fixed rate of interest over the entire term of the mortgage, with fixed payments. The loan contemplated by this Note is self-liquidating, meaning that the last payment will pay off the loan in full and without the need for a so-called "balloon" payment at the end.

This Mortgage Note also contains a "due on sale" provision. This provides that in the event of a sale of the property by the Mortgagor he must "satisfy" (pay off) his mortgage at or before the closing of the sale.

This form is presented with consumer protection laws and "plain language" laws in mind. It is similar to the one approved by both the Federal National Mortgage Administration (FNMA) and the Federal Home Loan Mortgage Corporation (FHLMC) and has been adopted by an increasing number of banks.

WARNING

A Note is the primary and only true evidence of a loan having been made. As with any Note, the Borrower should sign only one Mortgage Note, since multiple original Notes have the legal effect of multiple loans.

MORTGAGE NOTE (Fixed Rate)

1. The principal amount of the loan, in numbers.

   U.S.$_____[1]_____   _____[2]_____
                              _____[3]_____

2. The city and state in which the loan is made.

3. The date of signing the loan.

(Document continued on next page)

4. The address of the property.

5. The city and state in which the property is located.

6. The county in which the property is located.

Note: the information for Nos. 7 through 9 is typically found on the Seller's deed or the tax map of the property located in the office of the local tax authority.

7. The Section in which the property is located.

8. The Block in which the property is located.

9. The Lot(s) in which the property is located.

10. The principal amount of the loan, in words and numbers.

11. The name of the Lender.

12. The address of the Lender.

13. The annual percentage rate, in numbers, of the loan.

14. The month and year during which the first full monthly payment of principal and interest is to be made. (Note: interest is paid only after it is earned—the first full monthly payment will be made starting with the *second* month after the closing, but will be for the prior 30-day period. For example, if the closing is on April 21st, at the closing a payment of interest only will be made for the period April 21 through April 30 and the first full payment of both principal and interest will be made on June 1, with the interest portion of the June 1 payment being for the period May 1 through May 31.)

Property Address:

_____[4]_____

_____[5]_____

County of _____[6]_____

Tax Map Designation:

Section:_____[7]_____

Block: _____[8]_____

Lot(s) _____[9]_____

1. BORROWER'S PROMISE TO PAY - In return for a loan that I have received, I promise to pay the sum of _____[10]_____ U.S. Dollars ($_____) , which is called "Principal," plus interest, to the order of the Lender. The Lender is _____[11]_____, residing at _____[12]_____. I understand that the Lender may transfer this Note. The Lender or anyone who takes this Note by transfer and who is entitled to receive payments under this Note is called the "Note Holder."

2. INTEREST - Interest will be charged on unpaid principal until the full amount of principal has been paid. I will pay interest at a yearly rate of ___[13]___%.

The interest rate required by this Section 2 is the rate I will pay both before and after any default described in Section 6(B) of this Note.

3. PAYMENTS

(A) TIME AND PLACE OF PAYMENT - Except when this Note is dated the first (1st) day of the month, I will make a payment of interest only from the date of this Note to the first day of the following month. I will pay principal and interest by making payments every month. I will make my monthly payments on the first (1st) day of each month beginning with _____[14]_____, 19__. I will make these payments every month until I have paid all of the principal and interest and any other charges described below that I may owe under this Note. My monthly payments will be applied to interest before princi-

(Document continued on next page)

15. The month and year during which the last full payment of interest and principal is to be made.

16. The address where the payments are to be made or mailed.

17. The dollar amount of each monthly payment, in numbers.

18. The number of days, in words and numbers, of the allowed "grace" period (typically 15 days).

19. Choose one and fill in the amount. A late charge may be expressed as either a fixed dollar amount or as a percentage of the payment due.

pal. If, on the first (1st) of _____[15]_____, 19__, I still owe amounts under this Note, I will pay those amounts in full on that date, which is called the "Maturity Date."

I will make my monthly payments at _____[16]_____, or at a different place if required by the Note Holder.

(B) AMOUNT OF MONTHLY PAYMENTS - My monthly payments will be in the amount of U.S.$_____[17]_____.

4. BORROWER'S RIGHT TO PREPAY - I have the right to make payments of principal at any time before they are due. A payment of principal only is known as a "prepayment." When I make a prepayment, I will tell the Note Holder in writing that I am doing so. I may make a full prepayment or partial prepayments without paying a prepayment charge. The Note Holder will use all of my prepayments to reduce the amount of principal that I owe under this Note. If I make a partial prepayment, there will be no changes in the due date or in the amount of my monthly payments unless the Note Holder agrees in writing to those changes.

5. LOAN CHARGES - If a law, which applies to this loan and which sets maximum loan charges, is finally interpreted so that the interest or other loan charges collected or to be collected in connection with this loan exceed the permitted limits, then: (i) any such loan charge shall be reduced by the amount necessary to reduce the charge to the permitted limit; and (ii) any sums already collected from me which exceeded permitted limits will be refunded to me. The Note Holder may choose to make this refund by reducing the principal I owe under this Note or by making a direct payment to me. If a refund reduces principal, the reduction will be treated as a partial prepayment.

6. BORROWER'S FAILURE TO PAY AS REQUIRED

(A) LATE CHARGES FOR OVERDUE PAYMENTS - if the Note holder has not received the full amount of any monthly payment by the end of ___[18]___ (__) calendar days after the date it is due, I will pay a late charge to the Note Holder. The amount of the late charge will be *[19][$_____] OR [__%]* of my overdue payment of principal and interest]. I will pay this late charge promptly but only once on each late payment.

(Document continued on next page)

(B)   DEFAULT - If I do not pay the full amount of each monthly payment on the date it is due, I will be in default.

(C)   NOTICE OF DEFAULT - If I am in default, the Note Holder may send me a written notice telling me that if I do not pay the overdue amount by a certain date, the Note Holder may require me to pay immediately the full amount of principal which has not been paid and all the interest that I owe on that amount. That date must be at least 30 days after the date on which the notice is delivered or mailed to me.

(D)   NO WAIVER BY NOTE HOLDER - Even if, at a time when I am in default, the Note Holder does not require me to pay immediately in full as described above, the Note Holder will still have the right to do so if I am in default at a later time.

(E)   PAYMENT OF NOTE HOLDER'S COSTS AND EXPENSES - If the Note Holder has required me to pay immediately in full as described above, the Note Holder will have the right to be paid back by me for all of its costs and expenses in enforcing this Note to the extent not prohibited by applicable law. Those expenses include, for example, reasonable attorneys' fees.

7. GIVING OF NOTICES - Unless applicable law requires a different method, any notice that must be given to me under this Note will be given by delivering it or by mailing it by first class mail to me at the Property Address above or at a different address if I give the Note Holder a notice of my different address. Any notice that must be given to the Note Holder under this Note will be given by mailing it first class mail to the Note Holder at the address stated in Section 3(A) above or at a different place if I am given notice of that different address.

8. OBLIGATIONS OF PERSONS UNDER THIS NOTE - If more than one person signs this Note, each person is fully and personally obligated to keep all of the promises made in this Note, including the promise to pay the full amount owed. Any person who is a guarantor, surety or endorser of this Note is also obligated to do these things. Any person who takes over these obligations, including the obligations of a guarantor, surety or endorser of this Note, is also obligated to keep all of the promises made in this

(Document continued on next page)

MORTGAGE NOTE (Fixed Rate) *continued*

Note. The Note Holder may enforce its rights under this Note against each person individually or against all of us together. This means that any one of us may be required to pay all of the amounts owed under this Note.

9. WAIVERS - I and any other person who has obligations under this Note waive the rights of presentment and notice of dishonor. "Presentment" means the right to require the Note Holder to demand payment of amounts due. "Notice of Dishonor" means the right to require the Note Holder to give notice to other persons that amounts due have not been paid. Any guarantor, surety or endorser of this Note also waives these rights.

10. NOTE SECURED BY "SECURITY INSTRUMENT" - This Note is secured by a Mortgage, Deed of Trust or Security Deed (the "Security Instrument") dated the same day as this Note. In addition to the protections given to the Note Holder under this Note, the "Security Instrument" dated the same date as this Note protects the Note Holder from possible losses which might result if I do not keep the promises which I make in this Note.

That Security Instrument describes how and under what conditions I may be required to make immediate payment in full of all amounts I owe under this Note. Among those conditions are described as follows:

(Document continued on next page)

20. The name of the Witness to the signing of the Note printed below the line, with the Witness to sign above the line.

21. The name of the Borrower(s) printed below the line, with the Borrower(s) to sign above the line. Delete the second line if only one Borrower.

22. A Notary completes this section and affixes his stamp or seal.

TRANSFER OF THE PROPERTY OR BENEFICIAL INTEREST IN BORROWER - If all or any part of the Property or any interest in it is sold or transferred (or if a beneficial interest in Borrower is sold or transferred and Borrower is not a natural person) without Note Holder's prior written consent, Note Holder may, at its option, require immediate payment in full of all sums secured by the Security Instrument. However, this option shall not be exercised by the Note Holder if exercise is prohibited by federal law as of the date of the Security Instrument. If the Note Holder exercises this option, the Note Holder will give Borrower notice of acceleration. This notice shall provide a period of not less than 30 days from the date the notice is delivered or mailed within which Borrower must pay all sums secured by the Security Instrument. If Borrower fails to pay these sums prior to the expiration of this period, the Note Holder may invoke any of the remedies permitted by the Security Instrument without further notice or demand on Borrower.

Witness:

_____   _____
         [20]   [21]   Borrower

                                          _____
                                           [21]   Borrower

STATE OF _____[22]_____, COUNTY OF _____, ss.:

On _____[22]_____, 19__, before me a _____[22]_____ personally came _____[22]_____, to me known, and known to me to be the individual(s) described in and who executed the foregoing _____[22]_____, and duly acknowledged to me that (he)(she)(they) executed the same.

                                         _____
                                             Notary Public

MORTGAGE (2-27)

A Mortgage is an agreement to put up real estate as collateral to secure the repayment of a loan. The owner of the Property who is borrowing the money agrees that his real estate can be used as security for the repayment of the loan in the event of a default. He is called the "Mortgagor." The Lender who agrees to accept the real estate as security for repayment of the loan is called the "Mortgagee." At all times, legal title to the Property remains with the Mortgagor, the Borrower. The Mortgagee will record the Mortgage to alert the public that such collateral in the real estate exists.

This form is similar to the one approved by both the Federal National Mortgage Administration (FNMA) and the Federal Home Loan Mortgage Corporation (FHLMC) and has been adopted by an increasing number of banks. It is a "plain language" type of form.

WARNING

Since the Mortgage is only the security, and not evidence of the loan itself, the Mortgage must be used together with the preceding Mortgage Note.

MORTGAGE

1. The date of the Mortgage.

2. The name of the Borrower.

3. If the Borrower is a corporation, insert the state of incorporation. Otherwise delete.

4. The Borrower's address.

5. The name of the Lender.

6. If the Lender is a corporation, insert the state of incorporation. Otherwise delete.

7. The Lender's address.

8. The date of the Note. (Note: the date of the Note will most likely be the same as the date of the Mortgage, in No. 1 above, since the Note and the Mortgage are usually signed at the same time.)

9. The principal amount of the loan (the Note amount), in words.

10. The principal amount of the loan, in numbers.

11. The date on which the last payment on the loan is due (the maturity date).

WORDS USED IN THIS DOCUMENT

(A)   "Security Instrument" and "Mortgage:" This document, which is dated _____[1]_____, sometimes called either the "Security Agreement" or the "Mortgage."

(B)   "Borrower:" _____[2]_____ *[3][, a corporation organized under the laws of _____,]* sometimes called either "Borrower," "I" or "me." Borrower's address is _____[4]_____.

(C)   "Lender:" _____[5]_____ *[6][, a corporation organized under the laws of _____]* sometimes called "Lender." Lender's address is _____[7]_____.

(D)   "Note:" The Note signed by the Borrower and dated _____[8]_____ will be called the "Note." The Note shows that I owe Lender _____[9]_____ U.S. Dollars ($_____[10]_____), plus interest.

I have promised to pay this debt in monthly payments and to pay the debt in full by _____[11]_____.

(Document continued on next page)

12. The address of the Property being mortgaged.

13. The city in which the Property being mortgaged is located.

14. The county in which the Property being mortgaged is located.

15. The state in which the Property being mortgaged is located.

16. On a separate sheet, headed "Schedule A," set forth the so-called "metes and bounds" describing the Property being mortgaged by feet and compass direction—which is the best description of the Property. This description and the ones called for in Nos. 17 through 20 are typically found in the Property's original deed. The information should be copied from the Property's original deed EXACTLY.

17. The district number in which the Property is located.

18. The section number in which the Property is located.

19. The block number in which the Property is located.

20. The lot number(s) in which the Property is located.

(E) "Property:" The Property that is described below in the section titled "Description of the Property," will be called the "Property."

(F) "Sums secured:" The amounts described below in the section titled "Borrower's Transfer to Lender of Rights in Property" sometimes will be called the "sums secured."

BORROWER'S TRANSFER TO LENDER OF RIGHTS IN PROPERTY - I mortgage, grant and convey the Property to Lender subject to the terms of this Security Instrument. This means that, by signing this Security Instrument, I am giving Lender those rights that are stated in this Security Instrument and also those rights the law gives to lenders who hold mortgages on real property. I am giving Lender these rights to protect Lender from possible losses if I fail to:

(A) Pay all the amounts that I owe Lender as stated in the Note;

(B) Pay, with interest, any amounts that Lender spends under Paragraphs 2 and 7 of this Security Instrument to protect the value of the Property and Lender's rights in the Property; and

(C) Keep all of my other promises and agreements under this Security Instrument.

DESCRIPTION OF THE PROPERTY - I give Lender rights in the Property described in (A) through (J) below:

(A) The Property which is located at
_____[12]_____, in the City of
_____[13]_____, County of _____[14]____,
State of _____[15]_____.

The Property has the legal description which is more fully stated on the attached [16] SCHEDULE A and as well has the following tax map designation:

District No.: ____[17]____
Section No. ____[18]____
Block No.: ____[19]____
Lot(s) No.: ____[20]____

(Document continued on next page)

21. If the state in which the Property being mortgaged taxes mortgages, the borrower initials the appropriate parentheses for the type of building on the Property. Or add a brief description of the type of building after the word "Other," for example: "Three story commercial property," or the like. Otherwise delete the section.

22. Delete if the mortgage is NOT used to enable the borrower to purchase the Property (if for example, this mortgage is a "refinance," equity loan, second mortgage or the like).

[21][FOR MORTGAGE TAX PURPOSES, Borrowers represent that the within Property is improved by:

(   ) A legal one/two family residence
(   ) A legal three/four family residence
(   ) Other:_____

(HAVE BORROWERS INITIAL THE APPROPRIATE BOX)]

[22][BEING the same Property which was conveyed to the Borrower by deed delivered and intended to be recorded simultaneously with this Mortgage. This Mortgage is a purchase money mortgage given to secure a portion of the consideration expressed in said deed.]

(B)   All buildings and other improvements that are located on the Property described in subparagraph (A) of this section;

(C)   All rights in other property that I have as owner of the Property described in subparagraph (A) of this section. These rights are known as "easements, rights and appurtenances attached to the Property";

(D)   All rents or royalties from the Property described in subparagraph (A) of this section;

(E)   All mineral, oil, gas rights and profits, water rights and stock that are part of the Property described in subparagraph (A) of this section;

(F)   All rights that I have in the land which lies in the streets or roads in front of, or next to, the Property as described in subparagraph (A) of this section;

(G)   All fixtures that are now or in the future will be on this Property described in subparagraph (A) of this section;

(H)   All of the rights and property described in subparagraphs (B) through (G) of this section that I acquire in the future;

(I)   All replacements of or additions to the Property

(Document continued on next page)

described in subparagraphs (B) through (H) of this section; and

(J)   All of the amounts that I pay to Lender under Paragraph 2 below.

BORROWER'S RIGHT TO MORTGAGE THE PROP-ERTY AND BORROWER'S OBLIGATION TO DE-FEND OWNERSHIP OF THE PROPERTY - I promise that: (i) I lawfully own the Property; (ii) I have the right to mortgage, grant and convey the Property to Lender; and (iii) there are no outstanding claims or charges against the Property, except for those which are of public record.

I give a general warranty of title to Lender. This means that I will be fully responsible for any losses which Lender suffers because someone other than myself has some of the rights in the Property which I promise that I have. I prom-ise that I will defend my ownership of the Property against any claim of such rights.

IN CONSIDERATION OF A LOAN MADE TO ME BY THE LENDER, I promise and I agree with Lender as follows:

1.   BORROWER'S PROMISE TO PAY - I will pay to Lender on time principal and interest due under the Note and any prepayment and late charges due under the Note.

2.   MONTHLY PAYMENTS FOR TAXES AND INSURANCE

(A)   BORROWER'S OBLIGATIONS - I will pay to Lender all amounts necessary for taxes, assessments, leaseholds payments or ground rents (if any), and hazard insurance on the Property and mortgage insurance (if any). I will pay those amounts to Lender unless Lender tells me, in writing, that I do not have to do so, or unless the law requires otherwise. I will make those payments on the same day that my monthly payments of principal and interest are due under this Note.

Each of my payments under this Paragraph 2 will be the sum of the following: (i) One-twelfth of the estimated yearly taxes and assessments on the Property which under the law may be superior to this Security Instrument; plus (ii) One-twelfth of the estimated yearly leasehold payments

(Document continued on next page)

or ground rents on the Property, if any; plus (iii) One-twelfth of the estimated yearly premium for hazard insurance covering the Property; plus (iv) One-twelfth of the estimated yearly premium for mortgage insurance (if any).

Lender will estimate from time to time my yearly taxes, assessments, leasehold payments or ground rents and insurance premiums, which will be called "escrow items." Lender will use existing assessments and bills and reasonable estimates for future assessments and bills. The amounts that I pay to Lender for escrow items under this Paragraph 2 will be called the "Funds."

(B)　　LENDER'S OBLIGATIONS - Lender will keep the Funds in a savings or banking institution which has deposits or accounts insured by a federal or state agency. If Lender is such an institution, Lender may hold the Funds. Except as described in this Paragraph 2, Lender will use the Funds to pay the escrow items. Lender will give to me, without charge, an annual accounting of the Funds. That accounting must show all additions to and deductions from the funds and the reason for each deduction.

Lender may not charge me for holding or keeping the Funds, for using the Funds to pay escrow items, for analyzing my payment of Funds, or for receiving, verifying and totalling assessments and bills. However, Lender may charge me for these services if Lender pays me interest on the Funds and if the law permits Lender to make such a charge. Lender will not be required to pay me any interest or earnings of the Funds unless either (i) Lender and I agree in writing, at the time I sign this Security Instrument, that Lender will pay interest on the funds; or (ii) the law requires that the Lender pay interest on the Funds.

(C)　　ADJUSTMENT TO THE FUNDS - If Lender's estimates are too high or if taxes and insurance rates go down, the amounts that I must pay under this Paragraph 2 will be too large. If this happens at a time when I am keeping all of my promises and agreements made in this Security instrument, I will have the right to have the excess money promptly repaid to me as direct refund or credited to my future monthly payment of Funds. There will be excess amounts if, at any time, the sum of (i) the amount of Funds which Lender is holding or keeping, plus (ii) the amount of the monthly payments of Funds

(Document continued on next page)

which I must still pay between that time and the due dates of escrow items is greater than the amount necessary to pay the escrow items when they are due. If, when payments of escrow items are due, Lender has not received enough Funds to make those payments, I will pay to Lender whatever additional amount is necessary to pay the escrow items in full. I must pay that additional amount in one or more payments as Lender may require.

When I have paid all of the sums secured, Lender will promptly refund to me any Funds that are then being held by Lender. If, under Paragraph 20 below, Lender either acquires the Property or the Property is sold, then immediately before the acquisition or sale, Lender will use any Funds which Lender is holding at that time to reduce the sums secured.

3. APPLICATION OF BORROWER'S PAYMENTS - Unless the law requires otherwise, Lender will apply each of my payments under the Note and under Paragraphs 1 and 2 above in the following order and for the following purposes: first, to pay late charges due under the Note; next, to pay prepayment charges due under the Note; next, to pay the amounts due to Lender under Paragraph 2 above; next, to pay interest due; and last, to pay principal due.

4. BORROWER'S OBLIGATION TO PAY ALL CHARGES, ASSESSMENTS AND CLAIMS - I will pay all taxes, assessments and any other charges and fines that may be imposed on the Property and that may be superior to this Security Instrument. I will also make payments due under my lease if I am a tenant on the Property and I will pay ground rents (if any) due on the Property. I will do this either by making the payments to Lender that are described in Paragraph 2 above or, if I am not required to make payments under Paragraph 2, by making the payments on time to the person owed them. (In this Security Instrument, the word "person" means any person, organization, governmental authority or other party.) If I make direct payments, then promptly after making any of those payments I will give Lender a receipt which shows that I have done so. If I make payment to Lender under Paragraph 2, I will give Lender all notices or bills that I receive for the amounts due under this Paragraph 4.

Any claim, demand or charge that is made against property because an obligation has not been fulfilled is

(Document continued on next page)

known as a "lien." I will promptly pay or satisfy all liens against the Property that may be superior to this Security Instrument. However, this Security instrument does not require me to satisfy a superior lien if: (i) I agree in writing to pay the obligation which gave rise to the superior lien and Lender approves the way in which I agree to pay that obligation; or (ii) in good faith, I argue or defend against the superior lien in a lawsuit so that, during the lawsuit, the superior lien may not be enforced and no part of the Property must be given up; or (iii) I secure from the holder of that other lien an agreement, approved in writing by Lender, that the lien of this Security Instrument is superior to the lien held by that person. If Lender determines that any part of the Property is subject to a superior lien, Lender may give Borrower a notice identifying the superior lien. Borrower shall pay or satisfy the superior lien or take one or more of the actions set forth above within 10 days of the giving of the notice.

5.   BORROWER'S OBLIGATION TO MAINTAIN HAZARD INSURANCE - I will obtain hazard insurance to cover all buildings and other improvements that now are or in the future will be located on the Property. This insurance must cover loss or damage caused by fire, hazards normally covered by "extended coverage" hazard insurance policies and other hazards for which Lender requires coverage. The insurance must be in the amounts and for periods of time required by the Lender. I may choose the insurance company, but my choice is subject to the Lender's approval. Lender may not refuse to approve my choice unless the refusal is reasonable.

All of the insurance policies and renewals of those policies must include what is known as a "standard mortgage clause" to protect Lender. The form of all policies and renewals must be acceptable to Lender. Lender will have the right to hold the policies and renewals. If Lender requires, I will promptly give Lender all receipts of paid premiums and renewal notices that I receive.

If there is a loss or damage to the Property, I will promptly notify the insurance company and Lender. If I do not promptly prove to the insurance company that the loss or damage occurred, then Lender may do so.

The amount paid by the insurance company is called "proceeds." The proceeds will be used to repair or to

(Document continued on next page)

restore the damaged Property unless: (i) it is not economically feasible to make the repairs or restoration; or (ii) the use of the proceeds for that purpose would lessen the protection to Lender by this Security Instrument; or (iii) Lender and I have agreed in writing not to use the proceeds for that purpose. If the repair or restoration is not economically feasible or if it would lessen Lender's protection under this Security Instrument, then the proceeds will be used to reduce the amount that I owe to Lender under the Note and under this Security Instrument. If any of the proceeds remain after the amount that I owe to Lender has been paid in full, the remaining proceeds will be paid to me.

If I abandon the Property, or if I do not answer, within 30 days, a notice from Lender stating that the insurance company has offered to settle a claim, Lender may collect the proceeds. Lender may use the proceeds to repair or restore the Property or to pay the sums secured. The 30-day period will begin when the notice is given.

If any proceeds are used to reduce the amount of principal which I owe to Lender under the Note, that use will not delay the due date or change the amount of any of my monthly payments under the Note and under Paragraphs 1 and 2 above. However, Lender and I may agree in writing to those delays or changes.

If Lender acquires the Property under Paragraph 19 below, all of my rights in the insurance policies will belong to Lender. Also, all of my rights in any proceeds which are paid because of damage that occurred before the Property is acquired by Lender or sold will belong to Lender. However, Lender's rights in those proceeds will not be greater than the sums secured immediately before the Property is acquired by Lender or sold.

6.   BORROWER'S OBLIGATION TO MAINTAIN THE PROPERTY AND TO FULFILL ANY LEASE OBLIGATIONS - I will keep the Property in good repair. I will not destroy, damage or substantially change the Property, and I will not allow the Property to deteriorate. If I do not own but am a tenant on the Property, I will fulfill my obligations under my lease. I also agree that, if I acquire the fee title to the Property, my lease interest and the fee title will not merge unless Lender agrees to the merger in writing.

(Document continued on next page)

7.   LENDER'S RIGHT TO PROTECT ITS RIGHTS IN THE PROPERTY (MORTGAGE INSURANCE) - If either: (i) I do not keep my promises and agreements made in this Security Instrument, or (ii) someone, including me, begins a legal proceeding that may significantly affect Lender's rights in the Property (such as a legal proceeding in bankruptcy, in probate, for condemnation or to enforce laws or regulations), Lender may do and pay for whatever is necessary to protect the value of the Property and Lender's rights in the Property. Lender's actions may include appearing in court, paying reasonable attorneys' fees and entering on the Property to make repairs. Lender must give me notice before Lender may take any of these actions. Although Lender may take action under this Paragraph 7, Lender does not have to do so.

I will pay to Lender any amounts, with interest, which Lender spends under this Paragraph 7. I will pay those amounts to Lender when Lender sends me a notice requesting that I do so. I will also pay interest on those amounts at the Note rate. Interest on each amount will begin on the date that the amount is spent by Lender. However, Lender and I may agree in writing to terms of payment that are different from those in this paragraph. This Security Instrument will protect Lender in case I do not keep this promise to pay those amounts with interest.

If Lender has required mortgage insurance as a condition of making the loan that I promise to pay under the Note, I will pay the premiums for that mortgage insurance. I will pay the premiums until the requirement for mortgage insurance ends according to my written agreement with Lender or according to law. Lender may require me to pay the premiums in the manner described in Paragraph 2 above.

8.   LENDER'S RIGHT TO INSPECT THE PROPERTY - Lender, and others authorized by Lender, may enter on and inspect the Property. They must do so in a reasonable manner and at reasonable times. Before or at the time an inspection is made, Lender must give me notice stating a reasonable purpose for the inspection.

9.   AGREEMENTS ABOUT CONDEMNATION OF THE PROPERTY - A taking of property by any governmental authority by eminent domain is known as "condemnation." I give to Lender my right: (i) to proceeds of

(Document continued on next page)

all awards or claims for damages resulting from condemnation or other governmental taking of the Property; and (ii) to proceeds from a sale of the Property that is made to avoid condemnation. All of those proceeds will be paid to Lender.

If all of the Property is taken, the proceeds will be used to reduce the sums secured. If any of the proceeds remain after the amount that I owe to Lender has been paid in full, the remaining proceeds will be paid to me. Unless Lender and I agree otherwise in writing, if only a part of the Property is taken, the amount I owe to Lender will be reduced only by the amount of proceeds multiplied by the following fraction: the total amount of the sums secured immediately before the taking, divided by the fair market value of the Property immediately before the taking. The remainder of the proceeds will be paid to me.

If I abandon the Property, or I do not answer, within 30 days, a notice from Lender stating that a governmental authority has offered to make a payment or to settle a claim for damages, Lender has the authority to collect the proceeds. Lender may then use the proceeds to repair or restore the Property or to reduce the sums secured. The 30-day period will begin when the notice is given.

If any proceeds are used to reduce the amount of principal which I owe to Lender under the Note, that use will not delay the due date or change the amount of monthly payments under the Note and under Paragraph 1 and 2 above. However, Lender and I may agree in writing to those delays or changes.

10.   CONTINUATION OF BORROWER'S OBLIGATIONS AND OF LENDER'S RIGHTS

(A)   BORROWER'S OBLIGATIONS - Lender may allow a person who takes over my rights and obligations to delay or to change the amount of the monthly payments of principal and interest due under the Note or under this Security Instrument. Even if Lender does this, however, that person and I will both still be fully obligated under the Note and under this Security Instrument.

Lender may allow those delays or changes for a person who takes over my rights and obligations, even if Lender is requested not to do so. Lender will not be re-

(Document continued on next page)

quired to bring a lawsuit against such a person for not fulfilling obligations under the Note or under this Security Instrument, even if Lender is requested to do so.

(B) LENDER'S RIGHTS - Even if Lender does not exercise or enforce any right of Lender under this Security Instrument or under the law, Lender will still have all of those rights and may exercise or enforce them in the future. Even if Lender obtains insurance, pays taxes, or pays other claims, charges or liens against the Property, Lender will have the right under Paragraph 19 below to demand that I make immediate payment in full of the amount that I owe to the Lender under the Note and under this Security Instrument.

11. OBLIGATIONS OF BORROWER AND OF PERSONS TAKING OVER BORROWER'S RIGHTS OR OBLIGATIONS - Any person who takes over my rights or obligations under this Security Instrument will have all of my rights and will be obligated to keep all of my promises and agreements made in this Security Instrument. Similarly, any person who takes over Lender's rights of obligations under this Security Instrument will have all of Lender's rights and will be obligated to keep all of Lender's agreements made in this Security Instrument.

If more than one person signs this Security Instrument as Borrower, each of us is fully obligated to keep all of Borrower's promises and obligations contained in this Security Instrument. Lender may enforce Lender's rights under this Security Instrument against each of us individually or against all of us together. This means that any one of us may be required to pay all of the sums secured. However, if one of us does not sign the Note: (i) that person is signing this Security Instrument only to give that person's rights in the Property to Lender under the terms of this Security Instrument; and (ii) that person is not personally obligated to pay the sums secured; and (iii) that person agrees that Lender may agree with the other Borrowers to delay enforcing any of the Lender's rights or to modify or make any accommodations with regard to the terms of this security Instrument or the Note without that person's consent.

12. LOAN CHARGES - If the loan secured by this Security Instrument is subject to a law which sets maximum loan charges, and that law is finally interpreted so that

(Document continued on next page)

the interest or other loan charges collected or to be collected in connection with the loan exceed permitted limits: (i) any such loan charge shall be reduced by the amount necessary to reduce the charge to the permitted limit; and (ii) any sums already collected from the Borrower which exceeded permitted limits will be refunded to Borrower. Lender may choose to make this refund by reducing the principal owed under the Note or by making a direct payment to Borrower. If a refund reduces principal, the reduction will be treated as a partial prepayment without any prepayment charge under the Note.

13.   LEGISLATION AFFECTING LENDER'S RIGHTS - If a change in applicable law would make any provision of the Note or Security Instrument unenforceable, Lender may require immediate payment in full of all sums secured by this Security Instrument as that phrase is defined in Paragraph 19 below. If Lender requires immediate payment in full under this Paragraph 13, Lender will take the steps and may act as specified in the last paragraph of Paragraph 17 below.

14.   NOTICES REQUIRED UNDER THIS SECURITY INSTRUMENT - Any notice that must be given to me under this Security Instrument will be given by delivering it or mailing it by first class mail unless applicable law requires the use of another method. The notice will be addressed to me at the address stated in the section above titled "Description of Property." A notice will be given to me at a different address if I give the Lender a notice of a different address. Any notice must be given to Lender under this Security Instrument will be given by mailing it to Lender's address stated in paragraph (C) of the section above "Words Used in This Document." A notice will be mailed to Lender at a different address if Lender gives me notice of the address. A notice required by this Security Instrument is given when it is mailed or when it is delivered according to the requirements of this Paragraph 14 or of applicable law.

15.   LAW THAT GOVERNS THIS SECURITY INSTRUMENT - This Security Instrument is governed by federal law and the law that applies in the place where the Property is located. If any term of this Security Instrument or of the Note conflicts with the law, all other terms of this Security Instrument and of the Note will still remain in effect if they can be given effect without the conflicting

(Document continued on next page)

23. Delete these two paragraphs if the Lender will NOT require immediate payment in full of the loan on a sale or transfer of the Property.

24. Delete these three paragraphs if the Lender will NOT permit an assumption of the Note and Mortgage by another.

term. This means that any terms of this Security Instrument and of the Note which conflict with the law can be separated from the remaining terms, and the remaining terms will still be enforced.

16.   BORROWER'S COPY - I will be given one conformed copy of the Note and of this Security Instrument.

17.   AGREEMENTS ABOUT LENDER'S RIGHTS IF THE PROPERTY IS SOLD OR TRANSFERRED OR ANY RIGHTS IN THE PROPERTY ARE SOLD OR TRANSFERRED

[23][(A)   "DUE ON SALE" - Lender may require immediate payment in full, as this term is described in this Mortgage, of all sums secured by this Security Instrument if all or any part of the Property, or if any right in the Property, is sold or transferred without Lender's prior written permission. Lender also may require immediate payment in full if a beneficial interest in Borrower is sold or transferred and Borrower is not a natural person. However, Lender shall not require immediate payment in full if this is prohibited by federal law on the date of this Security Instrument.

*   If Lender requires immediate payment in full under this Paragraph 17, Lender will give me a notice which states this requirement. The notice will give me at least 30 days to make the required payment. The 30-day period will begin on the date the notice is mailed or delivered. If I do not make the required payment during that period, Lender may act to enforce its rights under this Security Instrument without giving me further notice or demand for payment.]*

[24][(B)   ASSUMPTION OF MORTGAGE - If I sell or transfer all or any part of the Property or sell or transfer any rights in the Property, any person to whom I sell or transfer the Property or any rights to the Property may take over all of my obligations and rights under the Mortgage. This is called an "assumption of the Mortgage." The Lender may, but need not, give its consent. The Lender may charge a different rate of interest that will be paid on the remaining principal balance due, either higher or lower. An assumption of the Mortgage will be permitted if: (i) I give the Lender notice of the sale or transfer and (ii) if Lender agrees that the credit of the person that I wish to sell or transfer to is satisfactory; and (iii) that person

(Document continued on next page)

25. Delete this paragraph if the Lender will NOT permit any second, junior, subordinate, or inferior mortgage on the Property.

Note: change the paragraph letters (A, B and C) if you have deleted any of the paragraphs described in Nos. 24 through 26.

agrees, in writing: (a) to pay all amounts due to Lender under the Note and Mortgage at whatever rate of interest the Lender shall then require and (b) the person signs an agreement of assumption of the Mortgage in the form acceptable to the Lender and which states that that person agrees to assume the Mortgage and agrees to be obligated to fulfill all of the Borrower's obligations as stated in the Note and Mortgage. If all of these conditions are met and the Lender agrees to permit an assumption of the Mortgage, the Lender will also agree to release me from all of my obligations under the Note and this Mortgage.

If I sell or transfer all or any part of the Property or my rights and the above conditions (i) through (iii)(b) of this paragraph 17(B) are not met, I will still be obligated under the Note and this Mortgage and the Lender may require immediate payment in full as that term is defined in this Mortgage.

The Lender will not have the right to require Immediate Payment in Full in the event of either of the following transfers: (i) rights in household appliances (but only to a person who provides me with money to buy those appliances and in order to protect that person against loss); (ii) to surviving co-owners, following the death of a co-owner, when such transfer is automatic according to law; or (iii) a lease of the Property for a term of less than three (3) years and in the event that such lease does not give to tenant an option to buy the Property.]

[25][(C)   OTHER LIENS, MORTGAGES OR EN-CUMBRANCES - Other than the lien created by this Mortgage, I will not create nor allow the creation of any liens, mortgages or encumbrances, including any that may be junior, second or subordinate or inferior to the lien created by this Mortgage, without the written consent of the Lender on such terms as the Lender may require.]

18.   BORROWER'S RIGHT TO HAVE LENDER'S ENFORCEMENT OF THIS SECURITY INSTRUMENT DISCONTINUED - Even if Lender has required immediate payment in full, I may have the right to have enforcement of this Security Instrument discontinued. I will have this right at any time before sale of the Property under any power of sale granted by this Security Instrument or at any time before a judgment has been entered enforcing this Security Instrument if I meet the following conditions:

(Document continued on next page)

(A)   I pay to Lender the full amount that would have been due under this Security Instrument and the Note if Lender had not required immediate payment in full; and

(B)   I correct my failure to keep any of my other promises or agreements made in this Security Instrument; and

(C)   I pay all of Lender's reasonable expenses in enforcing this Security Instrument including, for example, reasonable attorneys' fees; and

(D)   I do whatever Lender reasonably requires to assure that Lender's rights in the Property, Lender's rights under this Security Instrument, and my obligations under the Note and this Security Instrument continue unchanged.

If I fulfill all of the conditions in this Paragraph 18, then the note and this Security Instrument will remain in full effect as if immediate payment in full had never been required. However, I will not have the right to have Lender's enforcement of this Security Instrument discontinued if Lender has required immediate payment in full under Paragraph 13 or 17 above.

19.   LENDER'S RIGHTS IF BORROWER FAILS TO KEEP PROMISES - Except as provided in Paragraphs 13 and 17 above, if all of the conditions stated in subparagraphs (A), (B) and (C) of this Paragraph 19 are met, Lender may require that I pay immediately the entire amount then remaining unpaid under this Note and under this Security Instrument. Lender may do this without making any further demand for payment. This requirement is called "immediate payment in full."

If Lender requires immediate payment in full, Lender may bring a lawsuit to take away all of my remaining rights to the Property and have the Property sold. At this sale Lender or another person may acquire the Property. This is known as "foreclosure and sale." In any lawsuit for foreclosure or sale, Lender will have the right to collect all costs allowed by law.

Lender may require immediate payment in full under this Paragraph 19 only if the following conditions are met:

(Document continued on next page)

(A)   I fail to keep any promise or agreement made in this Security Instrument, including the promise to pay when due all sums secured.

(B)   Lender sends to me, in the manner described in Paragraph 14 above, a notice that states: (i) the promise of agreement that I failed to keep; (ii) the action that I must take to correct the default; (iii) a date by which I must correct the default (and the date must be at least 30 days from the date on which the notice is given); (iv) that if I do not correct the default by the date stated in the notice, Lender may require immediate payment in full, and as well Lender or another person may acquire the Property by means of foreclosure and sale; (v) that if I meet the conditions stated in Paragraph 18 above, I will have the right to have Lender's enforcement of this Security Instrument discontinued and to have the Note and this Security Instrument remain fully effective as if immediate payment in full had never been required; and (vi) that I have the right in any lawsuit for foreclosure and sale to argue that I did keep my promises and agreements under the Note and under this Security Instrument, and to present any other defenses that I may have.

(C)   I do not correct the default stated in the notice from Lender by the date stated in that notice.

20.   LENDER'S RIGHTS TO RENTAL PAYMENTS AND TO TAKE POSSESSION OF THE PROPERTY - If Lender requires immediate payment in full, or if I abandon the Property, then Lender, persons authorized by Lender, or a receiver appointed by a court at Lender's request may: (i) collect the rental payments, including overdue rental payments, directly from tenants; (ii) enter on and take possession of the Property; (iii) manage the Property; and (iv) sign, cancel and change leases. If Lender notifies the tenants that Lender has the right to collect rental payments directly from them under this Paragraph 20, I agree that the tenants may make those rental payments to Lender without having to ask whether I have failed to keep my promises and agreements under this Security Instrument.

If there is a judgment for Lender in a lawsuit for

(Document continued on next page)

foreclosure and sale, I will pay to Lender reasonable rent from the date the judgment is entered for as long as I occupy the Property. However, this does not give me the right to occupy the Property.

All rental payments collected by Lender or by a receiver, other than the rent paid by me under this Paragraph 20, will be used first to pay the costs of collecting rental payments and or managing the Property. If any part of the rental payment remains after those costs have been paid in full the remaining part will be used to reduce the sums secured. The cost of managing the Property may include the receiver's fees, reasonable attorneys' fees and the cost of any necessary bonds.

21.   BORROWER'S USE OF PROPERTY, COMPLI-ANCE WITH LAW AND ALTERATIONS

(A)   USE OF PROPERTY, COMPLIANCE WITH LAW - Borrower agrees to use and maintain the Property so as to be in compliance with all laws, ordinances, regulations and requirements of any governmental body applicable to the Property. Borrower agrees that the Property shall be used only as permitted by law or zoning classification on the date of signing of this Security Instrument and agrees not to use or to seek, agree to or make or permit any change in the use of the Property without the written consent of the Lender.

(B)   ALTERATIONS - Borrower agrees not to remove, demolish, destroy or materially alter or permit any other person to remove, demolish, destroy or alter the Property or any buildings or improvements located on the Property without the written consent of the Lender.

22.   LENDER'S OBLIGATION TO DISCHARGE THIS SECURITY INSTRUMENT - When Lender has been paid all amount due under the Note and under this Security Instrument, Lender will discharge this Security Instrument by delivering a certificate stating that this Security Instrument has been satisfied. I will not be required to pay Lender for this discharge, but I will pay all costs of recording the discharge in the proper official records.

(Document continued on next page)

26. The name of the the Borrower if a corporation. Otherwise delete the line.

27. The name of the Witness to the signing of the Note printed directly below the line, with the Witness to sign above the line.

28. If the Borrower is an individual, delete "BY" and print the Borrower's name directly below the line, with the Borrower to sign above the line. If the Borrower is a corporation, print the name and title of the individual acting for the corporation directly below the line, with that person to sign above the line.

29. Insert the Notary Statement for an Individual or Notary Statement for a Corporation, found elsewhere in this book, depending upon whether the Borrower is an individual or a corporation. The Notary will complete the Notary Statement.

BY SIGNING THIS MORTGAGE AND ACCEPTING THE LOAN FROM LENDER, Borrower accepts and agrees to the promises and agreements contained in this Security Instrument and in any rider(s) executed by Borrower and recorded with this Security Instrument.

Witness:

_____*[26]*_____

_____ BY_____
           [27]   [28]   Borrower

[29] [Notary Statement for Borrower]

ASSIGNMENT OF MORTGAGE (2-28)

This form is used when the Seller of real estate does not want to pay off his existing Mortgage but rather would like to assign his existing mortgage to the Buyer. Note: the Seller must very carefully review the terms of his Note and Mortgage to determine whether an assignment is permitted and if so, whether the Lender has the right to impose new repayment terms.

ASSIGNMENT OF MORTGAGE

1. The name of the Buyer of the Property, the person who will take over (assume) the existing mortgage (the Assignee).

2. If the Buyer is a corporation, insert the state of incorporation. Otherwise delete.

3. The Buyer's address.

4. The name of the Seller of the Property (the Assignor).

5. If the Seller is a corporation, insert the state of incorporation. Otherwise delete.

6. The Seller's address.

7. The address of the Property.

8. The city in which the Property is located.

9. The county in which the Property is located.

10. The state in which the Property is located.

11. On a separate sheet, headed "Schedule A," set forth the so-called "metes and bounds" that describe the property being mortgaged by feet and compass direction—which is the best description of the property. This description and the ones called for in Nos. 12 through 19 are typically found on the Property's original deed. The information should be copied from that deed EXACTLY.

1. WORDS USED IN THIS DOCUMENT

(A) "BUYER:" _____[1]_____, *[2][a corporation organized under the laws of _____,]* whose address is _____[3]_____, sometimes called either "Buyer" or "Assignee."

(B) "SELLER:" _____[4]_____, *[5][a corporation organized under the laws of _____,]* whose address is _____[6]_____, sometimes called either "Seller" or "Assignor."

(C) "PROPERTY:" located at _____[7]_____, in the City of _____[8]_____, County of _____[9]_____, State of _____[10]_____, and which has the legal description which is more fully stated on the attached SCHEDULE A [11] and as well has the following

(Document continued on next page)

12. The district number in which the Property is located.

13. The section number in which the Property is located.

14. The block number in which the Property is located.

15. The lot number(s) in which the Property is located.

16. The title of the city, county, district or state office responsible for recording deeds.

17. Choose one.

18. The number of the "Liber" (book) or "Reel" (microfilm) where the Seller's deed was recorded.

19. The Page Number of the Liber or Reel where the Seller's deed was recorded.

20. The name of the Lender.

21. Choose one. (Note: the Note and the Mortgage will state whether the Lender, typically a bank, is chartered under the laws of the United States or under state law.)

22. The state of incorporation of the Lender.

23. The address of the Lender.

24. The date of the Seller's Note.

25. The principal amount, in numbers, of the Seller's Note.

26. The annual interest rate, in numbers, due on the Seller's Note.

27. The amount, in numbers, of monthly payments due on the Seller's Note.

28. The date of the first payment due on the Seller's Note.

tax map designation: District No.: __[12]__, Section No. __[13]__, Block No.: __[14]__, Lot(s) No.: _____[15]_____, and together with all buildings and improvements and the fixtures, equipment and personal property located on the Property, and intended to be the Property sold and transferred to Seller by deed recorded in the Office of _____[16]_____ at *[17][Liber]* **OR** *[Reel]* __[18]__, Page __[19]__, sometimes called the "Property."

(D)   "LENDER:" _____[20]_____, *[21][an association formed and which exists under the laws of the United States of America.]* **OR** *[a corporation organized under the laws of ____[22]____.]* Lender's address is _____[23]_____.

2.   SELLER'S REPRESENTATIONS

(A)   SELLER'S LOAN - As evidenced by Note dated _____[24]_____, Seller borrowed the principal sum of $_____[25]_____ from Lender and that this principal amount was to be repaid with interest at the rate of __[26]__% per year with monthly payments in the amount of $_____[27]_____ commencing _____[28]_____ with a maturity date of

(Document continued on next page)

29. The maturity date of the Seller's Note.

30. A brief description of any prepayment terms that are contained in the Seller's Note, such as penalties or accelerated payments.

31. Choose one.

32. Choose one.

33. The title of the city, county, district or state office responsible for recording Mortgages.

34. Choose one.

35. The number of the "Liber" (book) or "Reel" (microfilm) where the Seller's Mortgage and Note were recorded. This and No. 36 are found in the Seller's Mortgage and Note.

36. The Page Number of the Liber or Reel where the Seller's Mortgage and Note were recorded.

37. Delete if the Note and/or Mortgage do not require the maintenance of any escrow funds for real estate taxes or the like, and skip to No. 39.

38. Insert any other escrow funds required by the Note and/or Mortgage.

39. The principal amount, in numbers, remaining due on Seller's Note.

_____[29]_____ . The Note provided that prepayment could be made _____[30]_____ *[31][with]* **OR** *[without]* penalty. The Note also provided that the Seller's promise to repay the loan could be assigned by the Seller and assumed by another *[32][with]* **OR** *[without]* the consent of the Lender.

(B) SELLER'S MORTGAGE - In order to secure the repayment of Seller's Loan, Seller, as Mortgagor, gave and Lender, as Mortgagee, accepted a Mortgage of the Property which was recorded in the Office of _____[33]_____ at *[34][Liber]* **OR** *[Reel]* ___[35]___, Page ___[36]___.

(C) SELLER'S PAYMENTS - Seller has timely made all payments of principal and interest *[37][and all required payments to any escrow funds for real estate taxes, insurance and _____[38]_____]* required by the Note and the Mortgage and there remains due the principal amount of $_____[39]_____.

(D) SELLER'S TRANSFER OF THE PROPERTY - By written contract, the Seller has agreed to sell and Buyer has agreed to purchase the Property for valuable consideration but contingent upon the Lender's consent to this assignment and release of the Seller from the obligations stated in the Note and Mortgage. Upon the consent of the Lender, Buyer agrees to pay any additional money due towards the purchase price of the Property and to assume the Note and Mortgage. Seller agrees to deliver a deed to the Property in recordable form to Buyer.

3. SELLER'S ASSIGNMENT OF NOTE AND MORTGAGE - Upon the consent of the Lender on such terms as the Lender may require to this assignment and Lender's release of the Seller, for value received, Seller hereby assigns to Buyer the Note and Mortgage and all of Seller's obligations as stated in the Note and Mortgage.

4. BUYER'S ASSUMPTION OF THE NOTE AND MORTGAGE - For value received, Buyer assumes the

(Document continued on next page)

40. Delete if there are no additional terms or conditions, and skip to No. 42.

41. Insert any other terms or conditions that are imposed by the Lender in order to give its consent.

42. The name of the Seller if a corporation. Otherwise delete the line.

Note and Mortgage in place and instead of Seller, and Buyer agrees to assume all of Seller's obligations stated in the Note and Mortgage. Buyer further agrees to be bound by all of the terms and conditions of the Note and Mortgage and any additional or different terms and conditions that the Lender may have required in exchange for giving its consent to this assignment by Seller and assumption by Buyer.

5.   LENDER'S CONSENT - By this agreement, Lender consents to: (i) the assignment of the Note and Mortgage to Buyer; (ii) the release of the Seller from any further obligation or liability under either the Note or the Mortgage; (iii) Buyer's assumption of the Note and Mortgage and all of the obligations and liabilities under both the Note and the Mortgage *[40][; and (iv) Buyer's additional promise to* _____*[41]*_____ *].*

        Seller, Buyer and Lender agree to all of the above terms.

_____*[42]*_____

(Document continued on next page)

43. If the Seller is an individual, delete "BY" and print the Seller's name directly below the line, with the Seller to sign above the line. If the Seller is a corporation, print the name and title of the individual acting for the corporation directly below the line, with that person to sign above the line.

44. The name of the Buyer if a corporation. Otherwise delete the line.

45. If the Buyer is an individual, delete "BY" and print the Buyer's name directly below the line, with the Buyer to sign above the line. If the Buyer is a corporation, print the name and title of the individual acting for the corporation directly below the line, with that person to sign above the line.

46. The name of the Lender if a corporation. Otherwise delete the line.

47. If the Lender is an individual, delete "BY" and print the Lender's name directly below the line with, the Lender to sign above the line. If the Lender is a corporation, print the name and title of the individual acting for the corporation directly below the line, with that person to sign above the line.

48. Insert a Notary Statement, found elsewhere in this book, for the Seller, either an Individual or Corporate form as appropriate.

49. Insert a Notary Statement, found elsewhere in this book, for the Buyer, either an Individual or Corporate form as appropriate.

50. Insert a Notary Statement, found elsewhere in this book, for the Lender, either an Individual or Corporate form as appropriate.

*BY*_____
[43]   (Seller)

_____*[44]*_____

*BY*_____
[45]   (Buyer)

_____*[46]*_____

*BY*_____
[47]   (Lender)

[48] [Notary Statement for Seller]

[49] [Notary Statement for Buyer]

[50] [Notary Statement for Lender]

SATISFACTION OF MORTGAGE (2-29)

This form is used to acknowledge that a Note and Mortgage have been paid in full ("satisfied"). It is signed by the Lender and given to the Borrower. The Borrower will want this document recorded with the government office which recorded his Mortgage since it is necessary to "clear the record." Note: a recorded document is never removed from the files or records; rather it is cleared by the recording of a subsequent document with the same office.

SATISFACTION OF MORTGAGE

1. The name of the Lender.

2. Choose one depending on whether the Lender is a corporation.

3. The Lender's address, if the Lender is an individual.

4. The state in which the Lender is incorporated, if the Lender is a corporation.

5. The Lender's address.

6. Choose one depending on whether the Mortgage has been assigned and the assignment recorded.

7. The name of the Borrower.

8. The date of the Mortgage.

9. The principal amount of the loan, in numbers.

10. The title of the city, county, district or state office responsible for recording mortgages.

11. Choose one. (See No. 12 for an explanation.)

12. The number of the "Liber" (book) or "Reel" (microfilm) where the Mortgage was recorded. This information and for Nos. 13 through 21 are found in the property's Mortgage.

13. The page number of the Liber or Reel where the mortgage was recorded.

KNOW ALL MEN BY THESE PRESENTS:

_____[1]_____, [2][residing at _____[3]_____,] OR [a corporation organized under the laws of _____[4]_____ with its principal office at _____[5]_____,] as owner and holder does acknowledge and certify that the following Note and Mortgage, which [6][has] OR [has not] been assigned of record, is fully satisfied, paid and discharged and does direct the Clerk to cancel of record the mortgage given by _____[7]_____ to _____[1]_____ dated _____[8]_____ in the principal sum of $_____[9]_____ recorded in the office of _____[10]_____ at [11][Liber] OR [Reel] __[12]__, Page __[13]__ and securing certain promises and obligations upon property located at

(Document continued on next page)

14. The address of the property.

15. The city in which the property is located.

16. The county in which the property is located.

17. The state in which the property is located.

18. The district number in which the property is located.

19. The section number in which the property is located.

20. The block number in which the property is located.

21. The lot number(s) in which the property is located.

22. The name of the Lender if a corporation. Otherwise delete the line.

23. If the Lender is an individual, delete "BY" and print the Lender's name directly below the line, with the Lender to sign above the line. If the Lender is a corporation, print the name and title of the individual acting for the corporation directly below the line, with that person to sign above the line.

24. Insert a Notary Statement, found elsewhere in this book, for the Lender, either for an Individual or a Corporation as appropriate.

_____[14]_____, in the City of
_____[15]_____, County of _____[16]_____, State of
_____[17]_____ and which is designated on the tax map
as: District No. __[18]__, Section No. __[19]__, Block No.
__[20]__, Lot(s) No. ____[21]____.

_____*[22]*_____

BY_____
[23]

[24] [Notary Statement for Lender]

GRANT OF EASEMENT OF RIGHT OF WAY (2-30)

Ownership of property is considered to continue underneath the land to the center of the Earth (mineral rights, etc.), and above the land to the end of the universe (air rights). An owner may not want to sell his rights either above or below his land but may agree to sell the right to enter on or walk over or string cables over a portion of the land. For example, suppose someone owns lakefront property. He may wish to grant to his neighbor the right to cross his land (to trespass) to gain access to the lake. Or suppose the power company wants to run its cables over a portion of the land. The landowner grants to his neighbor or to the power company the right, in effect, to trespass, which is called an Easement.

WARNING

An Easement is a grant of a right or interest in land. The Grantee (the one receiving the right) is strongly urged to record the Easement just as he would any deed.

GRANT OF EASEMENT OF RIGHT OF WAY

1. The date of signing the agreement.

2. The name of the owner of the property, the party who is granting the Easement (the Grantor).

3. If the Grantor is a corporation, insert the state of incorporation. Otherwise delete.

4. The name of the party who is being granted the Easement (the Grantee).

5. If the Grantee is a corporation, insert the state of incorporation. Otherwise delete.

6. Delete if the property owned is land only and does not have any improvements on it such as buildings.

7. The city in which the property is located.

8. The county in which the property is located.

INDENTURE, made as of _____[1]_____, 19__, by and between _____[2]_____ *[3][, a _____ corporation]* ("Owner" or "Grantor"), and _____[4]_____ *[5][, a _____ corporation]* ("Grantee").

1. GRANTOR'S REPRESENTATION - Grantor is the owner of the real property *[6][including all buildings and improvements on and to said property]* located in the City of _____[7]_____, County of _____[8]_____, State of

(Document continued on next page)

9. The state in which the property is located.

Note: the information for Nos. 10 through 20 is typically found on the Seller's deed or the tax map of the property located in the office of the local tax authority.

10. Delete through No. 15 if your locality does not use a "block and lot" system of identifying property.

11. The name of the town, county or district where the tax map referred to is filed.

12. Identify the specific tax map by the date of its filing.

13. The Section in which the property is located.

14. The Block in which the property is located.

15. The Lot(s) in which the property is located.

16. The address of the property.

17. The title of the city, county, district or state office responsible for recording deeds.

18. Choose one (see the explanation in No. 19 below).

19. The number of the "Liber" (book) or "Reel" (microfilm) where the Grantor's deed was actually recorded.

20. The Page Number of the Liber or Reel where the Grantor's deed was actually recorded.

_____[9]_____, *[10][identified on the Tax Map of* _____[11]_____, *dated* _____[12]_____ *as Section* ___[13]___, *Block* ___[14]___, *Lot(s)* ___[15]___*]*, known by the street address _____[16]_____ and intended to be the same property conveyed to Seller by Deed recorded in the Office of _____[17]_____ at *[18][Liber]* **OR** *[Reel]* __[19]__, Page __[20]__ (the "Premises").

(Document continued on next page)

21. Choose one. Some states require that all deeds to be recorded state the full amount (the consideration) actually paid for the Easement (for the state's use in computing any real estate transfer or sales taxes). If your state does require this, choose the second alternative.

22. The amount, in words and numbers, paid for the Easement.

23. Choose one depending on whether the Easement being granted is exclusive to the Grantee or granted to others as well.

24. Choose one and either on a separate sheet headed "Schedule A" attach a copy of the survey showing the exact location of the Easement, or insert the legal description (the so–called "metes and bounds") of the Easement.

25. The purpose of the Easement. For example: "For the sole purpose of obtaining access to Lake _____" or "For the purpose of constructing, erecting and maintaining electrical power lines" or "For the sole purpose of installing and maintaining water pipes," or the like.

26. Delete if not appropriate and also delete "; and" from the end of the previous paragraph.

2. AGREEMENT - In consideration of the sum of *[21][Ten Dollars ($10.00), lawful money of the United States and other valuable consideration]* **OR** *[_____[22]_____ Dollars ($_____) lawful money of the United States]* paid by Grantee, the receipt of which is acknowledged, Owner as Grantor does by this Indenture grant, release and forever quit-claim to Grantee, and Grantee's heirs, successors, assigns and grantees and their grantees, *[23][a non-exclusive]* **OR** *[an exclusive]* EASEMENT OF RIGHT OF WAY to pass and repass over that portion of Grantor's land as more particularly described *[24][on Schedule A annexed to and made part of this Grant of Easement of Right of Way.]* **OR** *[as follows: beginning at a point _____*
_____.]

3. PURPOSE OF PERMITTED EASEMENT -
_____[25]_____
_____
_____.

4. COVENANT TO RUN WITH THE LAND - This Easement and the rights granted shall run with the land and any sub-division(s) of the land and pass to Grantee's heirs, successors, assigns and grantees and their grantees. This Easement and the rights granted are IRREVOCABLE and shall be granted and construed to be granted and incorporated by reference by this Indenture into each and every respective deed, indenture and conveyance affecting the Premises, subject only and always to the following conditions:

(i) any and all present and future local, state and/or federal regulations, ordinances or laws affecting the use of the Premises as may be promulgated by competent authority having jurisdiction; *and*

[26] (ii) *any temporary disruption or suspension of the use of said access because of construction or related activities.*

5. INDEMNITY - By accepting this Easement of Right of Way, Grantee, Grantee's heirs, successors, assigns and grantees and their grantees agree to indemnify and hold harmless Grantor and Grantor's heirs, successors and assigns from any and all claim for damages or liability of

(Document continued on next page)

27. The name of the Grantor if a corporation. Otherwise delete the line.

28. If the Grantor is an individual, delete "BY" and print the Grantor's name directly below the line, with the Grantor to sign above the line. If the Grantor is a corporation, print the name and title of the individual acting for the corporation directly below the line, with the Grantor to sign above the line.

29. The Grantor's Taxpayer Identification Number (which for an individual is his Social Security Number).

30. The name of the Witness to the signing of the contract printed below the line, with the Witness to sign above the line.

31. The name of the Grantee if a corporation. Otherwise delete the line.

32. If the Grantee is an individual, delete "BY" and print the Grantee's name directly below the line, with the Grantee to sign above the line. If the Grantee is a corporation, print the name and title of the individual acting for the corporation directly below the line, with the Grantee to sign above the line.

33. Grantee's Taxpayer Identification number.

34. Insert a Notary Statement for the Grantor—either for an Individual or for a Corporation as appropriate. The Notary Statements are found elsewhere in this book. The Notary completes this part of the form.

35. Insert a Notary Statement for the Grantee—either for an Individual or for a Corporation as appropriate. The Notary completes this part of the form.

any kind on the part of any person by reason of Grantee's acts.

    IN WITNESS WHEREOF, this contract has been duly executed by the parties on the date first written above.

_____[27]_____

BY_____
                [28]

Grantor's Taxpayer
Identification No.:_____[29]_____

Witness:
_____   _____[31]_____
        [30]

BY_____
                [32]

Grantee's Taxpayer
Identification No.:_____[33]_____

[34][Notary Statement for Grantor]

[35][Notary Statement for Grantee]

APPLICATION FOR RESIDENTIAL LEASE (2-31)

This form is used to obtain information about a potential tenant for a Residential Lease. It should be given to any potential tenant before agreeing to lease to that tenant.

APPLICATION FOR RESIDENTIAL LEASE

The form is self-explanatory; add or delete as appropriate or necessary for your rental.

Name _____

Present Address _____
_____

Telephone # _____

Social Security # _____

Driver's Lic. # and State_____

Employer _____   Telephone # _____

Address _____   Length of Employment _____
_____

Position _____   Annual Income _____

Amount and Source of Any Additional Income:
_____
_____

Banks:
Checking A/C #_____   Bank _____
_____
Savings A/C #_____   Bank _____
_____

Credit Cards:
(List Card Issuer and Account No.)
_____
_____

Business Reference _____   Telephone # _____
_____

Business Reference _____   Telephone # _____
_____

Business Reference _____   Telephone # _____
_____

(Document continued on next page)

Pets (kind and number) _____

Number of People Who Will Occupy This Dwelling: _____

Reason(s) for Moving _____

Number of Months/Years at Present Address _____

Has Applicant Ever Been Evicted?_____

Applicant(s) and references must be satisfactory to the Landlord. Landlord will not be bound and possession will not be given until lease is signed by Landlord and delivered to Applicant. Landlord assumes no responsibility to the applicant for delay or failure to give possession due to failure of present occupant to vacate or any other reason.

Applicant acknowledges that Landlord is relying on the statements made above. Applicant warrants that any and all information and statements made on this application are true.

Applicant(s) signature _____ Date_____

Applicant(s) signature _____ Date_____

RESIDENTIAL LEASE (2-32)

A Residential Lease is the document by which the owner of real estate (the Landlord) gives the right of possession and occupancy for its use as a residence or dwelling to someone else (the Tenant) in exchange for payment (Rent). The Landlord gives this right for a stated length of time (the Term) and for a specific amount of rent, but usually (except in the case of seasonal or short-term Leases) permits the Tenant to pay that amount in monthly installments.

WARNING

Most states (and cities) have laws for the protection of Tenants that restrict the rights of Landlords. Therefore, because laws vary widely from state to state and, in some cases, even from city to city within the same state, every Landlord should consult his local housing authority or an attorney who is familiar with local laws.

RESIDENTIAL LEASE

1. The date of signing the Lease.

2. The name of the Landlord.

3. Choose one depending on whether the Landlord is a corporation.

4. The address of the Landlord.

5. The state of incorporation of the Landlord.

6. The address of the Landlord corporation's principal office.

7. The name of the Tenant.

8. Choose one depending on whether the Tenant is a corporation.

9. The address of the Tenant.

10. The state of incorporation of the Tenant.

11. The address of the Tenant corporation's principal office.

12. Choose one.

LEASE, made the _11_ [1] _/_ day of _NOV_, 19 _96_ between _L. Sam_ [2]_____, [3][residing at _____ [4]_25 s Ma sc_] **OR** [a _____ [5]_____ corporation with its principal office at _____ [6]_____], as "Landlord" and _____ [7]_____, [8][residing at _Delaware_ [9] _pelton_] **OR** [a _____ [10]_____ corporation with its principal office at _____ [11]_____], as "Tenant."

1.   PREMISES/TERM/USE - Landlord agrees to lease to Tenant the [12][house located at] **OR** [apartment known _property located at for a term of 1 year_

(Document continued on next page)

13. The apartment number, condominium unit or cooperative apartment number being rented.

14. The address of the house or the building in which the apartment, condominium unit or cooperative apartment is located.

15. The number of years or months of the Lease, in words.

16. Choose one.

17. The starting date of the Lease.

18. The ending date of the Lease.

19. The party or parties that may use the premises, such as "Tenant and Tenant's immediate family."

20. Choose one. If this is to be a typical Lease (where the rent will be paid monthly), choose the first alternative. If the Lease is for a seasonal rental (such as the summer beach season or the winter skiing season) where the custom is for the entire rent to be paid in advance in full, choose the second alternative and skip to No. 23.

21. The total rent due, in numbers.

22. The monthly rent, in numbers.

23. The total rent due, in numbers.

24. The amount, in numbers, of any deposit advanced by Tenant.

25. The balance of total rent due, in numbers.

as _____ [13] _____ in the building located at] OR [condominium unit known as _____ [13] _____ in the building located at] OR [cooperative apartment _____ [13] _____ in the building located at] _____ [14] _____
(the "Premises") for a term of __[15]__ [16][years] OR [months] beginning on _____[17]_____ and ending on _____[18]_____ for use and occupancy by _____[19]_____ as a strictly residential dwelling.

2.   RENT - [20][The rent for the term is $_____[21]_____ payable in advance without demand or notice, in equal monthly installments of $_____[22]_____ on the first day of each and every month during the term.] OR [The rent for term is $_____[23]_____ payable by the Tenant to the Landlord upon the signing of this Agreement. The parties acknowledge that $_____[24]_____ has been paid in advance, leaving a balance of $_____[25]_____ due upon execution.]

(Document continued on next page)

26. Delete this paragraph if this is NOT to be a typical Lease where the purpose of the security deposit is primarily to guaranty payment of the rent.

27. The amount, in numbers, of the security deposit (typically, an amount equal to one month's rent for each year of the Lease term).

28. Choose one, depending on whether state or local housing laws require the payment of interest on rent security deposits.

29. Choose one, depending on whether state or local housing laws require deposit in a bank and depending on whether such laws require that separate accounts be maintained.

30. The name and address of the bank to which the Tenant's security deposit has been deposited.

31. The number of days, in numbers, in which the Landlord will return the Tenant's security deposit.

32. Delete this paragraph if the Lease is NOT for a seasonal rental where the purpose of the security deposit is primarily for repairs.

33. The amount, in numbers, of the seasonal security deposit.

[26][3. SECURITY - Landlord acknowledges receipt from Tenant of the sum of $_____ [27]_____ as security deposit, which [28][shall] OR [shall not] bear interest, [29][need not be kept separate from other monies belonging to Landlord] OR [shall be deposited to _____ [30]_____ and shall not be commingled with other monies belonging to Landlord], and shall be returned to Tenant within __[31]__ days of the peaceful termination of the full term of this lease and surrender of possession, less the cost of any repairs which shall have been made necessary by acts of the Tenant.]

[32][3. SECURITY - Tenant has deposited with the Landlord the sum of $_____ [33]_____ upon signing of this lease, said sum to be held by the Landlord for a period of thirty (30) days after termination of this Lease, said deposit money to be used by the Landlord in the event of damage or loss resulting to either the real or personal property contained in said demised Premises not properly repaired or replaced by Tenant within twenty (20) days of termination, said sum of money to be used to clean, repair or replace same, said sum of money also to be used to pay for any unpaid utilities, services, fuels and supplies, to the extent that there are any, for which the Tenant is responsible; however, said deposit does not release Tenant from the obligation to pay for same when bills are presented, and the balance, if any, shall be returned to the Tenant within thirty (30) day of the termination of this Lease. The Tenant hereby authorizes the Landlord to pay out of the aforesaid deposit such charges and expenses herein set forth.]

4.   OCCUPANCY AND USE - The Premises shall be used solely as a private dwelling for Tenant and his immediate family and for no others except with written permission of Landlord. Tenant agrees not to use or permit the use of the Premises for unlawful or immoral purposes. Tenant shall keep the grounds in neat order, to remove ashes, waste and refuse from the Premises and to dispose of same only in accordance with all local laws, rules and regulations. Tenant agrees to keep Premises clean, sanitary and in good order, and agrees not to hamper, disturb or interfere with other tenants in the building, nor to create or suffer any nuisances in the Premises affecting the rights of others, and agrees to comply with all laws, ordinances, rules, regulations and directions of governmental authorities and the Board of Fire Underwriters. Upon termination of this lease, Tenant agrees to surrender possession in as

(Document continued on next page)

34. Delete if NOT a condominium unit.

35. The name of the condominium.

36. Delete if NOT a cooperative apartment.

37. The name of the Cooperative Apartment Corporation.

38. Add or delete items as appropriate.

39. Add or delete items as appropriate.

good condition and repair as when received, ordinary wear and tear excepted.

[34]   [(A)   It is specifically understood by the parties that this Lease is made in connection with a Condominium Unit and is presented in this form for convenience only. This lease and the rights of Landlord, as owner of the Condominium Unit, and Tenant are subject and subordinate to all covenants and restrictions contained in the Master or Unit Owner's Deed to the _____[35]_____ and the by-laws and "house rules" of the Condominium Association as they may exist from time to time.]

[36]   [(A)   Tenant understands and acknowledges that the Building in which the Apartment is located is a cooperative apartment building and that the Owner is the owner of shares of stock of _____[37]_____ (the Apartment Corporation) appurtenant to the Apartment and entitled to occupancy of the Apartment pursuant to a proprietary lease for the Apartment. Accordingly, it is agreed that this instrument is a sub-lease and that it is subject to and subordinate to Owner's Proprietary Lease, and "house rules" and the by-laws of the Apartment Corporation, as they may exist from time to time.]

(i) The parties acknowledge and agree that this sublease and the occupancy of the Apartment by the Tenant named herein is subject to the consent of the Board of Directors of the cooperative apartment corporation.

(ii) Tenant agrees to abide by the terms and conditions of the Proprietary Lease, the "house rules" and the by-laws of the Apartment Corporation and further agrees that a violation of any of the terms and conditions of the Proprietary Lease, the "house rules" and the by-laws as they apply to Tenant shall be deemed a material violation of this sublease.]

5.   EQUIPMENT/APPLIANCES - The Premises is furnished by the Landlord with a *[38][range, refrigerator, disposal, dishwasher]* among other mechanical installations and *[39][furniture, furnishings, bedding supplies, including blankets, bed-linens, towels, kitchen supplies, including utensils]*. Tenant agrees to use and maintain all such equipment, and plumbing fixtures and all other equipment, furniture, furnishings and supplies with which Premises is

(Document continued on next page)

40. Add or delete items as appropriate.

furnished, in accordance with manufacturers' specifications and the regulations of the Landlord now or hereafter provided, and to be responsible for all repairs and any damages to the Premises brought about by misuse or neglect of such equipment by the Tenant. All repairs to equipment furnished by Landlord shall be made by licensed persons approved by Landlord. Should Tenant fail or refuse to make repairs after reasonable notice from Landlord, Landlord may cause same to be done and the cost thereof shall be additional rent immediately due from Tenant to Landlord.

6.   ALTERATIONS/ADDITIONS/IMPROVE-MENTS - Tenant agrees not to make any alterations, additions, improvements or changes in the Premises, interior or exterior, or to the equipment and fixtures provided by Landlord or to install any major appliances in the Premises without written consent of the Landlord.

7.   SERVICES/UTILITIES - Tenant acknowledges that Owner has no obligation to provide *[40][electrical service, heating/cooking fuel/oil, telephone service]* and that no part of the rent is for such service or services. Tenant shall make such separate arrangement with the local utility providing such service as may be required, shall have accounts with said suppliers in Tenant's name, shall timely pay all bills therefore and will not suffer or permit any charges for such services to become a lien against the Premises or separate account of the Landlord.

(A)   Interruption of Service - Interruption or failure of any service maintained for the Premises, if due to causes beyond Landlord's control, shall not entitle Tenant to any claim against Landlord or to any reduction in rent, and shall not constitute constructive eviction unless Landlord shall fail to take such measures as may be reasonable in the circumstances to restore the service without undue delay.

8.   ASSIGNMENT - No assignment or sub-lease of the Premises shall be binding upon the Landlord or confer any rights on the proposed assignee or sub-lessee without the written consent of Landlord. No assignment or sub-lease shall release Tenant from the obligations of this lease.

9.   POSSESSION/DELAY IN TENDER OF POSSESSION - Taking of possession of the Premises by Tenant

(Document continued on next page)

41. Choose one.

42. Identify, by kind and number, any permitted pets.

43. The time period in days, in numbers, during which the Landlord can show the leased space to prospective Tenants.

shall be conclusive evidence against Tenant that he received the Premises in good condition. If Landlord is unable to give possession on the commencement date, rent shall abate until possession is given, and Tenant shall pay a fractional part from the date of possession up to the first day of the next month following date of possession. Tenant waives all damages by reason of Landlord's failure to give possession on the commencement date. Delay in tendering possession shall not extend the termination date of this lease.

10. RELEASE OF LIABILITY - The Tenant assumes all risk of any damage to person or property that may occur by reason of water or the bursting or leaking of any pipes or waste about said Premises or from any act of negligence of any co-tenants or occupants of the building or of any other person, or fire or hurricane or other act of God or from any cause whatsoever, provided that Landlord shall make necessary repairs to prevent further damage upon reasonable diligence after notice given to it, and the Tenant agrees to give the Landlord prompt written notice of any accident to or defect in the water pipes, electricity or of any plumbing, heating or cooling apparatus or device.

11. PETS - It is the specific understanding of Landlord and Tenant that *[41][no pets]* **OR** *[the _____ [42]_____ presently owned by the Tenants shall be allowed in the Premises, but no other animals or pets]* shall be permitted.

12. TENANT'S PROPERTY - If, upon the termination of this lease or abandonment of the Premises by Tenant, Tenant abandons or leaves any property in the Premises, Landlord shall have the right, without notice to Tenant, to store or otherwise dispose of the property at Tenant's cost and expense, without being liable in any respect to the Tenant.

13. PARKING - Tenant shall use only that parking space designated for his use by the Landlord, and the Tenant shall see to it that Tenant's guests use only the parking space provided for guest parking.

14. RIGHT OF ENTRY - Landlord shall have the right to enter the Premises at all times which are necessary to make needed repairs, and this right shall exist whether or not Tenant or other occupant shall be on the Premises at such time. During the last __[43]__ days of the term of the

(Document continued on next page)

44. The amount of fire/theft insurance coverage, in numbers, required to be maintained by the Tenant.

45. The amount of liability insurance coverage, in numbers, required to be maintained by the Tenant.

46. The amount, expressed as a percentage of the monthly rental, in numbers, of any late charge to be assessed by the Landlord (typically five percent of the rent).

47. The number of days' notice, in words and numbers, which the Landlord will give for the Tenant to cure any default (typically ten or more, but not more than thirty).

48. The number of days' notice, in words and numbers, which the Landlord will give for termination of the Lease based upon failure to cure a default after notice (typically ten days).

lease, Landlord shall have the right to enter the Premises at reasonable hours to show the same to prospective tenants.

15.   FIRE AND CASUALTY - If the Premises is damaged by fire or other casualty, Landlord may cause the damage to be repaired and the rent will be abated from such period of time as Premises remain untenantable, but if the Premises is destroyed or so damaged that Landlord shall decide that it is inadvisable to repair same, this lease shall cease and terminate, and rental shall be adjusted to the date when such fire or casualty occurred. Tenant agrees to release Landlord from any and all claims for loss, damage or inconvenience arising from such fire or casualty.

16.   INSURANCE - Tenant shall obtain and maintain a homeowner's insurance policy with a qualified insurance company with respect to the Premises and Tenant's personal property therein with minimum coverage for fire and theft in the amount of no less than $_____[44]_____ and personal liability claims in an amount of no less than $_____[45]_____.

17.   LATE CHARGE - Tenant understands that timely payment of rent is of the essence of this agreement. Tenant agrees to pay as additional rent a late charge equal to __[46]__ percent of any rent payment received by Owner more than ten (10) days after it is due.

18.   DEFAULT - If Tenant shall fail to pay the rent or any other charge required to be paid by Tenant, or if Tenant shall breach any of the terms of this lease or the rules attached hereto, if any, or enacted from time to time, then as to every default or breach, except non-payment of rent, Landlord may give Tenant ____[47]____ (__) days' written notice thereof, and if such default has not been cured within such period, then Landlord may give Tenant ____[48]____ (__) days' notice of the termination of this lease, and this lease shall expire accordingly and Tenant shall surrender possession to Landlord, but Tenant shall remain liable as hereinafter provided. If the Premises becomes vacant or abandoned, this lease shall expire and terminate and Landlord may re-enter and may take possession of the Premises in the manner provided by law. In case Landlord shall recover possession of the Premises, Landlord may, but shall not be required to remove the property of Tenant and store the same at Tenant's expense, or he may dispose of said property, and Tenant agrees that in no respect shall Land-

(Document continued on next page)

49. Delete if there are no "House Rules" governing the use of the Premises. Then renumber paragraph 20 as paragraph 19 and delete No. 54. (Note: if the Premises being rented is a condominium unit or cooperative apartment, it is likely that the owner, the Landlord, will himself be subject to so-called "House Rules," in which event these same rules should be made part of any Lease so that the Tenant will be bound by them as well.

lord be responsible in damages for any action in entering said Premises or removing and disposing of Tenant's property, with or without process of law. Notwithstanding anything stated herein, Tenant agrees that whether possession is taken or this lease is cancelled by Landlord, the entire unpaid balance of rent shall accelerate and immediately become due and payable and Tenant shall be responsible for all costs, including attorneys' fees incurred by Landlord in enforcing this and any other provision of this lease.

In the event of a default by Tenant, Landlord shall not be required to return any part or portion of the security deposit but may retain all or any part or portion of the security deposit as liquidated damages or apply all or any part or portion of the security deposit against actual damages sustained by reason of Tenant's default. The retention of the security deposit shall not be the only remedy to which Landlord is entitled but Landlord shall have all recourse against Tenant provided by this lease and by law, and all remedies shall be cumulative and non-exclusive. Tenant agrees to pay Landlord's reasonable attorneys' fees and expenses incurred in and about enforcing any of the terms of this lease, in collecting past due rent, and in and about recovering possession from Tenant, should the services of an attorney be retained by Landlord in so doing.

19.   [49][RULES AND REGULATIONS - There are attached hereto certain Rules and Regulations which are made a part of this lease. Tenant agrees to comply with all current rules and regulations, together with any subsequent reasonable rules and regulations which may be adopted by the Landlord for the general benefit of all tenants in the building. Any violation of these rules or any one of them shall be cause for termination of this lease at the option of the Landlord.]

20.   QUIET ENJOYMENT - In the event that Tenant pays the rent as provided for herein and otherwise performs all of the covenants and conditions to be performed by the Tenant and abides by all of the rules and regulation as set forth herein and referred to, Tenant shall have peaceful and

(Document continued on next page)

50. The name of the Landlord if a corporation. Otherwise delete the line.

51. If the Landlord is an individual, delete "BY" and print the Landlord's name directly below the line, with the Landlord to sign above the line. If the Landlord is a corporation, print the name and title of the individual acting for the corporation directly below the line, with that person to sign above the line.

52. The name of the Tenant if a corporation. Otherwise delete the line.

53. If the Tenant is an individual, delete "BY" and print the Tenant's name directly below the line, with the Tenant to sign above the line. If the Tenant is a corporation, print the name and title of the individual acting for the corporation directly below the line, with that person to sign above the line.

Note: if the Tenant is a corporation, the Landlord may want to consider requiring that the Tenant corporation's Lease obligations (particularly the payment of rent) be personally guaranteed by an officer of the corporation. A Personal Guaranty form is found elsewhere in this book.

54. A typical set of "House Rules" is set forth. Rules can be added, deleted or modified to fit a particular situation. For example, if the Premises does not have an elevator, delete those rules which refer to an elevator. It is also suggested that a copy of any "House Rules" be attached to the Lease and initialed by the Tenant (to prove his receipt). Delete if paragraph 19 was deleted. (See instruction No. 49.)

quiet enjoyment of all the demised Premises for the term of this lease.

  IN WITNESS WHEREOF, the Landlord and Tenant have executed this lease the day and year first above written.

_____*[50]*_____

BY_____
                    [51] (Landlord)

_____*[52]*_____

BY_____
                    [53] (Tenant)

[54]RULES AND REGULATIONS

1.   *Public halls and stairways shall not be obstructed or used for any purpose other than for ingress to, and egress from, the apartments.*

2.   *Passenger and service elevators shall be operated only by employees of the Landlord, without any interference whatsoever by the Tenants, members of their families, or their agents, servants or visitors.*

3.   *No Tenant shall make or permit any disturbing noises in the building by himself, his family, agents, servants or visitors; nor do, nor permit any of such persons to do, anything that will interfere with the rights, comforts or convenience of other Tenants. No Tenant shall play upon, or suffer to be played upon or operated, any musical instrument, phonograph, radio or other like device in the demised premises between the hours of eleven o'clock P.M. and the following eight o'clock A.M., if the same shall disturb or annoy other occupants of the building.*

4.   *Tenants, their families, agents, servants and visitors*

(Document continued on next page)

shall not throw anything whatever out of the windows or doors, or in the halls of the building.

5. *Supplies, goods and packages of every kind shall be delivered to Tenants at the entrance provided for deliveries, through service elevators; and the Landlord shall not be responsible for loss of, or damage to, any such property, notwithstanding such loss or damage may occur through the carelessness or negligence of employees of the Landlord. Landlord shall not be responsible for any article left with any employee.*

6. *All garbage and refuse must be sent to the basement from the apartments and kitchens, at such times as may be directed, and in accordance with the Landlord's superintendent.*

7. *No baby carriages, tricycles, or bicycles will be allowed in passenger elevators, or in the halls, passageways, areas or courts of the building.*

8. *Baggage must be taken in and out through the service entrance.*

9. *Each Tenant shall keep the premises leased in a good state of preservation and cleanliness and shall not sweep or throw or permit to be swept or thrown from the premises leased, any dirt or other substance into any of the corridors, halls, elevators or stairways of the building, or into any of the light shafts or ventilators of it.*

10. *No garbage can, kitchen supplies, or other article, shall be placed in the halls or on the staircase landings, nor shall anything be hung from the windows or balconies, or placed upon any window sill or ledge. Nor shall any article be shaken or hung from any of the windows or doors.*

11. *The obstruction of the fire escapes is prohibited by the Fire Department as well as by the Landlord.*

12. *The water-closets and other water apparatus shall not be used for any purposes other than those for which they were constructed. Any resulting damage*

(Document continued on next page)

from misuse shall be borne by the Tenant by whom, or upon whose premises, it shall have been caused.

13. *Children shall not play in the public halls, stairways or elevators, nor be permitted in the service elevators.*

14. *No sign, signal, advertisement or illumination shall be inscribed or exposed on or at any window, or other part of the building, except such as first shall have been approved in writing by the Landlord, nor shall anything be projected out of any window without such written consent.*

15. *No shades, awnings or window guards shall be used except such as shall have been first approved in writing by the Landlord.*

16. *No dogs or other animals shall be kept or harbored in the leased premises.*

17. *The Landlord reserves the right to make such other rules and regulations, from time to time, as may be deemed needful for the safety, care and cleanliness of the premises and for securing the comfort and convenience of all Tenants.*

18. *Each Tenant, without charge, shall have the use of a reasonable portion of the storeroom space to be designated by the Landlord, provided that the Landlord shall not be liable for any loss or damage to property left, placed or stored in such storeroom.*

EXTENSION/RENEWAL
OF RESIDENTIAL LEASE (2-33)

A Residential Lease Extension/Renewal is typically less complex than one for commercial property. This form is to be used when the only change in the Residential Lease is a new rent (and payment of additional security based on the higher rental).

This form also provides for the Tenant, or for one of the Tenants in the case of Joint Tenants, to indicate his desire not to extend or renew his lease.

WARNING

Many states regulate residential housing by law. It is recommended that you consult your local housing authority to determine any local requirements such as the length of an extension or renewal that **must** be offered to a Tenant not in default as well as the maximum permitted rent increase.

EXTENSION/RENEWAL
OF RESIDENTIAL LEASE

1. The name of each Tenant as it appears on the Lease.

2. The date of the Lease being extended.

3. Identify the leased premises by apartment number, street address, etc.

4. The expiration date of the existing Lease or Extension.

5. The commencement date of this Extension.

6. The annual rent, in numbers, to be charged during the Extension period.

7. The monthly rent, in numbers, to be charged during the Extension period.

8. The length of the Extension period in years or months, in words, for example "two years."

9. The ending date of the Extension period.

10. The amount, in numbers, of additional security required.

11. The total security that will be held upon payment of the additional security.

Tenant(s): _____[1]_____   Re: Lease
           _____[1]_____   Dated: ____[2]____, 19__
Premises: _____[3]_____   Expires:___[4]___, 19__
           _____

Dear Tenant(s):

The Lease referred to above expires shortly. If you wish to extend this Lease, the annual rent for the Premises commencing on _____[5]_____, 19__, will be $_____[6]_____ payable $___[7]___ monthly in advance, for an extended term of _____[8]_____ ending on _____[9]_____, 19__.

If you elect to extend your Lease, additional security will be required in the amount of $___[10]___, making the total security $___[11]___.

All other terms, covenants and conditions of the Lease shall remain in full force and effect for the duration of the extended term. HOWEVER, IF PRIOR TO THE COMMENCEMENT OF THE EXTENDED TERM YOU DEFAULT IN ANY OF THE TERMS, COVENANTS AND CONDITIONS OF THIS LEASE, THIS AGREEMENT OF EXTENSION SHALL, AT THE OPTION OF THE LANDLORD, BE NULL AND VOID.

Each Tenant named on the original Lease who wishes to extend the term of the original Lease must sign this agreement where indicated (X) and return two (2) copies to the Landlord together with a check in the amount

(Document continued on next page)

12. The number of days, in numbers, prior to the expiration date by which the Tenant must sign and return the Extension.

13. The name of the Tenant wishing to extend and renew his Lease printed directly below the line, with the Tenant to sign above the line.

14. The name of the Landlord if a corporation. Otherwise delete the line.

15. If the Landlord is an individual, delete "BY" and print the Landlord's name directly below the line, with the Landlord to sign above the line. If the Landlord is a corporation, print the name and title of the individual acting for the corporation directly below the line, with that person to sign above the line.

16. The name of the Tenant wishing to vacate (and NOT extend and renew his lease) printed directly below the line, with the Tenant to sign above the line.

of the additional security not less than __[12]__ days BEFORE the expiration date noted above. If any Tenant named on the original Lease intends to vacate the Premises, each such Tenant should sign his name under the words "Tenant(s) will vacate the Premises at the end of the present term" and return a copy to the Landlord.

(Sign here to extend Lease)
Tenant(s):

This EXTENSION AGREEMENT does not become binding until the return to you of a copy signed by Landlord.

X_____
     [13] (Tenant)

_____*[14]*_____

X_____
     [13] (Tenant)

BY_____
     [15] (Landlord)

Tenant(s) will vacate the Premises at the end of the term:

X_____
     [16] (Tenant)

X_____
     [16] (Tenant)

APPLICATION FOR COMMERCIAL LEASE (2-34)

This form is used to obtain information about a potential tenant for a Commercial Lease. It should be given to any potential tenant before agreeing to lease space to that tenant.

APPLICATION FOR COMMERCIAL LEASE

The form is self-explanatory; add or delete as appropriate or necessary.

Name of Business _____

Contact Person _____

Present Address _____ Telephone # _____
_____

Federal Taxpayer ID No. _____

Date Business Established _____

Type of Business: _____

No. of Employees to Be at This Location _____

Special Operating Permits Required _____
_____

Banks:
Checking A/C #_____ Bank _____
_____

Checking A/C #_____ Bank _____
_____

Bank Reference _____ Telephone # _____
_____

Bank Reference _____ Telephone # _____
_____

Personal Reference _____ Telephone # _____
_____

Personal Reference _____ Telephone # _____
_____

No. of Parking Spaces Required and
Other Special Requirements
_____

Reason(s) for Moving _____
_____

Number of Months/Years at Present Address _____

(Document continued on next page)

Has Applicant Ever Been Evicted?_____

Applicant(s) and references must be satisfactory to the Landlord. Landlord will not be bound and possession will not be given until lease is signed by Landlord and delivered to Applicant. Landlord assumes no responsibility to the applicant for delay or failure to give possession due to failure of present occupant to vacate or any other reason.

Applicant acknowledges that Landlord is relying on the statements made above. Applicant warrants that any and all information and statements made on this application are true.

Applicant(s) signature _____ Date_____

Applicant(s) signature _____ Date_____

COMMERCIAL LEASE (2-35)

At its simplest level, a Lease is an agreement by an owner of property (the Landlord) to allow another (the Tenant) to use, occupy and possess (but not own) that property for a particular period of time (the Term) and for the Tenant to pay for that use (Rent). Note that the contract between the Landlord and the Tenant is essentially one in which the rent charge is permitted to be paid over time (that is, over the term of the Lease). But in reality the entire, total rent is what the Landlord is entitled to as the consideration for permitting the use and occupancy by the Tenant. Thus, if the Tenant defaults at some time during the term of the Lease, he is still obligated for the total rent less whatever he paid prior to the default.

The extent to which a "modern" Lease deals with matters other than the bare-bones use, rent and term issues is a reflection of the fact that a Landlord wants to pass through to the Tenant any increase in operating costs during the term of the Lease or expenses that may be caused by the Tenant's use of the property. This is particularly so for Commercial Leases which typically are not subject to regulation (unlike Residential Leases which are regulated in most states) based on the theory that a businessman probably needs less protection from the Landlord than does an individual renting a home.

Note that while the current real estate tax is reflected in the rent, this Lease provides that any increase will be paid by the Tenant. A Landlord should always be aware of costs that are likely to increase over the term of a Lease and should provide in the Lease for passing these on to the Tenant. Additionally, a Landlord should consider any other financial exposure, based on the type of business that will be conducted by the Tenant, and protect himself accordingly in the Lease.

COMMERCIAL LEASE

1. The name of the Landlord.

2. Choose one depending on whether the Landlord is a corporation.

3. The address of the Landlord.

4. The state of incorporation of the Landlord.

5. The address of the Landlord corporation's principal office.

6. The name of the Tenant.

7. Choose one depending on whether the Tenant is a corporation.

8. The address of the Tenant.

9. The state of incorporation of the Tenant.

LEASE, between _____[1]_____, *[2][residing at _____[3]_____] OR [a _____[4]_____ corporation with its principal office at _____[5]_____]*, as "Landlord" and _____[6]_____, *[7][residing at _____[8]_____] OR [a _____[9]_____ corpo-*

(Document continued on next page)

10. The address of the Tenant corporation's principal office.

11. A description of the leased space, for example "a suite," "a room," "a floor," etc.

12. Identify the specific space being leased, such as the suite number, room number or floor number.

13. If only a portion of a building is being leased (such as part of one floor), it is recommended that plans be made a part of the Lease (annexed) to identify exactly which space is being leased. Otherwise delete.

14. The address of the building.

15. The city in which the space being leased is located.

16. The county in which the space being leased is located.

17. The state in which the space being leased is located.

18. The number of years or months, in words, of the term of the Lease.

19. Choose one.

20. The first day of the term of the Lease (the "commencement date").

21. The last day of the term of the Lease.

22. The use of the space which is permitted by the Landlord.

ration with its principal office at
_____*[10]*_____*],* as "Tenant."

1.   PREMISES, TERM AND USE - Landlord agrees to lease to Tenant _____[11]_____ known as _____[12]_____ *[13][and more particularly described on the plan annexed to and made part of this Lease]* in the building located at _____[14]_____ in the City of _____[15]_____, County of _____[16]_____, State of _____[17]_____ (the "Premises"), for a term of ___[18]___ *[19][years]* **OR** *[months]* beginning on _____[20]_____ and ending on _____[21]_____ for use and occupancy as _____[22]_____.

(Document continued on next page)

23. The annual rent being charged, in words and numbers.

24. If the rent will automatically increase during the term of the Lease, insert the increased amounts along with the starting and ending dates of each increase. Otherwise delete.

25. The day of the month on which rent must be paid (typically the 1st).

26. The amount of the security deposit, in numbers. (In some areas, the custom is for the security to equal one or two month's rent, in other areas the custom is an amount equal to one month's rent for each year of the Lease.)

27. Choose one. (Note: some states require the payment of interest on rent security deposits while others do not. In addition, some states prohibit combining security deposits with the Landlord's own monies.)

2.   RENT - Tenant shall pay the annual rental of
_____[23]_____ Dollars ($_____)
*[24][*_____
_____*]*
paid in equal monthly installments in advance on the
__[25]__ day of each and every month during the term of
this Lease.

3.   SECURITY - Tenant has deposited with Landlord
$_____[26]_____ as security for the faithful performance
by Tenant of all the terms, covenants and conditions of this
Lease on Tenant's part to be performed. Provided Tenant
has fully and faithfully carried out all of said terms, covenants and conditions on Tenant's part to be performed, this
security deposit shall be returned to Tenant after the expiration of this Lease *[27][with]* **OR** *[without]* interest.

        (A)   In the event of a bona fide sale, subject to
this Lease, Landlord shall have the right to transfer the
security to the buyer for the benefit of Tenant. Landlord,
upon notice to Tenant of such sale and assignment of the
security deposit to the buyer, shall be released from all
liability for the return of such security. Tenant agrees to
look solely to the new Landlord for the return of the said
security, and it is agreed that this shall apply to subsequent
transfer or assignment of the security to any new Landlord.

        (B)   The security deposited under this Lease shall
not be mortgaged, assigned or encumbered by the Tenant
without the written consent of the Landlord.

4.   CARE OF PREMISES, ALTERATIONS, ETC. -
Tenant shall take good care of the Premises and any fixtures which are and shall remain the property of the Landlord which may be located or situated on, in or made a part
of the Premises and shall, at Tenant's own cost and expense
make all repairs to the Premises and fixtures other than
structural repairs. At the end of the term of this Lease,
Tenant shall deliver the Premises in good order and condition, damages by the elements excepted.

        (A)   The Tenant shall promptly execute and
comply with all statutes, ordinances, rules, orders, regulations and requirements of any governmental or quasi-
governmental authority, including departments, bureaus
and the like, having jurisdiction applicable to the Premises,
for the correction, prevention, and abatement of violations,

(Document continued on next page)

28. Add or delete as appropriate depending on exactly what services the Landlord is providing. (For example, a two story building is unlikely to have an elevator, in which case the reference to elevator service should be deleted. On the other hand, if the building does have an elevator which is not self–service the Landlord should specify what time the elevator will be attended to avoid a Tenant's claim of a so-called constructive eviction if he should be working late at night and the elevator is not in operation.)

nuisances or other grievances, in, upon, or connected with the Premises during the term of this Lease, at the Tenant's own cost and expense.

(B)   Tenant's, Tenant's successors, heirs, executors or administrators shall not make any alterations to the Premises without the Landlord's consent in writing; or occupy, or permit or suffer the same to be occupied for any business or purpose deemed disreputable or extra-hazardous on account of fire, under the penalty of damages and forfeiture, and in the event of a breach thereof, the term herein shall immediately cease and terminate at the option of the Landlord as if it were the expiration of the original term.

(C)   Tenant will not do anything in or to the Premises, or bring anything into the Premises, or permit anything to be done or brought into or kept in the Premises, which will in any way increase the rate of fire insurance on said Premises, nor use the Premises or any part thereof, nor allow or permit its use for any business or purpose which would cause an increase in the rate of fire insurance on said building, and the Tenant agrees to pay as additional rent the cost of any increase in fire insurance on demand by Landlord.

(D)   Tenant shall not encumber or obstruct the sidewalk in front of, entrance to, or halls and stairs of said Premises, nor allow the same to be obstructed or encumbered in any manner.

(E)   Landlord is exempt from any and all liability for any damage or injury to person or property caused by or resulting from steam, electricity, gas, water, rain, ice or snow, or any leak or flow from or into any part of said building or from any damage or injury caused by or due to the negligence of the Landlord.

5.   SERVICES PROVIDED BY LANDLORD - As long as Tenant is not in default of any of the terms and conditions of this Lease, Landlord agrees to provide the following services:

[28]   [(A)   *Heat, when and as required by law and except for holidays, Monday through Friday from _____ A.M. to _____ P.M. and Saturdays from _____ A.M. to _____ P.M.*

(Document continued on next page)

(B)   Air conditioning/cooling/ventilation, except for holidays from May 15th through September 30th from _____ A.M. to _____ P.M. and Saturdays _____ A.M. to _____ P.M.

(C)   Elevator except for holidays, Monday through Friday from _____ A.M. to _____ P.M. and Saturdays from _____ A.M. to _____ P.M.

(D)   Water for ordinary lavatory purposes, except that if, in the sole determination of Landlord, Tenant shall use or consume water for any other purpose or in unusual quantities, Tenant shall pay to Landlord the rent or charge which may, during the term of this Lease, be assessed or imposed for the water used or consumed in or on the said Premises, whether determined by meter or otherwise, as soon as and when the same may be assessed or imposed and will also pay the expenses for the installation, setting and maintenance of a water meter in the said Premises should a meter be required by Landlord. Tenant shall pay Tenant's proportionate part of the sewer rent or charge imposed upon the building. All such rents or charges or expenses shall be paid as additional rent when billed by Landlord.

(E)   Electrical service at all times except that if the Premises shall not be separately metered, Tenant agrees to pay as additional rent ___% of the electric bill as Landlord may determine based upon a survey of the consumption and equipment used by Tenant (or such additional percentage as may be determined by Landlord based upon changes in consumption by Tenant) and if the Premises shall be separately metered, Tenant agrees to make its own arrangements with the utility company providing electricity and to pay all bills in its own name.

(F)   Cleaning services on business days provided that the Premises are kept in order by Tenant. Tenant shall pay as additional rent the cost of removal of Tenant's rubbish or refuse. Window cleaning shall be at Landlord's sole cost and expense and at such times as Landlord may determine, it being understood and agreed that Tenant is strictly forbidden and prohibited from cleaning any window from the outside.]

6.   NO ABATEMENT OF RENT OR ADDITIONAL RENT - Landlord shall not be liable for failure to give

(Document continued on next page)

possession of the Premises upon commencement date by reason of the fact that the Premises are not ready for occupancy or because a prior tenant or any other person is wrongfully holding over or is in wrongful possession, or for any other reason. The rent shall not commence until possession is given or is available, but the term herein shall not be extended.

(A)   This lease and the obligation of Tenant to pay rent hereunder and perform all of the other covenants and agreements hereunder on part of Tenant to be performed shall in no way be affected, impaired or excused because Landlord is unable to supply or is delayed in supplying any service expressly or impliedly to be supplied or is unable to make, or is delayed in making any repairs, additions, alterations or decorations or is unable to supply or is delayed in supplying any equipment or fixtures if Landlord is prevented or delayed from so doing by reasons of government preemption in connection with a National Emergency or in connection with any rule, order or regulation of any department or subdivision thereof of any governmental agency or by reason of the conditions of supply and demand which have been or are affected by war or other emergency.

(B)   No diminution or abatement of rent, or other compensation, shall be claimed or allowed for inconvenience or discomfort arising form the making of repairs or improvements to the building or to its appliances, nor for any space taken to comply with any law, ordinance or order of a government authority. In respect to the various "services" if any, herein expressly or impliedly agreed to be furnished by Landlord to Tenant, it is agreed that there shall be no diminution or abatement of the rent, or any other compensation, for interruption or curtailment of such "service" when such interruption or curtailment shall be due to accident, alteration or repairs desirable or necessary to be made or to inability or difficulty in securing supplies or labor for the maintenance of such "service" or to some other cause, nor gross negligence on the part of Landlord. No such interruption or curtailment of any such "service" shall be deemed a constructive eviction. Landlord shall not be required to furnish, and Tenant shall not be entitled to receive any "services" during any period when Tenant shall be in default in respect to the payment of rent. Neither shall there be any abatement or diminution of rent because of making of repairs, improvements or decorations to the

(Document continued on next page)

COMMERCIAL LEASE *continued*

29. If the Tenant is leasing part of the building, insert the percentage leased (usually based on square footage). Otherwise delete.

Premises after the date above fixed for the commencement of the term, it being understood that rent shall, in any event, commence to run at such date so above fixed.

7. REAL ESTATE TAXES - *[29][Tenant acknowledges that the Premises comprise approximately ____% of the building and which shall be defined as "Tenant's share."]* In the event that real estate taxes due and owing by Landlord for the building shall be increased above those charges during the base year (which is defined as the tax or fiscal year used by the governmental authority assessing such taxes in effect on the commencement date of this Lease), Tenant agrees to pay as additional rent within thirty (30) days of receipt of notice from Landlord, an amount equal to such additional real estate taxes or Tenant's share of additional real estate taxes.

8. DAMAGE TO THE PREMISES - Tenant must give Landlord prompt notice of fire, accident, casualty, damage or dangerous or defective condition. If the Premises can not be used because of fire or other casualty, Tenant is not required to pay rent for the time the Premises are unusable. If part of the Premises can not be used, Tenant must pay rent for the usable part. Landlord shall have the right to decide which part of the Premises is usable. Landlord need only repair the damaged structural parts of the Premises. Landlord is not required to repair or replace any equipment, fixtures, furnishings or decorations unless originally installed by Landlord. Landlord is not responsible for delays due to settling insurance claims, obtaining estimates, labor and supply problems or any other cause not fully under Landlord's control.

(A) If the fire or other casualty is caused by an act or neglect of Tenant, Tenant's employees or persons on the Premises with permission of Tenant, or at the time of the fire or casualty Tenant is in default in any term of this Lease, then all repairs will be made at Tenant's expense and Tenant must pay the full rent with no adjustment. The cost of the repairs will be added to the rent.

(B) Landlord has the right to demolish or rebuild the building if there is substantial damage by fire or other casualty. Landlord may cancel this Lease within 30 days after the substantial fire or casualty by giving Tenant notice of Landlord's intention to demolish or rebuild. The Lease will end 30 days after Landlord's cancellation notice to Tenant. Tenant must deliver the Premises to Landlord on

(Document continued on next page)

or before the cancellation date in the notice and pay all rent due to the date of the fire or casualty. If the lease is cancelled, Landlord is not required to repair the Premises or building. The cancellation does not release Tenant of liability in connection with the fire or casualty.

9.   INSPECTION AND ENTRY BY LANDLORD - Tenant agrees that Landlord and Landlord's agents and other representatives shall have the right to enter into and upon the Premises, or any part hereof, at all reasonable hours for the purpose of examining the same, or making such repairs or alterations therein as may be necessary for the safety and preservation of the Premises.

(A)   Tenant also agrees to permit Landlord or the Landlord's agents to show the Premises to persons wishing to lease or purchase the Premises. Tenant further agrees that on and after the sixth month preceding the expiration of the term of this Lease, Landlord or Landlord's agents shall have the right to place notices on the front of said Premises, or any part thereof, offering the Premises "To Let" or "For Sale" and the Tenant agrees to permit the same to remain thereof without hindrance or molestation.

(B)   If the Premises, or any part thereof shall be deserted or become vacant during the term of this Lease, or if Tenant shall default in the payment of rent or any part thereof or shall default in the performance of any of the covenants herein contained, Landlord or its representatives may re-enter the Premises by force, summary proceeding or otherwise, and remove all persons therefrom, without being liable to prosecution therefor, and Tenant hereby expressly waives the service of any notice in writing of intention to re-enter, and Tenant shall pay at the same time as the rent becomes payable under the terms hereof a sum equivalent to the rent herein, and the Landlord may rent the Premises on behalf of the Tenant, reserving the right to rent the Premises for a longer period of time than fixed in the original lease without releasing the original Tenant from any liability, applying any moneys collected, first to the expense of resuming or obtaining possession, second to restoring the Premises to a rentable condition, and then to the payment of the rent and all other charges due and to become due to the Landlord, any surplus to be paid to the Tenant, who shall remain liable for any deficiency.

10.   GLASS - Landlord may replace, at the expense of Tenant, any and all broken glass in and about the Premises.

(Document continued on next page)

30. The limits of insurance the Tenant must maintain. It is recommended that the Landlord discuss this with his insurance agent.

Landlord may insure, and keep insured, all plate glass in the Premises for and in the name of Landlord. Bills for the premiums therefor shall be rendered by Landlord to Tenant at such times as Landlord may elect, and shall be due from and payable by Tenant when rendered, and the amount thereof shall be deemed additional rental. Damage and injury to the said Premises, caused by the carelessness, negligence or improper conduct on the part of Tenant or Tenant's agents or employees shall be repaired as speedily as possible by Tenant at Tenant's own cost and expense.

11.   SIGNS - Tenant shall neither place, nor cause nor allow to be placed, any sign or signs of any kind whatsoever at, in or about the entrance to said Premises or any part of same, except in or at such place or places as may be indicated by the Landlord and upon written consent by Landlord. In the event Landlord or Landlord's representatives shall deem it necessary to remove any such sign in order to paint the Premises or the building wherein same is situated or make any repairs, alterations, improvements in or upon the Premises or the building or any part of the Premises or the building, Landlord shall have the right to do so, providing any sign be removed and replaced at Landlord's expense whenever the said repairs, alterations or improvements shall be completed.

12.   INSURANCE - Tenant agrees to maintain in full force and effect during the entire term of this Lease, liability insurance insuring Landlord against any loss or damage sustained or to which Landlord may be subject by reason of Tenant's occupancy and use of the Premises, which policy shall have the following limits of liability:
_____[30]_____. Tenant agrees to furnish to Landlord, prior to the effective date of this Lease, a binder or other such certificate evidencing such insurance coverage.

(A)   Tenant agrees that it will, at its own cost and expense, keep its furniture, fixtures, equipment, records, and personal property insured against loss or damage by fire or other peril normally covered by "extended coverage" endorsements, and shall deliver to Landlord prior to the effective date of this Lease, a binder or other such certificate of such insurance coverage.

13.   SUBLETTING OR ASSIGNMENT - Neither the Premises nor any portion of the Premises may be sublet,

(Document continued on next page)

31. The number of days, in words and numbers, that the Tenant would have to cure his Lease violation.

32. The number of days, in words and numbers, after which the Lease would automatically expire and the Tenant could legally be evicted.

nor may this Lease be assigned without the express written consent of Landlord upon such terms and conditions as Landlord may require.

14.   DEFAULT - If Tenant defaults in fulfilling any of the terms and conditions of this Lease other than the payment of rent or additional rent; or if the Premises becomes vacant or deserted; or if any execution or attachment shall be issued against Tenant or any of Tenant's property located or situated at or on the Premises whereby the Premises shall be taken or occupied by someone other than Tenant; or if this Lease shall be rejected under any applicable provision of the bankruptcy laws; or if Tenant shall fail to take possession within fifteen (15) days of the commencement of this Lease; and upon Landlord serving written notice to Tenant specifying the nature of the default, Tenant shall have ___[31]____ (__) days from the date of receipt of such notice to cure the default (or if such default cannot be cured within such period, Tenant must diligently and in good faith proceed to cure the default). If Tenant shall have failed to cure or proceed to cure the default within such period, Landlord may serve a ____[32]____ (__) day notice of cancellation of this Lease upon Tenant and upon the expiration of the cancellation period this Lease shall terminate and expire and Tenant shall quit and surrender the Premises to Landlord but Tenant shall remain liable as provided in this Lease.

        (A)   If after default in payment of rent or violation of any other provision of this Lease, or upon the expiration of this Lease, Tenant moves out or is dispossessed and fails to remove any trade fixtures or other property prior to such said default, removal, expiration of Lease, or prior to the issuance of the final order or execution of the warrant, then and in that event, the said fixtures and property shall be deemed abandoned by the said Tenant and shall become the property of Landlord.

15.   NO WAIVER BY LANDLORD - The failure of Landlord to insist upon a strict performance of any of the terms, conditions and covenants herein shall not be deemed a waiver of any rights or remedies that Landlord may have, and shall not be deemed a waiver of any subsequent breach or default in the terms, conditions and covenants herein contained. This instrument may not be changed, modified, discharged or terminated orally.

(Document continued on next page)

33. The date of signing the Lease.

34. The name of the Landlord if a corporation. Otherwise delete the line.

35. If the Landlord is an individual, delete "BY" and print the Landlord's name directly below the line, with the Landlord to sign above the line. If the Landlord is a corporation, print the name and title of the individual acting for the corporation directly below the line, with that person to sign above the line.

36. The name of the Tenant if a corporation. Otherwise delete the line.

37. If the Tenant is an individual, delete "BY" and print the Tenant's name directly below the line, with the Tenant to sign above the line. If the Tenant is a corporation, print the name and title of the individual acting for the corporation directly below the line, with that person to sign above the line.

Note: if the Tenant is a corporation, the Landlord may want to consider requiring that the Tenant corporation's Lease obligations (particularly the payment of rent) be personally guaranteed by an officer of the corporation. A Personal Guaranty form is found elsewhere in this book.

16.   LEASE NOT A LIEN - This Lease shall not be a lien against the Premises in respect to any mortgage that may now or in the future be placed against said Premises, and that the recording of such mortgage or mortgages shall have preference and precedence and be superior and prior in lien of this Lease, irrespective of the date of recording, and the Tenant agrees to execute without cost any such instrument which may be deemed necessary or desirable to further effect the subordination of this Lease to any such mortgages, and a refusal to execute such instrument shall entitle the Landlord, or the Landlord's assigns and legal representative to the option of cancelling this Lease without incurring any expenses or damages and the term hereby granted is expressly limited accordingly.

17.   QUIET POSSESSION - Landlord covenants that Tenant, on paying the rent and additional rent, and faithfully performing the covenants required or imposed upon Tenant, shall and may peacefully and quietly have, hold and enjoy the Premises for the term of this Lease, provided however, that this covenant shall be conditioned upon the retention of title to the Premises by the Landlord.

18.   BINDING EFFECT - It is mutually understood and agreed that the covenants and agreements contained in this Lease shall be binding upon the parties hereto and upon their respective successors, heirs, executors and administrators.

    IN WITNESS WHEREOF, the parties have set their hand and seal this __[33]__ day of _____, 19__.

_____[34]_____

BY_____
              [35] (Landlord)

_____[36]_____

BY_____
              [37] (Tenant)

EXTENSION/RENEWAL
OF COMMERCIAL LEASE (2-36)

This form may be used when a Landlord or Tenant wishes to extend or renew an existing Commercial Lease with only minor changes (such as a new expiration date, a new rent or the like) without the necessity of preparing a new Lease. Both the Landlord and the Tenant must be careful however, since this form carries forward all terms and conditions of the original Lease except those specifically changed. On the other hand, with an Extension/Renewal both parties are protected from the problems that might arise by having mistakenly forgotten to carry forward certain terms from the original Lease into a new Lease.

EXTENSION/RENEWAL
OF COMMERCIAL LEASE

1. The date of signing the Agreement.

2. The name of the Landlord.

3. Choose one depending on whether the Landlord is a corporation.

4. The address of the Landlord.

5. The state of incorporation of the Landlord.

6. The address of the Landlord corporation's principal office.

7. The name of the Tenant.

8. Choose one depending on whether the Tenant is a corporation.

9. The address of the Tenant.

10. The state of incorporation of the Tenant.

11. The address of the Tenant corporation's principal office.

EXTENSION/RENEWAL AGREEMENT, made on _____[1]_____, 19__, between _____[2]_____, *[3][residing at _____[4]_____] OR [a _____[5]_____ corporation with its principal office at _____[6]_____]*, as "Landlord" and _____[7]_____, *[8][residing at _____[9]_____] OR [a _____[10]_____ corporation with its principal office at _____[11]_____]*, as "Tenant."

(Document continued on next page)

12. A description of the leased space, for example "a suite," "a room," "a floor," etc.

13. Identify the specific space being leased, such as the suite number, room number or floor number.

14. If only a portion of a building is being leased (such as part of one floor), it is recommended that plans be made a part of the Lease (annexed) to identify exactly which space is being leased. Otherwise delete.

15. The address of the building.

16. The city in which the space being leased is located.

17. The county in which the space being leased is located.

18. The state in which the space being leased is located.

19. The number of years or months, in words, of the term of the Lease.

20. Choose one.

21. The last day of the term of the Lease.

22. The nature of any default by either party. Otherwise delete.

23. The amount, in numbers, charged by the Landlord for consenting to the extension/renewal. If none, insert "0."

24. The length of the extension in years and months and the last date of the extended period, for example "for two additional years ending December 31, 1994."

1.   LEASE - Landlord and Tenant acknowledge that they have previously entered into a lease for a
_____[12]_____ known as _____[13]_____ *[14][and more particularly described on the plan annexed to and made part of this Lease]* in the building located at
_____[15]_____ in the City of
_____[16]_____, County of _____[17]_____, State of
_____[18]_____ (the "Premises"), for a term of ___[19]___ *[20][years]* **OR** *[months]* ending on _____[21]_____ (the "Lease").

(A)   Landlord and Tenant acknowledge that neither party is now in default of any of the obligations imposed upon the other under the terms and conditions of the Lease *[22][except* _____
_____ *].*

2.   EXTENSION/RENEWAL OF LEASE - In consideration of the payment of $_____[23]_____ by Tenant, the receipt of which is acknowledged, Landlord and Tenant agree to extend and renew the Lease as follows:

(A)   Term - _____[24]_____
_____.

(Document continued on next page)

25. The amount, in numbers, of rent to be charged during each year of the extension/renewal period, including any automatic increases and when such increases will begin.

26. The amount, in numbers, of the present security deposit.

27. The amount, in numbers, of any additional security deposit required. Otherwise delete. (Note: since the rental during the extension/renewal period is most likely greater than during the initial period, the Landlord should consider requesting such additional security as may be necessary to keep the total security deposit held equal to the same monthly rent multiple as originally charged.)

28. The "base year" to be used for calculation of escalation provisions during the extension/renewal period.

29. Any changes, modifications, alterations, additions or deletions to the terms of the original Lease. If none, delete.

(B)   Rent - _____[25]_____
_____.

(C)   Security - The parties acknowledge that Landlord is presently holding the sum of $_____[26]_____ as a security deposit for the faithful performance of the obligations of Tenant under the Lease and Landlord will continue to hold this sum as security during the period of this extension/renewal. *[Tenant agrees to deposit with Landlord as additional security $_____[27]_____.]*

(D)   "Base Year for Escalations" - The base year for the calculation of all escalations shall be ___[28]___.

[29]   [(E) _____
_____
_____.]*

3.   RATIFICATION OF LEASE - In all other respects, Landlord and Tenant ratify, extend and renew the Lease and agree that the Lease shall be deemed a part of this extension/renewal and incorporated by reference into this extension and renewal with the same force and effect as if set forth in its entirety in this agreement of extension and renewal.

(Document continued on next page)

30. The name of the Landlord if a corporation. Otherwise delete the line.

31. If the Landlord is an individual, delete "BY" and print the Landlord's name directly below the line, with the Landlord to sign above the line. If the Landlord is a corporation, print the name and title of the individual acting for the corporation directly below the line, with that person to sign above the line.

32. The name of the Tenant if a corporation. Otherwise delete the line.

33. If the Tenant is an individual, delete "BY" and print the Tenant's name directly below the line, with the Tenant to sign above the line. If the Tenant is a corporation, print the name and title of the individual acting for the corporation directly below the line, with that person to sign above the line.

Note: if the Tenant's obligations under the original Lease were personally guaranteed, the Landlord should require a new, personal guaranty of the Extension/renewal Agreement since the law in most states is that a change in the terms of the agreement being guaranteed releases the person giving the guarantee. A Personal Guaranty form is found elsewhere in this book.

IN WITNESS WHEREOF, the parties have set their hand and seal this __[1]__ day of _____, 19__.

_____[30]_____

BY_____
[31] (Landlord)

_____[32]_____

BY_____
[33] (Tenant)

ASSIGNMENT AND ASSUMPTION OF COMMERCIAL LEASE (2-37)

This form is used when an existing Commercial Lease is to be assigned by the Tenant (the Assignor) to another party (the Assignee) who agrees to assume all of the obligations of the Lease. This form assumes a typical situation in which payment is made to the Landlord for obtaining his approval for assigning the Lease.

The Lease to be assigned must be reviewed carefully to determine the rights of the Tenant to assign the Lease and the rights of the Landlord in the event of a request to assign the Lease.

ASSIGNMENT AND ASSUMPTION OF COMMERCIAL LEASE

1. The date of signing the Assignment.

2. The name of the Landlord.

3. Choose one depending on whether the Landlord is a corporation.

4. The address of the Landlord.

5. The state of incorporation of the Landlord.

6. The address of the Landlord corporation's principal office.

7. The name of the Tenant.

8. Choose one depending on whether the Tenant is a corporation.

9. The address of the Tenant.

10. The state of incorporation of the Tenant.

11. The address of the Tenant corporation's principal office.

12. Choose one.

13. A description of the leased space, for example "a suite," "a room," "a floor," etc.

14. Identify the specific space being leased, such as the suite number, room number or floor number.

AGREEMENT OF ASSIGNMENT AND AS-SUMPTION OF LEASE made on _____[1]_____, 19__, between _____[2]_____, *[3][residing at _____[4]_____] OR [a _____[5]_____ corporation with its principal office at _____[6]_____]*, as "Assignor" and _____[7]_____, *[8][residing at _____[9]_____] OR [a _____[10]_____ corporation with its principal office at _____[11]_____]*, as "Assignee."

1.   LEASE - Assignor acknowledges that *[12][he] OR [it]* has previously entered into a lease for a ____[13]____ known as _____[14]_____ in the building located at

(Document continued on next page)

15. The address of the building.

16. The city in which the space being leased is located.

17. The county in which the space being leased is located.

18. The state in which the space being leased is located.

19. The number of years or months, in words, of the term of the Lease.

20. Choose one.

21. The last day of the term of the Lease.

22. Delete if the lease is not available. However, it is strongly recommended that a copy be attached to preclude the Assignee from later claiming that he was unfamiliar with all of its terms.

23. The nature of any default by the Assignor. If none, delete.

24. The amount, in words and numbers, paid by the Assignee to the Assignor for the Assignment.

25. The date the Assignment is to begin.

_____[15]_____ in the City of _____[16]_____, County of _____[17]_____, State of _____[18]_____ (the "Premises"), for a term of ___[19]___ *[20][years]* **OR** *[months]* ending on _____[21]_____ *[22][, a true and complete copy of which is attached to and made a part of this Agreement]* (the "Lease").

(A)   Assignor represents to Assignee and Landlord:

(i)   that Assignor is not in default of any of the obligations imposed upon Assignor under the terms and conditions of the Lease *[23][except _____ _____];*

(ii)   that Assignor has not done or suffered anything to be done which might impose any liability upon Landlord or Assignee; and

(iii)   that there are no claims, security interests or liens against the Premises, the Lease or any equipment, fixtures or personal property installed by Assignor in or attached to the Premises.

(B)   Assignee represents to Assignor and Landlord that Assignee has examined the attached Lease and is familiar with all of its terms and conditions.

(C)   Assignor and Assignee represent to each other and to Landlord that Landlord's consent to this Assignment and assumption is necessary and may be conditioned upon such additional terms and conditions as Landlord may require. In the event that Landlord shall have failed or refused to give its consent, this agreement shall be null and void and neither party shall have any further obligation to the other.

2.   ASSIGNMENT BY ASSIGNOR - Assignor, in consideration of the sum of _____[24]_____ Dollars ($_____) to be paid by Assignee upon receipt by Assignee of a copy of this Assignment consented to by the Landlord, does hereby assign to Assignee the Lease from and after _____[25]_____, 19__, (the "Effective Date") for all the rest and remainder of the term of the Lease and any renewals or extensions of the Lease subject only to the

(Document continued on next page)

26. The amount, in numbers, of the previously paid security deposit.

27. Choose one depending on whether the security deposit is to be returned to the Assignor.

28. Choose one.

29. The amount, in numbers, of the new security to be paid by the Assignee.

30. The payment, in numbers, required by the Landlord for giving his consent to the Assignment.

31. The party paying money to the Landlord for giving his consent to the Assignment, typically the Assignee or Assignor.

32. A description of any additional conditions imposed by the Landlord. If none, delete.

33. The name of the Assignor if a corporation. Otherwise delete the line.

34. If the Assignor is an individual, delete "BY" and print the Assignor's name directly below the line, with the Assignor to sign above the line. If the Assignor is a corporation, print the name and title of the individual acting for the corporation directly below the line, with that person to sign above the line.

covenants, conditions and limitations contained in the Lease.

(A) Assignor agrees that the security deposit of $_____[26]_____ previously paid by Assignor, together with interest earned but unpaid, if any, shall be *[27][similarly assigned to Assignee and Assignor waives any claim or interest in the security deposit.]* **OR** *[refunded and returned to Assignor.]*

3. ASSUMPTION BY ASSIGNEE - Assignee assumes the Lease and all the terms, covenants and conditions imposed by the Lease upon the Tenant and agrees to perform and comply with all of the terms, covenants, and conditions imposed upon Tenant by the Lease on or after the Effective Date as if Assignee had originally executed the Lease.

(A) Assignee acknowledges that the security deposit in the sum of $_____[26]_____ *[28][previously paid by Assignor shall be assigned to the account of and for the benefit of Assignee.]* **OR** *[shall be returned and refunded to Assignor in which event Assignee shall pay to Landlord the sum of $_____[29]_____ as and for security for the faithful performance of the term, covenants and conditions of the Lease by Assignee.]*

4. CONSENT BY LANDLORD - In consideration of the payment of $___[30]___ by _____[31]_____, the receipt of which is hereby acknowledged, and upon Assignee's assumption of all of the terms, covenants and conditions imposed upon Tenant in the Lease, Landlord consents to the Assignment of the Lease *[32][upon the following additional conditions:* _____
_____*].*

IN WITNESS WHEREOF, the parties have set their hand and seal on the date written above.

_____[33]_____

*BY*_____
[34] (Assignor)

(Document continued on next page)

35. The name of the Assignee if a corporation. Otherwise delete the line.

36. If the Assignee is an individual, delete "BY" and print the Assignee's name directly below the line, with the Assignee to sign above the line. If the Assignee is a corporation, print the name and title of the individual acting for the corporation directly below the line, with that person to sign above the line.

Note: if the Assignee is a new corporation or one without a tested credit history, the Landlord should consider requiring a personal guaranty of the Lease terms being assumed by the Assignee. A Personal Guaranty is found elsewhere in this book.

37. The date through which all rent, additional rent and other charges imposed by the Lease have been paid.

38. The date of signing the consent by the Landlord.

39. The name of the Landlord if a corporation. Otherwise delete the line.

40. If the Landlord is an individual, delete "BY" and print the Landlord's name directly below the line, with the Landlord to sign above the line. If the Landlord is a corporation, print the name and title of the individual acting for the corporation directly below the line, with that person to sign above the line.

_____[35]_____

BY_____
[36] (Assignee)

CERTIFICATION AND CONSENT BY LANDLORD

Landlord certifies that: (i) all rent, additional rent and other sundry charges under the Lease are paid through _____[37]_____, 19__; (ii) that the Lease is in full force and effect and that Landlord has not been notified of any lien, pledge or encumbrance upon or against the Lease; and (iii) that there is no known existing default of any of the terms, covenants or conditions imposed upon Assignor as Tenant under the Lease.

Upon the foregoing, Landlord hereby consents to the Assignment of the Lease by Assignor and the Assumption of the Lease by Assignee as of the Effective Date.

Dated: _____[38]_____, 19___

_____[39]_____

BY_____
[40] (Landlord)

SUBLEASE AGREEMENT (2-38)

A Sublease Agreement is used when a Tenant wants to Lease all or a portion of his space to another party while retaining his interest (either in the rest of the space or in the entire space if the Tenant expects to return). The Tenant is called the "Over–Tenant" and the Tenant's Lease with the Landlord is called the "Over-Lease." The party subleasing the space is called the "Under-Tenant." This Sublease provides for obtaining the consent of the Landlord. A copy of the original Lease is to be attached (annexed) to the Sublease Agreement.

This Sublease can be used for both Commercial and Residential Leases. Note that in most states, the Landlord's consent is usually not required in a Commercial Lease but is most likely required in a Residential Lease. Also, state and local laws will likely govern subleasing and you are therefore urged to consult your local housing authority.

SUBLEASE AGREEMENT

1. The name of the Over-Tenant (the original Tenant).

2. The address of the Over-Tenant.

3. The name of the Under-Tenant (the party subleasing the space).

4. The address of the Under-Tenant.

5. The name of the Landlord.

6. The address of the Landlord.

7. The date of signing the Over-Lease (the original Lease).

8. The commencement date of the Over-Lease.

9. The ending date of the Over-Lease.

The parties agree as follows:

Parties to this Sublease:

A. Over-Tenant: _____ [1] _____

    Address: _____ [2] _____
    _____

B. Under-Tenant: _____ [3] _____

    Address: _____ [4] _____
    _____

Information From Over-Lease, a complete copy of which is annexed to and made a part of this Sublease:

A. Landlord: _____ [5] _____

    Address: _____ [6] _____
    _____

B. Over-Tenant: _____ [1] _____

    Address: _____ [2] _____
    _____

C. Date, Term of
    Over-Lease: ____[7]____, 19__, commencing on _____[8]___, 19__ and ending on _____[9]___, 19__.

1. SUBLEASE - Over-Tenant agrees to sublet to

(Document continued on next page)

10. A description of the leased space, such as a "suite," "apartment," "room," "floor," etc.

11. Identify the specific space being leased, such as the suite number, apartment number, room number or floor number.

12. The address of the building in which the space being subleased is located.

13. The city in which the space being subleased is located.

14. The county in which the space being subleased is located.

15. The state in which the space being subleased is located.

16. The number of years or months, in words, of the Sublease.

17. Choose one.

18. The commencement date of the Sublease.

19. The ending date of the Sublease.

20. The use of the space which is permitted by the Landlord.

21. The amount, in numbers, of monthly rent to be paid.

22. The amount, in numbers, of the security deposit to be paid by the Under-Tenant.

23. Choose one.

24. A description detailing rent escalation charges that are being passed through to the Under-Tenant. Include references to the specific paragraph numbers of the Over-Lease. If none, delete.

Under-Tenant and Under-Tenant agrees to sublet _____[10]_____ known as ____[11]_____ in the building located at _____[12]_____ in the City of _____[13]_____, County of _____[14]_____, State of _____[15]_____ (the "Premises"), for a term of ___[16]___ *[17][years]* **OR** *[months]* commencing on _____[18]_____, 19__ and ending on _____[19]_____, 19__ on the following terms:

     (A)   Use of the Premises - _____[20]_____.

     (B)   Monthly Rent - $_____[21]_____ payable in advance on the first day of each month.

     (C)   Security - Under-Tenant shall pay to Over-Tenant the sum of $_____[22]_____ as security for the faithful performance of Under-Tenant's obligations which *[23] [will]* **OR** *[will not]* be deposited to an interest bearing account.

[24]   *[(D)   Additional Rent -*

_____

_____*.]*

2.   OVER-TENANT'S DUTIES - The Over-Lease sets forth the duties of the Landlord. Over-Tenant is not obligated to perform the duties of Landlord. If Landlord fails or refuses to perform its duties, Under-Tenant must advise Over-Tenant and upon receipt of such notice, Over-Tenant will promptly request Landlord to perform Landlord's duties under the Over-Lease. Over-Tenant's duties in this regard are limited to promptly requesting that Landlord perform its duties. The parties acknowledge that Under–Tenant may not pay rent directly to Landlord and has no authority to contact or make any agreement with Landlord.

(*Document continued on next page*)

25. A description of any other duties of the Over-Tenant. If none, delete this paragraph and renumber the remaining paragraphs.

26. Insert the appliances to be furnished. If none, delete.

27. A description of any other duties of the Under-Tenant. If none, delete.

[25]   [(A)   Over-Tenant's Additional Duties -

_____

_____*.]*

      (B)   Under-Tenant acknowledges that Over-Tenant has no obligation to supply or provide heat, hot water, electricity or telephone service and that no part of the rent is for such service. Under-Tenant shall make such separate arrangements with the utility company customarily providing any such service as may be required, shall have accounts with any such supplier in his own name, shall timely pay all bills and will not suffer or permit any charges for such service to become a lien against the Premises or any separate account(s) of Over-Tenant.

[26]   [(C)   Under-Tenant acknowledges that the Premises is equipped and furnished with

_____*,*

collectively called "the Appliances," that Under-Tenant has inspected the Appliances and that they are in working order. Under-Tenant agrees to take good care of the Appliances and return them at the end of this Sublease in the same or similar condition, ordinary wear and tear excepted. Under-Tenant agrees to pay to Over-Tenant the replacement or repair cost of any Appliance lost or damaged through Under-Tenant's negligence or failure to act.]

      3.   UNDER-TENANT'S DUTIES - Under-Tenant agrees to pay directly to Over-Tenant rent, additional rent and other charges as required by this Sublease and to do everything required of Under-Tenant by this Sublease. The parties acknowledge that Under-Tenant may not pay rent directly to Landlord and has no authority to contact or make any agreement with Landlord.

[27]   [(A)   Under-Tenant's Additional Duties -

_____

_____*.]*

      4.   SUBJECT TO OVER-LEASE - This Sublease is subject to the Over-Lease and to any agreement to which the Over-Tenant is subject. The provisions of the Over-Lease are made a part of this Sublease and all provisions binding on the Over-Tenant are binding on the Under-Tenant who has read the Over-Lease and agrees not to violate it in any way. Over-Tenant shall have all the rights and remedies against Under-Tenant that Landlord has

(*Document continued on next page*)

28. The number of days, in numbers, by which the Landlord's consent must be received.

29. The date of signing the Sublease Agreement.

30. The name of the Over-Tenant if a corporation. Otherwise delete the line.

31. If the Over-Tenant is an individual, delete "BY" and print the Over-Tenant's name directly below the line, with the Over-Tenant to sign above the line. If the Over-Tenant is a corporation, print the name and title of the individual acting for the corporation directly below the line, with that person to sign above the line.

32. The name of the Under-Tenant if a corporation. Otherwise delete the line.

33. If the Under-Tenant is an individual, delete "BY" and print the Under-Tenant's name directly below the line, with that individual to sign above the line. If the Under-Tenant is a corporation, print the name and title of the individual acting for the corporation directly below the line, with that person to sign above the line.

Note: if the Under-Tenant is a new corporation or one without a tested credit history, the Over-Tenant should consider requiring a Personal Guaranty of the Sublease by the Under-Tenant, found elsewhere in this book.

against Over-Tenant for breach of the Over-Lease or a default by Over-Tenant. If Over-Tenant is found to have breached its obligation to the Landlord as a result of any breach of Under–Tenant's obligation to Over-Tenant, or if such breach by Over-Tenant was caused by Under-Tenant then Under-Tenant shall fully indemnify Over-Tenant for any and all losses, including but not limited to legal and other professional fees, disbursements and costs suffered or incurred as a result of Under-Tenant's breach.

5.   CONSENT OF LANDLORD - If Landlord's consent to this Sublease is required, this consent must be received within __[28]__ days from the date of this Sublease. If Landlord's consent is not received within such time, this Sublease shall be null and void; any payments made by Under-Tenant shall be refunded and each party shall be released from any further liability or obligation to the other.

6.   ASSIGNMENT OR FURTHER SUBLETTING - Under-Tenant shall not be permitted to assign this Sublease or further sublet the Premises without the express written consent of the Over-Tenant and Landlord (if Landlord's consent for this Sublease was required) on such other or additional terms as either Over-Tenant or Landlord may require.

IN WITNESS WHEREOF, the parties have set their hand and seal this __[29]__ day of _____, 19__.

_____*[30]*_____

*BY*_____
[31] (Over-Tenant)

_____*[32]*_____

*BY*_____
[33] (Under-Tenant)

(Document continued on next page)

SUBLEASE AGREEMENT *continued*

34. Delete the remainder of the form if the Landlord's consent is NOT required for the Sublet.

35. The date of signing the consent by the Landlord.

36. The name of the Landlord if a corporation. Otherwise delete the line.

37. If the Landlord is an individual, delete "BY" and print the Landlord's name directly below the line, with the Landlord to sign above the line. If the Landlord is a corporation, print the name and title of the individual acting for the corporation directly below the line, with that person to sign above the line.

[34] [CONSENT BY LANDLORD

Landlord hereby consents to the Sublease.

Dated: _____[35]_____, 19___

_____[36]_____

BY_____
        [37] (Landlord)]

Buying and Selling Goods 3

Whether purchasing something tangible, like an automobile, or intangible, like a license to sell someone else's product, buying and selling are the lifeblood of commerce. The common thread that runs through the agreements in this chapter is the requirement to accurately and completely describe what is being bought and sold.

Selling Personal Property Personal property is any property other than real estate. This section provides forms that can be used by individuals to sell property. The forms also may be used by businesses for the sale of items that are not sold in the ordinary course of that business. For example, if a business is selling a computer because it is no longer needed, the Bill of Sale—Personal Property form in this section is applicable. However, if the business sells computers as its regular business, it should use a form in the next section.

Selling and Leasing—Business It is important to decide exactly what is to be bought or sold and how it is to be paid for before deciding which of the contracts for sale of goods to use. For example, if a seller wishes to limit his merchandise warranties, the Contract for Sale of Goods—Warranties should be considered. An Equipment Lease is also provided, since many businesses lease rather than purchase.

Assignments and Licenses An Assignment is used by one party to transfer his rights to another. Several Assignment forms are found in this section, including those for assigning trademarks, copyrights and literary works. Often a sale does not involve the transfer of a product, but rather the right to manufacture or sell that product, which is a license. This section offers licensing forms for both trademarks and general use.

BILL OF SALE—AUTOMOBILE (3-01)

This Bill of Sale establishes a change of ownership of an automobile (or truck), and of any added accessories such as an audio system, from the current owner (the Seller) to a new owner (the Buyer). Additionally, this form satisfies federal law requiring certain statements by sellers of used cars regarding odometer readings (mileage) and odometer alterations.

BILL OF SALE—AUTOMOBILE

1. The name of the Seller.

2. The address of the Seller.

3. The selling price, in words.

4. The selling price, in numbers.

5. The name of the Buyer.

6. The address of the Buyer.

7. The model year of the automobile, for example "1981."

8. The manufacturer of the automobile, for example "Alfa Romeo."

9. The "V.I.N." (Vehicle Identification Number), for example "ZARAA6695B121." (Note: on most automobiles, the V.I.N. can be found stamped on a metal plate visible from the outside of the car in the corner of the windshield on the driver's side.)

10. The engine serial number if it is not the original engine. Otherwise delete.

11. The model name or type, for example "GTV-6/2.5."

12. The body type, for example "two door sedan."

13. The color.

14. Insert descriptions and serial numbers, if available, for all accessories added after the original purchase that will be included in the sale, for example "Alpine radio, serial no. ____." If none, delete.

_____[1]_____, residing at _____[2]_____ ("Seller"), in consideration of the sum of _____[3]_____ Dollars ($_____[4]_____) received from _____[5]_____, residing at _____[6]_____ ("Buyer"), receipt of which is acknowledged, hereby sells, transfers and conveys the following automobile:

Model Year: __[7]__, Manufacturer/Make: _____[8]_____, ("V.I.N.") Vehicle Identification No.: _____[9]_____, *[10][Engine Serial No.: _____]*, Model: _____[11]_____, Body Type: ____[12]____, Color: ___[13]___, *[14][together with the following accessories: _____,]* (the "Automobile").

Seller warrants to Buyer the following: (i) Seller is the owner of the Automobile; (ii) Seller has the legal right to sell the Automobile; (iii) the Automobile is free and

(Document continued on next page)

15. Insert the name of any lender, such as a bank, for which there may be an outstanding loan and the amount owed. If none, delete.

16. If the odometer reading was reset to "0000" or it is a replacement unit, insert the previous mileage, in numbers.

17. The odometer reading, in numbers.

18. Choose one.

19. The date of signing the Bill of Sale by the Seller.

20. The name of the Seller printed directly below the line, with the Seller to sign above the line.

clear of all liens and encumbrances *[15][except:*
_____*]*; and (iv) Seller will defend title of the Automobile against any claim or demand except any lienholder disclosed in this Bill of Sale.

BUYER HAS EXAMINED OR HAS HAD AN OPPORTUNITY TO EXAMINE THE AUTOMOBILE. THE AUTOMOBILE IS SOLD AND DELIVERED IN A STRICTLY "AS IS" CONDITION AND SELLER EXPRESSLY DISCLAIMS ALL WARRANTIES, EXPRESS OR IMPLIED, OF MERCHANTABILITY OR FITNESS FOR A PARTICULAR PURPOSE.

Seller certifies that while the Automobile was in Seller's possession, the odometer was (check one box ONLY):

( )   not altered or disconnected;

( )   altered for repair/replacement and that the mileage registered is the same as before the repair/replacement;

( )   reset to 0000 miles/kilometers and that the registered mileage before such repair/replacement was ____[16]____.

Seller certifies that the odometer reading is ____[17]____ *[18][miles]* **OR** *[kilometers]* and that to the best of Seller's knowledge the foregoing odometer reading (check one box ONLY):

( )   reflects the actual mileage.

( )   reflects the actual mileage in excess of 99,999 miles/kilometers.

( )   is NOT the actual mileage.

Dated: _____[19]_____   _____
                                          [20]   (Seller)

(Document continued on next page)

21. The Notary Public completes this part of the form, and signs and seals it by affixing his stamp or seal.

STATE OF _____[21]_____, COUNTY OF _____[21]_____, ss.:

On _____[21]_____, 19__, before me _____[21]_____ personally came _____[21]_____, to me known, and known to me to be the individual(s) described in and who executed the foregoing _____[21]_____, and duly acknowledged to me that (he)(she)(they) executed the same.

_____
Notary Public

BILL OF SALE—PERSONAL PROPERTY (3-02)

This Bill of Sale is used to establish a change in ownership of personal property, as distinguished from real property (land and buildings) for which there are different requirements (see the real estate forms elsewhere in this book). Care should be taken to identify each item of property as completely as possible to distinguish the property being bought from other, similar items.

BILL OF SALE—PERSONAL PROPERTY

1. The name of the Seller.

2. Choose one depending on whether the Seller is a corporation.

3. The address of the Seller.

4. The state of incorporation of the Seller.

5. The address of the Seller corporation's principal office.

6. The selling price, in words.

7. The selling price, in numbers.

8. The name of the Buyer.

9. Choose one depending on whether the Buyer is a corporation.

10. The address of the Buyer.

11. The state of incorporation of the Buyer.

12. The address of the Buyer corporation's principal office.

13. Choose one. If the use of a "Schedule A" is chosen, on a separate sheet of paper headed "Schedule A" list the names of the items to be sold and their serial numbers, if any.

14. A description of each item of property and its serial number, if any.

_____[1]_____, *[2][residing at _____[3]_____] **OR** [a _____[4]_____ corporation with its principal office at _____[5]_____* ("Seller"), in consideration of the sum of _____[6]_____ Dollars ($_____[7]_____) received from _____[8]_____, *[9][residing at _____[10]_____] **OR** [a _____[11]_____ corporation with its principal office at _____[12]_____* ("Buyer"), receipt of which is acknowledged, hereby sells, transfers and conveys the *[13][personal property listed on the attached Schedule A]* **OR** *personal property: _____[14]_____]* ("Property").

Seller warrants to Buyer the following: (i) Seller is the owner of the Property and each item of property listed; (ii) Seller has the legal right to sell the Property and each item of property listed; (iii) the Property and each item of property is/are free and clear of all liens and encumbrances

(Document continued on next page)

15. On a separate sheet headed "Schedule A", or on Schedule A if it was already created in No. 13 above, insert the names of any parties who have liens against the property being sold and the amount owed to each.

16. The date of signing the Bill of Sale.

17. The name of the Seller if a corporation. Otherwise delete the line.

18. If the Seller is an individual, delete "BY" and print the name of the Seller directly below the line, with the Seller to sign above the line. If the Seller is a corporation, print the name and title of the person acting for the corporation directly below the line, with that person to sign above the line.

19. Insert a Notary Statement, found elsewhere in this book, for the Seller, either an Individual or Corporate form, as appropriate. The Notary will complete the form.

except as shown on the attached Schedule A[15]; and (iv) Seller will defend title of the Property and of each item of property against any claim or demand except any lienholder disclosed in this Bill of Sale.

BUYER HAS EXAMINED OR HAS HAD AN OPPORTUNITY TO EXAMINE THE PROPERTY AND EACH ITEM OF PROPERTY SOLD. THE PROPERTY AND EACH ITEM OF PROPERTY IS SOLD AND DELIVERED IN A STRICTLY "AS IS" CONDITION AND SELLER EXPRESSLY DISCLAIMS ALL WARRANTIES, EXPRESS OR IMPLIED, OF MERCHANTABILITY OR FITNESS FOR PARTICULAR PURPOSE.

Dated: _____[16]_____   _____*[17]*_____

                              *BY*_____
                                          [18]   (Seller)

[19] [Notary Statement]

CONTRACT FOR SALE OF GOODS—
GENERAL (3-03)

As a general rule, a Contract relating to the Sale of Goods whose value is more than $500 cannot be enforced unless the agreement is in writing and signed by both the Buyer and Seller. Therefore, this Contract should be used when buying or selling goods whose value is in excess of that amount.

A Contract for the Sale of Goods may contain any terms to which the parties agree but should, at the very least, include a description of exactly what is being sold and the price and delivery terms. Additional contract clauses are found elsewhere in this book and may be inserted as necessary.

A cautionary note: nobody likes to consider what would happen in the event that one of the parties defaulted. The guiding principal should be to "hope for the best, but plan for the worst." This Contract deals with that issue.

CONTRACT FOR SALE OF GOODS—
GENERAL

1. The date of signing the Contract.

2. The name of the Seller.

3. If the Seller is a corporation, insert the state of incorporation. Otherwise delete.

4. The address of the Seller.

5. The name of the Buyer.

6. If the Buyer is a corporation, insert the state of incorporation. Otherwise delete.

7. The address of the Buyer.

8. A detailed description of the goods being purchased, for example "5,000 cases of widgets, 12 per case, on pallets of 100 cases each."

9. On a separate sheet of paper headed "Schedule A" list the specifications (size, weight, etc.) of the goods being purchased.

10. The price, in numbers, of the goods being purchased.

11. The location at which title (ownership) to the goods passes to the Buyer, for example: "Seller's loading dock" or "Buyer's loading dock."

AGREEMENT made this __[1]__ day of _____, 19__ by and between _____[2]_____ *[3][, a* _____ *corporation,]* with its office at _____[4]_____ ("Seller") and _____[5]_____ *[6][, a* _____ *corporation,]* with its office at _____[7]_____ ("Buyer").

1.   SALE - Seller has agreed to sell and Buyer has agreed to purchase _____[8]_____ in accordance with the plans and specifications set forth on the attached Schedule A.[9]

2.   PRICE - The total price for the goods is $_____[10]_____ at _____[11]_____, it being

(Document continued on next page)

12. Choose one, depending on whether the price includes freight and insurance.

13. Choose one depending on the desired payment schedule. If the third alternative is chosen, skip to instruction No. 18. (Note: the choices shown are examples only. The method and timing of payment can be upon whatever terms the parties agree.)

14. The number of days, in numbers, after receipt of the items by which payment must be made. Then skip to instruction No. 19.

15. The amount, in numbers, of any deposit or down-payment made by the Buyer.

16. The amount, in numbers, due upon the Buyer's receipt of each shipment.

17. The amount, in numbers, of any unpaid balance remaining due.

18. Any other payment terms agreed upon by the parties.

19. Choose one, and if the use of a "Schedule B" is chosen, on a separate sheet of paper headed "Schedule B" list the the delivery schedule and skip to instruction No. 27. If the third alternative is chosen, skip to instruction No. 26. (As with the terms of payment, so too the delivery schedule can contain any terms to which the parties agree.)

understood that the price *[12][does not include freight, shipping and delivery and insurance costs, which shall be the sole responsibility of Buyer.]* **OR** *[includes freight, shipping and delivery and insurance costs.]*

 (A) Payment shall be made as follows: *[13][the entire amount due shall be paid in full not later than __[14]__ days after receipt by Buyer of the items purchased.]* **OR** *[$___[15]____ upon signing of this Agreement, $___[16]___ upon receipt of each shipment and the balance of $__[17]___ upon receipt of the shipment containing the balance of the items purchased.]* **OR** _____[18]_____.]*

3. DELIVERY/SHIPPING/ACCEPTANCE -
 (A) Delivery of the goods purchased shall be *[19][as set forth in the attached Schedule B.]* **OR**

(Document continued on next page)

20. The quantity of the first shipment.

21. The date by which the first shipment must be received.

22. The quantity of the second shipment.

23. The date by which the second shipment must be received.

24. The quantity of the final shipment.

25. The date by which the final shipment must be received.

26. Any other delivery schedule agreed upon by the parties.

27. The specific shipping terms agreed upon, including the method (such as via the Seller's trucks, independent motor carrier, rail, air or a combination) and who will pay the costs of shipping and insurance. Be sure to be consistent with your choice in No. 12 above.

28. The number of days, in numbers, after receipt by which the Buyer must notify the Seller of rejection of any item.

29. The party who will pay the costs of shipping rejected items back to the Seller.

30. The number of days, in numbers, by which rejected items must be returned to the Seller.

[___[20]___ on or before _____[21]_____,
___[22]___ on or before _____[23]_____ and the
balance of ___[24]___ not later than _____[25]_____.]
OR [_____[26]_____.]

(B)   Shipment of the goods purchased shall be
_____[27]_____.

(C)   Buyer shall examine each shipment promptly upon receipt and will advise Seller in writing of the number or quantity accepted and rejected and the reason(s) for rejection within __[28]__ days of receipt of each shipment. All items not accepted shall be returned to Seller at _____[29]_____ expense and any item not returned within __[30]__ days of notification to Seller shall be deemed accepted.

(Document continued on next page)

31. A description of the Seller's obligations to continue to perform the terms of the contract (essentially to continue to manufacture and ship the goods) and Seller's remedies in the event of a default by the Buyer. For example, the Seller may not wish to continue to produce or deliver goods if the Buyer has defaulted in making a payment. To protect himself, the Seller may wish to provide that "Seller is not obligated to deliver goods if any payment is not received within 10 days after the date due."

32. A description of the Buyer's obligations to continue to perform the terms of the contract (essentially to continue to pay) and the Buyer's remedies in the event of a default by the Seller. For example, where a Buyer is relying on the delivery of a continuous "stream" of goods from the Seller, to protect himself the Buyer may wish to provide for a monetary damage penalty. Note: in many cases, such damages may not be easy to calculate. Therefore, the parties may agree on a specific dollar amount to be included in the contract (called "liquidated damages," the language for which is found in the Contract for Sale of Goods— "Custom Made" with Liquidated Damages found elsewhere in this chapter).

33. It is suggested that the Seller very carefully consider what, if any, warranties will be given to the Buyer. This paragraph states that there is no warranty. If a warranty is to be given, replace this paragraph with one stating the terms of the warranty.

4.   BUYER'S DEFAULT - _____[31]_____
_____.

5.   SELLER'S DEFAULT - _____[32]_____
_____.

[33][6. SELLER'S WARRANTIES - It is understood and agreed by the parties that Seller does not warrant the Buyer's use of the items purchased and does not warrant to Buyer or any other that the items are merchantable or fit for any particular purpose.]

(Document continued on next page)

34. The name of the Seller if a corporation. Otherwise delete the line.

35. If the Seller is an individual, delete "BY" and print the Seller's name directly below the line, with the Seller to sign above the line. If the Seller is a corporation, print the name and title of the person acting for the corporation directly below the line, with that person to sign above the line.

36. The name of the Buyer if a corporation. Otherwise delete the line.

37. If the Buyer is an individual, delete "BY" and print the Buyer's name directly below the line, with the Buyer to sign above the line. If the Buyer is a corporation, print the name and title of the person acting for the corporation directly below the line, with that person to sign above the line.

IN WITNESS WHEREOF, the parties have signed this Agreement on the date first written above.

_____*[34]*_____

BY_____
　　　　　[35]　(Seller)

_____*[36]*_____

BY_____
　　　　　[37]　(Buyer)

CONTRACT FOR SALE OF GOODS—
"BUYER'S REQUIREMENTS" (3-04)

A "Buyer's Requirements" contract is one in which the Seller agrees to supply all of the Buyer's Requirements, usually for a stated period of time. This differs from a General Contract of Sale in which the parties agree to a specific number of units at a fixed price to be delivered on a fixed date or dates. A "Buyer's Requirements" contract typically, but not always, gives the Seller the right to adjust the unit price based on factors that are not within the Seller's control such as changes in materials costs or the like. The Buyer would like the contract to permit no price modifications but may be forced to agree to such a provision in order to secure a source of supply. With such a contract, the Buyer knows that the Seller cannot raise his price to increase his profit.

A "Buyer's Requirements" contract may contain any terms to which the parties agree but should, at the very least, include a description of exactly what is being sold and the price and delivery terms. Additional contract clauses are found elsewhere in this book and may be inserted as necessary.

A cautionary note: nobody likes to consider what would happen in the event that one of the parties defaulted. The guiding principal should be to "hope for the best but plan for the worst." This Contract deals with that issue.

CONTRACT OF SALE OF GOODS—
"BUYER'S REQUIREMENTS"

1. The date of signing the Contract.

2. The name of the Seller.

3. If the Seller is a corporation, insert the state of incorporation. Otherwise delete.

4. The address of the Seller.

5. The name of the Buyer.

6. If the Buyer is a corporation, insert the state of incorporation. Otherwise delete.

7. The address of the Buyer.

8. A thorough description of the goods being purchased, for example "5,000 cases of widgets, 12 per case, on pallets of 100 cases each."

9. The starting date of the Seller's shipments of the goods.

10. The ending date of the Seller's shipments of the goods.

AGREEMENT made this __[1]__ day of _____, 19__ by and between _____[2]_____ *[3][, a* _____ *corporation,]* with its office at _____[4]_____ ("Seller") and _____[5]_____ *[6][, a* _____ *corporation,]* with its office at _____[7]_____ ("Buyer").

1.   SALE - Seller has agreed to sell and Buyer has agreed to purchase from Seller Buyer's entire requirement of _____[8]_____ which Buyer requires for actual use in Buyer's business from _____[9]_____, 19__ to _____[10]_____, 19__ (the "Term" of this agreement) in accordance with the

(Document continued on next page)

11. On a separate sheet of paper headed "Schedule A" list the specifications (size, weight, etc.) of the goods being purchased.

12. Choose one. Enter the price for each item either in the Contract or on a separate sheet of paper headed "Schedule B."

13. The price, in numbers, for each item supplied.

14. Choose one depending on whether the price includes freight and insurance.

15. A description of the circumstances under which the Seller may raise its price, such as an increase in the Seller's materials costs. The event that "triggers" any such increase should be some factor that is both outside of the Seller's control and independently verifiable by the Buyer.

16. Choose one depending on the desired payment schedule. If the third alternative is chosen, skip to instruction No. 21. (Note: the choices shown are examples only. The method and timing of payment can be upon whatever terms the parties agree.)

17. The number of days, in numbers, after receipt of the items by which payment must be made. Then skip to instruction No. 22.

18. The amount, in numbers, of any deposit or down-payment made by the Buyer.

19. The amount, in numbers, due upon the Buyer's receipt of each shipment.

20. The amount, in numbers, of any unpaid balance remaining due.

plans and specifications and quantities set forth on the attached Schedule A.[11]

2.   PRICE - During the Term of this agreement, the price for each item shall be *[12][$___[13]___] OR [as set forth on the attached Schedule B]*, it being understood that the price *[14][does not include freight, shipping and delivery and insurance costs which shall be the sole responsibility of Buyer.] OR [includes freight, shipping and delivery and insurance costs.]*

        (A)   Adjustment in Price - The price may, at the option of Seller, be adjusted in accordance with _____[15]_____.

        (B)   Payment shall be made as follows: *[16][the entire amount due shall be paid in full not later than __[17]__ days after receipt by Buyer of the items purchased.] OR [$_____[18]_____ upon signing of this Agreement, $_____[19]_____ upon receipt of each shipment and the balance of $_____[20]_____ upon receipt of*

(Document continued on next page)

21. Any other payment terms agreed upon by the parties.

22. Choose one depending on the delivery schedule desired. If the first alternative is chosen, on a separate sheet of paper headed "Schedule C" (or headed "Schedule B" if there is no previous "Schedule B" from No. 12) list the delivery schedule and then skip to instruction No. 30. If the third alternative is chosen, skip to instruction No. 29.

23. The quantity of the first shipment.

24. The date by which the first shipment must be received.

25. The quantity of the second shipment.

26. The date by which the second shipment must be received.

27. The quantity of the final shipment.

28. The date by which the final shipment must be made.

29. Any other delivery schedule agreed upon by the parties.

30. The specific shipping terms agreed upon, including method (such as Seller's trucks, independent motor carrier, rail, air or combination) and who will pay the costs of shipping, insurance and the like. Be sure to be consistent with the choice in No. 14.

31. The number of days, in numbers, after receipt by which the Buyer must notify the Seller of rejection of any item received.

32. The party who will pay the costs of shipping any rejected items back to the Seller.

the shipment containing the balance of the items purchased.] OR [_____[21]_____.]

3.   DELIVERY/SHIPPING/ACCEPTANCE -
    (A)   Delivery of the goods purchased shall be *[22][as set forth in the attached Schedule C.] OR [____[23]_____ on or before _____[24]_____, _____[25]_____ on or before _____[26]_____ and the balance of _____[27]_____ not later than _____[28]_____.] OR [_____[29]_____ _____.]*

    (B)   Shipment of the goods purchased shall be _____[30]_____.

    (C)   Buyer shall examine each shipment promptly upon receipt and will advise Seller in writing of the number or quantity accepted and rejected and the reason(s) for rejection within __[31]__ days of receipt of each shipment. All items not accepted shall be returned to Seller at _____[32]_____ expense and any item not

(Document continued on next page)

33. The number of days, in numbers, by which rejected items must be returned to the Seller.

34. A description of the Seller's obligations to continue to perform the terms of the contract (essentially to continue to manufacture and ship the goods) and the Seller's remedies in the event of a default by the Buyer. For example, the Seller may not wish to continue to produce or deliver goods if the Buyer has defaulted in making a payment. To protect itself, the Seller may wish to provide that "Seller is not obligated to deliver goods if any payment is not received within 10 days after the date due."

35. A description of the Buyer's obligations to continue to perform the terms of the contract (essentially to continue to pay) and the Buyer's remedies in the event of a default by the Seller. For example, where a Buyer is relying on the delivery of a continuous "stream" of goods from the Seller, to protect itself the Buyer may wish to provide for a monetary damage penalty. Note: in many cases, such damages may not be easily calculated. Therefore, the parties may agree on a specific dollar amount to be included in the contract (called "liquidated damages," the language for which is found in the Contract for Sale of Goods— "Custom Made" with Liquidated Damages elsewhere in this chapter).

36. It is suggested that the Seller very carefully consider what, if any, warranties will be given to the Buyer. This paragraph states that there is no warranty. If a warranty is to be given, replace this paragraph with one stating the terms of the warranty.

returned within __[33]__ days of notification to Seller shall be deemed accepted.

4.   BUYER'S DEFAULT - _____[34]_____
_____.

5.   SELLER'S DEFAULT - _____[35]_____
_____.

[36][6. SELLER'S WARRANTIES - It is understood and agreed by the parties that Seller does not warrant the Buyer's use of the items purchased and does not warrant to Buyer or any other that the items are merchantable or fit for any particular purpose.]

(Document continued on next page)

CONTRACT FOR SALE OF GOODS—
"BUYER'S REQUIREMENTS" *continued*

37. The name of the Seller if a corporation. Otherwise delete the line.

38. If the Seller is an individual, delete "BY" and print the Seller's name directly below the line, with the Seller to sign above the line. If the Seller is a corporation, print the name and title of the person acting for the corporation directly below the line, with that person to sign above the line.

39. The name of the Buyer if a corporation. Otherwise delete the line.

40. If the Buyer is an individual, delete "BY" and print the Buyer's name directly below the line, with the Buyer to sign above the line. If the Buyer is a corporation, print the name and title of the person acting for the corporation directly below the line, with that person to sign above the line.

IN WITNESS WHEREOF, the parties have signed this Agreement on the date first written above.

_____*[37]*_____

BY_____
 [38] (Seller)

_____*[39]*_____

BY_____
 [40] (Buyer)

CONTRACT FOR SALE OF GOODS—
WARRANTIES (3-05)

Generally, a business can give Warranties for its own products as it wants or feels it must to remain competitive, or it can chose to give no Warranties at all. However, if the Seller is a merchant, that is, he deals in goods of a particular kind, holds himself out as having knowledge or skill related to goods of a particular kind, or if he employs a broker or agent who has such knowledge or skills, the law will consider the Seller to give certain implied Warranties unless specifically disclaimed in writing.

This Contract gives an example of a Seller's Warranty limited to his own materials and workmanship (areas that a Seller who is also the manufacturer can control) and also gives examples of disclaimers of Warranties.

CONTRACT FOR SALE OF GOODS—
WARRANTIES

1. The date of signing the Contract.

2. The name of the Seller.

3. If the Seller is a corporation, insert the state of incorporation. Otherwise delete.

4. The address of the Seller.

5. The name of Buyer.

6. If the Buyer is a corporation, insert the state of incorporation. Otherwise delete.

7. The address of the Buyer.

8. A detailed description of the goods being purchased, for example "5,000 cases of widgets, 12 per case, on pallets of 100 cases each."

9. On a separate sheet of paper headed "Schedule A" list the specifications (size, weight, etc.) of the goods being purchased.

10. The price, in numbers, of the goods being purchased.

11. The location at which title (ownership) to the goods passes to the Buyer, for example: "Seller's loading dock" or "Buyer's loading dock."

AGREEMENT made this __[1]__ day of _____, 19__ by and between _____[2]_____ [3][, a _____ corporation,] with its office at _____[4]_____ ("Seller") and _____[5]_____ [6][, a _____ corporation,] with its office at _____[7]_____ ("Buyer").

1. SALE - Seller has agreed to sell and Buyer has agreed to purchase _____[8]_____ in accordance with the plans and specifications set forth on the attached Schedule A.[9]

2. PRICE - The total price for the goods is $_____[10]_____ at _____[11]_____, it being

(Document continued on next page)

12. Choose one, depending on whether the price includes freight and insurance.

13. Choose one depending on the desired payment schedule. If the third alternative is chosen, skip to instruction No. 18. (Note: the choices shown are examples only. The method and timing of payment can be upon whatever terms the parties agree.)

14. The number of days, in numbers, after receipt of the items by which payment must be made. Then skip to instruction No. 19.

15. The amount, in numbers, of any deposit or down-payment made by the Buyer.

16. The amount, in numbers, due upon the Buyer's receipt of each shipment.

17. The amount, in numbers, of any unpaid balance remaining due.

18. Any other payment terms agreed upon by the parties.

19. Choose one, and if the use of a "Schedule B" is chosen, on a separate sheet of paper headed "Schedule B" list the the delivery schedule and then skip to instruction No. 27. If the third alternative is chosen, skip to instruction No. 26. (As with the terms of payment, so too the delivery schedule can contain any terms to which the parties agree.)

20. The quantity of the first shipment.

21. The date by which the first shipment must be received.

understood that the price *[12][does not include freight, shipping and delivery and insurance costs, which shall be the sole responsibility of Buyer.]* **OR** *[includes freight, shipping and delivery and insurance costs.]*

(A)   Payment shall be made as follows: *[13][the entire amount due shall be paid in full not later than __[14]__ days after receipt by Buyer of the items purchased.]* **OR** *[$___[15]____ upon signing of this Agreement, $___[16]___ upon receipt of each shipment and the balance of $__[17]___ upon receipt of the shipment containing the balance of the items purchased.]* **OR** *[_____[18]_____.]*

3.   DELIVERY/SHIPPING/ACCEPTANCE

(A)   Delivery of the goods purchased shall be *[19][as set forth in the attached Schedule B.]* **OR** *[___[20]___ on or before _____[21]_____,*

(Document continued on next page)

22. The quantity of the second shipment.

23. The date by which the second shipment must be received.

24. The quantity of the final shipment.

25. The date by which the final shipment must be received.

26. Any other delivery schedule agreed upon by the parties.

27. The specific shipping terms agreed upon, including the method (such as via the Seller's trucks, independent motor carrier, rail, air or a combination) and who will pay the costs of shipping and insurance. Be sure to be consistent with your choice in No. 12 above.

28. The number of days after receipt by which the Buyer must notify the Seller of rejection of any item.

29. The party at whose expense it will be to ship rejected items back to the Seller, for example "Seller's."

30. The number of days by which rejected items must be returned to the Seller.

31. If the agreement of the parties is that the goods are being sold in a so-called "as is" condition and without any Warranties, use this paragraph and delete paragraphs 32 and 33.

32. If the Seller is generally disclaiming all Warranties, use this paragraph and delete paragraphs 31 and 33.

___*[22]___ on or before _____[23]_____ and the balance of ___[24]___ not later than _____[25]_____.]*
***OR* [_____[26]_____.]**

 (B) Shipment of the goods purchased shall be _____[27]_____.

 (C) Buyer shall examine each shipment promptly upon receipt and will advise Seller in writing of the number or quantity accepted and rejected and the reason(s) for rejection within __[28]__ days of receipt of each shipment. All items not accepted shall be returned to Seller at _____[29]_____ expense and any item not returned within __[30]__ days of notification to Seller shall be deemed accepted.

4. SELLER'S WARRANTIES

[31] [Buyer acknowledges that Buyer has or has had the opportunity to make a full and complete inspection of the goods. IT IS UNDERSTOOD AND AGREED THAT THE GOODS SOLD TO BUYER ARE SOLD STRICTLY "AS IS" AND "WITH ALL FAULTS" AND BUYER ACKNOWLEDGES THAT THERE ARE NO WARRANTIES, EITHER EXPRESS OR IMPLIED OF EITHER MERCHANTABILITY OR FITNESS FOR ANY PARTICULAR PURPOSE.]

[32] [IT IS UNDERSTOOD AND AGREED THAT SELLER NEITHER GIVES NOR MAKES ANY WARRANTIES, EITHER EXPRESS OR IMPLIED, AS TO DESCRIPTION OF GOODS, QUALITY OF GOODS, MERCHANTABILITY OR FITNESS FOR ANY PARTICULAR PURPOSE OR ANY OTHER MATTER. BUYER ACKNOWLEDGES THAT SELLER SHALL IN NO WAY BE RESPONSIBLE OR LIABLE TO BUYER OR ANY OTHER PARTY FOR ANY USE OR PROPER USE OF THE GOODS. BUYER ACKNOWLEDGES THAT BUYER HAS NOT AND DOES NOT RELY ON SELLER'S SKILL OR JUDGMENT WITH REGARD TO THE SELECTION OF THE GOODS AS FIT OR SUITABLE FOR ANY PARTICULAR PURPOSE. NOTWITHSTANDING ANYTHING CONTAINED IN THIS AGREEMENT, BUYER WAIVES ALL RIGHT OF REFUSAL OR RIGHT TO RETURN THE GOODS OR ANY ITEM THEREOF.]

(Document continued on next page)

33. If the Seller warrants the parts and workmanship to be free from defect but makes no other Warranties, use this paragraph and delete paragraphs 31 and 32.

34. If the goods sold are for a particular use or environment, describe the use, for example "home, non-commercial" or "office, non-industrial use."

35. The duration of the Warranties, in words and numbers, for example "Thirty (30) days," "Ninety (90) days," "one (1) year."

36. A description of the Seller's obligations to continue to perform the terms of the contract (essentially to continue to manufacture and ship the goods) and the Seller's remedies in the event of a default by the Buyer. For example, the Seller may not wish to continue to produce or deliver goods if the Buyer has defaulted in making a payment. To protect himself, the Seller may wish to provide that "Seller is not obligated to deliver goods if any payment is not received within 10 days after the date due."

[33]   [Seller warrants to Buyer, or if Buyer is a dealer only, to the original purchaser, the goods manufactured by Seller to be free from defects in material and workmanship under normal _____[34]_____ for a period of ____[35]____ from the date of sale to the Buyer or from the date of installation by the original purchaser. In the event of such defect in material or workmanship, Seller's obligations under this warranty shall be limited to repair or replacement, at the sole option of Seller, of any defective part(s). THE FOREGOING WARRANTY IS EXPRESSLY MADE IN LIEU AND IN PLACE AND STEAD OF ALL OTHER WARRANTIES EXPRESS OR IMPLIED INCLUDING ANY WARRANTY OF MERCHANTABILITY OR FITNESS FOR ANY PURPOSE AND OF ANY OTHER LIABILITY OR OBLIGATION. THE FOREGOING WARRANTY SHALL NOT APPLY TO ANY GOODS OR PARTS WHICH HAVE BEEN SUBJECT TO IMPROPER INSTALLATION, ACCIDENT, NEGLIGENCE, ALTERATION, ABUSE OR MISUSE. BUYER ACKNOWLEDGES THAT BUYER HAS NOT AND DOES NOT RELY ON SELLER'S SKILL OR JUDGMENT WITH REGARD TO THE SELECTION OF THE GOODS AS FIT OR SUITABLE FOR ANY PARTICULAR PURPOSE.]

5.   BUYER'S DEFAULT - _____[36]_____
_____.

(Document continued on next page)

37. A description of the Buyer's obligations to continue to perform the terms of the contract (essentially to continue to pay) and the Buyer's remedies in the event of a default by Seller. For example, where a Buyer is relying on the delivery of a continuous "stream" of goods from the Seller, to protect himself the Buyer may wish to provide for a monetary damage penalty. Note: in many cases, such damages may not be easy to calculate. Therefore, the parties may agree on a specific dollar amount to be included in the contract (called "liquidated damages," the language for which is found in the Contract for Sale of Goods— "Custom Made" with Liquidated Damages found elsewhere in this chapter).

38. The name of the Seller if a corporation. Otherwise delete the line.

39. If the Seller is an individual, delete "BY" and type the Seller's name below the signature line with that individual to sign above the line. If the Seller is a corporation, type the name and title of the person acting for the corporation below the line with that person to sign above the line.

40. The name of the Buyer if a corporation. Otherwise delete the line.

41. If the Buyer is an individual, delete "BY" and type the Buyer's name below the signature line with that individual to sign above the line. If the Buyer is a corporation, type the name and title of the person acting for the corporation below the line with that person to sign above the line.

6.   SELLER'S DEFAULT - _____[37]_____
_____.

    IN WITNESS WHEREOF, the parties have signed this Agreement on the date first written above.

_____[38]_____

BY_____
        [39] (Seller)

_____[40]_____

BY_____
        [41] (Buyer)

CONTRACT FOR SALE OF GOODS—
"CUSTOM MADE"
WITH LIQUIDATED DAMAGES CLAUSE (3-06)

In the normal course of business, if a Buyer defaults (for example, fails to pay the Seller), the Seller can usually recoup a portion, if not all, of his damages (his losses) by sale of the goods to another party, since one Buyer is usually as good as another. However, goods that have been produced to the unique plans and specifications of a particular Buyer present special problems for the Seller since he cannot sell these goods to another Buyer. Where goods have been "custom made" it is typical for the parties to agree to an amount of damages (called "Liquidated Damages") so that the injured Seller does not have to establish the exact amount of his damages in any subsequent law suit. The parties should be careful to establish a reasonable amount as the Liquidated Damages.

CONTRACT FOR SALE OF GOODS—
"CUSTOM MADE"
WITH LIQUIDATED DAMAGES CLAUSE

1. The date of signing the Contract.

2. The name of the Seller.

3. If the Seller is a corporation, insert the state of incorporation. Otherwise delete.

4. The address of the Seller.

5. The name of the Buyer.

6. If the Buyer is a corporation, insert the state of incorporation. Otherwise delete.

7. The address of the Buyer.

8. A detailed description of the goods being purchased, for example "5,000 cases of widgets, 12 per case, on pallets of 100 cases each."

9. On a separate sheet of paper headed "Schedule A" list the specifications (size, weight, etc.) of the goods being purchased.

10. The price, in numbers, of the goods being purchased.

11. The location at which title (ownership) to the goods passes to the Buyer, for example: "Seller's loading dock" or "Buyer's loading dock."

AGREEMENT made this __[1]__ day of _____, 19__ by and between _____[2]_____ [3][, a _____ corporation,] with its office at _____[4]_____ ("Seller") and _____[5]_____ [6][, a _____ corporation,] with its office at _____[7]_____ ("Buyer").

1. SALE - Seller has agreed to sell and Buyer has agreed to purchase _____[8]_____ in accordance with the plans and specifications set forth on the attached Schedule A.[9]

2. PRICE - The total price for the goods is $_____[10]_____ at _____[11]_____, it being

(Document continued on next page)

12. Choose one, depending on whether the price includes freight and insurance.

13. Choose one depending on the desired payment schedule. If the third alternative is chosen, skip to instruction No. 18. Note: the choices shown are examples only. The method and timing of payment can be upon whatever terms the parties agree.

14. The number of days, in numbers, after receipt of the items by which payment must be made. Then skip to instruction No. 19.

15. The amount, in numbers, of any deposit or down-payment made by the Buyer.

16. The amount, in numbers, due upon the Buyer's receipt of each shipment.

17. The amount, in numbers, of any unpaid balance remaining due.

18. Any other payment terms agreed upon by the parties.

19. Choose one depending on whether damages will be a fixed amount or a percentage of the sale.

20. The dollar amount, in numbers, of the damages as agreed to by the parties (Liquidated Damages).

21. The percentage, in numbers, of the damages agreed to by the parties (Liquidated Damages) as calculated on the total sale price of the goods.

understood that the price *[12][does not include freight, shipping and delivery and insurance costs, which shall be the sole responsibility of Buyer.]* **OR** *[includes freight, shipping and delivery and insurance costs.]*

(A)   Payment shall be made as follows: *[13][the entire amount due shall be paid in full not later than __[14]__ days after receipt by Buyer of the items purchased.]* **OR** *[$___[15]____ upon signing of this Agreement; $___[16]___ upon receipt of each shipment and the balance of $__[17]___ upon receipt of the shipment containing the balance of the items purchased.]* **OR** _____[18]_____.]*

3.   CUSTOM MADE GOODS - The parties acknowledge that the goods are to be produced at the specific request, insistence and behest of Buyer and only in accordance with plans, specifications and standards prepared by Buyer and furnished to Seller by Buyer and set forth on the attached Schedule A. Buyer acknowledges that it has freely selected Seller only for the purpose of manufacturing the goods and that it has not relied on any representations of Seller, Seller's agents or employees or any other party. Buyer acknowledges that the goods are unique and are "custom made" for Buyer and only for Buyer and that other than Buyer, there is no market or other potential purchaser for the goods.

(A)   Based upon the foregoing, the parties acknowledge that it will be difficult if not impossible to adequately ascertain damages to Seller in the event of default by Buyer. It is expressly understood and agreed that in the event that Buyer shall fail or refuse to comply with any of the terms and conditions contained in this Agreement imposed on Buyer, Buyer shall pay to Seller *[19][the sum of $_____[20]_____]* **OR** *[an amount equal to __[21]__% of the total sale price set forth above]* as liquidated and agreed damages. In addition, Buyer acknowledges that Seller may elect to enforce any other remedies which Seller may have at law or equity.

(Document continued on next page)

22. Choose one, and if the use of a "Schedule B" is chosen, on a separate sheet of paper headed "Schedule B" list the the delivery schedule and then skip to instruction No. 30. If the third alternative is chosen, skip to instruction No. 29. As with the terms of payment, so too the delivery schedule can contain any terms to which the parties agree.

23. The quantity of the first shipment.

24. The date by which the first shipment must be received.

25. The quantity of the second shipment.

26. The date by which the second shipment must be received.

27. The quantity of the final shipment.

28. The date by which the final shipment must be received.

29. Any other delivery schedule agreed upon by the parties.

30. The specific shipping terms agreed upon, including the method (such as via the Seller's trucks, independent motor carrier, rail, air or a combination) and who will pay the costs of shipping and insurance. Be sure to be consistent with your choice in No. 12 above.

31. The number of days, in numbers, after receipt by which the Buyer must notify the Seller of rejection of any item.

32. The party at whose expense it will be to ship rejected items back to the Seller, for example "Seller's."

4.   DELIVERY/SHIPPING/ACCEPTANCE

(A)   Delivery of the goods purchased shall be *[22][as set forth in the attached Schedule B.] OR [___[23]___ on or before _____[24]_____, ___[25]___ on or before _____[26]_____ and the balance of ___[27]___ not later than _____[28]_____.] OR [_____[29]_____.]*

(B)   Shipment of the goods purchased shall be _____[30]_____.

(C)   Buyer shall examine each shipment promptly upon receipt and will advise Seller in writing of the number or quantity accepted and rejected and the reason(s) for rejection within __[31]__ days of receipt of each shipment. All items not accepted shall be returned to Seller at _____[32]_____ expense and any item not re-

(Document continued on next page)

33. The number of days, in numbers, by which rejected items must be returned to the Seller.

34. It is suggested that the Seller very carefully consider what, if any, warranties will be given to the Buyer. This paragraph states that there is no warranty. If a warranty is to be given, replace this paragraph with one stating the terms of the warranty.

35. The name of the Seller if a corporation. Otherwise delete the line.

36. If the Seller is an individual, delete "BY" and print the Seller's name directly below the line, with the Seller to sign above the line. If the Seller is a corporation, print the name and title of the person acting for the corporation directly below the line, with that person to sign above the line.

37. The name of the Buyer if a corporation. Otherwise delete the line.

38. If the Buyer is an individual, delete "BY" and print the Buyer's name directly below the line, with the Buyer to sign above the line. If the Buyer is a corporation, print the name and title of the person acting for the corporation directly below the line, with that person to sign above the line.

turned within __[33]__ days of notification to Seller shall be deemed accepted.

[34][5. SELLER'S WARRANTIES - It is understood and agreed by the parties that Seller does not warrant the Buyer's use of the items purchased and does not warrant to Buyer or any other that the items are merchantable or fit for any particular purpose.]

IN WITNESS WHEREOF, that parties have signed this Agreement on the date first written above.

_____[35]_____

BY_____
        [36] (Seller)

_____[37]_____

BY_____
        [38] (Buyer)

CONSIGNMENT SALES AGREEMENT (3-07)

A Consignment Sale is defined as the act of shipping, transferring or depositing goods with a merchant, agent or factor for sale by the merchant, agent or factor. Products are deposited with a merchant (the CONSIGNEE) for sale to others but for the account of the seller (the CONSIGNOR). In consignment sales, the merchant does not take ownership of the products; the merchant makes a commission when he makes the sale of the CONSIGNOR's products. Since the merchant is the agent of the seller (rather than the owner of the products himself), the merchant, as CONSIGNEE, is placed in a position of trust with respect to the products and must account to the seller.

CONSIGNMENT SALES AGREEMENT

1. The date of the Agreement.

2. The name of the seller of the goods or products (the CONSIGNOR).

3. If the CONSIGNOR is a corporation, insert the state of incorporation. Otherwise delete.

4. The address of the CONSIGNOR.

5. The name of the merchant, agent or factor (the CONSIGNEE).

6. If the CONSIGNEE is a corporation, insert the state of incorporation. Otherwise delete.

7. The address of the CONSIGNEE.

8. A description of the products placed with the CONSIGNEE for sale.

AGREEMENT made as of _____[1]_____ 19__, between _____[2]_____, [3][a _____ corporation,] with a place of business at _____[4]_____ ("CONSIGNOR") and _____[5]_____, [6][a _____ corporation,] with a place of business at _____[7]_____ ("CONSIGNEE").

1. Consignment of Products: CONSIGNOR shall, subject to causes beyond its control, ship to CONSIGNEE, on consignment, _____[8]_____ ("Products") in such quantity as CONSIGNOR may determine. CONSIGNEE shall accept the Products and shall store them either at CONSIGNEE's place of business or at such other locations specified in writing. Shipments shall be F.O.B. place of manufacture or CONSIGNOR's place of business. The Products shall be held by CONSIGNEE for sale to others. CONSIGNEE shall perform all acts required by law to protect the rights of CONSIGNOR to the consigned Products, including but not limited to segregation of the Products from other goods of CONSIGNEE and identification of the Products as consigned goods of CONSIGNOR, wherever and whenever possible. CONSIGNEE, after receipt of the Products, shall pay all expenses incident to the Products, including all expenses of storage, insurance, selling and delivering to customers, and all taxes and other charges which may be assessed or levied on the Products while in CONSIGNEE's possession.

2. Title to Products: The consigned Products shall remain the property of CONSIGNOR until sold by CONSIGNEE, and title to the proceeds of the sales of Products shall vest in and belong to CONSIGNOR until accounted for and paid over to CONSIGNOR.

(Document continued on next page)

9. The date of the month by which the CONSIGNEE must prepare its report (accounting) to the CONSIGNOR.

10. The date of the expiration of the Agreement.

3. Loss or Damage to Products: CONSIGNEE shall be responsible to and shall reimburse CONSIGNOR for all loss and expense to CONSIGNOR resulting from theft of, damage to or destruction of the consigned Products, or from levy or attachment by any process or lien thereon while in CONSIGNEE's possession and until such time as title passes by reason of the sale of the Products and the proceeds of the sale have been accounted for and remitted to CONSIGNOR. CONSIGNEE shall keep the consigned Products fully insured, at CONSIGNEE's expense, for the benefit of CONSIGNOR and shall provide CONSIGNOR with a Certificate of Insurance naming CONSIGNOR as an additional insured with a loss payable to CONSIGNOR provision.

4. Report of Sales and Payment: On the ___ [9]___ day of each month, CONSIGNEE shall report to the CONSIGNOR sales of Products made by CONSIGNEE since the last report. CONSIGNEE shall make payment to CONSIGNOR for all sales at the time of the report. Every six (6) months a physical inventory of consigned Products shall be taken by CONSIGNEE. CONSIGNOR reserves the right to have a representative present and report the inventory to CONSIGNOR. If consigned Products are found missing CONSIGNEE shall immediately pay CONSIGNOR for missing Products.

5. Term: This Agreement shall terminate on _____[10]_____, at which time all sold Products shall be accounted and paid for. At CONSIGNOR's sole option unsold Products may be returned, freight prepaid, or paid for by CONSIGNEE. Notwithstanding the foregoing, CONSIGNOR may terminate this Agreement without prior notice if CONSIGNEE violates any term of this Agreement or in the event that CONSIGNOR, in its sole determination, becomes dissatisfied with the financial stability of CONSIGNEE.

6. Authority to Act for CONSIGNOR: CONSIGNEE shall conduct the entire business of selling CONSIGNOR's Products in CONSIGNEE's name and at CONSIGNEE's cost and expense. Nothing in this Agreement shall authorize or empower CONSIGNEE to assume or create any obligation or responsibility whatsoever, express or implied, on behalf of or in the name of CONSIGNOR, or to bind CONSIGNOR in any manner, or make any representation, warranty, or commitment on behalf of

(Document continued on next page)

11. The state whose laws will govern the Agreement, typically the state in which the CONSIGNOR is located.

12. The city in which arbitration will take place.

13. The state in which arbitration will take place, typically the state in which the CONSIGNOR is located.

CONSIGNOR, this Agreement being limited solely to the consignment of Products.

7.   Indemnity: CONSIGNEE shall indemnify and hold CONSIGNOR harmless against any loss or damage caused by acts of the CONSIGNEE not authorized by this Agreement.

8.   Financing Statement: CONSIGNEE agrees to sign and deliver to CONSIGNOR such financing statements, security agreements or continuation statements, in a form satisfactory to CONSIGNOR, as CONSIGNOR may from time to time reasonably request. CONSIGNOR may, at its expense, file the statements with the appropriate government agency.

9.   Benefit: This Agreement shall be binding upon and inure to the benefit of the parties hereto, and their respective successors and assigns. This Agreement may not be assigned by CONSIGNEE without the express written consent of the CONSIGNOR.

10.   Controlling Law: This Agreement shall be governed by and construed under the laws of the State of _____[11]_____.

11.   Arbitration: Any controversy or claim arising out of or relating to this Agreement, or the breach thereof, shall be settled by arbitration, in the City of ___[12]____, State of ____[13]____, in accordance with the Commercial Arbitration Rules of the American Arbitration Association, and judgment upon the award rendered by the arbitrator(s) may be entered in any court having jurisdiction thereof.

(Document continued on next page)

14. The name of the CON-SIGNOR if a corporation. Otherwise delete the line.

15. If the CONSIGNOR is an individual, delete "BY" and print the CONSIGNOR's name directly below the line, with the CONSIGNOR to sign above the line. If the CONSIGNOR is a corporation, print the name and title of the individual acting for the corporation directly below the line, with that person to sign above the line.

16. The name of the CON-SIGNEE if a corporation. Otherwise delete the line.

17. If the CONSIGNEE is an individual, delete "BY" and print the CONSIGNEE's name directly below the line, with the CONSIGNEE to sign above the line. If the CONSIGNEE is a corporation, print the name and title of the individual acting for the corporation directly below the line, with that person to sign above the line.

12.   Notice: All notices shall be sent by certified mail, return receipt requested, to the party to be notified, at the addresses stated above, or at such other address as either party shall designate in writing.

IN WITNESS WHEREOF, the parties have executed this Agreement.

_____*[14]*_____

BY_____
[15]

_____*[16]*_____

BY_____
[17]

EQUIPMENT LEASE (3-08)

       Businesses increasingly rely on equipment and machinery ranging from computers to photocopiers to package handling equipment to lathes and milling machines. The outright purchase of such equipment diverts capital from other uses such as payroll (for people to operate the equipment and machinery) or raw materials (necessary to produce whatever the business sells). One solution to this problem is to lease equipment so that the supplier or dealer of the equipment retains title (ownership) but allows the customer to use the equipment during a stated time period. The owner of the equipment is the Lessor, the user is the Lessee, the stated time period is referred to as the Term of the Lease and the "rental" payment for use of the equipment is the monthly Lease payment.

EQUIPMENT LEASE

1. The name, address and telephone number of the Lessor (the owner of the equipment who is leasing it to another).

2. The name, address and telephone number of the Lessee (the party leasing the equipment from the owner of the equipment).

3. The quantity of each piece of equipment.

4. The name of the manufacturer or supplier and a description (model, type or the like) of each piece of equipment.

5. The serial number of each piece of equipment.

6. The location where each piece of equipment will be installed and kept. Or list on a separate sheet headed "Schedule of Equipment."

7. The initial term of the Lease in months, in numbers.

8. The dollar amount, in numbers, of each monthly Lease payment.

9. The dollar amount, in numbers, of the advance payment.

LESSOR: _____[1]_____ LESSEE: _____[2]_____
_____ _____
_____ _____
Tel. _____ Tel. _____

QTY.	DESCRIPTION OF EQUIP.	SERIAL NO.
__[3]__	_____[4]_____	____[5]____
__[3]__	_____[4]_____	____[5]____
__[3]__	_____[4]_____	____[5]____
__[3]__	_____[4]_____	____[5]____
__[3]__	_____[4]_____	____[5]____

EQUIPMENT LOCATION:
_____[6]_____
_____

INITIAL TERM	MONTHLY PAYMENT	ADVANCE PAYMENT
__[7]__ Months	$_____[8]_____	$____[9]____

     THIS LEASE CANNOT BE CANCELLED EXCEPT AS EXPRESSLY PROVIDED. THIS LEASE SHALL BECOME EFFECTIVE UPON SIGNING BY LESSOR AND LESSEE.

1.   TERMS AND CONDITIONS - Lessor agrees to lease and Lessee leases from Lessor the equipment described above and on any attached Schedule (the "Equipment") in accordance with the terms and conditions stated in this Lease Agreement. Lessee authorizes Lessor to insert in this Equipment Lease Agreement (the "Lease") serial numbers and other identification information when deter-

(Document continued on next page)

10. The number of days, in numbers, permitted for the Lessee to give notice that the leased equipment does not perform as promised.

mined by Lessor. This Lease constitutes the full and entire agreement between the Lessor and Lessee in connection with the Equipment and merges any and all other understandings. Neither party relies on any other statement or representation made by the other or any third party. This Lease can neither be cancelled nor modified except by written agreement signed by both Lessor and Lessee. Lessee's acceptance of the Equipment shall be irrevocable unless Lessor and Vendor each receive Lessee's written notice of substantial non-conformance of the Equipment within __[10]__ days after acceptance of the Equipment.

2.   PAYMENT - Lessee agrees to make all monthly Lease payments in advance on the 1st day of each and every month commencing with the first full month after delivery of the Leased Equipment, and to pay such other charges as provided in this Agreement. Lease payments shall be increased by any cost or expense Lessor incurs to preserve the Equipment or to pay any taxes, assessments, fees, penalties, liens or encumbrances. Each payment received will be applied to the oldest charge due under this Lease. Lessee agrees to make payments regardless of any problems Lessee might or may have with the Equipment including its operations, capability, installation or repair and regardless of any claim, set-off, counterclaim or defense Lessee might or may have against the Vendor or Manufacturer (the "Supplier"), Salesperson or other Third Party. Without Lessor's prior written consent, any payment to Lessor of a smaller sum than due at any time under this Agreement shall not constitute release or an accord or satisfaction for any greater sum due or to become due regardless of any restrictive endorsement. An advance payment shall be held by Lessor as a security deposit for the faithful performance of this Lease.

3.   TAXES/ASSESSMENTS/FEES - Lessee agrees: to pay all licensing, filing and registration fees reasonably required; to keep the Equipment free of all liens and encumbrances; to show the Equipment as "Leased Equipment" on Lessee's tax returns; to pay Lessor for all personal property taxes assessed against the Equipment; to pay all other taxes, assessments, fees and penalties which may be levied or assessed with respect to the Equipment, its use or any interest thereon or any lease payments, including but not limited to all federal, state and local taxes however designated, levied or assessed whether upon Lessee or Lessor of the Equipment or upon any sale, ownership, use or op-

(Document continued on next page)

11. The percentage, in numbers, of the monthly Lease payment that the Lessor will charge as an escrow for taxes.

12. The amount, in numbers, to be charged by the Lessor for the preparation and filing of any Financing Statements permitted by the Uniform Commercial Code ("U.C.C."), credit searches and the like.

eration excepting any income taxes levied on the lease payments to Lessor. Lessor may, at its option, collect from Lessee an escrow fee of up to __[11]__ percent of the Equipment cost per month for a tax escrow fund. Lessor will pay on Lessee's behalf such taxes and other amounts and file applicable returns. In addition, Lessee authorizes Lessor to file at Lessor's option informational financing statements without Lessee's signature and if a signature is required by law, Lessee appoints Lessor as Lessee's attorney-in-fact to execute such financing statements. Lessee agrees to pay Lessor a fee of $_____[12]_____ to reimburse Lessor's expenses of preparing such financing statements and of making credit checks and analysis of Lessee's and guarantor's financial status and of Lessor's other administrative costs. Lessee and any guarantor agree to reimburse Lessor for reasonable costs incurred in collecting taxes, assessments or fees for which Lessee is liable and any collection charges attributable thereto including reasonable attorneys' fees. Lessee agrees that Lessor is entitled to all tax benefits resulting from ownership of the Equipment including any investment tax credit and depreciation. Lessee agrees that should any of such tax benefits be disallowed, Lessee shall indemnify Lessor for such loss by paying Lessor an amount equal to the value of the lost benefits as stipulated and liquidated herein.

4.   LESSEE'S AND GUARANTOR'S WARRANTIES TO LESSOR - Lessee and any guarantor expressly warrant to Lessor and Lessor relies on the fact that Lessee and any guarantor: (a) have read and understood this Lease before it was signed; (b) have selected and are fully satisfied with both the Equipment and the Supplier who sold the Equipment to Lessor for the purposes set forth in this Lease; (c) will authorize Lessor to pay for the Equipment only after Lessee has received and accepted the Equipment as fully operable for Lessee's purposes; (d) have freely chosen to lease, not buy, from Lessor only after having considered other means of obtaining the use of the Equipment; (e) freely acknowledge that neither the manufacturer nor the supplier of the Equipment nor any of its salespersons are, or have acted as, Lessor's agents or employees; (f) have provided accurate and correct financial information and other statements and same will be updated upon Lessor's request during the term of the Lease; (g) are currently meeting all debts as such come due; (h) will use the Equipment exclusively for Lessee's business purposes and not for personal, family or household purposes; (i) have

(Document continued on next page)

unrestricted power to enter into this Lease, have duly authorized the person executing it and certify that all signatures are authentic; and (j) will pay all costs connected with the Equipment including taxes, insurance, repairs, shipping, collection costs and other expenses normally paid in a net lease.

5.   LESSEE'S WAIVER OF DAMAGES AND WARRANTIES FROM LESSOR - Lessee acknowledges that it has selected the Equipment and each piece of the Equipment and that in doing so Lessee has not relied upon any statements of Lessor, Lessor's salespeople, agents or employees. Lessee further acknowledges that: (a) Lessee leases the Equipment from Lessor in a strictly "AS IS" condition; Lessor makes absolutely no warranties express or implied, including any warranty of merchantability for fitness for a particular purpose; (b) if the Equipment is not properly installed, does not operate as represented or warranted by the manufacturer or supplier, or is unsatisfactory for any reasons whatsoever, Lessee shall make any claim on account thereof solely against the manufacturer or supplier and Lessee hereby waives any such claim against Lessor (all warranties from the Supplier to Lessor are hereby assigned to Lessee for the term of the Lease for Lessee's exercise at Lessee's expense); (c) Lessee shall hold Lessor harmless and shall be responsible for any loss, damage or injury to persons or property caused by the Equipment; (d) no representation or warranty by the manufacturer, supplier or salesperson is binding on Lessor nor shall breach of such warranty relieve Lessee of Lessee's obligations to Lessor; and (e) in no case shall Lessor be liable to Lessee for special, indirect or consequential damages.

6.   OWNERSHIP AND TITLE - Lessor is the sole owner of the Equipment, has sole title to the Equipment, has the right to inspect the Equipment and has the right to affix and display notice of Lessor's ownership thereon. The Equipment shall remain Lessor's personal property whether or not affixed to realty and shall not be part of any real property on which it is placed. All additions, attachments and accessories placed on the Equipment become part of the Equipment and Lessor's property. Lessee agrees to maintain the Equipment so that it may be removed from the property or building where located without damage.

(Document continued on next page)

7.   OPERATION AND TERMINATION - Lessee shall be solely responsible for the installation, operation, and maintenance of the Equipment, shall keep it in good condition and running order and shall use and operate the Equipment in compliance with applicable law. Lessee agrees to keep and use the Equipment only at the business address specified above ("Equipment Location"), to never abandon or move the Equipment from that address, nor relinquish possession of the Equipment except to Lessor's agent. At the end of the Lease Term, Lessee must contact Lessor who will designate the return location within the continental United States, and Lessee shall at Lessee's expense, immediately crate, insure and return the Equipment to the designated location in as good a condition as when Lessee received it, excepting only reasonable wear and tear. Until Lessor actually receives the Equipment at the return location, the Lease renews automatically from month to month and Lessee agrees to continue to make lease payments at the last effective rate under the Lease.

8.   RISK OF LOSS AND INSURANCE - Until Lessee has returned the Equipment to the designated location, Lessee bears the entire risk of loss or damage to the Equipment regardless how arising. Lessee shall immediately notify Lessor of the occurrence of any loss or other occurrence affecting Lessor's interests and shall make repairs or corrections at Lessee's expense. In such event, Lessee agrees to continue to meet all payment and other obligations under the Lease. Lessee agrees to keep the Equipment insured at Lessee's expense against risk of loss or damage from any cause whatsoever. Lessee agrees that such insurance shall be not less than the greater of the unpaid balance of the rentals due or the then-current fair market value of the Equipment. Lessee also agrees that the insurance shall be in such additional amount as is reasonable to cover Lessor for public liability and property damage arising from the Equipment or Lessee's use of it. Lessee agrees to name Lessor as the loss payee. Each policy shall provide that the insurance cannot be cancelled without thirty (30) days prior written notice to Lessor. Upon request by Lessor, Lessee agrees to furnish proof of each insurance policy including a certificate of insurance and a copy of the policy. The proceeds of such insurance shall be applied at Lessor's sole election toward the replacement or repair of the Equipment or payment towards Lessee's obligations. Lessee appoints Lessor as attorney-in-fact to make any claim for, receive payment of, or execute or endorse all

(Document continued on next page)

documents, checks or drafts for loss or damage or return of premium under such insurance. Because of increased credit risks to Lessor when not insured by Lessee, Lessee agrees to pay to Lessor each month a risk charge stipulated and liquidated at 25% of Lessor's original equipment cost until Lessee provides proof of compliance with insurance requirements. In spite of such risk charge, Lessee has no right to any insurance benefits from Lessor. Lessee is still liable for all losses and such risk charge is not in lieu of the insurance requirements of this Lease.

9.   INDEMNITY - Lessee agrees to indemnify and hold Lessor harmless from and against any and all losses, damages, injuries, demands and expense (a "Claim"), including any and all attorneys' fees and legal expenses, arising from or caused directly or indirectly by any actual or alleged use, possession, maintenance, condition (whether or not latent or discoverable), operation, location, delivery or transportation of any item of Equipment. Should Lessee be entitled under applicable law to revoke its acceptance of the Equipment, Lessee agrees to pay and indemnify Lessor for any payment by Lessor to the manufacturer or supplier of the Equipment.

10.   COLLECTION CHARGES AND ATTORNEYS' FEES - If any part of any sum due to Lessor is not received by Lessor within ten (10) days of the due date or if any sum paid by check shall be dishonored or returned to Lessor on account of uncollected funds or for insufficient funds, Lessee agrees to pay Lessor: (a) a one-time late charge to compensate Lessor for collecting and processing the late sum, equal to the greater of 15% of any delayed sum or $25.00, plus (b) an interest charge for every month after the first month in which the sum is late to compensate Lessor for the inability to reinvest the sum, such interest charge stipulated and liquidated at 1 1/2% per month or the maximum allowed by applicable law, whichever is less.

11.   LESSEE AND ANY GUARANTOR AGREE TO PAY LESSOR'S REASONABLE ATTORNEYS' FEES AS DAMAGES AND NOT COSTS - In all proceedings arising under this lease, such proceedings including any arbitration, bankruptcy proceeding, civil action, mediation or counterclaim on which Lessor prevails seeking relief from stay in bankruptcy or post-judgment action or appeal with respect to any of the foregoing, reasonable attorneys' fees

(Document continued on next page)

are stipulated and liquidated at not less than the greater of $500.00 or 25% of Lessor's total amount in collection.

12.   DEFAULT - Lessee shall be in default of this Lease on any of the following events: (a) Lessee fails to pay any month's rent within ten (10) days after it first becomes due; (b) Lessee assigns, moves, pledges, subleases, sells or relinquishes possession of the Equipment or attempts to do so, without Lessor's prior written authorization; (c) Lessee breaches any of its warranties or other obligations under this Lease or any other agreement with Lessor and fails to cure such breach within ten (10) days after Lessor sends Lessee a notice of the existence of such breach; (d) any execution or writ of process is issued in any action or proceeding to seize or detain the Equipment; (e) Lessee or any guarantor gives Lessor reasonable cause to be insecure about Lessee's willingness or ability to perform obligations under the Lease or any other agreement with Lessor; (f) Lessee or any guarantor dies, becomes insolvent or unable to pay debts when due, stops doing business as a going concern, consolidates, merges, transfers all or substantially all of its assets, makes an assignment for the benefit of creditors, appoints a trustee or receiver or undergoes a substantial deterioration of financial health; or (g) Lessor or any guarantor fails to reaffirm this lease obligation within thirty (30) days of the filing of any petition for protection under the United States Bankruptcy Code.

13.   REMEDIES - Should Lessee default, Lessor has the right to exercise any or all of the following: Lessor may without notice accelerate all sums under the Lease and require Lessee to immediately pay Lessor all sums that are already due and the discounted value of those that will become due and (i) require the immediate return of the Equipment to Lessor or (ii) if Lessee agrees after Lessee pays all other sums under the Lease, sell the Equipment to Lessee at the estimated lease-end fair market Equipment value discounted to the date of sale. Such estimated lease-end fair market Equipment value is stipulated and liquidated as the Lessor's cost of the Equipment less 2% per month during the first 12 months of the Lease and less 1% per month thereafter up until the date of acceleration. Lessor has the right to immediately retake possession of the Equipment without any court or other process of law and for such purpose may enter upon any premises where the Equipment may be and remove the same. Lessor has the right to exercise any remedy at law or equity, notice thereof

(Document continued on next page)

13. The city and state in which any arbitration hearing is to be held, typically the state in which the Lessor is located.

14. The state whose laws will govern the contract, typically the state in which the Lessor is located.

being expressly waived by Lessee and any guarantor; Lessor's action or failure to act on any one remedy constitutes neither an election to be limited thereon nor a waiver of any other remedy nor a release of Lessee from the liability to return the Equipment or for any Loss or Claim with respect thereto. The provisions of this Lease are severable and shall not be affected or impaired if any one provision is held unenforceable, invalid or illegal. Any provision held in conflict with any statute or rule of law shall be deemed inoperative only to the extent of such conflict and shall be modified to conform with such statute or rule.

14.   ARBITRATION - Lessor may, at its option, submit any matter arising out of this Lease Agreement, including any claim, counterclaim, setoff or defense to binding arbitration by the American Arbitration Association in the City of _____[13]_____, State of _____[13]_____ irrespective of the fact that neither the Lessee, any guarantor or the Equipment may be located in that City now or then. The decision and award of the arbitrator(s) shall be final and binding and may be entered as rendered in any court having jurisdiction thereof.

15.   CONSENT TO JURISDICTION, VENUE AND NON-JURY TRIAL - Lessee and any guarantor consent, agree and stipulate that: (a) this Lease shall be deemed fully executed and performed in the State of _____[14]_____ and shall be governed by and construed in accordance with the laws thereof; and (b) in any action, proceeding, or appeal on any matter related to or arising out of this lease, Lessor, Lessee and any guarantor: (i) shall be subject to the personal jurisdiction of the State of _____[14]_____ including any state or federal court sitting therein and all court rules thereof; (ii) shall accept venue in any federal or state court in _____[14]_____; and (iii) expressly waive any right to a trial by jury so that trial shall be by and only to the court. Nothing contained herein is intended to preclude Lessor from commencing any action hereunder in any court having jurisdiction thereof.

16.   CONSENT TO SERVICE OF PROCESS - Lessee and any guarantor agree that any process served for any action or proceeding shall be valid if mailed by Certified Mail, return receipt requested, with delivery restricted to

(Document continued on next page)

EQUIPMENT LEASE *continued*

15. The date of signing the Lease by the Lessee.

16. The name of the Lessee if a corporation. Otherwise delete the line.

17. If the Lessee is an individual, delete "BY" and print the Lessee's name directly below the line, with the Lessee to sign above the line. If the Lessee is a corporation, print the name and title of the person acting for the corporation directly below the line, with that person to sign above the line.

18. The date of signing the Lease by the Lessor.

19. The name of the Lessor if a corporation. Otherwise delete the line.

20. If the Lessor is an individual, delete "BY" and print the Lessor's name directly below the line, with the Lessor to sign above the line. If the Lessor is a corporation, print the name and title of the person acting for the corporation below the line, with that person to sign above the line.

21. The date of signing the Statement of Acceptance by the Lessee.

22. The name of the Lessee if a corporation. Otherwise delete the line.

23. If the Lessee is an individual, delete "BY" and print the Lessee's name directly below the line, with the Lessee to sign above the line. If the Lessee is a corporation, print the name and title of the person acting for the corporation directly below the line, with that person to sign above the line.

either the addressee, its registered agent or any agent appointed in writing to accept such process.

Dated: _____[15]_____

_____[16]_____

BY_____
[17]   (Lessee)

ACCEPTED:
Date of Acceptance: _____[18]_____

_____[19]_____

BY_____
[20]   (Lessor)

===

LESSEE'S STATEMENT OF ACCEPTANCE OF LEASE EQUIPMENT

Lessee acknowledges that all of the items set forth above (the "Leased Equipment") have been received by Lessee; that all required installation, preparation, set-up and other work has been performed; and that in all respects, the Lease Equipment is satisfactory and is hereby accepted by Lessee.

Dated: ____[21]____

_____[22]_____

BY_____
[23]   (Lessee)

RECEIPT (3-09)

At its simplest, a receipt is nothing more than an acknowledgement of having received something. As our society has grown more complex, and more people pay for items upon delivery (as opposed to at the time of the sale) and pay by credit card, more information is required to facilitate delivery. This Receipt contains the necessary information for such deliveries.

RECEIPT
FROM

1. The name of the seller or party making the delivery.

_____[1]_____

2. The date of the delivery.

DEL. DATE: _____[2]_____

3. The home telephone number of the party receiving the delivery.

HOME PHONE #: _____[3]_____

4. The business telephone number of the party receiving the delivery.

BUSINESS PHONE #: _____[4]_____

5. The name and address to which the delivery is being made.

DELIVER TO: _____[5]_____ Apt.#____

_____

_____

DESCRIPTION

6. The number of pieces being delivered.

7. A description, model number or the like of each item being delivered.

No.	Item
__[6]__	_____[7]_____
__[6]__	_____[7]_____
__[6]__	_____[7]_____
__[6]__	_____[7]_____

PAYMENT

8. The amount of payment made by cash or certified check.

C.O.D. _____[8]_____
cash or certified check

9. The account number of the credit card being used for payment.

CREDIT CARD
( ) VISA   ( ) MC   ( ) AMEX   ( ) DINERS

10. The expiration date of the credit card used for payment.

CARD #_____[9]_____

11. The dollar amount, in numbers, being charged.

EXP. DATE:____[10]_____

12. The credit card charge authorization number received.

AMOUNT OF CHARGE (TOTAL) $_____[11]_____

AUTH.#_____[12]_____

(Document continued on next page)

13. The billing address of the credit card being used for payment.

14. The name of the person receiving (signing for) the goods printed directly below the line, with that person to sign above the line. (If a credit card is used, the name and signature of the credit card holder.)

15. Insert any directions as to the place of delivery, special handling, delivery or pick-up instructions.

BILLING
ADDRESS_____[13]_____
_____
_____

CARDHOLDER NAME _____

YOUR SIGNATURE CONSTITUTES ACCEPTANCE OF ALL MERCHANDISE AND INDICATES 100% SATIS-FACTION AS PER ORDER. ALL SALES ARE FINAL.

X _____
                              [14]

FOR CREDIT CARDS ONLY: The issuer of the card identified on this item is authorized to pay the amount shown as TOTAL upon proper presentation. I promise to pay such TOTAL (together with any other charges due thereon) subject to and in accordance with the Agreement governing the use of such card.

DIRECTIONS/OTHER DELIVERY OR PICK-UP IN-STRUCTIONS:
_____[15]_____
_____
_____

DOOR-TO-DOOR SALES/
3-DAY CANCELLATION NOTICE (3-10)

The Federal Trade Commission and most states require that the buyer of a product sold in the home be offered the opportunity to cancel the purchase within 3 business days after the date of the sale ("the cooling-off period"). In addition to leaving two copies of the written Notice with the buyer, the seller must orally inform the buyer of his right to cancel.

The Federal Trade Commission defines a Door-to-Door Sale as:

A sale, lease or rental of consumer goods or services with a purchase price of $25 or more, whether under single or multiple contracts, in which the seller or the seller's representative personally solicits the sale, including those in response to or following an invitation by the buyer, and the buyer's agreement or offer to purchase is made at a place other than the place of business of the seller.

Some states have a slight variation in language for the Notice (Iowa, for example) and if business is conducted in only one state, that state's language should be followed. Some states include Saturday as a business day and some exclude it. As a general rule Saturday, Sunday and legal holidays should not be counted as business days.

DOOR-TO-DOOR SALES
3-DAY CANCELLATION NOTICE

1. This statement must be printed in 10 point bold type on the face of the contract of sale.

2. The entire Notice of Right to Cancel must be printed in 10 point bold type. The Notice may be part of the contract of sale or a separate sheet attached to the contract of sale.

3. The date of the sale.

[1]   You, the buyer, may cancel this transaction at any time prior to midnight of the third business day after the date of this transaction. See the attached notice of cancellation form for an explanation of this right.

[2] NOTICE OF RIGHT TO CANCEL

Date of Transaction _____[3]_____

You may cancel this transaction, without any penalty or obligation, within 3 business days from the above date.

If you cancel, any property traded in, any payments made by you under the contract of sale, and any negotiable instrument executed by you will be returned within 10 business days following receipt by the seller of your cancellation notice, and any security interest arising out of the transaction will be cancelled.

If you cancel, you must make available to the seller at your residence, in substantially as good condition as when received, any goods delivered to you under

(Document continued on next page)

4. The name of the company making the sale.

5. The address of the company.

6. The date by which the Notice must be sent.

7. The date the Notice is sent by the buyer.

8. The buyer's name printed directly below the line, with the buyer to sign above the line.

this contract of sale; or you may, if you wish, comply with the instructions of the seller regarding the return shipment of the goods at the seller's expense and risk.

If you do make the goods available to the seller and the seller does not pick them up within 20 days of the date of your notice of cancellation, you may retain or dispose of the goods without any further obligation. If you fail to make the goods available to the seller, or if you agree to return the goods to the seller and fail to do so, then you remain liable for performance of all obligations under the contract.

To cancel this transaction, mail or deliver a signed and dated copy of this cancellation notice or any other written notice or send a telegram to _____[4]_____ at _____[5]_____ not later than midnight of _____[6]_____.

I hereby cancel this transaction.

Date: _____[7]_____

_____
[8] (Buyer)

ASSIGNMENT AND ASSUMPTION OF
LIMITED PARTNERSHIP INTEREST (3-11)

Virtually anything, tangible or intangible, can be sold or transferred for value to someone else. An interest in an existing Limited Partnership is no different except that one does not sell such an interest but rather assigns his interest. The limited partner is the "Assignor" and he assigns his interest to the "Assignee." As part of the transaction (usually required to obtain the consent of the Limited Partnership), the Assignee also agrees to assume all of the risks and obligations of the Assignor. An Assignee is said to "stand in the shoes of the Assignor." This form is the Assignment by the Assignor to the Assignee and the Assignee's Agreement to assume the obligations of the Assignor.

WARNING

This form should be used only after a thorough review of the Limited Partnership Agreement and relevant financial information concerning the partnership. The Limited Partnership Agreement must be examined to ascertain whether or not this particular Limited Partnership permits one of its partners to assign his interest and, if so, under what circumstances and conditions.

ASSIGNMENT AND ASSUMPTION
OF LIMITED PARTNERSHIP INTEREST

1. The amount paid for the Assignment, in words and numbers.

2. The name of the Limited Partner making the Assignment (the Assignor).

3. The legal name of the Limited Partnership.

4. The name of the person or entity paying the money and receiving the Assignment of interest (the Assignee).

5. The percentage interest of the Limited Partnership being purchased, in words and numbers.

6. The specific title of the Limited Partnership Agreement being assigned.

In consideration of the sum of _____[1]_____ Dollars ($____[1]____), receipt of which is hereby acknowledged, _____[2]_____ ("Assignor") as a Limited Partner in _____[3]_____ LIMITED PARTNERSHIP (the "Company"), hereby assigns to _____[4]_____ ("Assignee") Assignor's interest as a Limited Partner in the Company to the extent of ____[5]____ Percent (____%) of One Hundred Percent (100%) of Net Profits in the Company as defined in the _____[6]_____, a copy of which Assignee acknowledges having received and read.

Said assignment is solely out of the share of Net Profits owned by the Assignor as a Limited Partner in the Company.

Subject to the acceptance of this assignment and assumption by the Company, Assignee shall become: (i) a substitute Limited Partner in the Company to the extent of the assignment; (ii) entitled to receive from the Company (at the time, in the manner, and upon the conditions set forth in the Partnership Agreement) repayment as a contribution to the Company of the aforesaid sum paid to Assignor; and (iii) entitled to receive payment of an amount equal to ____[5]____ Percent (____%) of the Net Profits of the Company.

(Document continued on next page)

7. The date of the Assignment.

8. The name of the Assignor printed below the line, with the Assignor to sign above the line.

9. The name of the Assignee printed below the line, with the Assignee to sign above the line.

10. The address of the Assignee.

11. The Social Security number or Federal Taxpayer Identification Number of the Assignee.

The Assignee, by execution hereof, agrees to assume Assignor's proportionate share of the obligations of the Assignor as a Limited Partner of the Company under the Partnership Agreement, to the same extent as if the Assignee had been an original Limited Partner and agrees to pay all of the liabilities and obligations imposed upon a Limited Partner of the Company under the Partnership Agreement, including the obligation to repay, in the manner set forth in the Partnership Agreement and any contributions returned or Net Profits distributed to any Limited Partner of the Company.

IN WITNESS WHEREOF, the parties have executed this agreement as of the __[7]__ day of _____[7]_____, 19__.

BY_____   BY_____
　　　　　　[8]　　　　　　　　　　　　　　　[9]

Address of Assignee
_____ [10] _____
_____

Federal I.D. Number of Assignee
(or S.S. No.) _____[11]_____

(Document continued on next page)

12. The name of the General Partner (or other person authorized by the Limited Partnership Agreement to bind and sign for the Limited Partnership) printed below the line, with that person to sign above the line.

13. The Notary Public will complete these sections acknowledging the signatures of the Assignor and Assignee, and sign his name and affix his stamp or seal.

ACCEPTED AND AGREED:

_____[3]_____

BY_____
          [12]

On the __[13]__ day of _____, 19__, before me personally came _____[2]_____, to me known and known to me to be the individual described in and who executed the foregoing instrument and he acknowledged to me that he executed the same.

_____[13]_____
Notary Public

On the __[13]__ day of _____, 19__, before me personally came _____[4]_____, to me known and known to me to be the individual described in and who executed the foregoing instrument and he acknowledged to me that he executed the same.

_____[13]_____
Notary Public

ASSIGNMENT OF TRADEMARK (3-12)

A Trademark is an asset which may be sold in the same manner as any other asset. To formalize the transfer, an assignment must be filed with the U.S. Patent & Trademark Office so that the new owner becomes the registered owner of record. This Assignment of Trademark form is acceptable to the U.S. Patent & Trademark Office.

The Trademark Office address is: U.S. Department of Commerce, Patent and Trademark Office, Washington, D.C. 20231.

ASSIGNMENT OF TRADEMARK

1. The name of the registered owner of the Trademark (the Assignor).

2. If the registered owner is a corporation, insert the state of incorporation. Otherwise delete.

3. The address of the registered owner.

4. The registered Trademark.

5. The registration number assigned by the U.S. Trademark & Patent Office.

6. The name of the buyer (the Assignee).

7. If the buyer is a corporation, insert the state of incorporation. Otherwise delete.

8. The address of the buyer.

9. The amount, in numbers, being paid.

WHEREAS _____[1]_____, *[2][a* _____ *corporation,]* having a principal place of business at _____[3]_____, has adopted and used the mark "_____[4]_____" which mark is registered in the United States Patent & Trademark Office under the Registration No. _____[5]_____; and

WHEREAS _____[6]_____, *[7][a* _____ *corporation,]* having a principal place of business at _____[8]_____, is desirous of acquiring the mark "_____[4]_____," the registration and the goodwill associated with the mark;

NOW, THEREFORE, in consideration of the payment of $____[9]____, the receipt of which is hereby acknowledged, _____[1]_____ does hereby assign unto _____[6]_____, all right, title and interest in and to the mark "_____[4]_____," Registration No._____[5]_____, together with the goodwill of the

(Document continued on next page)

10. The name of the registered owner if a corporation. Otherwise delete the line.

11. If the registered owner is an individual, delete "BY" and print the registered owner's name directly below the line, with that individual to sign above the line. If the registered owner is a corporation, print the name and title of the person acting for the corporation directly below the line, with that person to sign above the line.

12. Insert a Notary Statement, found elsewhere in this book, for the registered owner, either an Individual or Corporate form as appropriate. The Notary will complete the form.

business symbolized by the mark and the registration.

_____*[10]*_____

*BY*_____
[11]

[12] [Notary Statement]

ASSIGNMENT OF COPYRIGHT (3-13)

Copyright is a protection provided to the authors of "original works of authorship" including literary, dramatic, musical, artistic and certain other intellectual works, for example, advertisements. Copyright protection exists from the time the work is created. Notice and registration is not needed to gain protection but if registered with the Copyright Office within 3 months of creation, additional significant advantages are gained.

For complete information and forms contact: Copyright Office, Library of Congress, Washington, D.C. 20559.

Mere sale or possession of a copyrighted work does not give the physical owner Copyright ownership. That ownership remains with the creator of the work unless formally transferred. This Assignment meets the requirements of a transfer of Copyright and should, if the Copyright has been registered, be recorded with the Copyright Office.

ASSIGNMENT OF COPYRIGHT

1. The name of the owner of the Copyright.

2. If the owner is a corporation, insert the state of incorporation. Otherwise delete.

3. The address of the owner.

4. A description of the work, for example "a book entitled 'Divorce Made Easy'."

5. Choose one. If the work has been registered with the Copyright Office use the first alternative; otherwise use the second alternative.

6. The number of The Registration Certificate issued by The Copyright Office.

7. The year of first publication of the work.

8. The Copyright notice. A Copyright notice takes the form: Copyright © 1991 Round Lake Publishing Company. The year is the year of first publication of the work (the same as in No. 7 above). The name is the owner of the copyright (the same as in No. 1 above). The word "Copyright" and the © symbol must precede the year to insure both U.S. and foreign (Universal) copyright protection.

WHEREAS _____[1]_____, *[2][a _____ corporation,]* having a principal place of business at _____[3]_____, is the copyright owner of _____[4]_____, *an original work [5][registered with the Copyright Office bearing Certificate No. _____[6]_____]* **OR** *[created in _____[7]_____ and bearing the copyright notice _____[8]_____]*; and

(Document continued on next page)

9.   The name of the buyer.

10. If the buyer is a corporation, insert the State of incorporation. Otherwise delete.

11. The address of the buyer.

12. The amount, in numbers, being paid.

13. The number of the Registration Certificate. Delete if not registered.

14. The date of the Assignment.

15. The name of the owner if a corporation. Otherwise delete the line.

16. If the owner is an individual, delete "BY" and print the owner's name directly below the line, with the owner to sign above the line. If the owner is a corporation, print the name and title of the person acting for the corporation directly below the line, with that person to sign above the line.

17. Insert a Notary Statement, found elsewhere in this book, for the owner, either an Individual or Corporate form, as appropriate. The Notary will complete the form.

WHEREAS _____[9]_____, *[10][a* _____ *corporation,]* having a principal place of business at _____[11]_____, is desirous of acquiring the copyright ownership of _____[4]_____, the registration therefor, and all other incidence thereof;

NOW, THEREFORE, in consideration of the payment of $_____[12]_____, the receipt of which is hereby acknowledged, _____[1]_____ does hereby assign unto _____[9]_____ all rights, title and interest in and to the copyright for _____[4]_____ *[, Certificate No. _____[13]_____].*

Dated: _____[14]_____

_____[15]_____

BY _____
[16]

[17] [Notary Statement]

ASSIGNMENT OF LITERARY WORK (3-14)

An Assignment of Literary Work is used when an Author sells a book that is already written to a publisher or other promoter of literary properties. The Agreement requires an advance payment against future royalties and a flat percentage of sales as a royalty. Royalties are usually negotiated. Rights are typically assigned by type of usage such as paperback rights, television rights, movie rights, stage dramatization, etc.

ASSIGNMENT OF LITERARY WORK

1. The date the Agreement is signed.

2 The name of the Author of the Work.

3. The name of the Company receiving the assignment.

4. If the Company receiving the assignment is a corporation, insert the state of incorporation. Otherwise delete.

5. The title of the Literary Work.

6. This form is found elsewhere in this chapter.

Agreement made this __[1]__ day of _____, 19__, by and between _____[2]_____ ("Author") and _____[3]_____ *[4][, a _____ corporation]* ("Company").

Author is the owner of an original work (the "Work") entitled "_____[5]_____"; and

Company is desirous of obtaining all rights of the Author to the Work.

In consideration of the mutual terms, conditions and covenants hereinafter set forth, Author and Company agree as follows:

1.   Author sells, assigns, grants, transfers, sets over, and delivers to the Company, its successor and assigns, all right, title and interest to the Work.

2.   Author shall, simultaneously with the execution of this Agreement execute an Assignment of Copyright [6] in the form as annexed hereto as Exhibit A and such other documents as are reasonably requested by Company to transfer the ownership in and to all rights to the Work.

3.   Author warrants that the Work does not violate any copyright law, nor unlawfully infringes or interferes in any way with any literary property of another, nor contains any libelous matter, and in such event agrees that Author will forever warrant and defend the Company at Author's own expense against any alleged infringement of copyright or property rights based upon publication of the Work and against all claims, demands, suits, losses, costs, damages and expenses the Company may sustain or incur by reason of any libelous matter contained or alleged to be contained in the Work.

(Document continued on next page)

7. The amount of the advance, in numbers.

8. The royalty percentage, in numbers.

4. Company shall pay to Author a royalty for the Work as follows:

(a) Author shall receive, upon the execution of this Agreement, a non-refundable advance, to be applied against earned royalties, in the amount of $_____[7]_____.

(b) Company shall pay to Author a royalty representing __[8]__% of Company's net sales of the Work. Payments shall be based upon actual cash received. "Net Sales" shall be defined as gross sales less commissions, discounts, rebates, freight, postage and handling, returns, refunds and reshipments. Net sales shall not include sales of subsidiary rights; e.g. movie or television dramatizations of the Work, which shall be negotiated separately. "Actual cash Received" shall be defined as payment received for net sales.

(c) Payments shall be made to Author without any deductions for federal, state or local income tax or social security.

5. Company shall prepare royalty reports covering quarterly periods in the following manner.

(a) The quarterly royalty periods shall end on March 31, June 30, September 30 and December 31 of each year. The first royalty period shall be from the date of publication of the Work to the end of the next quarterly royalty period. Reports thereafter will cover each succeeding period of three (3) months.

(b) Each royalty report shall disclose the net sales of the Work, if any, during the reporting period and the amount of royalties calculated upon those net sales. The report shall also show the amount and general nature of all charges debited against the Author's account during the reporting period. The amount due the Author under the royalty report shall be the difference between its earned royalties and the charges debited against it as shown on the report. A deficit balance on any royalty report shall be carried forward as a debit on succeeding reports until fully offset by future royalties.

(c) Such royalty reports may, from time to time, contain negative sales figures. Such negative sales figures

(Document continued on next page)

9. The address of the Company.

10. The address of the Author.

will reflect sales which were credited to the Author's account during a preceding reporting period and returns of the Work in the current reporting period. Where such returns exceed the sales during the current reporting periods, a negative figure will result which will be charged against the Author's royalties for that period.

        (d)   Company shall provide Author with the royalty report within thirty (30) days of the end of each quarterly period and shall enclose therewith payment of any amounts due thereunder.

6.   Author, or its representative, shall have the right to inspect, at the Company or such other location as the Company may designate, the books, records, reports and accounts of the Company with respect to the sales of the Work, upon forty-eight (48) hours' written notice to the Company, during normal business hours.

7.   Author consents to the use of Author's name, signature, likeness, and biographical material concerning Author, on and with published copies, and in publicity, promotional material and advertising concerning the Work and the Company.

8.   All notices required or permitted to be given hereunder shall be in writing and may be delivered personally or by Certified Mail - Return Receipt Requested, postage prepaid. Notice shall be addressed:

        To Company: _____ [9] _____

        _____

        To Author: _____ [10] _____

        _____

(Document continued on next page)

11. The state whose laws will govern the Agreement, typically the state in which the Company is located.

12. The name of the Company if a corporation. Otherwise delete the line.

13. If the Company is not a corporation, delete "BY" and print the individual's name directly below the line, with that person to sign above the line. If the Company is a corporation, print the name and title of the person acting for the corporation directly below the line, with that person to sign above the line.

14. The name of the Author printed directly below the line, with the Author to sign above the line.

9. Any controversy or claim arising out of or relating to this Agreement, or the breach thereof, shall be settled by arbitration in accordance with the Commercial Arbitration Rules of the American Arbitration Association, and judgment upon the award rendered by the arbitrator(s) may be entered in any court having jurisdiction thereof.

10. This Agreement shall be construed in accordance with and governed by the laws of the State of _____[11]_____, irrespective of the fact that a party hereto may not be a resident of that State.

11. It is agreed between the parties hereto that there are no other agreements or understandings between them relating to the subject matter of this Agreement. This Agreement supersedes all prior agreements, oral or written, between the parties and is intended as a complete and exclusive statement of the agreement between the parties. No change or modification of this Agreement shall be valid unless the same be in writing and signed by the parties.

INTENDING TO BE LEGALLY BOUND, the parties have executed this Agreement as of the date first above written.

_____*[12]*_____

BY_____
[13]   (Company)

_____
[14]   (Author)

TRADEMARK LICENSING AGREEMENT (3-15)

A Trademark may be licensed to another party. For example, Coca-Cola® licenses its Trademark for the manufacture of memorabilia. A license allows the owner of a Trademark to maintain control over the manner in which the Trademark is used by permitting the owner of the Trademark to monitor the quality of the manufactured products bearing the Trademark.

TRADEMARK LICENSING AGREEMENT

1. The date the Agreement is signed.

2. The name of the owner of the Trademark (the Licensor).

3. If the Licensor is a corporation, insert the state of incorporation. Otherwise delete.

4. The address of the Licensor.

5. The name of the party receiving the license (the Licensee).

6. If the Licensee is a corporation, insert the state of incorporation. Otherwise delete.

7. The address of the Licensee.

8. The Trademark.

9. Choose one.

10. A description of the territory in which the Licensee may use the Trademark, for example "North America."

11. A description of the products for which the license is granted, such as "tee shirts," "golfing equipment" or "plush toys."

12. The term of the License, in words and numbers, for example "three (3) years."

Agreement made this __[1]__ day of _____, 19__ by and between _____[2]_____, *[3][a _____ corporation,]* having a principal place of business at _____[4]_____ ("Licensor") and _____[5]_____, *[6][a _____ corporation,]* having a principal place of business at _____[7]_____ ("Licensee").

Licensor is the registered owner of the mark "_____[8]_____" together with the goodwill associated with the mark; and

Licensor desires to permit Licensee to use the mark; and

In consideration of the mutual terms, conditions and covenants hereinafter set forth, the parties agree as follows:

1. Licensor grants to Licensee *[9][exclusive]* **OR** *[non–exclusive]* license to use the mark "_____[8]_____" in _____[10]_____ in connection with the manufacture and sale of _____[11]_____.

2. The term of the license shall be _____[12]_____ unless sooner terminated.

(Document continued on next page)

13. A description of the license fee, which can take many forms such as a single payment: "$25,000," a payment per unit: "$.05 per unit," or payment based upon sales: "5% of gross sales of Licensee."

14. When payments are to be made, for example "on the 15th day of the month for sales made in the prior month."

15. The number of days, in words and numbers, upon which the Agreement can be cancelled.

16. The name of the Licensor if a corporation. Otherwise delete the line.

17. If the Licensor is an individual, delete "BY" and print the Licensor's name directly below the line, with the Licensor to sign above the line. If the Licensor is a corporation, print the name and title of the person acting for the corporation directly below the line, with that person to sign above the line.

18. The name of the Licensee if a corporation. Otherwise delete the line.

19. If the Licensee is an individual, delete "BY" and print the Licensee's name directly below the line, with the Licensee to sign above the line. If the Licensee is a corporation, print the name and title of the person acting for the corporation directly below the line, with that person to sign above the line.

3.   Licensee shall pay to Licensor a license fee of _____[13]_____ payable _____[14]_____.

4.   Licensee agrees that Licensor shall have full control over the manner in which Licensee uses the licensed mark. Licensee agrees that it will not use the mark in connection with the sale or advertising of any goods or in a manner which has not been approved by Licensor in writing.

5.   Licensee agrees to permit representatives of Licensor to inspect the facilities of Licensee, during normal business hours but without advance notice, to insure that the requirements of paragraph 4 are fulfilled. If Licensor determines that the requirements have been violated, it may, at its sole option, declare this Agreement to be terminated.

6.   Licensee shall have the right to terminate this Agreement upon _____[15]_____ (__) days' notice to Licensor sent via U.S. Mail, Postage Prepaid, Certified Mail, Return Receipt Requested.

7.   If the Agreement is terminated for any reason, Licensee will immediately cease and desist from further use of the licensed mark and will deliver to Licensor all unused material containing the licensed mark, or will make a showing, to the satisfaction of Licensor, that such items have been destroyed.

    INTENDING TO BE LEGALLY BOUND, the parties have signed this License Agreement as of the date first above written.

_____*[16]*_____

BY_____
                [17]   (Licensor)

_____*[18]*_____

BY_____
                [19]   (Licensee)

LICENSING AGREEMENT—GENERAL (3-16)

A Licensing Agreement is used when one party receives a license from another party to manufacture or market a product. The Agreement requires the party receiving the license to market the Product in a specified territory and to purchase or manufacture a minimum quantity of the Product. A Licensing Agreement differs from a franchise in that with a Licensing Agreement there are no fees to be paid to the Licensor other than for Product purchased or manufactured.

LICENSING AGREEMENT—GENERAL

1. The date the Agreement is signed.

2. The name of the party giving the license (the Licensor).

3. If the Licensor is a corporation, insert the state in which incorporated. Otherwise delete.

4. The name of the party receiving the license (the Licensee).

5. If the Licensee is a corporation, insert the state in which incorporated. Otherwise delete.

6. Insert either "manufacture" or "market."

7. A description of the Product being licensed.

8. Insert either "manufacture" or "market."

9. Insert either "exclusive" or "non-exclusive."

10. Insert either "manufacturer" or "market."

11. A description of the territory for which the license is granted, for example "North America."

12. The date the license is to begin.

13. The number of years, in numbers, of the license.

14. The number of years, in numbers, for renewal of the license.

Agreement made this __[1]__ day of _____, 19__ by and between _____[2]_____ *[3][, a _____ corporation]* ("Licensor") and _____[4]_____ *[5][, a _____ corporation]* ("Licensee").

Licensor has the exclusive rights to _____[6]_____ the _____[7]_____ ("Product"); and

Licensee is desirous of obtaining a license to _____[8]_____ the product; therefore

In consideration of the mutual terms, conditions and covenants hereinafter set forth, Licensor and Licensee agree as follows:

1. (a) Licensor grants to Licensee the ____[9]____ and non–transferable right to _____[10]_____ the product in _____[11]_____ for a period commencing on _____[12]_____ (the "Effective Date") and ending __[13]__ years from the Effective Date (the "Initial Term") unless sooner terminated pursuant to the provisions of this Agreement.

(b) It is mutually agreed that either party may terminate this Agreement at the end of the Initial Term by giving the other party written notice thereof at least six (6) months prior to the end of the Initial Term. Should either party fail to give such notice, this Agreement shall continue upon the same terms and conditions in force immediately prior to the expiration of the Initial Term, for an additional period of __[14]__ years. After the Initial Term, either party may terminate the renewal of the Agreement by giving six months' written notice of its intention to terminate at any time prior to the expiration of the then current term.

(Document continued on next page)

15. Insert either "manufacture" or "market."

16. Choose one.

17. Insert either "manufacture" or "market."

18. Insert the number of units of the Product the Licensee must manufacture or sell each year.

19. Insert either "manufactured" or "sold."

20. If the Licensee is to manufacture the Product, delete this paragraph.

21. Choose one depending on whether the Licensee is to buy or manufacture the Product.

22. Insert the agreed upon royalty rate expressed as a percentage, in numbers, typically of the wholesale price of the Product, and when royalties are to be paid, such as "calendar quarterly" or "semiannually."

23. Insert either "of all royalties" or "for all Product purchased from Licensor," depending on whether the Product is to be manufactured or purchased from the Licensor.

24. The amount of product liability insurance, in numbers, to be carried.

25. The period of non-competition, in numbers. It is advisable not to exceed three years. (Note: in some states, for example California, non-competition restrictions are prohibited by law. Check your state's law before including this provision.)

26. A description of the territory in which the Licensee may not compete, such as "the states of New York and New Jersey."

27. The state in which any arbitration will take place, typically the state in which the Licensor is located.

28. The state whose laws will govern the Agreement, typi-

2.   (a)   Licensee hereby accepts the right to
_____[15]_____ the Product and agrees to do so in accordance with this Agreement.

(b)   Licensee shall *[16][purchase all of the Licensee's requirements for Product only from Licensor, and not directly or indirectly from any other person, firm or corporation.]* **OR** *[manufacture the Product in strict conformity with the specifications and standards provided to Licensee by Licensor. Licensor reserves the right to amend the specifications and standards from time to time.]*

3.   Licensee is an independent contractor and nothing contained in this Agreement shall be deemed or interpreted to constitute Licensee to be the agent or legal representative of Licensor for any purpose whatsoever. Licensee is not granted any right or authority to assume or create any obligation or responsibility, express or implied, on behalf of or in the name of Licensor, or to bind Licensor in any manner or fashion whatsoever.

4.   Commencing with the Effective Date, Licensee shall _____[17]_____ _____[18]_____ units of Product per twelve month period. Licensee may consider the total units of Product _____[19]_____ in any twelve month period over and above the specified volume as cumulative, to be carried forward to the succeeding twelve month periods.

[20][Licensor shall fill all orders from Licensee with reasonable promptness, except that in case of fire, riots, strikes or accidents or other conditions, whether or not similar in character to those specifically named, which unavoidably stop the making of deliveries contracted for, orders may be cancelled or partially cancelled, as the case may require, upon written notice or telegraph notice to Licensee. Such interruption of deliveries, however, shall not invalidate the remainder of this Agreement, but upon removal of the cause of the interruption, delivery shall continue as before. During the period of interruption, the Licensee's obligations to purchase the minimum units shall abate and, if required to meet Licensee's obligations, Licensee may obtain inventory and goods from such other source as required to mitigate any damages Licensee might sustain by virtue of the interruption.]

(Document continued on next page)

21. Choose one depending on whether the Licensee is to buy or manufacture the Product.

22. Insert the agreed upon royalty rate expressed as a percentage, in numbers, typically of the wholesale price of the Product, and when royalties are to be paid, such as "calendar quarterly" or "semi-annually."

23. Insert either "of all royalties" or "for all Product purchased from Licensor," depending on whether the Product is to be manufactured or purchased from the Licensor.

24. The amount of product liability insurance, in numbers, to be carried.

25. The period of non-competition, in numbers. It is advisable not to exceed three years. (Note: in some states, for example California, non-competition restrictions are prohibited by law. Check your state's law before including this provision.)

26. A description of the territory in which the Licensee may not compete, such as "the states of New York and New Jersey."

27. The state in which any arbitration will take place, typically the state in which the Licensor is located.

5.   Licensee shall pay to Licensor *[21][a royalty for each unit of Product manufactured as follows: _____[22]_____.] OR [upon the usual trade terms of Licensor, the wholesale price of Product plus freight. Licensor shall not charge Licensee a higher price than any other Licensee purchasing equal quantities and making payment on the same terms.]*

6.   The provisions of Paragraph 1(a) and 1(b) notwithstanding, in the event that Licensee shall default in the performance of the terms and conditions of this Agreement on Licensee's part to be kept, performed and observed, including without limiting the generality of the foregoing, prompt payment _____[23]_____ and other obligations incurred under the terms of this Agreement, this Agreement shall be subject to cancellation by Licensor upon fourteen (14) days' written notice by Certified Mail, Return Receipt Requested, to Licensee, during which period of fourteen (14) days Licensee shall have the right to remedy such default. Upon the remedying of such default, the cancellation notice shall have no further force or effect.

7.   Licensee agrees that it will obtain and maintain during the term of this Agreement and any renewal thereof product liability insurance in the amount of $____[24]____.

8.   In the event of the termination of this Agreement, whether voluntary or involuntary, Licensee agrees that Licensee will not, for a period of __[25]__ years from the effective date of termination, engage in the manufacture, sale or distribution of product similar to Product in the _____[26]_____.

9.   It is agreed between the parties hereto that there are no oral or other agreements or understandings between them relating to the selling or servicing of Product. This Agreement supersedes all prior agreements between the parties, and is intended as a complete and exclusive statement of the full agreement between the parties.

10.   In the event of any dispute between Licensor and Licensee arising under or pursuant to the terms of this Agreement, the same shall be settled only by Arbitration in the State of _____[27]_____, under the then pertaining rules and regulations of the American Arbitration Association. The determination of the arbitrators shall be final and

(Document continued on next page)

28. The state whose laws will govern the Agreement, typically the state in which the Licensor is located.

29. The name of the Licensor if a corporation. Otherwise delete the line.

30. If the Licensor is an individual, delete "BY" and print the Licensor's name directly below the line, with the Licensor to sign above the line. If the Licensor is a corporation, print the name and title of the person acting for the corporation directly below the line, with that person to sign above the line.

31. The name of the Licensee if a corporation. Otherwise delete the line.

32. If the Licensee is an individual, delete "BY" and print the Licensee's name directly below the line, with the Licensee to sign above the line. If the Licensee is a corporation, print the name and title of the person acting for the corporation directly below the line, with that person to sign above the line.

binding upon the parties and may be enforced in any court of appropriate jurisdiction.

11. This Agreement shall be construed in accordance with and governed by the Laws of _____[28]_____.

INTENDING TO BE LEGALLY BOUND, the parties hereto have caused the License Agreement to be executed as of the date first above written.

_____[29]_____

BY_____
[30] (Licensor)

_____[31]_____

BY_____
[32] (Licensee)

Borrowing and Lending Money 4

The flow of capital, money, is the grease that lubricates the wheels of commerce. Over the years, important rights and protections have been developed to ensure that this flow is continuous and uninterrupted.

Promissory Notes Promissory Notes are essentially promises to repay borrowed money. The times, rates and numbers of payments can be varied, depending on the particular form chosen.

Loan Agreements and Letters of Credit These forms provide different options to deal with what will happen if a loan is not repaid. The section also contains an application for a Letter of Credit.

Guarantees These forms set up various ways of providing for another person to repay a debt if the borrower cannot—or for another person to put up collateral if the borrower is unable to.

Demands This series of forms provides the necessary first legal steps to getting payment from a borrower who has not paid his loan, or from the party that guaranteed the loan.

Financing Forms for two ways of raising money for a business are provided in this section.

PROMISSORY NOTE—FIXED INTEREST
WITH INSTALLMENT PAYMENTS (4-01)

This type of Promissory Note is used when payment is to be made in equal amounts. Interest is computed on the remaining balance due as of the date of payment.

PROMISSORY NOTE—FIXED INTEREST
WITH INSTALLMENT PAYMENTS

1. The dollar amount of the loan, in numbers.

2. The yearly interest rate, in numbers.

3. The date the loan is given and the Note is signed.

4. The name of the borrower.

5. If the borrower is a corporation, insert the state of incorporation. Otherwise delete.

6. The name of the lender.

7. If the lender is a corporation, insert the state of incorporation. Otherwise delete.

8. The address where payment is to be made.

9. The amount of the loan, in words.

10. The amount of the loan, in numbers.

11. The yearly rate of interest, in words.

12. The yearly rate of interest, in numbers.

13. The amount of each payment, in words.

14. The amount of each payment, in numbers.

15. The date the first payment is due.

16. If the last payment is unequal add "and a final payment of _____ Dollars ($_____)", in words and numbers.

$ _____[1]_____   __[2]__% Interest Per Annum
                               _____[3]_____ , 19___

In installments, as set forth, for value received, the undersigned, _____[4]_____ _[5][, a _____ corporation]_ promises to pay to _____[6]_____ _[7][, a _____ corporation]_ or order at _____[8]_____ , the sum of _____[9]_____ Dollars ($_____[10]_____), together with interest from the date above on the unpaid principal balance due at the rate of ___[11]___ percent (__[12]__%) per annum. Principal shall be payable monthly in installments of _____[13]_____ Dollars ($___[14]___) on the first day of _____[15]_____ , 19___ and on the first day of each month thereafter [16] until the sum of _____[9]_____ Dollars ($_____[10]_____) is paid in full, and interest accrued to the date of payment shall be payable on such dates.

Should interest not be paid when due it shall thereafter bear interest at the same rate as the principal, but such unpaid interest so compounded shall not exceed an amount equal to the maximum rate of interest permitted by law computed on the unpaid principal balance. All payments shall be payable in lawful currency of the United States of America. The undersigned agrees to pay all costs of collection including reasonable attorneys' fees.

(Document continued on next page)

228   *BORROWING AND LENDING MONEY*

17. If the Note cannot be prepaid, delete this paragraph.

18. If the Note is part of another agreement, identify the parties to that agreement and the date of that agreement. Otherwise delete.

19. If the Note is part of a Security Agreement, identify the parties to the Security Agreement and the date of the Security Agreement. Otherwise delete.

20. The name of the borrower if a corporation. Otherwise delete the line.

21. If the borrower is an individual, delete "BY" and print the borrower's name directly below the line, with the borrower to sign above the line. If the borrower is a corporation, print the name and title of the individual acting for the corporation directly below the line, with that person to sign above the line.

[17][This Note may be prepaid at any time or from time to time in whole or in part without penalty, premium or permission. Any partial payment under this Section shall be applied to the installments of the Note in the inverse order of their maturities.]

[18][This Note is the Note referred to in a certain Agreement between _____ and _____ dated the _____ day of _____, 19___ and is subject to all of the terms and provisions of the Agreement.] [19][This Note is secured pursuant to and as more specifically set forth in a certain Security Agreement between _____ and _____ dated the _____ day of _____, 19___ and is subject to all of the terms and provisions of the Security Agreement.]

_____*[20]*_____

BY _____
    [21]

PROMISSORY NOTE—DEMAND (4-02)

This type of Promissory Note is used when payment is to be made upon demand in a single payment. The form can be modified so that it becomes a Note due on a specific date or on demand, whichever the lender chooses. To make this change, for the opening phrase "On Demand" substitute "On ____(date)____ or upon Demand."

PROMISSORY NOTE—DEMAND

1. The dollar amount of the loan, in numbers.

2. The annual interest rate, in numbers.

3. The date the loan is given and the Note is signed.

4. The name of the borrower.

5. If the borrower is a corporation, insert the state of incorporation. Otherwise delete.

6. The name of the lender.

7. If the lender is a corporation, insert the state of incorporation. Otherwise delete.

8. The address where payment is to be made.

9. The amount of the loan, in words.

10. The amount of the loan, in numbers.

11. The annual interest rate, in words.

12. The annual interest rate, in numbers.

13. If the Note cannot be prepaid, delete this paragraph.

14. If the Note is part of another agreement, identify the parties to that agreement and the date of that agreement. Otherwise delete.

15. If the Note is part of a Security Agreement, identify the parties to the Security Agreement and the date of the Security Agreement. Otherwise delete.

$ _____[1]_____   ___[2]___% Interest Per Annum
                           _____[3]_____, 19__

On Demand, the undersigned, _____[4]_____ *[5][, a _____ corporation]* promises to pay to _____[6]_____ *[7][, a _____ corporation]* or order at _____[8]_____, the sum of _____[9]_____ Dollars ($_____[10]_____), together with interest thereon at the rate of ___[11]___ percent (__[12]__%) per annum from the date above.

All payments shall be payable in lawful currency of the United States of America. The undersigned agrees to pay all costs of collection, including reasonable attorneys' fees.

[13][This Note may be prepaid at any time or from time to time in whole or in part without penalty, premium or permission. Any partial payment under this Section shall be applied to the installments of the Note in the inverse order of their maturities.]

[14][This Note is the Note referred to in a certain Agreement between _____ and _____ dated the ____ day of _____, 19__ and is subject to all of the terms and provisions of the Agreement.] [15][This Note is secured pursuant to and as more specifically set forth in a certain Security Agreement between _____ and _____ dated the

(Document continued on next page)

16. The name of the borrower if a corporation. Otherwise delete the line.

17. If the borrower is an individual, delete "BY" and print the borrower's name directly below the line, with the borrower to sign above the line. If the borrower is a corporation, print the name and title of the individual acting for the corporation directly below the line, with that person to sign above the line.

_____ *day of* _____, *19___ and is subject to all of the terms and provisions of the Security Agreement.]*

_____[16]_____

BY _____
       [17]

PROMISSORY NOTE—SERIES (4-03)

This type of Promissory Note is to be used when a debt is to be repaid in install-ments that are not equal in amount or payable at uniform time intervals.

PROMISSORY NOTE—SERIES

1. The dollar amount of the loan, in numbers.

2. The annual rate of inter-est, in numbers.

3. The date the loan is given and the Note is signed.

4. The number of days in which payment is due, i.e.: thirty, forty-five. Or an actual date may be substituted by using "on or before (date), the undersigned..."

5. The name of the borrower.

6. If the borrower is a cor-poration, insert the state of in-corporation. Otherwise delete.

7. The name of the lender.

8. If the lender is a corpora-tion, insert the state of incor-poration. Otherwise delete.

9. The address where pay-ment is to be made.

10. The amount of this Note, in words.

11. The amount of this Note, in numbers.

12. The annual rate of inter-est, in words.

13. The annual rate of inter-est, in numbers.

14. The number of this par-ticular Note (one, two, twelve, etc.).

15. The total number of Notes in this series (twelve, twenty, etc.).

$ _____[1]_____   __[2]__% Interest Per Annum
                                    _____[3]_____, 19__

___[4]___ days after date, the undersigned _____[5]_____ [6][, a _____ corporation] promises to pay to _____[7]_____ [8][, a _____ corporation] or order at _____[9]_____, the sum of _____[10]_____ Dollars ($____[11]____), together with interest at the rate of _____[12]_____ percent (___[13]___%) from the date above.

Payment shall be payable in lawful currency of the United States of America.

The undersigned agrees to pay all costs of collection, including reasonable attorneys' fees.

This Note is No. __[14]__ of a series of __[15]__

(Document continued on next page)

16. The total dollar amount of the entire series of Notes, in words.

17. The total dollar amount of the entire series of Notes, in numbers.

18. The name of the borrower if a corporation. Otherwise delete the line.

19. If the borrower is an individual, delete "BY" and print the borrower's name directly below the line, with the borrower to sign above the line. If the borrower is a corporation, print the name and title of the individual acting for the corporation directly below the line, with that person to sign above the line.

Notes due on successive dates and totalling
_____[16]_____ Dollars ($___[17]___). Upon default in the payment of any Note in this series, the remaining Notes and outstanding balance shall immediately become due and payable, without notice to the undersigned.

_____*[18]*_____

*BY*_____
[19]

PROMISSORY NOTE—BALLOON PAYMENT (4-04)

This type of Promissory Note is used when payment is to be made in equal payments of principal and interest but the total amount does not fully pay off the loan. The remaining unpaid balance is due in one final payment (the "balloon").

PROMISSORY NOTE—BALLOON PAYMENT

1. The dollar amount of the loan, in numbers.

2. The yearly interest rate, in numbers.

3. The date the loan is given and the Note is signed.

4. The name of the borrower.

5. If the borrower is a corporation, insert the state of incorporation. Otherwise delete.

6. The name of the lender.

7. If the lender is a corporation, insert the state of incorporation. Otherwise delete.

8. The address where payment is to be made.

9. The amount of the loan, in words.

10. The amount of the loan, in numbers.

11. The yearly interest rate, in words.

12. The yearly interest rate, in numbers.

13. The amount of each payment, in words.

14. The amount of each payment, in numbers.

15. The month the first payment is due.

16. If the Note cannot be prepaid, delete this paragraph.

17. If the Note is part of another agreement, identify the parties to that agreement and the date of that agreement. Otherwise delete.

$_____[1]_____ \qquad \_\_[2]\_\_% Interest Per Annum$
$_____[3]_____ , 19\_\_$

    In installments, as set forth, for value received, the undersigned, _____[4]_____ *[5][, a* _____ *corporation]* promises to pay to _____[6]_____ *[7][, a* _____ *corporation]* or order at _____[8]_____, the sum of _____[9]_____ Dollars ($\_\_\_\_\_[10]\_\_\_\_\_), together with interest from the date above on the unpaid principal balance due at the rate of \_\_\_\_[11]\_\_\_\_ percent (\_\_\_[12]\_\_\_%) per annum. Payment shall be made in consecutive monthly installments of _____[13]_____ Dollars ($_____[14]_____) on the first day of _____[15]_____ , 19__ and on the first day of each month thereafter except that the final installment shall be in the amount of the balance of the principal and accrued interest then remaining unpaid on this Note.

    All payments shall be payable in lawful currency of the United States of America.

    The undersigned agrees to pay all costs of collection, including reasonable attorneys' fees.

    [16][This Note may be prepaid at any time or from time to time in whole or in part without penalty, premium or permission. Any partial payment under this Section shall be applied to the installments of the Note in the inverse order of their maturities.]

    [17][This Note is the Note referred to in a certain Agreement between _____ *and* _____

(Document continued on next page)

18. If the Note is part of a Security Agreement, identify the parties to the Security Agreement and the date of the Security Agreement. Otherwise delete.

19. The name of the borrower if a corporation. Otherwise delete the line.

20. If the borrower is an individual, delete "BY" and print the borrower's name directly below the line, with the borrower to sign above the line. If the borrower is a corporation, print the name and title of the individual acting for the corporation directly below the line, with that person to sign above the line.

dated the _____ day of _____, 19__ and is subject to all of the terms and provisions of the Agreement.] [18][This Note is secured pursuant to and as more specifically set forth in a certain Security Agreement between _____ and _____ dated the _____ day of _____, 19__ and is subject to all of the terms and provisions of the Security Agreement.]

_____[19]_____

BY _____
[20]

LOAN AGREEMENT (4-05)

When the terms of a Loan are more complex than can be contained in a simple Promissory Note, a Loan Agreement is useful. If the Loan is to be guaranteed by a third party, add a Guaranty (either Personal or Corporate, as appropriate, found elsewhere in this chapter) to the end of this form—after the signatures of the Borrower and Lender. Forms for Exhibits A and B, referenced in this Agreement, are to be found as separate documents in this chapter.

LOAN AGREEMENT

1. The date the Loan Agreement is signed.

2. The name of the Borrower. If the Borrower is a corporation, add ", a _____ corporation" inserting the state in which incorporated.

3. The name of the Lender. If the Lender is a corporation, add ", a _____ corporation" inserting the state in which incorporated.

4. The date the money is to be loaned.

5. The amount of the loan, in words.

6. The amount of the loan, in numbers.

7. The yearly interest rate, in words.

8. The yearly interest rate, in numbers.

9. A multiple in which partial payment is to be made, i.e. $100, $1,000.

10. The minimum payment, in numbers, the Lender will accept.

11. Insert either "360" or "365." Note: most banks still typically use a 360-day year to compute interest.

Loan Agreement made this __[1]__ day of _____, 19__, by and between _____[2]_____ ("Borrower") and _____[3]_____ ("Lender").

In consideration of the mutual terms, conditions and covenants hereinafter set forth Borrower and Lender agree as follows:

1. LOAN: Subject to and in accordance with this Agreement, its terms, conditions and covenants Lender agrees to lend to Borrower on _____[4]_____ (the "Closing" date) the principal sum of _____[5]_____ Dollars ($_____[6]_____).

2. NOTE: The Loan shall be evidenced by a Note in the form attached hereto as Exhibit A (the "Note") executed by the Borrower and delivered to Lender on Closing.

3. INTEREST: The Loan shall bear interest on the unpaid principal at an annual rate of _____[7]_____ percent (__[8]__%). In the event of a default in payment the aforesaid interest rate shall apply to the total of principal and interest due at the time of default.

4. PAYMENT: Payment shall be in accordance with the terms contained in the Note. The Note may, at any time and from time to time, be paid or prepaid in whole or in part without premium or penalty, except that any partial prepayment shall be (a) in multiples of $_____[9]_____, (b) a minimum of $_____[10]_____, applied to any installments due under the Note in the inverse order of their maturity. Upon the payment of the outstanding principal in full or all of the installments, if any, the interest on the Loan shall be computed and a final adjustment and payment of interest shall be made within five (5) days of the receipt of notice. Interest shall be calculated on the basis of a year of __[11]__ days and the actual number of days elapsed.

(Document continued on next page)

12. The grace period for making payment, in words.

13. The grace period, in numbers.

5.   SECURITY: Borrower agrees to secure the repayment of the Loan by executing those security documents attached hereto as Exhibit B and shall deliver said security documents on Closing. From time to time Lender may demand, and Borrower shall execute, additional loan documents which are reasonably necessary to perfect Lender's security interests.

6.   REPRESENTATIONS AND WARRANTIES: Borrower represents and warrants: (i) that the execution, delivery and performance of this Agreement, and the Note and Security Documents have been duly authorized and are proper; (ii) that the financial statement submitted to Lender fairly presents the financial condition of the Borrower as of the date of this Agreement knowing that the Lender has relied thereon in granting the Loan; (iii) that the Borrower has no contingent obligations not disclosed or reserved against in said financial statement, and at the present time there are no material, unrealized or anticipated losses from any present commitment of Borrower; (iv) that there will be no material adverse changes in the financial condition of the Borrower at the time of Closing; (v) that Borrower will advise of material adverse changes which occur at any time prior to Closing and thereafter to the date of final payment; and (vi) that Borrower has good and valid title to all of the property given as Security hereunder. Borrower represents and warrants that such representations and warranties shall be deemed to be continuing representations and warranties during the entire life of this Agreement.

7.   DEFAULT: Borrower shall be in default: (i) if any payment due hereunder is not made within ____[12]____ (_[13]_) days of the date due; (ii) in the event of assignment by Borrower for the benefit of creditors; (iii) upon the filing of any voluntary or involuntary petition in bankruptcy by or against Borrower; or (iv) if Borrower has breached any representation or warranty specified in this Agreement.

8.   GOVERNING LAW: This Agreement, Note(s) and Security Documents shall be governed by, construed and

(Document continued on next page)

LOAN AGREEMENT *continued*

14. The state whose laws will govern the Agreement, typically the state in which the Lender is located.

15. The name of the Borrower if a corporation. Otherwise delete the line.

16. If the Borrower is an individual, delete "BY" and print the Borrower's name directly below the line, with the Borrower to sign above the line. If the Borrower is a corporation, print the name and title of the individual acting for the corporation directly below the line, with that person to sign above the line.

17. The name of the Lender if a corporation. Otherwise delete the line.

18. If the Lender is an individual, delete "BY" and print the Lender's name directly below the line, with the Lender to sign above the line. If the Lender is a corporation, print the name and title of the individual acting for the corporation directly below the line, with that person to sign above the line.

enforced in accordance with the laws of the State of
_____[14]_____.

INTENDING TO BE LEGALLY BOUND, the parties hereto have caused this Loan Agreement to be executed as of the date first above written.

_____[15]_____

BY_____
[16]

_____[17]_____

BY_____
[18]

EXHIBIT A

Attach a copy of the Note.

EXHIBIT B

Attach a copy of a Security Agreement or Pledge Agreement.

PLEDGE OF PERSONAL PROPERTY (4-06)

A Pledge Agreement is used in conjunction with a Loan Agreement where the Borrower pledges tangible personal property (i.e. stocks, bonds, certificates of deposit, jewelry, etc.) that can be delivered to the Lender to hold as security for the Loan. A Pledge Agreement may also be used, with modification, to secure a past due debt. In such a case, references to the Loan Agreement would be eliminated and the Loan would be termed the "Debt." This differs from the following Security Agreement in that in a Pledge of Personal Property, the Lender actually holds the property or security.

PLEDGE OF PERSONAL PROPERTY

1. The date the Pledge Agreement is signed.

2. The name of the Borrower. If the Borrower is a corporation, add ", a _____ corporation" inserting the state in which incorporated.

3. The name of the Lender. If the Lender is a corporation, add ", a _____ corporation" inserting the state in which incorporated.

4. The date of the Loan Agreement.

5. The amount of the Loan, in numbers.

Pledge Agreement made this __[1]__ day of _____, 19__, by and between _____[2]_____ ("Borrower") and _____[3]_____ ("Lender"), and is made with reference to the following facts:

A.   Borrower and Lender have entered into a Loan Agreement dated _____[4]_____ for a Loan in the amount of $_____[5]_____.

B.   Pursuant to the Loan Agreement Borrower is to pledge certain personal property as collateral to secure repayment of the Loan which personal property is listed on Schedule A attached hereto (the "Collateral").

C.   Lender would not have extended credit to Borrower pursuant to the Loan Assignment and Note but for the Borrower's execution of this Pledge Agreement.

THEREFORE, in order to induce Lender to loan to Borrower, Borrower agrees:

1.   SECURITY INTEREST: As security for the Loan, Borrower hereby pledges, assigns, transfers and grants to Lender a security interest in and to the personal property described in Schedule A attached hereto.

2.   DELIVERY TO AND DUTIES OF LENDER: In furtherance of the pledge, assignment, transfer and grant Borrower shall deliver to Lender the personal property described in Schedule A attached hereto together with such assignments or powers necessary at the time of Closing. Borrower agrees that Lender shall have no liability of any kind or nature whatsoever with respect to the Collateral, other than to hold, release or dispose of the same in accordance with the terms and provisions of this Pledge Agreement.

(Document continued on next page)

6. The name of the Borrower if a corporation. Otherwise delete the line.

7. If the Borrower is an individual, delete "BY" and print the Borrower's name directly below the line, with the Borrower to sign above the line. If the Borrower is a corporation, print the name and title of the individual acting for the corporation directly below the line, with that person to sign above the line.

8. The name of the Lender if a corporation. Otherwise delete the line.

9. If the Lender is an individual, delete "BY" and print the Lender's name directly below the line, with the Lender to sign above the line. If the Lender is a corporation, print the name and title of the individual acting for the corporation directly below the line, with that person to sign above the line.

3. COSTS: Borrower shall pay or reimburse Lender for all costs and expenses advanced or incurred by Lender in connection with the perfection and protection of the security interest granted herein or the preservation or disposition of the Collateral, or any part thereof.

4. TITLE: Lender is the legal and beneficial owner of all the Collateral, has and will have good and marketable title to the Collateral free and clear of any security interest, lien, pledge, option, claim, lease or other encumbrance unless otherwise indicated on Schedule A attached hereto.

5. INSURANCE and RISK OF LOSS: Borrower shall keep the Collateral insured for its full value at all times and retains the risk of loss of such Collateral.

6. NOTIFICATION: The parties shall promptly notify each other in writing of any event which affects the value of the Collateral.

INTENDING TO BE LEGALLY BOUND, the parties hereto have caused this Pledge Agreement to be executed as of the date first above written.

_____*[6]*_____

BY_____
[7]

_____*[8]*_____

BY_____
[9]

SCHEDULE A

Quantity	Description of Property	Liens or Encumbrances (if any)

SECURITY AGREEMENT (4-07)

A Security Agreement is used in conjunction with a Loan Agreement or a Note representing a debt. In a Security Agreement, the Lender is given a secured interest in the form of personal property. The Uniform Commercial Code requires the filing of a "Financing Statement" (Form U.C.C.-1) as notice to the world that the Lender has the secured interest. These forms are available at all stationery and office supply stores. Unless the forms are filed with the state in which the Borrower does business, the security interest is not "perfected" and could be lost.

SECURITY AGREEMENT

1. The date the Security Agreement is signed.

2. The name of the Borrower. If the Borrower is a corporation, add ", a _____ corporation" inserting the state in which incorporated.

3. The name of the Lender. If the Lender is a corporation, add ", a _____ corporation" inserting the state in which incorporated.

4. Delete those categories of personal property in which a security interest is not being granted and renumber the sections.

5. The date of the Loan Agreement.

6. The amount of the Loan, in numbers.

Security Agreement made this __[1]__ day of _____ ,19__, by and between _____[2]_____ ("Borrower") and _____[3]_____ ("Lender").

In consideration of the mutual terms, conditions and covenants hereinafter set forth, Borrower and Lender agree as follows:

1. SECURITY: The Borrower hereby assigns and grants to Lender a security interest in the following described personal property (the "Collateral").

   [4][1.1 Accounts. All present and future accounts, chattel paper, debts of any kind and collateral therefore, documents, notes, drafts, or other forms of obligations to Borrower.

   1.2 Inventory. All present and hereafter acquired inventory wherever located, including, but not limited to, raw materials, works in progress and finished goods.

   1.3 Intangibles. All general intangibles, including but not limited to, trade-names, service marks, goodwill, trademarks, copyrights, patents, patent applications, inventions, royalties or commissions.

   1.4 Equipment. All present and hereafter acquired equipment wherever located.]

   1.5 Proceeds. This security interest shall apply to the above described Collateral and to the proceeds thereof.

2. DEBTS: The Security Interest herein granted shall secure the Loan granted to the Borrower by Lender pursuant to a Loan Agreement or Note between the parties dated _____[5]_____ for the Loan in the amount of $____[6]_____.

(Document continued on next page)

7.   The state whose laws will govern the Security Agreement, typically the state in which the Lender is located.

8.   The name of the Borrower if a corporation. Otherwise delete the line.

9.   If the Borrower is an individual, delete "BY" and print the Borrower's name directly below the line, with the Borrower to sign above the line. If the Borrower is a corporation, print the name and title of the individual acting for the corporation directly below the line, with that person to sign above the line.

10.   The name of the Lender if a corporation. Otherwise delete the line.

11.   If the Lender is an individual, delete "BY" and print the Lender's name directly below the line, with the Lender to sign above the line. If the Lender is a corporation, print the name and title of the individual acting for the corporation directly below the line, with that person to sign above the line.

3.   DUTIES OF BORROWER: Borrower will maintain and care for the Collateral, defend the Collateral against all claims and demands, insure the Collateral for its full value against all hazards and will keep the Collateral free and clear of all liens, claims, security interest and encumbrances.

4.   SALE OF COLLATERAL: Borrower will not sell or otherwise dispose of any of the of the Collateral except in the ordinary course of Borrower's business.

5.   WAIVER: Any waiver, express or implied, of any provision of this Agreement or Loan Agreement or any failure or delay to enforce any provision shall not be deemed a continuing waiver of that or any other provision.

6.   ADDITIONAL DOCUMENTS: Lender may request and Borrower shall execute such other agreements, documents or interests in connection with this Security Agreement in a form and substance satisfactory to Lender as Lender may reasonably deem necessary.

7.   U.C.C.: All terms not defined in this Security Agreement shall be governed by, construed and enforced in accordance with the Uniform Commercial Code of the State of _____[7]_____.

8.   COSTS: Borrower agrees to promptly pay all costs and expenses, together with reasonable attorneys' fees, incurred by Lender to enforce this Security Agreement, protect Lender's security interest or to protect or preserve the Collateral.

INTENDING TO BE LEGALLY BOUND, the parties hereto have caused this Security Agreement to be executed as of the date above first written.

_____[8]_____

BY_____
[9]

_____[10]_____

BY_____
[11]

INSTALLMENT AGREEMENT TO PAY DEBT (4-08)

An Installment Agreement is used when there is an existing debt that is past due and the Debtor is unable to make payment. This form creates an Installment loan for the outstanding balance of the loan.

INSTALLMENT AGREEMENT TO PAY DEBT

1. The date the Agreement is signed.

2. The name of the Debtor. If the Debtor is a corporation, add ", a _____ corporation" inserting the state in which incorporated.

3. The name of the Creditor. If the Creditor is a corporation, add ", a _____ corporation" inserting the state in which incorporated.

4. The amount of the debt, in numbers.

5. The annual rate of interest, in numbers, to be applied to the debt.

6. The amount of each installment payment, in numbers.

7. The date the first payment is due.

8. The day of the month that each subsequent payment is due.

9. The amount of the debt with interest, in numbers.

Agreement made this __[1]__ day of _____, 19__, by and between _____[2]_____ ("Debtor") and _____[3]_____ ("Creditor").

Debtor is presently indebted to Creditor in the principal sum of $_____[4]_____, which debt is now due and payable. In consideration of Creditor not pursuing legal action to seek payment, Creditor agrees to the payment of the debt as follows:

In installments, together with interest from the date above on the unpaid principal balance due at the rate of __[5]__% per annum. Payment shall be made in consecutive monthly payments of $_____[6]_____ on the __[7]__ day of _____, 19___ and on the __[8]__ day of each month thereafter until the sum of $_____[9]_____ is paid in full, and interest accrued to the date of payment shall be payable on such dates.

Should interest not be paid when due it shall thereafter bear interest at the same rate as the principal, but such unpaid interest so compounded shall not exceed an amount equal to the maximum rate of interest permitted by law computed on the unpaid principal balance. All payments shall be payable in lawful currency of the United States of America. The undersigned agrees to pay all costs of collection including reasonable attorneys' fees.

This Note may be prepaid at any time or from time to time in whole or in part without penalty, premium or permission. Any partial prepayment under this Section shall be applied to the installments of the Note in the inverse order of their maturities.

Should Debtor default in the payment of any installment or interest due hereunder, the amount of principal and any accrued but unpaid interest then remaining unpaid may be declared immediately due and

(Document continued on next page)

10. The annual rate of interest, in numbers, to be applied after default.

11. The name of the Debtor, if a corporation. Otherwise delete the line.

12. If the Debtor is an individual, delete "BY" and print the Debtor's name directly below the line, with the Debtor to sign above the line. If the Debtor is a corporation, print the name and title of the individual acting for the corporation directly below the line, with that person to sign above the line.

13. The name of the Creditor, if a corporation. Otherwise delete the line.

14. If the Creditor is an individual, delete "BY" and print the Creditor's name directly below the line, with the Creditor to sign above the line. If the Creditor is a corporation, print the name and title of the individual acting for the corporation directly below the line, with that person to sign above the line.

payable and shall bear interest at the rate of __[10]__% per annum until paid.

_____[11]_____

BY_____
[12]

_____[13]_____

BY_____
[14]

APPLICATION FOR LETTER OF CREDIT (4-09)

A Letter of Credit is a promise by a bank or other financial institution to pay a specific amount of money at the request of, and in accordance with, the instructions of its customer, to a third party (supplier or manufacturer) for merchandise to be shipped—provided that the required documentation is presented. A Letter of Credit is commonly used when merchandise is shipped to the United States from a foreign destination. Banks and other financial institutions use their own forms for Letters of Credit. This form is an Application submitted for the issuance of a Letter of Credit.

A "Notation Letter of Credit," for which this form is an Application, has the running (declining) balance recorded ("notated") on the back of each draft of the Letter of Credit. Each draft, or a writing attached to the draft, must indicate that the notation has been made on the Letter of Credit. The notation must be attached to the last draft when the amount of the Letter of Credit has been used up. The draft would be endorsed on the back: "Noted to Letter of Credit dated _____." The Letter of Credit would be endorsed: "Draft dated _____ in the amount of $_____."

APPLICATION FOR LETTER OF CREDIT

1. The name and address of the bank or other financial institution issuing the Letter of Credit.

2. The name and address of the party requesting the Letter of Credit.

3. The name and address of the party to whom the Letter of Credit will be delivered (the supplier or manufacturer of the merchandise).

4. The number of days, in numbers, after the presentation that the draft against the Letter of Credit is to be honored. Note: this is to be negotiated with the bank but will usually be determined by the bank.

5. The expiration date of the Letter of Credit.

6. The total amount of the Letter of Credit, in numbers.

TO: _____ [1] _____

FROM: _____ [2] _____

You are herewith requested to issue a Letter of Credit as follows:

1. The Credit is to be irrevocable and nontransferable.

2. The Credit is to be a Notation Credit.

3. The beneficiary is to be _____ [3] _____.

4. Drafts against the Credit are to be drawn at ___[4]___ days sight and presented for payment before the expiration of the Credit on _____ [5] _____.

5. The total of all drafts drawn against the Credit shall not exceed $ _____ [6] _____.

(Document continued on next page)

7. A description of the merchandise being purchased, i.e. Dresses.

8. The name and address of the supplier or manufacturer.

9. The name and address of the recipient of the merchandise.

10. The last date on which the merchandise can be shipped.

11. The state whose laws shall govern the Letter of Credit.

12. The name of the party requesting the Letter of Credit if a corporation. Otherwise delete the line.

13. If the party requesting the Letter of Credit is an individual, delete "BY" and print the party's name directly below the line, with that party to sign above the line. If the party requesting the Letter of Credit is a corporation, print the name and title of the individual acting for the corporation directly below the line, with that person to sign above the line.

6.   To cover the full cost of merchandise described in the accompanying invoices as _____[7]_____ which are to be delivered from _____[8]_____ to _____[9]_____ on or before _____[10]_____, which merchandise is to be insured by the buyer.

7.   The following documents are required: invoice in duplicate, insurance policies or certificates covering not less than full invoice cost, bills of lading made to the issuer's order.

8.   The Credit shall be governed by, construed and enforced in accordance with the Uniform Commercial Code of the State of _____[11]_____.

_____*[12]*_____

*BY*_____
[13]

PERSONAL GUARANTY OF PAYMENT OF THE DEBTS OF ANOTHER (4-10)

A Lender may not feel secure with the collateral it is holding and may have greater requirements if it is to make a loan. The Lender may suggest that another person (the Guarantor) be liable for payment if the Borrower defaults. The Guarantor agrees with the Lender to make the payments of the Borrower if the Borrower is in default and cannot meet the loan payments. The Lender must first seek payment from the Borrower before he turns to the Guarantor for payment.

PERSONAL GUARANTY OF PAYMENT OF THE DEBTS OF ANOTHER

1. The name of the Lender.

2. The name of the Borrower.

3. The name of the Guarantor.

4. The name of the Witness printed directly below the line, with the Witness to sign above the line.

5. The name of the Guarantor printed directly below the line, with the Guarantor to sign above the line.

In consideration of and as an inducement to _____[1]_____ ("Lender") to extend credit to _____[2]_____ ("Borrower"), and in further consideration of the sum of One Dollar ($1.00) paid to the undersigned, the receipt and sufficiency of which are hereby acknowledged,

I, _____[3]_____ ("Guarantor") hereby guaranty to Lender, the prompt payment, when due, of each and every claim which Lender may have against Borrower. This continuing guaranty shall remain in force until revoked by the undersigned by written notice to Lender but any such revocation shall be effective only as to any claims which may arise out of transactions entered into after receipt of notice of revocation. This guaranty shall be effective as to the renewal of any claims guaranteed hereby or extensions of time of payment, and shall not be affected by the surrender or release by Lender of any other or additional security Lender may hold for any claim hereby guaranteed. The Lender shall be under no obligation to give the undersigned notice of renewals or extensions of existing loans.

In the event of default by Borrower in the making of any payment when due, the undersigned hereby agrees to pay on demand all sums then due and all losses or expenses which may be incurred by Lender, including but not limited to reasonable attorneys' fees, without Lender having first or prior thereto proceeded against Borrower.

Witness:

_____   _____
[4]   [5]

CORPORATE GUARANTY OF PAYMENT OF THE DEBTS OF ANOTHER (4-11)

A Lender may not feel secure with the collateral it is holding and may have greater requirments if it is to make a loan. The Lender may suggest that a corporation (the Guarantor) be liable for payment if the Borrower defaults. The Guarantor agrees with the Lender to make the payments of the Borrower if the Borrower is in default and cannot meet the loan payments. The Lender must first seek payment from the Borrower before he turns to the Guarantor for payment.

CORPORATE GUARANTY OF PAYMENT OF THE DEBTS OF ANOTHER

1. The name of the Lender.

2. The name of the Borrower.

3. The name of the corporation (the Guarantor).

4. The state of incorporation of the corporation.

5. The date of the resolution of the corporation's Board of Directors authorizing the giving of the Guaranty.

In consideration of and as an inducement to _____[1]_____ ("Lender") to extend credit to _____[2]_____ ("Borrower"), and in further consideration of the sum of One Dollar ($1.00) paid to the undersigned, the receipt and sufficiency of which are hereby acknowledged,

_____[3]_____, a _____[4]_____ corporation ("Guarantor"), hereby guarantees to Lender, the prompt payment, when due, of each and every claim which Lender may have against Borrower. This continuing guaranty shall remain in force until revoked by the undersigned by written notice to Lender but any such revocation shall be effective only as to any claims which may arise out of transactions entered into after receipt of notice of revocation. This guaranty shall be effective as to the renewal of any claims guaranteed hereby or extensions of time of payment, and shall not be affected by the surrender or release by Lender of any other or additional security Lender may hold for any claim hereby guaranteed. The Lender shall be under no obligation to give undersigned notice of renewals or extensions of existing loans.

In the event of default by Borrower in the making of any payment when due, the undersigned hereby agrees to pay on demand all sums then due and all losses or expenses which may be incurred by Lender, including but not limited to reasonable attorneys' fees, without Lender having first or prior thereto proceeded against Borrower.

The guaranty was duly authorized by resolution of the Board of Directors of _____[3]_____, dated _____[5]_____ whereby the undersigned as

(Document continued on next page)

6.   The title of the officer of the corporation authorized to sign the Guaranty.

7.   The Secretary of the corporation to sign above the line.

8.   The name and title of No. 6 above printed directly below the line, with that person to sign above the line.

_____[6]_____ was authorized and directed to execute this guaranty and to affix the corporate seal hereto.

Attest: _____[3]_____

_____[7]_____   BY_____
        Secretary   [8]

CONTINUING GUARANTY AGREEMENT (4-12)

A Continuing Guaranty Agreement is used when a corporation or individual (the Customer) wishes to buy merchandise from the Seller but has neither the cash nor the credit to do so. A credit-worthy corporation or individual will guarantee the payment for the merchandise. The Guaranty is not restricted to a specific dollar amount or time period. Termination of the Guaranty requires notification and covers purchases made only after the receipt of the notice.

Note that in a Continuing Guaranty, the Guarantor is liable for the Customer's default of all obligations, including present or future obligations, until the Guarantor notifies the creditor (the Seller) of his revocation of the Guaranty as to future obligations.

CONTINUING GUARANTY AGREEMENT

1. The name of the Seller. If a corporation, add ", a _____ corporation" inserting the state of incorporation of the Seller.

2. If the Seller is an individual, insert "a residence." If a corporation, insert "a place of business."

3. The address of the Seller.

4. The name of the Customer. If a corporation, add ", a _____ corporation" inserting the state of incorporation of the Customer.

5. If the Customer is an individual, insert "a residence." If a corporation, insert "a place of business."

6. The address of the Customer.

7. The name of the party guaranteeing the debt (the Guarantor). If a corporation, add ", a _____ corporation" inserting the state of incorporation of the Guarantor.

8. If the Guarantor is an individual, insert "a residence." If a corporation, insert "a place of business."

9. The address of the Guarantor.

10. The interest rate, in numbers, to be applied to past due amounts.

To induce _____[1]_____ (the "Seller") having _____[2]_____ at _____[3]_____ to extend credit in such sum and upon such terms as Seller may deem best to _____[4]_____ (the "Customer") having _____[5]_____ at _____[6]_____, the undersigned _____[7]_____ (the "Guarantor") having _____[8]_____ at _____[9]_____, guarantees prompt performance and payment by the Customer when due, or at any time thereafter with interest at __[10]__% per annum, of all obligations heretofore or hereafter incurred by the Customer if not performed or paid promptly by the Customer when due.

This guaranty is an absolute, unconditional, present and continuing guarantee of payment and not of collectability and is in no manner conditional or contingent upon any attempt to collect from the Customer or upon any other condition or contingency.

If the Customer shall fail to perform or pay promptly any of its obligation to Seller or shall file a petition in bankruptcy, reorganization or arrangement or shall consent to a petition in bankruptcy filed against it or not obtain a dismissal of any such petition within twenty (20) days after it has been filed, or shall make an arrangement for the benefit of creditors, or shall take advantage of any insolvency act, Seller may accelerate the performance or payment of Customer's obligations.

Guarantor waives: (i) notice of the acceptance by Seller of the Guaranty Agreement; (ii) notice of all transactions with Customer; (iii) notice of the conversion of any indebtedness to promissory notes and any requirements

(Document continued on next page)

11. The state whose laws will govern the Agreement, usually the state where the Seller is located.

12. The date of signing the Guaranty Agreement.

13. The name of the Guarantor if a corporation. Otherwise delete the line.

14. If the Guarantor is an individual, delete "BY" and print the Guarantor's name directly below the line, with the Guarantor to sign above the line. If the Guarantor is a corporation, print the name and title of the individual acting for the corporation directly below the line, with that person to sign above the line.

15. Insert the Notary Statement, found elsewhere in this book, for an Individual or for a Corporation, as appropriate, for the Guarantor. The Notary will complete the Notary Statement.

for presentment, protest and notice of protest and non-payment.

This Guaranty Agreement may be terminated by Guarantor only by written notice given to Seller by personal service or Certified Mail, Return Receipt Requested and shall be effective only as to credit given to or obligations incurred by Customer subsequent to receipt of the written notice to Seller.

Guarantor will pay all costs and expenses, including but not limited to reasonable attorneys' fees, incurred by Seller in enforcing the obligations of the Customer and Guarantor.

Seller may, if it assigns the underlying debt or any portion thereof of Customer to Seller, assign the rights granted hereunder as they apply to the assigned debt or portion thereof.

This Guaranty Agreement shall be governed by and construed in accordance with the laws of the State of _____[11]_____.

Dated: _____[12]_____

_____[13]_____

*BY*_____
[14]

[15] [Notary Statement]

LIMITED GUARANTY AGREEMENT (4-13)

In contrast to the preceding Continuing Guaranty Agreement, a Limited Guaranty Agrement is restricted to a specific dollar amount and to obligations that arise within a specified period of time.

LIMITED GUARANTY AGREEMENT

1. The name of the party guarantying the debt (the Guarantor). If the Guarantor is a corporation, add ", a _____ corporation" inserting the state of incorporation of the Guarantor.

2. If the Guarantor is an individual, insert ", a residence." If a corporation, insert " a place of business."

3. The address of the Guarantor.

4. The name of the party giving the credit (the Lender). If the Lender is a corporation, add ", a _____ corporation" inserting the state of incorporation of the Lender.

5. If an individual insert ", a residence." If a corporation, insert ", a place of business."

6. The address of the Lender.

7. The name of the party receiving the credit (the Borrower). If a corporation, add ", a _____ corporation" inserting the state of incorporation of the Borrower.

8. If an individual, insert ", a residence." If a corporation, insert "a place of business."

9. The address of the Borrower.

10. The date the Guaranty will expire.

11. The dollar limit, in numbers, of the Guaranty.

Guaranty given by _____[1]_____ (the "Guarantor") having _____[2]_____ at _____[3]_____ to _____[4]_____ ("the Lender") having _____[5]_____ at _____[6]_____ to induce Lender to extend credit to _____[7]_____ (the "Borrower") having _____[8]_____ at _____[9]_____.

In consideration of the foregoing, the Guarantor hereby guarantees to the Lender, its successors and assigns the prompt payment by the Borrower to the Lender at maturity of any order for the payment of money, claim or indebtedness in connection with which the Borrower is or shall become liable to the Lender from this date to _____[10]_____. The liability of the Guarantor shall not during the lifetime of this Guaranty exceed the sum of $_____[11]_____ with interest thereon, plus all attorneys' fees, costs and expenses of collection incurred by the Lender in connection with this Guaranty.

Upon default by the Borrower in any payment due to Lender, Guarantor agrees to pay such amounts on

(Document continued on next page)

12. The date of signing the Guaranty Agreement.

13. The name of the Guarantor if a corporation. Otherwise delete the line.

14. If the Guarantor is an individual, delete "BY" and print the Guarantor's name directly below the line, with the Guarantor to sign above the line. If the Guarantor is a corporation, print the name and title of the individual acting for the corporation directly below the line, with that person to sign above the line.

15. Insert the Notary Statement, found elsewhere in this book, for an Individual or a Corporation, as appropriate, for the Guarantor. The Notary will complete the Notary Statement.

demand, subject to the above limitations as to time and amount. Guarantor hereby waives notice of all transactions subject to this Guaranty, protest and non-payment.

Dated: _____[12]_____

_____*[13]*_____

*BY*_____
[14]

[15] [Notary Statement]

REVOCATION OF GUARANTY AGREEMENT (4-14)

Because a Guaranty Agreement guarantees the debts of another, the Revocation or termination of that Guaranty should be documented. Whether or not the Guaranty Agreement requires notification by Certified Mail—Return Receipt Requested, it should be sent that way to provide proof of receipt. A copy must also be sent to the party whose debt is being guaranteed.

REVOCATION OF GUARANTY AGREEMENT

1. The date of signing the Revocation.

2. The name and address of the party who granted the credit (the Lender).

3. The date of the Guaranty Agreement.

4. The name of the party whose debt was guaranteed (the Borrower).

5. The name of the Guarantor if a corporation. Otherwise delete the line.

6. If the Guarantor is an individual, delete "BY" and print the Guarantor's name directly below the line, with the Guarantor to sign above the line. If the Guarantor is a corporation, print the name and title of the individual acting for the corporation directly below the line, with that person to sign above the line.

7. The name and address of the Borrower.

_____[1]_____

TO: _____[2]_____

_____

_____

Gentlemen:

On _____[3]_____ I executed a Guaranty Agreement guaranteeing certain of the debts of _____[4]_____. Pursuant to the terms of the Guaranty Agreement, the Guaranty is herewith terminated as to all credit or obligations incurred by _____[4]_____ as of this date.

By a copy of this revocation I have notified _____[4]_____ that the Guaranty has been terminated.

Very truly yours,

_____[5]_____

BY_____
[6]

cc: [7]_____

_____

DEMAND FOR SECURITY COLLATERAL (4-15)

Upon the default in the payment of a debt which has been secured by collateral (any property used as security), a formal Demand for the delivery of the collateral should be made by the Lender. If either the Security Agreement or the underlying Loan Agreement provides for a method of giving Notice, that procedure must be followed. In any event, it is good practice to use a means that provides the Lender with a receipt signed by the Borrower, such as sending the Notice via Certified Mail—Return Receipt Requested.

DEMAND FOR SECURITY/COLLATERAL

1. The date of the Notice.

_____[1]_____

2. The name and address of the holder of the collateral (the Borrower).

TO: _____[2]_____

_____

3. The date of the Security Agreement.

_____

4. The name and address where the collateral is to be delivered.

Gentlemen:

5. The date the collateral is to be delivered.

On _____[3]_____ you executed a Security Agreement wherein you granted a security interest in the following collateral to secure an indebtedness. The debt having become due and payable and your having defaulted in the payment, demand is herewith made that the collateral be delivered to _____[4]_____ on _____[5]_____ at _____[6]_____.

6. The time of day when the collateral is to be delivered.

7. A detailed list of the collateral so that it may be identified without the possibility of confusion.

8. The name of the party making the Demand (the Lender) if a corporation. Otherwise delete the line.

[7] Collateral:

Very truly yours,

9. If the Lender is an individual, delete "BY" and print the Lender's name directly below the line, with the Lender to sign above the line. If the Lender is a corporation, print the name and title of the individual acting for the corporation directly below the line, with that person to sign above the line.

_____[8]_____

BY_____
[9]

DEMAND FOR PAYMENT (4-16)

A Demand for Payment is used when a debt has become due and the Borrower has failed to make payment. Many states require that a Demand for Payment be made before instituting legal action to collect. If a document pertaining to the Loan provides for a method of making demand for payment, that procedure must be followed. In any event, it is good practice to use a means that provides the Lender with a receipt signed by the Borrower, such as sending the Notice via Certified Mail—Return Receipt Requested.

DEMAND FOR PAYMENT

1. The date of the Notice.

           _____[1]_____

2. The name and address of the Borrower.

    TO: _____[2]_____

3. The date of the Note.

    _____

4. The amount of the Note, in numbers.

    _____

5. If partial payments have been made, include this language. Otherwise delete.

    Gentlemen:

6. The balance now due on the Note, in numbers.

        On _____[3]_____ you executed a Note in the amount of $_____[4]_____ *[5][of which $ ____[6]____ is outstanding]*. The Note was payable on _____[7]_____. Payment has not been received and you are now in default.

7. The date the Note was payable.

8. The amount now due, in numbers. Note: this amount may include late payment penalties or accelerated future payments, depending on the terms of the original loan agreement or Note.

        Payment in the amount of $ _____[8]_____ together with interest thereon at __[9]__% per annum in the

9. The interest rate on the Note, in numbers.

(Document continued on next page)

10. The amount of interest due, in numbers.

11. The name and address of the party who is to receive payment.

12. The date when payment is to be made.

13. The name of the party making the Demand (the Lender) if a corporation. Otherwise delete the line.

14. If the Lender is an individual, delete "BY" and print the Lender's name directly below the line, with the Lender to sign above the line. If the Lender is a corporation, print the name and title of the individual acting for the corporation directly below the line, with that person to sign above the line.

amount of $_____[10]_____ is herewith demanded. Payment should be delivered to _____[11]_____ on or before _____[12]_____ by cash or bank check.

Very truly yours,

_____*[13]*_____

BY_____
[14]

DEMAND UPON GUARANTOR (4-17)

This form is used when a Borrower defaults in the payment of a loan or fails to make payments on a credit purchase, either of which has been guaranteed by another party. If the Note or Guaranty Agreement provides for a method of making the Demand upon the Guarantor, that procedure must be followed. In any event, it is good practice to use a means that provides a receipt for the Demand, such as sending the Demand via Certified Mail—Return Receipt Requested.

DEMAND UPON GUARANTOR

1. The date of the Demand.

2. The name and address of the party who guaranteed the payment (the Guarantor).

3. The date of the Guaranty.

4. The name of the party (the Borrower) whose payment or performance was guaranteed.

5. The name or description of the document which contained the guaranty, i.e. "Promissory Note," "Guaranty Agreement," etc.

6. The name of the Borrower.

7. The unpaid balance, in numbers.

8. The name of the party to whom payment was to be made.

9. The date payment was due.

10. The amount of principal, in numbers, now due.

11. The interest rate, in numbers, if any, to be applied to the amount now due. If none, delete.

_____[1]_____

TO: _____[2]_____

_____

_____

Gentlemen:

On _____[3]_____ you guaranteed the performance and payment by _____[4]_____ pursuant to a _____[5]_____.

Although performance and payment were duly demanded, _____[6]_____ has failed to pay the indebtedness of $_____[7]_____ to _____[8]_____ on _____[9]_____.

Pursuant to the _____[5]_____, demand is herewith made for payment in the amount of $_____[10]_____, *together with interest at __[11]__% per annum on the unpaid balance of $_____[7]_____*. Payment

(Document continued on next page)

12. The total amount, in numbers, now due including principal and interest.

13. The date that payment is to be made.

14. The name and address of the party to whom payment is to be made.

15. The name of the party making the Demand, if a corporation. Otherwise delete the line.

16. If the party making the Demand is an individual, delete "BY" and print the the party's name directly below the line, with the party to sign above the line. If the party is a corporation, print the name and title of the individual acting for the corporation directly below the line, with that person to sign above the line.

of $_____[12]_____ is to be made on or before _____[13]_____ to _____[14]_____.

Very truly yours,

_____*[15]*_____

*BY*_____
        [16]

NOTICE OF DEFAULT (4-18)

Agreements may contain provisions for a Default which would trigger a termination of the agreement. If there is a Default, the defaulting party must receive Notice of the Default in order for the payment to be due, for the agreement to be terminated, or for whatever consequences are provided for in the contract's Default provisions to take effect. If the agreement provides for a method of giving Notice, that procedure must be followed. In any event, it is good practice to use a means that provides a receipt for the Notice, such as sending the Notice via Certified Mail—Return Receipt Requested.

NOTICE OF DEFAULT

1. The date of the Notice.

_____[1]_____

2. The name and address of the party who defaulted and who is receiving Notice.

TO: _____[2]_____

_____

_____

3. The date of the agreement containing the provision(s) which has been violated.

4. The name of the other party to the agreement, typically the party sending the Notice.

Gentlemen:

On _____[3]_____ you entered into an Agreement with _____[4]_____ which provided that you would be in default if _____ [5]_____

5. The exact language from the agreement that sets forth the terms of Default.

_____.

6. The number of days, in words and numbers, in which a cure of the Default may be made.

You are now in default.

You have __[6]__ (__) days to cure the default by

7. A detailed description of how the Default may be cured.

_____[7]_____

_____

_____.

(Document continued on next page)

8. A description of the consequences of the termination, i.e. "payment of $_____ will be due and payable," "the obligation of ABC Corporation to manufacture widgets will be terminated," etc.

9. The name of the party giving the Notice, if a corporation. Otherwise delete the line.

10. If the party giving the Notice is an individual, delete "BY" and print the the party's name directly below the line, with the party to sign above the line. If the party is a corporation, print the name and title of the individual acting for the corporation directly below the line, with that person to sign above the line.

If you fail to cure this default, the Agreement between us will terminate and _____[8]_____ _____.

Very truly yours,

_____*[9]*_____

BY_____
[10]

ASSIGNMENT OF PROMISSORY NOTE (4-19)

This form is used to transfer a Lender's interest in a Promissory Note to another.

ASSIGNMENT OF PROMISSORY NOTE

1. The date of the Assignment.

2. The name of the party assigning the Promissory Note (the Assignor). If the Assignor is a corporation, add ", a _____ corporation" inserting the state in which incorporated.

3. The name of the party accepting the assignment (the Assignee). If the Assignee is a corporation, add ", a _____ corporation" inserting the state in which incorporated.

4. The name of the party (the Borrower) who signed the Promissory Note.

5. The name of the Assignor.

6. The date of the Promissory Note.

7. The amount of the Promissory Note, in numbers.

8. The annual rate of interest, in numbers, of the Promissory Note.

9. A description of how the Promissory Note is payable, i.e. "On Demand," "in installments of $_____ commencing _____," etc.

Assignment made this __[1]__ day of _____. 19__ by _____[2]_____ ("Assignor") to _____[3]_____ ("Assignee").

For valuable consideration, the receipt of which is hereby acknowledged, Assignor hereby assigns to Assignee the entire interest of Assignor in a Promissory Note from _____[4]_____ to _____[5]_____, dated _____[6]_____, for the payment of $_____[7]_____ with interest at the annual rate of __[8]__% per annum which Promissory Note is payable _____[9]_____.

Assignor warrants and represents that the Promissory Note arose out of a loan by _____[2]_____ to _____[4]_____, that the Promissory Note has not matured and has not been paid in part or in full, that Assignor will do nothing to discharge

(Document continued on next page)

10. The name of the Assignor if a corporation. Otherwise delete the line.

11. If the Assignor is an individual, delete "BY" and print the the Assignor's name directly below the line, with the Assignor to sign above the line. If the Assignor is a corporation, print the name and title of the individual acting for the corporation directly below the line, with that person to sign above the line.

12. Insert the Notary Statement, found elsewhere in this book, for an Individual or Corporation, as appropriate for the Assignor. The Notary will complete the Notary Statement.

the Promissory Note or hinder its collection, and that there are no offsets or defenses to the underlying debt.

In Witness Whereof the Assignor has executed this Agreement.

_____*[10]*_____

BY_____
[11]

[12] [Notary Statement]

ASSIGNMENT OF ACCOUNTS RECEIVABLE (4-20)

This Assignment is used when a business assigns all or a portion of its Accounts Receivable either for cash or in payment of a debt owed to a third party. The Assignment may be for the full face value of the accounts or may be discounted. This type of Assignment is different from "factoring" in that it is a one-time assignment rather than a continuing relationship.

Note: on a separate sheet of paper, headed "Schedule A", list all of the accounts being assigned and the value ("face amount") of each.

ASSIGNMENT OF ACCOUNTS RECEIVABLE

1. The date of the Assignment.

2. The name of the party assigning the accounts (the Assignor). If the Assignor is a corporation, add ", a _____ corporation" inserting the state in which incorporated.

3. The name of the party accepting the assignment (the Assignee). If the Assignee is a corporation, add ",a _____ corporation" inserting the state in which incorporated.

4. The total face amount of the accounts being assigned. If the accounts are being transferred for less than full face value, add either " ____ % of face value," i.e 80%; or "$_____," the actual discounted payment being made.

Assignment made this __[1]__ day of _____ ,19__ by _____[2]_____ ("Assignor") to _____[3]_____ ("Assignee").

For valuable consideration, the receipt of which is hereby acknowledged, Assignor hereby assigns to Assignee the accounts set forth in Schedule A attached hereto, having an aggregate value of _____[4]_____, together with: all amounts due or to become due upon the accounts; title to the goods represented by the accounts whether or not received, rejected, returned or reconsigned; and title to any new account, including amounts to become due, created by a subsequent resale and not received, rejected, returned or reconsigned.

Concurrent with the execution of this Assignment, Assignor delivers to Assignee, receipt of which is hereby acknowledged, all invoices and shipping documents representing the goods and accounts receivable herein assigned. Assignor agrees to deliver and execute such other documents as are reasonably requested by Assignee with respect to this Assignment.

Assignor herewith warrants and represents to Assignee:

1. Schedule A attached hereto is a true and accurate statement of open accounts now owing to Assignor, that all sales are bona fide sales and that said goods have been shipped as ordered, received and accepted.

2. Schedule A attached hereto reflects the true

(Document continued on next page)

5. This paragraph is a "recourse" clause. If the accounts are being transferred "without recourse" (the Assignor is not required to buy back the account if the Assignee is not paid by the buyer of the goods) then substitute the following for this paragraph: "The assignment and transfer of accounts receivable herein is without recourse to the Assignor."

6. The name of the Assignor if a corporation. Otherwise delete the line.

7. If the Assignor is an individual, delete "BY" and print the Assignor's name directly below the line, with the Assignor to sign above the line. If the Assignor is a corporation, print the name and title of the individual acting for the corporation directly below the line, with that person to sign above the line.

8. Insert the Notary Statement, found elsewhere in this book, for an Individual or Corporation as appropriate for the Assignor. The Notary will complete the Notary Statement.

net balances and payment history of each account and the date payment of each account is due.

3. All accounts are free of any lien, security interest or any encumbrance and payment is not subject to any contingency not yet performed by any party.

4. Assignor had at the time of the delivery of the goods free and clear title to the goods and Assignor has the full legal right to make this assignment.

5. Any payments received by the Assignor for the accounts herein transferred shall be received by the Assignor on behalf of and as the property of the Assignee and shall be immediately transferred to the Assignee, subject to collection, or properly endorsed.

[5][In the event of default in the payment of any account herein transferred and upon demand by Assignee the Assignor shall repurchase the defaulted account at the value paid for that account.]

Assignor acknowledges that Assignee has relied on Assignor's warranties and representations in taking this Assignment.

In Witness Whereof the Assignor has executed this Assignment.

_____*[6]*_____

*BY*_____
[7]

[8] [Notary Statement]

FINDER'S AGREEMENT (4-21)

At some point a business may look for an outside source of capital by finding an investor. This Agreement sets forth the basic understanding between a business and a "middle-man" or FINDER who locates that source of capital. Of critical importance in such an Agreement is a determination as to the moment in time when the FINDER's fee is earned and becomes payable.

FINDER'S AGREEMENT

1. The date of signing the Agreement.

2. The name of the business seeking capital.

3. The name of the FINDER of the capital.

4. If the business seeking capital is a corporation, insert the state of incorporation. Otherwise delete.

5. The address of the business seeking capital.

6. If the FINDER of the capital is a corporation, insert the state of incorporation. Otherwise delete.

7. The address of the FINDER.

AGREEMENT made on _____[1]_____, 19__, by and between _____[2]_____ and _____[3]_____.

1. THE PARTIES

1.1 _____[2]_____, *[4][a corporation organized under the laws of the State of _____] * with its principal office at _____[5]_____.

1.1.1 The person executing this Agreement on behalf of _____[2]_____ represents to _____[3]_____ that he has full and complete authority to do so and has been designated to do so by the directors and/or owners of _____[2]_____.

1.2 _____[3]_____, *[6][a corporation organized under the laws of the State of _____] * with its principal office at _____[7]_____ ("FINDER").

2. THE AGREEMENT

2.1 _____[2]_____ seeks a purchaser of all or part of its stock and/or assets and/or trade name and goodwill and/or an investor to invest cash, credits or other tangible or intangible assets in or on behalf of _____[2]_____. Such purchase and/or investment may take the form, without limitation, of a purchase of assets, or of stock of _____[2]_____, for cash or a combination of cash, notes and stock, but in any event on terms and conditions satisfactory to _____[2]_____, as a result of any introduction made through FINDER and as a result of negotiations with any such purchaser and/or investor. FINDER will not, and is not required to, take part in any of such negotiations.

2.2 _____[2]_____ shall be under no obligation to pay any fee or other monies whatsoever to FINDER on account of this Agreement until any purchase

(Document continued on next page)

8. Note: the fee schedule shown in this Finder's Agreement is only an example to indicate where the agreed upon fee should appear. The example shown is a sliding fee based upon the total amount of the ultimate investment.

of and/or investment in _____[2]_____ contemplated by this Agreement has closed with any purchaser and/or investor and has resulted exclusively from the introduction by FINDER to _____[2]_____ of the purchaser and/or investor. FINDER shall not be entitled to any fee or other monies until _____[2]_____ has entered into a binding arrangement with the purchaser and/or investor. For purposes of this Agreement, the total amount of the fee due FINDER shall be due and payable on the date of the closing or, in the event that any such purchase and/or investment shall be of payments over time, on the date of the first payment made by such purchaser and/or investor.

2.3 Nothing contained in this Agreement shall be construed to give FINDER any exclusive rights, it being understood and agreed that FINDER shall be entitled to a fee only in connection with the entry by _____[2]_____ into a binding agreement with a purchaser and/or investor introduced by FINDER.

3. THE FEE

3.1 The fee for introduction by FINDER to _____[2]_____ of any such purchaser and/or investor, to be paid to FINDER by _____[2]_____ pursuant to this Agreement, shall be a sum computed on the total purchase and/or investment price as follows:

[8]less than $1,000,000.00	*5%*
$1,000,000.00 but less than $2,000,000.00	*4%*
$2,000,000.00 but less than $3,000,000.00	*3%*
$3,000,000.00 but less than $4,000,000.00	*2%*
$4,000,000.00 or more	*1%*

3.2 FINDER shall not be entitled to any fee or other monies until _____[2]_____ has entered into a binding arrangement with any purchaser and/or investor.

4. OTHER

4.1 Any arrangements made by FINDER with any broker or other persons with whom FINDER is or may be involved are the total responsibility of FINDER. Upon payment made by _____[2]_____ to FINDER of the finder's fee, FINDER will hold _____[2]_____ free and harmless from any and all claims, liabilities, com-

(Document continued on next page)

9. The city in which arbitration will take place.

10. The state in which arbitration will take place.

11. The state whose laws will govern the Agreement.

missions, fees or expenses in connection with the transaction from any party who alleges a relationship with or through FINDER and the purchaser and/or investor.

4.2 It is specifically understood and agreed that the dominant purpose of this Agreement is the entry by _____[2]_____ into a contract of purchase of and/or investment in _____[2]_____ and a transfer of any interest in or to real estate is merely incidental to this dominant purpose. It is further understood that this dominant purpose shall not be defeated or diminished by the inclusion in any such purchase and/or investment in _____[2]_____ by the transfer of any interest in real estate from _____[2]_____ and related companies to any such purchaser and/or investor. Despite the foregoing it is understood that the value (or present value) of any interest in real estate shall be included in determining the amount upon which the fee is computed.

4.3 In the event of any dispute between _____[2]_____ and FINDER arising under or pursuant to the terms of this Agreement, or any matters arising under the terms of this Agreement, the same shall be settled only by arbitration in the City of ____[9]_____, State of _____[10]_____, in accordance with the rules and regulations of the American Arbitration Association. The determination of the arbitrators shall be final and binding upon _____[2]_____ and FINDER and may be enforced in any court of appropriate jurisdiction.

4.4 This Agreement shall be construed by and governed under the laws of the State of ____[11]_____.

4.5 This Agreement contains the entire agreement between FINDER and _____[2]_____ concerning the introduction of a purchaser and/or investor to _____[2]_____ and correctly sets forth the rights

(Document continued on next page)

12. The name of the business if a corporation. Otherwise delete the line.

13. If the business is not a corporation, delete "BY" and print the owner's name directly below the line, with the owner to sign above the line. If it is a corporation, print the name and title of the individual acting for the corporation directly below the line, with that person to sign above the line.

14. The name of the FINDER if a corporation. Otherwise delete the line.

15. If the FINDER is an individual, delete "BY" and print the FINDER's name directly below the line, with the FINDER to sign above the line. If the FINDER is a corporation, print the name and title of the individual acting for the corporation directly below the line, with that person to sign above the line.

and duties of each of the parties to each other concerning that matter as of this date. Any agreement or representation concerning the subject matter of this Agreement or the duties of FINDER to _____[2]_____ in relation thereto, not set forth in this Agreement, is null and void.

   IN WITNESS WHEREOF, the parties have signed this Agreement on the date first written above.

_____[12]_____

BY_____
                [13]

_____[14]_____

BY_____
                [15]

INVESTMENT OF CAPITAL
FROM AN OUTSIDE SOURCE (4-22)

This agreement is typically used when a company needs additional capital and normal lending channels are not open to it. The agreement is written for the protection of the Investor.

INVESTMENT OF CAPITAL
FROM AN OUTSIDE SOURCE

1. The date the Investment agreement is signed.

2. The name of the Investor.

3. If the Investor is a corporation, insert the state in which incorporated. Otherwise delete.

4. The name of the Company in which the investment is made.

5. If the Company is a corporation, insert the state in which incorporated. Otherwise delete.

6. A general description of the business's activities, i.e. "manufacturing," "retailing," etc.

7. The amount, in numbers, being invested.

8. The date the money is to be given to the Company.

9. A description of the purposes for which the investment is to be used, such as "general," "raw materials," "inventory," "advertising."

10. The date the Investment is to be repaid. It may be a specific date or "upon demand" or "___ days after demand."

AGREEMENT made this __[1]__ day of _____ 19__, by and between _____[2]_____ *[3][, a _____ corporation]* ("Investor") and _____[4]_____ *[5][, a _____ corporation]* ("Company").

Company is in the business of _____[6]_____ and requires the investment of capital in the Company; and

Investor desires to invest capital in the Company and to participate in the profits of the Company.

In consideration of the mutual terms, conditions and covenants hereinafter set forth the parties agree as follows:

1.   Investor shall advance to the Company the sum of $_____[7]_____ on _____[8]_____, which Investment shall be used for _____[9]_____ purposes only, which sum shall be repayable by the Company to Investor on _____[10]_____.

2.   The Company shall have no right of repayment of the Investment without the written consent of the Investor, which consent shall be at the sole discretion of the Investor.

3.   During the period of the Investment the Company shall not: increase the compensation of any officer, director or employee; pledge, assign or encumber any asset, tangible or intangible, of the Company; borrow any funds; sell or transfer any asset of the Company other than in the normal course of business; or otherwise conduct the business that preceded this Agreement without the prior written consent of the Investor.

(Document continued on next page)

11. The name(s) of the shareholders or principals (owners) of the Company. Add or delete spaces as required to accommodate the actual number of names.

12. Insert "Shareholders" if the Company is a corporation or "Principals" if not a corporation.

13. The date the Investor will receive the first financial statement.

14. The interval at which financial statements will be issued; i.e. month, quarter.

15. Insert either "Shareholders" or "Principals." (See No. 12.)

16. A description of the property in which a security interest is given, such as "accounts receivable," "inventory."

17. The frequency with which the Investor is to receive the share of profits, i.e. monthly, quarterly.

18. The percentage, in numbers, of profits to be paid to the Investor.

19. A number of days that is reasonable, in words and numbers, such as three (3).

4. _____[11]_____, _____[11]_____ and _____[11]_____, being all of the _____[12]_____ of the Company hereby subrogate any and all loans heretofore made to the Company and any and all claims for past due compensation to the advance made pursuant to this Agreement and such loans and claims shall not be paid without the prior written consent of the Investor.

5. The Company shall, commencing _____[13]_____ and every ___[14]___ thereafter, submit to Investor a financial statement indicating the profit/loss for the preceding period and year to date.

6. The books, records, reports and accounts of the Company shall be kept at all times so as to accurately reflect the business and financial condition of the Company. Investor shall, at all times during normal business hours, have access to and may inspect said books, records, reports and accounts.

7. The Company and the _____[15]_____ guarantee the repayment of the Investment to the Investor and shall grant to the Investor a security interest in _____[16]_____, shall execute a Guaranty in favor of the Investor in a form as attached to this Agreement and shall execute all documents reasonably required and necessary to perfect the security interest.

8. No less often than ____[17]____ during the period of the Investment, the Company shall pay to Investor __[18]__% of the net profit, as determined by standard accounting practices, for that period. Losses shall be carried forward to the next period and shall not under any circumstances be applied retroactively to prior periods.

9. All notices required or permitted to be given hereunder shall be in writing and may be delivered personally or by U.S. Mail, Certified Mail - Return Receipt Requested, postage prepaid. Receipt of notice shall be deemed to have been given upon receipt if personally delivered or within ___[19]___ (__) days after being deposited in the U.S. Mails. Notice shall be addressed:

(Document continued on next page)

20. The name and address of the person to receive notices on behalf of the Company.

21. The name and address of the person to receive notices on behalf of the Investor.

22. The name of the state whose laws will govern the agreement.

If to Company: _____[20]_____

_____

_____

If to Investor: _____[21]_____

_____

_____

10.   Any controversy or claim arising out of or relating to this contract, or the breach thereof, shall be settled by arbitration in accordance with the Commercial Arbitration Rules of the American Arbitration Association, and judgment upon the award rendered by the arbitrator(s) may be entered in any court having jurisdiction thereof.

11.   This Agreement shall be construed in accordance with and governed by the laws of the State of _____[22]_____, irrespective of the fact that a party hereto may not be a resident and/or maintain an office in that state.

(Document continued on next page)

23. The name of the Company if a corporation. Otherwise delete the line.

24. If the Company is not a corporation, delete "BY" and print the individual's name directly below the line, with the individual to sign above the line. If the Company is a corporation, print the name and title of the person acting for the corporation directly below the line, with that person to sign above the line.

25. The name of the Investor if a corporation. Otherwise delete the line.

26. If the Investor is an individual, delete "BY" and print the Investor's name directly below the line, with the Investor to sign above the line. If the Investor is a corporation, print the name and title of the person acting for the corporation directly below the line, with that person to sign above the line.

27. Insert either "Shareholders" or "Principals." (See No. 12.)

28. The name of each shareholder or principal printed directly below the line, with that person to sign above the line. Add or delete lines as required to accommodate the actual number of names.

29. Insert a Personal or Corporate Guaranty, as appropriate, for the Company. The Guaranties are found elsewhere in this book.

INTENDING TO BE LEGALLY BOUND, the parties hereto have caused this Agreement to be executed as of the date first above written.

_____[23]_____

BY_____
[24]   (Company)

_____[25]_____

BY_____
[26]   (Investor)

The undersigned, being all of the _____[27]_____ of the Company hereby agree to the foregoing.

_____
[28]

_____
[28]

_____
[28]

[29] [Guaranty]

Starting a Business 5

New businesses, like new babies, fill us with hope and promise. As the "newborn" emerges, the proud "parents" make long range plans. The first step in realizing long range goals is to build a strong foundation. The forms in this chapter will put a new business on a solid foundation, whether it is a partnership, joint venture or corporation.

Partnerships and Joint Ventures When two or more individuals or companies go into business on a continuing basis as co–owners, equally sharing profits and losses, it is called a partnership. When two or more individuals or companies go into business for a specific situation or for a fixed period of time it is called a joint venture. Forms for both types of associations are found in this section.

Corporations One or more individuals may decide to enjoy the benefits of ownership with the added protection of limiting loss to the amount of each participant's investment. A corporation presents this type of protection. Pre-incorporation, stock subscription, shareholders agreements and organizational meeting forms are presented in this section to set a corporation on the right path.

PARTNERSHIP AGREEMENT (5-01)

A Partnership exists when two or more parties conduct business on a continuing basis. It is not the Partnership Agreement that creates the Partnership relationship, but the parties' voluntary and continued intention to conduct business as co-owners. A written Agreement is advisable, however, because it permits the parties to define the rights and obligations of the Partnership in conformance with their wishes. In the absence of such an agreement, the Uniform Partnership Act will apply. That legislation may not, however, reflect the parties' desires.

A Partnership differs from a Joint Venture, which is usually a relationship covering a single business situation. This Partnership Agreement purposely has been kept general, with the specifics of the operation of the Partnership to be determined by the action of the Partners at a Partnership meeting.

PARTNERSHIP AGREEMENT

1. The date the Partnership Agreement is signed.

2. The name of each Partner (add or delete spaces as necessary).

3. The purpose of the Partnership, for example "real estate investment" or "the practice of accounting."

4. The name of the Partnership.

5. The location where the Partnership initially will conduct business.

6. The county and state where the Partnership initially will conduct business.

Partnership Agreement made this __[1]__ day of _____,19__ by and between _____[2]_____, _____[2]_____ and _____[2]_____, (individually the "Partner" and collectively the "Partners").

In consideration of the mutual terms, conditions and covenants hereinafter set forth, the Partners agree as follows:

I. GENERAL

1.1 The purpose of the Partnership shall be _____[3]_____.

1.2 The name of the Partnership shall be _____[4]_____, (the "Partnership").

1.3 The initial address of the Partnership shall be _____[5]_____, which address may be changed from time to time by the Partners.

1.4 The Partners shall execute the necessary documents to register the Partnership name and existence with the proper governmental offices in the County of _____[6]_____, State of _____[6]_____.

1.5 The Partnership shall continue until, and dissolve upon, the first happening of:

    a)   The death of one Partner; or

    b)   The withdrawal, by written notice, of one Partner; or

(Document continued on next page)

7. The dollar amount, in numbers, of each Partner's initial capital (cash) contribution.

8. The Partnership interest of each Partner expressed as a percentage, in numbers. (Note: unless there are extenuating circumstances, i.e. the Partnership business is the unique concept of one Partner for which that Partner is to receive a disproportionate share, the Partnership interest typically will be the percentage of a Partner's capital contribution to the total capital of the Partnership.)

c)   The affirmative vote of a majority in interest of the Partners.

II. CAPITALIZATION

2.1   The Partners shall contribute to the Partnership in the following amounts which shall reflect their Partnership interest:

_____[2]_____ $____[7]____   __[8]__%

_____[2]_____ $____[7]____   __[8]__%

_____[2]_____ $____[7]____   __[8]__%

2.2   No Partner shall receive interest on his capital contribution.

2.3   A separate "Capital Account" shall be maintained for each Partner.

a)   A Capital Account shall be increased by (i) the contribution to the capital of the Partnership, including the initial contribution (Paragraph 2.1. above) and (ii) the distributive share of the Net Profits of the Partnership; and decreased by (i) distributions, (ii) the distributive share of Net Losses of the Partnership and (iii) the distributive share of expenditures of the Partnership not deductible in computing Net Profits/Losses and not properly treated as capital expenditures.

b)   Distributions in kind shall be valued at fair market value less any liability which the Partner assumes on the distribution or to which the asset distributed is subject.

2.4   If in the opinion of the majority in interest of the Partnership additional capital is needed for the proper conduct of the business of the Partnership, each Partner shall contribute pro rata in accordance with his interest.

2.5   Each Partner shall be indemnified by the other Partners as to excess over the Partner's interest in the Partnership in the event a Partner is compelled to pay and does pay any Creditor of the Partnership in satisfaction of

(Document continued on next page)

9. The percentage of the Partnership, in numbers, necessary to call a meeting.

10. The date of the first Partnership meeting.

11. The location of the first Partnership meeting.

12. The time of the first Partnership meeting, such as 5:00 PM.

13. The fiscal year of the Partnership, for example "calendar year," or "July 1 to June 30."

an obligation of the Partnership. It is the intent and purpose of this provision that all of the Partners shall pay their pro rata share of the Partnership debts, regardless of whether a creditor of the Partnership recovers payment from some but not all of the Partners.

III. MANAGEMENT

3.1   All matters to be determined by the Partners shall be determined by affirmative vote of a majority in interest of the Partners at a meeting. All matters determined by the Partners shall be recorded in a Minute Book reflecting the date, matter discussed and the action taken.

3.2   The Partners shall meet at least once each year. Additional meetings may be held at the request of __[9]__% of the Partnership by interest. All meetings shall be by written notice reasonably in advance so that each Partner may be present either in person or by written proxy authorization.

3.3   At the first meeting of the Partnership to be held on _____[10]_____, at _____[11]_____, at __[12]__ __M, the Partnership shall determine:

a)   the manner in which the business of the Partnership shall be managed;

b)   the hiring of employees;

c)   salaries to be paid to employees and the Partner(s) who participate in the day-to-day management of the business of the Partnership;

d)   banking procedures; and

e)   any other matters which may properly come before the Partnership.

3.4   The fiscal year of the Partnership shall be _____[13]_____.

3.5   Each Partner shall have the right to inspect the books, records, reports and accounts of the Partnership during normal business hours, which books, records, reports and accounts shall be kept at the Partnership's place

(Document continued on next page)

of business or at such other place as determined from time to time by the Partnership.

IV. PROHIBITIONS

4.1   No Partner shall sell, assign, mortgage, hypothecate or encumber his interest in the Partnership without the express written permission of all the remaining Partners, without regard to interest.

4.2.   All Partners shall meet their personal obligations and debts as they become due and each agrees to save and hold the remaining Partners and the Partnership harmless from all costs, claims and demands with respect to such obligations and debts.

4.3.   No Partner shall, except upon the approval of the Partnership by affirmative vote:

      a)   lend any Partnership funds;

      b)   incur any obligation in the name of or on the credit of the Partnership;

      c)   lend any of the Partner's funds to the Partnership, with or without interest;

      d)   sell, assign, mortgage, hypothecate or encumber any asset of the Partnership;

      e)   make an assignment of the assets of the Partnership for the benefit of creditors of the Partnership;

      f)   execute any guarantee on behalf of the Partnership;

      g)   release, assign or transfer a Partnership claim or any asset of the Partnership;

      h)   borrow in the name of the Partnership;

      i)   submit any Partnership claim or liability to arbitration;

(Document continued on next page)

14. The state in which the Partnership is located.

15. The city and state where arbitration is to take place, typically the state in which the Partnership is located.

j)   initiate, conduct or settle litigation in the name of or pertaining to the Partnership; or

k)   invest Partnership funds or other assets.

4.4   Any Partner who commits a prohibited act shall be individually liable to the remaining Partners, pro rata to their Partnership interest, for any loss caused by the prohibited act.

V. PROFITS/LOSSES AND DISTRIBUTIONS

5.1   Net Profits/Losses shall be determined in accordance with good accounting principles and shall be as finally determined for federal income tax purposes.

5.2   Net Profits/Losses shall be apportioned pro rata among the Partners' capital account according to each Partner's interest.

5.3.   Distribution shall be made upon the affirmative vote of the Partners as provided for in paragraph 3.1. herein.

VI. ADDITIONAL PARTNERS/DISSOLUTION

6.1   The Partnership may admit additional Partners upon the affirmative vote of the Partners, as provided for herein. Additional Partners shall then be admitted upon payment of a contribution to capital as determined by the Partnership and each Partner's interest in the Partnership as provided for in paragraph 2.1 shall be redetermined.

6.2   In the event of the dissolution of the Partnership for any reason, the affairs of the Partnership shall be wound up and the proceeds of the Partnership distributed in accordance with the terms of this Agreement and the laws of the State of ____[14]____.

VII. MISCELLANEOUS

7.1   Arbitration. If any controversy or claim arising out of this Agreement cannot be settled by the Partners, the controversy or claims shall be settled by arbitration in the City of ____[15]___, State of ____[15]___, in accordance with the rules of the American Arbitration Association then in effect, and judgment on the award may be entered in any court having jurisdiction.

(Document continued on next page)

16. The state whose laws will govern the Agreement, typically the state in which the Partnership is located.

17. The name of each partner printed directly below the line, with each partner to sign above the line.

7.2   Governing Law. This Agreement shall be enforced and construed under and shall be subject to the laws of the State of _____[16]_____. If any provision of this Agreement shall be unlawful, void or unenforceable, that provision shall be deemed separate from and in no way shall affect the validity or enforceability of the remaining provisions of this Agreement.

7.3   Notices. All notices required to be given under this Agreement shall be either (i) personally delivered to the party to whom addressed or (ii) sent by U.S. Mail, postage prepaid, Certified Mail, Return Receipt Requested, addressed to the Partner at the last address for that Partner as maintained by the Partnership.

7.4   Entire Agreement. This Agreement contains the full and complete understanding of all of the Partners with reference to the Partnership and supersedes all prior agreements and understandings, whether written or oral. This agreement may not be amended except in writing and upon the consent of all of the Partners then existing of the Partnership.

7.5   Successors. This Agreement shall be binding on and inure to the benefit of the respective successors, permitted assigns, executors, administrators, personal representatives and beneficiaries of the Partners.

7.6.   Subject Headings. The subject headings used in this Agreement are for convenience only and shall not be deemed to affect the meaning or construction of any of the provisions of this Agreement.

Executed by the Partners as of the date first above written.

_____
[17]

_____
[17]

_____
[17]

JOINT VENTURE AGREEMENT (5-02)

A Joint Venture Agreement is typically used for a single business situation, in contrast to a Partnership, which is a continuing relationship. Partners intend to remain together—for better or for worse. Joint Venturers intend to stay together only until the completion of a particular project. The Joint Venturers may limit their liability to a stated contribution (cash or services). The Venture Manager may be one of the Joint Venturers, an outside agent, or an employee with expertise in the area.

This form assumes that there are two parties (Venturers) in the Joint Venture. More may be added by changing the appropriate sections below.

JOINT VENTURE AGREEMENT

1.   The date the Joint Venture Agreement is signed.

2.   The name of the first party to the Joint Venture (the Venturer).

3.   If the first Venturer is a corporation, insert the state in which incorporated. Otherwise delete.

4.   The name of the second Venturer.

5.   If the second Venturer is a corporation, insert the state in which incorporated. Otherwise delete.

6.   The purpose for which the Joint Venture is formed.

7.   The name of the Joint Venture.

8.   The location at which the Joint Venture will conduct business.

9.   The term of the Joint Venture, for example "three years" or "from January 1, 1991 to December 31, 1993."

10. The county and state from which the Joint Venture will conduct business.

11. The total amount of capital, in numbers, for the Joint Venture.

12. The amount, in numbers, to be contributed by the first Venturer.

Joint Venture Agreement made the __[1]__ day of _____, 19__ by and between _____[2]_____ *[3][, a _____ corporation]* and _____[4]_____ *[5][, a _____ corporation]* (individually the "Venturer" and collectively the "Joint Venturers").

In consideration of the mutual terms, conditions and covenants hereinafter set forth, the Joint Venturers agree as follows:

1.   The Joint Venturers hereby form a "Joint Venture" for the purposes of _____[6]_____ and shall conduct business under the name _____[7]_____ at _____[8]_____.

2.   The term of the Joint Venture shall be _____[9]_____.

3.   The Joint Venturers shall execute the necessary documents to register the Joint Venture with the proper governmental offices in the County of _____[10]_____, State of _____[10]_____.

4.   The Capital of the Joint Venture shall consist of $_____[11]_____. _____[2]_____ shall contribute $_____[12]_____ and _____[4]_____ shall

(Document continued on next page)

JOINT VENTURE AGREEMENT *continued*

13. The amount, in numbers, to be contributed by the second Venturer.

14. The bank where an account will be maintained for the benefit of the Joint Venture.

15. The name of the person or entity who will manage the Joint Venture (the Venture Manager).

16. The salary of the Venture Manager, in numbers.

17. The frequency with which the salary will be paid, for example "per month."

contribute $_____[13]_____, which shall be deposited in _____[14]_____ and shall be disbursed only upon the signature of the Joint Venturers.

5.   The profits and losses of the Joint Venture shall be determined in accordance with good accounting practices and shall be shared among the Joint Venturers in proportion to their respective capital contributions.

6.   _____[15]_____ shall have the sole discretion, management and entire control of the conduct of the business of the Joint Venture as the "Venture Manager."

7.   As compensation for his services the Venture Manager shall be paid $_____[16]_____ per ____[17]____ during the duration of the Joint Venture and shall be reimbursed for all reasonable expenses incurred in the performance of his duties as Venture Manager.

8.   Each Joint Venturer shall be bound by any action taken by the Venture Manager in good faith under this Agreement. In no event shall any Joint Venturer be called upon to pay any amount beyond the liability arising against him on account of his capital contribution.

9.   The Venture Manger shall not be liable for any error in judgment or any mistake of law or fact or any act done in good faith in the exercise of the power and authority as Venture Manager but shall be liable for gross negligence or willful default.

10.   The relationship between the Joint Venturers shall be limited to the performance of the terms and conditions of this Agreement. Nothing herein shall be construed to create a general partnership between the Joint Venturers, or to authorize any Venturer to act as a general agent for another, or to permit any Venturer to bind another other than as set forth in this Agreement, or to borrow money on behalf of another Venturer, or to use the credit of any Venturer for any purpose.

11.   Neither this Agreement nor any interest in the Joint Venture may be assigned, pledged, transferred or hypothecated without the prior written consent of the Joint Venturers hereto.

12.   This Agreement shall be governed by and inter-

(Document continued on next page)

18. The state whose laws will govern the Joint Venture, typically the state in which the Joint Venture is located.

19. The city and state where arbitration is to take place, typically the state in which the Joint Venture is located

20. The name of the first Venturer if a corporation. Otherwise delete the line.

21. If the first Venturer is an individual, delete "BY" and print the Venturer's name directly below the line, with the Venturer to sign above the line. If the Venturer is a corporation, print the name and title of the individual acting for the corporation directly below the line, with that person to sign above the line.

22. The name of the second Venturer if a corporation. Otherwise delete the line.

23. If the second Venturer is an individual, delete "BY" and print the Venturer's name directly below the line, with the Venturer to sign above the line. If the Venturer is a corporation, print the name and title of the individual acting for the corporation directly below the line, with that person to sign above the line.

preted under the laws of the State of _____[18]_____. Any controversy or claim arising out of or relating to this Agreement, or the breach thereof, shall be settled by arbitration in accordance with the Commercial Arbitration Rules of the American Arbitration Association in the City of _____[19]_____, State of _____[19]_____, and judgment upon the award rendered by the arbitrator(s) may be entered in any court having jurisdiction thereof.

13.   Any and all notices to be given pursuant to or under this Agreement shall be sent to the party to whom the notice is addressed at the address of the Venturer maintained by the Joint Venture and shall be sent Certified Mail, Return Receipt Requested.

14.   This Agreement constitutes the entire agreement between the Joint Venturers pertaining to the subject matter contained in it, and supersedes all prior and contemporaneous agreements, representations, warranties and understandings of the parties. No supplement, modification or amendment of this Agreement shall be binding unless executed in writing by all the parties hereto. No waiver of any of the provisions of this Agreement shall be deemed, or shall constitute, a waiver of any other provision, whether similar or not similar, nor shall any waiver constitute a continuing waiver. No waiver shall be binding unless in writing signed by the party making the waiver.

The parties hereto, intending to be bound, have signed this Agreement as of the date and year first above written.

_____[20]_____

BY_____
[21]

_____[22]_____

BY_____
[23]

TERMINATION NOTICE (5-03)

The preceding forms, Partnership Agreement and Joint Venture Agreement, provide for Termination by written Notice. This form fulfills the Notice requirement for those Agreements.

Note that the Notices should be sent via Certified Mail—Return Receipt Requested.

TERMINATION NOTICE

1. The name and address of the party to whom the Termination Notice must be sent.

2. The date of the Termination Notice.

3. The name of the party to whom the Notice is addressed, or use "Gentlemen" if it is not an individual.

4. Insert either "Partnership" or "Joint Venture."

5. The date of the Agreement.

6. The name of the Partnership or Joint Venture.

7. The state whose laws govern the Agreement, as stated in the Agreement.

8. The name of the terminating party if a corporation. Otherwise delete the line.

9. If the terminating party is an individual, delete "BY" and print the terminating party's name directly below the line, with the terminating party to sign above the line. If the terminating party is a corporation, print the name and title of the individual acting for the terminating party directly below the line, with that person to sign above the line.

TO: _____[1]_____   ____[2]____, 19__
_____
_____

Dear _____[3]_____:

Pursuant to the terms of the _____[4]_____ Agreement dated _____[5]_____, 19__ the undersigned hereby gives notice that the undersigned desires to terminate participation in the _____[4]_____, "_____[6]_____."

The _____[4]_____ should immediately commence to wind up its business and dissolve the _____[4]_____ as provided in the Agreement and the laws of the State of _____[7]_____. Should my assistance be required, please advise.

Very truly yours,

_____[8]_____

BY_____
[9]

PRE-INCORPORATION AGREEMENT (5-04)

A Pre-Incorporation Agreement is used when two or more parties desire to start a business and have elected the corporate form of organization. The Agreement provides for the money needed to form the Corporation and sets forth the procedures for its operation. After the Corporation is formed, the information contained in the Agreement becomes the basis for the By-Laws and Shareholders Agreements found in this chapter. A Certificate of Incorporation, which is to be filed with the Secretary of State, has not been included in this book because each state has its own requirements that are available from the office of the Secretary of State in each state's capital.

PRE-INCORPORATION AGREEMENT

1. The date the Agreement is signed.

2. The name of each party who is forming the Corporation.

3. The main business in which the Corporation will be engaged, for example "restaurant," "auto-leasing," "landscaping."

4. The name the Corporation is to have. Note: the name desired by the parties may not always be available for use. It is recommended that the Organizers agree on alternative names.

5. The state in which the Corporation will be formed.

6. The number of shares authorized.

7. Insert either "no par" or "$___ par" with the value, in numbers, to be inserted. (Note: most small corporations have "no par value" shares.

8. The number of days after registering with the Secretary of State in which the shares must be purchased.

9. The names of the Organizers (the parties forming the Corporation).

10. Adjacent to each name the number of shares to be purchased by that Organizer.

Agreement made this __[1]__ day of _____, 19__ by and between _____[2]_____, _____[2]_____ and _____[2]_____ to engage primarily in the _____[3]_____ business, in accordance with the following:

1.   The name of the Corporation shall be _____[4]_____.

2.   The Corporation shall be organized pursuant to the laws of and registered in the State of _____[5]_____. The authorized shares of stock shall be ___[6]___ shares of ____[7]_____ value common stock.

3.   The Organizers agree to purchase shares of stock within __[8]__ days after the formation of the Corporation as follows:

_____[9]_____   ___[10]___ shares

_____[9]_____   ___[10]___ shares

_____[9]_____   ___[10]___ shares

4.   The Organizers shall be the first directors of the Corporation.

(Document continued on next page)

11. The names of the officers of the Corporation. (Each state has separate requirements regarding the number of officers that are required. As a general rule, if there is more than one shareholder the minimum requirement is two officers, a President and a Secretary/Treasurer.)

12. The amount each Organizer will contribute to pay the expenses of forming the Corporation.

13. Depending upon whether the contribution in No. 12 is to be considered a loan to the Corporation, insert either "a loan to the Corporation to be repaid with interest at ____% per annum" and the percent, or "applied toward purchase of stock."

14. The name of each Organizer to be employed by the Corporation.

15. The corporate title of each Organizer in No. 14.

16. The salary and pay period of each Organizer named in no. 14, for example "$15,000 per year."

17. The name of each Organizer printed directly below the line, with that person to sign above the line.

5.　The officers of the Corporation shall be as follows:

_____[11]_____　President

_____[11]_____　Secretary

_____[11]_____　Treasurer

6.　　The Organizers shall upon the execution of this Agreement advance on behalf of the Corporation $___[12]____ each to carry out the intents and purposes of this Agreement. Upon its formation the advance shall be deemed to be _____[13]_____.

7.　　The following shall be employed by the Corporation and receive compensation in the amount stated. Compensation may be revised by the Board of Directors from time to time.

_____[14]_____　_____[15]_____　____[16]____

_____[14]_____　_____[15]_____　____[16]____

_____[14]_____　_____[15]_____　____[16]____

　　INTENDING TO BE LEGALLY BOUND, the parties hereto have caused this Pre-Incorporation Agreement to be executed as of the date first above written.

_____
[17]

_____
[17]

_____
[17]

STOCK SUBSCRIPTION AGREEMENT (5-05)

The organizers of a corporation that has already been formed may determine that they need additional capital before the corporation begins operation. This Agreement is used to obligate a Subscriber to purchase the stock of a corporation when issued by the corporation and at a predetermined price. Each Subscriber executes a separate Agreement.

WARNING

It is crucial that the corporation determine if the sale of its stock is regulated by either federal or state securities laws. If the stock sale is regulated, it is recommended that an attorney specializing in securities law be engaged to prepare the Agreement and monitor the sale for compliance with the law.

STOCK SUBSCRIPTION AGREEMENT

1. The date the Agreement is signed.

2. The name of the purchaser of the stock (the Subscriber).

3. If the Subscriber is a corporation, insert the state in which incorporated. Otherwise delete.

4. The name of the corporation selling the stock.

5. The state in which the corporation is incorporated.

6. The date of incorporation.

7. The number of shares of stock, in numbers, the Certificate of Incorporation authorizes to be issued.

8. Insert either "no par" or "$____ par" with the value, in numbers, to be inserted.

9. The number of shares of stock, in numbers, issued to the organizers.

10. The names of the organizers.

11. The number of shares of stock, in numbers, to be purchased by the Subscriber.

Agreement made this __[1]__ day of _____, 19__ by and between _____[2]_____ *[3][, a _____ corporation]* ("Subscriber") and _____[4]_____, a _____[5]_____ corporation ("Corporation").

The Corporation has been organized on _____[6]_____ having been authorized to issue ___[7]___ shares of ___[8]___ value common stock and has issued ___[9]___ shares of the stock to _____[10]_____ as "Founders" of the Corporation.

The Corporation desires to raise additional capital by this issuance of stock.

The Subscriber desires to be a Shareholder in the Corporation and agrees to purchase shares.

AGREED

1. The Corporation will issue to the Subscriber ___[11]___ shares of the common stock of the Corporation and the Subscriber shall purchase from and pay to the

(Document continued on next page)

12. The price per share, in numbers, to be paid by the Subscriber. (This may be different from the price paid by the organizers.)

13. The date on which the price will be paid and the shares issued.

14. The name of the incorporation papers, a copy of which is to be attached to the Agreement. (Note: some states have a different title for the incorporation papers; i.e. "Certificate of Incorporation," "Articles of Incorporation," "Charter" etc. This title is readily ascertainable from the document itself.)

Corporation $___[12]___ for each share of common stock on _____[13]_____.

2.   The Corporation represents and warrants, which representations and warranties shall survive the purchase date, that:

a)   The Corporation has been duly formed and is in existence and has operated in conformity with all laws and regulations applicable to its operation;

b)   The issuance of the shares of common stock contemplated herein is in conformance with all laws and regulations applicable to the issuance of the shares;

c)   Attached hereto are true copies of the _____[14]_____, By-laws and all Agreements and Resolutions of the Board of Directors or Shareholders that are applicable to Shareholders; and

d)   The Corporation has duly authorized the sale and issuance of the shares to the Subscriber.

(Document continued on next page)

15. The name of the Subscriber if a corporation. Otherwise delete the line.

16. If the Subscriber is an individual, delete "BY" and print the Subscriber's name directly below the line, with the Subscriber to sign above the line. If the Subscriber is a corporation, print the name and title of the individual acting for the corporation directly below the line, with that person to sign above the line.

17. The address of the Subscriber.

18. The Federal Taxpayer Identification Number (Social Security Number if an individual) of the Subscriber.

19. The date the corporation accepts the Subscription.

20. The name and title of the officer acting for the corporation offering the stock printed directly below the line, with that person to sign above the line.

INTENTING TO BE LEGALLY BOUND, the parties hereto have caused this Agreement to be executed as of the date first above written.

_____*[15]*_____

BY_____
[16] (Subscriber)

_____ [17]_____
_____

Subscriber's Taxpayer
Identification No.:

_____[18]_____

ACCEPTED

Date _____[19]_____

_____[4]_____

BY_____
[20]

SHAREHOLDERS AGREEMENT (5-06)

When a non-publicly traded corporation is formed, it is advisable to have an Agreement among the Shareholders as to how the corporation will be organized and operate. The Agreement is used in addition to the By-laws of the corporation and should be accompanied by a Buy-Sell Agreement, also found in this chapter, governing the conditions under which a Shareholder may sell his interest in the corporation. Just as with the Buy-Sell Agreement, it is strongly urged that corporate governing procedures be established and memorialized in a written Shareholders Agreement at the time of, or soon after, the formation of the corporation when all concerned find it relatively easy to agree. Later, when matters may not be proceeding quite so smoothly, it may be less likely that agreement can be reached.

SHAREHOLDERS AGREEMENT

1.   The date the Agreement is signed.

2.   The name of each Shareholder (add or delete spaces as necessary).

3.   The state in which incorporated.

4.   The name of the corporation.

5.   The number of shares of stock authorized to be issued, as stated in the Certificate of Incorporation or Charter of the corporation.

6.   Insert either "no par" or "$____ par" with the value, in numbers, to be inserted.

Agreement made this __[1]_ day of _____, 19__ by and between _____[2]_____, _____[2]_____ and _____[2]_____, all of whom are hereinafter collectively referred to as the "Shareholders" and individually as a "Shareholder."

The Shareholders have caused to be formed a _____[3]_____ corporation whose name is _____[4]_____ ("The Corporation").

The Shareholders desire to provide: for the ownership of the shares, the voting of shares, the election of directors, the voting of the Board of Directors and the election of officers, among other provisions.

In consideration of the premises and the mutual covenants of the parties hereinafter set forth, it is

AGREED

1.   FORMATION OF CORPORATION

1.1   The parties have caused to be formed a corporation, _____[4]_____, organized under the laws of the State of _____[3]_____ and agree to execute all necessary documents.

1.2   The Corporation shall maintain a place of business within the State of _____[3]_____.

1.3   The Corporation is authorized to issue ___[5]___ shares of ____[6]____ value stock.

(Document continued on next page)

7. The name of each Share-holder and adjacent to it the number of shares each owns.

8. The name of each director of the corporation (add or delete spaces as necessary).

2. SHARES OF STOCK

2.1 The respective Shareholders shall own shares of stock in the Corporation according to the following schedule.

_____[7]_____   _____ shares

_____[7]_____   _____ shares

_____[7]_____   _____ shares

2.2 Any plan for an increase in the number of shares which the Corporation shall be authorized to issue shall require the unanimous consent of the Shareholders who are the parties to this Agreement, or their successors.

2.3 All shares now or hereafter owned by the Shareholders or prospective shareholders or transferors shall be subject to the provisions of this Agreement and the certificates representing same shall bear the following legend:

The sale, transfer or encumbrance of this Certificate is subject to an agreement dated as of ____[1]____, between _____[2]_____, _____[2]_____ and _____[2]_____. A copy of the Agreement is on file at the principal office of the Corporation. The agreement provides, among other things, for certain prior rights to purchase and certain obligations to sell the shares of stock evidenced by this Certificate, as well as for voting rights of Shareholders and Directors. By accepting this Certificate, the holder agrees to be bound by said agreement.

3. DIRECTORS

3.1 The initial Board of Directors shall consist of:

_____[8]_____,

_____[8]_____,

_____[8]_____,

(Document continued on next page)

9. The name of each person elected as officer of the corporation. (Note: each state has separate requirements as to the officers that are required. As a general rule, if there is more than one shareholder, the minimum requirement is two officers, a President and a Secretary/Treasurer.)

and they shall hold office until their successors are duly elected.

3.2 In all matters requiring the vote of the Board of Directors a majority shall suffice.

4. OFFICERS

4.1 The following shall serve as officers of the Corporation until their successors are duly elected:

President: _____[9]_____

Secretary: _____[9]_____

Treasurer: _____[9]_____

5. SALE OF STOCK

5.1 Each of the Shareholders covenants and agrees that he will not sell, assign, transfer, donate or otherwise dispose of, or pledge, hypothecate or otherwise encumber any of the shares of the Corporation's stock except upon the prior written consent of the remaining Shareholders.

6. COMPENSATION

6.1 Base Compensation. The compensation of all employees shall be fixed by the Board of Directors.

7. MISCELLANEOUS

7.1 Applicable Law. This Agreement shall be construed pursuant to the Laws of the State of _____[3]_____.

7.2 Notices. All notices provided for by this Agreement shall be made in writing either (i) by actual delivery of the notice into the hands of the parties thereunto entitled, or (ii) by mailing of the notice in the United States mails to the last known address of the party entitled thereto by Certified Mail - return receipt requested. If any notice is mailed, it shall be deemed to have been received five (5) days from the date postmarked on the envelope.

7.3 Headings. The headings have been inserted

(Document continued on next page)

10. The name of each Share-holder printed directly below the line, with that person to sign above the line.

as a matter of convenience to the parties and shall not affect the constructions or meaning thereof.

7.4   Binding Effect. This Agreement is binding upon and inures to the benefit of the Corporation, its successors, and assigns, and to the Shareholders and their respective heirs, personal representatives, successors and assigns.

7.5   Amendments. No waiver, modification or discharge of the terms hereunder shall be valid unless in writing and signed by the party or parties to be charged and only to the extent therein set forth.

7.6   Severability. If any part, section, phrase or term of this Agreement be deemed invalid, by operation of law or otherwise, it is the intention of the parties hereto that the remaining parts, sections, phrases and/or terms stand and continue in effect, to carry out the intent and purposes of the parties to this Agreement, to the extent permitted by the laws of the State of _____[3]_____.

7.7   Enforcement. Each of the parties hereto and the Corporation recognizes that the corporate stock herein contemplated to be purchased is unique, and each of them for themselves, their heirs, successors or assigns agrees and consents to the specific enforcement of this Agreement.

8.   CORPORATION TO BE BOUND

8.1   It is understood and agreed by and between the Shareholders that the Corporation shall be bound by all of the terms and conditions of this Agreement.

INTENDING TO BE LEGALLY BOUND, the parties hereto have caused this Shareholders Agreement to be executed as of the date first above written.

_____
[10]

_____
[10]

_____
[10]

BUY-SELL AGREEMENT (5-07)

When a non-publicly traded corporation is formed it is advisable to have an Agreement to establish the terms and conditions under which the shares owned by each Shareholder may be sold (Voluntary Transfer), transferred due to bankruptcy of the Shareholder (Involuntary Transfer) or purchased upon the death of a Shareholder. The Buy-Sell Agreement is usually executed at the same time as the Shareholders Agreement, also found in this chapter, and the two may be combined into a single agreement. Just as with the Shareholders Agreement, it is strongly urged that Buy-Sell procedures be established and memorialized in a written Buy-Sell Agreement at the time of, or soon after, the formation of the corporation when all concerned find it relatively easy to agree. Later, when matters may not be proceeding quite so smoothly, it may be less likely that agreement can be reached.

BUY-SELL AGREEMENT

1. The date the Agreement is signed.

2. The names of the Shareholders.

3. The name of the corporation.

Agreement made this __[1]__ day of _____, 19__ by and between _____[2]_____, _____[2]_____ and _____[2]_____, being all of the "Shareholders" of _____[3]_____ (the "Corporation").

The Shareholders desiring to set forth the terms and conditions under which their shares of stock in the Corporation may be transferred,

AGREE

1.   RIGHT OF FIRST REFUSAL-VOLUNTARY TRANSFER

1.1   Terms of the Offer, Offer Notice. It is understood and agreed that a Shareholder shall not be permitted to sell only a portion of his shares except as specifically provided herein. If any Shareholder shall desire to sell all the shares of the Corporation's stock owned by him (such Shareholder being hereinafter referred to as the "Offeror" and such shares being hereinafter referred to as the "Offered Shares"), then the Offeror shall give concurrent notice (the "Offer Notice") to the Corporation and to the other Shareholders (the Corporation and the other Shareholders being hereinafter referred to as the "Offerees"). The Offer Notice shall:

(a)   State the name and address of the person (the "Proposed Purchaser") to whom the Offeror proposes to sell the Offered Shares and the price at and the terms upon which he proposes to sell the Offered Shares to the Proposed Purchaser (and shall have attached thereto a commitment letter setting forth the substantial terms of the sale to the Proposed Purchaser); and

(Document continued on next page)

(b)   Constitute an offer to sell to the Offerees all, but not less than all of the Offered Shares at the same price and upon the same terms as the Offeror proposes to sell the Offered Shares to the Proposed Purchaser.

1.2   Acceptance of the Offer. The Offerees shall have a period of thirty (30) days after the date of the giving of the Offer Notice in which to accept the offer. Acceptance shall be made by giving concurrent notice thereof, within the thirty (30) day time limit, to the Offeror. In determining whether the Corporation shall accept such Offer the Offeror shall abstain from voting as a shareholder or director.

1.3   Priority Among Offerees. If all or any of the Offerees shall accept the offer made by the Offer Notice, then:

(a)   If the Corporation shall have accepted such offer, the Offeror shall sell and the Corporation shall purchase all or such portion of the Offered Shares as it desires of the Offeror's shares, at the price, upon the terms and in the manner set forth in the Offer Notice.

(b)   If the Corporation shall not have accepted such offer or it shall have accepted only as to a portion of the Offeror's Shares, the Offeror shall sell to the other accepting Offeree(s) and they shall purchase all of the balance of the Offered Shares.

1.4   Failure of Offerees to Accept. If none of the Offerees, within the required time, accepts the Offer made by the Offer Notice, the Offeror shall thereafter within sixty (60) days of giving of the Offer Notice have the right to sell all, but not less than all, of the Offered Shares, but only to the Proposed Purchaser at the price, upon the terms and in the manner set forth in the Offer Notice. If the Offeror shall not so sell the Offered Shares within such period, the Offer shall be deemed to have lapsed and the Offeror shall continue to hold the Offered Shares subject to the provisions of the Agreement. After such a lapse any offer or attempt to sell the shares shall be treated as an original offer under this article.

(Document continued on next page)

2.   INVOLUNTARY TRANSFER

2.1   If, other than by reason of a Shareholder's death, shares are transferred by operation of law to any person other than the Corporation (such as, but not limited to, a Shareholder's trustee in bankruptcy, a purchaser at any creditor's or court sale or the guardian or conservator of an incompetent Shareholder), the Corporation within sixty (60) days, or the remaining Shareholders within seventy (70) days of the Corporation's receipt of actual notice of the transfer, may notify such transferee of its desire to purchase all, but not less than all, of the shares so transferred ("Notice of Intent to Purchase"). In such a case, the purchase price shall be determined in accordance with the book value of the Corporation's stock as reflected on the most recent balance sheet.

3.   PURCHASE OBLIGATIONS UPON DEATH

3.1   Purchase by Corporation. Upon the death of a shareholder, his estate shall sell and the Corporation shall, as soon as practicable, purchase the shares which are owned by the deceased Shareholder at his death for the price and upon the terms hereinafter provided.

3.2   Determination of Price, Certificate of Value. For the purposes of determining the price to be paid under paragraph 3.1 hereof, the Shareholders agree to cause the Corporation to execute a Certificate of Value not less than annually, as of January 1 of each year (or such other date as may from time to time be determined by the Shareholders), computed in accordance with generally accepted accounting principles.

3.3   Alternative Purchase by Shareholders. To the extent that the Corporation is prevented by law from purchasing all or any portion of the shares owned by the deceased Shareholder's estate, the surviving Shareholders shall be entitled to purchase such shares pro rata at a price fixed in accordance with paragraph 3.2 hereof. Any shares purchased under this article by the Corporation shall then be retired or held as treasury stock as determined by the surviving Shareholders.

3.4   Freedom of Estate to Sell. If the Corporation is prevented by law from purchasing all or any portion of the shares owned by a deceased Shareholder hereunder, and if the remaining Shareholders fail or refuse to purchase

(Document continued on next page)

4. The state in which incorporated.

the remaining shares, then the estate shall be entitled to make such disposition of its shares as it may determine in its sole discretion.

4.   MISCELLANEOUS

        4.1   Applicable Law. This Agreement shall be construed pursuant to the Laws of the State of _____[4]_____.

        4.2   Notices. All notices provided for by this Agreement shall be made in writing either (i) by actual delivery of the notice into the hands of the parties thereunto entitled, or (ii) by mailing of the notice in the United States mails to the last known address of the party entitled thereto, by certified mail, return receipt requested. If any notice is mailed, it shall be deemed to have been received five (5) days from the date postmarked on the envelope.

        4.3   Headings. The headings have been inserted as a matter of convenience to the parties and shall not affect the construction or meaning thereof.

        4.4   Binding Effect. This Agreement is binding upon and inures to the benefit of the Corporation, its successors, and assigns, and to the Shareholders and their respective heirs, personal representatives, successors and assigns.

        4.5   Amendments. No waiver, modification or discharge of the terms hereunder shall be valid unless in writing and signed by the party or parties to be charged and only to the extent therein set forth.

        4.6   Severability. If any part, section, phrase or term of this Agreement be deemed invalid, by operation of law or otherwise, it is the intention of the parties hereto that the remaining parts, sections, phrases and/or terms stand and continue in effect, to carry out the intent and purposes of the parties to this Agreement, to the extent permitted by the laws of the State of _____[4]_____.

        4.7   Enforcement. Each of the parties hereto and the Corporation recognizes that the corporate stock herein contemplated to be purchased is unique, and each of them for themselves, their heirs, successors or assigns agrees and consents to the specific enforcement of this Agreement.

(Document continued on next page)

5. The name of each Share-holder printed directly below the line, with that person to sign above the line.

5. CORPORATION TO BE BOUND

5.1　It is understood and agreed by and between the Shareholders that the Corporation shall be bound by all of the terms and conditions of this Agreement.

INTENDING TO BE LEGALLY BOUND, the parties hereto have caused this Buy-Sell Agreement to be executed as of the date first above written.

_____
[5]

_____
[5]

_____
[5]

STOCK PURCHASE OPTION AGREEMENT (5-08)

A Stock Purchase Option is granted to key employees or others who may be providing the corporation with a benefit, such as a supplier who is extending credit, a party providing services at no charge or reduced charge, or a creditor who has loaned money to the corporation.

WARNING

Consultation with a local attorney is recommended to be sure that offering Stock Options in the company does not require the company to be registered either with the state or with the Securities and Exchange Commission.

STOCK PURCHASE OPTION AGREEMENT

1. The date the Agreement is signed.

2. The name of the corporation granting the Option.

3. The state of incorporation of the corporation granting the Option.

4. The name of the party receiving the Option (the Purchaser).

5. If the Purchaser is a corporation, insert the state of incorporation. Otherwise delete.

6. The number of shares, in words, that may be purchased.

7. The number of shares, in numbers, that may be purchased.

8. The price of each share, in numbers.

9. The date by which the purchase must be made.

10. The total number of shares, in numbers, that the corporation is authorized to issue.

11. The number of shares, in numbers, issued as of the date of the Agreement.

Agreement made this __[1]__ day of _____, 19__ by and between _____[2]_____, a _____[3]_____ corporation ("Corporation) and _____[4]_____ [5][, a _____ corporation] ("Purchaser").

1.   In consideration of Ten Dollars ($10.00) in hand paid, receipt of which is hereby acknowledged, the Corporation hereby grants to the Purchaser an Option, subject to the terms and conditions hereof, to purchase from the Corporation up to ____[6]____ (__[7]__) shares of its Common Stock at the price of $___[8]___ per share.

2.   The Option shall expire at 5:00 p.m. on _____[9]_____.

3.   The Option granted hereunder shall be exercisable by the giving of not less than seven (7) days' written notice of exercise to the Corporation specifying the number of Shares to be purchased with payment of the full purchase price accompanying such notice. Within fifteen (15) days after written notice from the Purchaser, the Corporation will deliver to the Purchaser a stock certificate representing the shares of stock purchased.

4.   By accepting this Option, the Purchaser agrees that any and all shares purchased upon the exercise of this Option shall be subject to a Shareholders Agreement and Buy-Sell Agreement executed by the Shareholders prior to the date of this Option Agreement and on file in the office of the Corporation.

5.   The Corporation represents that its authorized capital stock consists of __[10]__ shares of which ____[11]____ have been issued.

(Document continued on next page)

6. Neither the Purchaser nor Purchaser's legal representatives shall be or have any of the rights or privileges of a Shareholder of the Corporation in respect of any of the Shares issuable upon the exercise of this Option unless and until certificates representing such Shares shall have been issued and delivered.

7. In the event of the liquidation, dissolution or winding up of the Corporation, a notice of such anticipated liquidation, dissolution or winding up shall be mailed to the Purchaser in which event this Option shall expire on the service of such notice. Failure to give such notice or any defect therein shall not affect the legality or validity of the liquidation, dissolution or winding up, or any distribution in connection therewith.

8. All notices provided for by this Option shall be made in writing, either (i) by actual delivery of the notice into the hand of the party entitled or (ii) by mailing of the notice in the United States mails at the last known address of the party entitled thereto, by Certified Mail, return receipt requested.

9. Except as otherwise herein provided, this Option and the rights and privileges conferred hereby may not be transferred, assigned, pledged or hypothecated in any way (whether by operation of law or otherwise) and shall not be subject to execution, attachment or similar process. Upon any attempt to transfer, assign, pledge, hypothecate or otherwise dispose of this Option or any right or privilege conferred hereby, contrary to the provisions hereof, or upon the levy of any attachment or similar process on the rights and privileges conferred hereby, this Option shall immediately become null and void.

(Document continued on next page)

12. The name of the corporation granting the Option.

13. The name and title of the individual acting for the Corporation printed directly below the line, with that person to sign above the line.

14. The name of the Purchaser if a corporation. Otherwise delete the line.

15. If the Purchaser is an individual, delete "BY" and print the Purchaser's name directly below the line, with the Purchaser to sign above the line. If the Purchaser is a corporation, print the name and title of the individual acting for the corporation directly below the line, with that person to sign above the line.

INTENTING TO BE LEGALLY BOUND, the parties hereto have caused this Stock Purchase Option Agreement to be executed as of the date first above written.

_____[12]_____

BY_____
          [13]

ACCEPTED:

_____*[14]*_____

BY_____
          [15]

NOTICE OF ORGANIZATIONAL MEETING
OF INCORPORATORS (5-09)

The laws of most states provide that when there are two or more Incorporators the Organizational Meeting may be called at the request of any Incorporator upon written Notice given to the other Incorporators. The time required and the method of delivery of the Notice varies, so the corporation laws of your state should be consulted. For example, New York requires at least five days' notice by mail to each of the other Incorporators.

NOTICE OF ORGANIZATION MEETING
OF INCORPORATORS

1. The name of the corporation.

2. The date of the Meeting.

3. The time of the Meeting.

4. Choose one.

5. The address where the Meeting will be held.

6. The city and state where the Meeting will be held.

7. A brief description of any other matters that will be considered by the Incorporators, such as the issuance of stock certificates and the like.

8. The date of the Notice.

9. The name of the Incorporator calling for the Meeting printed directly below the line, with the Incorporator to sign above the line.

PLEASE TAKE NOTICE that the organizational meeting of the incorporators of _____[1]_____ will be held on _____[2]_____ at __[3]__ *[4][A.M.] OR [P.M.]* at _____[5]_____, _____[6]_____.

The purpose of the meeting will be the adopting of By-Laws for the governing and operation of the corporation, the election of directors to hold office until the first annual meeting of shareholders, _____[7]_____ and such other business as may regularly come before the meeting.

The meeting is open to all incorporators or their designees.

Dated _____[8]_____

_____
[9]   (Incorporator)

WAIVER OF NOTICE OF
ORGANIZATIONAL MEETING (5-10)

Scheduling problems may prevent timely notice of the Organizational Meeting from being sent so as to give each person sufficient notice. If each incorporator or subscriber waives such notice in writing, the Meeting can still be held as scheduled.

WAIVER OF NOTICE OF
ORGANIZATIONAL MEETING
of
_____[1]_____

1.   The name of the corporation.

2.   The time of day and date
of the Meeting.

3.   The address, city and
state where the Meeting will
be held.

4.   The date of signing the
Waiver.

5.   The name of the incorporator or shareholder printed
directly below the line, with
that person to sign above the
line.

The undersigned incorporator/subscriber for shares of stock of _____[1]_____ agrees and consents that the organizational meeting of _____[1]_____ be held as stated below and does waive all notice of the meeting and of any adjournment.

Time/Date of Meeting:_____[2]_____

Location of Meeting: _____[3]_____

_____[3]_____

Dated: _____[4]_____

_____
[5]

MINUTES OF ORGANIZATIONAL MEETING—
SOLE INCORPORATOR (5-11)

The most important benefit of forming a business as a corporation (as opposed to a sole proprietorship or a general partnership) is the protection of limited liability offered to the participants. With rare exception, a participant's potential loss is limited to his investment in the corporation. While offering the flexibility needed to accommodate large numbers of participants, a corporation need not have a cast of thousands, or even hundreds or tens. Most states recognize that a corporation can be formed by just one person. This form is used to record the Minutes of the Organizational Meeting of the Sole Incorporator.

Even though the sole incorporator effectively is the corporation, clear, concise and complete Minutes are still essential.

Note that the Sole Incorporator is likely to be the sole shareholder and is permitted to hold several officer's positions. Whatever the number of directors, the authors strongly urge that the number be an odd one because experience has taught that an even number of directors invites deadlock.

WARNINGS

The laws of most states give the power to recognize a corporation to the state alone and not to the town, city, county or federal government. Therefore, to be recognized and valid, the Charter/Articles of Incorporation/Certificate of Incorporation must be filed with the state government. The terms "Charter," Articles of Incorporation," and "Certificate of Incorporation" designate the same thing. All refer to the incorporating document whose name varies from state to state.

By filing the Charter/Articles of Incorporation/ Certificate of Incorporation with your state government, you have created a legal entity which the law will regard as perpetual unless formally dissolved. The creation of a corporation and its filing with your state government should not be undertaken lightly.

A word about taxes. Just as you have a Social Security number or Taxpayer Identification Number, under which your income tax returns are filed, so too your new corporation, your new legal entity, must also obtain a Taxpayer Identification Number by filing "Form SS-4—Application for Employer Identification Number" (even if you do not have, or plan to have, employees). This form can be obtained from any Internal Revenue Service office.

MINUTES OF ORGANIZATIONAL MEETING

of

_____[1]_____

1. The name of the corporation.

The undersigned, as the sole incorporator and shareholder of _____[1]_____, held an organizational meeting at the place and on the date stated below. At the meeting action was taken and it was:

(Document continued on next page)

2. Choose the appropriate name for the incorporating document depending on the name given to such document by the state in which the document is filed.

3. Delete if the state of filing merely accepts the document for filing but does not issue a receipt.

4. The name of the particular department of the state government in which the corporate documents are filed, typically but not necessarily the Department of State.

5. The state of incorporation.

6. The name of the attorney(s) who prepared the By-Laws. Delete if an attorney did not prepare the By-Laws.

7. The name of the each director who has accepted the appointment, printed above the line. (Note the commentary above as to the number of directors.)

8. The signature of each director.

9. The address, city and state of the principal office of the corporation (where the books and records will be kept).

10. The city and state where the Meeting was held.

11. The name of the sole incorporator printed directly below the line, with the sole incorporator to sign above the line.

12. The date of the Meeting.

"RESOLVED, that a copy of the *[2][Charter]* **OR** *[Articles of Incorporation]* **OR** *[Certificate of Incorporation]* setting forth the permitted corporate purposes *[3][, and the filing receipt issued by the Secretary of* _____*[4]*_____ *of* _____*[5]*_____ *showing the payment of the filing or organization fee or tax as fixed by law and the date of payment of such tax or fee]* be annexed to these Minutes."

"RESOLVED, that the By-Laws stating the regulations and rules adopted by the Corporation for its governing and operating, *[6][as prepared by* _____ *, as counsel for the Corporation]* are adopted in the form annexed to these Minutes."

"RESOLVED, that the persons whose names appear below were nominated and appointed as directors of the Corporation and by their signatures adjacent to their respective names, accepted such appointment:"

_____[7]_____   _____[8]_____

_____[7]_____   _____[8]_____

_____[7]_____   _____[8]_____

"RESOLVED, that the principal office of the Corporation be located at _____[9]_____."

_____[10]_____   _____
                                          [11]

Dated: _____[12]_____

MINUTES OF ORGANIZATIONAL MEETING—
TWO OR MORE INCORPORATORS (5-12)

The most important benefit to forming a business as a corporation (as opposed to a sole proprietorship or a general partnership) is the protection of limited liability offered to the participants. With rare exception, a participant's potential loss is no more than his investment in the corporation. While offering the flexibility needed to accommodate large numbers of participants, a corporation need not have a cast of thousands, or even hundreds or tens. This form is used to record the Minutes of the Organizational Meeting of two or more Incorporators.

The authors urge that the number of directors of a small (in terms of number of shareholders) or closely held corporation should be an odd number. Experience has taught that an even number of directors invites deadlock.

WARNINGS

The laws of most states give the power to recognize a corporation to the state alone and not to the town, city, county or federal government. Therefore, to be recognized and valid, the Charter/Articles of Incorporation/Certificate of Incorporation must be filed with the state government. The terms "Charter," Articles of Incorporation," and "Certificate of Incorporation" designate the same thing. All refer to the incorporating document whose name varies from state to state.

By filing the Charter/Articles of Incorporation/ Certificate of Incorporation with your state government, you have created a legal entity which the law will regard as perpetual unless formally dissolved. The creation of a corporation and its filing with your state government should not be undertaken lightly.

A word about taxes. Just as you have a Social Security number or Taxpayer Identification Number, under which your income tax returns are filed, so too your new corporation, your new legal entity, must also obtain a Taxpayer Identification Number by filing "Form SS-4—Application for Employer Identification Number" (even if you do not have, or plan to have, employees). This form can be obtained from any Internal Revenue Service office.

MINUTES OF ORGANIZATIONAL MEETING
of
_____[1]_____

1. The name of the corporation.

2. The time of the Meeting.

3. Choose one.

4. The date of the Meeting.

5. The address where the Meeting was held.

6. The city and state where the Meeting was held.

The organizational meeting of the incorporators of _____[1]_____ was held at ___[2]___ *[3][A.M.] OR [P.M.]* on _____[4]_____ at _____[5]_____, _____[6]_____.

(Document continued on next page)

7. The names of all the people present at the Meeting. Add or delete lines as necessary.

8. The name of the incorporator who called the meeting to order.

9. The name of the the incorporator elected to act as Chairman of the Meeting.

10. The name of the the incorporator elected to act as Secretary of the Meeting.

11. The name of any incorporator attending by proxy. Delete if there were no proxies submitted.

12. Choose the appropriate name depending on the name given to such document by the state in which the document is filed.

13. The name of the particular department of the state government in which the corporate documents are filed, typically, but not necessarily, the Department of State.

14. Delete if the state of filing merely accepts the document for filing but does not issue a receipt, then skip to No. 18.

15. The state of incorporation.

16. Delete if No. 14 was deleted.

17. The name of the attorney(s) who prepared the By-Laws. Delete if an attorney did not prepare the By-Laws.

The following incorporators were present:

_____[7]_____   _____[7]_____
_____[7]_____   _____[7]_____
_____[7]_____   _____[7]_____
_____[7]_____   _____[7]_____

Incorporator _____[8]_____ called the meeting to order. Upon motion duly made, seconded and carried, _____[9]_____ was elected as Chairman of the Meeting and _____[10]_____ was elected Secretary of the Meeting and each accepted his respective office.

The Secretary then read the form of Waiver of Notice of Organizational Meeting duly signed by all of the incorporators. Upon motion duly made, seconded and carried, the Secretary was directed to attach a copy of each executed Waiver to these Minutes. *[11][The Secretary examined and approved the proxy submitted by Incorporator _____. Upon motion duly made, seconded and carried, the Secretary was directed to attach a copy of each approved proxy to these Minutes].* The Secretary noted that the incorporators attending either in person or by proxy constituted a quorum.

The Chairman read the *[12][Charter]* **OR** *[Articles of Incorporation]* **OR** *[Certificate of Incorporation]* setting forth the permitted corporate purposes and noted that said document was filed with the Department of _____[13]_____ *[14][, and that the filing receipt was issued by the Secretary of _____[13]_____ of _____[15]_____ showing the payment of the filing or organization fee or tax as fixed by law and the date of payment of such tax or fee].* The Secretary was directed to attach a copy *[16][of each]* to these Minutes.

The Chairman then presented the proposed By-Laws stating the regulations and rules for the governing and operating of the Corporation, *[17][as prepared by _____, as counsel for the Corporation].* The By-Laws were read and discussed article by article. Upon motion duly made, seconded and carried, the By-Laws were adopted as the By-Laws of the Corporation and the Secretary was directed to attach a copy to these Minutes.

(Document continued on next page)

18. The name of each director. (Note the commentary above as to the number of directors.)

19. The signature of each director who has accepted the appointment signed above the line adjacent to his printed name.

20. The address, city and state of the principal office of the corporation (where the books and records of the corporation will be kept).

21. The time of adjournment of the Meeting.

22. The name of the Secretary of the Meeting printed directly below the line before the word "Secretary," with that person to sign above the line.

23. The name of the Chairman of the Meeting printed directly below the line before the word "Chairman," with that person to sign above the line.

The Chairman stated that election of directors was then in order. Nominations were called for and each person nominated was seconded. Upon motion duly made, second and carried, the following were elected as directors of the Corporation and by their signatures adjacent to their respective names, accepted their election and agreed to serve the term provided in the By–Laws of the Corporation:

_____[18]_____   _____[19]_____

_____[18]_____   _____[19]_____

_____[18]_____   _____[19]_____

The Chairman then stated that certain incorporators had previously signed subscriptions for shares of stock of the Corporation when issued. Upon motion duly made, seconded and carried, the directors were authorized to direct the officers of the Corporation, upon their appointment to issue shares of stock of the Corporation in the respective amounts to the subscribers and to direct the Secretary to prepare and keep a shareholders' list and transfer journal.

Upon motion duly made, seconded and carried the principal office of the Corporation was determined to be located at _____[20]_____.

There being no further business, on motion duly made, seconded and carried, the Meeting was adjourned at ____[21]____.

_____
[22] Secretary

Approved:

_____
[23] Chairman

Operating a Corporation 6

Once a corporation is formed, certain procedures must be followed to keep it running smoothly. The owners of the corporation, the shareholders, must meet at least annually. One purpose of the shareholders' meeting is to elect directors.

Directors typically meet monthly, their function being to make the financial and other policy decisions necessary to operate the corporation in the best interest of all of the shareholders. Additionally, the directors appoint officers to make the day-to–day business decisions. The discussions at both the shareholders' meetings and the directors' meetings are preserved in the corporate minutes. The actions of both shareholders and directors taken at these meetings are set forth in resolutions which are contained in these minutes.

Notices and Minutes of Shareholders' and Directors' Meetings
These sections provide forms for giving proper notice of meetings of shareholders and directors plus forms for minutes of those meetings.

Corporate Resolutions These forms provide guidance in preparing resolutions that deal with some of the more common organizational issues corporations encounter. Those that are used are to be inserted into the book of corporate minutes.

Stock The last section of this chapter deals with issues related to stock certificates, such as the endorsement of a stock certificate when it is sold or transferred (a stock power), how stock is voted by a shareholder who cannot personally attend a shareholders' meeting (a proxy), and how corporations and shareholders can protect themselves if a stock certificate is lost (by affidavit of lost certificate).

NOTICE OF ANNUAL MEETING
OF SHAREHOLDERS (6-01)

The by-laws of most corporations provide that specific Notice of Annual Meetings must be given in writing to each Shareholder, typically (if time allows) by mail. The Notice should state the time, location and the matters that will be presented to the Shareholders, for example: the election of Board members or the like. Most states mandate minimum and maximum times for Notice. Your state's corporation law should be consulted to determine the applicable time required. For example, New York law requires that Notice be given not less than 10 nor more than 50 days before the scheduled date of the Meeting.

NOTICE OF ANNUAL MEETING OF
SHAREHOLDERS
of
_____[1]_____

1. The name of the corporation.

2. The date of the Meeting.

3. The time of the Meeting.

4. Choose one.

5. The address where the Meeting will be held.

6. The city and state where the Meeting will be held.

7. A brief description of the purpose of the Meeting.

8. The last day by which shareholders must be "of record" for attendance at the Meeting.

9. The date of the Notice.

10. The name and title of the officer (typically the Secretary) giving the Notice printed directly below the line, with that person to sign above the line.

PLEASE TAKE NOTICE that the annual meeting of shareholders of _____[1]_____ will be held on _____[2]_____ at __[3]__ *[4][A.M.] OR [P.M.]* at _____[5]_____, _____[6]_____.

The purpose of the meeting will be _____[7]_____ and such other business as may regularly come before the shareholders.

The meeting is open to all shareholders of record, or their designees, as of the close of business on _____[8]_____.

Dated:_____[9]_____   _____[1]_____

BY:_____
                [10]

NOTICE OF SPECIAL MEETING
OF SHAREHOLDERS (6-02)

During the life of any corporation events may arise that must be brought to the attention of the shareholders and that require their vote, but that cannot wait until the next regularly scheduled or annual meeting. Such events may require that a Special Meeting be called, the Notice of which must be in writing.

Since a Special Meeting is usually called in response to a specific, unique set of circumstances, the Notice should state the specific purpose.

Most states mandate minimum and maximum times for Notice. Your state's corporation law should be consulted to determine the applicable time required. For example, New York law requires that Notice be given not less than 10 nor more than 50 days before the scheduled date of the Meeting.

NOTICE OF SPECIAL MEETING
OF SHAREHOLDERS
of
_____[1]_____

1. The name of the the corporation.

2. The date of the Meeting.

3. The time of the Meeting.

4. Choose one.

5. The address where the Meeting will be held.

6. The city and state where the Meeting will be held.

7. A brief description of the purpose of the Meeting.

8. The last day by which shareholders must be "of record" for attendance at the Meeting.

9. The date of the Notice.

10. The name and title of the officer (typically the Secretary) giving the Notice of the Meeting printed directly below the line, with that person to sign above the line.

PLEASE TAKE NOTICE that a special meeting of shareholders of _____[1]_____ will be held on _____[2]_____ at __[3]__ *[4][A.M.]* **OR** *[P.M.]* at _____[5]_____, _____[6]_____ for the purpose of _____[7]_____.

This special meeting is open to all shareholders of record, or their designees, as of the close of business on _____[8]_____.

Dated: _____[9]_____   _____[1]_____

BY:_____
          [10]

AFFIDAVIT OF MAILING OF NOTICE
OF MEETING OF SHAREHOLDERS (6-03)

The Secretary (or other officer) of the corporation responsible for mailing a Notice of a Meeting should give a statement under oath as to the date of mailing and the name and address of each shareholder to whom Notice was sent.

AFFIDAVIT OF MAILING OF
NOTICE OF *[1][ANNUAL]* **OR** *[SPECIAL]* MEETING
OF SHAREHOLDERS
of
_____[2]_____

1. Choose one.

2. The name of the corporation.

3. The state in which the statement is given.

4. The county in which the statement is given.

5. The name of the person giving the statement.

6. The title of the person giving the statement.

7. The date of mailing the Notices.

8. The state in which the Notices were mailed.

9. The name of the person giving the statement printed directly below the line, with that person to sign above the line.

10. A Notary Public fills in the date, and signs and seals the form by affixing his stamp or seal.

STATE OF _____[3]_____)
COUNTY OF _____[4]_____) ss.:

_____[5]_____ being duly sworn deposes and says:

    I am the _____[6]_____ of _____[2]_____, that on _____[7]_____ I deposited in an official depository maintained under the exclusive care and custody of the United States Postal Service located in the State of _____[8]_____, a true and complete copy of the Notice of *[1][Annual* **OR** *[Special]* meeting of the shareholders of _____[2]_____, each enclosed in a sealed, postage paid wrapper to each shareholder whose name appears on the attached list at the respective address adjacent to each name.

_____
[9]

Sworn to before me this

__[10]__ day of _____, 19__

_____
Notary Public

WAIVER OF NOTICE OF
MEETING OF SHAREHOLDERS (6-04)

Circumstances such as scheduling or even clerical oversight may prevent Notice of a regular or special meeting of Shareholders from being sent so as to give Shareholders the advanced notice required by either the corporate by-laws or state law. If each Shareholder waives such notice in writing, the Meeting can still be held as scheduled.

WAIVER OF NOTICE OF
MEETING OF SHAREHOLDERS
of
_____[1]_____

1. The name of the corporation.

2. Choose one.

3. The time of day and date of the Meeting.

4. The address, city and state where the Meeting will be held.

5. The date of signing the Waiver.

6. The name of the shareholder printed directly below the line, with the shareholder to sign above the line.

7. The number of shares held by the person signing.

The undersigned shareholder of _____[1]_____ agrees and consents that the *[2][regular] OR [special]* meeting of shareholders be held as stated below for the purpose of such business as may lawfully come before such meeting and does waive all notice of the meeting and of any adjournment.

Time/Date of Meeting:_____[3]_____

Location of Meeting: _____[4]_____

_____[4]_____

Dated: _____[5]_____   _____
                                    [6]

Number of shares: _____[7]_____

MINUTES OF SHAREHOLDERS' MEETING (6-05)

The purpose of taking Minutes at a Shareholders' Meeting is to provide a lasting record of the proceedings, to record the people present (to ensure a quorum), and to record the actions (the "resolutions") taken. The wise Secretary of the Meeting will take the time necessary to make notes in order to be able to reconstruct, for the Minutes, the background discussion and comments concerning the matters discussed. Such complete Minutes may prove invaluable in the future. Because of this, the duties of the Secretary of the Meeting are not to be taken lightly.

While there is no required or correct form for recording proceedings of Shareholders' Meetings, history and tradition have developed a recognized, consistent approach. The particular style, length and depth of Minutes will depend on the needs and desires of the corporation and its Shareholders.

MINUTES OF SHAREHOLDERS' MEETING
of
_____[1]_____

1. The name of the corporation.

2. Choose one.

3. Delete if the Meeting is held at a location other than the office of the corporation.

4. The address, city and state where the Meeting was held.

5. The date of the Meeting.

6. The time of the Meeting.

7. The title of the person acting as Chairman of the Meeting (typically, but not necessarily, the president of the corporation).

8. The title of the person acting as Secretary of the Meeting (typically, but not necessarily the secretary of the corporation.)

9. Choose one. If a Waiver of Notification of Meeting was issued, choose the second alternative.

10. The date of the last Shareholders' Meeting.

MINUTES of *[2][annual]* **OR** *[special]* meeting of the shareholders of _____[1]_____, held at *[3][the office of the Corporation,]* _____[4]_____, on _____[5]_____ at ____[6]____.

The meeting was called to order by the President who stated the purpose of the *[2][annual]* **OR** *[special]* meeting. The _____[7]_____ of the Corporation acted as Chairman of the Meeting. The _____[8]_____ of the Corporation acted as Secretary of the Meeting.

Upon noting the presence of shareholders, either in person or by valid proxy, the Secretary stated that a quorum of shareholders was present. [9][The Secretary submitted the form of Notice of Meeting and the Affidavit of Mailing of Notice of Meeting together with the list of shareholders attached and then read the roll of stockholders as they appear on the books of the Corporation. Upon motion duly made, seconded and carried, the Secretary was directed to attach a copy of the Notice and Affidavit to these Minutes.] OR [The Secretary then read the form of Waiver of Notice of Meeting duly signed by all shareholders. Upon motion duly made, seconded and carried, the Secretary was directed to attach a copy of the Waiver of Notice of Meeting to these Minutes.]

Upon request by the Chairman, the Secretary read the Minutes of the Meeting of the Shareholders held on _____[10]_____, which were approved.

(Document continued on next page)

11. The names of the people elected as directors of the corporation. (The form provides five spaces; however care should be taken to review the by-laws of the corporation since the by-laws will state the number permitted for that corporation.)

12. List all other matters discussed at the Meeting, who initiated each discussion, the substance of each discussion, the recommendations made and by whom, and any resolutions voted upon (even if rejected).

13. The time of adjournment of the Meeting.

14. The name of the Secretary of the Meeting printed directly below the line, with that person to sign above the line. (Note: It should be the same as No. 8.)

Upon request by the Chairman, the Treasurer presented his report. After discussion, the report was approved and on motion duly made and seconded, the Secretary was directed to attach a copy of the report to these Minutes.

The following were duly nominated and were, upon affirmative vote, elected as directors of the Corporation to serve the term set forth in the By-Laws of the Corporation or until their successors are elected:

_____[11]_____   _____[11]_____

_____[11]_____   _____[11]_____

_____[11]_____

After discussion and due deliberation by the shareholders, upon motion duly made, seconded and carried by affirmative vote it was

"RESOLVED, that all of the decisions made and acts and action taken by the Board of Directors and the officers of the Corporation since the last meeting of the shareholders are ratified and approved."

_____[12]_____
_____
_____.

There being no further business, on motion duly made, seconded and carried, the Meeting was adjourned at ____[13]____.

_____
[14] Secretary

NOTICE OF MEETING OF DIRECTORS (6-06)

Generally the shareholders of a corporation are absentee owners. They elect Directors to operate the business in their absence but on their behalf. The elected Directors determine policy. The Directors in turn appoint officers as the day-to-day managers of the corporation to carry out the policy decisions made by the board.

Directors meet regularly, perhaps as frequently as monthly but certainly no less than annually (and usually immediately after the annual Stockholders' Meeting). Notices of Meetings of Directors should be in writing, as this form provides.

NOTICE OF MEETING OF DIRECTORS
of
_____[1]_____

1. The name of the corporation.

2. The date of the Meeting.

3. The time of the Meeting.

4. Choose one.

5. The address where the Meeting will be held.

6. The city and state where the Meeting will be held.

7. The date of the Notice.

8. The name and title of the officer (typically the Secretary) giving the Notice printed directly below the line, with that person to sign above the line.

PLEASE TAKE NOTICE that a regular meeting of the Board of Directors of _____[1]_____ will be held on _____[2]_____ at __[3]__ *[4][A.M.] **OR** [P.M.]* at _____[5]_____, _____[6]_____, for such business as may properly come before the Board.

Dated: _____[7]_____   _____[1]_____

BY: _____
            [8]

NOTICE OF SPECIAL MEETING
OF DIRECTORS (6-07)

        Just as unforeseen events may require the attention of and vote by shareholders, so events which cannot wait for the next regularly scheduled meeting may require the attention of and vote by the Directors. Such an event may require calling a Special Meeting. Notice of this meeting must be in writing to the Directors.

        Since a Special Meeting is usually in response to specific, unique circumstances, the Notice should state the specific purpose for the Meeting.

NOTICE OF SPECIAL MEETING
OF DIRECTORS
of
_____[1]_____

1. The name of the the corporation.	PLEASE TAKE NOTICE that a special meeting of the Board of Directors of _____[1]_____ will be held on _____[2]_____ at __[3]__ *[4][A.M.]* **OR** *[P.M.]* at _____[5]_____, _____[6]_____, for the purpose of _____[7]_____.
2. The date of the Meeting.	
3. The time of the Meeting.	
4. Choose one.	
5. The address where the Meeting will be held.	Dated: _____[8]_____ _____[1]_____
6. The city and state where the Meeting will be held.	BY: _____
7. A brief description of the purpose of the Meeting.	[9]
8. The date of the Notice.	
9. The name and title of the officer (typically the Secretary) giving the Notice of the Meeting printed directly below the line, with that person to sign above the line.	

WAIVER OF NOTICE OF
MEETING OF DIRECTORS (6-08)

Circumstances such as scheduling problems or even clerical oversight may prevent Notice of a regular or special meeting of the Board of Directors from being sent so as to give the Directors sufficient advanced notice required by either the corporate by-laws or state law. If each Director waives such Notice in writing, the Meeting can still be held as scheduled.

WAIVER OF NOTICE OF
MEETING OF DIRECTORS
of
_____[1]_____

1. The name of the the corporation.

2. Choose one.

3. The time of day and the date of the Meeting.

4. The address, city and state where the Meeting will be held.

5. The date of signing the Waiver.

6. The name of the director printed directly below the line, with the director to sign above the line.

The undersigned director of _____[1]_____ agrees and consents that the *[2][regular]* **OR** *[special]* meeting of the Board of Directors of _____[1]_____ be held as stated below for the purpose of such business as may lawfully come before such meeting and does waive all notice of the meeting and any adjournment.

Time/Date of meeting: _____[3]_____

Location of meeting: _____[4]_____

_____[4]_____

Dated: _____[5]_____   _____

[6]

MINUTES OF DIRECTORS' MEETING (6-09)

The purpose of taking Minutes at a Directors' Meeting is to provide a lasting record of the proceedings, to record the people present and the actions (the "resolutions") taken. The wise Director or Secretary of the Meeting will take the time necessary to make notes in order to be able to reconstruct, for the Minutes, the background discussion and comments concerning the matters discussed. Such complete Minutes may prove invaluable if, in the future when a particular Director may no longer be associated with the corporation, the corporation needs to establish the "business judgment" behind a particular resolution or to establish the fiduciary obligations of any individual Director to the corporation. Because of this, the duties of the Secretary of the Meeting are not to be taken lightly.

Resolutions are recorded in the Minutes of the meeting. The Corporate Resolutions later in this chapter contain resolutions for commonly encountered situations.

While there is no required or correct form for recording proceedings of Directors' Meetings, history and tradition have developed a recognized, consistent approach. The particular style, length and depth of Minutes will depend on the needs and desires of the corporation and its Directors.

MINUTES OF DIRECTORS' MEETING
of
_____[1]_____

1. The name of the corporation.

2. Choose one.

3. Delete if the Meeting is held at a location other than the office of the corporation.

4. The street address, city and state where the Meeting was held.

5. The date of the Meeting.

6. The time of the Meeting.

7. The name of each director attending the Meeting. (The form provides five spaces; however the number of directors for a particular corporation is determined by its by-laws.)

8. Choose one depending on whether all directors were present.

9. If any other person attended, state his name and any title such as "accountant," "legal counsel" or the like. Otherwise delete.

MINUTES of a *[2][regular]* **OR** *[special]* meeting of the Board of Directors of _____[1]_____, held at *[3][the office of the Corporation]*, _____[4]_____, on _____[5]_____ at ____[6]____.

The following directors were present:

_____[7]_____   _____[7]_____

_____[7]_____   _____[7]_____

_____[7]_____

being *[8][a quorum in accordance with the By-Laws of the Corporation]* **OR** *[all of the directors of the Corporation]*. *[9][Also present by invitation of the Board:*

_____

_____ *.]*

(Document continued on next page)

10. The name of the person acting as Chairman of the Meeting (typically, but not necessarily, the president of the corporation).

11. The corporate title, if any, of the Chairman of the Meeting, such as "Director," "President" or the like.

12. The name of the person acting as Secretary of the Meeting (typically, but not necessarily, the secretary of the corporation).

13. The corporate title, if any, of the Secretary of the Meeting.

14. Choose one depending on whether a Waiver of Notice of Meeting was issued.

15. Choose one depending on whether Waivers of Notice were received.

16. The date of the last Meeting of the Board.

17. The name of the director who initiated any discussion.

18. List any other matters discussed by the Board, the substance of each discussion, the recommendations made and by whom, and any resolutions voted upon (even if rejected).

19. Fill in the name of each officer elected.

20. The time of adjournment of the Meeting.

21. The name of the Secretary of the Meeting plus the title "Secretary" printed directly below the line, with that person to sign above the line. (Note: it should be the same as No. 12.)

_____[10]_____, _____[11]_____ of the Corporation, acted as Chairman of the Meeting. _____[12]_____, _____[13]_____ of the Corporation, acted as Secretary of the Meeting. The Chairman noted the presence of a quorum.

The Secretary *[14][presented the form of Notice of Meeting and proof of mailing of the Notice to the Directors.]* **OR** *[presented written Waivers of Notice signed by all directors of the Corporation.]* On motion duly made and seconded, the Secretary was directed to attach the *[15][Notice of Meeting and proof of mailing]* **OR** *[Waivers of Notice]* to these Minutes.

The Secretary read the Minutes of the Meeting of the Board held on _____[16]_____ which were approved.

The Treasurer presented his report. After discussion, the report was approved and on motion duly made and seconded, the Secretary was directed to attach the report to these Minutes.

Upon motion made by Director _____[17]_____, seconded and carried, the Board opened a discussion concerning the issue of _____[18]_____ _____ _____.

The following were duly nominated and were, upon unanimous vote, elected as officers of the Corporation to serve the term set forth in the By-Laws of the Corporation or until their successors are elected:

[19]   President: _____

Vice President: _____

Secretary: _____

Treasurer: _____

There being no further business, on motion duly made, seconded and carried, the Meeting was adjourned at ____[20]____.

_____
[21] Secretary

RESIGNATION OF DIRECTOR OR OFFICER (6-10)

While a verbal exchange of "I quit"/"You're fired" is common, tradition, custom and simple courtesy require a written letter of Resignation, particularly if the person resigning is a Director or Officer of a business. A Resignation should be kept simple. The date on which the Resignation becomes effective (either immediately or on some particular date in the future) is the most important element.

RESIGNATION OF DIRECTOR OR OFFICER

1. The name and address of the business.

2. The date of the Resignation letter, which may or may not be the same as the date the Resignation becomes effective.

3. The name of the individual to whom the Resignation is to be directed.

4. The name of the company.

5. Choose one.

6. The resigning person's title.

7. Choose one.

8. The date the Resignation is to take effect.

9. The name and title of the person resigning printed directly below the line, with that person to sign above the line.

_____[1]_____   _____[2]_____

_____

_____

_____

Attention: _____[3]_____

Gentlemen:

    Please be advised that I hereby tender my resignation from _____[4]_____ *[5][as a Director]* **OR** *[and the office of _____[6]_____] effective [7][immediately]* **OR** *[as of _____[8]_____].*

                              Very truly yours,

                              _____
                                          [9]

CORPORATE RESOLUTION—AMENDING THE ARTICLES
OF INCORPORATION OR CORPORATE BY-LAWS (6-11)

This Corporate Resolution is to be used in the Minutes of Directors' Meeting.

Over its life, a corporation may determine that its interests can be better served by doing things differently or doing different things. Such changes may require amending the corporation's Articles of Incorporation (its charter) or its By-laws—or both. Typical of the changes would be a change in the corporate structure such as the kind of stock it issues or the number or term of its directors, the corporations permitted purpose or powers, or even its name.

The recognition of the need for such change may originate either with the shareholders or with a director, but the directors must recommend the changes. If a change is such that the Articles of Incorporation (also called Certificate of Incorporation) or the By-laws must be amended, a vote of the shareholders will be necessary. If, and only if, the directors determine that the proposed change is in the best interests of the corporation, the directors must propose a specific resolution and direct that it be submitted to the shareholders, either at the next regular meeting or at a special meeting.

Note: an Amendment of the Articles of Incorporation will require a filing with the appropriate state agency (typically, the Secretary of State), because it is considered a public document. On the other hand, an Amendment of the By-laws will not require such a filing because By-laws are not public documents.

CORPORATE RESOLUTION—AMENDING THE
ARTICLES OF INCORPORATION OR
CORPORATE BY-LAWS

1. The name of the director making the motion.

2. The issue or change to be discussed.

3. The substance of the discussion.

4. The name of the director making the motion.

5. Choose one.

6. A description of the proposed change.

7. Choose one.

8. The date of the meeting.

Upon motion made by Director _____[1]_____, seconded and carried, the Board opened a discussion concerning the issue of _____[2]_____.
_____[3]_____
_____
_____.

Upon motion made by Director _____[4]_____, seconded and carried, it is

"RESOLVED, that the Board recommend to the shareholders that the *[5][Articles of Incorporation]* **OR** *[By-Laws]* be amended to provide: ___[6]___
_____
_____,

and further

RESOLVED, that such recommendation be presented to the shareholders at the next *[7][special]* **OR** *[regular]* meeting of the shareholders to be held on _____[8]_____."

CORPORATE RESOLUTION—
SMALL BUSINESS CORPORATION
(SUB-CHAPTER S CORPORATION) (6-12)

This Corporate Resolution is to be used in the Minutes of Directors' Meeting.

Certain corporations which, among other requirements, have less than 35 stockholders, have only one class of stock, and whose stockholders are individuals, estates or certain trusts, none of whom are non-resident aliens may, together with their shareholders, derive tax benefits from treatment as a "small business corporation" (also referred to as an "S Corporation" or a "Sub-Chapter S corporation").

Note: this election for treatment as a small business corporation is valid only if made upon the consent of all the shareholders on the day the election is made.

CORPORATE RESOLUTION—
SMALL BUSINESS CORPORATION
(SUB-CHAPTER S CORPORATION)

1. The name of the director making the motion.

2. The name of the director making the motion.

3. The name of the tax authority of the state in which the corporation files its state tax returns.

4. The state in which the corporation files its state tax returns.

Upon motion made by Director _____[1]_____, seconded and carried, the Board opened a discussion concerning the issue of an election by the Corporation to be treated as a "small business corporation" for income tax purposes. The Secretary noted that the holders of all of the issued stock of the Corporation have consented to such election and presented forms of written consent to such an election. The Chairman directed that the forms of written consent be attached to these Minutes. The Treasurer of the Corporation advised that such election was also recommended by the accountant for the Corporation. Upon motion made by _____[2]_____, seconded and carried, it was

"RESOLVED, the appropriate officers of the Corporation are hereby authorized and directed to take all reasonable and necessary action to comply with the rules and regulations of the Internal Revenue Service and the _____[3]_____ of _____[4]_____ to make the election for treatment as a Sub-Chapter S Corporation pursuant to Internal Revenue Code, Sec. 1361, et seq."

CORPORATE RESOLUTION—INTERNAL REVENUE
CODE SEC. 1244 STOCK (6-13)

This Corporate Resolution is to be used in the Minutes of Directors' Meeting.

Every stockholder of a new corporation would like to believe that the new venture will become a huge success. He would rather not think that its shares may, in the future, be sold at a loss. Unfortunately, that can happen. With advanced planning, a corporation may ease the pain and at the same time make itself significantly more attractive to investors if it can offer beneficial tax treatment on the investors' personal tax returns in the event of sale of the stock at a loss.

This form is included for the purpose of alerting the reader to the need for advanced planning. It provides the by-laws provision necessary to set up the corporate mechanism so that some tax benefits may be realized in the event of a future sale at a loss. However, since this book is not meant to be a tax treatise, it is strongly urged that the reader consult his own accountant or tax preparer for a further discussion of Internal Revenue Code Sec. 1244.

CORPORATE RESOLUTION—INTERNAL REVENUE
CODE SEC. 1244 STOCK

1. The name of the director making the motion.

2. The name of the director making the motion.

Upon motion made by Director _____[1]_____, seconded and carried, the Board opened a discussion concerning the desirability of raising capital from investors in the Corporation and how the Corporation's attractiveness to investors would be enhanced if the Corporation were to be organized and operated as a small business corporation as defined in Internal Revenue Service Code Sec. 1244 and so that the shares issued by the Corporation are "Sec. 1244 Stock." It was noted that such a decision would permit the shareholders to treat any loss arising out of the sale or exchange of the Corporation's stock as "ordinary loss" on the shareholder's personal income tax return. Upon motion made by _____[2]_____, seconded and carried, it was

"RESOLVED, that the sale and issuance of stock of the Corporation be made in compliance with Internal Revenue Code Sec. 1244 such that the shareholders of the Corporation receive the benefits of such tax treatment and to that end, the appropriate officers of the Corporation are hereby authorized and directed to take all reasonable and necessary action to comply with the rules and regulations of the Internal Revenue Code Sec. 1244 and to issue stock in the Corporation such that the amount of money and other property received by the Corporation for stock, as a contribution to capital and paid in surplus, does not exceed $1,000,000 at the time of issuance of the stock, and it is further

RESOLVED, that the appropriate officers of the Corporation are authorized and directed to place any appropriate legends or notations on all such stock certificates if required."

CORPORATE RESOLUTION—MEDICAL CARE
COST REIMBURSEMENT PLAN (6-14)

This Corporate Resolution is to be used in the Minutes of Directors' Meeting.

High medical costs are a fact of life that must be faced by any individual or corporation. Competent, skilled employees have come to expect that, in addition to their salary or wages, they will be assisted in meeting these high costs. The corporation that can offer such assistance is more likely to attract better qualified and motivated employees. This form sets up the corporation's authority to offer such assistance.

CORPORATE RESOLUTION—MEDICAL CARE
COST REIMBURSEMENT PLAN

1. The name of the director making the motion.

2. The name of the director suggesting.

3. The name of the director suggesting.

4. The length of employment required, for example "one year."

5. The name of the director suggesting.

6. The name of the director suggesting.

7. The dollar amount, in numbers, of the upper limit to be reimbursed.

8. The dollar amount, in numbers, of the upper limit to be advanced.

9. The name of the director suggesting.

Upon motion made by Director _____[1]_____, seconded and carried, the Board opened a discussion noting the high cost of adequate medical care and concerning the desirability of attracting and benefitting employees of the Corporation by the ability to reduce employee concerns over such high costs. Director _____[2]_____ acknowledging the high costs, stated that in his opinion the best interests of the Corporation might be better served by not offering unlimited reimbursement, but rather imposing an annual cap or ceiling and conditioning any reimbursement on reasonable eligibility standards. Director _____[3]_____ suggested that eligibility be limited to directors, officers and full-time employees with _____[4]_____ of service to the Corporation. Director _____[5]_____ questioned whether eligibility be extended to dependents of directors, officers or eligible employees as well. Director _____[6]_____ suggested that costs below a certain amount be reimbursed only and that costs above such amount would, upon written request, be advanced and that in either event, an annual limit of a certain amount per person be imposed. The Board agreed on $ _____[7]_____ and $ _____[8]_____ for the limits on reimbursements and annual advances respectively. Director _____[9]_____ suggested that any advance or reimbursement also be limited to amounts not provided by any health, accident or disability insurance covering any director, officer, eligible employee or dependent regardless of ownership of such policy. Upon motion made by

(Document continued on next page)

10. The name of the director making the motion.

_____[10]_____, seconded and carried, it was

"RESOLVED, that the Secretary be authorized and directed to take all reasonable and necessary steps to devise, approve and implement a plan of medical care cost reimbursement within the guidelines established by the Board, for all directors, officers and eligible employees having _____[4]_____ of service to the Corporation and all dependents, as defined in Internal Revenue Code Sec. 152, of the directors, officers and eligible employees. It is the intention of the Corporation that any benefits payable shall be excluded from the gross income of the recipient of such benefit."

CORPORATE RESOLUTION—
INSURANCE PLAN (6-15)

This Corporate Resolution is to be used in the Minutes of Directors' Meeting.

A corporation may realize that the death of a particular (key) corporate officer would threaten its very existence or that it might be required to pay a large sum to the widow of an officer. The corporation may elect to take out a life insurance policy on that officer. This form provides the authority to do so.

CORPORATE RESOLUTION—INSURANCE PLAN

1. The name of the director making the motion.

2. The title of the corporate officer to be insured.

3. The name of the corporate officer to be insured.

4. The name of the director making the motion.

5. The type of insurance, for example: term, straight or whole life or the like.

6. The dollar amount of the insurance, in numbers.

Upon motion made by Director
_____[1]_____, seconded and carried, the Board opened a discussion concerning the benefit received by the Corporation from the past and future services and contribution made by its _____[2]_____, _____[3]_____, and the loss to the Corporation that would result from the death while in office of _____[3]_____. Upon motion made by _____[4]_____, seconded and carried, it was

"RESOLVED, that the Corporation apply for, own, pay all premiums as and when due and be the irrevocable beneficiary of a policy of _____[5]_____ life insurance on the life of _____[3]_____ which will provide benefits payable to the Corporation upon the death of _____[3]_____ in the amount of $ _____[6]_____. _____[3]_____ is directed to make himself available and to submit to such medical examination as may, from time to time, be required."

CORPORATE RESOLUTION—CHANGE OF BANK
AND OTHER BANKING MATTERS (6-16)

This Corporate Resolution is to be used in the Minutes of Directors' Meeting.

Banking matters such as writing checks and borrowing money are vital to every business. Every corporation needs to establish clear and concise policies concerning the number of officers necessary to sign checks and the authority to borrow money. This form accomplishes those purposes while providing protection to the corporation by requiring that checks and loans in excess of a predetermined limit must have more than one signature.

CORPORATE RESOLUTION—CHANGE OF BANK
AND OTHER BANKING MATTERS

1. The name of the director making the motion.

2. The name of the director making the motion.

3. The name of the present bank.

4. The name of the new bank.

5. The address of the new bank.

6. The dollar amount, in numbers, for checks below a certain limit (for example $500) requiring the number of signature(s) specified in No. 7 (typically only one).

7. The number of signatures required, in numbers.

8. The dollar amount, in numbers, for checks above a certain amount (for example $500) requiring the number of signatures specified in No. 9 (typically two).

Upon motion made by Director _____[1]_____, seconded and carried, the Board opened a discussion concerning the growth of the Corporation having exceeded the capabilities of its present bank to serve the financial needs of the Corporation. Discussion continued as to the present banking needs of the Corporation and the authority needed by the officers to operate and manage the Corporation. The services offered by several competing banks were then discussed. Upon motion made by _____[2]_____, seconded and carried, it was

"RESOLVED, that the Treasurer or other appropriate officer of the Corporation is authorized and directed to close and terminate all accounts maintained at _____[3]_____ as soon as practicable and open and maintain such accounts in the name of and for the benefit of the Corporation as the Treasurer may determine to be necessary at _____[4]_____, with offices located at _____[5]_____, which is hereby designated as the depository of funds of the Corporation. The officers and agents of the Corporation are authorized and directed to deposit any monies of the Corporation in _____[4]_____, and it is further

RESOLVED, that any draft, check and other instrument or order for the payment of money drawn against any accounts of the Corporation with the depository for amounts not to exceed $ ____[6]____ shall be signed by any __[7]__ of the following officers of the Corporation and for amounts in excess of $____[8]____ shall

(Document continued on next page)

9. The number of signatures required, in numbers.

10. List by title all officers, assistants and others who may sign the corporation's checks.

11. The dollar amount, in numbers, for loans below a certain amount (for example $5,000) requiring the number of signature(s) specified in No. 12 (typically only one).

12. The number of signatures required, in numbers.

13. The dollar amount, in numbers, for loans above a certain amount (for example $5,000) requiring the number of signatures specified in No. 14 (typically two).

14. The number of signatures required, in numbers.

15. List by title all officers, assistants and others who may obligate the corporation by borrowing money for its needs.

be signed by any __[9]__ of the following officers of the Corporation:

_____[10]_____
_____
_____,

and it is further

RESOLVED, that the depository is authorized to place to the credit of the Corporation funds, drafts, checks or other property that may be delivered to the depository for deposit to the accounts of the Corporation, endorsed with the name of the Corporation, whether by stamp, facsimile, manual or mechanical or other signature, except that if any such item shall bear or be accompanied by direction for deposit to a specific account of the Corporation maintained at the depository, the deposit shall be to the credit of that specific account, and it is further

RESOLVED, that the Corporation borrow from time to time from the depository and that any drafts, notes, agreements, trust receipts or other similar documents for amounts not to exceed $ _____[11]_____ shall be signed by any __[12]__ of the following officers of the Corporation and for amounts in excess of $ ___[13]___ shall be signed by any __[14]__ of the following officers of the Corporation: _____[15]_____

_____
_____,

and it is further

RESOLVED, that the appropriate officers are authorized and directed to execute such resolutions, signature specimen cards and the like as may be reasonable and necessary to implement these resolutions of the Board."

CORPORATE RESOLUTION—RATIFICATION OF
OFFICERS' ACTS (6-17)

This Corporate Resolution is to be used in the Minutes of Directors' Meeting.

Periodically, the Officers of a corporation may undertake acts which are beyond the scope of their authority or are properly the responsibility of the Board of Directors. If such acts are in the best interests of the corporation, the directors wisely may choose to ratify the acts rather than reject them. This form provides the Directors' resolution to do so. If the Officers' acts are subsequently ratified by the Board of Directors, the granting of authority is done retroactively to the time of the transactions. Therefore, Ratification absolves the Officers from liability for the acts and transfers that liability to the corporation. This form is set up to provide Ratification of either disclosed acts by specific Officers or all acts by all Officers.

CORPORATE RESOLUTION—RATIFICATION OF OFFICERS' ACTS

1. The name of the director making the motion.

2. The title or name of the officer or officers who undertook the specific act(s).

3. The name of the director making the motion.

4. Choose one depending on whether certain specific acts, or all acts since the last meeting, are to be ratified.

5. The title or name of the officer or officers who undertook the specific act(s).

6. The specific act(s).

7. The titles of all officers whose act(s) the Board of Directors wishes to ratify.

Upon motion made by Director _____[1]_____, seconded and carried, the Board opened a discussion concerning certain acts having been undertaken by _____[2]_____. Discussion of certain specific acts prompted the Chairman to point out that while these acts properly may have required the affirmative vote of the Board of Directors, they were nevertheless undertaken as being in the best interests of the Corporation. Upon motion made by _____[3]_____, seconded and carried, it was

"RESOLVED, that *[4][the actions of* _____*[5]_____ taken with regard to* _____*[6]_____] OR [all acts and transactions of* _____*[7]_____ taken or made since the last meeting of the Board of Directors which have been disclosed to the Board at this meeting]* are hereby ratified and approved as actions of the Board of Directors."

CORPORATE RESOLUTION—
AUTHORITY OF OFFICER (6-18)

This Corporate Resolution is to be used in the Minutes of Directors' Meeting.

Since the primary responsibility of the Board of Directors of every corporation is to establish policy and then to appoint Officers to implement that policy, the directors must give Officers sufficient authority to act. This form provides either broad, general authority or specific authority.

CORPORATE RESOLUTION—
AUTHORITY OF OFFICER

1. The name of the director making the motion.

2. The title of the officer to be given authority.

3. The name of the director making the motion.

4. Choose one depending on whether general or specific authority is to be given.

5. The title of the officer to be given authority.

6. The name of the other party to a specific contract.

7. The terms of a specific contract, such as "entering into an agreement for the sale of the Corporation's widgets in Europe."

Upon motion made by Director _____[1]_____, seconded and carried, the Board opened a discussion concerning the authority of the _____[2]_____ to transact business on behalf of the Corporation. The Chairman pointed out the need to give the officers of the Corporation authority so that they could best manage the affairs of the Corporation. Upon motion made by _____[3]_____, seconded and carried, it was

"RESOLVED, *[4][that the _____[5]_____ is authorized to negotiate, enter into and execute and deliver in the name of and on behalf of the Corporation, any contract or agreement which said officer deems to be reasonable and necessary for the business of the Corporation without further or prior act of the Directors of the Corporation]* **OR** *[that the _____[5]_____ is authorized and directed to execute and deliver in the name of and on behalf of the Corporation a contract with _____[6]_____ for _____[7]_____]* and the Secretary is authorized and directed to affix the corporate seal thereto if so ordered by the officer executing the contract and without further or prior order of this Board."

CORPORATE RESOLUTION—
INDEMNIFICATION OF DIRECTORS (6-19)

This Corporate Resolution is to be used in the Minutes of Directors' Meeting.

Despite acting in the best interests of the corporation and in their honest exercise of business judgment, and properly exercising their fiduciary duties without any self-dealing, one or more of the Directors of a corporation may be sued, perhaps by a shareholder. Other shareholders of the corporation may decide that such a law suit is baseless and determine that the Directors should not have to "reach into their own pockets." The shareholders can resolve to indemnify the Directors for the amount of any judgment or settlement against the Directors, including their legal fees.

Note that the Directors cannot resolve to indemnify themselves. Rather the shareholders, as the owners of the corporation and on whose behalf the Directors run the corporation, must do so.

CORPORATE RESOLUTION—
INDEMNIFICATION OF DIRECTORS

1. The date of the Shareholders' Meeting.

2. The names of the directors to be indemnified.

3. The circumstances giving rise to the law suit.

Whereas, the shareholders of the Corporation at the meeting held on _____[1]_____ were advised that a legal action has been commenced against the Corporation and _____[2]_____ as Directors of the Corporation on account of certain actions of the Board of Directors, and

Whereas, the shareholders determined that said Directors were acting in their respective capacities as Directors of the Corporation, acting in the best interests of the Corporation, acting on the basis of their legitimate exercise of business judgment, and acting in accordance with the fiduciary duties imposed on them by law, and

Whereas, after due deliberation by the shareholders determined to constitute a quorum present at the meeting, upon motion duly made, seconded and carried by the affirmative vote of the shareholders, it was

"RESOLVED, that _____[2]_____ shall be indemnified by the Corporation for all reasonable, actual and necessary expenses, including attorneys' fees, which have or may be incurred by them or any of them in connection with the defense of a lawsuit commenced against them and the Corporation, whether by judgment, settlement or upon and after appeal, and arising out of _____[3]_____

_____

_____."

STOCK POWER (6-20)

A Stock Power is used whenever a stockholder sells shares of stock. A stock certificate is "negotiable" (that is, can be sold, assigned or transferred) only when accompanied by a Stock Power. The Stock Power is to a certificate for stock as the endorsement (on the back of a check) is to a check.

WARNING

In order for the Stock Power to be accepted by the transfer agent designated by the corporation, the Seller's signature must be *guaranteed* by an officer of a commercial bank or a licensed stock broker. This is *not* the same as having the Seller's signature notarized by a Notary Public, which will result in the Stock Power being rejected by the transfer agent.

STOCK POWER

1. The name of the Seller of the stock. (Note: the name on the Stock Power must be exactly the same as it appears on the stock certificate.)

2. The Seller's social security or taxpayer identification number.

3. The name of the Purchaser (if known). Otherwise, leave blank.

4. The Purchaser's Social Security or Taxpayer Identification number (if known). Otherwise, leave blank.

5. The number of shares being sold, in words.

6. The number of shares being sold, in numbers.

7. The type of stock, i.e.: common, preferred, etc.

8. The name of the corporation whose stock is being sold.

9. The certificate number(s) of the stock being sold.

10. The transfer agent will fill in this portion.

11. The date of the sale.

12. The name of the Seller printed directly below the line, with the Seller to sign above the line.

FOR VALUE RECEIVED, I,
_____[1]_____ (my social security/taxpayer identification no. is: _____[2]_____), hereby sell, assign and transfer unto _____[3]_____ (whose social security /taxpayer identification no. is: _____[4]_____) _____[5]_____ (___[6]___) shares of the _____[7]_____ capital stock of _____[8]_____ standing in (my)(our) name(s) on the books of said Corporation represented by Certificate(s) No(s) _____[9]_____, and do hereby irrevocably constitute and appoint _____[10]_____ as attorney to transfer said stock on the books of the Corporation with full power of substitution in the premises.

Dated:_____[11]_____

_____

[12]

PROXY (6-21)

A shareholder of a corporation might not be able to attend a shareholders' meeting but might nevertheless wish his vote to be counted. A Proxy provides written notice to the corporation that the shareholder has designated another to attend the meeting and authorizes that person to cast the shareholder's votes. The Proxy also requires the corporation to permit the attendance of the designee (the Proxy holder) at the meeting and to accept and record the designee's vote.

PROXY

1. The number of shares owned by the shareholder.

2. The name of the corporation.

3. The name of the designee (the Proxy holder).

4. The address of the designee.

5. The date of the shareholders' meeting.

6. The location of the shareholders' meeting.

7. The date of the Proxy.

8. The name of the witness printed directly below the line, with the witness to sign above the line.

9. The name of the shareholder giving the Proxy printed directly below the line, with the shareholder to sign above the line.

10. The address of the shareholder.

KNOW ALL MEN BY THESE PRESENTS that the undersigned shareholder of _____[1]_____ shares of _____[2]_____ does hereby appoint _____[3]_____, of _____[4]_____, or the bearer of this proxy, to be his true and lawful attorney-in-fact and agent to vote as proxy at the meeting of shareholders of _____[2]_____ to be held on _____[5]_____ at _____[6]_____ or any adjournment of such meeting and to act as fully as the undersigned could do if personally present at such meeting. By this proxy the undersigned does hereby revoke any proxy previously given.

Dated: _____[7]_____

WITNESS:

_____   _____
        [8]   [9]

                              _____[10]_____
                              _____[10]_____

AFFIDAVIT OF LOST STOCK CERTIFICATE (6-22)

Stock certificates sometimes get lost despite the best efforts to safeguard them. The Uniform Commercial Code provides that the issuing corporation must replace a stock certificate: 1) when the registered shareholder requests a replacement AND 2) before the issuing corporation receives notice that the security has been acquired by a bona fide purchaser (someone who has bought the stock certificate and does not know that the certificate had been lost). The owner may be required to file a sufficient indemnity bond with the issuing corporation (which usually can be obtained through the issuing corporation) and satisfy any other reasonable requests of the issuing corporation. This form provides written request to the issuing corporation.

An Affidavit is a statement made under oath before a Notary Public or similar person authorized by the laws of that state to administer oaths. The Affidavit must be signed in the presence of the Notary.

AFFIDAVIT OF LOST STOCK CERTIFICATE

1. The state in which the requesting owner of the lost certificate is located and in which he will make the Affidavit.

2. The county in which the requesting owner of the lost certificate is located.

3. The name of the person giving the Affidavit.

4. Choose one.

5. The name of the deceased owner of the lost certificate.

6. The number of shares represented by the lost certificate(s).

7. The name of the issuing corporation.

8. The name of the owner of the lost certificate.

STATE OF _____[1]_____)
COUNTY OF _____[2]_____) ss.:

_____[3]_____, being duly sworn, deposes and says:

I am *[4][the lawful owner]* **OR** *[the executor, administrator, representative or fiduciary of the Estate of* _____[5]_____ *who at the time of death was the lawful owner]* of ___[6]___ shares of _____[7]_____ registered in the name of _____[8]_____.

I believe the original certificate(s) representing said shares has been lost, stolen, destroyed or misplaced because I have made a diligent search of all available records and have been unable to locate the certificate(s). I believe that said certificate(s) were not endorsed, that said certificate(s) have not been sold, transferred, assigned, delivered, hypothecated, pledged or otherwise disposed of and that no person or entity other than the undersigned has any right, title, equity, claim or interest in or to said certificate(s) or the ownership interest represented by said certificate(s).

I agree that if said certificate(s) ever come into my custody or control, I will immediately, and without consideration, surrender and return said certificate(s) to _____[7]_____ for cancellation.

This affidavit is made for the purpose of inducing and requesting _____[7]_____ and its transfer agents to issue new certificate(s) in substitution and

(Document continued on next page)

9. The name of the company which will issue the indemnity bond (usually selected by the issuing corporation).

replacement of the lost certificate(s) and for the purpose of inducing _____[9]_____ to issue an indemnity bond assuming liability.

10. The name of the person giving the Affidavit printed directly below the line, with that person to sign above the line.

_____
[10]

11. A Notary Public fills in the date and signs and seals the form by affixing his stamp or seal.

Sworn to before me this

_[11]_ day of _____, 19__

_____
Notary Public

Buying and Selling A Business 7

Just as the goods or services produced by a business can be bought or sold, so too can a business *itself* or its parts be bought or sold.

Buying There are two basic ways to buy a business. One is to buy the assets of the company and the other, if the business is a corporation, is to buy its stock. The methods differ in terms of the legal consequences. In an asset purchase, the buyer assumes only those liabilities of the seller to which the buyer agrees. In a stock purchase, however, the buyer assumes *all* of the liabilities of the seller. Forms for both asset and stock purchases are found in this section.

Bulk Transfers This section provides the necessary forms to protect the buyer and the seller from the seller's creditors if the sale of the business is a sale of assets.

AGREEMENT FOR THE PURCHASE/
SALE OF A BUSINESS/ASSETS (7-01)

Essentially, there are two ways to purchase an existing business. The Assets, including goodwill, can be purchased or its stock, if a corporation, can be purchased. The determination should be made in consultation with a tax advisor as there are tax consequences to both the Buyer and Seller depending on the method chosen. Legally, the differences are that in an Asset Purchase the Buyer assumes only those liabilities of the Seller that the Buyer agrees to; in a Stock Purchase the Buyer assumes all of the liabilities and Assets of the Seller. (See also the Agreement for the Purchase/Sale of Corporate Stock which follows.)

Note: the Agreement requires that Schedules A, B and C be prepared listing the assets, accounts receivable and promissory notes respectively. To prepare these, create three separate sheets each headed with the proper schedule names (for example, "Schedule A") and list the required information on each. Follow the style shown at the end of this form. Further, the sale of assets may be considered a Bulk Transfer. See the Bulk Transfer forms later in this chapter, which are required for such a sale.

AGREEMENT FOR THE PURCHASE/
SALE OF A BUSINESS/ASSETS

1. The date the Agreement is signed.

2. The name of the Seller.

3. If the Seller is a corporation, insert the state in which incorporated. Otherwise delete.

4. The name of the Buyer.

5. If the Buyer is a corporation, insert the state in which incorporated. Otherwise delete.

6. The name under which the Seller conducts business.

7. The address at which the business is operated.

AGREEMENT made this __[1]__ day of _____ ,19__ by and between _____[2]_____ *[3][, a _____ corporation]* ("Seller") and _____[4]_____ *[5][, a _____ corporation]* ("Buyer").

Seller is the owner and operator of _____[6]_____ located at _____[7]_____ and desires to sell certain of the assets of _____[6]_____ ("Business").

Buyer desires to purchase from the Seller the aforesaid Business, as a going concern free of all obligations and liabilities and exclusive of cash and receivables.

In consideration of the mutual terms, conditions and covenants hereinafter set forth Seller and Buyer agree as follows:

1. Seller shall sell to Buyer the Business owned and operated by the Seller as a going concern. Such sale shall include the assets as shown on Schedule A attached hereto, which shall include but not be limited to: goodwill; assignment of trade names, trademarks and copyrights, if any; assignment of the lease for the premises at _____[7]_____; all furniture and fixtures, supplies and equipment located in the premises on the date of closing; all records pertaining to the operation of the Business; all contracts between the Business and third parties;

(Document continued on next page)

8. The total price, in numbers, for the sale of the business.

Note: Nos. 9, 10 and 11 should be arrived at in consultation with a tax advisor as there are specific tax consequences regarding the allocation which may change according to the current federal and state tax laws.

9. The amount, in numbers, attributed to the physical assets of Schedule A.

10. The amount, in numbers, attributed to the intangible assets, i.e. goodwill.

11. The amount, in numbers, attributed to the restrictive covenant (the non-compete provision).

12. The amount, in numbers, to be paid on signing the Agreement.

13. The amount, in numbers, to be paid on the closing date.

14. The amount, in numbers, to be paid by promissory notes.

all other assets necessary to the operation of the Business, and pre-paid expenses.

2.   This sale does not include any cash on hand or in banks at the date of closing. This sale does not include any accounts receivable due to Seller at the date of closing or those that accrue after the date of closing attributable to acts that occurred prior to or on the date of closing.

3.   All proceeds received by Buyer in payment of accounts receivable due to Seller as listed on Schedule B, attached hereto, shall upon receipt be immediately turned over to Seller in the form in which they are received. Seller covenants that these funds shall be deposited in a separate account and shall be first used to pay all accounts payable incurred by Seller in the conduct of the Business prior to the closing date.

4.   All accounts payable, liabilities and obligations incurred by Seller in the conduct of the Business up to the date of closing shall be paid by the Seller, and Seller shall hold the Buyer harmless against such amounts. Buyer is not acquiring, directly, any of Seller's liabilities by operation of law or otherwise.

5.   The purchase price for the assets transferred pursuant to the Agreement and Schedule A is $_____[8]_____ of which $_____[9]_____ is attributable to the physical assets on Schedule A, $_____[10]_____ is attributable to goodwill, trade name, and other intangible assets of the agency, and $_____[11]_____ is attributable to the restrictive covenants of paragraph 7 herein. Payment shall be made: $_____[12]_____ upon the signing of this Agreement; $_____[13]_____ in cash or certified check upon the closing date; and $_____[14]_____ represented by promissory note(s) as attached hereto as Schedule C.

6.   Until the closing date Seller agrees to conduct the Business in the same manner in which it has heretofore been conducted and shall not without the written consent of the Buyer increase the compensation or employee benefits to any employee or employees.

7.   Seller shall not for a period of two (2) years from the closing date through any entity in which Seller has an ownership or management interest or control:

(Document continued on next page)

(a)   Compete, either directly or indirectly, with the Business for the products and services provided by the Business within the geographic areas in which the Business operates as of the date of closing.

(b)   Solicit any individuals or businesses who were customers of the Seller prior to closing or disclose any information about said customers to any person, company or other legal entity.

(c)   Directly or indirectly induce, or attempt to influence, any employee of the Business to terminate their employment.

8.   Seller represents and warrants to Buyer:

(a)   All assets transferred pursuant to this Agreement, except as otherwise noted in Schedule A, are free of any and all liens, security interests, claims and encumbrances.

(b)   Seller is not in breach or default of any contract, lease or other commitment to be assigned pursuant to this Agreement and will not commit a breach or act of default to the date of closing.

(c)   Seller makes no representation or warranty as to the future conduct of the Business and the continued relationship with the customers of the Business.

(d)   Other than those attached to this Agreement there are no outstanding leases; employment agreements; employee pension, retirement or union agreements.

(e)   Seller has not engaged a broker for the sale represented by this Agreement. Each party hereto agrees to indemnify and hold the other harmless from any broker's or finder's fee or alleged broker's or finder's fee incurred by the other party, or any claim by any party that the other entered into an agreement calling for a broker's or finder's fee.

(f)   All inventory transferred herein is merchantable.

(Document continued on next page)

15. The date of the closing.

16. The time of the closing.

17. The location of the closing, typically the office of the Seller's attorney.

18. The name of the Seller if a corporation. Otherwise delete the line.

19. If the Seller is an individual, delete "BY" and print the Seller's name directly below the line, with the Seller to sign above the line. If the Seller is a corporation, print the name and title of the individual acting for the corporation directly below the line, with that person to sign above the line.

20. The name of the Buyer if a corporation. Otherwise delete the line.

21. If the Buyer is an individual, delete "BY" and print the Buyer's name directly below the line, with the Buyer to sign above the line. If the Buyer is a corporation, print the name and title of the individual acting for the corporation directly below the line, with that person to sign above the line.

(g)   All furniture, fixtures and equipment transferred by the Seller are in good condition and repair and free from any defect or condition that would materially affect their operation, excepting normal wear and tear.

(h)   No special consents are required to carry out the transactions contemplated by this Agreement.

(i)   Seller has complied with all applicable provisions for Bulk Transfers, U.C.C. Article 6.

The above representations and warranties shall survive closing.

9.   Buyer hereby agrees to assume the lease(s) for the premises at _____[7]_____ and hereby indemnifies and agrees to hold Seller harmless from any liability thereunder.

10.   Buyer agrees to indemnify and hold Seller harmless from any liability arising out of any agreement or commitment initiated by Seller and which is continued by Buyer after the date of closing.

11.   The closing shall take place on _____[15]_____ at ____[16]____ at the offices of _____[17]_____.

IN WITNESS WHEREOF, the parties have executed this Agreement.

_____[18]_____

BY_____
        [19]   (Seller)

_____[20]_____

BY_____
        [21]   (Buyer)

(Document continued on next page)

**AGREEMENT FOR THE PURCHASE/
SALE OF A BUSINESS/ASSETS** *continued*

SCHEDULE A

LIST OF ASSETS

PHYSICAL ASSETS

Quantity	Description and Location	Lien, Security Agreement,etc.

INTANGIBLE ASSETS

Description

SCHEDULE B

ACCOUNTS RECEIVABLE

Account Name	Date Due	Invoice No.	Amount

SCHEDULE C

PROMISSORY NOTES

Lender	Date Due	Amount

AGREEMENT FOR THE PURCHASE/
SALE OF CORPORATE STOCK (7-02)

This Agreement is used when the Stock of an existing corporation is purchased. In a Stock purchase, the Purchaser buys the existing company as a going concern with all of its assets and liabilities. The method of purchase chosen (Stock versus Assets) should be made in consultation with a tax advisor since each method has different tax consequences to both the Seller and Purchaser. This Agreement also requires a Stock Power which is found elsewhere in this book. (See also the preceding Agreement for the Purchase/Sale of A Business/Assets.)

Note that the Agreement also requires that any promissory notes be listed on Schedule A. Follow the style shown at the end of this form.

AGREEMENT FOR THE PURCHASE/
SALE OF CORPORATE STOCK

1. The date the Agreement is signed.

2. The names of the Sellers. This form assumes two Sellers (referred to in the singular as "Seller" in the form). Add or delete spaces as required to accommodate the actual number of names.

3. The name of the Purchaser.

4. If the Purchaser is a corporation, insert the state in which incorporated. Otherwise delete.

5. The name of the corporation whose stock is being sold.

6. The state of incorporation of the corporation whose stock is being sold.

7. The numbers of the stock certificates representing the shares of stock.

8. The total number of shares being sold, in numbers.

AGREEMENT made this __[1]__ day of _____ ,19__ by and between _____[2]_____ and _____[2]_____ (collectively the "Seller") and _____[3]_____ *[4][, a _____ corporation]* ("Purchaser").

Seller is the owner of all of the outstanding shares of stock of _____[5]_____, a _____[6]_____ corporation ("Corporation") and is desirous of selling its shares; and

Purchaser is desirous of purchasing all of the outstanding shares of the Corporation.

In consideration of the mutual terms, conditions and covenants hereinafter set forth Seller and Purchaser agree as follows:

1. Seller hereby sells to the Purchaser and the Purchaser hereby purchases from the Seller all of the outstanding shares of stock of the Corporation, represented by Certificates Numbers _____[7]_____, totaling _____[8]_____ shares of the Common Stock of the Corporation.

2. Seller warrants and represents that he is the owner of the shares of stock referred to in paragraph 1 above; that such shares constitute all of the outstanding shares of stock of the Corporation; that he owns all of the shares of stock free and clear of all mortgages, pledges, liens, encumbrances, charges and claims; that he has the right, power and authority to enter into this Agreement, and to transfer and deliver the shares of stock heretofore owned by him to

(Document continued on next page)

9. The price, in numbers, per share of stock being sold.

10. The price, in numbers, of all of the shares of stock being sold. (Note: the purchase price is usually arrived at by valuing the assets and adding an amount for the value of an ongoing, profitable business.)

11. The amount, in numbers, to be paid on signing the Agreement.

12. The amount, in numbers, to be paid on the closing date (the date the transaction is to be completed).

13. The closing date.

14. The amount, in numbers, to be paid by Promissory Note.

15. The name and address of the Escrow Agent who will hold the shares of stock and Stock Power, typically the attorney for the Seller.

the Purchaser; and that there are no actions, suits, claims or litigation pending or threatened against or affecting the ownership by him of the shares transferred or delivered to the Purchaser. He further warrants and covenants that the delivery by him of the Certificates for such shares accompanied by a Stock Power, as hereinafter provided for, is sufficient to and does transfer and convey full and clear title to all of the shares reflected by the Certificates to the Purchaser, and that he will make, execute and deliver such further instruments as may be required to confirm said transfer.

3. The purchase price for the shares shall be $__[9]__ per share for a total of $_____[10]_____. Payment shall be made: $_____[11]_____ upon the signing of this Agreement; $_____[12]_____ in cash or certified check upon the closing date, _____[13]_____; and $_____[14]_____ represented by promissory notes as attached hereto as Schedule A.

4. To secure the payment of the purchase price to the Seller by the Purchaser the shares of stock shall be delivered to _____[15]_____ ("Escrow Agent"), to be held in escrow, together with a Stock Power executed by Seller with his signature guaranteed by the Escrow Agent.

5. The Escrow Agent shall hold the shares in escrow and shall deliver them to the Purchaser upon payment to the Seller of the last payment. In the event that the Purchaser fails to make any of the above payments on the due date or within 60 days of demand thereafter, the Escrow Agent shall deliver said shares to the Seller. Upon delivery in either instance the Escrow Agent shall be relieved of all responsibility and liability.

6. Seller shall have the right, and may delegate such right to anyone of his choice, to inspect the books and records of the Corporation to verify any and all statements upon which the purchase price was based. Said inspection shall be on 48 hours' notice and is to be conducted during normal business hours at the Corporation's place of business.

7. Seller (and each of them if more than one), has heretofore been employed by the Corporation, and acknowledges that he has been paid and received all pay-

(Document continued on next page)

16. The most recent tax year for which the Sellers state that corporate taxes have been paid.

17. The most recent tax year for which the Sellers will protect the Purchaser from the payment of any taxes.

ments and compensation of any kind or character at any time due to him by reason thereof. He further warrants, represents and acknowledges that: (a) he has no claims of any kind whatsoever, whether as an employee, stockholder or otherwise, against the Corporation, or any of its officers, directors or stockholders; (b) he has not since the termination of his employment by the Corporation incurred any obligation for which the Corporation may be liable; (c) he knows of no fact which could justify or sustain the imposition of a liability on the Corporation other than the liabilities reflected on the Corporation's balance sheet.

8. Seller holds harmless and indemnifies the Purchaser for and on account of any loss, damage and expense incurred by the Purchaser by reason of the assertion by the Seller or on his behalf of any claim contrary to the terms of this Agreement, any breach of any of the foregoing warranties or any misrepresentation of the foregoing facts.

9. Seller confirms that as far as he is aware, all corporate taxes have been fully paid up to and including the calendar year __[16]__, and there is no reason for the imposition of any additional tax or penalty. In any event, Seller will indemnify and hold Purchaser harmless against any cost, expense or liability by reason of the imposition upon the Corporation of any additional income or other taxes and penalties (including interest) for the years up to and including __[17]__.

10. Seller agrees to cooperate with the Purchaser for an orderly transition of the business. Seller shall, simultaneously with the execution of this Agreement, deliver to Purchaser its resignation as officers and directors of the corporation.

11. Any notices to be delivered under the terms of this

(Document continued on next page)

18. The address where the Sellers are to receive notices.

19. The address where the Purchaser is to receive notices.

20. The name of the Escrow Agent printed directly below the line, with that person to sign above the line.

21. The name of each Seller printed directly below the line, with each Seller to sign above the line. Add or delete lines as required to accommodate the actual number of names.

22. The name of the Purchaser if a corporation. Otherwise delete the line.

23. If the Purchaser is an individual, delete "BY" and print the Purchaser's name directly below the line, with the Purchaser to sign above the line. If the Purchaser is a corporation, print the name and title of the individual acting for the corporation directly below the line, with that person to sign above the line.

Agreement shall be sent certified mail, return receipt requested to:

If to Seller: _____[18]_____

_____

_____

If to Purchaser: _____[19]_____

_____

_____

12.   This Agreement shall be binding upon the successors, heirs, executors, administrators and assigns of the parties hereto.

    IN WITNESS WHEREOF, the parties hereto have executed this Agreement as of the date first above written.

ESCROW ACCEPTED: _____
                                                 [21]   (Seller)

_____   _____
    [20] (Escrow Agent)   [21]   (Seller)

                                            _____*[22]*_____

                                       *BY*_____
                                            [23]   (Purchaser)

SCHEDULE A

PROMISSORY NOTES

Lender	Date Due	Amount

INTRODUCTION TO BULK TRANSFERS

A Bulk Transfer is a sale or transfer in bulk—meaning a sale or transfer: 1) of a major portion (more than 50%) of the materials, supplies, merchandise or other inventory of the seller, and 2) which is NOT in the ordinary course of the Transferor's (the seller's) business. If, for example, it is customary to sell off a wholesaler's entire inventory of summer merchandise before receipt of fall merchandise, such a sale is not a Bulk Transfer because it is in the ordinary course of the seller's business.

The purpose of the law of Bulk Transfers is to protect creditors from unknowingly losing rights in a debtor's assets by advising creditors that a Bulk Transfer is to take place. The following forms must be used to comply with the provisions of the Uniform Commercial Code. Failure to do so makes the buyer (Transferee) responsible for the seller's (Transferor's) debts related to the transferred assets.

The Bulk Transfer (also called Bulk Sale) of the assets is governed by the Uniform Commercial Code (the "U.C.C."), a set of uniform laws adopted by all states (except Louisiana and the Commonwealth of Puerto Rico). There are, however, slight variations from state to state and it is advisable to determine if the following forms are applicable for your state or if other forms are required. For example, New York State requires the filing of a form with the state tax authority (the New York State Department of Taxation and Finance) advising of a Bulk Transfer. Check with your tax advisor concerning such additional requirements.

There are statutory provisions exempting certain sales or transfers: (1) transfers given as security for the performance of an obligation; (2) general assignments for the benefit of creditors; (3) transfers made because of a security agreement or lien; (4) sales by executors, administrators, receivers, trustees in bankruptcy, or any public officer under court order; (5) sales made in the course of judicial or administrative proceedings for the dissolution or reorganization of a corporation in accordance with notice to all creditors and an order of the court or administrative agency; (6) sales or transfers to a person or corporation within the state who agrees to pay the debts of the transferor in full, and who gives public notice of that fact and is financially solvent; (7) transfers to a new business organized to take over and continue the old business, if public notice is given and the new business assumes the debts of the old business; and (8) transfers of property which are exempt from execution.

Note: the Agreement for the Purchase/Sale of a Business/Assets in this chapter may be a Bulk Transfer requiring the use of Bulk Transfer forms (however, see exemptions 6 and 7 above).

BULK TRANSFER—
SCHEDULE OF PROPERTY (7-03)

A Schedule of Property is required in a Bulk Transfer so that creditors who may have a lien or security interest in certain assets can be made aware of the assets being transferred. The party to whom the assets are to be transferred is required to keep the schedule for six months from the date of the transfer and must permit all creditors to inspect and/or copy the schedule. See the Demand for List of Creditors and Known Claimants that follows.

BULK TRANSFER—
SCHEDULE OF PROPERTY

1. Choose one.

2. The name of the party receiving the assets.

3. The name of the party selling, transferring or assigning the assets.

4. The date the transfer is to occur, which must be at least 10 days subsequent to delivery.

5. Choose one. If more space is required to list the items being transferred, on a separate sheet headed "Schedule A" list the items (see the example in No. 7 below) and then skip to No. 9.

The full and detailed inventory, including quantity, description and cost, so far as possible with the exercise of due diligence, of the assets to be *[1][sold]* **OR** *[transferred]* **OR** *[assigned]* to _____[2]_____ by _____[3]_____ on _____[4]_____ is *[5][as is more fully set forth on the annexed Schedule A.]* **OR** *[as follows:* _____ _____.]*

(Document continued on next page)

6.   Choose one.

7.   The quantity and description of the assets. Note: the description must sufficiently identify the goods depending on the type of business. For example, "30 gross, screws" would be insufficient for a machine shop or hardware store (which has vast quantities of assorted screws) but probably would be sufficient for a textile business. "30 gross, 1 1/4" No. 8 flat head screws" would be sufficient for a hardware store.

8.   The cost of the assets to the party selling, transferring or assigning.

9.   The city and state where the schedule is signed.

10.   The date the schedule is signed.

11.   If the sale, transfer or assignment is being made by a corporation, the name of the corporation. Otherwise delete the line.

12.   If the sale, transfer or assignment is being made by an individual, delete "BY" and print the seller's name directly below the line, with the seller to sign above the line. If the seller is a corporation, print the name and title of the individual acting for the corporation directly below the line, with the individual to sign above the line.

QUANTITY	*DESCRIPTION*	*[6][COST TO [SELLER] OR [TRANSFEROR] OR [ASSIGNOR]*
[7]	*[7]*	*[8]*
[7]	*[7]*	*[8]*
[7]	*[7]*	*[8]*
[7]	*[7]*	*[8]*
[7]	*[7]*	*[8]*
[7]	*[7]*	*[8]*

Dated: _____[9]_____

_____[10]_____, 19__   _____*[11]*_____

                                       BY_____
                                              [12]

BULK TRANSFER—
LIST OF CREDITORS AND
KNOWN CLAIMANTS (7-04)

In a Bulk Transfer, the party selling, transferring or assigning assets is required to provide to the party receiving the assets a complete List of Creditors and Known Claimants (people who have made a claim but which the selling, transferring or assigning party disputes). This document is typically prepared and served by an officer of the corporation, an accountant from the corporation, or another party having knowledge of the Creditors.

BULK TRANSFER—
LIST OF CREDITORS AND
KNOWN CLAIMANTS

1. The state where the document is signed.

2. The county where the document is signed.

3. The name of the individual signing the document.

4. Delete through No. 6 if the party selling, transferring or assigning the assets is an individual and skip to No. 7.

5. The title of the corporate officer signing the document.

6. The name of the corporation selling, transferring or assigning the assets.

7. The name of the party receiving the assets.

8. The name of the individual or corporation selling, transferring or assigning the assets.

9. The name of the creditor.

10. The business address of the creditor.

11. The amount of the creditor's claim.

12. The name of the claimant.

13. The business address of the claimant.

14. The amount of the disputed claim.

STATE OF _____[1]_____)
COUNTY OF _____[2]_____) ss.:

_____[3]_____, being duly sworn, deposes *[4][and states that he is the _____[5]_____ of _____[6]_____]* and certifies to _____[7]_____ and to all whom it may concern:

The following is a full, accurate and complete list of the creditors of _____[8]_____ and the indebtedness to each, to the best of the information and belief of deponent as they appear on the books and records of _____[8]_____, and all other persons known to assert a claim against _____[8]_____:

CREDITOR	BUSINESS ADDRESS	AMOUNT OF INDEBTEDNESS
[9]	[10]	[11]
[9]	[10]	[11]
[9]	[10]	[11]
[9]	[10]	[11]
[9]	[10]	[11]
[9]	[10]	[11]

CLAIMANT	BUSINESS ADDRESS	AMOUNT OF DISPUTED CLAIM
[12]	[13]	[14]
[12]	[13]	[14]
[12]	[13]	[14]
[12]	[13]	[14]

(Document continued on next page)

BULK TRANSFER—
LIST OF CREDITORS AND
KNOWN CLAIMANTS *continued*

15. Choose one.

16. The date of sale, transfer or assignment of the assets.

17. The name of the person in No. 3 printed below the line, with that person to sign above the line.

18. The Notary Public completes this part of the form, and signs and seals it by affixing his stamp or seal.

This certificate is made and intended to comply with Section 6-104 of the Uniform Commercial Code in connection with the *[15][sale]* **OR** *[transfer]* **OR** *[assignment]* of assets by _____[8]_____ to _____[7]_____ on _____[16]_____, 19__.

_____
[17]

Sworn to before me this

_[18]_ day of _____, 19__

_____
Notary Public

BULK TRANSFER—
DEMAND FOR LIST OF CREDITORS AND
KNOWN CLAIMANTS (7-05)

It is recommended that the party receiving the assets from a Bulk Transfer make a formal written request for the names of all the creditors and claimants. The purpose of this Demand is to assure the buyer that he has the names of all Creditors and Known Claimants.

BULK TRANSFER—
DEMAND FOR LIST OF CREDITORS AND
KNOWN CLAIMANTS

1. The name and address of the party selling, transferring or assigning the assets.

TO: _____[1]_____

_____

_____

2. The name of the party receiving the assets.

3. The date of the Demand.

4. If the Demand is being made by a corporation, the name of the corporation. Otherwise delete the line.

5. If the Demand is being made by an individual, delete "BY" and print the individual's name directly below the line, with the individual to sign above the line. If a corporation, print the name and title of the person acting for the corporation directly below the line, with that person to sign above the line.

PLEASE TAKE NOTICE that pursuant to Section 6-104 of the Uniform Commercial Code the undersigned, _____[2]_____, hereby demands a list of your creditors and known claimants, together with their last known business address and either the amount of the indebtedness or claim (even if disputed) of each. Said list is to be certified, under oath as provided for by statute.

Dated: _____[3]_____

_____[4]_____

BY_____
[5]

BULK TRANSFER—
NOTICE TO CREDITORS AND KNOWN CLAIMANTS (7-06)

This form should be sent to all Creditors and Claimants of the party selling, transferring or assigning the assets in a Bulk Transfer. If the Notice is not sent to each Creditor and known Claimant, the Bulk Transfer will not be binding on them and each may sue for payment from both the party selling, transferring or assigning the assets and from the party receiving the assets. The Notice should be delivered personally or sent by Certified Mail—Return Receipt Requested at least ten days before possession of the goods or payment for the goods, whichever occurs first.

BULK TRANSFER—
NOTICE TO CREDITORS AND KNOWN CLAIMANTS

1. The name of the party selling, transferring or assigning the assets (the Transferor).

2. The name of the party receiving the assets (the Transferee).

3. The date the transfer is to become effective.

4. A general description of the assets.

5. The address where the Schedule of Property and list of creditors will be kept.

6. The address of the Transferor.

7. The address of the Transferee.

8. Any other name or address used by the Transferor. Note: if there is none, insert the word "none."

9. Choose one.

10. The name and address where creditors are to send their bills for payment.

TO: Creditors and Claimants of _____[1]_____, Transferor:

    PLEASE TAKE NOTICE that you and each of you are HEREBY NOTIFIED pursuant to Sections 6-105 and 6-107 of the Uniform Commercial Code as follows:

1.   The Transferor, _____[1]_____, is to transfer to _____[2]_____, Transferee, on _____[3]_____, in bulk the _____[4]_____, all of which are listed and described in a Schedule of Property which, with a list of the creditors and claimants, is available for inspection and copying by any creditor or claimant during normal business hours at the office of the Transferee located at _____[5]_____.

2.   The name and business addresses of the Transferor and Transferee are:

Transferor: _____[1]_____   Transferee: _____[2]_____
       _____[6]_____   _____[7]_____
       _____   _____

3.   All other business names and addresses of the Transferor used within the past three (3) years are: _____[8]_____.

4.   *[9][All of the debts of the Transferor are to be paid in full as they fall due as a result of this transaction and creditors should send their bills to: _____[10]_____ _____.] OR [The debts of the Transferor are not to be paid in full as they fall due as a result of this transaction.] OR [The Transferee is in doubt if the debts of*

(Document continued on next page)

11. The location where the assets are to be found and a general description of the assets.

12. The dollar amount, in numbers, of the estimated total of the Transferor's debts.

13. The location where the Schedule of Property and the list of creditors is to be kept.

14. Choose one. If "is not to pay existing debts" is chosen then delete the remainder of the paragraph through No. 16.

15. The name of each creditor who will be paid.

16. The dollar amount of the claim to be paid, in numbers.

17. Choose one. If no payment (new consideration) is to be made, skip to No. 21.

18. The dollar amount, in numbers, of the payment being made upon the transfer.

19. The date the payment will be paid.

20. The location where the payment will be made.

21. The date of the Notice.

22. If the Notice is being sent by a corporation, the name of the corporation. Otherwise delete the line.

23. If the Notice is being sent by an individual, delete "BY" and print the individual's name directly below the line, with the individual to sign above the line. If a corporation, print the name and title of the person acting for the corporation directly below the line, with that person to sign above the line.

the Transferor will be paid in full as a result of this transaction.]

(a)   The location and general description of the assets to be transferred is
_____[11]_____
_____
and the estimated total of the Transferor's debts is
$_____[12]_____.

(b)   The Schedule of Property and List of Creditors and Known Claimants is located at:
_____[13]_____.

(c)   The Transfer *[14][is not to pay existing debts.]* **OR** *[is to pay existing debts and the amount of such debt and to whom owing is:*

CREDITOR   *AMOUNT*

[15]   *[16]*
[15]   *[16]*
[15]   *[16]*

(d)   The Transfer *[17][is not for new consideration.]* **OR** *[is for new consideration of*
$_____[18]_____ *to be paid on* _____[19]_____
at _____[20]_____.*]*

Dated: _____[21]_____   _____[22]_____

                              *BY*_____
                                        [23]

BULK TRANSFER—
NOTICE OF INTENDED BULK TRANSFER
BY AUCTION SALE (7-07)

       If a Bulk Transfer is made by sale at Auction, the Auctioneer must send notice to all creditors and claimants. The failure to do so will result in the Auctioneer being liable to the creditors up to the amount realized at the auction even if the money generated by the Auction is to be paid to the Transferor. A separate notice must be sent to each creditor or claimant, either by personal delivery or by Certified Mail—Return Receipt Requested at least ten days before the Auction.

BULK TRANSFER—
NOTICE OF INTENDED BULK TRANSFER
BY AUCTION SALE

1. The name and address of the creditor or known claimant.

2. The name of the Auctioneer.

3. The name and address of the Transferor.

4. Any other name or address used by the Transferor. If there is none, insert the word "none."

5. The address of the location of the auction.

6. The city in which the auction will be held.

7. The county in which the auction will be held.

8. The state in which the auction will be held.

9. The time of the auction.

10. Choose one.

11. The date of the auction.

12. The location of the assets being auctioned.

13. A general description of the assets to be auctioned.

TO: _____[1]_____
_____
_____

      PLEASE TAKE NOTICE that pursuant to Section 6-108 of the Uniform Commercial Code:

1.   _____[2]_____, Auctioneer, will sell at public auction certain property of _____[3]_____, Transferor.

2.   To the best of Auctioneer's knowledge, the Transferor has not used any business name or address, except as above, during the past three (3) years other than:
_____[4]_____.

3.   The auction will be held at _____[5]_____, City of _____[6]_____, County of _____[7]_____, State of _____[8]_____, at ___[9]___ *[10][A.M.] OR [P.M.]* on _____[11]_____, 19__.

4.   The property to be sold is located at _____[12]_____ and is described as follows:
_____[13]_____
_____.

(Document continued on next page)

14. The estimated dollar amount, in numbers, of the Transferor's debts.

15. The location of the Schedule of Property and the List of Creditors and Known Claimants.

16. The date by which creditors and known claimants must file their claims.

17. The name and address where claims are to be filed.

18. The date of the Notice.

19. If the auctioneer is a corporation, the name of the corporation. Otherwise delete the line.

20. If the auction will be conducted by an individual, delete "BY" and print the individual's name directly below the line, with the individual to sign above the line. If the auction will be conducted by a corporation, print the name and title of the person acting on behalf of the corporation directly below the line, with that person to sign above the line.

5.   The estimated total of Transferor's debts is
$_____[14]_____.

6.   The Schedule of Property and list of creditors and known claimants may be inspected at
_____[15]_____.

7.   Creditors of the Transferor must file their claims in writing on or before _____[16]_____ with
_____[17]_____.

Dated: _____[18]_____

_____[19]_____

BY_____
[20]

General Contract Clauses 8

This chapter contains general clauses that are advisable to include in most contracts. The clauses deal with issues that are not specific to any particular kind of transaction but rather are applicable to most transactions. These clauses should be reviewed to determine which should be included in a contract. Without the so-called "boilerplate" provisions contained in this chapter, problems may arise after a contract has been signed.

CONTRACT CLAUSE—INDEMNIFICATION/
HOLD HARMLESS (8-01)

In many types of agreements one party will agree to indemnify and hold the other party harmless (not responsible) in the event of a lawsuit or claim by a third party (any person who is not a party to the agreement) relating to the subject of the agreement. An agreement to Indemnify/Hold Harmless can be either a free-standing agreement (such as the form found elsewhere in this book) or it can be made part of an agreement.

CONTRACT CLAUSE—INDEMNIFICATION/
HOLD HARMLESS

1.   The number of this paragraph when inserted into a contract.

2.   The name of the party giving the Indemnification.

3.   The name of the party being indemnified.

4.   Insert either "the subject matter of this agreement" or describe what the Indemnification is for; i.e. "the sale of widgets."

[1]   INDEMNIFICATION/HOLD HARMLESS - _____[2]_____ irrevocably covenants, promises and agrees to indemnify _____[3]_____ and to hold _____[3]_____ harmless from and against any and all losses, claims, expenses, suits, damages, costs, demands or liabilities, joint or several, of whatever kind or nature which _____[3]_____ may sustain or to which _____[3]_____ may become subject arising out of or relating in any way to _____[4]_____ including, without limitation, in each case attorneys' fees, costs and expenses actually incurred in defending against or enforcing any such losses, claims, expenses, suits, damages or liabilities.

CONTRACT CLAUSE—AUDIT OF BOOKS
AND RECORDS (8-02)

In a partnership or joint venture agreement, or in an agreement that involves payment of commission or royalty, it is important to have the ability to inspect and Audit the Books to verify the condition of the business and to insure proper payments.

CONTRACT CLAUSE—AUDIT OF BOOKS
AND RECORDS

1. The number of this paragraph when inserted into a contract.

2. The name of the company, partnership, joint venture, etc.

3. The address where the books, etc. are to be kept.

4. A time period, in words and numbers, i.e. forty-eight (48) hours, three (3) business days, etc.

[1]   AUDIT OF BOOKS AND RECORDS - The books, records, reports and accounts of the _____[2]_____ shall be kept at all times so as to accurately reflect the business and financial condition of the _____[2]_____. Said books, etc. shall be kept at _____[3]_____ or at such other location as may be mutually agreed upon in writing. Upon _____[4]_____ written notice, given to the other(s), any party may audit and inspect said books, records, reports and accounts during normal business hours.

CONTRACT CLAUSE—NOTICE PROVISION (8-03)

Almost every agreement requires notification to one or the other of the parties regarding specific events (for example, the change of address for the sending of payments). Such notification is referred to as giving Notice.

CONTRACT CLAUSE—NOTICE PROVISION

1. The number of this paragraph when inserted into a contract.

2. A number of days, in words and numbers, that is reasonable for Notice sent by mail to be received, i.e. five (5).

3. The name and address of each party who would be entitled to receive Notice under the agreement.

[1]   NOTICE PROVISION - All notices required or permitted to be given hereunder shall be in writing and may be delivered personally or by U.S. Mail, postage prepaid. Receipt of notice shall be deemed to have been given upon receipt if personally delivered or within ____[2]____ (__) days after being deposited in the U.S. Mails. Notice shall be addressed:

If to: _____[3]_____

              _____[3]_____

              _____[3]_____

If to: _____[3]_____

              _____[3]_____

              _____[3]_____

CONTRACT CLAUSE—ARBITRATION
(Covering the Entire Agreement) (8-04)

The parties to a contract may decide that in the event of a dispute, resolution through the usual means (lawyers and the court system) would take too long and be too costly. The alternative is an agreement to submit disputes to the American Arbitration Association.

The decision by the parties to submit any dispute to Arbitration must be clearly spelled out in the contract. Because Arbitration will eliminate a party's opportunity to have his day in court, the law will insist on a clear, unequivocal written expression of this wish in the agreement.

This is the standard Arbitration clause recommended by the American Arbitration Association for commercial Arbitration. For a list of regional offices and a copy of the Commercial Arbitration Rules contact:

American Arbitration Association
140 West 51st Street
New York, NY 10020-1203
Tel: (212) 484-4000
Fax: (212) 765-4874

CONTRACT CLAUSE—ARBITRATION

1. The number of this paragraph when inserted into a contract.

[1]   ARBITRATION - Any controversy or claim arising out of or relating to this contract, or the breach thereof, shall be settled by arbitration in accordance with the Commercial Arbitration Rules of the American Arbitration Association, and judgment upon the award rendered by the arbitrator(s) may be entered in any court having jurisdiction thereof.

CONTRACT CLAUSE—ARBITRATION CLAUSE
(Covering Specific Parts of the Agreement) (8-05)

This Arbitration clause is specific as to what portions of an agreement are subject to Arbitration. It also requires the Arbitration to be in a specific location. For example, if you are in Philadelphia and the other party is in Los Angeles, it would be to your advantage to have the Arbitration in Philadelphia.

For a list of regional offices and a copy of the Commercial Arbitration Rules contact:

American Arbitration Association
140 West 51st Street
New York, NY 10020-1203
Tel: (212) 484-4000
Fax: (212) 765-4874

CONTRACT CLAUSE—ARBITRATION

1. The number of this paragraph when inserted into a contract.

2. A list of the paragraphs of the contract that are to be subject to Arbitration.

3. The city and state where Arbitration will take place, typically the location of one of the parties.

[1]   ARBITRATION - Any controversy or claim arising out of or relating to _____[2]_____ of this contract shall be settled by arbitration in _____[3]_____, in accordance with the Commercial Arbitration Rules of The American Arbitration Association, and judgment upon the award rendered by the arbitrator(s) may be entered in any court having jurisdiction thereof.

CONTRACT CLAUSE—GOVERNING LAW (8-06)

If the parties to an agreement are from different states, the agreement should contain a clause setting forth which state's laws should control the legal interpretation of the contract.

CONTRACT CLAUSE—GOVERNING LAW

1. The number of this paragraph when inserted into a contract.

2. The name of the state whose laws will govern.

[1]   GOVERNING LAW - This Agreement shall be construed in accordance with and governed by the laws of the State of _____[2]_____, irrespective of the fact that a party hereto may not be a resident of or maintain a place of business in that State.

CONTRACT CLAUSE—JURISDICTION
FOR COURT ACTION (8-07)

The purpose of this provision is to set forth where any lawsuit or action will be filed. It prevents one party from commencing a suit or action in a state that is inconvenient to the other.

CONTRACT CLAUSE—JURISDICTION
FOR COURT ACTION

1. The number of this paragraph when inserted into a contract.

2. The state in which the suit or action is to be filed.

3. There may be more than one federal district court in a state; therefore name the city and state to eliminate any doubt.

[1]   JURISDICTION FOR COURT ACTION - The court and authorities of the State of _____[2]_____ or the federal district court having venue for _____[3]_____ shall have jurisdiction over all controversies that may arise with respect to this Agreement, the parties hereby waiving any other venue to which they might be entitled by virtue of domicile or otherwise. Should either party initiate or bring a suit or action before any other courts, it is agreed that upon application any such suit or action shall be dismissed, without prejudice, and may be filed in accordance with this provision. The party bringing the suit or action before a court not agreed to herein shall pay to the other party all the costs of seeking dismissal including reasonable attorneys' fees.

CONTRACT CLAUSE—TRADE SECRETS (8-08)

If the subject matter of an agreement requires divulging information that would be regarded as a trade secret, i.e. a customer list, method of manufacture or the like, this clause should be considered.

CONTRACT CLAUSE—TRADE SECRETS

1. The number of this paragraph when inserted into a contract.

2. The name of the party who will be restricted.

3. The name of the business to be protected.

4. A number of years, in words and numbers. It has to be reasonable in duration, i.e. two (2) or three (3) years.

[1]   TRADE SECRETS - _____[2]_____ shall not divulge to any person, firm or firms, corporation or corporations, any trade secret having to do with the business of _____[3]_____ that shall come to the knowledge of _____[2]_____ by reason of this Agreement and the relationship of _____[2]_____ and _____[3]_____ created by this Agreement, during the term of this Agreement and for _____[4]_____ (__) years after the termination of this Agreement.

CONTRACT CLAUSE—CORPORATE AUTHORITY
TO ENTER INTO AGREEMENT (8-09)

If a corporation is a party to an agreement and the agreement contemplates an act that would require approval of the Board of Directors, then this clause should be part of the agreement. This would include such matters as the sale of an asset or hiring a consultant, but not an act in the normal course of business, such as the sale of manufactured goods.

Note: most extraordinary matters, such as a merger, would require shareholder approval in addition to Board authorization.

CONTRACT CLAUSE—CORPORATE AUTHORITY
TO ENTER INTO AGREEMENT

1. The number of this paragraph when inserted into a contract.

2. The name of the corporation.

[1]   CORPORATE AUTHORITY -
_____[2]_____ has the full corporate power, authority and right to enter into this Agreement and to perform the acts contemplated herein. The Board of Directors of _____[2]_____ has taken all necessary action to duly authorize the execution, delivery and performance of this Agreement which actions are reflected in the minute book of the corporation.

CONTRACT CLAUSE—WAIVER NOT TO BE CONSTRUED AS WAIVER OF SUBSEQUENT DEFAULTS (8-10)

The concept of a Waiver refers to a person giving up rights to which he would otherwise be entitled. The inclusion of this provision permits the Waiver of a breach or default of an agreement without setting a precedent as to future breaches or defaults. If, for example, a contract provides that the other party is to make monthly payments to you by a certain date, and you choose not to object if a payment is late, this clause will prevent the other party from using your lack of objection as an indication that future late payments will be acceptable under the contract.

CONTRACT CLAUSE—WAIVER NOT TO BE CONSTRUED AS WAIVER OF SUBSEQUENT DEFAULTS

1. The number of this paragraph when inserted into a contract.

[1]   NO WAIVER OF DEFAULTS - No waiver of any term, provision or condition of this Agreement, the breach or default thereof, by conduct or otherwise, in one or more instances shall be deemed to be either a continuing waiver or a waiver of a subsequent breach or default of any such term, provision or condition of this Agreement.

CONTRACT CLAUSE—FORCE MAJEURE (8-11)

In agreements where performance may be affected by events beyond the control of a party, for example a fire at a manufacturing plant, this provision will afford protection.

CONTRACT CLAUSE—FORCE MAJEURE

1. The number of this paragraph when inserted into a contract.

2. The name of the party agreeing to the Force Majeure.

3. The name of the party being protected.

[1]   FORCE MAJEURE - _____[2]_____ agrees that _____[3]_____ shall not be liable for: any (i) losses; (ii) damage, including consequential damages; (iii) detention; (iv) delay or failure to perform in whole or in part resulting from causes beyond the control of _____[3]_____ including but not limited to: acts of God; acts or omissions of _____[2]_____; fires; strikes; insurrections; riots; embargoes; delays in transportation; inability to obtain supplies; or requirements or regulations of the United States government or any other civil or military authority. Delays or non-performance excused by this provision shall not excuse payment of any amount due hereunder owed at the time of the occurrence.

CONTRACT CLAUSE—ASSIGNMENT (8-12)

Agreements based on the personal contribution or expertise of one party should not be assigned (transferred) to someone with whom the other party might not want to do business. On the other hand, an agreement to sell a specific item would not normally require this type of protection.

CONTRACT CLAUSE—ASSIGNMENT

1. The number of this paragraph when inserted into a contract.

2. The name of the party to be prohibited from assigning; i.e. licensee, agent.

3. The name of the party to be protected; i.e. licensor.

4. Insert either: "which consent shall not be unreasonably withheld" or "at the sole discretion of _____[2]_____," depending on whether the party to be protected wishes absolute control over the party to be assigned.

[1]   ASSIGNMENT - This Agreement and any rights granted hereunder shall not be assigned by _____[2]_____ to any person, firm or corporation without the prior written consent of _____[3]_____, _____[4]_____.

CONTRACT CLAUSE—
ENTIRE AGREEMENT/MODIFICATIONS
TO BE IN WRITING (8-13)

It is recommended that this clause be a part of every agreement. It prevents one party from claiming that there were "side" agreements, either written or oral, or subsequent verbal changes to an agreement.

CONTRACT CLAUSE—
ENTIRE AGREEMENT/MODIFICATIONS
TO BE IN WRITING

1. The number of this paragraph when inserted into a contract.

[1]   ENTIRE AGREEMENT - It is agreed between the parties hereto that there are no other agreements or understandings between them relating to the subject matter of this Agreement. This Agreement supersedes all prior agreements, oral or written, between the parties and is intended as a complete and exclusive statement of the Agreement between the parties. Neither this Agreement, nor its execution, have been induced by any reliance, representation, stipulation, warranty, agreement or understanding of any kind other than those herein expressed. No change or modification of this Agreement shall be valid unless the same be in writing and signed by the parties.

CONTRACT CLAUSE—HEADINGS/CAPTIONS (8-14)

If an agreement contains Headings or Captions to introduce provisions, i.e. such words as TERMS, ROYALTIES, TERMINATION, etc., this clause should be included, indicating that the Headings or Captions are merely labels and have no impact on the meaning of the contract.

CONTRACT CLAUSE—HEADINGS/CAPTIONS

1. The number of this paragraph when inserted into a contract.

[1]   HEADINGS/CAPTIONS - The headings and captions contained in this Agreement are for convenience purposes only and are not determinative nor are they to be considered in construction of the terms or provisions herein.

Employees and Representatives 9

In a perfect world, we could conduct business as we do personal relationships, relying on verbal agreements and handshakes. But business cannot be conducted in this manner. An area where misunderstandings can occur with frequency is in employer-employee relationships. It is because of this possibility that it is especially critical to put everything in writing.

Hiring This section provides an Employment Application form which asks the applicant for his work history and other information. The Request for Employee Verification and Authorization enables an employer to verify the information and history submitted by the applicant.

Employment Agreements Employee contracts, compensation and tuition reimbursement forms are presented. In addition, protection for the employer in the form of non-competition and and non-disclosure agreements are offered.

Employment Notices Any employer who must deal with a problem employee will find the warning and termination notices in this section particularly helpful.

Independent Contractors This section relates to the hiring of sales representatives, consultants and others as independent contractors.

EMPLOYMENT APPLICATION (9-01)

This form has been designed to comply with state and federal fair employment laws which prohibit discrimination in employment. The form is self-explanatory.

EMPLOYMENT APPLICATION

1. The name of the company.   _____[1]_____ is an Equal Opportunity Employer.

Date:_____

Last Name_____ First Name_____ Middle Initial____
Address _____ Social Security No. _____
_____ Phone # (___)_____

Are you 18 years or older? Yes ___ No___

The Age Discrimination in Employment Act of 1967 prohibits discrimination on the basis of age with respect to individuals who are at least 40 years of age.

Are you a U.S. Citizen or an alien authorized to work in the United States? Yes___ No___

What type of work are you applying for? _____
_____

What skills or qualifications do you have?_____
_____

What (office) (factory) machines can you operate? _____
_____

EDUCATION:

	School	Course	Did you Graduate? If Yes, Year
Grammar	_____	_____	_____
High	_____	_____	_____
College	_____	_____	_____
Other	_____	_____	_____

(Document continued on next page)

EMPLOYMENT APPLICATION *continued*

EXPERIENCE:

(The last two companies worked for)

Company _____

Address _____

Phone # (____)_____

Supervisor _____

Dates Employed: From _____ To _____

Reason for leaving _____

Company _____

Address _____

Phone # (____)_____

Supervisor _____

Dates Employed: From _____ To _____

Reason for Leaving _____

MILITARY SERVICE:

Branch_____ Discharge Date_____

Rank_____

National Guard/Reserve Yes_____ No___

Date Obligation Ends _____

REFERENCES:

Name _____

Company _____

Address _____

Phone # (____)_____

Name _____

Company _____

Address _____

Phone # (____)_____

I acknowledge that the Company is relying on the information given and I certify that the information in this form is true to the best of my knowledge. I authorize the company to obtain information from any person named above, and I release all concerned from any liability in connection with obtaining and releasing such information.

Signature of Applicant _____ Date_____

REQUEST FOR EMPLOYMENT
VERIFICATION AND AUTHORIZATION (9-02)

This form should be completed by each prospective employee being considered for Employment. It requests and authorizes the release of prior Employment information.

The Request should be printed on company stationery.

REQUEST FOR EMPLOYMENT
VERIFICATION AND AUTHORIZATION

1. The date of the request.

_____[1]_____

2. The name and address of the former employer.

TO: _____[2]_____
_____
_____

3. The name of the employee.

4. The employee's social security number.

Re: Employment of _____[3]_____
Soc. Sec. No. _____[4]_____

5. Choose one.

Gentlemen:

6. The position the employee held at the former company.

_____[3]_____ has applied for a position with our company and has advised us that *[5][he]* **OR** *[she]* was employed by you as _____[6]_____ from _____[7]_____ to _____[7]_____. It would be appreciated if you would verify the employment and provide the final salary. Additional comments regarding your evaluation of this applicant would be most helpful.

7. The dates of the former Employment.

8. The name and title of the person sending the letter printed directly below the line, with that person to sign above the line.

9. The name of the employee printed directly below the line, with the employee to sign above the line. (Note: while a release by the employee is not necessary, it puts the employee on notice that his Employment history is likely to be verified and gives the prior employer comfort in knowing that he can release to the proposed new employer the truth, "warts and all.")

Very truly yours,

_____
[8]

I hereby authorize the release of all information regarding my employment.

_____
[9]

EMPLOYMENT AGREEMENT (9-03)

This Employment Agreement is for use with middle management employees. As the level of management increases, the Employment Agreement becomes more sophisticated to deal with increasingly complex issues. The language should be carefully worded so that there can be no misunderstanding as to its intent. Wherever possible, examples should be used, as in paragraph 4 where the present language could be followed by "as an example: a private corner office, desktop computer and a private secretary." Also see the Non-competition Agreement, the Non–disclosure Agreement and Employee Invention forms in this chapter, which may be used as separate agreements or incorporated into this Agreement.

EMPLOYMENT AGREEMENT

1. The date the Agreement is signed.

2. The name of the Employer.

3. If the Employer is a corporation, insert the state of incorporation. Otherwise delete.

4. The name of the Employee being hired.

5. The beginning and ending dates of the Employment period.

6. The amount of the salary and time period it will cover, in numbers, for example "$5,000 per month."

7. The frequency with which the salary is to be paid, for example "weekly" or "semi-monthly."

8. A description of the Employee's duties and his title, if any.

9. The agreed upon number of weeks of paid vacation, in numbers.

10. Delete if there is to be no reduction in salary during a prolonged illness and renumber the remaining paragraphs.

Employment Agreement this __[1]__ day of _____, 19__ by and between _____[2]_____ *[3][, a _____ corporation]* ("Employer") and _____[4]_____ ("Employee").

Employer employs the Employee and the Employee accepts employment, upon the terms conditions and covenants as follows:

1. The term of employment shall be from _____[5]_____ to _____[5]_____.

2. Employee shall receive, for all services rendered, a salary of $_____[6]_____ per ___[6]___, payable _____[7]_____. Salary payments shall be subject to withholding and other applicable deductions.

3. The duties of Employee shall be _____ [8] _____ _____. The Employee shall devote his full and entire time and attention to the Employer's business.

4. Employee shall have an office, facilities and services that are suitable to the position and appropriate for the performance of Employee's duties.

5. Employer shall reimburse Employee for all reasonable expenses incurred in the performance of Employee's business, e.g. entertainment, travel, etc. Employee will be reimbursed upon submission of an itemized account of such expenditures with receipts where practicable.

6. Employee shall be entitled to __[9]__ weeks of paid vacation each year.

[10][7. If Employee is unable to perform Employee's

(Document continued on next page)

11. The number of weeks of paid sick leave, in numbers.

12. The reduced salary during a prolonged illness, in numbers, and the period it will cover.

13. Since no Employer can continue to pay an Employee indefinitely when the Employee is unable to work, determine and insert a cut-off time. Note: if the Employee is female, be sure to consult your State Department of Labor as to state law regarding maternity leave and make reference to such law in this paragraph as follows: "This provision is subject to _____ regarding pregnancy and maternity leave" and insert the appropriate statutory reference, for example "New York Executive Law, Section 296."

14. The number of days' notice, in words and numbers, upon which either party may cancel the Agreement.

15. If there is to be severance pay, insert the amount, for example "one week of salary for every year of employment." If not, delete the last two sentences of the paragraph and replace with: "Employee shall receive salary up to the last day of employment and under no circumstances shall there be severance pay."

16. If there is to be a death benefit, insert the amount, in numbers. If not, delete from "and as a death benefit..." to the end of the sentence.

17. The city and state where arbitration is to be conducted, typically the location of the Employer.

duties by reason of illness or incapacity for a consecutive period of more than ___[11]___ weeks, the compensation payable after the aforesaid period shall be $____[12]_____ per _____[12]_____. Upon return to full employment, full compensation shall be reinstated.]

8. Notwithstanding any provision in this Employment Agreement to the contrary, if Employee is unable to perform or is absent from employment for a period of more than __[13]__ months, Employer may terminate this Employment Agreement, without further cause, and all obligations of Employer hereunder shall terminate.

9. This Employment Agreement may be terminated, at will, at any time and without cause, by either party upon ____[14]____ (__) days' written notice to the other. *[If Employer elects to terminate, Employer shall pay to Employee on the last day of employment severance pay of _____[15]_____, subject to withholding and deductions. If Employee elects to terminate, Employee shall receive salary up to the last day of employment but no severance pay.]*

10. In the event Employee dies during the term of Employment, Employer shall pay to Employee's estate the salary that would otherwise be payable to the end of the month in which the Employee died *[and as a death benefit a sum equal to $_____[16]_____].*

11. Any controversy or claim arising out of, or relating to this Employment Agreement, or the breach thereof, shall be settled by arbitration in the City of ____[17]____, State of ____[17]____, in accordance with the then governing rules of the American Arbitration Association. Judgment upon the award rendered by the arbitrator(s) may be entered in any court of competent jurisdiction.

12. Any notice required to be given shall be either: (i) personally delivered, or (ii) sent by U.S. Postal Service, postage pre-paid, Certified Mail, Return Receipt Requested to the Employer at the place of employment and to the Employee at the last residence address given to and on file with the Employer.

13. A waiver of a breach of any provision of this Employ-

(Document continued on next page)

18. The name of the Employer if a corporation. Otherwise delete the line.

19. If the Employer is an individual, delete "BY" and print the Employer's name directly below the line, with the Employer to sign above the line. If the Employer is a corporation, print the name and title of the person acting for the corporation directly below the line, with that person to sign above the line.

20. The name of the Employee printed directly below the line, with the Employee to sign above the line.

ment Agreement shall not operate or be construed as a waiver of any subsequent breach.

14. The services of Employee are personal and unique and therefore Employee may not assign this Employment Agreement nor delegate the duties and obligations hereunder except in the normal course of business.

15. This Employment Agreement contains the entire understanding of the parties, except as may be set forth in writing signed by the party against whom enforcement may be sought, simultaneously with or subsequent to the execution of this Employment Agreement.

INTENDING TO BE LEGALLY BOUND, the parties have executed this Employment Agreement as of the date first above written.

_____*[18]*_____

*BY*_____
                [19] (Employer)

_____
                [20] (Employee)

INCENTIVE COMPENSATION AGREEMENT (9-04)

This Agreement provides for the payment of a cash bonus by an Employer to an Employee. It may be incorporated into the Employment Agreement found in this chapter.

A stock option provision was not not made part of this Agreement for two reasons. First, the Stock Purchase Option Agreement elsewhere in this book may be used. Second, consultation with a local attorney is recommended to be sure that offering stock options does not require the company to be registered either with the state or with the Securities and Exchange Commission.

INCENTIVE COMPENSATION AGREEMENT

1. The date the Agreement is signed.

2. The name of the Company.

3. If the Company is a corporation, insert the state in which incorporated. Otherwise delete.

4. The name of the Employee.

5. Choose one. If the second alternative is chosen skip to No. 9.

6. The percentage of pre-tax profits, in words.

7. The percentage of pre-tax profits, in numbers.

8. The number of days, in numbers, after the close of the company's fiscal year by which the Incentive Compensation will be paid.

9. The minimum amount of Incentive Compensation to be paid, in numbers. (Note: if no minimum amount is promised, end the paragraph after the words "sole discretion.")

10. The time period for which Incentive Compensation is paid, for example "per month."

Agreement made this __[1]__ day of _____, 19__, by and between _____[2]_____ *[3][, a _____ corporation]* ("Company") and _____[4]_____ ("Employee").

Company desires to grant to Employee an incentive for the performance of Employee's duties. Company hereby grants to Employee as follows:

[5][In addition to Employee's regular salary, Employee shall receive compensation equal to _____[6]_____ (__[7]__%) percent of the Company's pre-tax profits, as determined by the Company's accountants, in accordance with generally accepted accounting principles. Such additional compensation shall be determined, and paid to Employee within __[8]__ days of the end of the Company's fiscal year.] **OR** *[In addition to all other compensation, Employee shall receive bonus compensation in such form and amounts and at such times as the Company shall determine in its sole discretion, but in any event no less than $ _____[9]_____ per ____[10]____.]*

(Document continued on next page)

11. The name of the Company if a corporation. Otherwise delete the line.

12. If the Company is not a corporation, delete "BY" and print the individual's name directly below the line, with the individual to sign above the line. If the Company is a corporation, print the name and title of the person acting for the corporation directly below the line, with that person to sign above the line.

13. The name of the Employee printed directly below the line, with the Employee to sign above the line.

INTENDING TO BE LEGALLY BOUND, the parties hereto have caused this Incentive Compensation Agreement to be executed as of the date first above written.

_____*[11]*_____

BY_____
[12] (Company)

_____
[13] (Employee)

TUITION REIMBURSEMENT AGREEMENT (9-05)

To encourage the development of an Employee, a company may assist the Employee in obtaining additional education (either for general educational purposes or for specific purposes relating to job performance) and to provide tuition reimbursement. This Agreement permits the Employer to monitor the Employee's performance both at school and on the job to determine if the Tuition Reimbursement should continue.

TUITION REIMBURSEMENT AGREEMENT

1. This Agreement should be on Company stationery.

2. The name of the Company.

[1] [COMPANY STATIONERY]

_____[2]_____, believing that it is to the benefit of the Company to further the formal eduction of its employees, agrees with the undersigned Employee as follows:

1.   The Company shall reimburse the Employee for tuition expenses incurred by the Employee for educational courses taken at a recognized learning institution leading to a high school diploma, high school equivalency certificate, associate degree, college degree or graduate degree or as otherwise approved by the Company, provided the Employee:

(A)   submits to the Company a program of study from the learning institution indicating the courses to be taken and the diploma, certificate or degree that will result; and

(B)   submits to the Company paid receipts for tuition; and

(C)   maintains a satisfactory work record with the Company; and

(D)   maintains a passing grade average for all courses taken under this program.

2.   Reimbursement shall be made at the commencement of each course, provided however, that if reimbursement has been made for prior courses, the Employee has received passing grades for those courses.

3.   Employee agrees that the cost of books, transportation and other incidental expenses shall be borne by the Employee.

(Document continued on next page)

3. The name of the Company if a corporation. Otherwise delete the line.

4. If the Company is not a corporation, delete "BY" and print the individual's name directly below the line, with the individual to sign above the line. If the Company is a corporation, print the name and title of the individual acting for the corporation directly below the line, with that person to sign above the line.

5. The date the Agreement is signed by the Employee.

6. The name of the Employee printed directly below the line, with the Employee to sign above the line.

4.   The Company reserves the right to terminate this program at will except as to courses for which the Employee shall have paid tuition prior to the termination date.

_____*[3]*_____

*BY*_____
[4]

ACCEPTED

Date: _____[5]_____

_____
[6] (Employee)

NON-COMPETITION AGREEMENT (9-06)

Non-competition Agreements are common when an Employee is hired for a sensitive position and a change of employment to a competitor would prove injurious to the Employer's business. Non-competition agreements have usually been upheld by the court if they meet two criteria: they must be reasonable in length of time and reasonable in geographic area. For example, an Employer cannot prevent a former Employee from ever working throughout the entire United States.

WARNING

Some states, for example California, prohibit Non-competition Agreements. Therefore, be sure to check your state's employment laws before using this form.

NON-COMPETITION AGREEMENT

1. The date the Agreement is signed.

2. The name of the Employer.

3. If the Employer is a corporation, insert the state of incorporation. Otherwise delete.

4. The name of the Employee being hired.

5. The period of non-competition. As a general rule this should not exceed three years.

6. The geographic area to be prohibited, such as "in the state of Illinois." As a general rule this should not go beyond the states bordering the state in which the company is located.

7. The name of the Employer if a corporation. Otherwise delete the line.

8. If the Employer is an individual, delete "BY" and type the Employer's name directly below the line, with the Employer to sign above the line. If the Employer is a corporation, print the name and title of the person acting for the corporation directly below the line, with that person to sign above the line.

9. The name of the Employee printed directly below the line, with the Employee to sign above the line.

Agreement made this __[1]__ day of _____, 19__ by and between _____[2]_____ *[3][, a _____ corporation]* ("Employer") and _____[4]_____ ("Employee").

Employee has this day accepted employment offered by Employer and in consideration of the employment agrees as follows:

1. During the period of employment, Employee shall not engage in any other business activity, directly or indirectly, regardless of whether it is for profit, gain or otherwise that is similar to the business activity of Employer.

2. In the event of the termination of employment, whether voluntary or involuntary, Employee agrees that Employee will not for a period of _____[5]_____ from the effective date of termination engage in a business activity similar to that of Employer _____[6]_____.

INTENDING TO BE LEGALLY BOUND, the parties have executed this Agreement as of the date first above written.

_____*[7]*_____

BY _____
        [8] (Employer)

_____
        [9] (Employee)

NON-DISCLOSURE AGREEMENT (9-07)

A Non-disclosure Agreement is similar to a Non-competition Agreement but it is not limited in scope or geographic location. As its name implies, the Agreement prevents an Employee from disclosing information learned on the job to the Employer's competitors.

NON-DISCLOSURE AGREEMENT

1. The date the Agreement is signed.

2. The name of the Employer.

3. If the Employer is a corporation, insert the state of incorporation. Otherwise delete.

4. The name of the Employee being hired.

5. A description of the information to be protected, for example "customer lists," "product development information," "computer software," etc.

Agreement made this __[1]__ day of _____, 19__ by and between _____[2]_____ *[3][, a _____ corporation]* ("Employer") and _____[4]_____ ("Employee").

Employee has this day accepted employment offered by Employer and in consideration of the employment agrees as follows:

1. During the course of employment, Employee shall become aware of certain methods, practices and procedures with which Employer conducts its business, including but not limited to: _____[5]_____, all of which Employer and Employee agree are proprietary information and as such are trade secrets.

2. Employee will not at any time, either during his/her employment or thereafter divulge, furnish, or make available, either directly or indirectly, to any person, firm, corporation or other entity any proprietary information used by Employer. Employee agrees that all such matters and information shall be kept strictly and absolutely confidential.

3. Employee, upon the cessation of his/her employment, irrespective of the time, manner or reason of termination, will immediately surrender and deliver to Employer all lists, books, records, memoranda and data of every kind relating to all proprietary information and all property belonging to Employer.

4. Employee acknowledges that a breach of any of the provisions of this Agreement may result in continuing and irreparable damages to Employer for which there may be no adequate remedy at law and that Employer in addition to all other relief available to Employer shall be entitled to the issuance of an injunction restraining Employee from committing or continuing any breach of this Agreement.

(Document continued on next page)

NON-DISCLOSURE AGREEMENT *continued*

6. The state whose laws will goven the Agreement, typically the state in which the Employer is located.

7. The name of the Employer if a corporation. Otherwise delete the line.

8. If the Employer is an individual, delete "BY" and print the Employer's name directly below the line, with the Employer to sign above the line. If the Employer is a corporation, print the name and title of the person acting for the corporation directly below the line, with that person to sign above the line.

9. The name of the Employee printed directly below the line, with the Employee to sign above the line.

5. Wherever used "Employer" shall mean _____[2]_____, its subsidiaries and/or affiliates.

6. If any provision of this Agreement shall be determined, by a Court having jurisdiction, to be invalid, or illegal or unenforceable, the remainder of this Agreement shall not be affected but shall continue in full force and effect as though such invalid, illegal or unenforceable provision were not originally a part of this Agreement.

7. This Agreement shall be construed in accordance with and governed by the laws of the State of _____[6]_____, irrespective of the fact that a party hereto may not be a resident of that State.

INTENDING TO BE LEGALLY BOUND, the parties have executed this Agreement as of the date first above written.

_____[7]_____

BY _____
[8] (Employer)

_____
[9] (Employee)

EMPLOYEE INVENTION/
"WORK FOR HIRE" AGREEMENT (9-08)

This Agreement gives to an Employer ownership of anything an Employee creates during the term of his Employment or while "on company time" that relates to his employment. For example, a new computer software program that facilitates doing a particular task within the company is a "work created for hire" and the Employer should not have to involuntarily or additionally compensate the Employee for its creation nor should the Employee be permitted to claim ownership of it.

EMPLOYEE INVENTION/
"WORK FOR HIRE" AGREEMENT

1. The date the Agreement is signed.

2. The name of the Employer.

3. If the Employer is a corporation, insert the state of incorporation. Otherwise delete.

4. The name of the Employee being hired.

5. Change or expand these categories to suit the particular business. As a general rule they can be anything that can be patented or copyrighted.

Agreement made this __[1]__ day of _____, 19__ by and between _____[2]_____ _[3][, a _____ corporation]_ ("Employer") and _____[4]_____ ("Employee").

Employee has this day accepted employment offered by Employer and in consideration therefore agrees as follows:

1. Employee agrees that _[5][all inventions, computer programs and products]_ created by Employee either for use by Employer or which could be used by Employer in furtherance of Employer's business activity, which are created or conceived during the course of employment by Employer, shall be considered as Works Made For Hire and all rights to said Works shall and do vest in Employer.

2. Employee further agrees that said Works are proprietary information not to be divulged, furnished or made available, either directly or indirectly, to any person, firm or corporation or any other entity. Employee agrees that all such proprietary information shall be kept strictly and absolutely confidential.

3. Employee, upon the cessation of his/her employment, irrespective of the time, manner or reason of termination, will immediately surrender and deliver to Employer all data, information and models of every kind and in any stage of progress relating to the Works.

4. Employee acknowledges that a breach of any of the provisions of this Agreement may result in continuing and irreparable damages to Employer for which there may be no adequate remedy at law and that Employer, in addition to all other relief available to Employer, shall be entitled to the issuance of an injunction restraining Employee from committing or continuing any breach of this Agreement.

(Document continued on next page)

6. The state whose laws will goven the Agreement, typically the state in which the Employer is located.

7. The name of the Employer if a corporation. Otherwise delete the line.

8. If the Employer is an individual, delete "BY" and print the name of the Employer directly below the line, with the Employer to sign above the line. If the Employer is a corporation, print the name and title of the person acting for the corporation directly below the line, with that person to sign above the line.

9. The name of the Employee printed directly below the line with the Employee to sign above the line.

5. Wherever used herein "Employer" shall mean _____[2]_____, its subsidiaries and/or affiliates.

6. If any provision of this Agreement shall be determined, by a Court having jurisdiction, to be invalid, illegal or unenforceable, the remainder of this Agreement shall not be affected thereby but shall continue in full force and effect as though such invalid, illegal or unenforceable provisions were not originally a part of this Agreement.

7. This Agreement shall be construed in accordance with and governed by the laws of the State of _____[6]_____, irrespective of the fact that a party hereto may not be a resident of that State.

INTENDING TO BE LEGALLY BOUND, the parties have executed this Agreement as of the date first above written.

_____[7]_____

BY _____
[8] (Employer)

_____
[9] (Employee)

EMPLOYEE WARNING NOTICE (9-09)

To avoid charges of discrimination, unfair dealing or the like, it is advisable to record Warnings given to an Employee for improper conduct. The matter should be discussed with the Employee and a notation made of the date and topic discussed. When the conduct has reached the level where a written Warning must be made, this Notice should be used. The Notice should be prepared in duplicate with one copy given to the Employee and the other to be signed by the Employee to acknowledge receipt and then retained by the company in the Employee's personnel file.

EMPLOYEE WARNING NOTICE

1. The Notice should be on company stationery.

2. The name of the Employee.

3. The date of the conversation with the Employee in which the charges were discussed.

4. A detailed statement of the charges by category and specifics, for example "Lateness, April 1, 1990 arrived 10:15, April 2, 1990 arrived 11:30."

5. The name of the Employer if a corporation. Otherwise delete the line.

6. If the Employer is not a corporation, delete "BY" and print the Employer's name directly below the line, with the Employer to sign above the line. If the Employer is a corporation, print the name and title of the individual acting for the corporation directly below the line, with that person to sign above the line.

7. The date the Employee receives the Notice.

8. The name of the Employee printed below the line, with the Employee to sign above the line.

[1] [COMPANY STATIONERY]

TO: _____[2]_____

This will confirm our conversation of _____[3]_____ and will constitute a formal written notice concerning _____[4]_____.

The above practice is not acceptable to the Company and its continuation may result in suspension from or termination of employment.

This notice is being made a part of your permanent employment record.

_____*[5]*_____

BY_____
[6]

RECEIVED

Date: _____[7]_____

_____
[8] (Employee)

EMPLOYEE SUSPENSION NOTICE (9-10)

This form should be used after sending an Employee Warning Notice or used in its place if the conduct is serious enough to warrant immediate suspension. The Employee Suspension Notice becomes part of the record justifying a subsequent termination. The Notice should be prepared in duplicate with one copy given to the Employee and the other to be signed by the Employee to acknowledge receipt and then retained by the company in the Employee's personnel file.

1. The Notice should be on company stationery.

2. The name of the Employee.

3. The date of the warning notice, or if there was no warning notice, delete the paragraph and replace with: "On __(date)__ you __(describe the incident)__. This conduct is not acceptable and warrants suspension from employment." Then skip to No. 5.

4. A description of the incident in detail.

5. The period of suspension, for example "one week."

6. The date suspension is to begin.

7. The name of the Employer if a corporation. Otherwise delete the line.

8. If the Employer is not a corporation, delete "BY" and print the Employer's name directly below the line, with the Employer to sign above the line. If the Employer is a corporation, print the name and title of the individual acting for the corporation directly below the line, with that person to sign above the line.

9. The date the Employee receives the Notice.

10. The name of the Employee printed below the line, with the Employee to sign above the line.

EMPLOYEE SUSPENSION NOTICE

[1] [COMPANY STATIONERY]

TO: _____[2]_____

You have received informal notices that your conduct has been found to be unsatisfactory. On _____[3]_____ a formal Warning Notice was placed in your permanent employment record. The unacceptable conduct was continued by you in that _____[4]_____.

You are herewith suspended from work for a period of ____[5]____ commencing _____[6]_____. Suspension shall be without pay; however, your health benefits shall continue during the suspension providing you return to work immediately following the suspension period.

YOU MAY BE SUBJECT TO TERMINATION IN THE FUTURE IF YOU CONTINUE TO VIOLATE COMPANY POLICY.

_____[7]_____

BY_____
[8]

RECEIVED

Date: _____[9]_____

_____
[10] (Employee)

EMPLOYEE TERMINATION/
INVOLUNTARY DISCHARGE NOTICE (9-11)

There are many reasons for terminating the employment of an Employee. This form deals with two possible causes: employee misconduct or layoff due to poor business conditions. Choose the paragraph that applies.

EMPLOYEE TERMINATION/
INVOLUNTARY DISCHARGE NOTICE

1. The Notice should be on company stationery.

[1] [COMPANY STATIONERY]

2. The name of the Employee.

TO: _____[2]_____

3. Choose one, depending on why the Employee is being terminated.

[3][On _____[4]_____ we discussed your employee performance record, [_____[5]_____,] and you were advised that your performance was not satisfactory for continued employment.

4. The date the Employee was personally notified that he was terminated.

5. Insert if appropriate: "and issued a warning notice and/ or suspension to you on _____" and state the dates. Otherwise delete.

Your employment will be terminated on _____[6]_____ and you shall receive all compensation due to you at that time. In accordance with Federal Regulations you shall be notified of your options to continue in the Company health plan.]

6. The date employment ceases.

OR

7. The name of the Employer if a corporation. Otherwise delete the line.

[On _____[4]_____ we discussed your continued employment with the Company and the market conditions under which the Company is now operating. Under the circumstances your position has been necessarily eliminated.

8. If the Employer is not a corporation, delete "BY" and print the Employer's name directly below the line, with the Employer to sign above the line. If the Employer is a corporation, print the name and title of the individual acting for the corporation directly below the line, with that person to sign above the line.

Your employment will be terminated on _____[6]_____ and you shall receive all compensation due to you at that time. In accordance with Federal Regulations you shall be notified of your options to continue in the Company health plan.]

Very truly yours,

_____[7]_____

BY_____
[8]

SALES REPRESENTATIVE AGREEMENT (9-12)

Rather than hire employees to sell its products (thereby obligating the company to pay salary, benefits, social security, etc.), a company may instead hire independent Sales Representatives who work strictly on a commission basis. This Agreement contains the necessary elements for maintaining Sales Representatives as independent contractors rather than as employees.

SALES REPRESENTATIVE AGREEMENT

1. The Agreement should be on company stationery.

2. The name and address of the Sales Representative.

3. The name of the Sales Representative.

4. A description of the products to be sold.

5. A description of the geographic limitations of the sales territory, for example "The New England states and Pennsylvania."

[1] [COMPANY STATIONERY]

_____ [2] _____

_____

_____

Dear _____ [3] _____ :

The purpose of this letter is to set forth our agreement with respect to the terms and conditions upon which you agree to act as a direct seller of products distributed by the undersigned:

1. Effective as of the date of execution of this Agreement, you are engaged by the undersigned as a non-exclusive direct seller for _____ [4] _____ in _____ [5] _____ .

2. In such capacity, you will pursue such leads as you may obtain or that we may supply to you for the sale to such individuals who are interested in purchasing the undersigned's products. All sales will be at such purchase price as shall be mutually agreed upon by you and the undersigned.

3. You will use your best efforts to promote the sales and obtain orders for the undersigned and shall at all times maintain the good will between the undersigned and its customers.

4. You will determine the methods of carrying out your obligations hereunder and the number of hours that you will work. At all times you will maintain standards of performance and behavior established by the undersigned and will conduct your activities in accordance with standards and directions of the undersigned. You may employ such individuals as

(Document continued on next page)

6. On a separate sheet headed "Schedule A" state the commission structure.

7. Typically, the state in which the company has its place of business.

you may desire on such terms and conditions that you may establish, and you alone will be solely responsible for the payment of salaries and/or other compensation to your employees and for the payment of federal, state and local tax obligations with respect to such payments.

5. In consideration for the services to be rendered by you, you will receive commissions in accordance with the Schedule which is attached hereto and is set forth as Schedule A [6]. Such Schedule of Payment is subject to change by the undersigned upon prior written notice. Such commissions will be payable upon delivery of the products sold.

6. It is agreed that you will not be treated as an employee of the undersigned for federal and state tax purposes. Rather, you will be an independent contractor and will be solely responsible for payment of all federal, state and local tax obligations with respect to all amounts paid to you by the undersigned.

7. This agreement will continue until terminated by either of us at will.

8. Any controversy or claim arising out of or relating to this Agreement, or the breach thereof, shall be settled by arbitration in accordance with the then obtaining rules of the American Arbitration Association in the State of ____[7]____, and a judgment upon any award rendered by the arbitrator(s) may be entered in any court having jurisdiction thereof.

If the foregoing accurately contains the terms and conditions of our Agreement, kindly execute the enclosed

(Document continued on next page)

8. The name of the company if a corporation. Otherwise delete the line.

9. If the company is not a corporation, delete "BY" and print the name of the individual sending the letter directly below the line, with the individual to sign above the line. If the company is a corporation, print the name and title of the individual acting for the corporation directly below the line, with that person to sign above the line.

10. The date the Sales Representative signs the Agreement.

11. The name of the Sales Representative printed directly below the line, with the Sales Representative to sign above the line.

copy of this letter Agreement where indicated and return it to the undersigned.

Very truly yours,

_____*[8]*_____

BY _____
[9]

ACCEPTED

Date _____[10]_____

_____
[11]

SALES AGENCY AGREEMENT (9-13)

This Agreement is similar to the preceding Sales Representative Agreement but is broader in application, covering a wider range of products and giving the Agent more latitude.

SALES AGENCY AGREEMENT

1. The date the Agreement is signed.

2. The name of the Principal (the party contracting with the Agent).

3. If the Principal is a corporation, insert the state in which incorporated. Otherwise delete.

4. The name of the Agent.

5. If the Agent is a corporation, insert the state in which incorporated. Otherwise delete.

6. Insert either "exclusive" or "non-exclusive."

7. On a separate sheet headed "Schedule A" list the products, with their prices, to be sold by the Agent.

8. A description of the territory in which the Agent may sell, for example "the New England states and Pennsylvania."

Agreement made this __[1]__ day of _____, 19__, by and between _____[2]_____ *[3][, a _____ corporation]* ("Principal") and _____[4]_____ *[5][, a _____ corporation]* ("Agent").

In consideration of the mutual terms, conditions and covenants hereinafter set forth, Principal and Agent agree as follows:

1. Principal appoints Agent as its _____[6]_____ sales representative to sell the products of the Principal as listed in the attached Schedule A [7].

2. Agent accepts the appointment and agrees to promote, market and sell the products of the Principal at the prices set forth in Schedule A.

3. The parties agree that the list of products and/or prices may be amended from time to time. Principal may unilaterally remove products from the list or change prices. Additions to the product list shall be by mutual agreement.

4. Agent's territory to sell products shall be _____[8]_____ (the "Territory"), which may be amended by mutual written agreement.

5. With Principal's prior written consent, Agent may attempt to sell product outside Agent's Territory or at prices different from those on Schedule A. Principal's consent shall be on an individual sale basis only and shall not be construed to expand Agent's territory or to amend Schedule A.

6. Principal shall furnish to Agent all sales material for the products listed on Schedule A and shall keep the material up-to-date.

7. Agent shall use its best efforts to promote, market and sell the products of Schedule A within the allocated territory, devote such time and attention as may be reasonably necessary, and abide by the Principal's policies.

(Document continued on next page)

SALES AGENCY AGREEMENT *continued*

9. The number of years, in numbers, after the Agreement ends, during which the Agent will not compete with the Principal. It is advisable not to exceed three years. (Note: in some states, for example California, non-competition restrictions are prohibited by law. Check your state's law before including this provision.)

10. On a separate sheet headed "Schedule B" list the commission schedule. Include sales quotas if desired.

11. The number of years, in numbers, of the Agreement.

12. The number of days, in words and numbers, of advance notice of termination.

8.   Agent agrees that during the term of this Agreement and for a period of __[9]__ years thereafter, Agent, either directly or indirectly, shall handle no products that are competitive with those products listed in Schedule A within the Territory.

9.   Agent shall obtain, at its own expense, all necessary licenses and permits to permit Agent to conduct business as contemplated herein. Agent represents and warrants that Agent shall conduct business in strict conformity with all local, state and federal laws, rules and regulations.

10.   Principal agrees that Agent may employ representatives in furtherance of this Agreement and Agent agrees that Agent shall be solely responsible for the payment of wages or commissions to those representatives and that under no circumstances shall Agent's representatives be deemed employees of Principal for any purpose whatsoever.

11.   Principal shall pay to Agent a commission on the sale of products as set forth on Schedule B [10], which commission may be amended from time to time by mutual agreement. Principal shall be responsible for the granting of credit to customers and shall pay commissions to Agent on the 15th date of the month for all merchandise shipped by Principal in the preceding month.

12.   This Agreement shall be for a period of __[11]__ years unless sooner terminated by either party upon _____[12]_____ (__) days' written notice, without cause.

13.   Upon termination Agent shall be entitled to receive commissions for all orders accepted by Principal prior to the date of termination. Payment to be made upon shipment.

14.   Agent is an independent contractor and nothing contained in this Agreement shall be deemed or interpreted to constitute the Agent as a partner or employee of the Principal, nor shall either party have any authority to bind the other in any respect, it being understood and agreed that all orders submitted by Agent are subject to acceptance by Principal in its sole discretion.

15.   It is agreed between the parties that there are no

(Document continued on next page)

13. The state whose laws will govern the Agreement, typically the state in which the Principal is located.

14. The name of the Principal if a corporation. Otherwise delete the line.

15. If the Principal is an individual, delete "BY" and print the Principal's name directly below the line, with the Principal to sign above the line. If the Principal is a corporation, print the name and title of the person acting for the corporation directly below the line, with that person to sign above the line.

16. The name of the Agent if a Corporation. Otherwise delete the line.

17. If the Agent is an individual, delete "BY" and print the Agent's name directly below the line, with the Agent to sign above the line. If the Agent is a corporation, print the name and title of the person acting for the corporation directly below the line, with that person to sign above the line.

other agreements or understandings between them relating to the subject matter of this Agreement. This Agreement supersedes all prior agreements, oral or written, between the parties and is intended as a complete and exclusive statement of the agreement between the parties. No change or modification of this Agreement shall be valid unless the same be in writing and signed by the parties.

16.   This Agreement shall not be assigned by Agent without the prior written consent of Principal.

17.   All notices required or permitted to be given hereunder shall be in writing and may be delivered personally or by Certified Mail - Return Receipt Requested, postage prepaid, addressed to the party's last known address.

18.   This Agreement shall be construed in accordance with and governed by the laws of the State of _____[13]_____.

INTENDING TO BE LEGALLY BOUND, the parties hereto have caused this Agreement to be executed as of the date first above written.

_____[14]_____

BY_____
          [15] (Principal)

_____[16]_____

BY_____
          [17] (Agent)

AGENCY AGREEMENT (9-14)

An Agency Agreement is used to appoint an Agent as a Venture Manager (see the Joint Venture Agreement elsewhere in this book) or for other types of business situations where an "employee" or "consultant" arrangement is not desirable.

AGENCY AGREEMENT

1. The date the Agreement is signed.

2. The name of the party granting the Agency (the Company).

3. If the Company is a corporation, insert the state of incorporation. Otherwise delete.

4. The name of the Agent.

5. If the Agent is a corporation, insert the state of incorporation. Otherwise delete.

6. A description of the business in which the Company is engaged, for example "the purchase and resale of souvenirs commemorating Custer's Last Stand."

7. A description of the purpose for which the Agent is being engaged, for example "managing the Joint Venture known as Custer's Commemorative."

8. A description of the duties of the Agent, for example "design, have manufactured and conduct wholesale sales of souvenirs commemorating Custer's Last Stand."

9. The amount of time the Agent is to devote to the agency, for example "such time and efforts as is required," "___ hours per week," "all of its time and effort."

10. The termination date of the Agreement.

11. The number of days, in words and numbers, for Notice.

Agency Agreement made this _[1]_ day of _____, 19__ by and between _____[2]_____ *[3][, a _____ corporation]* (the "Company") and _____[4]_____ *[5][, a _____ corporation]* (the "Agent").

The Company is engaged in the business of _____[6]_____ and desires to engage the Agent in furtherance of that business.

In consideration of the mutual terms, conditions and covenants hereinafter set forth, the parties agree as follows:

1. The Company engages the Agent for the purposes of _____[7]_____.

2. The duties of the Agent shall be _____[8]_____ and the Agent shall devote _____[9]_____.

3. This Agreement shall continue in full force and effect until _____[10]_____ but may be terminated by either party upon __[11]__ (__) days' written notice to the other, Certified Mail, Return Receipt Requested.

4. For the services performed hereunder the Agent

(Document continued on next page)

12. The commission rate agreed upon, in numbers.

13. The name of the Company if a corporation. Otherwise delete the line.

14. If the Company is not a corporation, delete "BY" and print the individual's name directly below the line, with the individual to sign above the line. If the Company is a corporation, print the name and title of the individual acting for the corporation directly below the line, with that person to sign above the line.

15. The name of the Agent if a corporation. Otherwise delete the line.

16. If the Agent is an individual, delete "BY" and print the individual's name directly below the line, with the individual to sign above the line. If the Agent is a corporation, print the name and title of the individual acting for the corporation directly below the line, with that person to sign above the line.

shall receive compensation at the rate of __ [12]__% of wholesale sales, net of freight, discounts and returns. Commissions shall be deemed earned when goods are shipped and invoices paid.

5.   The Agent shall not represent any company or product engaged in the same business as the Company during the lifetime of this Agreement nor for a period of twelve (12) months thereafter if the Agent terminates this Agreement prior to its expiration date.

6.   The Agent may employ any employee it deems necessary to accomplish the purposes of this Agency but such employee(s) shall not be deemed to be employee(s) of the Company and they shall look only to the Agent for compensation.

7.   Nothing contained in this Agreement shall be construed to constitute the Agent as a partner, joint venturer, principal or employee of the Company, it being intended that the Agent is an independent contractor responsible for its own actions.

      INTENDING TO BE LEGALLY BOUND, the parties have signed this Agency Agreement as of the date first above written.

_____*[13]*_____

BY_____
      [14] (Company)

_____*[15]*_____

BY_____
      [16] (Agent)

CONSULTING AGREEMENT (9-15)

A Consultant typically is called upon when special skills are required for a specific period of time or for a specific project. This Consulting Agreement covers the basic issues in contracting for the services of such a party.

CONSULTING AGREEMENT

1. The date the Agreement is signed.

2. The name of the Company employing the Consultant.

3. If the Company is a corporation insert the state in which incorporated. Otherwise delete.

4. The name of the Consultant.

5. If the Consultant is a corporation, insert the state of incorporation. Otherwise delete.

6. The starting date of the Agreement.

7. The ending date of the Agreement.

8. The number of days, in words and numbers, of advance notice of termination.

9. The amount, in numbers, to be paid to the Consultant.

10. The time period for which the amount in No. 8 is to be applied, for example "per month."

11. The frequency of payment, for example "quarterly."

12. A description of the services to be performed by the Consultant.

Agreement made this __[1]__ day of _____, 19__ by and between _____[2]_____ *[3][, a _____ corporation]* ("Company") and _____[4]_____ *[5][, a _____ corporation]* ("Consultant").

Consultant is an independent contractor willing to provide certain skills and abilities to the Company that the Company has need for.

In consideration of the mutual terms, conditions and covenants hereinafter set forth, Company and Consultant agree as follows:

1. The Company hereby employs the Consultant as an independent contractor, and the Consultant hereby accepts employment.

2. The term of this Agreement shall commence on _____[6]_____ and shall terminate on _____[7]_____. After the first thirty (30) days of the term, either party may, without cause, terminate this Agreement by giving _____[8]_____ (__) days' written notice to the other.

3. Company shall pay to Consultant and Consultant shall accept from the Company as compensation for all services to be provided pursuant to this Agreement, the sum of $_____[9]_____ per _____[10]_____ payable ____[11]____.

4. Consultant shall provide on an "as needed" basis the following services: _____[12]_____. Consultant shall devote such time, attention and energies as required.

5. Consultant is an independent contractor and may engage in other business activities provided, however, that Consultant shall not during the term of this Agreement solicit Company's employees or accounts on behalf of Consultant or another entity.

(Document continued on next page)

13. The state whose laws will govern the Agreement, typically the state in which the Company is located.

14. The name of the Company if a corporation. Otherwise delete the line.

15. If the Company is not a corporation, delete "BY" and print the individual's name directly below the line, with the individual to sign above the line. If the Company is a corporation, print the name and title of the person acting for the corporation directly below the line, with that person to sign above the line.

16. The name of the Consultant if a corporation. Otherwise delete the line.

17. If the Consultant is an individual, print the Consultant's name directly below the line, with the Consultant to sign above the line. If the Consultant is a corporation, print the name and title of the person acting for the corporation directly below the line, with that person to sign above the line.

6.   If Consultant becomes unable to perform services pursuant to this Agreement by reason of illness, incapacity or death, compensation shall cease upon the happening of the event.

7.   Neither party may assign this Agreement without the express written consent of the other party.

8.   Consultant is an independent contractor and nothing contained in this Agreement shall be deemed or interpreted to constitute the Consultant as a partner, agent or employee of the Company, nor shall either party have any authority to bind the other.

9.   It is agreed between the parties that there are no other agreements or understandings between them relating to the subject matter of this Agreement. This Agreement supersedes all prior agreements, oral or written, between the parties and is intended as a complete and exclusive statement of the agreement between the parties. No change or modification of this Agreement shall be valid unless the same be in writing and signed by the parties.

10.   All notices required or permitted to be given hereunder shall be in writing and may be delivered personally or by Certified Mail - Return Receipt Requested, postage prepaid, addressed to the party's last known address.

11.   This Agreement shall be construed in accordance with and governed by the laws of the State of _____[13]_____.

        INTENDING TO BE LEGALLY BOUND, the parties hereto have caused this Agreement to be executed as of the date first above written.

_____*[14]*_____

*BY*_____
                    [15] (Company)

_____*[16]*_____

*BY*_____
                    [17] (Consultant)

Releases, Powers of Attorney and Notary Statements 10

This chapter contains legal forms that are used in a broad range of situations.

Releases These forms should be used whenever a person or a business is asked to give up a right it may have. There are General Releases (giving up the right to sue in court), for both individuals and corporations, a Model/Photographer's Release (giving up the right to prevent others from using your photo), and a Customer Testimonial Release (giving up the right to prevent others from using your testimonial).

Powers of Attorney This section provides a Power of Attorney and related forms used to authorize others to act for an individual when he is not present to act.

Notary Statements A Notary Public attests to the authenticity of a signature through the use of a Notary Statement. Two such statements are presented in this section, one for an individual's signature and the other for the signature of a person signing on behalf of a corporation.

GENERAL RELEASE (From an Individual) (10-01)

The General Release is one of the most commonly used legal documents. This form and the one following, General Release (From a Corporation), are used whenever a dispute is resolved between two parties. The type of dispute can include the amount of a bill, an employment contract, an exchange of merchandise, the termination of a contract, etc. The rule to follow is: exchange releases whenever you resolve a dispute.

GENERAL RELEASE (From an Individual)

1. The name of the person giving the Release in exchange for receiving money or other consideration (the RELEASOR).

2. The address of the RELEASOR.

3. The dollar amount, in words, being paid. If there is no money being paid, or the consideration is the promise not to sue, enter "Ten."

4. The dollar amount, in numbers.

5. The name of the party paying the money and getting the Release (the RELEASEE).

6. Identify the RELEASEE by entering his address if an individual, or if a corporation by entering the state in which the RELEASEE is incorporated and its current office address; i.e. "a _____ Corporation with offices at _____.

7. A description of the facts that gave rise to the dispute; i.e. "a purchase order dated _____,19__," "contract of employment between _____ and _____ dated _____,19__."

_____[1]_____ residing at _____[2]_____ as RELEASOR, in consideration of the sum of _____[3]_____ Dollars ($____[4]____) and other good and valuable consideration received from _____[5]_____, _____[6]_____ as RELEASEE, receipt whereof is hereby acknowledged hereby agrees to release and discharge the RELEASEE, RELEASEE'S heirs, executors, administrators, successors and assigns from any and all actions, causes of action, suits, charges and obligations, debts, dues, sums of money, accounts, reckonings, bonds, bills, specialties, covenants, contracts, controversies, agreements, promises, variances, trespasses, damages, judgments, extents, executions, claims, and demands whatsoever, in law, admiralty or equity, which against the RELEASEE, the RELEASOR, RELEASOR'S heirs, executors, administrators, successors and assigns ever had, now have or hereafter can, shall or may have for, upon, or by reason of any matter, cause or thing whatsoever from the beginning of time to the date of this RELEASE, more specifically:_____[7]_____ _____.

Wherever the sense of this RELEASE requires, a singular number shall be construed to be plural and vice versa, and words of the masculine gender shall be construed to be feminine and vice versa.

This RELEASE may only be changed in writing signed by both RELEASOR and RELEASEE.

(Document continued on next page)

GENERAL RELEASE (From an Individual) *continued*

8. The date the Release is given.

9. The name of the WITNESS printed directly below the line, with the WITNESS to sign above the line.

10. The name of the RELEA-SOR printed directly below the line, with the RELEASOR to sign above the line.

11. The Notary Public completes this part of the form, and signs and seals it by affixing his stamp or seal.

IN WITNESS WHEREOF, the RELEASOR has executed this RELEASE on the __[8]__ day of _____, 19 —.

WITNESS:

_____   _____
        [9]   [10]

STATE OF ____[11]____, COUNTY OF ___[11]___, ss.:

On _____[11]_____, 19__ before me _____[11]_____ personally came _____[11]_____ to me known, and known to me to be the individual(s) described in, and who executed the foregoing RELEASE, and duly acknowledged to me that (t)(s)he(y) executed the same.

_____
               Notary Public

GENERAL RELEASE (From a Corporation) (10-02)

The General Release (From a Corporation) is the companion to the preceding General Release (From an Individual.). The General Release (From a Corporation) should be used whenever a dispute is resolved by a corporation giving the Release.

GENERAL RELEASE (From a Corporation)

1. The name of the corporation giving the Release in exchange for receiving money or other consideration (the RELEASOR).

2. The state in which the RELEASOR is incorporated.

3. The address of the corporation.

4. The dollar amount, in words, being paid. If there is no money being paid, or the consideration is a promise not to sue, enter "Ten."

5. The dollar amount, in numbers.

6. The name of the person or entity paying money or giving other consideration and getting the Release (the RELEASEE).

7. A brief description of the facts giving rise to the dispute, i.e. "a purchase order dated _____," "a contract between _____ and _____."

_____[1]_____, a corporation organized under the laws of the State of _____[2]_____ whose principal place of business is located at _____[3]_____, as RELEASOR, in consideration of the sum of _____[4]_____ Dollars ($____[5]____) received from _____[6]_____, as RELEASEE, the receipt of which is hereby acknowledged, agrees to release and discharge the RELEASEE, RELEASEE's heirs, executors, administrators, successors and assigns from any and all actions, causes of action, suits, charges and obligations, debts, dues, sums of money, accounts, reckonings, bonds, bills, specialties, covenants, contracts, controversies, agreements, promises, variances, trespasses, damages, judgments, extents, executions, claims and demands whatsoever, in law, admiralty or equity, which against the RELEASEE, the RELEASOR, RELEASOR's heirs, executors, administrators, successors and assigns ever had, now have or hereafter can, shall or may have for, upon or by reason of any matter, cause or thing whatsoever from the beginning of time to the date of this RELEASE, and more specifically:_____[7]_____
_____.

Wherever the sense of this RELEASE requires, a singular number shall be construed to be plural and vice versa, and words of the masculine gender shall be construed to be feminine and vice versa.

This RELEASE may only be changed in writing signed by both RELEASOR and RELEASEE.

(Document continued on next page)

GENERAL RELEASE (From a Corporation) *continued*

8. The date the Release is given.

9. The name of the WITNESS printed directly below the line, with the WITNESS to sign above the line.

10. The name and title of the person acting for the corporation printed directly below the line, with that person to sign above the line.

11. The Notary Public completes this part of the form, and signs and seals it by affixing his stamp or seal.

IN WITNESS WHEREOF, the RELEASOR has executed this RELEASE on the __[8]__ day of ———————, 19__.

WITNESS:

————[9]————   ———— [1]————

BY————————
[10]

STATE OF ___[11]___, COUNTY OF ___[11]___, ss.:

On ————[11]————, 19__, before me ————————[11]———————— personally came ————————[11]———————— to me known, who duly sworn, did depose and say that (s)he resides at ————————[11]———————— , that deponent is the ———[11]——— of ————[11]————, the corporation described in and which executed the foregoing RELEASE, that deponent knows the seal of the corporation, that the seal affixed to the RELEASE is the corporate seal, that it was affixed by order of the Board of the corporation, and that deponent signed (his)(her) name thereto by like order.

———————————————————
Notary Public

MODEL RELEASE (10-03)

This form should be used by a photographer to secure the right to use the likeness (the photograph) of any model whose picture will be taken.

MODEL RELEASE

1. The name of the MODEL.

2. The fee paid to the MODEL.

3. The name of the PHOTOG-RAPHER taking the pictures.

4. Indicate the length of time of the permission being granted to use the photographs, and if such period is other than "unlimited" or "one year," check the last box and insert the expiration date of the permission.

5. The date the photographs are taken.

6. The name of the MODEL printed directly below the line, with the MODEL to sign above the line.

7. The address of the MODEL.

8. The name of the WITNESS printed directly below the line, with the WITNESS to sign above the line.

9. The name of the MODEL's parent or legal guardian (to be used if the MODEL is a minor). If the MODEL is not a minor, delete.

10. The name of the parent/ legal guardian printed directly below the line, with that person to sign above the line. If the MODEL is not a minor, delete.

_____[1]_____, the MODEL, in consideration of the sum of $_____[2]_____, the receipt of which is hereby acknowledged, sells, assigns and grants to _____[3]_____, PHOTOGRAPHER, the right and permission to use photographs of me taken this day. This right is granted for art, advertising, trade or any similar lawful purpose, except the following which are subject to separate negotiations and written consent of the model: television, motion pictures, billboards, posters, product packaging and point-of-purchase displays.

This right shall expire on (check one):

( ) unlimited; ( ) one year from today; ( ) ____[4]____

Accordingly, I hereby release and discharge the PHOTOGRAPHER and persons acting for or on behalf of PHOTOGRAPHER from any liability by virtue of any blurring, distortion, alteration, optical illusion or use in composite form that may occur or be processed in the taking of these photographs or in the processing of these photographs through the completion of the finished product.

I hereby warrant that I am of full age, or that if I am a minor that I and my legal guardian have every right to contract in my name in the above regard. I further state that (I)(we) have read this RELEASE prior to its execution, and that (I)(we) are fully familiar with its contents.

DATED:_____[5]_____   _____
                                            [6]

WITNESS: ADDRESS:_____
                                            [7]

_____   _____
        [8]

I, _____[9]_____, am the guardian of the above named MODEL and I do hereby consent to the execution of this RELEASE and agree to all of its terms.

_____
            [10]

CUSTOMER TESTIMONIAL/ENDORSEMENT RELEASE (10-04)

This form is used to secure permission to use customer testimonials or endorsements of a product or service.

CUSTOMER TESTIMONIAL/ENDORSEMENT RELEASE

1. The name of the person or business seeking the permission to use the Testimonial or Endorsement.

In consideration of the payment to me of TEN DOLLARS ($10.00) and other valuable consideration received by me, I hereby give _____[1]_____ (the "PUBLISHER"), the absolute and irrevocable right and permission, with respect to any photograph(s) taken of me or in which I may be included with others, direct quotes or portions of direct quotes made by me or all or any portions of statements, details, events or recountings of events in which I participated (the "MATERIAL"): (a) to copyright the same in PUBLISHER'S own name or any other name that the PUBLISHER might choose; (b) to use, re-use, publish and re-publish the same in whole or in part, individually or in conjunction with other similar MATERIAL, in any medium and for any purposes whatsoever, including (but not by way of limitation) illustration, promotion and advertising, and trade; and (c) to use my name in conjunction therewith if PUBLISHER so chooses.

I hereby waive any right that I may have to inspect or approve the finished product or products or the advertising copy or printed matter that may be used in connection therewith or the use to which it may be applied.

I hereby release PUBLISHER from any liability by virtue of any blurring, distortion, alteration, optical illusion, or use in composite form that may occur or be produced in the reproduction, use, processing, printing or publication of the MATERIAL.

This authorization and RELEASE shall also inure to the benefit of the legal representatives, licensees, and assigns of the PUBLISHER as well as the photographer(s) and others who compiled the MATERIAL.

I hereby warrant that I am of full age, or that if I am a minor that I and my legal guardian have every right to contract in my name in the above regard. I further state that

(Document continued on next page)

2. The date the permission is granted.

3. The name of the customer giving the Testimonial or making the Endorsement printed directly below the line, with the customer to sign above the line.

4. The address of the customer.

5. The name of the WITNESS to the signing of the Release printed directly below the line, with the WITNESS to sign above the line.

6. The name of the customer's parent or legal guardian (to be used if the customer is a minor). If the customer is not a minor, delete.

7. The name of the parent/legal guardian printed directly below the line, with that person to sign above the line. If the customer is not a minor, delete.

(I)(we) have read this RELEASE prior to its execution, and that (I)(we) are fully familiar with its contents.

DATED:_____   _____
       [2]   [3]

WITNESS: ADDRESS:_____
                                          [4]

_____   _____
       [5]   [4]

I,_____[6]_____, am the guardian of the above named minor and I do hereby consent to the execution of this RELEASE and agree to all of its terms.

_____
[7]

POWER OF ATTORNEY (10-05)

A Power of Attorney is used to give another person or entity (attorney-in-fact) authority to act for you if for some reason you cannot be present to act (for example, you have moved to California from New York and you need someone to be present at the sale of your home in New York).

You may at some time need to use a Power of Attorney while outside the United States. Should it be necessary, consult that country's diplomatic mission in the United States before you leave for that country's "notarial" requirements. Conversely, you may be outside the United States at a time you need to give a Power of Attorney. In that event, have the form "notarized" by the the U.S. Consul in that country's United States consulate.

While a Power of Attorney generally relates to delegating authority to act with respect to property, some states, New York for example, specifically permit the use of a Power of Attorney to authorize the attorney-in-fact to provide such things as medical care for a spouse or child. The laws of your state should be consulted before using this form for that purpose.

POWER OF ATTORNEY

1. The name of the person giving the Power of Attorney.

2. The address of the person giving the Power of Attorney.

3. The name of the party (attorney-in-fact) who will act for you.

4. The address of the party who will act for you.

Note: you may name more than one party. If you want these parties to act together, enter the word "jointly" after the word "act." If you want these parties to act independent of one another, enter the word "severally" after the word "act."

5. The area in which you are granting authority. It may be general, for example "Banking Transactions" or specific, "Banking transactions regarding Bank Account No. 124-8976 at New York Trust and Savings." If the Power of Attorney is to be used for a person, describe the authority being given such as "medical, surgical and hospital treatment and care" and identify the person to receive the care by full name and date of birth.

I, _____[1]_____, residing at _____[2]_____, do hereby appoint _____[3]_____, of _____[4]_____, my attorney(s)-in-fact to act in my name, place and stead in any way which I myself could do if I were personally present, with respect to _____[5]_____, to the extent I am by law permitted to act through an agent.

This Power of Attorney shall not be affected by my subsequent disability or incompetence.

To induce any third party to act under this Power of Attorney, I agree that any third party receiving an executed copy or facsimile of this Power of Attorney may act hereunder and that no revocation or termination of this Power of Attorney shall be effective as to any third party unless and until such third party shall have received actual notice or knowledge of such revocation or termination. I and for my heirs, executors, legal representatives and assigns, do indemnify and hold harmless any such third party from and against any and all claims that may arise against such third party by reasons of such third party having relied on this Power of Attorney.

(Document continued on next page)

6. The date you grant the Power of Attorney.

7. The name of the person giving the Power of Attorney printed directly below the line, with that person to sign above the line.

8. The Notary Public completes this part of the form, and signs and seals it by affixing his stamp or seal.

I have hereunto signed my name this __[6]__ day of _____, 19__.

_____
[7]

STATE OF ____[8]____, COUNTY OF ____[8]____, ss.:

On _____[8]_____, 19__ before me _____[8]_____ personally came _____[8]_____ to me known, and known to me to be the individual(s) described in, and who executed the foregoing, and duly acknowledged to me that (t)(s)he(y) executed the same.

_____
Notary Public

AFFIDAVIT—POWER OF ATTORNEY
IN FULL FORCE (10-06)

When a Power of Attorney is presented for use, the attorney-in-fact (the one authorized to act) may be asked to sign an Affidavit stating that the Power remains valid and effective and has not been revoked or terminated. It is to be signed before a Notary Public.

AFFIDAVIT—POWER OF ATTORNEY
IN FULL FORCE

1. The state and county where the Affidavit is signed.

2. The name of the attorney-in-fact.

3. The name of the person who gave the Power of Attorney.

4. The date the Power of Attorney was given.

5. A description of the document or transaction for which the Power of Attorney is being used.

6. The date on which the Power of Attorney is being used.

7. The name of the party accepting the Power of Attorney.

8. The name of the attorney-in-fact to be printed directly below the line, with the attorney-in-fact to sign above the line.

9. The date of the Affidavit.

10. The signature and stamp of the Notary Public taking the signature of the attorney-in-fact.

STATE OF ___[1]___, COUNTY OF _____[1]_____ ss.:

_____[2]_____, being duly sworn, deposes and says that: The Power of Attorney granted to me by _____[3]_____, on _____[4]_____, a true copy of which is annexed hereto is in full force and effect; that at the time of the execution of _____[5]_____, on _____[6]_____, I had no knowledge of or actual notice of the revocation or termination of the Power of Attorney by death or otherwise.

I make this affidavit for the purpose of inducing _____[7]_____ to accept the above described instrument as executed by me as attorney-in-fact knowing that in accepting the aforesaid instrument they will rely upon this affidavit.

_____
[8]

Sworn to before me this

__[9]__day of _____

_____[10]_____
Notary Public

REVOCATION OF POWER OF ATTORNEY (10-07)

Because a Power of Attorney permits another person or entity to act for you, the Revocation and termination of that Power of Attorney should be documented. It would be wise not only to communicate the Revocation verbally but to confirm it by the use of this form sent to the attorney-in-fact by Certified Mail—Return Receipt Requested.

REVOCATION OF POWER OF ATTORNEY

1. The name of the person who gave the Power of Attorney.

2. The address of the person who gave the Power of Attorney.

3. The date of the Revocation.

4. The name of the attorney-in-fact.

5. The address of the attorney-in-fact.

6. The date of the Power of Attorney.

7. How the notice of Revocation was given, i.e. "in person" or "telephone to (212) 555-1234."

8. The name of the person who gave the Power of Attorney printed directly below the line, with that person to sign above the line.

9. The Notary Public completes this part of the form, and signs and seals it by affixing his stamp or seal.

I, _____[1]_____, residing at _____[2]_____, do this date _____[3]_____, hereby revoke and terminate the Power of Attorney granted by me to _____[4]_____, of _____[5]_____ on _____[6]_____ and declare that it is no longer in force or effect.

I have advised _____[4]_____ of this revocation and termination on _____[3]_____, by _____[7]_____.

_____
[8]

STATE OF ____[9]____, COUNTY OF ___[9]___, ss.:

On _____[9]_____, 19__ before me _____[9]_____ personally came _____[9]_____ to me known, and known to me to be the individual(s) described in, and who executed the foregoing, and duly acknowledged to me that (t)(s)he(y) executed the same.

_____
Notary Public

INDEMNIFICATION/
HOLD HARMLESS AGREEMENT (10-08)

If there is a risk that you might be sued in the performance of an act for another, it would be advisable to use an Indemnification Agreement to protect yourself.

INDEMNIFICATION/
HOLD HARMLESS AGREEMENT

1. The name of person who will be indemnified.

2. A description of what the Indemnification is for, i.e. "sale of widgets to XYZ Company," "transportation of car from _____ to _____."

3. The date the Agreement is signed.

4. The name of the WITNESS printed directly below the line, with the WITNESS to sign above the line.

5. The address of the WIT-NESS.

6. The name of the party giving the Indemnification if a corporation. Otherwise delete the line.

7. If the party giving the Indemnification is an individual, delete "BY" and print the individual's name directly below the line, with that person to sign above the line. If the the party giving the Indemnification is a corporation, print the name and title of the individual acting for the corporation directly below the line, with that person to sign above the line.

8. The address of the party giving the Indemnification.

The undersigned does hereby irrevocably covenant, promise and agree to indemnify _____[1]_____ and to hold (it)(them)(him)(her) harmless from and against any and all losses, claims, expenses, suits, costs, demands, damages or liabilities, joint or several, of whatever kind or nature which _____[1]_____ may sustain or to which (it)(they)(he)(she) may become subject arising out of or relating in any way to _____[2]_____, including without limitation in each case attorneys' fees, costs and expenses actually incurred in defending against or enforcing any such losses, claims, expenses, suits, damages or liabilities.

Dated: _____[3]_____

WITNESS:

_____[4]_____   _____[6]_____

_____[5]_____   BY_____
                                  [7]
_____[5]_____   _____
                                  [8]
                             _____
                                  [8]

NOTARY STATEMENT
(ACKNOWLEDGEMENT)—INDIVIDUAL (10-09)

Many of the documents used throughout this book, and others from banks, government agencies, etc. require that the people who sign them have their signatures notarized by a Notary Public. Not all states use the title Notary Public. For example, in Pennsylvania this person is called a Prothonotary. But whatever name is used, it is always an individual who is licensed by the state to authenticate signatures.

NOTARY STATEMENT
(ACKNOWLEDGEMENT)—INDIVIDUAL

1. The state and county where the Acknowledgement is being taken.

2. The date of the Acknowledgement.

3. The title of the person notarizing the Acknowledgement, i.e. Notary Public.

4. The name of the person whose signature is being notarized.

5. A description of the document that has the signature, i.e. General Release, Power of Attorney, etc.

6. The signature, stamp or seal of the Notary Public.

STATE OF ___[1]___, COUNTY OF ____[1]____, ss.:

On _____[2]_____, 19__, before me _____[3]_____ personally came _____[4]_____, to me known, and known to me to be the individual(s) described in and who executed the foregoing _____[5]_____, and duly acknowledged to me that (he)(she)(they) executed the same.

_____

[6]

[SEAL]

NOTARY STATEMENT
(ACKNOWLEDGEMENT)—CORPORATION (10-10)

This Acknowledgement is used in the same manner and for the same purpose as the preceding Notary Statement (Acknowledgment)—Individual, except that this form is used when a corporation must have the signature of one of its officers notarized.

NOTARY STATEMENT
(ACKNOWLEDGEMENT)—CORPORATION

1. The state and county where the Acknowledgement is being taken.

2. The date of the Acknowledgement.

3. The title of the person taking the Acknowledgement, i.e. Notary Public.

4. The name of the person whose signature is being notarized (the Deponent).

5. The address of the person whose signature is being notarized.

6. The corporate title of the person in No.4, i.e. President, Controller, etc.

7. The name of the corporation.

8. A description of the document signed by the person in No. 4, i.e. General Release, Power of Attorney.

9. Delete if the document does not have the corporate seal and skip to No. 11.

10. The name of the governing body of the corporation, i.e. Directors, Trustees.

11. The signature, stamp or seal of the Notary Public.

STATE OF ___[1]___, COUNTY OF ____[1]____, ss.:

On _____[2]_____, 19__, before me _____[3]_____, personally came _____[4]_____, to me known, who by me duly sworn, did depose and say that deponent resides at _____[5]_____, that deponent is the _____[6]_____, of _____[7]_____, the corporation described in and which executed the foregoing _____[8]_____, *[9][that deponent knows the seal of the corporation, that the seal affixed is the corporate seal, that the seal was affixed by order of the Board of _____[10]_____ of the corporation]*, and that deponent signed his name to the foregoing by order of the Board of _____[10]_____.

_____
[11]

[SEAL]

Glossary

Acknowledgement A formal declaration made in the presence of a Notary Public that the statements contained in a document are true and that the signing of the document is the free act of the person making the statement. Also called a Notary Statement.

Affidavit A statement made under oath before a person, such as a Notary Public, qualified in that state to administer oaths.

Agent One who is authorized by another, called the "Principal," to act for or on behalf of the Principal.

Arbitration The process for resolution of dispute by one or more private, unofficial (non-governmental) persons whose selection is agreed to by the parties to the dispute, and which is outside of the judiciary processes (the courts). As used in this book, and as typically used, the word implies the use of the rules and regulations of the American Arbitration Association.

Assignee One who receives the title of ownership, right or interest from another who is the owner of that title, right or interest.

Assignment The act by an Assignor of transferring the Assignor's title of ownership, interest or right in real or personal property to another. The Assignor relinquishes his rights to, and his liabilities and responsibilities for, the property. The recipient of this transfer is called the Assignee.

Assignor One who transfers his title of ownership, right or interest to another.

Balloon Payment Loan A type of loan in which payments of either principal or interest do not pay off the loan completely by the maturity date, resulting in a single payment (a "balloon") on the maturity date.

Bankruptcy Loosely "insolvency," the inability to pay one's debts because one's debts and liabilities exceed one's income and assets. Also, legal proceedings brought in the United States Bankruptcy Court, which administers distribution of a bankrupt's assets to his creditors.

Beneficiary One who has or will receive a benefit, such as a person for whose benefit a trust has been created; any person entitled to all or any part of the estate of a deceased person under the terms of a will.

Breach An intentional or unintentional violation of an obligation, contract or promise.

Bulk Transfers (Also known as Bulk Sales) The transfer or sale of a major portion (more than 50%) of the materials, supplies, merchandise or other inventory of a business which is not in the ordinary course of the transferor's or seller's business, as governed by Article 6 of the Uniform Commercial Code.

By-Laws The rules and regulations establishing the governing structure of a corporation or association.

Closing (or Closing Date) The settlement date of all obligations of the seller and the buyer to each other, at which time title to property passes from the seller to the buyer.

Codicil A written supplement, modification or alteration of an existing Will, which must be signed and witnessed with the same formality as a Will.

Collateral Property given, designated or pledged as security or guaranty for the fulfillment or discharge of an obligation.

Consideration Any benefit given to one by another as an inducement to enter into a contract.

Consignee A merchant who receives goods for sale on a commission basis but who does not actually take ownership of the goods.

Consignment Sale A form of sale in which goods are deposited by the owner (the Consignor) with a merchant (the Consignee), with the merchant to receive a commission on each item actually sold. The Consignee does not own (take title to) the goods.

Consignor The owner of goods who leaves the goods with a merchant for sale on a commission basis.

Corporation An artificial entity created or recognized by a state, acknowledging an association of one or more people, which is separate and distinct from those people. Generally, individual shareholders enjoy the protection of limited liability in that each is liable and "at risk" only to the extent of his investment to purchase the stock of the corporation.

Custodian One who is entrusted, either by law or agreement, with the care, keeping, control or possession of a thing or person.

Damages Monetary compensation paid to a person who has suffered loss, detriment or injury to his person, property or rights through an act or omission of another.

Decedent A deceased person.

Declarant One who makes a declaration, generally not under oath and out of court.

Deed The term for any one of several types of documents signed by the seller (also known as the grantor or vendor) establishing the transfer or ownership (title) of real estate to the buyer (also known as the grantee or vendee).

Deed of Trust A document used in several states, in place of a mortgage, in which title to real estate is transferred to a trustee (who may be either the seller or a third party). The holder of the Deed of Trust cannot further encumber the property or make any improvements to the property without the consent of the buyer. If the buyer defaults in repayment, the holder of the Deed of Trust is entitled to take immediate possession of the property (see also Mortgage).

Default A failure or omission to meet a legal obligation.

Deponent A person who gives testimony under oath, which is then, typically, put in writing. (See also Affiant).

Designee One who has been designated by another.

Director (of a corporation) A person, appointed or elected by the shareholders of a corporation, who is authorized to direct and oversee the affairs of the corporation.

Domicile One's "home," the place where one ultimately intends to return. A person's domicile and residence may be, but are not always, the same. A person may have more than one residence but only one domicile.

Donee A person who receives a gift from another.

Donor A person who makes a gift to another.

Due On Sale A mortgage or loan provision requiring that the principal amount borrowed, and all interest accrued to the date of a sale of property, must be paid in full on or before the closing date of the sale.

Easement Permission or license, granted by the owner of real estate to another, to cross, trespass or use that property for a specific purpose.

Encumbrance A claim, charge, lien or interest in property, especially real estate.

Equity In real estate, the value of property over and above the total amount owed on any mortgages, liens or the like. The term is also used to refer to a legal doctrine of fairness—doing to others what one would want others to do to them.

Escalation (or Escalator) A contract clause permitting or providing for increases or decreases in price based upon fluctuations in underlying costs. It is is most commonly used in leases.

Escrow The delivery of money, a document or property by a buyer to a third person (typically referred to as the "Escrow Agent") to be held by that third person until a specific event occurs, and upon that occurrence, delivery to the seller. If the event does not occur, the money, document or property is returned to the seller.

Estoppel A legal doctrine which holds that one should be stopped from denying, disavowing or repudiating one's own statements or acts.

Estoppel Certificate (Mortgage Estoppel Certificate) A document in which a lender or holder of a mortgage (the Mortgagee) certifies the amount of unpaid principal and interest, the date of maturity and the rate of interest.

Exclusive Agency (Real Estate Brokerage Agreement) A form of real estate brokerage agreement in which the property owner agrees that a particular broker will be paid a commission in the event of any sale of the property, regardless of whether the buyer was procured by another broker. See also Exclusive Right to Sell and Open Listing.

Exclusive Right to Sell (Real Estate Brokerage Agreement) A form of real estate brokerage agreement in which the property owner agrees that a particular broker will be paid a commission in the event of any sale of the property, regardless of whether the buyer was procured by another broker *or even the property owner himself*. See also Exclusive Agency and Open Listing.

Execute To complete or make a document valid by signing and delivering it.

Executor The representative of the estate of a deceased person who has been approved by a court of probate and who is responsible for collecting the deceased person's assets, arranging for the payment of the deceased person's debts and estate taxes and for distributing the deceased person's property in accordance with his Will.

Executrix The feminine form of Executor.

Finder A "middle-man" engaged to locate an outside source of capital for a business venture or to locate a purchaser or seller for a business or personal property.

F.O.B. See Free On Board.

Force Majeure A force, event or occurrence which is beyond the control of the parties to a contract, such as a fire or strike.

Foreclosure Termination of a mortgage, in which the mortgage holder takes possession of the property by order of the court upon default by the borrower.

Free On Board A term meaning that the goods or subject matter of a sale is to be loaded for shipment without expense to the buyer.

Gift The act of transferring ownership of property or money to another, in which the person making the gift (the Donor) receives no payment or other consideration. Note that there must be "donative intent" (the Donor intends to make a gift, as opposed to making, for example, a loan) and there must be actual delivery of the gifted property to the person receiving the gift (the Donor).

Goodwill (Also Good Will) The intangible value added to a business resulting from its reputation among its customers and the market place.

Grant A transfer of property by gift, sale or lease.

Grantee One to whom a grant, especially of real estate, is made; the buyer of real estate.

Grantor One who makes a grant, especially of real estate; the seller of real estate.

Guarantee One to whom a guaranty is made or given.

Guarantor One who makes or gives a guaranty.

Guaranty A promise to be responsible for the debt of another in the event the other defaults.

Guardian One who has been lawfully charged with the duty to care for and to manage the property and affairs of another who, because of age or law, is considered to be incapable of managing his own property and affairs.

Hold Harmless See Indemnify.

Incumbrance See Encumbrance.

Indemnify The act of holding another not responsible for loss or damage. Also, the agreement to reimburse another for loss or damage from a third person's act or refusal to act.

Intangible That which cannot be touched. Intangible property means property which has no intrinsic or marketable value, such as goodwill or a trademark.

Intestate A person who dies without leaving a valid Will, or the condition of the estate of that person.

Irrevocable That which cannot be withdrawn, repealed, cancelled, annulled or changed.

Joint Venture A voluntary agreement between two or more people to conduct business for profit in a specific business situation and for a limited or fixed period of time. Typically, a Joint Venture is managed by a "Venture Manager" or "General Partner" who is liable for losses, and one or more other investing partners, referred to as "Limited Partners," each of whom is liable for losses only to the extent of his respective capital contribution to the Joint Venture.

Judgment The final decision of a court, which determines the rights and claims of the parties to a law suit.

Jurisdiction In the legal sense, the authority by which courts hear and decide cases and exercise their legal authority. The term also is used to refer to the sphere of territorial range of authority (usually divided along political boundaries such as towns, cities or states).

Last Will and Testament See Will.

Lease An agreement between the owner of property and another in which the owner retains title (ownership) of the property but grants to the other exclusive use and possession of the property for a fixed period of time and for a fixed fee. In a lease of real estate, the owner is usually referred to as "landlord" and the person receiving the rights of use and possession is usually referred to as "tenant." In a lease of personal property (property other than real estate), the owner is usually referred to as "lessor" and the person receiving the right of use and possession is usually referred to as "lessee."

Lessee See Lease.

Lessor See Lease.

Letter of Credit A promise by a bank, financial institution or other lender to pay a specific amount of money at the request of, and in accordance with, the instructions of its customer to a third party (such as a supplier or manufacturer of merchandise), provided that the required documentation is presented; usually used with regard to shipment of goods between countries.

Liability A comprehensive term referring to any and every hazard or responsibility.

License A permission or authority granted to another, or the certificate or other document which notes or attests to the granting of a permission or authority.

Lien A claim, charge, security or encumbrance upon the property of another as security for a debt.

Lien Holder One who owns or holds a lien upon the property of another.

Lienor See Lien Holder.

Liquidated Damages An agreed upon amount of damages (money) an injured party will be entitled to receive upon default or breach of an agreement by the other party, so that the injured party does not have to establish the exact amount of his actual damages in any subsequent lawsuit.

Litigant A party to a law suit.

Living Will A document used by an individual to clearly express his intentions regarding medical care and treatment during his lifetime in the event that he becomes unable to make or participate in the making of such decisions himself.

Metes and Bounds The exact legal description of a parcel of real estate which locates and defines the boundaries of the property in distance (in feet and inches) and compass direction (in degrees, minutes and seconds) and which is usually found on the deed.

Mortgage An interest given by the owner of real property (the Mortgagor) to secure repayment of a loan made by another (the Mortgagee). Despite making such a loan, title (ownership) remains in the name of the owner of the property and, in the event of a default in repayment, the lender must bring a legal proceeding known as "foreclosure" in order to sell the security to receive repayment of the loan. (See also Deed of Trust).

Mortgagee A lender who agrees to accept a lien on real estate as security for the repayment of a loan made to the owner of that real estate.

Mortgagor The owner of real estate who pledges his property as security for the repayment of a loan or debt.

Negligence The omission or failure to do something or to perform some act which a "reasonable man," guided by ordinary considerations, would do in the same or similar circumstances.

Notarize The acts performed by a Notary Public or other official authorized to administer oaths, especially the acts of signing and affixing his stamp or seal to a document.

Notary Public A person authorized by the laws of a state to administer an oath and witness signatures. A Notary Public attests only to the fact that the statements were made to him under oath on a certain date and place; he does not attest to the truth of those statements. See also Acknowledgement.

Notation Letter of Credit A type of Letter of Credit in which the running (declining) balance is recorded ("notated") on the back of the Letter of Credit.

Notice A formal declaration of intent, usually in writing, required to be given under the terms of an agreement, such as notice of a contract breach; also, the manner, method or means of communicating some fact or information to another.

Obligee The person in whose favor some act or obligation must be performed by an Obligor.

Obligor One who is required to perform some act or obligation.

Officer (of a corporation) A person appointed or elected by the directors of a corporation in accordance with the by-laws of the corporation and who is authorized to manage the day-to-day operations of the corporation (typically, the president, vice-president, secretary and treasurer).

Open Listing (Real Estate Brokerage Agreement) A form of real estate brokerage agreement in which the property owner is free to list the property with other brokers or to sell the property himself. The property owner is required to pay a brokerage commission only to the broker who procures the actual buyer. See also Exclusive Agency and Exclusive Right to Sell.

Option A contract in which the owner of property (the "Optionor") gives to another (the "Optionee") the exclusive right to purchase the property during a specific time period and on terms which have been agreed upon. The Optionor cannot revoke the Option and is required to sell the property if the Option is exercised. The Optionee can elect to purchase the property or not.

Optionee A person who receives an Option to purchase property.

Optionor The owner of property who gives an Option to purchase the property.

Over-tenant See Sub-lease.

Partner One who has formed a partnership with one or more others.

Partnership A voluntary agreement between two or more people or companies to conduct business for profit on a continuing basis as co-owners. Profits as well as losses are to be shared proportionally and each partner (and his assets) is liable and "at risk" for any losses incurred by the partnership.

Party A person or entity in a transaction, matter or proceeding who is obligated, as in a party to a contract, or is directly influenced by its outcome, as in a party (plaintiff or defendant) to a law suit.

Per Capita A formula for estate distribution in which all heirs divide property equally on a "per head" basis.

Personal Property That which can be moved, as distinguished from real property, which is land.

Per Stirpes A formula for estate distribution in which beneficiaries of the same degree of kinship are each to receive equal shares of the estate if each survives the Testator, but in which the children of each pre-deceased beneficiary divide only their parent's share.

Pledge The use of goods or other tangible property as security for a debt or other obligation. Possession of the goods is delivered to the creditor or lender who has a lien on the goods, but legal title (ownership) remains with the debtor or borrower.

Power of Attorney A document establishing the granting of authority to another person (called the "Attorney-In-Fact") to act in place of and on a behalf of a person if that person cannot be present to act for himself.

Pre-deceased One whose death precedes that of the maker of a Will or who dies before the probate of that Will.

Principal Any person or entity who grants authority to an agent or attorney-in-fact to act in its behalf.

Probate The act, process or court proceedings for proving or receiving official recognition that a document is, in fact, the Will of the deceased.

Proxy The person appointed to represent and act for another. The term also refers to the document establishing such appointment.

Purchase Money Mortgage A loan given by the seller of real estate to the buyer of the real estate to enable the buyer to purchase the property.

Quorum The number of members of a board, committee or the like which must be present at a meeting in order for the actions and resolutions of that meeting to be binding (to be "official") on all members; typically, a simple numerical majority of the total number of such members.

Ratify To approve, sanction, confirm or make valid.

Real Property Land, as distinguished from personal property.

Realty See Real Property.

Release The giving up of a right, claim or privilege, such as the right to sue, which one has or may in the future have against another. A "General Release" is the giving up of any and all rights, claims or privileges against another.

Releasee One who pays money or gives other consideration in order to be released.

Releasor One who gives a Release in exchange for money or other consideration.

Resolution A formal written statement or expression of opinion adopted by an official body or assembly, such as a Board of Directors.

Revocation The cancellation, annulment or repeal of some power or authority previously given or granted.

Rule Against Perpetuities With respect to Wills, a legal rule recognized in most states which prohibits holding property (the "alienation of property") in trust for a period longer than a "life in being plus 21 years" as measured from the date of the Testator's death (not the date of signing the Will).

S Corporation A "small business corporation" defined by Internal Revenue Code Sec. 1361 as a certain type of corporation which has no more than 35 shareholders, has no shareholders who are not individuals (except for a trust), has no shareholders who are nonresident aliens, has only one class of stock, and fulfills other requirements as well.

Security The pledge of property to guarantee payment of a loan (see Collateral).

Self-amortizing Loan A type of loan which by its terms provides that if all payments are made on time, principal and interest will have been repaid in full by the last scheduled payment (also known as a self-liquidating loan).

Shareholder An owner of all or a part of a corporation in whose name stock certificates are issued (also referred to as a "stockholder").

Signature Guarantee The certification of a signature as attested to by an officer of a commercial bank or stock exchange-registered stock brokerage firm. This is not the same as a Notary Statement (Acknowledgement).

Stock Power The endorsement of a stock certificate (whether on the back of the certificate itself or by a separate document) which allows the certificate to be sold or transferred. A stock power is to a stock certificate as an endorsement is to a check.

Sub-lease The transfer to another (known as "under-tenant") of all or part of one's interest in real property for a period of time ending no later than the ending date of one's own lease. The tenant, as "over-tenant," reserves for himself any rights to get the lease back and also remains ultimately liable to the landlord for performance of the terms of the original lease (also referred to as the "over-lease").

Subscriber A person or entity who agrees to purchase shares of stock of a corporation at a predetermined price on an indeterminate date in the future when the stock is issued.

Tangible That which can be touched, as opposed to intangible. Tangible property is property which has intrinsic value.

Term Length of time. When used in connection with a lease, term refers to the length or duration of permitted occupancy or possession, measured from the date of first permitted occupancy or possession (not the date of signing the lease).

Termination An end, severance or cessation of something, such as the termination of a contract.

Testator A person who makes a Will.

Testatrix The feminine term for a person who makes a Will.

Title Ownership or a claim of right of ownership, especially of real estate; a document proving ownership.

Transferee The buyer of property or rights, or the one to whom a transfer of property or rights is made.

Transferor The seller of property or rights.

U.C.C. See Uniform Commercial Code.

Under-Tenant See Sub-lease.

Uniform Commercial Code A body of uniform laws (with only slight variations) governing business, banking and commercial relationships, which have been adopted by all states (except Louisiana).

Vendee One who pays money or gives other consideration in order to receive title (ownership) of property. The buyer of real estate is usually referred to as the Grantee.

Vendor One who transfers or sells property to another; the seller. The seller of real estate is usually referred to as the Grantor.

Waive The act of exercising a waiver (see Waiver).

Waiver The voluntary, intentional relinquishing or giving up of some known right.

Warrantee One to whom a warranty is given.

Warranty A promise that a statement of fact is true.

Will A document signed during a person's lifetime which directs the disposition of that person's assets and property after his death.

Witness One who signs his name to a document, not as a party to the agreement, but rather for the purpose of establishing the authenticity of the signature of a party to the agreement.

Index by Title

A

B

C

Subject Index

Numbers in parentheses are document numbers found at the top of each document. They are followed by page numbers.

Tuition Reimbursement Agreement (9-05), 384

U

Uniform Commercial Code, 241, 349
Uniform Gifts to Minors Act, 31
Uniform Partnership Act 276

W

Waiver
    Not to be Construed as Waiver of Subsequent Defaults, Contract Clause for (8-10), 369
    of Notice of Meeting of Directors (6-08), 320
    of Notice of Meeting of Shareholders (6-04), 315
    of Notice of Organizational Meeting (5-10), 304
Warranties, Contract for the Sale of Goods with (3-05), 183
Will
    Administrator, 18
    Affidavit of Decedent's Domicile

    (1-05), 18
    Codicil to (1-04), 14
    Decedent, 18
    Executor, 2
    Living Will (1-06), 21
        Durable Power of Attorney for use with (1-07), 25
    purpose of, 2
    Simple, All to Spouse (1-01), 3
    Simple, All to Surviving Spouse and Alternative Bequest to Adult Child(ren) (1-02), 6
    Simple, All to Surviving Spouse and Child(ren) with Simple Trust If Any Child Is a Minor (1-03), 9
    Successor Executor, 2
    Testator, 2
    warnings concerning, 2
    witnesses to, 2
    wording of a, 2
"Work For Hire," Employee Invention, Agreement (9-08), 389

THEY RODE INTO EUROPE

Zue Innsprugg.

Das Tewtsch gestech

THEY RODE INTO EUROPE

*The Fruitful Exchange
in the Arts of Horsemanship
between East and West*

by

MIKLÓS JANKOVICH

Translated by

ANTHONY DENT

CHARLES SCRIBNER'S SONS

NEW YORK

To Ilona

A–4.73 (I)

Printed in Great Britain

Library of Congress Catalog Card Number 72–11324
SBN 684–13304–0

Author's Foreword to English Edition

This book was written in Hungarian but first published in German at Munich in 1968, as *Pferde, Reiter, Völkerstürme*. The present edition is a translation of that text, and has been rendered by Mr Anthony Dent, who is himself a writer on horses and their connection with history, and who has bred horses. He has supplemented the original text with his own interpolations (which are marked as such) in those passages which have a special bearing on conditions in Britain and North America. In thanking him for his valuable co-operation I am also expressing the conviction that together we can offer our English-speaking readers an original work on equestrian history that will satisfy a need wherever in the world horses are ridden and the English language spoken.

Original Foreword

Those important developments in the history of mankind which led in Europe to travel on horseback and to mounted warfare had their origin among the peoples of the steppes. Materials on their characteristic culture have been accumulated over the centuries abundantly in Hungarian archives. From a study of these, and from the results of research in the fields of history, ethnology, archaeology, and the study of horses I have been able to frame a coherent picture of the horseman's civilization and its diffusion throughout the world.

One fact alone has endowed the horse with historical significance: the horse enabled the Eurasians to travel overland from the Atlantic to the Pacific seaboards of the Old World, thus permitting contact between distant centres of civilization, and facilitating that exchange of ideas and inventions which is a fundamental requisite of human progress. Everything that we now revere as the triumph of the human spirit has been bought somewhere, at some time, not only with human blood and tears but also with the sweat of horses.

With the progress of technology the machine took the place of the animal as the source of power. The horse, which was the most loyal and self-sacrificing auxiliary of the human race, has vanished from our everyday life, within the memory of a generation still living, who can report from their own experience what life in the Equestrian Age was like. It is primarily to that generation that I dedicate this book.

But in it I have also something to say to the present generation, who live not only physically but also spiritually in the Machine Age. To them it often seems that bygones are bygones, and what is obsolete must be valueless. And yet youth is still drawn to animals, particularly to the horse. Hence we have in this mechanized generation a regeneration of riding for pleasure. And so this book is also dedicated to all those who are committed to sports on horseback. Sport is an inescapable function of civilization, and for them some knowledge of the equestrian past is an essential background element in their understanding of the horse–man relationship.

Lastly, the writing of this book has left me with the revived memory of many horses and many men—men with whom I have ridden and with whom I have served, for some of whom horses were a profession, for some a passion. I think now of many a horse whose footfall I would know again by ear after all the years, and of many a horse that has paid me its tribute of sweat under saddle or between the shafts. And for every word that I have written in the following pages, in memory I stroke them still, and pat their steaming necks.

M.J.

Translator's Preface

It is difficult for Europeans living west of the Rhine, and doubly difficult for the inhabitants of the British Isles, to appreciate the full force and significance of those waves of horsemen out of Asia that broke again and again on the (metaphorical) shores of Europe for centuries before the birth of the Roman Empire and for further centuries after its demise, reaching one of their peaks in the period following the death of Charlemagne, and finally turning to the ebb only with the unsuccessful siege of Vienna by the Turks. They left behind, on that last occasion, a useful piece of equine flotsam in the shape of the Byerly Turk, that magnificent Oriental stallion snatched from the undertow by a mercenary captain in the service of Prince Eugène, and brought home by him to serve as a charger at the battle of the Boyne, and become one of the Founding Fathers of the *General Stud Book*.

There you are; the maritime metaphor comes easiest to the lips of the Anglo-British islander. For us the Fury of the Norsemen is real enough; it is part of our history that sticks out like a sore thumb in every other place-name north of the Trent. The menace of the Blackamoors too has its place in our folklore here and there, as in the mummers' play of St George, simply because the last repercussions of the Turkish invasions were sea-borne, and the farthest range of the marauding galleys from the Barbary coast brought them now and again to the southern coasts of Britain, to snatch some luckless shepherd or fishwife from a lonely headland in Cornwall or Cork and haul them off to the slave-market of Tangier. But behind these pirates from the shores of Tripoli there stretched an unending chain of conquest and invasion, victory and defeat, a vortex of mounted strife that had its storm-centre far away in the steppes of Central Asia. There were brewed devastating gales that blew where they listed, sometimes to the south against Persia and India, sometimes to the east against the Chinese Empire—and one-third of the time against what came to be known as Christendom. Gaul and Iberia lay under the lee of steep mountains and thick forests that would diminish the force of such gales; only Britain lay behind salt water that would bring them to a dead stop.

Of all these terrible bowmen from the steppe, none learned, luckily for us, the art of combined operations, or how to transport light cavalry by sea. They were of many races and many tongues—Scythians, Sarmatians, Parthians, Huns, Alani, Tartars, Turks, Patzinaks, Mongols, and many more. Of such it was written by the prophet Habakkuk: "Their horses also are swifter than the leopards, and are more fierce than the evening wolves, and their horsemen shall spread themselves, and their horsemen shall come from afar: they shall fly as the eagle that hasteth to eat. They shall come all for violence." For all their diversity of racial origin, they had but one uniform way of life. There was no natural function that they could not and did not perform without dismounting—and one unnatural one. They could shoot

6

faster and straighter from the saddle than any Westerner on foot, though not so far.

In popular English speech we have only two memorials of these horse-borne (all but horse-born) raiders—to 'catch a Tartar', which is to have a bull by the horns, and the word 'ogre', which is the English adaptation of the Old French variant of *Hongrois*—Hungarian. Mr Jankovich knows all about ogres because his forefathers have lived among them since the seventeenth century, when they were displaced from Croatia (now Yugoslavia) by the invading Turks. During the past three hundred years there has been a Jankovich of every generation serving in the Hungarian Army as an officer of Hussars. In the middle of the tenth century Hungarian raiders reached the Atlantic coast at the mouth of the Loire, and then turned south away from it—while the English were barely aware of their presence.

Yet the indirect influence of these fast-shooting Eastern badmen, even on the inhabitants of sheltered Britain, was astonishingly widespread and powerful in every field of transport and communications before the first or steam-driven mechanical revolution. These were the people who invented the riding-saddle (though perhaps not the pack-saddle) and the stirrup. They also invented the relay system of mounted messengers which is the progenitor of every postal service in the world. Their type of saddlery was the cause (and also partly the effect) of a style of horsemanship which utterly displaced the Celtic method of equitation, that in antiquity had been almost universal in Europe, and was derived ultimately from the driving style of the charioteer. For these nomads had no heroic tradition of chariot-driving; only a tradition of mounted herdsmen and hunters and bow-bearing warriors. Yet when they did take to the wheel, using the wagon as a means of victualling the marauding horse-archers and transporting the abundant booty, they produced two more useful innovations—the free-turning fore-axle and the 'bogy' system that was early applied to the design of railway engines; that is, small wheels in front and larger 'driving' wheels behind. This was a feature of the characteristic Hungarian vehicle, the *kocsi*, from which in the seventeenth century both the word and the thing—the English 'coach'—were derived. Only a people intimately acquainted with the mechanics of equine power could have invented this system of large wheels behind and smaller wheels before; it is a mechanical imitation of the anatomy of the horse, whose massive hind-legs drive him forward at speed, while his lighter fore-legs merely assist in steering, and support his head and forepart.

In warfare the steppe-born art of mounted bowmanship was learned by few Western peoples, and the British were not among them. But some short time after 'villainous saltpetre' made its debut on the military stage the Hungarians began to specialize as mounted hand-gunners, known as hussars, doing what the mounted archer had done before them. A cruder and slower imitation of the hussar, made in Germany, soon spread through the West, and under the name of 'Reuters' were employed as mercenaries by Henry VIII. These pistoleers were the ancestors of the British dragoons, but, being mounted on the wrong type (and altogether the wrong quality) of horse, they never had the handiness or the speed of the genuine Magyar article. During the Seven Years War the combination of mobility and fire-power which this arm offered impressed itself on British commanders, and 'light dragoons' using Hungarian-type saddles and mounted on a better class of troop-horse began to appear in the Army List. As a result of the Napoleonic Wars these light dragoons reverted as near as might be to the original Danubian type, even going so far as to adopt the name Hussar; so much so that the Light Brigade of Balaclava fame had the clothing, the saddlery, and the accoutrements partly of Polish Ulani (in the Lancer regiments) and partly of Hungarian light horsemen.

Once the machine-gun and barbed wire between them had made nonsense of the horse as a vehicle for fighting-men, and the internal-combustion engine had robbed the coach-horse of what little utility the steam-engine had left it, the equine and the equestrian spheres of influence were confined more and more to ceremony and sport. As to ceremony, the major State occasions in the English-speaking world in the first four months of 1969 were the funeral of ex-President Eisenhower and the State reception of the Italian President at Windsor Castle. In the former not only was the coffin carried on the only horse-drawn 75 mm gun-carriage behind the only team of artillery horses that the U.S. Army has left, but a charger, fully accoutred and saddled, with jack-boots pointing backward in the stirrups, was led in the cortège. I once had the honour to serve under General of the Army Dwight D. Eisenhower, but I never saw him on horseback, and nobody else ever did either. It is just that horses are still inseparable from really first-class funereal pomp. The saddle-cloth on this horse was of the Hungarian pattern. At Windsor the ceremonial march-past was led by the bands of the Household Cavalry, which in turn was led by the drum-horse, accoutred in the Turkish manner and bearing brass kettle-drums ultimately of Turkish or Tartar design. Also on parade was the King's Troop, Royal Horse Artillery, in their full-dress uniform of Hussar (that is, Hungarian) pattern.

In the field of sport, horse-racing, which, as opposed to chariot-racing, is also probably an invention of the mounted nomads of the steppe, has never been so popular, and is diffused throughout the world. It depends on the thoroughbred racehorse, an amalgam of equine races evolved in England, but, as our author demonstrates, containing besides Arabian elements more than a measurable trace of Turkish and other Central Asiatic blood. Other equestrian spectacles, including Olympic events, dressage, and show-jumping in general, are a synthesis, in terms of the horses ridden and style of riding employed, of Eastern and Western elements. And the nodal point at which these traditions met and mingled is the lower Danube valley, among the Magyar horsemen.

The author is singularly well equipped to expound this highly original study of mobility in Eurasiatic societies before the advent of the machine, and its survivals today—first by reason of his access to records in the Magyar language which are beyond the reach of the West European student and layman alike, and second because in early life he himself herded colts on horseback on the Hungarian plains, in living contact with the traditions that go back to those of the earliest horse nomads. His work has opened a new vista for me on this far-reaching avenue of history, and I am glad that the opportunity has been afforded to reveal it to the eyes of an English-speaking public.

Contents

Part I Man and the Horse

Man as Breeder

In the course of prehistoric development it became ever clearer to man that he could exploit various animal species with less labour and peril than by hunting: by taming and breeding them. Of course, it was many thousands of years before all the implications of this were realized, and its realization took many different forms, depending on the parts of the world and species of animal concerned.

It is well known that the first animal to be domesticated was the dog. Even if there were no archaeological proof, this would be evident from the ease with which young puppies can be tamed, and from the fact that the dog eats the same sort of food as the diet of hunting and food-gathering men. Later we find hunting peoples who keep other animals of the cat and weasel tribe (cheetah, ferret) as well as falcons and eagles to hunt for them, and a few aquatic birds like the cormorant to fish for them. In such cases man and beast are only doing what both would do 'naturally' on their own account; only now side by side.

But when we come to the domestication of grazing animals and poultry a new element comes into play which tends to alter the life of the humans as well as the animals concerned. These animals are man's unrestricted and permanently available property, ensuring a supply of food and clothing and important raw materials for tool-making; some also provide a source of labour. So that many more new possibilities arise from the exploitation of these animals than by keeping auxiliary hunters such as hawk and hound.

But side by side with this potential, man is faced with new demands, primarily of a mental order. Now he is saddled with the care and protection of flocks and herds, with the provision of grazing in summer and fodder in winter, with protection against wild beasts and robbers. This amounts to much more work for the stock-keeper, involving also the division of labour and committedness. A balance had to be struck between the profits and the obligations of keeping animals—as it still has today. This was one of the most important stages in human progress.

Prehistorians up to now have been unable to form a clear and uniform picture of the earliest stages of domestication. In the absence of evidence they must have recourse to speculation, which is dangerous. It is generally assumed that the first grazing animal to be domesticated in Eurasia was the reindeer. In post-glacial times changes of climate and associated migrations of some animal species, and the extinction of others, led to a substantial spread of domestication, which became specialized, because independently developed, in different regions. Thus in the earlier phases of the history of domestic animals a limited number of wild species were tamed one by one.

Therefore in our view the archaeological material available up to now has only local relevance, and does not offer the basis of a comprehensive picture of the beginnings of stock-breeding. Such partial and local evidence is afforded, for instance, at Stellmoor, in North Germany, for domesticated reindeer in the eighth millennium B.C. or at Qualat Jarmo, in Iraq, for the keeping of sheep, cattle, and onagers in the fifth millennium.

We have no precise information about the earliest stages in the domestication of the horse. The one thing certain is that the earliest horse-keepers came from some hunting tribe in North Eurasia many thousands of years ago. The earliest archaeological find illustrating this in Northern Europe belongs to the end of the Neolithic—that is, between 4000 and 3000 B.C.

Man and the Evolution of Transport

As soon as man, by learning to walk upright, was sundered from the quadruped world he began to pay heavily for this privilege. It not only reduced his speed, but walking and running took up more of his energy. This was a grave disadvantage in the struggle for existence, for which only his increased mental capacity could compensate. Of course, the upright posture favoured his mental development. A man standing upright has a wider range of vision, his powers of observation are increased, he is able to absorb more experiences. This is allied to an increase in capacity and shape of the brain, and makes greater structural adaptability possible.

It took many hundreds of thousands of years to perfect this advance on the 'original' condition of man, and on this followed an improvement in human communications, travelling becoming less demanding in terms of effort, and more rewarding in proportion.

The great mountain ranges throughout the world acted as barriers between individual cultures, while waterways connected them. It is not by chance that the first traces of early civilizations are to be found on the banks of rivers or along sheltered stretches of coastline, where man found it easiest to provide for his daily needs, and to solve the problems of transport and communications. Even in primeval times men were able to take advantage of transport by water, to exploit the power of wind and tide; the raft, the dugout canoe, and at last the ship were what broke down the isolation of tribes and clans, enabling human contacts to be established over great distances. Thus larger human communities arose, and the exploitation of natural energy can be regarded as the first step in human progress.

The next step can be shown to depend directly on the further perfection of communications and the conquest of distance. Man used the energy of animals to facilitate transport by land. This led to contact between hitherto isolated communities.

In Europe and in those parts of Asia where wild Equidae lived, the horse for thousands of years held the primacy among those species of animals used for transport, until in very recent times the discovery of coal and oil and the way to exploit these new sources of energy opened up new possibilities in the field of transport and communications, undreamed of before. But even these possibilities are not the end of the road. In our day nuclear energy is shaping the beginning of a new era of transport.

The Beginnings of Horse-breeding

The single-hoofed animals grouped under the generic title of Equidae inhabited both the Old and the New World in pre-glacial times, or rather their ancestors did so. But at that time they still had more than one toe and were only the height of a dog. Apart from that, they bore little resemblance to the horse of today. It took some fifty to sixty million years before the emergence in North America of Plio-hippus, and another ten million before the true horse evolved. Severe conditions during the Ice Age tended to restrict rather than favour the spread of the race geographically. It is only a few thousand years since the last of the American horses died out or migrated into Siberia across what is now the Bering Strait. From then onward they were present only in the Old World.

Three original races of true Eurasian horses are known: the pony (*Equus abeli*); living on the fringes of the forest zone of Western Europe; the Tarpan of Eastern Europe of the border of forest and steppe (*Equus gmelini Antonius*); and the Asiatic wild horse, which may or may not be extinct, but was last seen wild in Djungaria, on the borders of Soviet Asia and Mongolia. This third race was called in the local languages Kertag or Tach or Taki, and its scientific name is *Equus przevalskii Poliakoff*. Whether or not it survives in the wild state, there are about a hundred specimens alive in the zoos of the world. The Tarpan has been extinct for the last century. There are no surviving herds of ponies which are wild, in the strict sense in which zoologists use the word.

These three races are closely allied to each other, in both their habits and bodily structure. None of them exceeds (or exceeded) 13 hands in height. It is difficult to assess the part played by the original wild pony and by the Tarpan as the foundation stock of domestic horses, because living specimens are not available for study.

The least evolved forms of Equidae are the two species of ass still found wild south of the Mediterranean; then come the Asiatic wild asses such as the Persian and Indian onagers and the Kulan and the Kiang of Turkestan and Tibet. Of these only the Mesopotamian sub-species of onager was domesticated in antiquity, but was displaced by the horse. They all inhabit the steppe region of Central Asia, and thus overlap the original habitat of the horse, but are adaptable to more arid zones.

A third group of Equidae still living wild in tropical and sub-tropical Africa are the various species of zebra. Of these the Grévy's Zebra is the largest, having a height of 15 hands, a greater stature than that of all the wild asses and horses. All species of zebra are prized as a source of meat by African tribes; but we know of no attempt by them to domesticate any of the species, although it has been demonstrated that both the zebra itself and the mule which is produced by crossing it with, for instance, the Basuto Pony, can be trained to work, and is easily kept.

Systems of classification of the ancestors of the domestic horse have been frequently revised since before the days of Darwin, and the current scheme, based on physical characteristics but also on feeding habits, is expounded in the various works of Dr Skorkowski in Poland, J. G. Speed in Scotland, and H. Ebhardt in Germany. It presents two wild species of pony and two wild species of horse, with different but overlapping habitats, and has replaced the threefold division mentioned above. Their characteristics shown in the accompanying sketches were as follows.

Pony Type I. Unspecialized, broad forehead, wide nostrils, straight (but in some northern varieties S-curved) facial profile, short ears, broad croup, height at withers 12 hands–12 hands 2 in. Approximately the Exmoor of today.

Pony Type II. Stoutly built, coarse, heavy head, pendulous lower lip, straight facial profile inclining to convex, ears of medium length, split up behind, height at

withers 14 hands–14 hands 2 in., reminiscent of modern northern cold-blooded types.
Horse Type III. Long in the back, long, narrow skull, Roman nose, very long ears, sloping croup, height at withers 14 hands 2 in.–15 hands, slab-sided.
Horse Type IV. Refined, short in the back, short head, wide nostrils, concave facial

Pony Type I   Pony Type II

Horse Type III   Horse Type IV

The Four Types of Wild Horse and Pony, according to H. Ebhardt
Drawn by E. Trumler

profile, small, short ears tufted at the tip, very narrow croup with the tail set on high. Height at withers 11 hands 2 in.–12 hands; represented today by the Arab type.

Although the scientific attitude to the question of ancestral horse types has not finally crystallized, we shall in the following pages argue along the lines laid down by Ebhardt, because they are supported by practical research, and because they

2　The Treasure of the Oxus
　Massagetic chariot-and-four, third century B.C.
　British Museum

3　Four-wheeled Wagon in Clay,
　excavated at Buda Kalasz, Hungary.
　Third millennium B.C.
　National Museum, Budapest

4   The Bayeux Tapestry. Horses transported by sea.

facilitate a decisive step forward in the solution of fundamental problems. The sole deviation from this classification that is justified is in connection with Arab and allied breeds, since today and in historical times they have been represented by a taller type of saddle horse.

In Eurasia these four types were initially bred by prehistoric man solely for meat, like his other domestic animals. This is brought out by the Scandinavian discoveries mentioned above, and by later discoveries from other parts of Eurasia. It was not until a later stage in the history of the animal-taming hunter that the horse entered on its historic role in the progress of mankind, by the exploitation of its strength. On the basis of the archaeological finds made up to the present, scientists have drawn the conclusion that initially the horse was only worked in harness, and not ridden for some thousand years after that. (But it must be taken into account that identifiable remains of carts and cart harness are much more likely to have been preserved over long periods than the rawhide bridle which probably constituted the sole equipment of the first riders.) The reindeer in harness first appeared in Eurasia in the third millennium B.C. The transition to the harness horse took place in the second millennium, and to the 'saddled' horse long after that.

The situation in Southern Eurasia and North Africa, collectively known as the Ancient East, was very different. As early as the fifth millennium, in various parts of the region, with its shared cultural traditions, the most important pack and draught animals were the ox, the onager, and the Nubian Ass (oxen carrying packs appear in early Saharan rock drawings; asses carrying packs in rock drawings in the Eastern Desert of Egypt about the same time; draught oxen, and later onagers harnessed to chariots, in early Mesopotamian art). In this region neither the reindeer nor the horse was found in the wild state. The use of the onager in harness ceased in Mesopotamia in the second millennium [but there are textual references to onager-drawn chariots among the Indian allies of the Persian Great King much later than that, and at least one wall painting of the Egyptian New Kingdom shows a chariot drawn by a pair that may be onagers or else mules, the progeny of an onager and a mare. Tr.]. Everywhere the onager was displaced as a harness animal by the horse, and its name was erased from the roster of domestic animals. Riding, as opposed to driving, did not become common throughout the Ancient East until the first millennium.

E. J. Ross in 1946 opened up a new archaeological perspective of the exploitation of animal tractive power, with his finds at Rana Gundai, in Northern Baluchistan, which showed domestic animals being kept between the fourth millennium and the middle of the first, including the horse derived from Central Asia and the ass derived from North Africa. This at a period in which such use had hitherto been considered impossible in that part of the world. Some scholars are still inclined to reserve judgment on this sensational discovery pending further assessment of the age of the bone material. [The presence of the horse and ass, both domesticated, would, of course, allow the possibility of mule-breeding then and there, but the first written mention of mules occurs later, and farther west, in the laws of the early Hittite kings—fifteenth century B.C. Tr.].

The only conclusion that we shall therefore draw from the Rana Gundai finds is that in the light of present knowledge the question of domestication of animals in Eurasia is still an open one, and must remain so for a long time. This is especially true of Central Asia, which is among the regions considered by scholars to have been the original home of mankind, but where archaeological research is still in its infancy, since the area is a very large one. The final answer to the question of the earliest farming and herdsmanship, both here and in the Afghan/Baluchi region, has yet to come.

For our solution to the problem of when and where animal tractive power was first exploited, we shall look to another quarter. Certainly it was response to an economic challenge, closely allied to the manner in which domestic animals were kept, and can best be studied in the light of practical experience. The choice before the primeval stock-keeper was either to graze his herds on the open range or to keep them in enclosed fields or stables. (This choice was open even to the pig-keeper; the swine could either be kept in styes or 'at pannage' in the forest.)

The difference between the two styles of agrarian life becomes sharpest in winter-time, when steppe nomads drive their cattle to what is called the winter pasture. Here in swamps and marshes or in the shelter of the woods they can always find something to eat. The forest trees provide shelter from the snow-storms. Herds thus are strangers to both halter and manger, and graze for themselves in summer and winter alike, just like wild animals—only that they are guided and guarded by herdsmen.

All over Eurasia where climate and terrain are suitable—that is, provide adequate winter pasture—we find traces of prehistoric herdsmanship in the forest and tundra of the sub-arctic zone with its reindeer-moss, swamps, and marshes for cattle (Camargue), low-lying meadows and deciduous woods for sheep, horses, and goats. This migration with the herds by which he gets his living makes no particular demands on the wandering stockman. There is no ceiling to the number of cattle he can breed, provided he has the sole use of the grazing-grounds.

The sedentary peasant, on the contrary, must spend at least part of the summer cultivating and harvesting fodder and forage for the winter, as well as crops for his own consumption; between grazing seasons—say from October to April—his cares are multiplied. He must bring his stock into stables and byres, or at least into a yard, and he must ration out his feed-stuffs. Even in normal seasons there is a limit to the number of head he can feed over the winter; after a hard winter and a late spring, when all the hay is eaten before the grass begins to grow, his lot is worse than that of the nomadic herdsman. Internal parasites are also a greater menace to the stock of the settled farmer than to that of the nomad. The latter can always move on when the grazing becomes tapeworm-infested or 'horse-sick'; the farmer cannot.

Climatic and topographical factors also play their part. The Russian scientist Popatov has established that the ox cannot be kept north of 51 degrees North. And for every animal that the nomad keeps or could keep there is a similar limit, both north and south. Thus for the horse 51 degrees is not the limit, north of which it must be stabled (it can winter out well to the north of the 60th parallel), but it cannot support life in some southern latitudes where cattle flourish, partly owing to the ravages of such plagues as African 'horse-sickness'.

The northern/southern limits between which the herding of grazing animals is practicable are identical with those between which the same animal was originally found in its wild state. Beyond these limits the animal must either be stabled or at least hand-fed (the classical example being the horse in Arabia). Theoretically there is no limit, geographically, to the 'artificial' keeping of grazing animals—at the beginning of this century Shackleton's expedition took Siberian ponies to the Antarctic. The only limits are economic ones. In time we shall be able, technically, to keep cows in interplanetary spaceships; but it will never pay to do so.

With the spread of settled agriculture and the stabling of cattle a significant breakthrough in agrarian economy took place—some animal species overstepped, as a result of domestication, the northern and southern bounds which Nature had set them in the wild—and this was to have the most important consequences for all mankind, as more and more tribes came into possession of poultry, cattle, pigs, goats, sheep—and horses.

This is by no means to imply that in the early stages of domestication animals were kept exclusively in herds in the open. [Obviously the dog was not, even though the Eskimo dog-team is a sort of wolf-pack, and does not sleep in the igloo. *Tr.*] The case is rather the contrary. The keeping of herds on free range is not more 'primitive' than the other method, nor is it more sophisticated. It is simply a quite different approach to the problem, which did not become widespread until after the rise of sedentary farming.

The above considerations about the keeping of livestock in general are also valid for the exploitation of animal-power by the two kinds of farmers—sedentary and pastoral. To begin with, the sedentary peasants used their animals only in harness, while the nomad herdsmen only rode them. (But probably both used them under the pack-saddle.)

This can be proved as follows. It is notorious that the "Battle-axe" people of Chalcolithic times, who perhaps can be equated with the Indo-European language group, did not ride but only drove carts or chariots, and the memory of such exclusive use of animals in draught is reflected in vocabulary and usage of some Indo-European languages, in historical times. Either they led the wagon team or drove it from the cart or the sled, and even when their cloven-footed cattle were replaced by single-hoofed equines they still did not ride, principally because their way of herdsmanship did not necessitate the risks inherent in riding. [That these risks were preserved in memory long after riding had become an everyday activity —at least of the aristocratic classes—is evident from one of the earliest Anglo-Saxon poems, the *Rune Poem*: "[*Rād*] *byþ on recyde rinca gehwylcum/sefte*..." "Riding seems easy to every warrior while he is indoors, and very courageous to him who traverses the highways on the back of a stout horse." *Tr.*]

Matters developed very differently among the wandering herdsmen. Animals only carried the rider or the pack among the peoples of Central Asia, with their Turkish or Mongolian way of life, in this first phase of exploitation of animal power. The herding and protection of half-wild bands of cattle and horses demanded more care and skill on the part of the herdsman than the winter-long care of stalled and hand-fed beasts. The only way to catch up and recover a herd which has panicked is to ride after them on something faster than they are, be it a camel, horse, donkey, reindeer, or even ox. But even droving requires judgment and practice.

Among wild or feral gregarious mammals it is mostly the older and more experienced individuals who are the leaders. The leader lays down the direction and the pace of march to pasture or water-hole, or of flight from enemies. This is especially noticeable in the case of sheep. The bell-wether leading the flock is proverbial.

The same principle applies to all other herd animals, but is less obvious among those which have long been domesticated and kept in enclosures.

The social life of horses has only a very scanty literature devoted to it. In the case of South America the English reader will think of W. H. Hudson's *A Little Boy Lost*, but G. Dadányi, a former cavalry officer of the Hungarian Army, also wrote a book about his experiences as a herdsman in Paraguay, in which he described how the half-wild bands of horses were led by a *mandrina* or bell-mare in the direction desired by the herdsmen. As a young boy I too was employed in herding colts, and have had similar experiences. (Note 1.)

In the case of domesticated horses the leadership function is commonly taken up by an elderly mare, usually conspicuous for her bad temper. If there are several contenders for the title a duel ensues. In the herd itself an interesting reflex action may be observed. If one of the horses is frightened it runs to the leader, while the others graze on unperturbed. But if the leading horse itself is alarmed, then the rest of the herd will gallop off after it.

But these observations are true only of domestic herds, from which stallions are usually absent. The bell-mare is a substitute, but in wild herds or herds which closely resemble the truly wild band of primeval horses (as on Exmoor) the most alert and aggressive adult stallion is the leader. [Only on Exmoor in the absence of an adult stallion the senior entire colt will not automatically succeed to the leadership, but some crafty and cantankerous old mare. *Tr.*] The Polish scholar W. Pruski (1959) in his book about the admixture of Tarpan blood in East European horses observes that domestic horses were often to be seen in the Tarpan herds, but these were all runaway mares, or mares that had been enticed away by Tarpan stallions. On the other hand, nobody had ever seen a runaway stallion take to the steppe and possess the Tarpan mares. Not only would the nearest wild stallion have torn him to shreds, but even if there were none present the wild mares would never accept him as a trustworthy leader of the herd, because he had lost the qualities essential to self-preservation which all born-wild horses possess, male and female alike.

The King Stallion's part does not consist only in holding the herd together and leading it to the best pasture and water. The duelling between stallions, the victor's mastery of the mares, is something essential for the natural selection of the best sire, and herd instinct was the force that created and maintained the communal life of horses in the wild. (Note 2.)

The foregoing explains why the early herdsman began to ride. It identified him, so to speak, physically with the equine leader, from whose back he could keep his herd together or lead it in the right direction rather than drive it, and this was so in the case of camels and cattle as well as horses. The roots of this procedure lie in the pleasure which young children take in romping with young animals. It was reported of the Huns that their children rode calves and foals, the smallest ones even sheep and goats. Thence to the mounting of adult animals by adults was but a step.

This is not to say that the nomad herdsman rode only stallions, and from the examples given above we see that this was not necessary. As the practice of our day demonstrates, the experienced horse-herder may employ the right sort of old mare for this purpose, especially if the herd is not only led but 'whipped-in' from the rear.

Thus riding and driving proceed from two different techniques of stock-keeping. Riding was a decisive aid to pasturing herds in the open country, and driving carts became necessary as permanent occupation of fields demanded more transport. As time went on the extreme forms of exclusive riding and exclusive driving became rarer. Transitional forms arose, in which the drivers occasionally rode their animals, and the riders occasionally harnessed theirs. And from this the point was reached in the history of transportation at which the Equestrian Era begins.

The Primary Centre of Nomadic Stock-breeding

The broad steppe region of Central Asia, which stretches north-west from the Great Wall of China to the mountain ranges of Outer Mongolia, is believed to be the place where nomad horse-breeding had its origin. This preliminary hypothesis rests neither on traditions of historical happenings nor on the fact that the last herds of truly wild horses survived there until recently. But the circumstance that this part of Asia has over the centuries been the storm-centre from which great swarms of horsemen have emerged means that horse-breeding there has been of great historical importance.

Down to our day the nomadic way of breeding horses is still practised in Mongolia, though now only a remnant of what it has been. Nature has provided extraordinary opportunities for stock-breeding, primarily because this was the habitat of three species of wild mammal of great importance to the human economy: the reindeer, the horse, and the camel.

A unique feature of the region is the presence of reindeer. [Only one such anachronistic pocket is known in Western Europe—in Caithness and Sutherland, in Northern Scotland, the reindeer survived into Viking times. *Tr.*] The natural territory of this animal in the wild lies between the 60th and 80th parallels of latitude. Its occurrence in the Sayan Mountains of Mongolia, along the 51st Parallel, is only to be explained by the fact that the highest mountains, rising to 6000 feet, of the Sayan range still support the characteristic flora of the Ice Age, including isolated colonies of reindeer-moss.

Reindeer-mounted Archer. Rock drawing from Tepsei, on the Upper Yenesei, first century B.C.
From Hančar, 1955

In our sketch above of Hančar's theory we have pointed out the crucial role of the reindeer in primitive stock-raising. How do scholars regard the progress of domestication of this deer? During the Ice Age the reindeer was widely distributed in what was then the cooler part of the North Temperate Zone, as is proved by numerous excavations and by the abundance of reindeer pictures in the cave art of France and Spain. Climatic changes at the end of this period led to a northward displacement as well as a shrinking of territory on the part of this and other Cervidae. The reindeer migrated northward to the border of the coniferous forests with the tundra, to which it is still confined, except for some herds in Scandinavia which migrate as far south as Hardanger Vidda. This hardy, abstemious, and easily tameable deer was, according to archaeological evidence, among the first animals to be domesticated.

The Sayan reindeer is, therefore, together with the moss on which it feeds, a survival from the Ice Age. In contrast to the archaeological evidence, written accounts of reindeer-keeping begin comparatively late, in the East. While the reindeer economy of Northern Scandinavia is mentioned in some detail by King Alfred in his translation of Orosius (round about A.D. 900), it is not until the thirteenth century that we have in Marco Polo's account of the Empire of Cathay and his journey to it by land some mention of tribes north of the Great Wall 'who ride on stags'. But other accounts did reach the West by different channels, as in Eden Richet's book published in 1555, where the forest-dwelling 'Scyths' along the wooded shores of Lake Baikal are described as riding cloven-hoofed animals the size of a mule which he calls 'reen'. [But as this is wooded country, as the reindeer is only the size of a rather small mule, and as the elk—the moose of North America —when it has no horns, as in the castrated male, looks much more like a mule, and is nearer to it in size than the reindeer, Richet's 'Scyths' may have been elk-borne. He is quoted by Carruthers in *Unknown Mongolia*, 1913. Incidentally, Peter the Great passed an edict against the capture alive and taming of elk; the reason for this *ukas* was that political exiles had been known to escape from Siberia on elk-back. *Tr.*] The attention of scholars was not drawn to this reindeer culture of Mongolia until rather late in the day, and these people are still little known to the ethnologist. Their way of life is that of primitive herders and hunters, at about the Neolithic level. What its significance is, in the development of pastoral and economic technique, we shall presently see. Russians made the first research into their language and way of life, but these descriptions, which were published early in the present century, aroused little interest. In 1911 Douglas Carruthers travelled from Minusinsk to Mongolia via the Sayan Mountains, and in the course of his journey met the mountaineers, in the forests. His journal contains a detailed ethnographical description of them. Unfortunately, two world wars and the intervening events hindered the continuation of his researches. In 1959 Miklós Gábori visited the reindeer-breeding hunters of the Khardyl-Sardik Mountains south of the Sayan. He published his findings in scientific periodicals, and in his account of Mongolia. Although these are not primarily concerned with reindeer-breeding, and do not give adequate answers to all the questions that arise in our inquiry into the history of transport, they will serve as a basis for a summary of the environment of the Sayan reindeer-herders.

These forest-dwellers, who call themselves Uryanchai, belong to the Altaic (Turkic-speaking) family of peoples and seem to be related, on linguistic grounds, to the neighbouring Soyets and South Siberian Karagasses. At the outset of this century there were 2000 of them or more; now there are only a few hundreds left.

They wander about in bands consisting of two or three families. They are chiefly occupied in hunting. Summer and winter they are out in the wooded Sayan hills, and the Khardyl-Sardik range. Their only domestic animal is the reindeer, which also occurs wild in the area; they milk it, ride it, and carry pack-saddles on it. They do not, like the Lapps, use sledges. They will eat reindeer meat only in the direst extremity.

Their stock-economy is of the Central Asian pattern. In summer the herds pasture on the grassy clearings of the upper slopes. On the march to fresh pastures the herdsman rides a reindeer at the head of the herd, while another mounted herdsman 'whips in' at the rear. They also use the reindeer for hunting elk, wild reindeer, chamois, and bear, since the boggy ground is for the most part impassable for horses, with their solid hoofs, but tolerable going for the reindeer, with its splayed cloven hoof. When they come within range they shoot the game with rifles from the saddle, but formerly they did so with the bow, according to Gábori.

The more characteristic nomad way of herding comes out more clearly in winter. When the upper slopes are covered with snow they do not drive their herds down the mountain but to exposed places where the wind sweeps the reindeer-moss clear of snow. From a historical point of view, this proves that their economy was limited by the occurrence of this moss. We shall have occasion later to refer to economic pressures of this nature.

The riding equipment of the Uryanchai herdsmen approximates to that of equestrian peoples, but is more primitive. They have neither bridle nor bit; the deer are steered by a thong which leads from the rider's hand to a loop round the neck. Their saddles, on the other hand, are a primitive variation—perhaps the original form—of the wooden saddles of equestrian peoples. The horizontal bars which rest on pads on either side of the animal's spine are not joined by arches, but

Mounted Archer, about 1200 B.C.
Rock drawing from Ladak, after C. Diem, 1941.

by two X-shaped forks, and the seat is a leather sling between these two forks. As in the horseman's saddle, the stirrup-leathers are attached to the bars on either side.

All signs indicate that thousands of years ago the transition from reindeer to horse as a riding animal took place here and under these special conditions. Proof is found not only in the typological development of the horse saddle from the reindeer saddle but also in the findings of archaeology and ethnology. In the shamanistic religion of people of Turkic/Mongolian culture the cult-ceremonies of the horse-sacrifice and the reindeer-sacrifice are very similar. The most striking evidence for the transition is in the change in the method of exploitation. In the whole polar zone of Eurasia, from Norway to the Bering Strait—that is, in the main body of its natural post-glacial habitat—the reindeer is used in draught, but it is not ridden, and where it is milked this can be shown to be due to the influence of neighbouring cattle-milkers to the south. In the Sayan, on the contrary, it is exclusively ridden and milked—so that the method of exploitation by nomadic horsemen and Uryanchai reindeer herdsmen is the same. Herodotus in the fifth century mentioned among other Scythian customs that of drinking mare's milk.

But in use for transport there is one other factor which points to a connection between the reindeer and the horse in this region, and perhaps here alone. The Lapps of Arctic Europe, and also the Voguls, Ostyaks, Samoyedes, Chukches, and Koryaks of Arctic Asia, all have a common history in the past of dog-drawn sleighs, dog-power having presumably first been used to supplement the tractive power of men (or more likely women) in sleigh harness. The dogs in turn were displaced by reindeer. Their methods of harnessing and guiding reindeer are all similar. The Tungus, neighbours of the Uryanchai, have been exposed to twin influences, those of riding and driving, so that they both ride their reindeer and use them in draught, as do the Yakuts.

As mentioned above, the Uryanchai only ride their reindeer and use them under the pack-saddle, never in harness. But a peculiar thing about their economy is that they have no dogs, a surprising lacuna among a hunting people. In the absence of the link, in northern latitudes, between the man-drawn sledge and the reindeer team an entirely different line of development was followed, and the possibility of riding and driving arising from a common source is excluded.

Now, to return to the traces of nomadic pastoralism as formerly practised in Mongolia. Besides horses, herds of camels and flocks of sheep were bred; these three species gradually became indispensable for life on the steppes. The only bovid was the Himalayan variety, the yak, imported from Tibet and also used for riding and pack traffic, the yak cows being milked. Later domestic cattle were introduced from China, bringing with them the two-wheeled ox-cart.

Mongolia, the original home of nomadic pastoralism, did not only stamp its impression on stock-breeding; its effect, however indirectly, on the political history of Eurasia was even more important. Knowledge of the evolution that led from nomadic reindeer-breeding through horse-keeping to the riding of the horse is the answer to the question why Mongolia over the centuries has been again and again the calm heart of the hurricane out of which the storms of horse archers have blown so devastatingly. When the economic factors are also taken into consideration, it becomes even more apparent that it was the mounted warrior who during that momentous period known as the Migration of Peoples was solely responsible for wrenching the world off its hinges.

"The Centre of the World"

Travellers in their descriptions of political and economic life among the Central Asian peoples during the nineteenth century are unanimous in emphasizing that the quarrels among the nomadic tribes who were then living under primeval conditions were principally due to economic causes. The historian and ethnologist Armin Vámberi says of the Turkomans in the heart of Turania during the seventies:

> Added to external pressure [he means conquest by Tsarist Russia] was internal strife, almost always about grazing grounds and irrigation canals branching off from perennial rivers. Water and grazing are here indispensable, and this explains the bitterness with which for instance Yomuds and Tekkes (near the Akhal oasis) fought each other for centuries . . .

The Swiss H. Moser said the same thing ten years later, though by 1888 the political independence of these nomadic tribes was vanishing. Only the final triumph of Tsarist power brought an end to these sanguinary struggles for water and grazing in Central Asia. Moser describes the traditions which individual tribes had inherited of the earlier migrations. Thus the Kirghiz still vividly remembered that they had once lived much farther east. When their stock was threatened by lack of grazing they set off westward, driving out the Kalmucks from the grounds which they then occupied.

Historical traditions of earlier periods are all of a piece with this. Thus Arab sources record the Seljuk Turks as having once run their herds on the grasslands round Bokhara, Khorasan, and Khoresmia, which they had gained by force. Again and again in Hungarian chronicles stress is laid on the importance of grazing and water. The scouts preceding the Magyar invaders were always on the lookout for good grass and abundant pure water, and this motif occurs in the legend of the White Horse, in which the Magyar chiefs ask Prince Sviatopolk in exchange for a splendidly caparisoned horse only a bundle of grass and a jug of Danube water. Later they interpreted this exchange of gifts to mean that the symbolic grass and water entitled them to graze their herds all over the Danubian plain and water them in the river—in practice, to take possession of Sviatopolk's country. The same procedure was repeated with the Bulgarian prince, asking of him water from the Tisza, sand, and grass from Alpar. The same motives kept the Huns on the move, as a Chinese source of the first century A.D. mentions them moving across the steppe in search of grazing and water.

The gain or loss of watering-places and pasture made a difference, for the nomad, between riches and poverty, even between life and death from famine. Their herds had increased, as shown above, in proportion as they learnt better animal husbandry by experience, but this very increase led to friction between flock-masters of the kind described often in the patriarchal chapters of the Old Testament. For instance:

> And the land was not able to bear them, that they [Lot and Abram] might dwell together; for their substance was great, so that they could not dwell together.
> And there was a strife between the herdmen of Abram's cattle and the herdmen of Lot's cattle: and the Canaanite and the Perizzite dwelled then in the land. (Genesis, xiii, 6, 7.)

[Here we have the added complication, which had its counterpart in Central Asia, of the settled farmers—the Canaanites and Perizzites whose demands on grazing would be less, but who at certain seasons would consume as much water as the herdsmen; moreover, their arable fields would lie along the river-banks. Such tensions arose between proprietors of 'great substance', because to pastoralists at this stage there is no such thing as over-stocking. One could, of course, have eaten or sold or exchanged the surplus cattle, but then that would be the end of one's reputation as 'the Man with a Thousand Cows', even though the remaining stock would have been in better condition. It is quantity of livestock, not quality, which confers prestige in such societies. *Tr.*]

The almost infinite perspective of early tribal wanderings in Central Asia has not yet been the subject of exhaustive research. Where historical and archaeological inquiry will not suffice, the findings of allied sciences may help the solution of some questions.

Before Columbus demonstrated the globular shape of the world and Magellan's crew came back from its first circumnavigation people thought of the earth as a plate-like disc: the centre of its surface, therefore, would be 'the middle of the world'. Although various rationalizations at different times and places attempted to locate it, this Navel of the World, even at the time when it was most seriously believed in, remained a mystical concept. It was possible to see it as the point of departure of centrifugal forces that for many thousands of years had determined human history. Just as a stone thrown into a pond sets up concentric rings of waves, so forces originating at the centre of the region where pastoral economy was first practised set up waves represented by the increase of herds and pressure on grazing facilities, which finally set in motion the Migration of Peoples. Neighbouring tribes came to blows, and in each case the loser had to vacate his pastures and his homestead, unless he were to face utter extermination. His only recourse was to drive his herds off, into the territory of some weaker pastoral tribe, which in turn he would displace and overpower. This pressure was not exercised solely on the tribes immediately involved, but its effects were apparent among distant peoples, especially among the weaker or less sophisticated.

It is highly probable that these movements originated among reindeer-breeders; but with the appearance of horse-breeders they reached their zenith. The nomad soon learned the advantages which being mounted on reindeer or horse brought, both in herding and in hunting, and he learned to apply these to warfare. As this mode of fighting was brought to perfection it became apparent that harmony between rider and mount was as important as the strength and valour of the rider. Thus a new chapter in the history of warfare came to be written.

The spread of nomadic pastoralism in prehistoric times was always governed by certain geographical and climatic limitations as to its direction. This is evident in the traces of migrations initiated by the reindeer-herders. The Uigurs, practising nomadic reindeer-breeding in the Sayan range, forced the Tungus out of their neighbouring hunting and grazing grounds, and the Tungus in turn drove the Siberian Yakuts northward, displacing the Samoyedes to the north-west and the Koryaks and Chukches to the east; the object of the displaced being all the time to find new winter pasture for their herds—that is, tracts of ground where the reindeer-moss grew. (Note 3.)

Here we come to another interesting fact: the Eskimo of North America came

6 The Taki or Mongolian Wild Horse

7 The same, believed to be the only one photo-
graphed under a rider. Askania Nova, 1907
Ziemsen Verlag Wittenberg

8 Detail from Fresco in Apse of Cathedral at
Aquileia: Knight with Pointed Shield and
Lance, pursuing . . .
Acta Archaeologica Hungarica

9 . . . Hungarian Raider mounted
on Gelding, armed with Bow
and Sabre, virtually without
Body-armour. *Twelfth century or
earlier*
Acta Archaeologica Hungarica

10
Uryanchai Girls riding
Reindeer bareback

11
Reindeer showing
Uryanchai Pattern of
Saddle

12   Mongol herding
Camels

13 Reindeer Mask from Pazyryk
Hermitage, Leningrad

from North-east Asia, the first of them in Mesolithic times, but in many waves since then, and these later crossings of the Bering Strait by Eskimo and Amerindian tribes may have been due to the pressure of the expanding reindeer-breeders of East Siberia. To this day the Eskimo practise a hunting and fishing economy, and their only domestic animal is the dog. The reindeer, in its American form of the caribou, was present in the new continent, but the fact that the Eskimo never attempted to domesticate it must point to their having crossed the Strait at a time before reindeer-herding had become general in Northern Siberia, and so they have remained specialized as hunters and fishermen. [At these callings they have reached a high level of technical skill. Like other North Eurasian hunting tribes since Mesolithic times, they used a composite (wood and horn or whalebone) bow, and before the introduction of firearms some tribes on the west side of Hudson's Bay used a crossbow of such penetrating power that it would even pierce the tough frontal bone of the musk-ox. Tr.] The southward migrations of the later waves of Eskimo, in their turn, touched off further migrations among other Amerindian tribes [but these were of a different kind, since flocks and herds were not involved; nor were the Eskimo warlike. Probably as hunters they were more efficient; they did not expel the Indian tribes by conquest; the latter just could not compete with them once the 'easier' meat animals had been killed off, and the Eskimo—but not other races—were able to make a living off what remained. Tr.]

The expansive force moving northward in the eastern part of Asia began to slow down when the reindeer-riders of the Mongolian region went over to horse-riding, since they could not then pass the northern limits of the natural habitat of the wild horse (see p. 16). Now the expansion had to take place east and west. Throughout historical time the pattern is the same—the swarms of horsemen, Huns, Ephthalites, Avars, Turks, and Mongols, from the Pacific to the Atlantic, only operated between certain parallels of latitude, which were a prolongation east and west of the home of Przewalski's Horse. Their entry on the agrarian scene brought a novelty, in the form of horse-breeding in herds on open ranges, to Eastern Europe.

[By contrast, it is worth noting that military conquest *by charioteers* overstepped the natural boundaries of the wild-horse habitat as early as the second millennium B.C. *Tr.*]

The pressure exercised by the equestrian tribes had its effect not only to the east and to the west but also to the north and to the south. This particularly affected people whose way of life was not materially affected by changes of climate. Among such were the Indo-European language group, which perhaps may be equated, archaeologically, with the "battle-axe" people who in the third millennium B.C. were moving out of the Central Asian region. Some of them turned south, and

MIGRATIONS OF HORSE-BREEDING PEOPLE

under the name of Aryans conquered India and Persia; the Hittites, Kassites, and Mitannians entered Asia Minor, while the Celts and later the Germans penetrated North and West Europe. All these were chariot-driving, not originally riding, aristocracies.

These movements in their turn all put to flight or subjected peoples of other stock and language. In the south the Dravidians who had originally peopled all India were driven down towards Ceylon, and even into the islands of the Indian Ocean. The Hittites pressing on into Anatolia subjugated the Sumerians, the Mitannians and Kassites overcame the Semitic tribes or drove them back into the Arabian peninsula, and this Semitic recoil had its repercussions among Hamitic peoples farther south. The advance of the Celts and Germans into Europe displaced the Finno-Ugric peoples towards the Baltic, who pushed the European Lapps into Northern Scandinavia.

The mounted herdsmen who were the prime cause of these migrations at last appeared on the scene of historically recorded events, but we do not know the actual date of their 'explosion'. We can only infer it by reference to the time when the sedentary farmers began to be displaced. But the Far East soon began to be the scene of new changes. The full weight of nomadic expansion turned westwards exclusively as soon as the Chinese Empire had become a great political power, in the second half of the first millennium, and was at last able to offer successful resistance to the Asiatic Huns. The hard-hitting Chinese armies and the Great Wall together barred the way to nomad peoples seeking expansion to the east and south-east. They recoiled in the direction of Europe, in the end penetrating as far as the Atlantic. This invasion left visible traces on the ethnographic map of Europe.

The last swarm of horsemen was the Mongol expansion under Jenghis Khan. Although the economic causes of these migrations had continued secondary effects, in that the search for grazing and water still led to war and unrest in the Oriental regions, after the Mongol invasions the displacements at last came to a halt. The superiority of the horseman in battle progressively lost momentum in the same measure as the peoples attacked adopted the technique and tactics of the invaders themselves, and began to use the horse as a weapon, or at least as a weapon-carrier. No longer was riding a monopoly of the warrior-herdsman.

The re-establishment of strategic equilibrium brought back order and stability to the disordered ranks of the Eurasian family of nations. The horse that once had borne the apocalyptic riders out of the heart of Nomad's Land had acted out the last line of his historical role. From now on horses were not only at the service of the warrior but the aides of creative man, supporting his advance to higher things.

Migrations and the Mounted Warrior

Tolstov called the social organization of the pastoral peoples a military state with the institution of slavery. The herdsmen were not only masters in their exploitation of animal resources; in the course of centuries of warfare they acquired more and more the taste for the exploitation of human labour. The mounted warrior's most valuable booty came to be the prisoner of war who could be enslaved. As the economic interests of many pastoral tribes widened they came to include an organized slave-trade.

Over the centuries of chronic war and migration riding technique had reached a high state of perfection. Among the nomads this high standard of horsemanship marked great advances in the arts of transport, communications, and warfare. The military superiority of equestrian nations was made manifest in the Migration of Peoples.

Among the nations first exposed to attack by mounted enemies, the predominant reaction was defensive. Its most impressive monument is the Great Wall of China, along the northern frontier. Remains of a similar defensive line have been found north-east of Kabul, on what was once the Bactrian frontier. It consists of a series of brick walls 17 metres broad traversing uninhabited territory, up hill and down dale, like similar defensive works of which traces have been found at intervals all the way from there to the Hungarian plain.

A self-contained defensive system has also been unearthed in the deserts of Kara-Kum and Kyzyl-Kum. This sterile wilderness was in antiquity, and still in the Middle Ages, a highly developed civilized region, dependent on irrigation canals which distributed water from the tributaries of the Amu-Darya as they flowed out of the Afghan mountains. The attention of scholars has only recently been directed to this ancient civilization. Air photography has supplemented the excavations by Soviet archaeologists before 1939. The plains are covered with drifted sand, underneath which are the remains of a dense network of irrigation channels and the settlements of the first Khoresmian farmers.

But the chief significance of this discovery is military. As well as displacing the agrarian population, the drifting sand has preserved the remains of a peculiar system of defensive works which are the relics of the wars between the Khoresmian settlers or Massagetes, and the nomads. The *Zend-Avesta*, or teaching of Zara-thustra, contains many traditions of the centuries-old Khoresmian civilization. According to it, the Massagetes lived in fortified settlements which are known in archaeological parlance as *gorodyishche*. These were so laid out that their four sides were used as living-quarters, while cattle were kept in the central courtyard. As a defence against repeated attacks by mounted enemies the outer walls contained loopholes for archery, and there were towers on them. Finally, from the first century B.C. onwards, fortresses were built whose sole purpose was defence.

The Massagetes were crop farmers at a high level of civilization. According to the *Avesta*, they were organized socially, about the second millennium B.C., in three classes; priests of fire, warriors, and commoners (farmers). The warrior caste was called *rataista*, a word which originally meant 'charioteer', and is derived from the common Indo-European root *rad-*, meaning wheel, though at this time we may assume that riding was gaining ground among them. Herodotus describes them as a heavily armed nation of horsemen, similar in costume and customs to the Scyths. They fought on foot and on horseback, their horses being armoured.

Riding spread to their western neighbours even later, the chariot still being in use in Eastern Europe at a time when the Massagetes were already fighting on horseback. In the lands about the Black Sea this was still true in the times of Herodotus, who says: "The limitless plains beyond the Lower Danube are peopled by the Sigynnes, who dress like the Medes. The winter coat of their horses is five fingers thick, but they are small; they are blunt-nosed and are only driven in harness, being too small to carry a man."

In the Carpathian basin, home of the Tarpan (p. 13) and still inhabited by its tame descendant the *Hucul* pony, riding can only be shown to have been practised after the time of the Sarmatians, and in more westerly regions later than that. According to Tacitus, some Germanic tribes still fought from the chariot in the first century A.D., and only gave up this technique on entering Roman employment as auxiliaries. In the century before that the British force which opposed Caesar's invasion consisted partly of mounted men, partly of chariots. [Chariots were still found in the Caledonian host which opposed the army of Agricola in A.D. 84, somewhere in the Scottish highlands. They were still in use in Ireland in the time of St Patrick. *Tr.*]

But the transference from the chariot to the saddle did not automatically give the newly converted squadrons parity with their adversaries, even in single combat. It took time to learn equitation, and to master the individual arms that went with horsemanship, as opposed to chariot-fighting, let alone the elements of squadron tactics. The Western equipment was rather defensive as opposed to the armament of the Eastern horsemen, which consisted of a short bow that could be used from the saddle, and a sabre. Horse and rider had to be armoured against the arrows.

Armourers came predominantly from the ranks of those peoples who were threatened by mounted enemies. Thus the armour made at Merv by Massagetic smiths was famed in antiquity, and much prized.

But it was precisely armour which impeded the adoption of the highly mobile tactics of nomad warfare. The pike and the javelin suitable for close combat remained in use after the agricultural levies had become mounted. However, in conformity with mounted service they were transformed into the lance, which was effective in the hands of massed armoured horsemen, but only if these were organized in large squadrons.

For a long time armoured mounted troops fought the mounted archers on equal terms, but in the end both armour and heavy non-missile weapons were laid aside, and the tactics of the Eastern cavalry adopted.

The Bactrian or Turanian Horse

Chinese sources are the first to mention this horse. In 126 B.C. Imperial envoys reported that in the distant land of Taiyuan marvellous blood-sweating 'heavenly' horses were bred.

This land of the wonderful horses was the Bactrian kingdom, at that time an important centre of central Asiatic civilization, on the northern slopes of the Afghan mountain ranges. That part of it which lay round the upper Syr-Darya river was called Ferghana, in Chinese Taiyuan; and the most important trade-route of antiquity, the Silk Road, traversed it from east to west. Bactra, the capital of the kingdom, had as its city badge a galloping horse, the symbol of traffic. Its lively trade with foreign countries had been since the fourth century in the hands of Greek (specifically Macedonian) colonists.

But the origin of Bactrian horse-breeding goes back further than that. When Alexander the Great was on his way to the conquest of India he remounted his cavalry on Bactrian horses, before the Chinese became aware of their existence. He also employed Bactrian mercenary cavalry. But even before that, in the time of the Achaemenid dynasty which began in 599, when Bactria had been a dependent satrapy of the Persian Empire, such Bactrian troopers served in the Persian army.

The Persian word *asp*—horse—is found at the time of the earlier independent Bactrian kings, the house of Kavanida, in the names of legendary heroes such as Aurvataspa and Vitaspa, and the ancient royal seat of Bactria was called Zariaspa. The tribal names Zariaspai and Arimaspai mean 'golden horses' and 'well-schooled horses' respectively.

Coin of King Eutractides of Bactria
From Rowland 1961

In the reign of King Yuë-chi (to give him his Chinese name) of Bactria the Chinese Emperor sent repeated embassies to him, seeking to buy horses, but in vain. At last he sent him a thousand gold pieces and a horse of solid gold, to help change his mind. But even this did not have the desired effect. Yuë-chi threw the envoys into prison and had them executed for attempting to escape. So now the Emperor Wu tried what force of arms would do. His first assault was beaten off. At the second attempt Yuë-chi was besieged in his palace. The spoils of this campaign included 30 blood-sweating horses, and 3000 half-bred mares and stallions. With this stock the Chinese Emperor set up stud-farms and covering centres, which according to Sven Hedin were the beginning of serious Chinese horse-breeding.

But the Chinese were not the only beneficiaries of this dispersal. Their records in the second century B.C. mention that the king of the Asiatic Huns, Tuman, possessed a 'thousand-mile' horse which after his death the people of Tung-hu demanded for themselves. We may assume that this horse was a widely known stallion with the conformation and characteristics of the 'heavenly' horses.

From this document, and from the anxiety of the Chinese to obtain horses of quality, we may conclude that the most dangerous enemies of the Chinese, the Huns, owed their superiority not to their valour but to the superior stamp of horse they rode. Eventually the Imperial forces were able to match the superiority of the Huns in matters of horsemanship. The Huns were turned westward largely because of the increased efficiency of Chinese cavalry, who came to be mounted on better horses once the remount studs began to feel the effect of better breeding-stock derived from exotic hot-blooded strains.

The Pazyryk Burial

There are still many uncertainties for archaeology to clear up concerning stock-breeding in early historical times, but so far as horse-breeding in Central Asia is concerned much valuable data has been obtained from one source alone.

Westward from Mongolia, in the high valley of Ulagan in the Altai mountains,

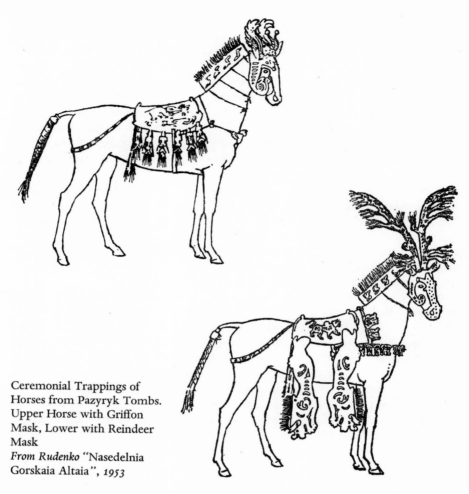

Ceremonial Trappings of
Horses from Pazyryk Tombs.
Upper Horse with Griffon
Mask, Lower with Reindeer
Mask
*From Rudenko "Nasedelnia
Gorskaia Altaia", 1953*

near Pazyryk, the graves of rich herd-owners who died in the middle of the first millennium B.C. were discovered by Russian explorers and fully described by S. I. Rudenko.[1] The tombs, known as *kurgans* or barrows, were shafts of rectangular section revetted with solid beams such as are used to build wooden houses in the same region today, and lined with felt hangings as the walls of the inmate's own houses must have been lined in life. By a strange and probably unrepeatable combination of climatic accidents, masses of ice formed in the tombs soon after interment, thus preserving organic material of all kinds in a deep-freeze. Corpses, leather, textiles, furs, horn, bone and wooden objects, food both human and animal, were preserved almost unaltered by decay. Thus where in other finds we only have bits and buckles, here we have whole bridles. Where elsewhere we have only the skeletons, and rarely the whole skeleton, of horses, here we have hair and hide and flesh. For anything between seven and fourteen horses were found in each grave-shaft. This unique find enabled 69 more or less perfect horse cadavers of the fifth century B.C. to be recovered, including even the stomach contents. The only comparable

[1] Published by J. M. Dent, 1969.

finds are the frozen mammoths of an earlier Siberian age, and the mummified corpses from the Danish bogs, which so far have been exclusively human, so that no contemporary European horses are available for comparison with those of Pazyryk.

The height of these at the withers varied from nearly 13 to 15 hands in the adult. [No foals were found, but some of the clothing was trimmed with foal-fur. *Tr.*] On the basis of stature and build they could be divided into four groups. Comparison of a horse from the first group with one from the fourth showed distinct evidence of the breeding of different types, one of which we should today call highly bred, the other a common sort of utility horse. The following peculiarities were noted, among others:

Group I was from 14 hands 3 in. high, to 15 hands. Their common characteristic was an impressive head, with concave profile and high neck carriage, short in the back, strong, 'dry' limbs with well-developed joints. The readiest comparison among present-day light-horse breeds is with the Arab, despite the coarser skeletal build of the Pazyryk horse. All were light-coloured, mostly golden dun, with black mane and tail. Since bridles and saddles were buried with them, they were obviously riding-horses. They correspond to Ebhardt's Type IV, though taller.

The height of horses in Group IV (Pazyryk), or the common horses, was about 13 hands 1½ in. They had short necks attached low to the body, long backs, with relatively short legs. They were buried with harness, and were intended to draw the four-wheeled living-wagon which had been used as a hearse. They resembled closely Ebhardt's Pony Type II. Examination of the stomach contents provided interesting results. They consisted partly of grain, showing that the horses had been kept in stables. The geldings had all been castrated before they were fully grown—evidence of systematic breeding.

This find tends to confirm the testimony of Chinese records, according to which the equine stock of Central Asia was up-graded by a highly bred strain. Furthermore, the remains prove that this up-grading took place shortly before the Hunnish on-slaught on China.

The saddles and bridles found were identical in pattern with that shown in the gold plate on Plate 20, which is Siberian, but not from the Pazyryk site. In general the scarcity of breakable objects such as pottery points to a nomadic tradition as does the general style of their equipment and accoutrements; the great plenty of felt and furs and leather goods of all kinds, especially saddle-bags; and the fact that all the textiles except felt can be shown to be imports. The Bactrian influence in horse-breeding, and hence on horsemanship, is demonstrably more recent than the wagon-borne way of life that lay in the immediate past of these Altaians. The historic role of the Bactrian horse appears all the clearer in the light of modern horse-breeding experience and practice.

Medieval and Modern Times

Very little is known about Bactria in the period following the reign of Yüe-chi. It is mentioned in the sixth century as forming part of the Ephthalite confederacy of states. This was a league of nomads that covered a vast area, but endured only until the years 563–567, when the Turks of Central Asia left their tribal territory and set up a new nomad empire in the area between the Great Wall and the Don. At this

14 Upper Palaeolithic *Art Mobilier*—Statuette of 'Quality' Horse from Lental in Württemberg

15 'Quality' Horses in the Cave Paintings of Altamira

16
Akhal-Tekke Stallion
from Turkmenistan

17
Mare from the Akhal
Oasis, Turkmenistan

18
Onager-drawn Quadriga
from Tell Agrab, about
2600 B.C.
Oriental Institute, Uni-
versity of Chicago

19   Assyrian War-chariot from Tell Agrab

20 Siberian Gold Plate, First
Millennium B.C.
Hermitage, Leningrad
(Peter the Great's Siberian collection)

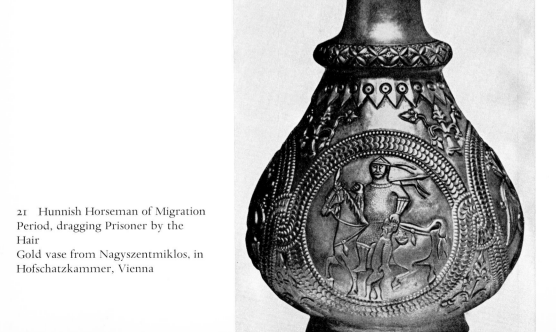

21 Hunnish Horseman of Migration
Period, dragging Prisoner by the
Hair
Gold vase from Nagyszentmiklos, in
Hofschatzkammer, Vienna

time Bactria split up into several independent principates. About the state of horse-breeding in these we have no immediate information. But the Turkmenian or Turanian horses bred in the adjoining territory of Turkestan prove the survival of this breed.

Both Bactria and Turkestan were conquered by the Arabs—or by the Muslim host, the nucleus of which was still Arab—during the eighth century. Arab travellers provide a rich source of information about Central Asian conditions at that time, and incidentally about the Turanian horse. At that time it enjoyed a great reputation, not only in the Far East but also in the West. Arabian journals of travel in the ninth and tenth centuries always emphasize the importance of the export of Bactrian horses from Kotal.

After the Seljuk Turks had advanced as far as Asia Minor—which led to the collapse of Arab power in Central Asia—the world was shaken by the ravages of Jenghis Khan's Mongol armies. This also struck a blow at Turanian horse-breeding, because all the most valuable stock in the conquered territories was haled off to Mongolia. Timur-i-leng or Tamerlane (1336–1405), founder of a new nomad dynasty, attempted to revive Turanian breeding by distributing five thousand brood mares among the Turkoman tribes.

That famous Venetian Marco Polo, who travelled through these countries in the late thirteenth century, says of horse-breeding there:

> They breed a great many excellent horses, very swift. They are never shod, though they run on the mountains and on stony ground, very bad roads, for their legs are superb and their hoofs very hard. They can carry their rider down slopes so steep that other horses will not face them or can only be got to do so with difficulty; but this they do at speed.

Marco Polo describes the extinction of the breed thus:

> It was told Messere Marco that in the province of Badasan [in Northern Afghanistan] there was until recently a breed of horses that were descended from Bucephalus, Alexander the Great's horse, and among them the foals were born with a star and a crescent moon on their foreheads, as if Bucephalus himself had covered the mares. Only the king's uncle possessed this strain. But as he refused even to let the king have some of them, the latter condemned him to death, and in revenge his widow destroyed the entire stud.

Contact was lost during the three hundred years of the Turkish menace, between Europe and Central Asia. The only news of it that reached Europe did so via Persian and thence Ottoman intermediaries, and only occasionally did a Turanian-bred horse reach a European stud (and then often under another name), as for example some foundation sires from Turkestan used at Trakehnen in the eighteenth and nineteenth centuries; but it is to them that that famous breed owes its reputation.

Reports from the nineteenth century, or the second half of it, give a more comprehensive picture of horse-breeding among the Turkomans. The pure Turanian breed had by then long been a thing of the past; and the 'heavenly heritage' of the blood-sweating golden horses of old Taiyuan only gleamed faintly here and there among Turkoman tribesmen and in some princely private studs in South Russia. But many attempts were made at a conscious revival of the old breed. For instance, Nasreddin, Shah of Persia, gave the Turkoman breeders six hundred mares. About the beginning of this century private studs in the Khanate of Karabakh tried to 'reconstruct' the ancient breed, which was near extinction, by a cross of Arab stallions on Turanian mares. Count G. Wrangel described the survivors of the old breed thus: "It is a peculiar feature of the Karabakh breed that it is very shortsighted and consequently uncommonly nervous. If it even suspects danger, it trembles all over and stands stock still, instead of taking to flight as other steppe horses do." [One might better say 'as all normal horses do'; this sounds like a typical manifestation of decadence, probably caused by inbreeding among the last representatives of a dying race. *Tr.*] A. Born said that on his journey to Bokhara in 1850 he observed something he would not have believed credible—that the neck arteries of Turkoman horses did in fact exude blood after severe exertion or when they were heated.

The horse-stock of Turania in the second half of the last century were known collectively as 'Turkoman' horses, but comprised many strains, which, however, differed little from each other: Jomud and Akhal-Tekke and Jomali horses, which to judge by their exceptional performances must have had the blood of the 'heavenly horses' in their veins. H. Moser, the Swiss traveller who journeyed in these parts in 1883, emphasizes the excellent qualities of the Akhal-Tekke race. According to him, the best of these were comparable with the English Thoroughbred. The clans living round the oasis of Akhal-Tekke who bred these horses lived by stock-raising and cattle-stealing. The outstanding performance of their horses on these raids, which they called 'Alaman', is well known. They could ride for twenty hours at a stretch, 200 versts. The very fine golden-dun coats of the horses looked magnificent, especially in bright sunshine.

Nineteenth-century Turkoman Horseman
Drawing by Evert van Muyden, 1886

In our day the breeding of the Turanian horse, once more on the verge of extinction, has been revived. Marshal Budenny took the initiative in establishing State farms, where a horse about 15½ hands of a uniform riding type has been bred. Today the coat varies considerably from the formerly universal golden colour, and includes silver-dun, dapple-grey, and even black. But reliable figures of performance are available. Times are recorded of 3400 km in 84 days (Askhabad to Moscow, 1935), and in 1949 one of their sprinters did 1000 metres in 66 seconds, which is on a par with the speeds attained by Thoroughbreds.

Origin of Hot-blooded Light-horse Breeding

All the available information about this breed of horse leads us to the evidence that Turania or Turkestan was for thousands of years the home of a fast horse of great quality and staying power. The question is, where did it come from, and when and under what circumstances was it first deliberately and systematically bred?

The specialist literature presents conflicting views. Hančar, it is true, adopts no decided position, but does point out the fact that the beginnings of Turanian horse-breeding lie further back in the past than the Pazyryk burials, and is inclined to think that tall horses of 'quality' appearance originated in this region. According to his view, this strain was represented in the horse-stock of antiquity in Central Asia, China, the Near East, and everywhere in the Roman Empire. V. O. Vitt considers the Pazyryk horses were a local product. He holds that in equines length of limb is inseparable from its thickness. Longer legs are always proportionately more slender, and short ones proportionately thicker. Thus he thinks of 'grading up' as a literal process of drawing the whole stature upward, at the same time drawing out the legs much finer, and holds that Groups 2 and 3 of the Pazyryk horses show different degrees of this development. [It is difficult to see how this concept could be applied to such breeds as the Clydesdale, whose legs are both long and thick. *Tr.*]

But this argument cannot be generalized. In comparing, say an Arab and a pony of Ebhardt's Type II or a Mongolian Wild Horse (Taki), it is impossible to speak of variant forms or of relative correspondence of proportions and dimensions. The Arab, with its small head, short back, and long legs, and the 'Forest' pony, with its big head, long back, and short legs, are original types in their own right, and they are as little amenable to the theory mentioned above as are animals derived from a cross of these types.

To make any progress at all we must check back on the available data about original wild stock, for it seems most unlikely that simply by means of crossing all or any two of the Taki, the Tarpan, and the European Pony together a hybrid could be produced which would so excel its wild congeners in speed and endurance. We have only to think of the riding exploits of the nomad breeders in their perpetual wars, with their forced marches and surprise attacks. This could hardly have been done on donkey-sized ponies of either Taki or Tarpan stock, which hardly weighed more than did the rider with his saddle and equipment. It is much more likely that the horses of the more sophisticated nomads were like the riding-horses in the Pazyryk barrows, among which the genetic influence of a high-bred strain is clearly visible.

The existence of such a 'wild blood-horse' is conceivable in the light of pictures occurring in Palaeolithic cave art. In Europe these pictures present among a variety of equine types, including recognizable Northern Pony and Tarpan types, not only some markedly 'cold-blooded' specimens such as this ram-headed 'earth-horse' from Combarelles but also a stamp of horse full of quality, 'hot-blooded' in modern European parlance. Such are seen among others on the walls of caves at Altamira and Lascaux, and must imply that in the Cantabrian region long before domestication there was a stamp of wild horse that has vanished. One such variety, apparently about the size of Grévy's zebra among modern equines, and perhaps striped (since some European pony breeds show vestigial stripes on the legs and blurred marks on the shoulder, in combination with an eel-stripe), represents the unknown factor in the ancestry of our domestic horses.

Wild Horse of Heavy Type,
with Roman Nose.
Drawing in the cave of
Les Combarelles, Dordogne

This very possibility is confirmed by folklore traditions in Bactria and Turania. The Turkomans used to say that their forefathers came by the finest foals by turning out 'horsing' mares at night in the mountains, so that they would be covered by wild stallions full of quality that came out of the mountains.

A Hungarian expedition found horses living wild in the Mongolian mountains north of Tienshan. These were obviously the last surviving band of Przewalski's Horse. The place from which they were observed at long range is called Takhin Shar Nuru—*i.e.*, "Yellow Horse Mountain". It is altogether possible that this place-name is a memorial of the golden-coated 'wild blood-horses'. The word *shar* means either 'yellow' or 'golden', and to this day the Turks call golden chestnut horses *sharylar* (in Hungarian *sarig*, or *sarga*). It cannot be a coincidence that this locality should also be the last refuge of the true wild (as opposed to feral) horses of our time, the brown-dun or sandy-bay Takis—a hilly, waterless wilderness, remote from all human settlement.

Chinese sources also speak of mysterious horses in Tienhansu, which lived wild on the mountains of Taiyuan. Persians travelling through this region in the ninth century said that these horses came 'out of the springs' [which brings us back to British folklore with its numerous Celtic legends, like that in the West of Ireland about the marvellously handsome horse that came up out of the sea and covered the poor man's mares, leaving magnificent foals. *Tr.*] The probability is that the rock-drawings from Ferghana (Aravan) which can be ascribed to the first millennium B.C., here reproduced, show such a coupling. It is accepted as part of the general history of domestication that at a certain stage, and especially with horses and cattle, herdsmen did not keep stallions—only mares and foals—and relied for the increase of their herds on this device of leaving the mare in season where the wild stallions could cover her, but so that she could not get away. [We have already explained why the reverse cross, that of tame stallion on wild mare, never happens. With this system of breeding the vigour of the wild sire, reimparted at every new generation, would do much to compensate for the debilitating effect of the first inefficient attempts at horsemastership by people with no long tradition of this branch of husbandry; but conversely there would be a steady loss of mares to the wild herds, despite all efforts to the contrary. *Tr.*]

All that we know of the origins of the Turanian horse tends to confirm the possibility that at the time of domestication such a 'wild blood-horse' did in fact still exist in Central Asia, with outstanding speed and endurance, high on the leg and with a 'dished face' and a highly developed nervous system quite different from other wild sub-varieties—as different as the modern Thoroughbred is from common horses. [Lady Wentworth believed implicitly in such a hypothesis, only her 'wild blood-horse' was domiciled in Central Arabia—specifically in the Nejd. *Tr.*]

The prepotency of such sires is the more credible in the light of modern biological knowledge. It is notorious that feral horses—the descendants of runaway domestic horses—after only a few generations lose the properties conferred by domestication and resume more and more those of their wild ancestors. Thus the mustang of the American plains, now itself on the road to extinction, lost no time in shedding the attributes of the pure-bred Andalusian, and acquired recognizably those of several different ancestral wild types. We may assume that its ancestors in the Old World had included Andalusian, Barb, and the *Asturión* or pacing pony of

Rock Drawings from Aravan,
near Ferghana, late first
century B.C.
From Hančar, 1955

Northern Iberia. All three in their turn were of composite wild ancestry. As these types once again began to 'separate out' in the process of wild breeding, natural selection again came into play, and 'survival factors' were the only forces that determined the ultimate constitution of mustang herds. Among them a type was thrown up, about $14\frac{1}{2}$ hands high, with 'Thoroughbred' features, such as might be sought in vain among Pony Type II or the Taki. The long-range influence alone of the Turanian horse, imparted drop by drop in Spanish horse-breeding of the pre-Conquistador centuries, can account for this. This influence is still at work among all domestic horses, throwing up once in so many thousand foalings the Turanian type but more frequently, of course, among 'hot-blooded' light-horse breeds.

Part II The Day of the Horseman

Distribution of the Bactrian Horse in Early Times

Even before the Asiatic Huns attacked China and the Emperor Wu determined to import Heavenly Horses from Taiyuan, the Bactrian Horse had appeared beyond the Iranian mountains to the south of Bactria as the chariot horse of the Ancient East. The countries famed in classical antiquity as ancient centres of civilization—the Nile, the Euphrates, the Tigris, and the Indus valleys—are the home of our oldest written traditions.

Although in the Asiatic part of these regions the only wild equine was the onager, and in the Nile valley only (possibly) one of the two African races of wild ass, these records provide valuable data on the beginnings of the horseman's way of life, in its earliest stages. In the fifth millennium B.C. oxen were the sole draught animals, but a thousand years later there is evidence that the onager had been harnessed. We have abundant illustrations of it from the third millennium. Pottery from the city of Mari shows these animals (*Hemionus onager*) harnessed and muzzled; this speaks much for the viciousness of the species, for which captive onagers are renowned among zoo-keepers. It was replaced in the second millennium by the horse, brought in from Central Asia. The first mention of the use of the horse belongs to the reign of Hammurabi, king and lawgiver of Babylonia (1728–1686 B.C.).

The Ancient East, apart from the numerous inscriptions, can also show many pictorial representations of horses. These sculptures and ceramics with their highly artistic and life-like portrayal allow us to draw certain conclusions about the type of horse then in use. They show—from the Nile to the Indus—a horse of noble bearing and all the attributes of quality, with a dished face, deeper in the body than the Pazyryk horses, but with the characteristic features of the Bactrian horse.

The distribution of the Central Asian horse throughout the Middle East is often associated with the advance of Indo-European language groups such as the Hittites, Mitannians, and Kassites towards Mesopotamia. But it is more likely to be due to the rise of commercial contacts, and probably took place primarily through peaceful channels initiated in the first place by Medes and Persians (whose lands bordered on Bactria to the north) through the kingdom of Urartu.

The Silk Road

We mentioned above that the most famous trade route of antiquity, the Silk Road, passed through these districts. From end to end it was some 6250 miles long, its eastern terminus being the Chinese Pacific coast, and its western Alexandria, on the Mediterranean. The middle sector, from Chinese Turkestan to Ecbatana, successively the capital of the Medes, of the Parthians, and later of the Sassanid dynasty, crossed the 13,000 ft. Terek Pass to Ferghana, thence traversed Bactria, and led into the heart of Iran.

We owe to the Swedish explorer Sven Hedin (who discovered the remains of the buried city of Lou-Lan near the dried up Lop-Nor lake in 1903) a clear picture of the importance of the Silk Road in economic history. Finds there indicated the kind of goods that had been traded along that road over the centuries. From the West came purple dye, spices, incense, precious metals, amber, and gold. The treasures of the East comprised principally silk, symbol of luxury and riches, sold in all the markets of the Ancient Orient and the Mediterranean. The caravans consisted of different animals on different stages of the route, according as the terrain and climate demanded. There were immeasurable difficulties to be overcome; the whirling sandstorms of the desert, icy snow-squalls in the Pamirs, attacks by robbers all along the way, took their toll of man and beast. The precious merchandise reached its destination only after years. Even in those days enterprise and the profit-motive were boundless. Caravan followed caravan, and according as the way lay through deserts, over mountains, or through the steppe, it demanded thousands of pack animals, be they camels, horses, asses, mules, or yaks. And despite prohibitions of export, a trade in draught animals sprang up along this route.

Having said all this, we may still wonder how the Bactrian Horse came to be distributed all along this route, when the trade between the Central Mediterranean and China was not developed until much later than the second millennium—not until the days of the Roman Empire.

Trade routes do not spring up from one day to the next, especially not when their exploitation depends on the collaboration between many nations and countries, and when not only natural obstacles but those of language and politics have to be overcome. It was centuries before the various sectors of the Silk Road, crossing many frontiers, could establish economic contact between innumerable states.

The connection between the Ancient Orient's many civilizations and those of Central Asia was of long standing. The finery recovered from the frozen tombs of Pazyryk includes objects of use and ornament from Persian as well as Chinese sources. Mesopotamian objects of art often have Central Asiatic motifs, and vice versa. A Kassite cylinder-seal shows a centaur shooting arrows backward, which is a further proof of the influence which the fighting technique of Asiatic mounted nomads had on decorative art.

Evidence of early contact along the Silk Road in its Persian-Bactrian sector is much older, and can be explained in the light of our knowledge of early stock-

DISTRIBUTION OF HOT-BLOODED HORSES

breeding. We mentioned above that in the region of the Upper Indus, in Rana Gundai, remains of camp-sites from the fourth to the first millennium had proved the employment side by side of horses (Asiatic) and asses (African) as pack-animals. The difficulties of crossing the Afghan mountains between Bactra and the Indian Ocean could only be overcome by using them or their hybrid, the mule.

We may assume that exchange of tools, animals, and objects of value took place along single stretches of the Silk Road in early historical times between Central Asia and the Ancient Orient. So the ass came to be distributed in Asia and the horse in North Africa, the latter along with the camel, which is also of Asiatic origin, and the traditional caravan pack-carrier. Once both had reached Asia Minor, their further distribution was inevitable.

The War-chariot

Documents of Sumerian, Kassite, Mitannian, Persian, Egyptian, Sanskrit, and Hebrew origin are all very revealing about the status of the horse once it had become established in the countries of the Near East. In the city of Mari, on the Euphrates, clay tablets with cuneiform inscriptions have been found, as at Tell Halaf, Nuri, and Susa, and we also have the book by Kikkuli on the care and training of the chariot team, documents in Egyptian hieroglyphics, and the Hindu *Rig-vedas* with their chronicles of ancient wars, all telling the same story—that the peoples of the Near and Middle East used the horse exclusively in harness in the second millennium.

Letters from the kings of the Kassites and the Mitannians to their brother-ruler

War-chariot of Rameses II at the Battle of Kadesh, 1296 B.C.
Low relief in Thebes Museum

Pharaoh all end with the traditional salutation: "We wish you, your country, your house, your womenfolk, your high officers and your horses and chariots the best of health and prosperity." Those dynasties all fought and hunted from the chariot (though whether such hunting was really in open country or in a game-preserve with prepared tracks for the chariot must remain an open question), and all of them patronized chariot-racing. The ideal masculine type of the period is portrayed in art driving a two-wheeled chariot to a pair of horses or four-in-hand. For centuries this was the image of majesty. Archaeological evidence all points the same way; from Persia, 2000 B.C.; from India, 2000 B.C.; from Ethiopia, 1500 B.C.; from Egypt, 1570 B.C.; from Palestine, 1000 B.C., etc.

The late appearance of the horse in Palestine is striking, but it has its historical reasons. The Jews brought no horses with them out of the Egyptian captivity. Moses forbade the Hebrews to keep or breed horses at all (Deuteronomy xvii, 14–16), and for long they hamstrung or killed captured horses (Joshua xi, 2–9). David is the first recorded Israelite king to give up this practice, and even he only kept a select proportion of such spoils, and he kept them for his personal use, and that of his close following. Solomon his son had impressive stables, which have been excavated, and imported horses both from Asia Minor and from Egypt (1 Kings iv, 26).

It often happens that mistrust so far prevails over common sense that a reasonable code of conduct is no longer possible, and so it must have been in this instance of the Mosaic law. Contempt for the hated enemy made the horse, symbol of Pharaonic power, anathema, so that the lawgiver would rather lame or destroy captured chariot horses than turn them to his own use. We shall find instances of similar behaviour later. [But the question does arise, where would Moses and Joshua have found drivers among the Jewish army, who were all accustomed only to handling pack-donkeys? In the conditions of stress obtaining during the prolonged rearguard-action which we call the Exodus, there would be little opportunity to train drivers, or rather for drivers to train themselves, to the standard required for active service. If you do not know how to load or fire a captured gun, you blow out the breech-block. *Tr.*]

Riding became naturalized in the Near East relatively late. All we know is that at the end of the second millennium it was no longer totally unknown, and that the first step to the great revolution had taken place. For the first time, in Babylon, riding-horses are mentioned in the reign of Nebuchadnezzar I, 1200 B.C. Three centuries later a relief was put up in the palace of Assurnasipal (884–859 B.C.) showing mounted nomads in their characteristic warlike posture—shooting backward. They are dressed in trousers, cross-belted, and shod with soft-topped boots—all items which show a Central Asiatic influence. The employment of horses as riding-animals had been forced on the inhabitants of these regions by the advance of the Medes and Persians from the north, as it had been on those of Khorasan and China by the inroads of the Asiatic Huns. Besides this, the appearance of mounted armies was the stimulus to the building of fortified cities and citadels. (See also Habakkuk i, 8: "Their horses also are swifter than the leopards.")

The Spread of Riding

A short survey of historical events sets the scene for the expansion of riding among the peoples of the Ancient Orient. The Medes inhabited the mountainous country in the northern part of what is now Persia, south of the Caspian. The earliest historical sources state that their country was conquered in the tenth or ninth century B.C. by the Bactrians from Central Asia. From that time onward the population of the country was mixed, the Median element paying tribute to the Bactrian ruling class. At length they fused to form one ethnic unit, which was the first in the Ancient Orient to adopt the riding tradition brought in from Central Asia. Understandably, they exploited their superiority, pressing onward to the south and conquering new territory. For centuries they struggled with their dourest enemies, the Assyrians, and according to Herodotus it was they who, in alliance with the Babylonians, destroyed Nineveh, the most considerable city of the Near East, in 612 B.C. The fame of the Nisaean horses bears witness to the high level of their horse-breeding. When the Assyrians temporarily got the upper hand they demanded a tribute of Nisaean horses, annually.

Oppian in his *Cynegeticon* describes the breed as follows: "The horses of Nisaea are the handsomest, fit only for mighty rulers. They are splendid, running swiftly under the rider, obeying the bridle willingly, with ram-nosed heads carried high, and streaming golden manes." Of the horses of the neighbouring Parthians he says: "These have great quality, with bright coats of splendid colours, having great courage". There can be little doubt that these horses were also of Bactrian origin, derived from Types III and IV in Ebhardt's classification.

The dominion of the Medes, which lasted more than three centuries, was broken by Cyrus, the ruler of the neighbouring Persians. He had once been a vassal of the Medes, but came to power as leader of a rebellion against them. According to Xenophon, up to that time the Persians had fought only from chariots, so that Cyrus must be regarded as the founder of the Persian cavalry.

On coming to power, Cyrus laid claim to the overlordship of the neighbouring principality of Bactria, but had no success. However, what rulers could not achieve by force of arms they often managed, then as now, by clever diplomacy or alliance. In this case, dynastic alliance; Cyrus married the daughter of the defeated Median king, Astyages, and as soon as this princess, Amythis, became his wife the Bactrians acknowledged his suzerainty.

The dowry which this lady with the euphonious name brought with her proved one of the most valuable acquisitions ever made by any ruler in antiquity; Cyrus having become master of the Bactrian cavalry, auxiliaries who helped him to the fruition of his ambitious plans for world dominion. His first campaign against the fabulously rich Croesus, ruler of Lydia, was won, according to Herodotus, because he placed camels in the forefront of his army and the Lydian horses panicked at the sight and smell of these unfamiliar creatures, throwing the host into disarray so that it could easily be overcome. After that Cyrus overran Mesopotamia and stormed Babylon. He expanded his empire in the east as far as the Oxus (Amu-Darya) and the Indus, and in the west to the Bosporus. His successor Cambyses conquered Egypt, thus bringing the whole of the Ancient Orient under Persian sway.

The horse even decided the enthronement of Darius I, great-nephew and son-in-law to Cyrus. Not that he seized the throne with the help of his cavalry—in this case his charger and his Master of the Horse sufficed of themselves.

When the candidates for the throne could not agree to elect a successor, they determined to leave the choice to their horses. The prince whose horse was first to neigh as they rode out of the city gates at dawn should be King of Kings. Oibares, Master of the Horse to Darius, was determined that his master should win the election, and thought of a trick; he touched a horsing mare and carefully kept that hand in a fold of his garment until the candidates rode up. Then he stepped forward to the horse of Darius, and held his hand under its nostrils, whereupon the stallion uttered a loud neigh. Herodotus says that in gratitude Darius had a statue erected to his horse and to his Master of the Horse.

The Persian kings throw some light on horsemastership and the techniques of warfare and commerce associated with it in the Ancient East. In his account of the Grecian campaigns of King Xerxes, Herodotus describes the Persian troopers in their bronze helmets and infantry weapons, the Sagartians, who were a race of herdsmen armed with lassos and daggers, the Medes, Bactrians, Caspians, and so on, also armed with infantry weapons. The Libyans of North Africa and the Indians fought from horse-drawn chariots, but some of the Indian chariots were drawn by onagers; so the onager was still being used in draught at that time.

The Arabian contingent was mounted on camels; and since these made the horses shy, they were drawn up in rear of the main body.

The Persian hegemony of the Near East was brought to an end by Alexander of Macedon (336–323 B.C.), the immortal hero of antiquity and one of the great captains of all time. He owed his military success largely to the newly created cavalry force bequeathed to him by his father, King Philip. When he came to the throne at the age of twenty he won his first cavalry victory, against the Thebans. Then he began to desire possession of the Ancient East; first he wrested from the Persians the satrapies of Asia Minor, then he turned southward to conquer Egypt. Not until then did he proceed to attack Darius himself.

But in any case by that time the power of the Persian monarchs was on the wane. The subject provinces of their empire, and primarily Bactria, at first delayed and then refused to support the King of Kings. But the open breach did not come until after the defeat of Darius by the Macedonians and his flight into Bactria, where the satrap turned on him and had him murdered.

Alexander followed the example of Cyrus. He consolidated his power in Bactria by marrying the daughter of the Bactrian king Oxyartes, Roxana. According to Arianes, the main body of his army already at this time contained mounted lancers and horse-archers, who took part in his Indian campaign.

Alexander's career mounted steeply to its climax, with his early death in 323. His army commanders partitioned the empire, founding new dynasties, but parts of it regained their independence. In 256 Bactria became an independent kingdom again, but now under a Greek dynasty.

Alexander was not only a famous commander but a genuine horseman, in the modern sense of the word, who knew the strategic worth of cavalry, and was an enthusiastic admirer of the true-bred Oriental horse. When his charger Bucephalus was killed at the battle of Hydaspes, he founded a city called Bucephala in memory of him. Bucephalus means 'ox-head', presumably because to European eyes the broad forehead, large round eyes, and concave profile of the 'Arab' type suggested bovine rather than equine features.

The horse was also highly esteemed by other nations of the Ancient Orient who had reached a high stage of equestrian culture. When Xerxes went to war the column was led by ten 'sacred' horses of the Nisaean breed, and a team of such horses also drew the royal chariot.

In the traditional literature of the Hebrews, a well-known passage from the Book of Job describes the horse thus, in praise of God's majesty:

Hast Thou given the horse strength? hast Thou clothed his neck with thunder?
Canst Thou make him afraid as a grasshopper? The glory of his nostrils is terrible.
He paweth in the valley, and rejoiceth in his strength. He goeth on to meet the armed men.
He mocketh at fear, and is not affrighted; neither turneth he back from the sword.
The quiver rattleth against him, the glittering spear and the shield.
He swalloweth the ground with fierceness and rage. (Auth. Version.)
Triumphantly he echoes the bugle's note. (Mgr. Knox.)

Now, this was the very people whose leaders had once held the horse in such abhorrence that they had forbidden Jews to keep them, and ordered the destruction of all captured stock. [But it is relevant to add that Job was not an Israelite; he dwelt in the land of Uz—that is, Edom, the modern Jordan—and his Book was originally a Bedouin saga, taken over by Hebrew literature on the strength of its high literary and religious merit. *Tr.*]

Horsemanship and Equitation in Classical Antiquity

As the art of riding began to spread through the Middle East, a new chapter was beginning in the history (partly in the prehistory) of the European peoples. In the Mediterranean the literate Classical Age is dawning, while north of the Alps the Age of Iron is succeeding the Age of Bronze. In both regions new possibilities in the fields of transport, of communications, and of warfare open up. Political life comes to be dominated by the mounted warrior rather than the charioteer. Mediterranean

Skulls of Arab (Kehailan) Horse and Shetland Pony compared
From J. E. Flade 1962

lands first felt the influence of fashions from the Near East, and thus the Mediterranean was the cradle of European equitation.

The wild-horse stock of Europe, the pony of the north-west and the Tarpan of the south-east, were both of low stature, which the early stages of domestication did nothing to increase. Indeed, rather the contrary. The height at the withers of horses in Gaul and Switzerland, to judge by skeletal remains dating from the La Tène period (beginning about 400 B.C.), was under 13 hands, and the average in Britain at that time lower still. The domesticated Tarpan of the Black Sea region was no bigger, and the horses of the Western Scythians were none of them as tall as the smallest horses buried in the frozen tombs of Pazyryk at that period.

The spread of riding is to be attributed to two events widely separated in space and time: the introduction of the Bactrian Horse from the Near East by the Greeks and the Romans, and the incursions of mounted nomads from Asia.

47

There is written evidence that about 630 B.C. some hundreds of Greek settlers established themselves on the African shore at the mouth of the river Cyre, where they founded the city of Cyrene, the nucleus of what is still called Cyrenaica, in Libya. This rapidly expanding colony became a great cultural and commercial centre in ancient Africa.

Herodotus says of the Cyrenian Greeks that the neighbouring Libyans took over from them the mode of harnessing four horses to a chariot (quadriga), and that they were principally occupied in breeding and breaking horses.

In the veins of the Cyrenaican horses coursed the blood of the Bactrian Horse, already naturalized in the Near East, as is abundantly shown by North African and Greek equestrian art, as well as by documentary evidence.

North Africa played a vital intermediary part in the further development of equestrian culture, though it did not come into its own as a land of horsemen until the westward expansion of Islam under the leadership of the Arabs, at a time when Arab enterprise in horse-breeding was profoundly affecting the material culture of the Near Eastern peoples.

So the Cyrenian colony played the same part in Greek history as had Bactria in the Persian. Its influence on horse-breeding in the Greek homeland persisted for centuries. Cyrenaica and Bactria had been connected, by way of the Silk Road, for centuries, so that it will have been possible at any time to reinforce the breeding-stock by a refreshing draught from the original source. When Darius of Persia conquered the town of Barka, in Cyrenaica, during his Egyptian campaign he transferred the population to Bactria. There those Greeks founded a city, likewise called Barka. The maintenance of their connections with the previous African settlement is very probable, even before the further settlement of Greeks in Bactria by Alexander the Great.

Hellenic horse-breeding soon became world-famous due to the importation of stock, both from Cyrenaica and from Asia Minor. When the Persian king Xerxes invaded Greece in 480, reaching Thessaly with his vast land army, he instituted a race between local horses and his own, in order to maintain the reputation of his own breed. In fact the 'sacred' Persian horses did win, which perhaps is not surprising in the light of breeding conditions of that day.

Many traditions bear witness to the high standard of horsemanship in Greece. The horse plays a prominent part in the mythology of Hellas. Thus the chariot of Ares, god of war, was drawn by four grey horses, as he went before the rising sun to announce daybreak. Heracles usually travelled in a two-wheeled chariot. The horse also figures largely in epics of the heroic age of Greece; the leading personalities in the Homeric poems drive chariots, but occasionally ride also. Beginning with the 25th Olympiad in 676 B.C., races between four-in-hand chariots were instituted, and from that time onward equestrian events were included in the Olympic programme, eventually also ridden events. Harness teams were driven only from the chariot; there were no outriders.

There is a striking Greek legend about riding: herds of wild cattle came down from Mount Pelion in the reign of King Ixion and laid waste the fields of Thessaly, spoiling the corn-lands of the whole plain. The King offered a great reward for the elimination of this plague, whereupon some bold youths took chariot horses

22 War-chariot and Four, from the Crater of Vix (Burgundy), made in Sicily or
Apulia
5th century B.C.

23 Assurbanipal of Assyria's Campaign against the Elamites
Relief from the palace of Nineveh, about 639 B.C.
British Museum

24
Detail from Parthenon Frieze, about 432 B.C., by Pheidias or his School

25
Roman Triumphal Car

26 Roman Tombstone from Pannonia, showing Saddle Horse and Draft Horses
Pannonia is approximately the modern Hungary.
National Museum, Budapest

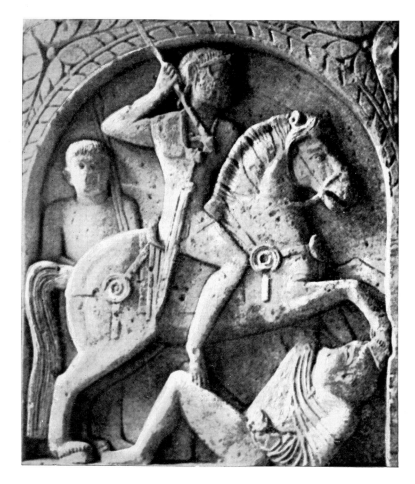

27
Tombstone of a Trooper
from a Roman Auxiliary
Cavalry Regiment
recruited in Noricum
(approximately the
modern Austria)
Altertumsmuseum, Mainz

28 The Stone of Hornhausen
Seventh-century Carvings of a
Saxon Horseman

29 West European ("Frankish")
Mounted Warriors of the
Ninth Century, without
Stirrups
The saddle is virtually
identical with the late Roman
pattern.

which had never been ridden before from under the yoke and drove off the dangerous herd of aurochs. The same youths then perceived the military value of the ridden horse, turned bandits, and attacked the King himself. The tradition of the mythological centaurs is connected with these early horsemen. The Thessalians, who had never before seen a man riding, took them for monsters with human trunks growing out of a horse's body.

Centaur with Nomad
Bow
Relief in Church of
Panagia Gorgopico,
Athens

Herodotus says that Greek armies in the days of the Persian wars consisted exclusively of infantry; there were only some mounted messengers. Riding did not become general until later. This is confirmed by Xenophon (434–359 B.C.) in his *Hippike*, which shows an extraordinary degree of technical knowledge, and is remarkable for its advice to the reader to deal gently with the horse—a principle still obtaining today, quietness and an absence of violence being the basis of successful horsemanship. Xenophon was himself a cavalry leader who conducted the retreat of the Greek auxiliaries from Mesopotamia after the battle of Cunaxa in 401 B.C. He describes this prolonged rearguard action in his *Anabasis*; a soldier of wide experience in the service of more than one state, the Mesopotamian campaign alone must have brought him into contact with mercenary cavalrymen of many Asiatic nations.

The Romans

Whereas in Greece the Bactrian horse was primarily responsible for the rise of equitation as an art, in Italy it served more utilitarian purposes, in both the commercial and the military field. The reason is that the main striking force of most Greek states was the navy, whereas in Rome armed force meant primarily the land army. In any case, cavalry was of no great military significance to the Romans until they came into conflict with the Carthaginians from Africa, by which time they were already a Great Power.

In the three Carthaginian campaigns in Italy, Sicily, and Spain which the Romans fought, the cavalry, including the African cavalry, swayed the balance. The fortunes of war favoured always that side on which the Numidian squadrons of light horse could be bribed or otherwise persuaded to fight. Hannibal triumphed over the Roman legions only until the day when the fickle Numidians turned against him—which was probably a triumph for Roman diplomacy. Once the scene of operations shifted to the African theatre this factor became more decisive, since more Numidians could be brought into action on the Roman side.

Naturally, the Punic wars had their influence on Roman military and transport technique, as is best shown by contemporary descriptions of Roman horsemanship during and before those wars.

The Romans had been a nation of charioteers, and were reluctant to mount the horse, especially for military purposes. This role they delegated to auxiliaries, drawn from the non-Roman inhabitants of the provinces. Polybius says that they engaged Hannibal's auxiliary Celtiberian cavalry at Cannae, both sides being dismounted. They tethered their horses to stakes to prevent them running away. At that time the Roman cavalry were equipped only with cuirasses of leather straps, thin leather shields, and light spears, in order not to be hindered in mounting. This was still very different from the arms and accoutrement of equestrian peoples. They had neither saddles nor stirrups, only a felt pad made fast with girth and breastplate. The lance was added to the javelin in time, and later armour, as a protection against arrows, was adopted.

The earliest Roman vehicle was the two-wheeled cart, in which the drivers sat. To begin with they employed a type of wagon of Near-Eastern pattern. It was very primitive, consisting essentially of two carts lashed one behind the other, having only the bed in common. Thus all its four wheels were of the same diameter, and consequently the vehicle did not turn easily, while as its loading surface was high above the wheel-base it was also unstable. The first Roman wagons were unmanoeuvrable, and their cross-country performance negligible.

The expansion of economic contacts and of traffic enhanced the importance of road-building. The cities of the Empire were connected by carefully paved roads, skilfully laid out, crossing rivers and ravines by bridges, in the construction of which the Romans soon reached a high degree of skill. Roads were also built behind the frontiers to provide lateral communication for the garrisons, as well as for trade purposes.

After the Punic Wars Roman horse-breeding received a great impetus. The appearance of the Numidian horse in Spain led to the production there of a more massive European type, Bactrian in origin. From then onward Iberia became the most important province as a source of remounts for the Roman cavalry arm, and also for the dissemination of good-quality horses throughout the western part of the Empire.

According to Tacitus, Rome provided all the new auxiliary cavalry regiments of European origin with Spanish horses. As Arrian, Strabo, and Caesar tell us, Gallic, British, and German horses were small, and Tacitus adds that the German horses were slow and ugly. These strains were primarily used as pack-animals and in harness, rather than for riding, but archaeological evidence confirms the greater stature of the Iberian horse. The finds in the Roman ampitheatre at Vindonissa (Switzerland) includes bones of horses up to 15 hands high, and horses of the same size are seen on a carved relief from Intercisa in Pannonia, which shows saddle-horses and harness-horses on the same register. This explains why the Romans called the riding-horse *materia generosa* ('quality') and the harness-horse *materia vulgaris* ('common'). The term 'quality' might well be applied to the Bactrian horse. About 70–60 B.C. the Roman forces on the eastern frontier made contact with a nation of horsemen whose mode of fighting they had not so far encountered. These Parthians, having left Khorasan, overran Persia and pressed on into the Roman province of Mesopotamia.

Pompeius Trogus, writing in the time of the Emperor Augustus, says of these people in his *Historiae Philippicae* (lost, but quoted by Justinus) that they were dressed like Medes and spoke a mixture of Median and Scythian. Their army consisted of slaves, whom they trained in the arts of riding and archery with the same care as they trained their own sons. The richer a man was, the more mounted archers he led under the banners of the king. Their method of fighting was novel. Often after an attack they turned about and feigned flight. Both they and their horses wore scale-armour.

According to the Greek geographer Strabo (63 B.C.–20 A.D.), the Parthians came from Bactria, and their rulers bore the proud title of Pahlavi, which means Bactrian.

The Roman consul Crassus was sent against the Parthians and in 53 B.C. he tried to bring them to a pitched battle in Mesopotamia. But they kept on drawing back into the desert, and did not begin fighting until the Romans were wearied by the pursuit, and thinking of retracing their steps.

Crassus, ignorant of Oriental tactics, insisted on forming a close hollow square, and this was his downfall. The Parthians charged, shot off their arrows, turned about, only to charge again, but never charged home; at last Crassus committed his own cavalry, which was outnumbered and worse-armed. They were destroyed, and once they were gone the Roman infantry was doomed; they took to flight, and the two legions were destroyed almost to a man.

Though Rome lamented the shame of this defeat and the loss of so many fine troops, no useful lessons were learned for a long time. In the days of Augustus, fifty years after the Parthian disaster, the Roman establishment consisted of twenty-five legions stationed in various provinces, each 5300 men strong, and each containing only one squadron of 120 mounted troops. Rome attempted to match the Parthian superiority in cavalry by groups of auxiliary cavalry in the provinces of Asia Minor, and along the Parthian frontier a defensive zone was created with fortified camps and systems of watch-towers. [But for two centuries an effective cavalry army, or one in which cavalry was the prevailing arm, could not be erected because the machinery of command did not exist. Only the legions had a staff and a hierarchy of officers through which orders could be quickly and effectively transmitted in action. The largest cavalry unit of the Roman army was the *ala millaria*, a regiment a thousand strong; but most of the cavalry units were only five hundred strong. Since convention demanded that auxiliaries be attached to and under command of a legion, even if a force were organized in which the number of cavalry equalled the number of legionary infantry, its commander would have to issue orders simultaneously to the officers commanding the infantry cohorts comprising the legion and the Tribunes or *praefecti* of up to ten *alae* of cavalry, without any intermediate echelon. An 'orders group' of this size is not a practical proposition, in any army in any age. Tr.]

This was so until the reforms of the Emperor Gallienus (A.D. 260–268). The pressure of Germanic tribes on the *Limes*, as well as a series of internal conflicts, brought the problem of an effective cavalry arm to a head. It had been conclusively proven that the striking power of the army could only be assured by a cavalry arm permanently organized and instantly ready for action, and capable of being brought into action tactically *en masse*. Gallienus provided the solution with the establishment of an independent corps of cavalry with its own chain of command, recruited and mounted by provinces. His successors Diocletian and Constantine continued the development of the cavalry, until Rome was on equal terms with her opponents, the mounted warriors of the East. The second-century Roman cavalry general Arrianus (a Greek by birth) shows in his tactical work *Acies contra Alanos* the limitations imposed on a Roman commander before the Gallienian reforms. He also says that the enemy (the Alani were not Germans, but spoke an Indo-European language allied to Persian) were all mounted, but armed only with throwing-spears, and thus more to be regarded as mounted infantry. According to Procopius, they did not adopt the essential tactic of mobile missile warfare—archery from the saddle at the gallop—until the sixth century.

Apart from this, the question arises, who were the mounted enemy on the eastern frontiers of Rome, since at this time the East Germanic tribes in general only drove horses in harness, without riding? When the Age of Migration entered its final stage the appearance of the Huns in Eastern Europe had become a reality. Now the process which had begun centuries before in Central Asia among peoples displaced by the nomads was repeated, or rather continued. Those Germanic tribes who were threatened by the Huns were already fighting on horseback, just as the Bactrians, Medes, Khoresmians, and Parthians had done at the time of their début on the stage of history. Their immediate contact with the Huns, which was more often peaceful than hostile, led to their adopting many Hunnish customs, and in the end the Hunnish method of warfare. (Note 4.)

The Huns

After the reform of army organization the Romans were quite capable of dealing with mounted Germanic hosts. At the battle of Strasbourg in 357 the Alemannic war-bands were shattered by the impact of the mail-clad Roman cavalry. But when the Huns appeared not much later, the tide turned again.

The Huns had caused the most recent and considerable migration on the part of the Goths, and in 376 they began to trespass on the Roman sphere of interest. They were conspicuous in the ranks of the Gothic host. In his summary of sources dealing with this equestrian people, Peter Váczy writes:

> Western authors are full of admiration for the skill of the Huns in horsemanship. Thus Claudianus says that nature herself has not welded the two parts of the centaur more firmly together than the Hun sits his horse. Sidonius points out that the children of the Huns, at an age when they cannot walk without the aid of their mothers, each have a horse to ride. It is as if they grew out of their horses. Other nations sit on horseback; the Hun lives there. *Equis prope adfixi*, as Ammianus puts it, adding: the Huns do not even dismount to perform their natural functions, and they transact all their affairs in the saddle, even eating and drinking there; they even sleep stretched out on the slender necks of their horses. They also hold important conferences on horseback. Ammianus Mar-

cellinus reported, credibly enough, that the Byzantine ambassadors negotiating a truce with the 'king of the Scyths' at Margus on the Danube, had to remain on their horses since the Huns would not dismount. Jordanes describes them as riders swift as the wind, who came up like a tornado and disappeared like a flock of birds. Their skill at archery commanded admiration everywhere, as Olympiodorus, Sidonius and Jordanes all affirm.

Chinese Brush-drawing of Mounted Hun

The first direct confrontation between the Romans on one side and the Goths and Huns on the other was at Adrianople in 378. Both sides had drawn up their array in depth, in the formation called *pugna stataria* in Roman tactical manuals. But the novelty consisted in the Hunnish tactics of repeated feint attacks which brought the ranks of their adversaries into such disorder that the battle ended in a devastating defeat for the Romans. This was regarded by contemporaries as the beginning of the end of Roman rule. And indeed from that time onward the Empire was no longer in a position to put in hand the necessary army reorganization.

The fate of Europe was finally decided in 451 at the battle of the Catalaunian Fields, the most gigantic cavalry engagement of all antiquity. Although the Romans had made some attempt to adapt their mounted troops to the demands of new conditions, it was in vain. They had, for instance, followed the example of the Huns and Alani by ceasing to wear armour on horseback, in the interests of mobility, according to sources of the late Empire quoted by Várady (1961).

It is said of the Catalaunian Fields that before the battle opened Attila had all the saddles collected and burnt. In the light of Western ideas this order is scarcely comprehensible. But perhaps it can be explained as follows: by doing this Attila would effectively dismount the non-Hunnish part of his force, who by their lack of skill might have endangered the success of the nomad riders who carried out their accustomed manœuvres like clockwork; at the same time he prevented the possibility of these less disciplined contingents spreading panic and perhaps flight throughout the host.

The battle began in the early afternoon and ended after dusk without any clear advantage to either side. Attila, disappointed after having been so confident of victory, withdrew his entire force from the battlefield, and although he was undefeated this withdrawal diminished his prestige, and the reputation for invincibility possessed by the Huns, as soon became apparent. The result, being seen as indecisive, encouraged the tributary peoples to try to regain their independence, and led to the rapid dissolution of the Hun empire after Attila's death in 453.

But on the Roman side too, this indecisive engagement had its effect on the attitude of subject peoples, and on the allies of the Romans. In practice, all that was left of the once mighty Roman empire was the name, and as for a long time the senior officers of the Praetorian Guard, and sometimes generals of the field army, had decided who should be the next Emperor, the consequence of those high offices being increasingly filled by German soldiers could be foreseen. At last, in 476, one of them, a Rugian officer called Odoacer, was elected King by the German mercenaries, and the Emperor Romulus Augustulus, the last actor in a charade presented on the Roman stage by managers who were anything but Roman, was deposed. The Roman Empire of the West had ceased to exist.

Now for a time the march of historical events came to a halt with the confrontation on equal terms of horsemen of the East and of the West. Now the past was buried and a new era was to begin, because a balance had been struck with the collision of two world Powers, each with a huge army of cavalry. The result was on the one hand the final fall of the Roman Empire and on the other a retreat by the forces from the steppe.

Decline and Renaissance of European Horsemanship

In the years after the fall of Rome, the focal point of equestrian affairs shifted to Eastern Europe. Once Attila was dead the Huns left their temporary home in the Carpathians and settled on the East European plains, living in a chronic state of warfare which had already been their lot for centuries, due to internal dissension and quarrels with neighbours which weakened the tribes. They now took part in the wars between Byzantium and Persia, sometimes on one side, sometimes on the other, according as their temporary advantage dictated.

The Byzantines mastered the art of employing these formidable horsemen in the most distant theatres of war, often overseas. Thus in 534–535 Count Belisarius broke the power of the Vandals in Africa with the aid of Hunnish mercenaries, and in 553 they helped to defeat the Ostrogoths before the walls of the now unimportant city of Rome. For a century after the collapse of the short-lived Hun empire their warriors, in foreign pay, still often dominated the battlefields of Europe.

The Avars

Eastern Europe, perpetually the scene of cavalry wars, presented in the sixth century signs of exhaustion, impoverishment, and decadence, just as Western Europe had done in the fifth. About the year 570 a nation of horsemen—the Avars—appeared on the scene, and were joined by some of the tribes of the Huns, such as the Utigures and Kutrigures; other Hun tribes became merged in the Bulgarians and Khazars. The Slavs began to settle wide tracts of Eastern Europe. The Arabs conquered Asia Minor and the Byzantine provinces of Africa, together with Persia. Only Constantinople itself withstood the alternate onslaughts of Slavs, Avars, Arabs, and Bulgars.

As the ethnic composition of Eastern Europe changed, so too did its civilization. New influences made themselves felt; the Avars were just one more wave of mounted nomads making their way into the heart of Europe. They had come originally from Mongolia, the homeland of wandering stock-breeders. Their Chinese neighbours mention them in the written sources under the name of Shwan-Shwan, describing at some length animal husbandry as practised in the Avar economy. The Chinese ruler T'ai-wu-Ti (of the T'o-pa dynasty from Sion-pi) declared during a council of war that the best time to launch a campaign against these northern barbarians was the summer, because then they would be grazing their herds in the north, around Lake Baikal. At this time their horses were not available for warfare, since the stallions were covering mares, and the mares were suckling foals. But in the autumn the barbarians drove their herds south, and spent the winter in harrying the Chinese border provinces. This description agrees with the account written five hundred years earlier of the Huns "migrating annually in search of water and grazing". (The northward movement of the nomads in summer—as is generally known—is done to avoid the plagues of midges, which also makes raiding difficult.)

The Avar dominion in Eastern Europe was short-lived, weakened as it was by the chronic feuding which was the curse of the mounted nomads, and inseparable from their way of life. Added to that was perpetual friction with the Slavs. The first of these to throw off the Avar yoke were the Czechs and Moravians in 623;

Mounted Archer
Illustration from a Chinese encyclopaedia of the sixteenth century

then it became the turn of the Croats. Charlemagne dealt the Avars the final blow in the years 791-796. The Avar nation disappeared without trace, and their territory was divided among the Slavonic tribes, under petty princes. The only traces remaining today of their rule in Central Europe (which lasted two and a half centuries) are the graves of their horsemen, from which stirrups—perhaps among the first seen in Europe—are often found. The saddle and the stirrup are what they bequeathed to European horsemanship.

The Byzantine army also learned much from them in the way of mounted tactics and skill at arms, being constantly threatened by Avar incursions. The Emperor Heraclius (610-641), who was perpetually having to contend on the one hand with the Avars, Slavs, and Persians, and on the other with the Arabs, wrote a tactical manual which was the basis of the later and better-known work by Leo the Wise, dealing mainly with the reorganization of cavalry units, in which he exploited experience gained in fighting the Avars as well as the Huns, and studying their methods. His cavalry were armed with Avar weapons, together with bows and arrows and swords, and his battle formations were based on the practice of the mounted nomads. These reforms proved so effective that the Byzantines were at last able to vanquish and destroy the Persians who had been a standing threat to their eastern frontier. This success was consolidated, according to the time-honoured practice, by diplomacy, alliances with the Khazars against the Persians and with the Bulgars against the Arabs being made.

The Advance of the Arabs

The half-nomadic Arabs had originally been anything but horsemen. In the army of Alexander the Great there had been Arab cameliers, and the Roman commander Gallus found no horsemen among them in 26 B.C. Some of them lived in towns, some of them were seafarers, trading in the Mediterranean, the Red Sea, the Persian Gulf. But the core of them, the Bedouin, to whom the generic term A'arab originally applied, were wandering stock-breeders in the desert, keeping a few cattle but more camels, sheep, and goats. In the time of Mahomet they still bred a lot of asses. Horses, like cattle, really require more water than the Bedouin grazing-grounds can provide, but in the days of the Prophet they did breed a few horses, and he himself kept some.

The tribes were by no means at one among themselves, either in politics or in religion, until the teaching of Mahomet united them in a brotherhood as the servants of the One God, in whose service they were inspired to fight by the promise of eternal life among the delights of Paradise for all those killed in action. The expansion of Islam, the concept of jihad—the Holy War—was not a mere excursion in search of plunder; its aim was the conversion of the world to the cult of the One True God.

In the beginning, the Arab armies were very different from those of the steppe nomads. At the battle of Mount Ohod between Mecca and Medina in 625 the victorious Meccan cavalry comprised only one-tenth of the army. The main body of the hosts of Islam still consisted of infantry, though on the march many of them rode pillion behind the horsemen and cameliers. But the mounted arm was of high quality, due to the excellence of their horses.

The Arab campaigns met with unparalleled success. One after another they conquered the most valuable provinces of the Byzantine Empire, Syria, Palestine, Mesopotamia, Armenia, and, between 639 and 643, North Africa. Once they had conquered the islands of the Mediterranean their fleet menaced Constantinople.

The campaigns waged simultaneously against Persia had quick success also. In 642 the main Persian army was destroyed, and that whole empire overcome. In their advance eastward, the Muslims reached the Indus valley in 664, and between 706 and 716 Khorasan, Bokhara, Samarkand, and Ferghana in Central Asia. Further progress was checked by the military might of the Chinese Empire.

ARAB CONQUESTS
632-827

The connection first brought about by Cyrus the Persian between the civilization of distant Bactria and the lands of the Mediterranean a thousand years earlier was revived by the Muslim advance. Traffic along the Silk Road, which had always depended on the balance of power, gained a new impetus. The steady importation of Turanian horses from Ferghana is now confirmed by written evidence. This strain thus reappears in the area from which more than a thousand years ago the horses of Cyrenaica, of Barka, Numidia, and Spain, had come to influence the destiny of Western peoples. Now this happened in the case of the Arabs. In a unique series of victories they conquered North Africa and crossed the Strait of Gibraltar to Spain. In 711 the kingdom of the Visigoths, weakened by internal discord, fell easily before them. After taking firm possession of the Iberian peninsula, they crossed the Pyrennees and pressed onward into Gaul.

The Frankish kingdom in Gaul was then ruled by the Merovingian dynasty. Eginhardus, contemporary and biographer of Charlemagne, says of the last Merovingian king that he used to travel in an ox-wagon. This is just one example of the retrograde development that had taken place in Gaul, the decay of the equestrian civilization, since the fall of Rome. When the Franks had invaded Italy, fighting against the Goths in 539 and 552, they had fought on foot, only the King's personal escort being mounted. (Note 4.) Repeated attacks by the Muslims at last caused Charles Martel, Mayor of the Palace to the Merovingian kings, to raise a force of cavalry. He rewarded his vassals for service on horseback with grants of land.

Meanwhile in neighbouring Spain the Muslims, known as Moors or Saracens, had taken a firm foothold. The Caliphate of Cordoba became the advanced bulwark of Islam as it pressed forward with fire and sword, but at the same time it was the centre of a new civilization. In Europe the turmoil of the Migration Period had left only ruins in its wake; the cultural riches of the antique world had been succeeded only by the foggy and clumsy speculations of the Nordic peoples. As the Arabs gained a footing in Europe—in Spain and Sicily—the fertilizing influence of the Near East was again felt; after all, it had been the source of the classical art and thought of antiquity. And so once more the clear light of the Mediterranean day was let in on the inhospitable castles and manor-houses of the West; comfort and elegance in dress and appurtenances, a more sophisticated style of living, became general in Iberia, and thence in Gaul. To this new way of life, for the upper classes at least, better communications were essential, and that meant faster horses—Oriental horses.

The Battle of Poitiers

Charles Martel ("the Hammer")'s efforts to improve his army were soon crowned with success. In 732 the Frankish armoured horsemen clashed with the Saracens for the first time, at Poitiers. After repulsing repeated attacks by the Muslims, the counter-attack by the Frankish armour was decisive. But it could not be fully exploited because the pursuit could not follow the fleeing Saracens fast enough.

This battle was a turning-point in the reawakening of Europe, and may be compared in importance with the battle of the Catalaunian Fields.

As to horse-breeding in Western Europe at that time, it has been established archaeologically that most of the stock was a pony type with strong bone and a height at the withers of 13 hands 2 in. or 14 hands. [In British terms, like the Fell or Highland pony of today. *Tr.*] Little is known of its origin. It is held that it had its origin in Flanders, whose heavy soil is conducive to the breeding of heavy horses. This theory is not entirely convincing, though often repeated, for the constitution of the soil is not the decisive factor in the development of a new breed of horses. It is also widely assumed that this ancestor of the heavy horse breeds such as the Belgian

Ardennais was itself descended from a wild type which early became extinct, and is known as *Equus robustus*.

Undoubtedly the heavy breeds of today do trace back to this ancestry, but it may also be assumed that many more early types figure in their pedigree, and primarily the Turanian horse, though not by the medium of direct introduction but as a cross among the horses bred in this region (Gallica Belgica, Germania Inferior) in antiquity. Nevertheless, we can perceive the influence of a third type, probably derived from the Central Asiatic Taki (*Equus Przewalskii* Poliakoff) brought in by the Huns, and corresponding to Ebhardt's Pony Type II.

Historical analogies point to this. Cold-blooded horses were not only bred in Western Europe. Long before the Central Asiatic nomads reached Europe, and with them these horses of Taki blood, both in the Far East and the Middle East larger horses with more bone had been bred, especially in China and in Persia. The latter country was particularly well situated, geographically, for horse-breeding. Breeding of cold-bloods began there in the last few centuries before our era; thus, after the appearance of the Huns. This fact of itself shows the connection between the breeding of cold-blooded types and the Hun horses. The horses of these nations who came swarming out of the homeland of nomadic stock-keeping are described even in late sources—such as Ammianus Marcellinus in the case of the Huns—as ugly and clumsy. This type is still widely distributed in Mongolia. The stocky build and the low-set massive head both show characteristic cold-blooded features. In the breeding of the West European heavy horse the crossing of the above wild types must have been the basis, but the decisive factor in their development was a fixed objective, aimed at through selection and refinement.

The Oriental horse, naturalized in Spain by the Saracens, was now brought into contact with the West European horse mentioned above, and interbred. The battle of Poitiers—together with many other and more recent proofs—had shown that armoured cavalry fighting in close order was an effective counter to Arab mounted attack. The proper horse to carry this 'wall of armour' was the cold-blood enlivened by some characteristics of Oriental origin. The strategic equilibrium which obtained for a time in Europe with the victories over the Avars and the Arabs was in part due to the employment of such horses.

The Battle on the Lech

But this equilibrium was maintained only until 887, when a new wave of mounted invaders hit Europe in the form of the Magyars. For half a century they were able to put Europe to the sword and the flames without let or hindrance, raising the dreaded ghost of Attila's hordes all over again. Where was the armoured host of the Franks, which had vanquished the Avars and the Arabs? In spite of these successes, Western chivalry was no match for the Magyars, in either numbers, armament, or horseflesh. In particular, the lack of remounts was probably the reason for the failure to raise adequate mounted forces, as witness a decree by Charles the Bald in 864, almost 150 years after the battle of Poitiers, obliging his vassals to take the field on horseback.

For all that, Western chivalry was not useless, even though it had no success against the Magyars within the Frankish frontiers. Other nations who were threatened by the same enemy took the Frankish knight as their model. Saxons, Swabians, and Bavarians had been, so to speak, taken unawares by the Magyar incursion. These nations still hardly ever fought on horseback; the army of Louis the Child, destroyed by the Hungarians at Bratislava in 907, was composed predominantly of infantry.

Now a remodelling along Frankish lines became urgent, and this did occur in a comparatively short time. At the battle of Riade on the Unstrut (near Merseburg) King Henry gained his first success by employing cavalry against the Hungarians in 933. According to the old Saxon chronicler Widukind, his army had been preparing for this battle for nine years. His son Otto I developed this plan further, and had at his disposal a considerable body of cavalry, with which he defeated the Hungarians decisively at the battle of the Lechfeld in 955, after the latter had ceased to reckon with any serious resistance.

Not that this victory broke the military power of the Hungarians. Nevertheless, this battle must rank with those of the Catalaunian Fields and Poitiers in the story of the newly awakening Europe. It was another victory of heavily armed cavalry restoring a parity of strength between East and West.

Its immediate effect was apparent, in that the Hungarians ceased from their raids and began to adapt themselves to the community of European nations. There was a further gain for the West, in that from now on Europe constituted a firmly united entity against Oriental aggression, with Hungary as its advanced guard. Against this united Europe the assaults of the Petchenegs, Uzes, Kumans, Mongols, and Osmanli Turks beat in vain.

Along the road which the mounted nomads had trod for centuries, wandering ever westward in the search for water and grazing for their herds, and more portable booty for themselves, there rode also the four apocalyptic horsemen—War, Famine, Pestilence, and Death—and yet this lamentable darkness was not unillumined by flashes of light: Europe would never have been able to play so great a part in the history of mankind if it had remained in isolation. By its contacts with the peoples of the East, it became familiar with distant civilizations, from which it adopted many things; often these were quite mundane, of no more aesthetic significance than the wheelbarrow, borrowed from China; but tools, weapons, customs—even words—taken together all added to the fullness of life in Europe. What we call 'European culture' as it has developed over thousands of years is the sum of such borrowings from many different quarters.

These peoples who have been famous in Europe for their horsemanship have contributed much to the solution of humanity's perennial problem: the perfection of transport and communications. The last phase of this solution falls within our own century; its equestrian stages began with the appearance of the Magyars and ended in the first decades of the 1900's.

Europe at the Time of the Last Eastern Mounted Invasions

A study of Chinese history cannot but emphasize the historical significance of communications technique, with the trenchant phrase "The state is founded on the horse's back". We might adapt it to apply to equestrian history in Eurasia, by saying that history itself takes shape from the back of a horse. Since the earliest appearance of the mounted nomads from Asia the course of history flowed always in the same direction; it followed the tracks of the high-bred horse. This theme can also be expressed in terms of European progress. Just as the historical centre of gravity shifted eastward with the departure of the Huns and the fall of the Western Empire, with the onset of the 'Dark Ages', so with the arrival of new peoples riding out of the East a new historical development began.

It also became apparent that a certain pattern or rhythm of events obtained. The avenues of invasion were determined by geographical limitations. The Black Sea and the Mediterranean, which divide the temperate zones of Europe and Africa, left two alternative routes open to westward migrants; one through the 'gateway of the East' between the Urals and the Caspian, the other south of the Caspian to the Mediterranean coasts and via North Africa to the Strait of Gibraltar, entering Europe via Spain. These highways were also the approach routes of the hot-blooded strains of horse. At this time the amount of traffic by other routes over the Bosporus or by other seaways was negligible.

Along these two approaches different equestrian traditions entered Europe, and they have played a decisive part in the evolution of military and economic techniques there. The line of demarcation between the two equestrian cultures has by and large coincided with the western boundaries of Hungary and Poland, and only varied as these frontiers have themselves varied over the centuries. (Note 5.) West of the line was the domain of the heavily armoured, heavily armed knight, while east of it the domain of the mounted archer stretched away to the borders of China. The only exception was in the lands of the Middle East. Here a third tradition, that of the Arabian horsemen, replaces the two aforesaid; this was a late development, but a highly characteristic one.

In the Polish sector the line of demarcation between East and West was at times blurred, but very clear-cut in the Hungarian sector. Here the frontier between the two cultures represented not merely an ethnic and economic break but also a political one, marked by obstacles and hedges which were great impediments to cultural exchange, either way. Isolation was also often artificially increased by the ban on exports which is characteristic of the hippocentric political structure. A state which enjoyed a superiority, real or fancied, in matters concerning the horse would make of the sale of horses across the frontier an indictable offence. [For centuries this rule obtained within the British Isles. Not only are there laws by the Anglo-Saxon kings forbidding the export of horses except by way of gift (which for practical purposes meant royal gift with a political motive), but the last of the statutes forbidding the sale of horses by Englishmen to Scots was not repealed until 1603. Tr.] One of the earliest Continental decrees on this subject was that of St Ladislaus, King of Hungary 1077–95. The motive in this as in all cases was primarily military; such laws remained in Hungary until the end of the Middle Ages.

The essential differences between the two equestrian traditions arose out of a different way of life in East and West. While in the East everybody, including women and children, was accustomed to handle and ride horses, in the West riding was for centuries the prerogative of the ruling class, and in some instances of the male sex. (Note 6.)

The Western Counter-attack

When the mounted warrior became the armoured knight this implied a uniform Western technique of riding. But the chivalrous way of life did not only represent a personification of the military virtues, it also embodied the highest ideals of the age.

The origin of this development, which had its religious components and can be broadly termed Franco-Norman, is also Oriental. The mounted archer of the Migration Period, who projected the life he had enjoyed beyond the frontier of death, and therefore took with him into the grave either a horse or something (a skull, a bit, a stirrup) to symbolize a horse, or the Roman for whom the equestrian statue stood for the memorial of courage and the military virtues, are all—together with the medieval knight—phenomena characteristic of the equestrian culture. The Man on Horseback, properly the knight, cavalier, chevalier, caballero, represents for that era the ideal superior human type, just as the technician does in popular esteem today.

The chivalrous social system became a source of expansive power. The West modified its tactics *vis-à-vis* the East, and passed to the offensive. Thus in Spain the era of the Reconquista dawned, with a general rising against the Moors. The Cid, national hero of Spain, took Valencia in 1094 and founded an order of chivalry whose task it was to protect the Christian faith. The most significant event of the two-hundred-year struggle was the joint triumph of the Kings of Castile and Aragon at Las Navas de Tolosa in 1212, which initiated the gradual decline of Saracen rule in Spain, and led eventually to the liberation of the whole peninsula.

At the Synod of Clermont in 1095 Pope Urban II called for the liberation of the Holy Land from the infidel, who, in the person of the Seljuk Turks, had conquered

Palestine in 1071. In 1097 the first Crusading army reached Asia Minor under Godfrey of Bouillon. The impetuous tactics of Western chivalry, hitherto unfamiliar to the Seljuks, led to the storming of Jerusalem in 1099.

The liberated Holy Land became the Kingdom of Jerusalem, which the newly founded orders of the Templars, the Knights Hospitalers, and the Teutonic Knights defended against repeated Turkish attacks. All these orders were founded in the

The Emperor Frederick I on Crusade
From a MS by Peter de Ebule

twelfth century. This was the furthest outpost of the Franco-Norman civilization, whose boundaries can be roughly equated with those of Romanesque architecture. But it had to struggle for existence, with shallow roots in an alien soil; it was scarcely viable without repeated subventions from the West, and had to endure the hostility or at best the indifference of the neighbouring Christian Great Power, Byzantium. As the relations of this eastern Rome became more and more exacerbated in regard to the 'Franks', zeal for the holy cause was drowned in a flood of jealousy and suspicion, and the Holy Land in whose defence the West had expended so much treasure, blood, and sweat fell again to the Muslims in 1187.

The expansion of the West, after the fire had gone out of the Crusading idea and its forces had been disengaged from the Levant, redirected itself to the north-east. The knights of the Teutonic Order, under pretext of spreading Christianity among the Slavonic and Baltic tribes, took possession of East Prussia, and later conquered Lithuania, Livonia, and Kurland (Esthonia), often overrunning these boundaries on the Polish side. This was the heyday of European chivalry. A martial spirit, new methods of warfare, and the means to practise it in the form of adequate horses of the right sort, weighed the scales in favour of the West. Thereby the equilibrium of forces between Western and Eastern Europe was jeopardized.

Jenghis Khan

This was the moment when yet again a swarm of horsemen came out of Mongolia. The mounted Mongol hordes under Jenghis Khan raged like a destructive thunderstorm right through Asia, reaching the Carpathians in 1240. Once more, as so often, the terror of the Four Deadly Horsemen paralysed Europe.

By all accounts the Mongolian horse of those days was not identical with the Tarpan-derived horse of Eastern Europe. Rogerius, Canon of Nagyvárad, was an eye-witness of the Tartar onslaught, and a chronicler of Hungarian events. He mentions that many Mongol horses came into possession of the Hungarians. Later documents also particularize 'Tartar' horses. This all goes to show that the horses of the Mongols could be easily distinguished from our own, probably because of their pronounced Przewalski features.

But the Mongols were also familiar with horses of Tarpan type with a dark eel-stripe. The unique source for the reign of Jenghis Khan, the *Secret History of the Mongols*, emphasizes every instance where this type is mentioned, as if it were something unusual. They also knew the Turanian horse. Ogedai Khan, when his people had forced Bagdad to surrender, demanded as ransom for the city not only jewels but also camels, pack-mules, and 'tall horses with long necks of western breed'. This means 'western' in relation to Mongolia, which lies east of Turania.

During the conquest of the Turkic tribes dwelling west of the Mongols the breeding of these Turanian or Turkestan horses had almost totally stopped, as was implied in the account of the Bactrian horse earlier. A more or less mixed blood-line of this race has since then been perceptible in the horse-stock of Asia Minor and North Africa.

It is worth noting that the *Secret History* also mentions the wild horses of Mongolia. They were hunted, like other game, on horseback. Jenghis Khan had a fatal accident out hunting, when a herd of these wild horses was unexpectedly put up. On sight of them his horse started and threw him on his back, and he died from spinal damage caused by this fall, in 1227.

The riding technique of the Mongols seems to be of Turkic origin; their horse-breeding, trading habits, and manner of warfare are also very similar to those of the Central Asiatic Turks. But other Turkish influences are also common among them, for instance in writing and vocabulary. These traditions too are mentioned in the *Secret History*, which traces the ancestry of Jenghis Khan to ancestors from the Uryanchai tribe among others.

Their ruthless attitude to horses is also reminiscent of Turkish practice. Whereas Western sources describe the Mongols as a savage mounted horde, they figure in Oriental writings as a disciplined army. According to Thomas, Archdeacon of Spalato (1268), the Mongols ride their tough little horses 'peasant-fashion', by which, apparently, he means in the Oriental manner, galloping them unshod over rocky, stony ground, as if they were chamois; and after three days on the march give them only a handful of inferior herbage. But the *Secret History* tells a very different story. It quotes a few lines from an order of the day by Jenghis Khan:

Take care of the led horses in your troop, before they lose condition. For once they have lost it, you may spare them as much as you will, they will never recover it on campaign. . . . You will encounter much game on the march. Do not let the men go after it. . . . Do not let the men tie anything to the back of the saddle. Bridles will not be worn on the march—the horses are to have their mouths free. If this is done, the men cannot march at a gallop. If an order has been given, then those who disobey it must be beaten and put under arrest. But as for those who have disobeyed my personal orders, send those who are

30 Contemporary Statuette of Charlemagne. Damaged, and restored in the sixteenth century, but it seems fair to assume that if the original had shown stirrups, the reproduction would have had them also

31   Persian Frieze showing Heavy Horses ridden by a King and a Deity

32   Asiatic Warrior extract-
ing Arrow from his
Horse
Note the method of
dressing mane. Hogged
short, so as not to
hamper the bow's use,
but locks left to assist
mounting. Tomb of the
Chinese Emperor
Tai-Tsong.
Musée Guimet

33 Magyar Marauders. Miniature from the Illuminated Vienna Chronicle.

34 King Béla IV of Hungary pursued by Mongols.
Miniature from Vienna Chronicle.

35
Kuman Archer.
Potsherd of the
thirteenth century.
National Museum,
Budapest

worth serious consideration to me. The rest, the unimportant ones, are to be beheaded on the spot. . . .

Was there ever a Western commander who ordered his troopers to take the bits off their horses on the march and reinforced his orders with such draconic sanctions? Scarcely; but then there was never a Western army that could point to such enormous feats of strategic marching on horseback.

Left Jenghis Khan, *right* Batu Khan. Chinese Portraits of the Manchu Era.
From a Hungarian edition of Secret History of the Mongols, 1962

Jenghis Khan's order is somewhat reminiscent of what the Emperor Leo the Wise says about the Magyars: "These people . . . suffer their superiors to punish them very severely for all transgressions, and they are held together not by affection but by fear". Old accounts of the Huns are similar; in their ranks were found many deserters. The art of war and the unsurpassed feats of long-distance horsemanship practised by the Oriental equestrian tribes had their roots, then, in the way of life of a warrior nation, who, hardened by centuries of fighting, had become accustomed to organization and iron discipline, and had made war their trade. What made the inexorable discipline bearable for the common trooper was the hope of rich booty, quickly won.

The observations of Archdeacon Thomas about the Mongol reserve horses are worth noting: "However many horses a man possesses, they are so trained that they follow him like dogs". A Hungarian bishop confirmed this on the evidence of Tartar prisoners: "They are followed by many riderless horses. One man riding in front and twenty or thirty horses after him". Now, this behaviour by the horses is not the result of training, as Thomas thought, but is the effect of the herd instinct which is the basis of nomadic horse-keeping, where horses are not driven but led to pasture in herds. Thus Leo the Wise writes of the Magyars: "Behind them follows a great troop of horses, both stallions and mares,[1] partly so that the horsemen can drink the mares' milk, partly to give the impression of a great host". The Pseudo-Maurikos had written almost exactly the same thing about the Avars nearly three hundred years earlier, and here we see how the supply system of the nomad armies worked, and this is the explanation of some of their marching feats: the spare horses followed the bell-mare, who was either ridden or led in hand, and were intended to be ridden in relays, and eventually eaten. The armies could thus move at a great pace over long stages, and supply was not the business of the army command, but of the individual soldier.

[As late as 1591 Giles Fletcher said of the Tartars in his *Of the Russe Commonwealth*: ". . . their souldiers to a certaine nomber, euery man with his two horse at the least, the one to ride on, the other to kill, when it commeth to his turne to haue his horse eaten. For their chiefe vittaile is horse flesh, which they eate without breade . . ." *Tr.*]

Thus the nomad's life presented no great contrast as between war and peace. In either case all their possessions and all their 'vittaile', as Fletcher says, was of animal origin, the only difference being that when on the warpath their customary food—milk, meat, and blood—was all derived from the horse, and no other animal. The blood was drawn by turns from the veins of living horses, kept in gut bags, thickened over the fire, and finally fried like a 'black pudding'. The number of horses involved seems to imply that several troopers would belong to a 'mess', the basis of which was twenty or thirty spare horses: and all the time the picture is the same, horses running after the man on the lead horse.

But the spare horses also had their tactical uses. According to Leo the Wise, the Magyars tethered their spare horses to each other before battle, and put them immediately in rear of the fighting-line so that their men could not be directly attacked from behind. Rogerius says that the Mongols used to mount dummy soldiers on the spare horses to give the impression of greater numbers. [Just as in the desert campaigns of the early 1940s the 1st British Cavalry Division—which no longer had any horses, and had not yet any tanks—was employed in simulating vast masses of armour by means of disguised vehicles. *Tr.*]

The organization of Oriental mounted forces can really only be understood in the light of the use made of spare horses. That is how the advance guard of Subotai's army in 1241 managed to cover the ground between the Verecke Pass on the Hungarian frontier to the walls of Pest in only three days, a distance of 300 miles.

When the Great Khan died in 1241, Europe was saved from further devastation. Since the new Great Khan would have to be elected by all the Mongol chiefs, the hordes turned about, after laying waste the lands of the Kumans, Russians, Poles, Hungarians, and some Balkan countries, and after their scouts had penetrated Silesia, and took the road to their distant home in the East, taking with them thousands of prisoners from Christendom. Hungary was hardest hit by the Mongol scourge, although it would appear from the foregoing that the Magyars stood the best chance of survival against such an enemy.

The rout of the Hungarian forces at the river Sajó, a tributary of the Tisza, in

---

[1] Curious that he does not mention geldings.

1241, is explained by many contemporaries as due to internal confusion, the under-mining of the royal prestige and mistakes in the command of the army. Even so, Chinese authorities state that the Mongols suffered the heaviest losses of their European campaign at the hands of the Magyars, in a night engagement on the eve of the Sajó battle. When the next incursion took place forty-four years later the Magyars had no difficulty in defeating the Golden Horde.

The battle at the Sajó was at the same time the scene of an equestrian feat of historic importance. King Béla IV broke out of his laager of wagons, which was surrounded by the Mongols, and was able by means of repeated changes of horse (which his self-sacrificing entourage put at his disposal) to outdistance his pursuers, though these were full of endurance and determined to capture him. Bearing in mind that this horse-race for life and death was run between scions of the two races who were the most accomplished horsemen in the world, and that all was at stake, then the escape of the King must rank as the most significant equestrian event the world has ever seen.

In the century of these last mounted incursions Europe underwent far-reaching changes based on the experience of the Mongolian inroads, castles and fortifications were reconstructed, just as they had been earlier in the history of cavalry raids, all along the line between the Wall of China and the headwaters of the Danube and the Rhine. This was combined with the organization of armed 'train-bands' of citizens to defend the fortified towns. But this drastic phlebotomy in Eastern Europe gave a new drive to Western expansion.

With the expansion of the Teutonic Order the Western way of life became cur-rent over more ground, and the frontier between the two Europes receded east-ward in the Polish sector. Hungary continued to fulfil her historic role as before, both politically and economically, by means of a closed frontier lined with fortifi-cations and a ban on certain exports, yet cultural influences were unmistakably at work, in two directions. These elements of the Eastern way of life which had become naturalized only under the stress of compulsion were now voluntarily adopted and imitated.

If the onslaught of the Mongols was the last recognizable wave of the Migration of Peoples, the undertow and the eddies took the form of much displacement, much resettlement. So long as all the populations of the Eastern region were not finally sedentary, some nations in Europe would be subject to pressure of westward-moving elements. New storm-clouds blew up in the form of settlement by the Tartars, on the steppes of eastern Europe, and then in the Ottoman Empire, where the revived fanaticism of Islam led to expansion by violence in Asia Minor.

The Turkish Peril

The Osmanlis belonged, as the Seljuks and Kumans had done, to the family of Oguz Turks who had left their homes under pressure from the Mongols in the thirteenth century. In all some thousands of them entered the service of the Seljuk Turkish sultan in Asia Minor. The Seljuk kingdom shortly became the scene of events that were to be repeated many times over among the splintered survivors of once united Turkish tribes: the prince of the small Osmanli minority, Osman I (1282–1326), became the founder of a dynasty, and ultimately ruler of an empire, and the Seljuk population, which had become more or less Persianized, adopted the name of Osmanli under his rule. This was the Turkish syndrome. Under the slogan of the spread of Islam, their first aim was the mastery of Constantinople.

The appearance of the Turks in Europe meant, for the Hungarians, the beginning of three hundred years of defensive warfare. In the whole eastern region the duel between two mounted antagonists began all over again. But now it was no longer a quarrel about pasture and waterholes: the Turks were interested only in power, the Hungarians in self-preservation. Besides these cardinal objectives, however, the counters were booty and prisoners, and it was the hope of these that brought recruits to the colours on both sides. On every campaign the Turks brought away thousands of peaceful inhabitants, to be sold as slaves to landowners in Anatolia, or in order to bring up the boys as mercenaries in the Janissary schools. In the hope of ransom, soldiers captured noblemen and their families. This happened also on the Hungarian side, though in a lesser degree, but apparently with the same financial success. The ransom of a Turkish soldier came to a respectable sum in cash, or the equivalent in Turkish horses. Volunteers marched with the armies, in the Hungarian ranks known as Heiducks, corresponding to the freebooters among the Turks. To such men every campaign was what the Turanian warriors called an *alaman*—an excursion in search of plunder.

The combat raged over Hungarian soil for nearly a hundred and fifty years, and finally led to exhaustion on both sides. At a time when the population of Western Europe was doubling itself, the four and a half million Magyars lost half their total strength. Loss of manpower in the Turkish Empire led to decadence at the end of these wars. All this served as a pretext for the house of Habsburg to expel the Turks at the end of the seventeenth century and establish their power in Hungary.

The Turkish wars had brought new experiences to the art of warfare on horseback; they led to the final abandonment of armour in Europe, so bringing Western practice nearer to the Asiatic norm. The greater emphasis on light cavalry led to the preponderance on the battlefield of the hot-blooded horse, and the breeding of half-blood horses, which in turn had beneficial effects on transport in general.

Apocalyptic Horsemen in the New World

While in Europe the Turkish wars saw the cavalry of East and West measured against each other, the European horseman in the Americas spread the same terror as his predecessors had once done in the Old World, as they swarmed out of Asia. Only the numbers were on a quite different scale.

The report by Hernán Cortez to the Emperor Charles V on the conquest of Mexico in 1519–21 tells an unvarnished tale of inhuman massacres perpetrated on the native population under the pretext of conversion to the True Faith, but actually inspired by immeasurable greed for wealth and power. Consciousness of their military superiority awakened in the Spaniards primarily the baser human passions.

The New World offered a re-enactment of previous historical events. The appearance of the mounted hidalgo paralysed the proven valour of the native population, as once the appearance of the 'centaurs' had robbed the astounded Europeans of their natural courage. The astonished aborigines lost their heads and fled, again and again, during the triumphal progress of the conquistadores. And yet the Mexican warriors were not really so defenceless. They had arrows and other missile weapons tipped with various metals (though no iron), and also obsidian and bone;

Aztec Temple stormed by Spanish Soldiers
From a sixteenth-century MS

but for the moral effect, they could easily have overwhelmed the handful of Spanish lancers.

The Mexican defensive measures showed themselves repeatedly in the same pattern: they dug deep pits as obstacles for the opposing cavalry, and these were effective, in so far as Cortez reports: "I continually admonished my men to make every handsbreadth of ground we won passable for the horses, for our cavalry were the decisive factor in the campaign". Whenever possible, these pits were filled in before the attack, even though it meant an embittered skirmish on foot, an escort fighting to protect the pioneers.

The horse, now an indispensable factor in the military and commercial life of Europe, played a decisive part in the further development of the fate of nations on the American continent, exactly as it had done in the Migration period. Wherever the White Man as soldier, hunter, pioneer, or farmer appeared with his horse, then it was time for the aborigine to fade away. The bounds of this new Migration of Peoples were set by climatic conditions. The icy North and the Tropic Zone—in neither of which can the horse flourish—were the last refuge of the autochthonous peoples. The same is true of Africa and Australia, except that one of these extremes is missing from both these continents.

Meanwhile in Europe that tract of the human story which had begun with the horsemen swarming out of Asia was drawing to its close, and as the Ottoman crescent waned the balance of power in East and Central Europe shifted once again, and in the new equilibrium the interests of the house of Habsburg and of the house of Romanov formed the counterweights. Gradually the line of demarcation between the two sectors of Europe, the two contrasting ways of life, was fading. And all this hastened the amalgamation of European horsemanship into a uniform standard.

Part III The Equestrian Civilization

The Threefold Turanian Legacy

The development of a uniform European standard of horsemanship was delayed, during the Middle Ages, by the same forces which had set bounds to it in the past. Custom, prejudice, and religious taboos and encumbrances put obstacle after obstacle in the way of people who were trying to make progress in various respects. It was not until the beginning of the nineteenth century that European horsemanship achieved its fullest development, even though the earliest traces of its development under various external influences were already evident in the Middle Ages.

But in order to treat of this historical process we must define what is meant by the 'equestrian civilization'.

It is determined by three factors: the man, the horse he rides, and the way he rides it. Yet all these together do not add up to an 'equestrian civilization'. Each of them must attain a certain standard, individually and collectively. So far as the man is concerned this standard is determined by the equestrian way of life, in the physical and mental sense. Of course, there are no hard-and-fast patterns. Different types of horsemen of different periods, different schools of riding and driving, can all be regarded as positively contributing to the equestrian civilization, presuming they are not only outwardly concerned, from motives of pleasure or display, but also inwardly committed, having the psychological attitude characteristic of the true horseman. Such a man sees in his horse not merely an animal that is of use to him, just some quadruped subject to his dominion, but regards it rather as a companion by whose help he can attain a higher way of life.

The second and passive partner is the horse, but not just any horse. The Good Horse, as such, stands out from the mass of *Equus caballus*, bearing in mind the special meaning which the word Good has in this context.

I am sure that many of my readers will have experienced that feeling which is so typical of the hippophile, at the moment when, after some strenuous journey, some dangerous ride, or the passing of some perilous obstacle, he gets down from the saddle or the driver's box and gratefully pats the neck of his horse, which has once again proved itself a reliable partner. Such gratitude has its roots in the reliance we place on the extraordinary capacities and high qualities associated with the 'good horse'.

In the past, and in part also today, that sort of horse embodied everything that went to make up the horseman's ideal.

But the outstanding qualities of a good horse depend not on its individual capabilities alone, but primarily on its breeding and pedigree. The part which the horse has been able to play, therefore, has been sustained thanks to its inheritance from Bactrian, Turanian, and Arabian ancestors, the *materia generosa* of the ancients. For thousands of years men have been trying to beg, borrow, buy, plunder, or steal horses of this kind, just because the attributes of the 'blood' horse are so highly prized. And this points to the real prerequisite of the equestrian civilization, which is a purposeful breeding policy whereby an adequate supply of the right sort of horse is ensured; and this demands much technical knowledge, and a heavy sacrifice of time, money, and patience.

As to the third and no less important factor—the actual techniques of riding and driving—one may regard this as part of the history of transport and communications, of war, or of sport, but in any case it does not require further elucidation at this stage.

In the art of horsemanship, as it had evolved in Europe by say 1800, the influence of three separate traditions was perceptible, all ultimately going back to Turania. The oldest of these was that of Central Asia, going back to the mounted nomads of that region, and it proved to be the one which exerted its influence latest on Western Europe. The second was the Arabian influence, exerted primarily during the campaigns of Moslem expansion through North Africa and against all the major peninsulas on the north shore of the Mediterranean. The third influence was internal, arising in Europe itself; here the West European institution of 'chivalry' (which originally had the same meaning as 'cavalry') grew up around the nucleus of a school of horsemanship that owed something to Near Eastern and much to Scandinavian influence. The knight of France-Norman pattern becomes the typical figure of Western Christendom in the Middle Ages.

We shall explore the history and achievements of these three equestrian civilizations in the following chapters, beginning with Western Europe and working backward via the world of the Arab horseman to Central Asia.

The West European Tradition

A deliberate horse-breeding policy became necessary, at the very latest, at the moment when German and French knights found it imperative to protect themselves and their horses from the hail of arrows discharged by the mounted bowmen of Central Asia; the horse must be able to carry the weight of armour over and above that of the rider and his weapons, and according to their ideas only a heavily built horse could carry heavy weights. (Note 7.) The Arabs, on the other hand, did not at this period shoot from the saddle, and indeed they did not adopt the stirrup until about 1150. They rode light horses, and the Christian knights of Mediterranean lands were able to oppose them on equally light horses.

France was the country in which the influence of Oriental stock brought home by the Crusaders, and used as sires to cover mares of local breeds such as the Ardennais and the Limousin, was important. Like all the North French breeds derived mostly from the mixture of Pony Type II, Horse Type III and Horse Type IV, (see p. 14) such races as the Percheron and the Boulonnais were big and slow and powerful, but after the twelfth century they acquired even more qualities of Oriental origin. They also began to be bred far outside the confines of France itself; not only in England (since 1066) but in Northern Italy and beyond the Rhine as far as Bohemia and Austria, in Denmark, and perhaps even in Sweden. The striking power of every Western army consisted of armoured knights on cold-blooded horses which had to be bred at home because all Western monarchs forbade the export of such horses on principle.

36 Mongolian Horses of Taki Strain

37
Mongolian Horse,
hobbled by Leading
Rein on Treeless Steppe

38   Sultan Soleiman's Army crossing the Drava.
Contemporary miniature.
Chester Beatty Library, Dublin

ANO · DNI · MCCCXXVIII

The breeding of heavy horses in the West was intended to produce the armour-carrying destrier (to adopt the Norman term; indeed, the word only occurs in Western languages). Derived from the Latin *dextrarius*, which means right-handed, this expression has been interpreted in different ways ever since medieval times; either it means that the groom or squire led it off the right hand, or the right hand is conceived of as being more powerful than the left (as it is in most people, but not in most horses). Thus a thirteenth-century chronicle compares the destrier as a type with Bucephalus as an individual, excelling all others in strength. It is significantly still the custom in Eastern Europe to harness the stronger horse on the right side of the pole—the dexter side, in terms of heraldry. There is documentary evidence that the destrier was exclusively an entire and specially trained stallion. It was accounted scandalous to use mares for military purposes. The dextrarius was in fact just the horse for the chosen method of fighting—charging in close order over comparatively short distances. It was not capable of a sustained gallop, but its very mass added weight to the impact. The aggressive instincts of the stallion were also exploited, but not always to the advantage of the rider, because horses which had been trained to be aggressive could only with difficulty be induced to go over to the defensive, or even to retreat. The care of destriers in camp was rendered more difficult by the fact that they could not be turned out to graze with other horses. (Note 8.)

They are first mentioned in connection with the struggle against the Moors or Saracens. It is recorded of the Emperor Otto II (973–983) that at the battle of Cotrone in Calabria (982), he was pursuing the Saracens after an initial success, but they lured him into an ambush and defeated him with crippling losses. The Emperor himself was barely able to escape capture on his marching-palfrey, after his destrier had been killed under him.

A Hungarian chronicle of about the same period tells us that Prince Béla of the Arpad dynasty, fighting in alliance with the Polish Prince Micislav, knocked his Pomeranian enemy out of the saddle of the destrier. Twelfth- and thirteenth-century documents often mention such chargers, notably in the records of the Hungarian King Béla IV for 1251, where this type of horse is described as the characteristic mount of the Western chivalry.

Detailed information about the breeding and care of horses in the West is available from the administrative accounts of the Teutonic Knights. In the archives of their headquarters at Marienburg a clear picture of the care and use of heavy horses is given. There are accounts of how horses were racked up in their stalls, about the building of stables and the fencing of paddocks, about rations of fodder and forage, about farriery, and so on. The general impression is one of similarity with modern practice. So also with breeding—the mares were put only to particular stallions, and we actually have a covering calendar with accurate entries of dates.

All of which goes to show that already there was a profound difference between stud practice East and West. The heavy horse as we know it is therefore not the result of natural selection but the result of systematic human interference. The overemphasis which was laid on breeding the type with the greatest body-weight of necessity led to the exaggeration of those disadvantages which go with such a conformation. The heavy horse, kept in the stable until it had become unaccustomed

(above)
he Condottiere
uidoriccio da
ogliano on a
acing Horse
y Simone Martini
280–1349), *in*
alazzo Pubblico,
ena

2 (below)
orsemen on
acing Palfreys,
welfth-century
resco from
hiesa dei Quattro
nti Coronati,
ome

to being turned out (even in the grazing season they spent far too little time at grass), did indeed attain a huge stature, but became soft and lethargic and unsuited to prolonged exertions. In the beginning of the Age of Chivalry, when this process of 'inflation' had barely begun, the 'heavy' characteristics were not nearly so conspicuous as they are in, say, the Shire or the Noriker of today, and indeed did not begin to predominate until the thirteenth century, as is apparent from the evidence of art alone.

[In the English context the Bayeux Tapestry makes this very plain. The war-horses at Hastings look like miniature Clydesdales, about the size of Welsh cobs. But they are not so hairy about the heels, and they are galloping in a way no Clydes-dale could ever move. *Tr.*]

There must certainly have been intermediate types between these and the common horses, as well as crosses between light and heavy strains.

On the march the destrier was led in hand, while the knight rode a light horse specially bred for this purpose to give a comfortable ride. This was the *palafridus*—palfrey in English. The knight did not change horses until the last moment before going into action; and the only parallel to this procedure is to be found among the Arabs.

It is therefore understandable that mounting the destrier—'getting on to one's high horse'—acquired a certain symbolic significance within the Order. The Emperor Frederick I's standing orders laid down that if a strange knight approaches the camp unarmed and shieldless on a palfrey (*in palafrido*), then he is to be peace-ably received, but if he rides up with slung shield on his fighting stallion (*in dextrario*), then he is to be attacked.

The Palfrey

The speciality of the palfrey was that it paced where other horses trotted. This gait is now largely obsolete in Europe, but it once lay at the foundations of a whole department of Western horsemanship.

Most quadrupeds at the walk and the trot put one fore- and one hind-foot forward simultaneously—or nearly so—but diagonally, that is, left fore and right hind or *vice-versa*. Even the erect biped human shows vestiges of this habit when he swings his arms on the march—as one leg goes forward the *opposite* arm swings forward. But in pacing the limbs on the same side of the body go forward together—left fore and left hind, then right fore and right hind.

This gait could either be induced by training, or to a certain extent by breeding, and it was prized because it was so comfortable for the rider. Mechanically, a stret-cher carried by two men marching in step gives the same sort of 'ride'. So does a camel.

The heavy horse which is incapable of a sustained gallop or canter can yet cover long distances at the trot, a gait which to the heavily armoured rider on a horse with the action that the destriers had would be sheer torture—and, indeed, Field Punishment Number One in the severe disciplinary code of the Teutonic Order consisted of trotting in full armour by the hour. For this reason the moment of changing horses was postponed as late as possible, and when the chivalry attacked they did so at a gallop, or more likely a slow canter, rather than a trot.

The palfrey was also the travelling horse for civilian purposes of all who could afford it in the West. From the Latin *paraveredus*, later *parafridus* and *palafridus*, are derived the French *palefroy* and the English 'palfrey'. Strangely, in the German language the old word *ross* for horse in general was displaced by an adaptation of *paraveredus—Pferd*. *Palefrenier* in French means a groom. So, originally, did the English surname Palfreyman. A slower, but also easy-going, type of horse was called in Latin *gradarius*, in French *ambleur*, and in English 'ambling pad'.

The other 'easy' gait, more showy and used more often in the West for civilian than for military purposes, was the rack, now almost exclusively practised in the United States and Iceland. It is a four-beat motion, in which the feet are set down in the series left hind, left fore, right hind, right fore, not in pairs but one after the other; and it can take place at any speed from that of a walk (which it much resembles) to the equivalent in m.p.h. of a fast gallop. [The sight and particularly the sound of a good racker accelerating from 3 to 20 m.p.h. without changing step is a unique experience. *Tr.*] According to Ursula Bruns, there are natural-born rackers, among some pony breeds of Western Europe, and such are highly prized for breeding purposes in Iceland.

[The fact that usage among Latin-writing clerks was not uniform from country to country in the West does not make historical investigation easier. Throughout the period the Vulgar Latin *tolutarius* was current, and was used in Scandinavia, and probably in England, to mean 'racker'. But since the French verb *trotter* is probably derived from *tolutare* it seems probable that by this Latin word the French clerk meant a trotting light horse of the kind called in English of the period a hakenay. This latter word is itself derived from the French *haquenée*, which meant some sort of soft-paced light horse, either pacing or racking. Thus the disciplines of etymology and semantics run dead contrary to the current of hippology! *Tr.*]

The Arts of War

In the revival of armoured cavalry there was necessarily an element of deliberate imitation of antiquity, since the Roman and more especially the Byzantine Empire had adopted this mode of warfare, and there was unbroken continuity between the armoured *infantry* of Roman legions and early medieval hosts. But the fighting power of the medieval armoured lancer in comparison with that of his counterpart in antiquity was much higher because, if his discipline was inferior, his equipment was superior.

This was primarily because of the saddle. The war-saddle was brought to perfection in the West, even though its origins lie somewhere in the East, probably among horse-breeders of the settled peasant rather than the nomadic herding tradition. Most likely the Arabs brought it to Europe. Its earliest form, as a true saddle, consists of a felt pad either side of the spine and united by wooden bows, as in the Pazyryk saddles discovered by Rudenko (1951). The saddle of chivalry was a very elaborate derivative of this, consisting of two enormous rigid 'bows', the hinder one of which 'embraced' the pelvis of the rider, united by wooden bars which are more like planks. The seat was stuffed, as was the inside of the saddle next to the horse. The high, wide pommel rose sheer in front of the rider's stomach, with only just room for him between it and the cantle. [Since, presumably, saddles were made to order for individual customers, it would in practice have been impossible for a thick-set knight to use his thin colleague's saddle—he would simply

Henry IV's War Saddle in
Westminster Abbey

not have been able to get into it. And that is the point—one rode *in*, not *on*, the medieval war-saddle. *Tr.*] Most saddles used on the march, for travelling and for hunting, seem to have been of the same pattern. They were not really practical or comfortable for either horse or rider, but in comparison with Roman models they did represent a technical advance.

The rider sat with a long, straight leg—the feet sticking forward in a style that was used for both military and civilian purposes. We think of this as the 'chivalrous' style, but it was not in fact peculiar to the armoured horseman, and it was practised both with and without stirrups, which had probably been introduced into Europe by the Avars: but their use became general only very slowly, especially when one considers their importance as an aid to riding. It was centuries before they had been adopted by all the Germanic tribes, even the Franks, who became the great equestrian champions of Europe. They cannot be definitely shown to have been used in the West until the defensive battles against the Magyars. Probably loathing and contempt for the enemy led here, as long ago in the case of the Jews *vis-à-vis* the Egyptians, to a reluctance to adopt his equipment and habits.

The tactical employment of the 'armoured wall' of knights demanded an open ground on which to ride down the enemy. The knight fighting alone or in small groups had so little effect that he was no match for the light cavalry, which would quickly overcome him, as can be seen in many historical instances. He was like a tank that has lost contact with its unit, or has blundered on to difficult going and become immobilized and more or less defenceless. Light cavalry, on the other hand, even when dispersed in open order, are still formidable individual opponents.

It did not take long for the vulnerable points of the 'armoured wall' to be detected, and more or less successful means to prise it apart to be devised. Ambush was the most common of these, in which connection the tactics of the White Huns against the Persian armoured cavalry, anticipating European tactics by about a thousand years, are of interest. (Note 9.)

The appearance of firearms solved at one blow the problem of how to break up the close array of armoured horsemen. More particularly this was the tactical role of artillery rather than hand-guns. The total collapse of heavy cavalry in the face of cannon-fire of necessity brought an end to the art of war as practised by chivalry—

and the end of chivalry as a practical military technique. The knight now survived in an unreal world, as is very evident from the literature of the sixteenth and seventeenth centuries, where he appears either as the central figure of an artificial pastoral romance (say Spenser's *Faerie Queene*) or as the butt of some satirical mock-epic (say *Don Quixote* or *Hudibras*). From the middle of the fifteenth century onward the light horseman replaced the armoured knight, just as he had done centuries before, in the armies of Khorasan, of Rome, and of Byzantium.

The Breeding of Half-bred Horses

With the decline of chivalry horse-breeding in the West took a new turn. Interest was focused on the Andalusian horse of Spain. The breed had been widely distributed in the Mediterranean (as far east as Cyprus) during the time when the cold-blooded heavy chargers were being bred up to their maximum size, and was esteemed (but scarce and expensive) in northern countries. The first recorded in England are the two black chargers ridden by William the Conqueror at Hastings. The Andalusian was as fast as Oriental horses, as handy, as pleasant to ride, and was up to weight. It was the first representative in the Western world of what in German are called 'warm-blooded' and in English 'Half-bred' or 'half-blood' horses—that is, a mixture of cold-blooded Great Horse elements with the Oriental (Barb, Arab, or Turk). In practice the Andalusian had all the properties of the best examples of such a mixture, but probably its genetic make-up was quite different. It was almost certainly descended from a breed indigenous to the southern part of the Iberian peninsula, and described in detail by the younger Pliny. It was the normal mount of Roman generals, with a straight facial profile, or a slightly convex one like that of the Nisaean horses of Persia.

The history of Spain and of the West generally is shot through and through with this breed. It was the great weapon of the Reconquista against the Moors, and of the conquistadores against the Incas; the mount of the Cid and of Pizarro. It was also the charger of the Christian armies of the Danube region confronting the Turks.

Its dispersal in the modern era was due to the rule of the House of Aragon over Naples and Sicily, and the House of Habsburg over Spain, but it had been widely distributed throughout Europe, at the top level only (because it was always expensive) from the early Middle Ages onward. [Indeed, one may say of the eleventh and twelfth centuries that the successful Western general was typically a Norman mercenary riding an Andalusian horse. *Tr.*] It was, of course, the stallions, not the mares, that were exported, and the pure race continued to be bred principally in Spain. Maximilian II brought Andalusian sires to the foundation of his studs at Lipizza, in Istria, and Kladrub, in Bohemia, and the famous breeds which bear these names are descended from the progeny of Spanish stallions out of mares of other races. Both became uniform throughout the extensive Habsburg domains, from the Danube to the Low Countries, as carriage horses and officers' chargers.

Half-blood breeding in France was on a somewhat different basis, and associated with the earlier rulers of the Bourbon dynasty. Henry IV (1589–1610) was a true horseman, and laid the foundations of French warm-blood breeding, on the basis of the light horse native to his homeland of Navarre. This Navarrese horse, close to the Limousin in type, and indeed to the regional varieties of South-west France generally, had many Oriental attributes which were no doubt the legacy of Moslem invasions in early Carolingian times. With such horses it was possible to practise an entirely new school of horsemanship. (Note 10.)

The abundant equestrian portraits of the period prove the widespread use of half-blood horses. Whether in battle, hunting, or on the march, the person of substance is always riding a horse of the same stamp, in Britain or on the Continent, and it is a horse with all the hallmarks of Iberian origin. [And this is the great difference between medieval and early modern times. The Western aristocrat down to about 1500 rode different types of horse in battle, out hunting, and on the road between one of his estates and another. But now he was able to use one stamp of horse for all these purposes—the Andalusian was indeed 'the horse for all seasons'. Tr.] The Andalusian, and more so its derivative the Neapolitan, was unmistakable with its 'presence', the high carriage of its head, often with Roman nose but never large, on a muscular neck, rather hollow back, very broad breast, sloping croup and luxuriant tail set on rather low. It figures prominently in pictures of the battles against the Turks, in which many painters and engravers with a good eye for a horse bring out very clearly the Oriental characteristics of the Turkish horses, in contrast to the Iberian features of what we must regard as 'the Occidental hot-blood'.

The Spanish High School

It is appropriate to mention here the High School or Spanish School of Vienna (ultimately of Naples). This is a particular branch of the art of training and riding horses, the ultimate goals of which are utterly contrary to the horse's nature, and which therefore demand an extraordinary degree of strength, intelligence, and perseverance. For this discipline the Spanish horse was well suited.

This decorative, spectacular mode of riding was not at first intended as a mere display of equestrian science. The various exercises at the walk and the trot lead to complete harmony between horse and rider, and in the literally higher branches (such as the 'airs above the ground') they preserve vestiges of a manner of mounted combat in which the horse was to some extent a weapon, used to ride down the enemy. A horse that had done this course of training was worth a great deal in difficult country, among obstacles, and in close-quarter fighting. This world-famous legacy of the horsemanship of former days now survives only in two centres; the Spanish High School of Vienna, and Saumur in France. Both schools as the preservers of a living tradition are of enormous historical worth, especially in the case of Vienna, which is horsed from its own stud of Lipizzaners (now at Piber), and directly descended from Maximilian's foundation stock. These horses, which are physically exactly suited to the task, carry out with baroque formality all the evolutions of the equestrian art as it was elaborated in the seventeenth century, in the dignified setting provided by the Emperor Charles VI, who in 1735 commissioned Fischer von Erlach to design the Spanish Riding School at the Hofburg.

Open-range Breeding in America

We have seen that the primary expansion of European horsemanship and horse-mastership in the New World was Spanish, and over the American continent as a whole the Spanish influence has been the predominant one, exerted alike on the

Indians, in so far as these took up horsemanship, and on Europeans of extra-Iberian origin. It was above all Spanish horses which, escaping from settlements in Mexico, California, Texas, Florida, soon populated the central plains with their feral descendants. Here the climate, soil, and herbage closely resembled that of the Eurasian steppe which had been the home of the horse before domestication. But this relapse into the primeval freedom did not entail also a physical recession to the original steppe type; the Mustang remained merely feral, merely a domestic horse run wild.

It was primarily with the aid of the mustang that the Plains Indians of the prairie region became mounted nomads, though probably the core of their horsemanship was formed by means of horses broken to ride and stolen from the Spaniards. The Indians invented nothing new in horsemanship or horsemastership so far as we know: what they did not learn by imitation of the Paleface horseman they learned empirically all over again—but nothing in excess of what was already known and practised. What is remarkable about the equestrian revolution among the Redskins is the speed with which it happened, and the absolute transformation of their way of life which the acquisition of the horse (far more so than the introduction of guns and whisky) brought about. Whole nations abandoned the practice of settled agriculture and became totally dependent on the horse, with the aid of which alone they could effectively hunt the bison all the year round. After the adoption of hunting as a way of life, war as a pastime and a prestige-giving occupation followed. Some tribes between 1720 and 1890 (when the 'horse-fever' had run its course) became quite sophisticated practitioners of line-breeding—for instance, the Nez Percé tribe, which produced the spotted Apaloosa breed, and became so emotionally bound up with its survival that after their war-bands had surrendered (severely outnumbered, and within sight of the Canadian frontier) to the U.S. Cavalry the American commanding officer perceived that the quickest way to achieve the complete psychological collapse of the red men was the immediate slaughter of their treasured spotted horses before their eyes. The desired effect was produced— there were no more Nez Percé risings—by this refinement of brutality, which hardly has its parallel even in the bloody chronicles of Eurasian mounted warfare.

On the grassy plains of the Americas, North and South, open-range horse-breeding on a large scale found a new home in the eighteenth and nineteenth centuries, alongside the extensive breeding of cattle and sheep. Apart from navigable rivers—mostly flowing from north to south, whereas the tide of migration ran from east to west—there was no alternative in transport and communications to the ox-wagon and the ridden or driven horse. The bell-mare as leader of the half-wild herds reassumed the key position she had occupied on the Eurasian steppe, and the conditions of nomadic stockbreeding were reproduced over again.

But only in terms of numbers and form. Otherwise American open-range breeding had little in common with the Central Asian prototype. Although the rough life of the prairies threw up a special type of man, the cowboy or gaucho, the horseman of the New World, whatever his ancestry, was dominated by Spanish tradition; his manner of breeding and breaking horses, style of riding, saddlery, accoutrements, all bore traces of Spanish origin, from the crown of his sombrero to the nails in his horseshoes (if his horse was shod at all). This is still evident in the United States, and even in Canada, in so far as the prairie way of life survives at all.

The breeding of heavy horses in modern times is an essential feature of the equestrian civilization. At the moment when the armoured mounted lancer left the military scene his horse took on a different role, primarily that of a harness horse. In England this change came about (though it was not fully completed) in the seventeenth century, and its crisis may be equated with the years following the Civil War. Here as in many European countries the ex-destrier displaced the smaller native breeds in the shafts of the cart, and the draught-ox before the plough. The release of the Great Horse from military service also made possible the increase in carriage traffic characteristic of the seventeenth and eighteenth centuries in the West. But the general trend of heavy-horse breeding was to an even heavier, even slower, animal of gigantic proportions with the pulling power of two oxen.

Pride of place in Europe as a whole still went to the North French breeds, from the Pas de Calais to Brittany. The Ardennais, widely known outside its native country simply as "the Belgian Horse", has contributed genetically to the foundations of every heavy-horse breed in Europe. In England, under the name of the Flemish Horse, it is an element in the foundation stock of the Clydesdale, the Shire, and even the Suffolk, the last of which probably owes much also to the Jutland breed of Denmark. Even in the Alps the influence of this lowland breed was felt, since the Austrian Pinzgau agricultural horse derives from a cross of the Ardennais on the indigenous mountain-bred Noriker.

The Arabian Tradition

The last sortie from the heartland of mounted nomadism reached the Near East in the thirteenth century. Crossing the mountains of Iran and Afghanistan, the Mongol hordes repeatedly plundered the Islamic lands. This brought about crises in the Near East which had fundamental changes as a consequence.

Cairo, which was then the seat of the Arab Caliphate, and with it the whole Islamic empire, suffered a like change in political direction. The Caliph's praetorian guard, which consisted of slaves, instituted a palace revolution in 1250, deposing the last of the Ayyubid Caliphs, Tur-in-Shah, taking power to itself. Now, this corps of guards, known as Mamelukes, consisted originally of Kipchak Turks who had been taken prisoner by the Mongols and bought from them by the Caliph El Malik el Saleh at some slave market on the Black Sea for his Cairene household. This take-over by Turks from Central Asia of Egyptian sovereignty brought with it many changes other than political. Turkish technique in military and transport fields took firm root in Egypt, and there now began that march of events which brought to the fore the Arab horse and the Arab style of horsemanship in that part of the world where the Cyrenaican and Barka horses had once had their being.

This Turkish influence was no isolated phenomenon in the Arab world of that time. Different elements of a Turkish realm that was disintegrating over a period of some centuries found a new home in the Arab world. Most of the Turks reached the Near East as mercenaries or as slave-soldiers, but they also appeared as conquerors, as for instance in the eleventh century, when the Seljuks left Central Asia, overran Asia Minor, and entered the Holy Land. The influence of Central

43 (above)   Sir Geoffrey Luttrell of Ingham, Lincolnshire, departing for the wars, *c.* 1340. From the Luttrell Psalter. *The British Museum*

44 (below left)   State Saddle in Ivory, made in 1396 and captured by the Turks from the Emperor Sigismund at the Battle of Nicopolis. *National Museum, Budapest*

45 (below right) Western Saddle of Baroque Period

Overleaf:

46 (above) Dressage on Black Andalusian Stallion, late Eighteenth Century
Engraving by J. Froschel junior

47 (below) Dressage Work on the Pillars, with Andalusian/Neapolitan Stallion, late Eighteenth Century
Engraving by J. Froschel junior

Overleaf:

48 (above)
The Spanish Riding
School, Vienna, in
1826
A. Kuntz

49 (below)
The Spanish Riding
School Today

50
French Light-horse Trooper
Early Seventeenth Century.
He is still wearing a cuirass,
the last vestige of armour.
From a lithograph by F.
Gerasch.
National Museum, Budapest

51
Austrian Dragoon of the
Early Nineteenth Century

Asia had therefore been preponderant in the Levant before the time of the Mameluke *putsch*.

This penetration over the centuries by Turks meant that from the ninth century onward a Turkish minority had been able to seize power now and again. The Ayyubid dynasty itself was of Turkish origin, and so had been that of the Tulunids (868–905). Like the Mamelukes themselves (who were to reign from 1250 to 1517), they brought many distinctively Turkish political and social influences to bear which reflected conditions of life in Central Asia, now to be imposed on the Arab society. The Fatimid Caliphs (969–1171) were supported by the Turks, and in other countries too the Turkish minorities managed to seize power. Thus in 1017 Mahmud of Ghazni, descendant of a slave bodyguard, became ruler of Afghanistan and Persia. Indeed, this syndrome of seizure of power by Turkish minorities amounts almost to a historical rule, so that historians have attributed a 'state-founding capacity' to this people. But if we take into account that the other nomadic stock-breeding peoples of Asia, such as Huns, Ephthalites, Mongols, have played a similar part in the history of India, of China, of Manchuria, etc., then this assumption can scarcely be valid for the Turks alone, but for all who practised the original Turkish way of life.

The prime reason for the important political function of the Turks lay simply in the fact that at that time the epitome of a ruling class was conceived of as a mounted warrior. We shall often have occasion to remark on the ideological side-effect of the equestrian civilization. It had occurred before and was to occur again, many times over.

These Mamelukes came from Central Asia, and their ancestors had migrated westward in successive waves until at the end of the twelfth century they were settled on the steppes east of the Carpathians. Their way of life and economic structure were no different from those of other mounted nomads; their own name for themselves was Kuman, but neighbouring peoples called them by many different names; in Greek, 'Turks', in Slavonic tongues 'Polovec', in German 'Falb', and in Hungarian 'Kun'. They made repeated attempts to cross the Carpathians and press on westward, but all were opposed by the Hungarian army, and frustrated.

The Mongols led by Batu Khan into Eastern Europe dealt a mortal blow to this steppe people in 1240. Part of the dispersed Kuman army under their prince Kuthen requested leave to pass into Hungary, and such of the remainder as had not been massacred or enslaved sought safety in alliance with the Mongols. Despite all their misfortunes, however, this nation of horsemen had preserved, together with their military virtues, a love of liberty. Just as they had been unable to reconcile this with life under the Mongols, so they found it impossible to adapt themselves either to the world of Islam, or to that of Christendom.

The admission of the Kumans to Hungary led to an internal political crisis, with tragic results, which were hastened by the battle on the Sajó mentioned above (p. 66). The reason was, once more, a dispute about grazing rights, a commonplace of nomadic history, but this time also about the slave trade and the kidnapping that went with it, combined also with religious intolerance. There were repeated armed clashes. Surprisingly, the Kumans gained a great influence in the political and social life of Hungary in a very short time; so much so that King Stephen V (1270–71) did not attempt—as the Arpad dynasty had done for so many centuries up to his time—to contract a marriage alliance with some royal house of Christendom, but married a Kuman girl and had her crowned queen. Their son Ladislas IV was called "The

Kuman", and when he succeeded to the crown of St Stephen (which he wore from 1272 to 1290), he adopted Kuman clothes, observing Turkish customs, and chose his immediate entourage from among the Kuman nobility. The Papal Legate sent urgent and repeated dispatches to Rome, reporting that the manners of the Kumans were gaining the upper hand, and that the Magyars were turning away from Christianity. But Kuman influence did not stop here; it extended, at least superficially, to the West, where the pointed Kuman cap and long cloak became fashionable.

In Egypt the Turkish conspiracy was touched off by the murder of Tur-in-Shah, heir presumptive to the Sultanate, and the last scion of the Ayyubid line. Like the Hungarian King Ladislas IV, he was the child of a Turkish mother, Chadjarat el Dur, by the Sultan Malik Shah. Events in Egypt and Hungary are paralleled also, in so far as in both cases the ruler was murdered by his Turkish subjects.

Tur-in-Shah's orphaned heir arrested Chadjarat el Dur, who had been implicated in the murder of her own son, and shared power with a Turk of noble birth as consort. But their reign was short, because the people would not tolerate a female ruler. The great period of Mameluke rule is undoubtedly represented by the reign of Sultan El Nasser (1291–1341), a son of El Mansour Kalaoun of the Bordj Ogly clan, a slave bodyguard who came to power in 1279. His nickname El Elfi ("Thousand") commemorates the price of one thousand gold pieces for which he changed hands as a slave [and reminds us that Mameluke means literally 'that which is bought and sold' Tr.]. Among the Turks this price was looked on as the measure of the wealth and noble descent of the prisoner, and this was the value all such prisoners retained so long as their identity was known, and they were not too far removed from the original scene of capture. While their status was still to some extent that of a hostage, and the possibility existed that their family would ransom them, the price paid really represented the option to obtain a much greater sum by way of ransom. [In this respect the slave-markets of the Turkish—or Turkish-dominated—world that eventually stretched as far west as Tangier, and always handled a certain proportion of West European—even British—'goods', differed radically from the slave markets of the ancient world, or even those of the Black Sea area, where in the early Middle Ages Varangian traders had brought Irish slaves for sale to the Arabs. In the old markets there had been no such 'fringe benefits', and the price of the anonymous slave was fixed solely by the potential of the man as, say, a swordsman or a wrestler, a labourer or a musician, and of the girl by her probable worth in bed. Tr.] The great sum paid for Kalaoun reflects the fortune which a feudal lord among these nomads possessed. It fell to the lot of that late scion of a highly respected Central Asian stock, El Nasser, to restore the Arab Empire, the legacy of the Prophet, to its ancient glory. But this involved also transplanting the equestrian civilization of Turkestan to an alien soil.

The best authorities for the reign of El Nasser are Ibn Batuta, Abu Bekr ibn Bedr, Makrizi, and El Damiri. The French author Perron made a special study of their contents in so far as they concern horsemanship, studying the relevant manuscripts in the library of Cairo at the beginning of the first century. His work has since been forgotten. The present writer found a digest of it in a German review of the 1850's. As such, the digest hardly fulfils the requirements of a source such as is demanded by the disciplines of modern scholarship; it nevertheless sheds much valuable light on Arab practice of the medieval period.

Horse-breeding by the Arabs, at any rate in terms of quantity, had not in El Nasser's time attained the standards of Central Asia. Even though the Bactrian horse had been acclimatized for two thousand years in the Near East and North Africa, so that the Roman Empire and later Western Europe had drawn their *materia generosa* from thence, this did not represent progress from the point of view of the Arab horseman. In general horse-breeding, riding and driving (there was very little driving) in this region, as well as fighting and games on horseback, were much the same as they had been in antiquity. One instance of this, among others, is the late adoption of the stirrup. Whereas Western horsemen had from the tenth century onward all adopted the stirrup, originally introduced by the Avars and again by the Magyars, the only people in the Arab world to use it were persons of Turkish origin, as late as the twelfth century. This may not seem so important today, but it has its significance in terms of world history, for at the time of the Arab expansion in Europe the West owed its military superiority to the more modern equipment of its cavalry, including stirrups. There can be no doubt at all that the political and cultural history of Europe would have taken quite another turn if Islam had then (say in the days of Charlemagne) got the upper hand.

The Arabs as Horse-breeders

The Arabs, like the Turks of Turkestan, were primarily nomad shepherds. The conspicuous difference is in the relatively small number of horses kept in proportion to other livestock. An Arab owning great herds of sheep and camels might have no more than four or five horses. Mahomet himself had a hundred sheep and sixty camels, but only seven horses. This is a consequence of the fact, mentioned earlier, that the Arab countries, including the Moghreb, lie outside the post-glacial boundaries of the wild-horse habitat.

For this reason even at the present day the manner of keeping horses, both in the Near East and in North Africa, is the manner characteristic of settled farmers, even though the Bedouin way of life is entirely nomadic. The Bedouin (and the Touaregs in the Sahara) keep their horses either near the tents or sometimes actually in the tents. They are hand-fed on cereals, gruel, milk, dates, even fish and meat, as well as the scraps of the master's meal. Meat as a food is considered especially important, because according to Arab ideas it induces courage.

Despite the wide difference between the Turkish and the Arab method of keeping horses—which is due primarily, of course, to the fact that the Turkish technique presupposes a supply of grass, which no pasture in the Arab world affords —signs of Central Asian influence appeared early. According to Islamic doctrine, it is an offence to sell a horse to an unbeliever, a foreigner, or any foe of Islam. This is on a par with the ban on horse exports by certain mounted nomad rulers. This dogma went so far that in Egypt down to the reign of Mehemet Ali (1805–46) no Frank and no Jew might ride a horse in public. The use of the Turkish loanword *at* in the enormous Arabic vocabulary of synonyms for 'horse' is also significant. The ordinary Arab word for horse in general, *faras*, is replaced by the Turkish term *atik* when referring to a well-bred animal, and the word has overtones suggesting purification and pure blood. A half-bred horse by a blood stallion is called *hedjin*, but if half-bred out of a blood mare, then *mukrif*. There are abundant sources to prove that these expressions were already current in Mahomet's day.

With the accession of El Nasser a new era in Arabian horse-breeding began. This far-sighted and highly gifted ruler was interested in everything that could be called progress. He was also an enthusiast in the matter of blood-stock, and open to new ideas that might be conducive to the improvement of cavalry technique, communications, and equestrian sports. The first years of his reign were devoted to warfare by way of consolidating his power. After seeing off the Mongol invaders and disposing of the Mameluke sultans, as traditional enemies, he began the re-organization of his kingdom. There is an old saying *cuius regio, huius religio* that is valid for the fifty-year reign of El Nasser. His reforms left abiding traces in many spheres of Arab life.

If his father and predecessor had preferred the Barka horse, El Nasser ibn Kalaoun promoted the use of those pure-bred Arab horses which were then bred principally by two Syrian desert tribes, the Beni Fadl and the Muhanna; both tribes came originally from Tajikistan, having migrated to Syria some three centuries earlier.

El Nasser devoted enormous energy and huge sums of money to the purchase of blood-horses. His agents were perpetually on tour, sending him regular reports of the stock available from horse-breeding tribes. He set high standards, being himself such a connoisseur of horses. If he once set his heart on an *atik*, he would stop at nothing to acquire it. Granted his enormous riches, and the extraordinary devotion of the Arabs to their horses, it is not surprising that some of the prices paid were astronomical. Kalaoun in his day had paid 5000 drachmae for an outstanding Barka horse, but El Nasser was to pay as much as seventy or eighty thousand; often, indeed, up to a hundred thousand. Mostly the money was paid in gold dirhems, and over and above this the vendor fitted out with a complete suit of clothes and his wives regaled with sweetmeats. There was hardly a tribe in all Arabia that could not boast of having sold this prince a horse.

He was especially interested in breeding problems, and made a point of visiting the leading sires at all the studs, witnessing the covering of the mares in person. If a mare were proved in foal he had to be the first to be notified, and he awaited the birth of the foal with almost childish impatience.

What is of supreme importance is that El Nasser set up a special department which maintained a register and Stud Book of pure-bred horses. So today strains of Arabian horse which are known under the collective term Kehailan, such as the O'Bayan, Seglawi, Hamdani, and Habdan, can trace their ancestry back to the days of El Nasser. Since his time it has become customary that the serving of a pure-bred mare should be witnessed by a committee, and witnesses are also summoned for the birth of a foal. Progeny of a mare which have been foaled other than before witnesses are not recognized as pure-bred, and are designated *kadisl*—that is, crossbred. It is by such means that the Arab horse has been able to preserve the eminent characteristics of its Turanian ancestors down to our own day.

Together with the expanded breeding of the pure strain of horses, there were other extraordinary developments in the field of horsemanship. Close by El Nasser's court at Cairo there was stabling on a luxurious scale for some three thousand horses. There were race-tracks with ornamental trees, fountains and grandstands, dressage arenas, and every facility for cavalry exercises and mounted sports. We may mention specifically the Maidan el Nasri for mounted spectacles and equestrian sports, the Maidan el Mahari for breaking colts, the Maidan el Kalah for horse-racing, and the Maidan el Kabak for cavalry exercises, which included archery from the saddle. Kabak is the Turkish word for a pumpkin. The target used was a gold or silver cage in the shape of a pumpkin, and containing a dove, which the competitors had to shoot at full gallop.

El Nasser took great pains to arouse interest in the Arab horse among his people. It was customary to brand yearlings in the nomad manner, and the operation took place with some solemnity, in public accompanied by the formal gift of some of the yearlings. It was a mark of especial favour to receive an Arab yearling, and most of them went to Mamelukes. Foreigners, and the less esteemed subjects of the Sultan, had to content themselves with Barka colts.

Facsimile of Arabian 'Pedigree'
This is not a pedigree in the Weatherby sense at all: more like an affidavit that the horse was bred in the stud of such and such a tribe.

Besides horse-breeding, this ruler also patronized camel-breeding, likewise favouring Turanian strains. Camel-breeding in the higher branches, as in the case of all domesticated animals, depends on the propagation of certain valued strains, and, for instance, in Central Asia down to this century a select 'Bactrian' two-humped camel has been bred for transport purposes alongside a one-humped riding camel, both by the Turkomans. Of the latter, a refined variant is dispersed through the Near East, known in Arabia as Mahran and in North Africa as Mehari. The racing camels bred by El Nasser and known as *Badjdah* could match horses for speed.

Here we may mention a curious fact in the history of warfare. The Arabs used their pure-bred horses just as the Western knights used the destrier—as a charger exclusively in battle—apart from its use as a racehorse. Generally the Arabian warrior rode a camel on the march and only mounted his horse immediately before going into action. The difference was that the Arab war horse was by custom a mare, because stallions made too much noise.

When El Nasser died there were 4800 horses and 5000 camels in his stables. Even though his immediate successors did not keep up his expensive hobby, they kept along the lines of his more important innovations.

The ascendancy of the Turkish Mamelukes did not in any case last long. In 1384 a new Turkish group, the Circassian Guard, seized power. One of them, Sultan Barkouk, known as 'El Malik el Zahar'—that is, "The Glorious King"—was the first of a dynasty of twenty-six Circassian Mamelukes to reign.

Under Barkouk's rule Central Asian traditions of horsemanship bloomed anew. His passion for stockbreeding is proved by his ownership of seven thousand horses and fifteen thousand camels. The codification of the rules of racing is also associated with his name. At that time the traditions of horsemanship had taken firm root in all ranks of Arab society, as is proved by the writings of the Arabic historian Makrizi (d. 1442) alone.

Early in the sixteenth century the Osmanli Turks put an end to the hegemony of the Circassians, and Sultan Selim I (1512–20) forced the last Mameluke prince to abdicate, so that Cairo and the whole Arab caliphate fell under the rule of Constantinople. In order to have done once and for all with the power of the Mamelukes which had endured for three centuries, their leaders were invited by the Turks to a feast and thereafter murdered—all except one who managed to mount his horse and, leaping over a high wall, made his escape. The memory of this feat lingered for many generations as a legend, and the same story was acted out again in the days of Mehemet Ali.

The Turks revoked the centuries-old Arab embargo on the export of horses, and henceforward Arabian horses were to be seen in the stables of the sultans of Constantinople, and of his pashas and beys. In the Turkish Empire Arabia figured as the reservoir of the noble *bedevi at* (Bedouin horse). With the Turkish expansion into Europe the Arab horse also won further renown in the West. Europe was then in a posture of defence *vis-à-vis* the advance of the Osmanlis, which involved changing over to light cavalry instead of chivalry, and this led to a great demand for 'Turkish' horses (by which was meant Turkish and also Arab horses).

The Arabian Horseman

In the mass of writing by Europeans who in the nineteenth century travelled in Arab lands in search of horses we find frequent mention of a peculiarity of Arab horsemanship, or rather horsemastership: to the Arab, his pure-bred horse was one of the family, and shared the tent with him. These animals are besides extraordinarily tame and intelligent, and deserve the care which is lavished on them. A high-bred horse is to the Arab a property whose worth can only be matched in refined gold, weight for weight, and on which all his pride is set. In it he sees the incarnation of all his skill in breeding. The Arab never has a rough word for his horse, and he could never bring himself to strike one.

Thus to him the horse is a domestic animal in the narrowest sense of the word; it shares his dwelling, whether this be a house or a tent, and is only to be compared, in Western terms, with the pet dog. It patiently allows the children to play between its feet, and when it lies down it allows its master to recline against it. It is also the watchdog of the black tents, and their inmates. Its acute senses apprise it at once of the approach of strangers, or of any danger, and it sounds the alarm by snorting, or by other conspicuous behaviour.

Of course, many anecdotes of miraculous performances by Arab horses are sheer fantasy, but many have been attested by reliable witnesses.

The Arab horse, with its utter emotional dependence on and loyalty to its master, is perfectly aware of what goes on when the owner is in treaty to sell it. It shows its unease by restless behaviour, threatening the buyer with teeth and hooves, so that he cannot approach it. But once the deal is clinched its behaviour alters; accepting the inevitable, it hangs its head and lets the new owner lead it away in all obedience. Cases have been known in which the rider has lain down in the shade of the horse to escape the singeing rays of the sun, while the horse stands rigid as a statue, watching over its resting master. There are horses, too, which in consideration for the squeamishness of the rider have refrained from performing their natural functions so long as he is in the saddle. But it is in perilous situations that the almost human intelligence of the Arab horse comes to the fore. Its spirit of sacrifice then becomes heroic. Whereas other horses wounded in battle run madly away in terror and pain, throwing their riders or rolling on the ground, the Arab horse endures to the last breath. According to one report, an Arab horse whose rider had fallen wounded to the ground picked him up with its teeth by his clothes and saved him out of the mêlée.

The legendary belief in the extraordinary powers of the Arab horse has also left traces in mystical belief. Thus the Arabs are convinced that no evil spirit can approach a man seated on a high-bred horse, or any house in which such a horse is stabled. Among this legendary lore coat-colour plays a large part. Greys are the mount of kings and princes, black horses are to be ridden at night, roans are the best for hunting, light bays are especially swift. Apart from colour, distinguishing marks—stars, blazes, socks, and the like—together with the partings of the hair, have a special significance. The Arab recognizes eleven such marks which have mysterious properties.

The very rare double, horn-like protuberance on the forehead is especially baneful, auguring misfortune and death to the rider. Horses born with this blemish are called *kabr maftuh* (open grave). Just as bad is the *bokh nikhan*, a horse with two hair-partings (vortices) on the cheek. White socks are thought to indicate the individual performance of the horse; three white legs are the most prized, but four mean that the horse is completely inferior.

After all that we have said above about the Arabs, their horses, and their tradition of horsemanship, it seems superfluous to adduce further proof of the enormous reserve of equestrian lore in the Near East and its ultimate origins in the traditions of Central Asia. Arab horsemanship fits in like a link in the chain of historical development whereby those long-dead nomadic herdsmen bequeathed their legacy of horsemanship to the Near East, and thence to all the world.

Horsemanship in Central Asia

After their settlement in the Carpathian region the Magyars were the most westerly of all nomadic herdsmen. The westward penetration of Oriental fashions in war and communications came primarily through Hungary. For our knowledge of the development of the equestrian civilization, therefore, Hungarian historical documents are invaluable.

The Magyars are the only pastoral people who possess written evidence of their centuries of nomadic stock-breeding. These documents have a bearing on the horseman's way of life, which was uniform throughout the vast area between the Great Wall of China and the river Leitha, and which is founded on the stock of the Sayan reindeer-culture. Hitherto historians (with some notable exceptions) have hardly taken account of the great significance for humanity of technical progress in the field of horse transport: and so it comes about that these documents have not yet been fully exploited, and the archaeological material that matches them has been somewhat neglected.

This material comes primarily from burial sites, dating from the era of settlement by the Magyar horsemen. It tells us much about their daily life, and also something of their beliefs, and hence of their intellectual life in general.

Ethnologically and linguistically, the Magyars belong to the Finno-Ugric family, and had a prehistory of hunting and fishing. Apparently their original home lay somewhere on the East European Plain, which was woodland interspersed with grassland. The horse would only be known to them as game. In the first centuries of the Christian era these people came in contact with Turkic tribes of pastoralists, the former probably becoming subject to the latter. There then began a process which has often been repeated in the history of mankind: the subject people took over the more advanced way of life from their overlords, but did not in the end adopt their language. The Hungarian tribes, having finally coalesced as one ethnic unit, became an equestrian people with a 'Turkish' pastoral culture but a Finno-Ugric language. Even today the anthropologist can trace these two threads in their make-up.

Attitude to the Horse

Traces of the fifteen-centuries-old Asiatic tradition of the Turks are hard to find today, due to the cultural attrition of the endless wars which the mounted warriors waged among themselves.

What few remain, either in the form of inscriptions or of folklore, tell us something not only of early Turkish history but of the mental attitude of the equestrian peoples. The oldest writing by Asiatic Turks, known as the Runestone of Orkon, is especially valuable (it is not, of course, a Runic inscription in the sense usually understood in a Scandinavian or West Germanic context).

In Mongolia, where nomadic pastoralism began, a prince of the Central Asian Turks, Kagan Bilge, raised a memorial to his brother Kül Tegin on the banks of the river Tola in the eighth century A.D. Inscriptions on the stone mention the Turkish campaigns and the deeds of Kül Tegin. The characteristic esteem of equestrian peoples for the horse shows clearly here. We learn the names of Kül Tegin's horses. In action against Chacha Sengün he rode his bay, Tadik Chur, and when it was killed under him he rode the grey Jamtar; after the loss of this again he fought on, in the saddle of the bright bay Kedimlig, property of Jeginsili Beg. Names are recorded of his grey horses, Basgu, Alp Salchi, Asman, and Ögsis, and his brown horse As. These 'runes' point clearly to the former connection between the Turks and the

Magyars, for such characters were still used for inscriptions by the Sekler of Transylvania in the sixteenth century.

A few lines of the ancient Turkish legend of Köroglu also deal with esteem of the horse. Oral versions of this legend were still current among all Turkish tribes from the Oxus to Syria in the second half of the nineteenth century. According to Vámbéri, it must go back to the time before the dispersal of the Turkish tribes. In it the hero laments the loss of his grey horse Kirat as follows:

> O thou whom I won in Turkestan,
> Come, Kirat, nourished with my life!
> Thou whom the hostile Tekke took from me,
> Come, Kirat, nourished with my life!
> O thou whose bit is heavy as a hundredweight,
> Who cravest no food after a three-day fast,
> Who tirest not after a forty-league march,
> Come, Kirat, nourished with my life!

The line about the bit is not meant to imply that the animal is hard or 'dead' in the mouth, but simply that it is so light-mouthed that the bit is a burden to it. This mental attitude is evident among Magyar horsemen as late as the eighteenth century; when the exiled adherents of Prince Rákóczi were passing through France on their way to Turkey, where they settled, one of them, Kelemen Mikes, kept a diary of his impressions in which he amended the seventeenth-century epigram about England and Italy to read "France is a paradise for women and a hell for horses; Turkey, a paradise for horses and a hell for women".

Of course, this is not quite accurate, since then at the French Court and among the upper classes generally horsemanship was of a high standard; the 'chivalrous' ideology of East and West has seldom been so trenchantly epitomized.

This mental attitude has survived in the East almost into our own day. Taboos of almost religious rigour surrounded it in Central Asia. Among the Siberian Yakuts it was not only forbidden to strike a horse but it was a misdemeanour to speak roughly to one. Among the Kirghiz, according to Radloff, striking another man's horse or making slighting remarks about it was as ill regarded as if the insult had been offered to the man himself. To them the horse was the pearl of creation, and the worth of a man could be expressed in terms of it alone. The dowry, or *Kalim*, was reckoned as so many head of horses, and so was the blood-price, which corresponded to the Anglo-Saxon *weregild*. Atonement for the death of a freeman cost 100 horses, what they called a whole *kun* (drove); for the death of a slave, a woman or a girl, half a kun; for that of a child under ten years, a quarter-kun; and so on. This reverential attitude extended also to mare's milk, to products derived from it, and even to horse-meat. It counted as an insult to set before a distinguished stranger anything but *kumis* (fermented mare's milk), and this had to be offered in a certain ceremonial form (as tea in China). Horse-flesh was chiefly eaten, as archaeological findings confirm, at religious ceremonies, and was part of the ritual of the funeral feast.

As among the Arabs, so among the Hungarians, belief in the supernatural powers of the horse flourished. Thus among the ruins of buildings in Hungarian villages dating to the eleventh century horse-skulls have been found fixed to the timbering of living-rooms; obviously as talismans against evil spirits. Both Hungarian and Arabian customs indicate a common origin in Central Asia.

This extraordinary esteem for the horse among the Turks and those people who took over their traditions hints at a further essential element in equestrian nomadic pastoralism; in the world of the nomad herdsman *mounted* nomadism was the 'higher' life, and for him the horse symbolized not only a superior standard of living, in war and in peace, but was an accessory of the 'superior person' in general.

Like other wandering herdsmen, the Magyars buried their dead with horse and saddlery, which is also a Central Asian custom. It was practised by the reindeer-breeders of Sayan, who used to sacrifice a white reindeer at the graveside. Ethnographic research has long since shown the connection between reindeer-sacrifice and horse-sacrifice. In both cases it is meant to provide the deceased with a mount for his journey in the next world.

This custom was similarly observed throughout the region traversed by the equestrian peoples, from the barrows of Pazyryk to the late medieval burials of Kuman Turks in Hungary. The grave-goods consisted above all of cavalry weapons and equipment: bow, arrows, quiver, valise, saddle, and so on. These are attested by surviving metal parts, such as sword-blades, arrowheads, snaffles, stirrups, as well as the metal ornaments that had once been fixed to saddlery, clothing, and accoutrements.

Among the Hungarians the manner of burying a horseman had its particular symbolism. The horse chosen for burial was beheaded, contrary to the custom observed by previous occupants of the country—Avars, Patzinaks, Uzes, Turks—and only the skull and cannon bones with the feet attached appear in the remains. It is probable they were left attached to the hide, which was stuffed with hay and the simulated horse disposed beside the corpse. Similar customs obtained in Central Asia, widely among breeders of reindeer and horses. Plano Carpini, who at the height of the Mongol invasions visited the Court of the Great Khan on behalf of Pope Innocent IV, described the horse-burials of the Mongols as follows.

> The dead man is laid in the earth with his tent, and provisions and mare's milk beside him. A mare with foal at foot and a saddled and bridled gelding are buried with him. Then they eat another horse, stuff the hide with straw and prop it up on two or four poles, so that in the next world the dead man shall have somewhere to live, a mare to provide milk, a foal to start another herd, and a horse to ride.

The partaking of horse-meat as part of a ritual meal has already been mentioned in connection with the Turks. It is notable that this custom was discarded by such equestrian peoples as were converted to Christianity (less consistently by those converted to Islam). Thus according to Eunodius the Bulgars in their pagan days ate horse-meat. Among the Magyars a reaction towards paganism which led to an uprising in 1063 was symbolized by ostentatious consumption of horse-flesh. [Farther north at exactly the same time the crisis of conversion to Christianity in Scandinavia often pivots on the same ritual point. In Norway an evangelizing king sitting down to feast at a harvest festival with his tenants is constrained, diplomatically, to inhale some of the steam from the cauldron of boiled horse-flesh which is a traditional item on the menu. Before that, missionaries in Anglo-Saxon England had classed hippophagy as equally sinful with idolatry, and 'disguising oneself as an animal'. The horse-meat taboo appears to be stronger the nearer one approaches to the north-west fringe of Europe. Among the ancient Irish and the Highlanders it was absolute in pagan days, and remains so today. *Tr.*]

In order to account for this phenomenon we must look back to the dietary laws embodied in the Old Testament. As codified by Moses, these forbade the eating of those beasts which had cloven hoofs but did not chew the cud; those with solid hoofs or claws; and those which walked on the soles of their feet. This excluded from their diet pigs, equines, dogs, cats, all rodents, monkeys, and bears. There were similar embargoes on the eating of certain species of fish, birds, reptiles, insects, and molluscs. And it was forbidden to drink blood of any origin.

These commandments, taken over by the Christian and Islamic world and very largely observed today, simply did not impinge on the pastoral peoples of the steppe so long as they retained their old shamanistic beliefs. Julianus, a Dominican monk, visiting those Hungarians who had not migrated from their former home in Eastern Europe, noted in 1237: "They do not plant crops, they eat horse and wolf and suchlike meats, they drink mares' milk and blood".

Over and above this there was an emotional current 'away from the horse'. When the horsemen from the East entered the stage of history they were figures of terror for the Western world, to such a degree that the folk-memory of the 'centaurs' was still alive at the time of later invasions, and simply served to reinforce the bogy-image of the Apocalyptic horsemen in the imagination of the now Christian Westerners who had to face them. [We may compare this with an English phenomenon, whereby any dreaded sea-raiders become, in folk-tradition, 'Danes', by analogy with the dreaded 'heathen men' of the ninth century. *Tr.*] It was this image of terror which caused Moses to forbid his people to keep, let alone eat, horses. The Christians who in part conformed to Mosaic law remained *selectively* antagonistic to the mounted archer, even though they were themselves horsemen of a different stamp. The physical image of the Devil in medieval art has certain features in common with the Avar or Magyar mounted archer of real life—aquiline nose, pointed beard and moustaches à la Mephistopheles and all—as the only begetter and model of all sins and vices. He is contrasted, in Western art, with angels symbolizing Christian piety whose physiognomy might be described, in terms of physical anthropology, as 'chocolate-box Nordic'.

Horse-breeding

As horse-breeders in the Carpathian region the Magyars had for centuries recourse to wild blood. This is almost inherent in the conditions of nomadic herd-breeding, since the life of domestic horses on open range is so little different from that of the wild herds, where these exist. As often as tame mares ran away, wild horses were caught, and, if not broken, used for breeding.

At Leka the steward of the Palatine, Thomas Nádasdy, writes to his master in 1537 that he is sending back the stallion drafted to the herd, for fear the wild mares will knock him about, and regrets it is not possible to catch the said mares as ordered. (Note 11.) Nearly forty years later, in 1576, the municipal accounts of Eperjes show payment of wages to certain men for taming and herding wild horses. (Note 12.) As late as 1647 the estate accounts of Sárvár show money paid out for snares for wild horses. (Note 13.)

Later on they are mentioned only in connection with gear made from wild-horse leather, or hair. The inventory of Count Szapáry in 1671 mentions ropes made of wild-horse hair. (Note 14.) Likewise at Lublo-Szepesvárer the effects of the deceased

Count Stephan Csáky in 1685 include a wild-horse tail, probably used as a fly-whisk.

The French knight, Bertrandon de la Broquière, has something to say of Hungarian horse-keeping methods, as he was on his way back from Constantinople in 1432. "[At Szegedin] I saw"—his diary notes—

a herd of wild horses brought in for sale, which are yet well able to be haltered and tamed, which made a remarkable sight. It was told us, that if any man had a mind to buy three or four thousand horses, in this town he might do it. Horses here are so cheap, that anyone can buy a fine stallion for ten Hungarian gulden. . . . From Szegedin I came to a town [Kecskemet?] and the way thither led all through a fair plain wherein the horses like wild game live quite free, one herd beside the other. This is the cause why so many are to be seen in the mart of Szegedin. . . . At Pest there is great plenty of horsedealers; if a man wished to buy two thousand good horses, surely he could buy them here. They are sold by the stableful—that is, ten at a time. Every stableful costs two hundred gulden. I also saw horses that would fetch this price between two or three of them. The most part of them come from the borders over against Transylvania, in the mountains. There is excellent pasture for them there. Their fault is, they are somewhat froward, and principally very awkward to shoe.

The Arab traveller Ibn Batuta describes the horse-stock of the Turks in Central Asia thus (fourteenth century): "This is a land most rich in horses . . . the kind called in Egypt *akadis* (cross-bred) is one of the sources of their husbandry. They have as many of them as we have sheep, if not more. Many a Turk has thousands."

Today it would be vain to search for traces of horse-breeding on such a vast scale in Hungary. The whole technique of stock-breeding has altered, so that there are no studs kept on open range, and there are hardly any horses left that winter out, or that could do so. We can nowadays speak only of the Asiatic influence on Hungarian horse-herding of former times.

Radloff, who in the mid-nineteenth century investigated the Kazakh and Kirghiz manner of horse-breeding, describes it thus: A herd amounts most often to fifty animals, of which nine or ten are mares, each with a foal less than a year old, the rest being their yearling and older followers. The stallion as leader keeps the herd together, and also stands sentry over it. He has no fear of wolves, and it is only rarely that they manage to snatch a foal from him. And it must be a bold wolf at that. The stallion is ready to fight not only predators, but also rivals. The arrival of a strange stallion is the signal for a fight to the death. The young colts of his own herd have to keep apart from the mares, in a group by themselves. The fillies do not stand to the stallion until their sixth year, but even so the instinctive aversion to inbreeding comes into play: when his own daughters come of age the stallion drives them out of the herd.

The composition of the herds seen by Broquière, we may assume, was similar to that observed by Radloff, because the life of wild and half-wild herds is determined inexorably by the instinct to survive and perpetuate themselves, without which these equines would not have survived for thousands of years. When he writes that in the great plains the herds on free range grazed side by side we can only assume that the majority of the stallions had been castrated, for we have no reason to doubt his credibility. Otherwise he would probably have reported that half the equine population of the *puszta* spent their time fighting each other, that he saw many sick and wounded horses driven out of the herd, and that the roadside was littered with the remains of dead colts. Not only was a surplus of stallions unwanted by the breeders, it was also, as is the case with American mustangs, a plague to the country-side. The unsuccessful ones, driven off the grazing-grounds, lured away mares from the farms, and those of travellers. For this reason they were treated as beasts of prey; hunted and shot. And so gelding became an indispensable procedure in this kind of breeding.

The earliest record of castrating colts comes likewise from the pen of a Western observer who had a good knowledge of the Hungarian horse-economy. Marx Fugger, who published a book in 1584 dealing with the reorganization of Western cavalry, did not, indeed, recommend the adoption of this custom, because he con-sidered geldings to be lacking in courage and unsuitable as chargers; yet he finds it necessary to mention that the Scythians and Sarmatians had once gelded their horses, as did the Turks in his day, as well as the Tartars and the Muscovites, and that on their campaigns the Magyars rode geldings almost exclusively.

The Chertomlyk Vase
     Frieze of Scythian herdsmen preparing to cast a colt for castration

It is fairly clear that this custom of the nomadic breeders also goes back to the reindeer-herdsmen. But among them the operation up to the most recent times was performed in the most primitive way—by severing the seminal cord with the teeth. The illustration on the famous Chertomlyk Vase from the Crimea, with its Hellenis-tic fringe showing Scythians preparing to cast a colt, quite in the modern manner, with ropes that are not shown in the engraving, does not show the actual orchi-dectomy, which was bloodless, being performed by crushing the cord with a wooden mallet. Just such tools are limned in the armorial bearings of István Várallyai in 1599: he was master colt-gelder to the Prince of Transylvania. (Note 15.)

Taxonomy of Hungarian Horses

We have hardly any usable descriptions of the Oriental rider or his horse dating from the period when the art of riding began to come into its own in the West, nor are they represented in the art of the period. Part of the reason may be that those circles, restricted in antiquity, which were masters of the arts of writing and drawing or sculpture were those furthest removed from the practice of horsemanship. Be that as it may, the representational art of the equestrian peoples—such as is evident, for instance, in the tombs of Pazyryk—was entering a declining phase, and would soon perish utterly, after going through a phase of the formally fantastic, rather than the naïve realism exemplified in Plate 5. After their adoption of Christianity, and therewith of Western cultural features, the Hungarians had to grope their way for a long time to full participation in the Occidental world of art and literature.

The written documents of the centuries after the settlement of Pannonia by the Magyars are the work of clerics with an alien point of view, and the visual art dating from this period, where it is relevant, has been painted and drawn and sculpted, engraved and beaten out in metal, by artists and craftsmen who were Westerners, from the outside. Disregard of this fact, especially as it affected and purported to depict the world of the Magyar horseman, has been the source of much error.

The Magyar horses were small, the average not exceeding 14 hands. They retained the lightly built frame characteristic of the half-bred horse, century after century, as is confirmed by archaeological evidence, as well as by medieval documents. The same tendency is indicated by the surviving bits and snaffles of medieval date, which by their dimensions were made for small horses with narrow jaws. This all points to the fact that during the Middle Ages the Magyars did not use a cross of heavy, 'cold' blood—did not ride the destrier of chivalry. Research has also established the Tarpan-type of the medieval Magyar horse, which was to be expected given the nature of the wild-horse population at that time. In the marginal area surrounding the Carpathians, especially in Carpatho-Ukraine and Eastern Transylvania, where before the Second World War the old, small stamp of 'native' horse was still being bred, horses with Tarpan characteristics often occurred, showing the skull-form, the dun colour, and dark eel-stripe of the Tarpan, as well as its general proportions.

Ebhardt considers the Tarpan a mixed form. The 'wild blood-horse' living close to the tropical zone was forced northward towards the end of the last interglacial (by drought?), at the same time as the pony types migrated southward. There thus occurred wild hybrids, leading to much wider distribution of the southern form, if diluted with northern blood. This state of affairs was obviously still in force after the domestication of the Pony, and was indeed assisted by deliberate human intervention.

Hungarian written sources establish that:

Among the gifts made by Hungarian princes and kings, mostly to foreign rulers, splendidly caparisoned horses, chiefly grey, figure. In medieval documents we often read of outstanding horses, far-famed, of great price, known by such epithets as *capitalis, electus, formosus, domino aptus*, etc. Now, what would be meant, in the context of the time, by these terms 'capital, hand-picked, handsome, fit for a lord' (*Urnok valo* in Hungarian)? A chronicle of the year 1380 describes the Magyar horses as small, strong, and swift, but those of the nobility are described as tall and handsome. (Note 16.)

These data fit in fascinatingly with facts arising from the results of recent archaeological research by the Russians. V. I. Calkin reported in 1966, in his work on the animal husbandry of Central Asia in the Scythian period, that the tall, 'quality' stamp of horse (which may be identified with the Akhal-Tekke breed of today, and occurred in the whole region between the Altai Mountains and the north littoral of the Black Sea) was the mount of the ruling class. But the great mass of horses were of another stamp, not being above 13 hands 3 in. in height, with much heavier bone.

The taxonomy of early Hungarian horses is on a par with that of the horses found

MAMALVCKE

II

Etching by Daniel Hofer (seventeenth century) in the National Museum, Budapest
Misleading illustration, common in early Western works, showing Mamelukes riding
cold-blooded horses of a type that did not exist in the Islamic world.

at Pazyryk. Here too the foundation stock was ponies, more or less graded-up by a greater or smaller dash of Turanian blood; only here the foundation of 'common' blood was Pony, not Taki. The Hungarian horse inherited overwhelmingly the conformation, the temperament, and the characteristics of both these original types in varying degrees according to the laws of heredity.

This means in practice that at the time of settlement in the Carpathian region most of the horses approached the average height of the Oriental races, and like the second and third groups found at Pazyryk had characteristics proper to both types. On the one hand there were to be found tall horses of general 'Turanian' appearance, assigned to the first group (by Vitt), and on the other, small Tarpans which correspond to Group Four.

In Hungarian horse-breeding there were—though to a lesser degree—other influences, and above all that of the Taki (the wild horse of Asia). As we have hinted earlier, this influence came into play during the Mongol invasions and those of the Kuman Turks. For a long time the documentary material cites this 'Kuman' type as the opposite of the Tarpan type. Miklós Oláh, historian of the sixteenth century, describes this horse as half-wild, with a big head, which points to a high proportion of Taki blood. But it has obviously left no trace behind it.

As the Osmanli Turks advanced westward the influence of the Arabian horse made itself felt. At the same time the Hungarian language was gaining ground, orally and in writing. The earlier Latin epithets *formosus, electus, capitalis*, and *principalis* were now replaced by the Hungarian word *főló*, which is the same as 'capital'. It implied a horse of quality, suitable for warfare, fit to carry a man-at-arms or a lord; it also meant the Turanian horse.

From the names used for horses in Hungary one can often deduce their origin or the identity of the former owner. Thus in the accounts of Ferenc Nádasdy for 1570 his horses are divided into three groups: 'Capital', 'Rackers', and 'Common'. The capital horses bear such names as Husain and Harambasha, whereas such names are not to be found among either the rackers or the common nags. (Note 17.)

The identity of the Oriental with the capital horse is most apparent in the letters of Ferenc Bebek. In answer to the request of Thomas Nádasdy to "send him two horses picked from the Turkish booty, one good racker and one capital" he says that among the loot there is nothing of that description, but "if we have nothing of the sort in hand, we have some Turkish prisoners for whom I can demand as ransom the stamp of horse required (capital)". (Note 18.) Ransom at this period was customarily asked in terms of horses.

In documents from Hungary at this time the demand for capital horses of Turkish breeding frequently occurs. So also in Poland. When the Polish prince Sigismund visited Buda in 1506 he brought with him 'badavia'—that is, *bedevi at* or Bedouin horses—from Poland, and these are shown in his account books. No doubt the reason was the shortage of capital horses of Hungarian breeding, one result of the war between the Hungarians and the Turks which lasted uninterrupted for decades. (Note 19.)

Besides Arabs from Turkish sources, these horses also reached Eastern Europe by a shorter route north from the Caspian and Black seas. As time went on the provenance of capital horses shifted farther and farther eastward. In the days of Broquière they still came from Transylvania, a hundred years later from Moldavia, then from Bessarabia, from Podolia, from Circassia, and from Tartary. Ad-

52 (above)
North American
Cowboys driving
Hereford Cattle
Railhead

53 (below)
Breeding Herds
Cattle and Horse
on the South
American Pampa

54 (right)
Argentine Gaucho

55 (below)
A good Western 'Cutting
Horse' at Work

56
An Arab stallion
from the Stud of
Abbas Pasha I,
Khedive of Egypt
1848–54.

57
Mameluke on Arab
stallion.
Lithograph by
Carle Vernet

58   Sultan Osman II, called "Genc Osman", on a Grey Arab Miniature from the
Seraglio, Istanbul

mittedly by then this stock was not nearly so uniform in type as it had been in the days when El Nasser with his deliberate breeding policy instituted his Stud Book for Arab horses, but still the high proportion of pure blood was unmistakable.

Marx Fugger describes such a horse, brought back from Poland by Henry III of France in 1574 and offered by him to Fugger for 2000 crowns. The object of this offer, which in its time attracted the attention of all Europe, is described by eye-witnesses as follows: "Turk mare, blaze on face, black mane, three white socks, eel-stripe." [The body colour most likely to occur in conjunction with the black mane and eel-stripe (which is a Tarpan feature) is dun. The white feet are characteristic of the modern Arab, but even more so of the modern *part-bred* Arab. Tr.]

We may also mention the purchases of horses made almost annually by the Transylvanian Prince George Rákóczi in Moldavia. He himself drew up the code of procedure for his agents when buying Turkish and Moldavian horses; its eight points taken together show what was expected of a quality horse then. (Note 20.)

The preference for Oriental stock is proved also by the inventory of Count Adam Batthyányi's horses, 1642. (Note 21.) Besides Hungarian-bred horses he owned Turkish, Moldavian, Podolian, Circassian and Tartar horses, as well as one or two 'Spanish'—no doubt among the earliest Andalusians in Eastern Europe. Evidence of direct importation from Turania was still to be found in the last century in some Hungarian and Transylvanian private studs. The Czindery establishment, noted for its excellent horses, boasted of its Turanian foundation stock. (Note 22.)

Summarizing, it can be established that the refreshment of Hungarian stock in the Middle Ages, contrary to what is often supposed, was exclusively of Oriental origin. The import of Western horses, and their use in breeding, as we shall show below, did not begin until the eighteenth century. More convincing is the verdict of a contemporary on Oriental and Occidental horses. When King Ferdinand of Naples sent one of his equerries, trained in the Spanish School, to Hungary, to introduce Western dressage methods at the royal Court, King Matthias (1458–90) sent him back with this message:

> With the horses which we trained ourselves we defeated the Getae [Turks], subjected Serbia, and vanquished all before us, honorably by means of our own horses. We have no desire for horses that hop about with bent hocks in the Spanish fashion, we do not want them even as a pastime, still less for serious business. What we want are horses that stride out and stand firm when required.

This is indeed a striking instance of the antithesis between the Eastern and Western conceptions of horsemanship.

Riding and Driving

But what gave Hungarian horsemanship its specifically Central Asian character was not breeding alone. East of the frontier between the two traditions that ran north and south through Europe, there was so much that pointed to the common heritage of nomadic pastoralism. All the accoutrements of riding and driving, transport technique and the art of war, have their roots in this common way of life, traces of which were to be seen in later centuries.

In an earlier chapter (1) we mentioned the origin of the wooden saddle of the Asiatic horseman, among the reindeer-breeders of Sayan. For the typological history of the two kinds of saddle and their relationship there is an objective unequivocal proof: George Almásy shows in his journal of travel the make of saddle in use among the Kazakhs and Kirghiz, which is a faithful copy of the reindeer-saddle—the difference is only in their use. Among the Kirghiz they were for children of two to five years old. It was possible to lash two rods to the crossed saddle-forks in such a way as to afford a safe seat for children. The same pattern of saddle was in use until recent times in Hungary among the shepherds, who called it a *tergenye* and used it on their pack-horses.

The archaeologist Gyula László dealt (1943) with the technical aspects of the saddles, remains of which were found in the horse-burials of Hungary, trying to reconstruct from them Avar and Magyar saddles. His attempts were very illuminating. From them it appeared, not only that the pattern of the Avar and the Hungarian saddles was identical, but that they also coincided with the make of saddle used by peoples of Turkic and Mongolian culture at the present day. László in his essay also has some interesting ethnological observations to make. He points out that this pattern of saddle has remained unmodified in Hungary since the time of the Settlement, and was still being turned out by craftsmen members of the traditional saddlers' guilds until the outbreak of the First World War. The last of these saddles was made in 1920, and has been preserved in the museum at Tisza-füred.

The essential components of the Oriental wooden saddle are the two bars which run parallel to the sides of the horse, joined by arches front and rear. The rider sat on a leather sling stretched between these arches. His feet were in two iron stirrups, the leathers of which were attached to the bars. The manner of saddling up the horse also remained unchanged for centuries. Its back was first covered with a felt rug or with a sheepskin, fleece uppermost; the saddle was made fast over it with a girth, and held in place by a breastplate before and a breeching or crupper behind. The seat was mostly reinforced with a cushion over which a fur (bearskin among the rich) was spread which afforded considerable comfort to the rider. Certainly the modern saddle is more pleasing to the eye, and perhaps more comfortable, but we can safely say that as regards practical utility and cheapness no saddle excels the Oriental wooden pattern, particularly taking into account that it avoids pressure on the spine of the horse. Its wide distribution shows its utility as an essential item of equipment for the extraordinary feats of horsemanship that have been performed by all the riding peoples of the East.

The Eastern style of riding was also utterly different from that of the West. Whereas the Western horseman, even when using the 'knight's' saddle, simply forced his extended legs outward and downward into the stirrups—that is to say, virtually stood in them—the Oriental horseman rode with a short leather and bent knee, literally *in* the saddle. The Vienna illuminated chronicle shows the difference between the two styles very strikingly, in those miniatures where Eastern and Western horsemen figure together.

However, realistic presentation of the posture of the Hungarian man-at-arms is somewhat dubious. Even among the Hungarian armoured cavalry, the stiffly extended leg was not customary. According to Broquière, the Hungarians rode with a short stirrup 'in the Turkish manner'. The master who illuminated the Vienna chronicle was probably at pains to emphasize the Christian—hence Western—quality of the Hungarian knight, even by exaggerating details.

Horse-stock, riding equipment, and the technique of equitation naturally all had their influence on performance. The horseman of the West was not as yet nearly capable of the long marches and the hours in the saddle which were common practice in the East. When in 1301 a Hungarian embassy offered the Crown to the Bohemian King Vaclav in Prague, he rejected it on the following grounds, according to the *Rhyming Chronicle* of Ottokar von Steier:

> Then said King Wenceslas:
> "And if I were to take it
> I should be robbing the Hungarians;
> For however I hastened
> So it seems most like to me,
> I am not the sort of man
> To go armed with a bow
> After the Hungarian manner
> And ride six leagues in a day . . ."

(Six Bohemian leagues is something over 35 miles.)

Accounts in later times are all in the same key. The cavalry of the Hungarian rebel leader Thököly in 1676 travelled twice as far in a day as did the Imperial horse, according to their commander, General Strassoldo. (Note 23.)

Better performance depended in part on the travelling pace. The natural gaits of Equidae are the walk and the gallop. They trot only when passing from the one to the other, more commonly when 'changing down' from the gallop to the walk than vice versa.

The Oriental horseman rode at a walk, canter, and gallop, the Westerner either pacing (earlier) or at a walk and trot. Long periods of trotting were not customary before the relatively late spread of the habit of 'posting' (known on the Continent as 'the English trot', having been invented in that country).

From fairly recent times there is abundant evidence of Oriental as opposed to Western practice. Thus according to the travel notes of Radloff, Vámbéri, Moser, and Almásy the Kirghiz and Turkomen rode only at a walk and a gallop; never trotting for long. If their horses did happen to break into a trot for a few paces they did not rise in the stirrups but just 'sat out' this unpleasant gait by leaning forward from the waist. The Turkomen also trained their horses to a sort of triple called *trapatka* in Russian. At this gait they would cover 200 versts, or about 133 miles, on their raids. [The English writer Blundeville, some three centuries earlier, no doubt meant just this when he said that the "Turk" horse went best at "a certain easy train". Tr.]

Travel on wheels was also different in East and West. Although some nomads took over the wagon at an early stage, for a long time riding held its pre-eminence among them. We may assume that guiding the draught animal from the saddle derives from the practice of wandering stockmen, being a transitional stage between riding and driving. The adoption of the wagon by 'riding' peoples, like the adoption of riding by peasants who for long had driven carts, was spread over a very long period.

Herodotus says that there were nomad herdsmen who had wagons as early as the last few centuries B.C., yet there were others who had none until the late Middle Ages. The Old Prussians, for instance. These Balts were introduced to the wagon in 1390, by the Teutonic Knights during their campaign against the Poles. And

Broquière says, too, that the Osmanli Turks in his time used horses, mules, and camels exclusively to ride, and for pack traffic. On the other hand, the Huns—and so also the Hungarians, who regard themselves as their descendants—first appeared in Europe complete with wagons; witness the wagon-laager of Attila at the battle of the Catalaunian Fields, and certain events concerning the Hungarians described in the *Annals of St Gall*.

Hungarian-style Harnessing of Five and Seven Horses to a Wagon
Drawn by Á. Garay

There is much evidence of quite sophisticated wagon traffic among the Hungarians, whose wagon-train followed the armies, in rear of which it formed up when they went into action, so as to cover the rear of the host. From the twelfth century onward they had a royal corps of wagoners, and the Master of the Train (*major plaustrorum*) was an officer of the Queen's, as also of the King's, household. (Note 24.) The widespread adoption of the Hungarian pattern of wagon in the late Middle Ages bears witness to its utility, recognized by many European peoples.

The Arab traveller Ibn Battuta, visiting the Caspian region in the fourteenth century, describes the vehicles of the local inhabitants as follows:

> They are called *araba* and have four wheels. According to the size of the load they are drawn by two or more horses, many being drawn by oxen and camels. One of the horses in a team is saddled, and on this the driver sits. He drives the horses on with his whip, and strikes them with a great staff if they swerve off the track.

This corresponds to the traditional method of harnessing, whereby the driver rode the wheeler. *Ductor currus* is the Latin name given to such a driver, and his special saddle is called in Hungarian *pajzán*. This rig was still common in East Hungary between the last two wars, especially in the Heiduck district.

Tibor Pettko-Szandtner, a noted whip and connoisseur of harness horses, described it in a book which Ákos Garay illustrated, and a drawing from which is reproduced here. These two rigs, rural five- and seven-in-hands, show an idea never current in the West at all. Peter Apor wrote in 1736: "At first horses were never driven from the box, but even princes' coachmen drove four-in-hand from the saddle".

Hungarian 'Peasant Coach'
Drawn by Á. Garay

Four-in-hand was the most popular rig for driving from the saddle. The driver was mounted on the near wheeler, and on the command *Tüled* ("From you") the horse on his right either drew or pushed the pole to the right, on the command *Hozzád* ("To you") he drew or pushed it to the left. The near fore-horse was called the leading trace horse because the driver, who rode behind him, had his reins in his hand. For the job a lively, active horse was preferred and his function was declared by a blanket on his back. The off trace horse had to be the steadiest, as his job was to keep the wagon rolling at the speed indicated by signals from the whip. More than four horses were harnessed together only for ceremonial purposes, especially on good roads, or when horses were being moved. The wagon with four wheels, all of equal size, was therefore what the Magyars brought with them out of the East. In the Middle Ages other types were used, the two-wheeled *kola* and *ajonca*, which on linguistic grounds may be assumed to have been taken over from the Slavs. The chroniclers tell of King Ladislas the Kuman being drawn in such a cart, whose destitute subjects pulled it for lack of draught horses themselves.

From the fifteenth century onward we hear of a new Hungarian vehicle, the *kocsi*. According to the travel journals of the Imperial ambassador Count Herberstein in 1517, it was so called after the place of its invention, the village of Kocs in Komorn county. The account by Broquière makes the difference between this and the old type of wagon clear: "They are very fair and lightly built", he says, "so that you would think one man could carry them away, wheels and body and all, on his back. The hind wheels are much higher than the fore wheels". Now the *kocsi* drivers were no longer mounted on the wheeler, but in the front of the body, if not yet on a box. Smaller fore-wheels occurred very early in the Orient. In the shaft-grave of the Sumerian king Abargi (third millennium B.C.) there was a wagon with 60 cm fore-wheels and 80 cm hind wheels.

There are many advantages to the small front pair of wheels. They make the vehicle easier to 'start', and reduce 'bucking' or pitching of the draught-pole on uneven ground or stony roads which reduced the tractive power of the horses. An even greater advantage is that it permits a fuller lock and a smaller turning-circle. It also brings the loading-surface lower, and therewith the centre of gravity, making for greater stability. It is faster and has better cross-country potential than vehicles with axles of the same height behind and before. Driving from the box is easier for the driver, and easier for the wheeler which he would otherwise ride: this is a consideration on long journeys.

A similar development is seen in the sixteenth-century Hungarian *hintó* (slung wagon), in which the body is carried on slings instead of springs. This also was four-wheeled. It was known in the West as a *calèche*. It was the combination of these two features which gave birth to the coach of Western Europe, and indeed 'coach' is only an anglicization of the old Hungarian name *kocsi*.

The coach was harnessed to the team in exactly the same way as were the country wagons of Hungary, as Broquière makes plain, however many horses were used. But in accordance with Central Asiatic practice it was still driven only at a walk or at a gallop. The Hungarian light horse, the Hungarian coach, and this manner of driving made communications inside Hungary rapid and comfortable up to the dawn of the railway era. Country wagons which are still to be seen east of the Leitha river differ little, even today, from the late medieval Hungarian *kocsi*.

The Art of War

The historical role of Central Asiatic horsemanship is most clearly evidenced in the military field. The early history of Hungarian mounted warfare is a much debated, and up to the present little clarified, problem.

However, historians are agreed on one thing: the Hungarians of the Settlement Period represented the Oriental type of 'warrior shepherd', and their fighting men were mounted archers. There is a difference of opinion as to when and to what degree the Western style of fighting was adopted. Perhaps it may be placed as far back as the eleventh century, and the decline of Oriental war-craft must be dated from then on. We incline to this view, with the reservation that armour is not a Western invention or early monopoly, but was known in antiquity and in the Middle Ages in Japan, in China, in India, and in Persia, while the Byzantine Empire employed among its manifold auxiliaries armoured Asiatic horse and foot. The fact that Germans also fought in the host of St Stephen does not by any means imply that it was from them that the Hungarians learned the use of armour; more likely the Hungarians borrowed it from either the Persians or the Byzantines, at least as the equipment of nobles and rich men and members of the princely retinue. In the period before the Mongol invasions the Hungarian man-at-arms was only distinguished from the light horseman by his wearing armour and carrying a lance. When tactically necessary, as A. Borosy emphasizes, he handled a bow also. The spread of Western armament falls chiefly in the time after the Tartar incursions, but the tactics of Hungarian heavy cavalry also had a certain Oriental character. This is shown by what Broquière says about the Hungarians: "taking part in tournaments on small horses with a saddle without high arches, dressed in fair garments according to local custom".

From contemporary accounts we get the impression of warfare waged in the style of the pastoral peoples. The first source is the Arabic historian and traveller Masudi, who described the campaign of 934 by the Magyars and Patzinaks against Byzantium.

> As day broke he [the king of the Patzinaks] formed up many bodies of horsemen on the right wing, and as many on the left. The engagement began with the horsemen of the right wing attacking the main battle of the Byzantines, showering it with arrows, and taking up a new position on the left. Then they of the left wing likewise advanced and shot against the Byzantine main battle, changing over to the right of the line. So the mounted bands kept wheeling across the Byzantine front, grinding away at it like millstones, while the Turkish main body was still not engaged. As the hail of arrows came shower after shower, the Byzantines in open order charged the Turkish main body, which till then had made no move. The horsemen did not impede them, but the Turks received them with such a shower of arrows that they recoiled. Their columns had remained drawn up in order of battle, and had not opened ranks. The mounted bands swarmed out from either flank. Now sabres were drawn. The heavens darkened and there was loud neighing of horses. . . .

The second comes after the Tartar invasion, being an abstract of Ottokar von Steier's *Rhyming Chronicle* (1312–18) concerned with the events of the defensive struggle against the Teutonic Order, who in 1286 crossed the western frontiers of Hungary. We render the somewhat pedestrian verse in prose and paraphrased:

The armoured horse of the Austrian host was some thousand strong, and composed of Austrian, Styrian, and Swabian knights. These last did not know how the Hungarians were accustomed to fight. On the news that the Hungarians were approaching, the Austrian commander wanted to sound the retreat, on the grounds that they could not be countered as one did the French (meaning that they opened fire at long range), since they would not come to close quarters. But the Swabians refused to withdraw, they formed up in close order, stirrup to stirrup, lance to lance. The Hungarians tried their usual tactics; like Turks, they rode at the enemy, yelling and shooting from the saddle, but did not close with their opponents. The battle lasted five hours, without the men-at-arms coming to grips. The Swabians took counsel what they should do. Should they disarm, to bring themselves on equal terms with the Hungarians who were fighting in their shirts? They would not take off their mail, since the Hungarians had even killed the herald who had been sent to them with an offer of peace. Men and horses were being hit by arrows, and the wounded beasts began to rage in delirium. The army, exhausted by the godless heathen, faced utter annihilation, against which it was powerless. When at last they surrendered the Hungarians approached, took away their weapons and armour, and divided the prisoners among themselves.

These two reports are by men who were not familiar with Central Asian tactics. They do not, therefore, give such insight as is afforded by the *Secret History of the*

Mongols, with Jenghis Khan's routine orders. We do not know in detail how these manœuvres were carried out, but we do know—from Villani's chronicle—that the signal to swerve aside was given by shaking a quiver, thus making a noise only audible at close quarters by the horses, when a feint was intended and the attack not to be pressed home. The horses reacted instantly, but how many men took part in each attack, and whether they discharged their arrows before or after turning away from the front, we do not know. Certain it is that this abrupt volte-face demanded a high degree of equestrian skill, for the whole squadron to turn as one man.

When we consider that the arrows were discharged at a fast gallop, throwing the reins to the horse, this is further proof of their skill in riding, their skill at arms, and not least of the state of training of their horses. There were certain risks inherent in this tactic; any confusion or hesitation among the thousands of galloping horsemen could have meant disaster in the face of an enemy who knew how to exploit it.

A hundred years later, under the Anjou dynasty, the armament of the armoured knights of the fourteenth century showed unequivocal Western influence, but the light horse still consisted of mounted archers. The Neapolitan chronicler Villani, describing the Italian campaign of Louis I (1342–82), calls the Hungarian horse lightly armed, invariably their weapons being bow, arrows, and a long sabre, their clothing being layer on layer of leather jerkins ('wambaces' in the English of the period) which acted as sort of 'poor man's armour'. Their strategic significance is stressed also in a later (1395) document of King Sigismund, in which he commanded every mounted lancer in his pay to provide also two mounted archers.

The appearance of the Osmanli Turks only increased the importance of this tried arm of the service. Rearmament against this new threat from the East became more urgent after the defeat at Nikopolis (1396). But that battle also demonstrates the difference between Eastern and Western military practice. King Sigismund of Hungary was also Holy Roman Emperor, and his campaign, which was of the nature of a belated Crusade, attracted many foreign volunteers, principally knights from France. Contemporary writers lay the blame for the defeat entirely on the French, who would let no-one deny them the honour of the first onslaught. They were the first to attack the Turks, which they did on foot, adopting what had now become the common Western practice imitated from the successful charge of the dismounted English chivalry at Crécy in 1346. In doing so they got in the way of the Hungarian light-horse skirmishers. According to the chronicle of Thuróczi, part of the Hungarian army was thrown into disarray when the horses of the dismounted French knights came into their lines and they, being unfamiliar with this procedure, thought that their riders must have been slain or unhorsed. [The question arises, what were the squires of the French knights doing? It is the duty of an esquire to take charge of the destrier at all times when the knight is not riding it. *Tr.*] It is easy to imagine what confusion would be caused by the irruption of the huge, pugnacious chargers among the ranks of Hungarian light horse, standing-to ready for action. This mishap led to a reorganization of the Hungarian army, the mounted archers being reinforced at the expense of the other arms. The Diet passed a law in 1397, whereby for the duration of hostilities against the Turks all landed gentry were to raise one mounted archer for every twenty farmsteads on their estates, and to bring him into the field. It is assumed that this was the origin of hussars. (Note 25.)

59
Hadban Enzahi, foaled in
1952, by Nazeer out of
Kamla. Standing at the
Marbach Arab stud.

60
Shari, foaled 1961, by
Hadban Enzahi out of
Hathor; Champion Arab
Female of Germany in 1968.

61
Tajar, Grey Arab Stallion,
once the Charger of a
Mameluke Officer
among those massacred by
Mehemet Ali. He was the
Foundation Sire of
Hungarian-bred Arabs

62/63 Tourney.
    Illumination from the Tournament Book of Duke William IV of Bavaria, first half of 16th century.
    State Library, Munich

64 Hungarian Csikos (Herdsman) with his Horse at a Cattle-trough in the the Hortogagy Puszta

65 (below) Uryanchai Girl milking Reindeer

66 (right)   Mongolian Girl milking Mare

But these horse-bowmen were not conscripted serfs. The latter constituted the so-called servile militia (infantry). The archers to be raised as a part of what in England would be called 'knight service' were all freemen, experienced soldiers. Many of them were impoverished gentlemen, often refugees from Turkish-occupied territory. And so whoever was bound to find a mounted archer or hussar had not only

Hungarian Hussar with Bow and Sabre
Sixteenth-century engraving from National Museum, Budapest

to recruit him but to pay him. Such easily hired masterless men had been a feature of Hungarian life before this, especially in the cavalry of Oriental style.

The professional soldier was heir to a tradition that went back to the ancient world, for both Rome and Byzantium had filled the ranks of their cavalry with Oriental mercenaries, and still in 1259 the army of Michael Palaeologos of Constantinople contained 1500 Hungarian and Kuman Turkish horse, who by 1298 were serving the Archduke Albert of Habsburg, and in the following century were in the pay of the Pope and of many Italian city-states. Things were not much different at home. Under Andrew III of Hungary (1290–1301) and the Anjou dynasty (1307–82) Kuman archers were permanently on the establishment.

As the Turkish wars progressed their numbers grew ever greater. Refugees from the Balkans—Raizes, Croats, Slovenes, and Hungarians—all found sanctuary in Hungary, among other lands. At this time the ranks of the hussars were full of them. At the accession of Ferdinand I (1526) it was said, with reference to warfare: "It is therefore necessary to have recourse to the swiftness of doughty hussars, who can easily be had from Hungary, Slavonia, Croatia or Transylvania".

The Yugoslavs who entered the hussar bands had no influence on the development of this arm. They simply adapted themselves to the model of the Magyar hussar, riding a Hungarian light horse, in the Hungarian manner on a Hungarian saddle, equally master of the sabre, the bow, and later the hand-gun. The Hungarian army thus did not become 'Balkanized', and its tactics continued to be overwhelmingly Central Asian in style.

There is contemporary evidence in a letter of King Matthias to Gabriel of Verona in 1481, from which we deduce that the traditional procedure was still used in battle: they stationed themselves on the field in rear of the main body and sallied out at the enemy whenever opportunity offered, and when they were tired or threatened they withdrew and reformed, ready for the next assault. (Note 26.)

Increased Turkish pressure on Hungary led of necessity to further reinforcement of the light cavalry. The Diet of 1435 stepped up the furnishing of one mounted archer from every twenty farmsteads to one for every ten. King Matthias, who kept a standing army in pay, describes the hussar in the letter quoted above as the intermediate arm between the armoured cavalry and the infantry. And at this point the hussar had attained the status in Central European armies that he was to hold for the next five centuries, as the model of a light-cavalryman.

A Setback to Hungarian Horse-breeding

The life-and-death struggle against the Turks bore hard on the horse-stock of Hungary. The horses captured from the Asiatics did not go far to replace casualties. The position became worse when the centuries-old embargo on the export of horses was lifted. Under the Habsburgs the country came into the economic orbit of Austria and of the German Empire, and now nothing could stop the drain of Hungarian horses westward.

A hundred years earlier Duke Frederick of Austria was not able to find, in Wiener-Neustadt market, any Hungarian horses, their importation having been rendered impossible by the King of Hungary. But now Ferdinand I and his successor Maximilian could direct the Chamberlain of Zips to obtain horses for the Court from Upper Hungary. (Note 27.) With the lively export trade an inflation of prices went hand in hand. Whereas at the beginning of the sixteenth century eight or ten gulden was the going price for an ordinary horse, now a useful draught horse cost 150 gulden. Fugger has this to say of the prices current in the 1580's: "If it please any man to travel to the Hungarian borders, there he shall find out what horses cost; yea it is now uncommon to be able to buy a rouncy or a saddle-nag less than a hundred talers." [Even insular England did not escape this general trend of live-stock and commodity prices in the sixteenth century. It was a long-range effect of the Spanish exploitation of the Americas, resulting in a disastrous fall in the price of precious metals. *Tr.*]

The demand for Oriental horses was enormous. Fugger writes:

> Now latterly they bring to us many horses, much more than was formerly the case, both from Transylvania and Hungary and Poland, and also Podolian, Croatian and Czech horses . . . but those from Transylvania, Hungary and Bohemia are commonly shy and fearful, yet a good part of them are strong and bold, apt to make a warhorse . . .

The increased demand, on top of the general inflation, for light cavalry horses and fast harness horses drove the price of half-blood horses very high. The Andalusian, never a cheap horse, was simply not in this market. It was now every horseman's dream to acquire a charger that would pass muster as a 'capital' horse.

The third reason for the shrinking supply of horses in Hungary was simply the decline of breeding itself. This was chiefly the case in Transdanubia and Upper Hungary, where the grazing-grounds round the frontier fortresses had been a theatre of war for so long. Two documents of the period show this decline. A report from Zips as late as 1592 says that the serfs around Mezönánás are chiefly occupied in breeding horses, and get their living by the sale of them. (Note 28.) But on the other hand as early as 1639 the steward of the Sárospatak estate reports to Prince George Rákóczi that he is unable to procure post-horses, because the servile tenants of the Crown lands not occupied by the Turks have no horses. (Note 29.)

In Turkish-occupied territory the situation was somewhat easier. The great expanses of pasture in the depopulated lowlands became 'ranches'. Here horse-breeding flourished anew. It was easier in time of danger to bring the herds out of harm's way than in the thickly populated Crown lands across the border, where every rood of land was occupied. Droves of horses and cattle were brought to islands in the swamps, or simply driven a long way off—say sixty miles. A measure of security was to be had by a form of 'homage'; a levy paid to the Turkish overlord for immunity from sequestration of stock by the Turks. The Hungarian horse-dealer of the seventeenth century bought most of his stock from this source. Both they and private buyers favoured the southern parts of the Turkish-held territory, and sold them on from there to foreign countries. For instance, the Palatine Wesse-lényi ordered the Chamber to procure remounts for the German dragoons from Jazygia and the Kecskemét district, both under Turkish occupation in 1661. (Note 30.) Even the Hungarian magnates often kept their studs in those areas—which, however, often had undesired results, as in the case of Count Valentin Balassa, a descendant of the famous poet, who wrote to Stephan Koháry in 1677:

> although I have paid tribute for my stud, Ibrahim Bey fell in love with my mares. He sent a guard of honour of Kuruzes to conduct them via Szécsén to

Hatvan where the marriage to the Bey took place. So that is all one gets for paying tribute in respect of farm and stock. You never can trust a Turk...

(Note 31.)

Recovery in terms of numbers was not possible after the liberation from Turkish rule. Even in terms of quality, the once far-famed Hungarian horse 'fit for a lord' was gone with the wind. In its place were little thrifty, durable farm horses, quite unsuitable for upper-class use, either to ride or to drive. The landowners turned their attention to the 'Spanish' horses (which by now had become the Neapolitan-Andalusian) that now begin to appear in inventories of noble households, even in Transylvania. Even pictures of hussars show them mounted on such horses.

Finally the national interest, in both the military and the civilian transport sphere, was so jeopardized that in 1766 Maria Theresa issued a proclamation entitled *Commissio in negotio propagationis equorum* with the object of breeding stronger horses. This State intervention followed the Seven Years War, which again had played havoc with the remount services, and hence with the stock in general. The Commission laid certain restrictions on privately-owned stallions at stud. Strong stallions in State ownership were made available to cover farmers' mares. They were of Western stamp. (Notes 32, 33.)

The results appear to have been catastrophic, because no account was taken of traditional methods and conditions. Through the use of unsuitable stallions, breeding by farmers was all but ruined. Captain Josef Csekonics made a report for the Emperor Joseph II on the reform of Hungarian horse-breeding; pointing out that remount-purchasing commissions were not able to find more than two or three suitable troop horses in three whole counties.

That energetic ruler, who had ideas in advance of his age, acted in character. He introduced Government stallion depots and covering stations, founding the Mezö-hegyes stud, with Csekonics in charge to start matters on the right lines. He also founded the stud at Radauti, in Bukovina. The captain, whose services to Hungarian horse-breeding are incalculable, chose his foundation stock with great skill. In accordance with Hungarian tradition, it consisted predominantly of imported Tartar and Circassian mares, the stallions being in part Thoroughbreds from England.

Along with this reanimation of Hungarian horse-breeding there went also a reflorescence of equitation, though now vitally different from the Central Asian origins. The line dividing East from West, of which the western frontier of Hungary had so long been a sector, had been slowly fading for three centuries. And now Hungarian practice became wholly European.

A summary of the factors governing stock-breeding and transport in Central Asia among the nomad herdsmen shows the same general picture as in Hungary. After the decline of the Turkish empire in Central Asia a deliberate grading-up of steppe horses with Turanian blood can be demonstrated. Jenghis Khan's order to take all blood-horses captured back to Mongolia to be used for breeding purposes, and then the patronage of Turkoman horse-breeding by Timur-i-Leng and Nasr-ed-Din, had the same object.

The same is true of transport technique. Riding, driving, saddlery, harness, vehicles—all go back to the same source. Likewise in the military sphere. The

IMPORTANT HORSE-BREEDING CENTRES AND AREAS OF EUROPE IN MODERN TIMES

Leningrad

Moscow

DON COSSACKS

CIRCASSIANS.

T A T A R S

Jerusalem

Cairo

Stockholm

Trakehnen

Marienburg

Warsaw

PODOLIA

ZAPOROZHE COSSACKS

MOLDAVIA

Besztercze

Torda

TRANSYLVANIA

WALLACHIA

Nikopolis

Istanbul

Demotika
Kandia
Rodosto

Athens

Salonika

Copenhagen
HOLSTEIN
Hamburg Strelsund's
Berlin
Celle

Elstermerida

Hanover
Dresden
Prague
Merseburg Kladrub

OLDENBURG
FRIESLAND
WESTPHALIA
Frankfurt

Amsterdam
Antwerp
Brussels
Ostend ARDENNES
Strasbourg
Chartres
Troyes

Augsburg

PINZGAU

Brno
Vienna
Wr. Neustadt

Lipizza

Venice

Rome

Naples
Taranto

Palermo

YORKSHIRE
SUFFOLK
Newmarket
London
Hastings

Rouen
Paris
Chantilly

NORMANDY
Saumur
Poitiers
Clermont-Ferrand
Montpellier

Nantes

Bordeaux
Tarbes
NAVARRE

IRELAND

GALICIA
ASTURIAS
Madrid
Valencia
Córdoba
ANDALUSIA

Eperjes

Veszto

Niskic

Belgrade

Mezőhegyes

Kisber (Szárp)
Bábolna
(Szárp)
Lad

Kopping
Mohács (Szárp)

Tuszafüred

N S

KINN

Uyárfán-vár

Vecsés

Augsburg

Cossacks in the service of the Tsar, who had originally been free-lances engaged for pay and the hope of booty, became in time troops of the line just like the hussars. Their horses, their equipment, their tactics were those of the hussars, the Cossack saddle and the hussar saddle were identical down to the last century, both being derived from the wooden saddle of the nomad herdsmen.

This equestrian culture, however, lasted longer in Central Asia than in Hungary —or the Ukraine. The last traces of it surrendered only yesterday to the overwhelming forces of the modern technical revolution.

Part IV A Uniform Europe

Contributions from East and West

Two fundamental elements of European horsemanship derive from opposite poles
—East and West. There is an almost unbroken chain of development lasting from
the beginning of the mounted invasions until some time in the nineteenth century,
in which the Hungarians acted as the catalytic agent.

The three-hundred-year sojourn of the Avars in Europe left deep impressions
behind it, more than appear to the superficial observer. It may be proved, for
example, by reference to East Prussia. This was once a backwater of Europe, left
almost undisturbed by the currents of the Migration Period; the civilization of the
Occident reached it comparatively late, and the indigenous peoples retained their
ancient customs all the longer. Our chief documentary source is the archives of the
Germans—in particular of the Teutonic Order of Knights. [It is as if, in terms of
English history, the last hundred years of the *Anglo-Saxon Chronicle* did not exist,
and we were entirely dependent on Norman accounts of England and the English.
Tr.] The specialist literature based on these archives which concerns us here is
principally the study by Fritz Rünger (1925) on the breeding and origin of the war-
horses used by the Order. As mentioned above, once the Order was free of its
commitments in the Holy Land, it annexed East Prussia in the thirteenth century,
for the furtherance of the Christian faith. In the territory between the Vistula and
the Memel they came in contact with the Old Prussians, a Baltic people known as
the Borussi or Pruthoni, the Central Asian origin of whose equestrian culture can
be shown in incontrovertible archaeological evidence.

The Avars and the Old Prussians

The Marienburg archives of the Order point to four typically Central Asian features
of the Old Prussian horse-husbandry: breeding on open range, method of castration,
branding as mark of ownership (Note 34), and the milking of mares, particularly
to provide kumiss, the use of which was restricted to the ruling class.

Transport and military equipment were also reminiscent of Central Asia. Their
horses were small, they waged war as mounted archers, and only used pack-horses.
Harness horses did not become common among them until the early fifteenth
century, after the Teutonic Order's campaign of 1390, for which it did not requisi-
tion any pack-horses, as such, from its Prussian vassals, but only draught horses for
the wagon-train.

So much for documentary evidence, which is substantiated by archaeological
findings. First among these is the custom of equestrian burial which was customary
only among the upper classes. Here Slavonic influence is perceptible; like the Slavs,
they cremated their dead, burying beside the ashes both horse and horseman's
gear. Gy. László points out that the Slavs of the Danube region, whose settlements
alternated with those of the Avars, also followed this custom.

In the realm of ideas, too, there are certain affinities with the nomadic horse-breeders. This is evident in the hanging up of horse-skulls in Prussian stables and in Hungarian dwelling-houses, and the decoration of gable-ends with horse-heads carved in wood, in East Prussia as elsewhere in the Germanic world.

Their horse-stock, too, is what we should expect of nomadic breeders. The Ambassador, Count Herberstein, in his journal of travel through East Prussia in 1557, as well as Marx Fugger, notes that the local horses were mouse-grey or ash-grey (dun), with a dark eel-stripe. They had either domed foreheads or Roman noses, a stiff upright mane, and 'zebra' stripes on the hocks. According to Ebhardt this would indicate a mixture of Pony Type I and Horse Type III (see p. 14). In the Old Prussian language the wild horse was called *paustocaican* and the domestic horse *schweike*. But in the records of the Order the *schweike* herds were called 'wild herds'. [This apparent contradiction is explained by the widespread use of the word 'wild' among medieval and indeed later authors to indicate the technique of breeding horses and ponies on open range, and it has nothing to do with the modern biologist's definition of a 'wild' animal. It is in this sense, not in the scientific sense, that, for instance, Welsh Mountain ponies are described as 'wild'. Tr.]. We may deduce that the indigenous East Prussian horse was kept in herds on the common grazing of the wastes, and was of pony size, if not exclusively of pony type.

After the war of extermination carried on by Charlemagne in 796 we find only one further mention of the Avars: about the year 805 they sent an embassy to the Frankish Court, asking the Emperor to grant them new lands, since owing to pressure from the Slavs life was becoming intolerable for them in their old home. The Russian Chronicle of Nestor states also "When the Vlachs" [that is, the Franks] "assailed the Slavs on the Danube, subduing them by force and planting settlements among them, some of the Slavs moved out and settled on the Vistula...."

Taken together, those two passages mean that Pannonia (Hungary) was the scene of repeated shifts of population in the early ninth century, and that some element of the population—either Slavs or Slavophone Avars—migrated to the Vistula basin. That there may well be some connection between the Pannonian Avars and the Prussians of the Vistula is to be assumed from the similarity of tribal names—e.g., Serb/Sorb, Abrodit/Brodnik, Prosto/Prussian.

This question can only be finally decided by a synthesis of research in the archaeological, ethnological, and linguistic fields. One thing is certain, however; that one of the routes by which the technique of Central Asiatic horsemastership reached Europe (and probably Scandinavia in particular) is through East Prussia. This made a fruitful contribution to material civilization, and probably even the practice of the Teutonic Order was influenced by its taking over, in the course of centuries of living side by side with the Old Prussians (so long as those survived at all), much of their legacy of mounted pastoralism. This may explain the community of outlook between the Hungarian landowner and his Prussian counterpart, the Junker, whose traditions seem to be derived not so much from his German forebears, whether these were Saxons or immigrants from "High Germany", as from the Old Prussian ruling class of Baltic speech and culture whom they had displaced.

The first hundred years following the advance of the Order into East Prussia were filled with continuous warfare. In the early stages the tactics of the Knights were rather primitive, and some of them still fought on foot. The Borussi, who were at the same time fighting the Poles on another front, held out heroically for a long

67 Evolution of the Saddle
(Top left) Reindeer saddle from Sayan Mountains. 68 (top right) Kirghiz saddle for
children. 69 (centre left) Mongol saddle. 70 (centre right) Nineteenth-century Turkish
saddle. 71 (bottom left) Reconstruction of Magyar saddle at time of settlement of
Danube plain. 72 (bottom right) Hungarian country saddle of nineteenth century.

er Anfall ist gewagt; die möchten mit angreiffen,
Es zappelt Mann und Pferd und ist schon auf dem flug,

Doch, da der fällt, hält Sie zuruk der kuglen pfeiffen,
Als die bey hiz und Muth zugleich auch schlau genug

73   Hungarian Hussars, Eighteenth Century
Engraving by G. P. Rugendas

74 Hungarian Coach, 1563. Engraving by J.
Schemel.
National Museum, Budapest

75 Kuman Peasant, Early Nineteenth Century
Drawing by Bikkesy.
National Museum

76 Hungarian Country-bred Horses
Early Nineteenth Century.
National Museum

77 Stag Headdress from the Pazyryk
Horse-burials
Hermitage, Leningrad

time. Rising after rising ended at last with the almost total extermination of their ruling class. The last of the Old Prussian nobility perished in the rebellion of 1322, after which the Order was able for the first time to set about the building up of a systematic economy. At this period they founded the studs of heavy horses to provide chargers, a characteristic manifestation of the Occidental 'Frankish' mode of military life, existing side by side with the Oriental practices of the indigenous population. In some respects tactics and equipment of the Teutonic Order resembled that of contemporary Hungary. On the wings of the heavily armed 'main battle', mounted on destriers, there were bodies of light horse drawn from the freemen among the subject Old Prussians, the *equites pruteni*, with an important tactical role. Besides its studs of heavy horses the Order also had herds of *schweiken* running in the woods and on the heaths. As might be expected, these latter provided them with palfreys. Every Brother of the Order had to maintain one destrier and two *schweiken*; their squires were mounted on light horses of the same stamp.

The Oriental influence already evident in the fields of transport and warfare spread into the social sphere of everyday life. Out of the constant necessity to maintain everything on a war footing there arose a way of life characteristic of the army-as-State or the State-as-army which has been the baleful legacy of the Asiatic equestrian warrior-peoples to posterity. For the individual, this meant the wholesale adaptation to the 'chivalrous' way of life, at a time when—in England, for instance —the rigid bonds of feudal society based on land held by military service and the 'knight's fee' were beginning to loosen. Even the obligatory embargo on horse-exports was introduced into the Order's dominions—a little late in the day, indeed —being first mentioned in a document of 1386. At first this law discriminated solely against the Polish enemy, but by 1414 it was also directed against the West. [The Prussia of the Teutonic Knights really represents an anachronism, and as such may have been welcome to certain elements outside Germany. Thus in the *Canterbury Tales*—actually composed in the 1380's—Chaucer's Knight, who is obviously somewhat ill at ease in the increasingly un-feudal atmosphere of contemporary England, and would have been happier in the days of Edward I, had actually served as a volunteer under the banners of the Order "in Lettow and in Pruce". Tr.]

From then onward Prussian horsemanship played a significant part in the events of the West, and still today the Prussian horseman and the Prussian horse are important in the international equestrian field.

The Vikings

We mentioned above that the East Prussians and other Balts who were in contact with the horse-culture of Central Asia had passed on a certain part of this technique to Scandinavia, among other places. [Archaeology shows that Sweden and Norway, far from being the home of a North Germanic language group living in isolation after one definitive migration, had since the Bronze Age—the Age of the Charioteers —been continuously refreshed culturally by a series of immigrations from the south shore of the Baltic which sometimes had their point of departure as far west as Mecklenburg, sometimes as far east as Estonia. Even as far east as Estonia, and as late as the ninth century, we have an account of the part played by horses in the social customs of the Baltic peoples by a Scandinavian traveller who contributed this item to King Alfred's English edition (it is more than a translation) of the *History* of Orosius. (Note 34a.) *Tr.*]

If the Northmen depended for communications principally on their superbly built ships and their skilful seamanship, they were no strangers to the horse, and it is significant that the sea-going ship begins to appear in Bronze Age rock-carvings of Scandinavia at the same time and in conjunction with the pair-horse chariot. Their ships took them to every coast where they had hopes of either profitable trade or still more profitable piracy. But when they came to the head of navigable water, whether in Ireland or Apulia, then they took to horse. "This year", says the *Anglo-Saxon Chronicle* so many times, "the heathen men went up on land and stole horses". In every capacity, as merchants, as pirates, as slave-dealers, as hired swordsmen, their calling brought them into contact with the great masters of the horse, such as the Moor in Andalusia and the Khazars and Turks of the Caspian region. The eastern branch of the Scandinavian expansion, mainly of Swedish origin, is known to us as Varangians, forming among other things the guard regiment of marine infantry at Constantinople—the Polekophoroi, or wielders of the two-handed axe. In this service they learnt, as infantry, the tactical lessons of co-operation with both heavy (Fancopouloi) and light (Turcopouloi) cavalry; but the Varangian—or Variag, as the Russians called him—was also a merchant doing business along the great inland waterways of the Kievan kingdom, and, less well-known to us in the West, in Hungary, where the place-name Varong occurs frequently. Those who came home to a wealthy and honoured retirement brought with them knowledge of Eastern horse-lore, and Norway and Denmark must be regarded as the entrepôt of equestrian knowledge, which by this northern route was passed on to the West. It contributed much to the last, most momentous, and yet most indirect of the Viking expeditions. When the clan of Tancred de Hauteville took service with the Pope in Southern Italy against the Emperor of Constantinople (or occasionally vice-versa, when the latter paid better wages) they set out not from Norway but from Seine Inférieure, and no longer as their forefathers had done as marine infantry who might out of tactical necessity now and again perform a strategic march on horse-back, but as knights armed and fighting in the 'Frankish' manner.

Equestrian burial with certain Asiatic elements was already an ancient institution in Scandinavia, well attested by archaeological evidence and mentioned in Northern literature as early as the days of the legendary Harald Hilditönn, slain in battle by Sigurd Ring (reputedly the father of the Viking Ragnar Hairy-Breeches who ravaged Northumbria in the first wave of westward expansion from the Fjords). Harald was an old man, who only went out to this last battle because his peasant subjects were about to offer him as a ritual sacrifice to ensure the fertility of their fields and flocks, and to take a younger and more vigorous prince as their sovereign. After the battle his enemy Sigurd Ring had him fittingly interred together with his horse, throwing his own saddle into the grave, so that his dead rival could make a fitting entry into Valhalla. [Horse-burial in the North is associated primarily with the devotees of Odin and of Freyr, and has many features in common with the funerary rites of the steppe horsemen as far east as the Altai. *Tr.*]

The Western Vikings sacked and burnt Antwerp in 836, Rouen in 841, Nantes in 843, Paris in 845, Hamburg in the same year, and Bordeaux in 847. They had in the same period destroyed the headquarters at Dorstad of their principal commercial rivals, the Frisians, who were also horse-breeders. The Duchy of Normandy, on the

Greenland 10th century
ICELAND c. 870
'Vinland' c.1000
•₀Faeröe c.700
802
793
795
798
878
875
862
859
1046
1066
891
911
882
882
880
842-43
844
860
862
844
1076
859
844
1098

south shore of the English Channel, was founded in 911, and thence was mounted not only the Sicilian adventure mentioned above but William the Bastard's Enterprise of England.

It was the Viking incursions which caused the Frankish King Charles the Bald to summon his vassals to take the field on horseback. They were among other things the challenge, a response to which was the Frankish institution of chivalry, which they so successfully adopted themselves. The core of the Crusading armies was formed of Franco-Norman knights or knights armed and operating in this manner —the most spectacular and prolonged confrontation of East and West that the world has seen.

Thus among European equestrian peoples we may say that three above all have spread the technique and the principles of Asiatic horsemanship and horsemastership through the breadth of this continent—the Avars, the Magyars, and the Norsemen (with their half-bred descendants the Normans). To this was added— principally in the Modern period—the Near Eastern or specifically the Arab element. Traces of all these legacies are still perceptible in the world of the Western horseman today.

Eastern Customs

Burial with Horses

The earliest indication of the spread of Oriental customs is in the religious sphere. It is typified in the survival of the Oriental custom of horse-burial in symbolic form. At the time of the Scyth invasions carts, wagons, and chariots were being buried along with the dead, at least as far west as Burgundy. The mode of entombment differed somewhat from the practice of the steppes, since though the corpse was often placed in a vehicle as in a bier, the wheels being detached and placed at the side of the burial pit, the horse or horses were usually interred outside the actual tomb-chamber, and the entire carcass was not invariably present. However, the intention is obviously the same—to provide the dead with the means of travel to the next world.

Vestiges of this custom were present in the funeral pomp of the Romans, in which the dead man's horse was led, though no longer to be sacrificed at the graveside. Signs of a more recently imported Oriental custom are to be seen in the mortuary dedication of a horse, customary in the West from Germany to England inclusive in the late Middle Ages. One German example will suffice:

The German anti-King, Johann Latomus Günther von Schwarzburg, was buried in 1349; records state that two torch bearers led five horses to the altar, where they were symbolically offered, and then bought back by the next-of-kin for four hundred gold pieces, which was paid to the Church. [English wills down to the Reformation often contain similar bequests. Tr.] Plainly the symbolic offering of the horses goes back to some kind of funerary sacrifice as at Pazyryk, while the burning torches may either be a reminder of cremation as practised by the pagan Prussians or an echo of classical mythology; Artemis, who was among other things the Queen of Night and of Death, is often represented as driving in a wagon with torch-bearers attendant. And she was also the patron goddess of horse and hound.

In the West this custom remained a privilege of the landowning class which the burghers were reluctant to recognize—perhaps a prolongation of the antithesis between nomadic pastoralists and settled husbandmen. Thus in 1356 the city of Frankfurt passed a by-law specifically forbidding its citizens to claim this privilege. "Nyman vor keiner lych keyn roz adir pherd lazsen fueren mit eyme gewapetin mane"—No man is to have led before the corpse a destrier (roz) or palfrey (pherd) by an armed man. [The charger was led, at English funerals, by a man in full armour as late as the seventeenth century, as notably in the cortège of Sir Philip Sydney, of which contemporary pictures exist. The continued use so late as this, in Germany, of the word Pherd (parafridus) in its restricted sense of ambling palfrey, and not in the more general sense of horse, is interesting. Tr.]

If a Frankfurter wished to bequeath a horse to the Church he might do so, but it was to remain in ecclesiastical hands, and the family were forbidden to buy it back on pain of a fine equal to the price of the horse.

It is not yet clear by what means this Asiatic custom became diffused through the West, but it may well be the combined effect of Avar, Magyar, and Viking influence.

It may be helpful to refer to Hungarian practice. We may begin from the horse-burial as found in Hungary. The Hungarians themselves had this custom until the days of St Ladislas (1065–95), but later waves of invaders from the East—notably Patzinaks and Kumans—kept it up until the fourteenth century. Joinville, in his life of St Louis, says of the Kumans who were settled in Egypt that they were wont to bury their chief men together with their horses, but with this cruel variation, that the living horse and a groom, also living, were buried or walled up along with the dead. These Turks were nominally Muslims, and such elaborate practices are diametrically opposed to the bare simplicity of orthodox Mahomedan burial.

Both history and archaeology confirm that among the Kumans of Hungary this procedure did not apply, yet some elements of it persisted into the mid-fourteenth century. Another French source quotes a letter from the Abbot of St Geneviève at Paris to the parents of a Hungarian youth by the name of Bethlehem (Bethlen?) who died there in 1180; among the list of presents sent by the bereaved to the church where their son was buried he mentions a white horse and a lance.

A Hungarian will of about 1270 by Bezter, son of Demetrius, commands his body to be buried in the chapel of the Franciscan abbey at Ofen; he left his best horse, with saddle, accoutrements, and arms, to the Church. At the funeral of King Charles I of Hungary in 1342 three horses trapped in black were led in the cortège, carrying his arms and armour. The will of his widow Elizabeth, proved in 1380, desired that six of her twelve carriage horses should be led in the funeral procession. [This is also significant in another context. The earliest mention of carriages *at all* in English documents is in 1381! *Tr.*] (Note 35.)

Symbolic horse-offerings occur regularly in Hungarian wills of the fifteenth century. As in Germany, the importance of the offertory is emphasized by the quality of the horses and arms concerned. Not only are the horses made over to the Church, but the amount for which they are to be redeemed is specified. Johan Ernuszt, who rose from obscure circumstances to become a high dignitary (he was, incidentally, of Jewish origin), points out in his will that the offering of a horse is obligatory on persons of baronial rank.

A German ballad on the funeral of King Albert, who died in 1439, shows how important this horse-offering was in royal obsequies. It blames the Hungarians for the King's early death, and reproaches them for showing their spite by not bringing out either chargers or armour in his funeral cortège.

Pomp of all kinds, including the funeral, reached its height in the Age of Baroque and the funerals of Hungarian landowners of this period were no exception. See p. 118 for a panoramic view of the cortège of four sons of the house of Esterházy killed at the battle of Vezekény against the Turks in 1652—a veritable equestrian spectacle. Even now, three centuries later, many people find it goes against the grain to accept the motorized hearse.

Still very occasionally a horse is led in some funeral procession (usually a State funeral) with the boots fixed in the stirrups, the toes pointing backward. The reason for this lies far back in the past, among the beliefs of the steppe herdsmen, who thought of life in the next world as the reverse of this one, and used to put the saddle on the funeral horse back to front with this significance.

Panorama of Funeral Cortège at the Obsequies of Four Members of the House of Esterházy, killed in Action against the Turks, 1652

Copper engraving in Library of Academy of Sciences, Budapest

Oriental influence was not confined to the mental attitude of the horseman, but also to the technique of driving. The adoption of the Hungarian style of harness represents a diffusion of Eastern technique.

West European harness in the early Middle Ages differed little from that of the Romans. Vehicles were the single-axle cart and the four-wheeled wagon having fore- and hind-wheels of the same size. When driven from the vehicle itself, these equipages were clumsy, and only suitable for good roads. There were few good roads, and fast wheeled traffic did not exist.

The earliest indication of adoption by the West of driving from the saddle is our Plate 81, the journey of St Elizabeth. This Hungarian princess, a daughter of King Andreas II of the House of Arpad, went to visit her father, accompanied by her husband, the Margrave of Thuringia, in 1225. The picture dates from the early fourteenth century, and though it still shows fore- and hind-wheels of the same size, the driver is mounted on one of the wheelers, in Danubian fashion. The tubular tilted wagon-cover is of a type still used in Hungary until recently, and is mentioned both by Ibn Batuta and by Broquière as typically Hungarian. During the next century driving from the saddle became much more widely diffused.

According to the historian Domanovszky (1917), distribution of the sprung carriage also began from Hungary, and followed the same route. The first such vehicle in France is mentioned in the *Grande Encyclopédie* as having been brought by Isabella of Bavaria on her way to her wedding with King Charles VI. The second to be seen was in 1457, sent by King Ladislaus V of Hungary to the Queen of France, when sueing for the hand of her daughter, the Princess Madeleine, in marriage.

There is much evidence of the capabilities of Hungarian wainwrights during the next century. A letter from Count Ferenc Batthyány of 1559 mentions one who would deliver an iron-tyred sprung wagon to Count Arco for 25 gulden. (Note 36.) At that time the sprung wagon was used only by royalty and nobility. It was usually driven six-in-hand. (Note 37.)

The next development was the diffusion of the Hungarian *kocsi* throughout Europe. In a previous chapter we traced its origin to Oriental prototypes, and drew attention to the peculiarity of this Hungarian speciality in having smaller fore-wheels. Furthermore, it was no longer driven from the saddle but from the box, which may be regarded as a concession to Western custom.

While in Hungary the great advantage of this novel vehicle lay chiefly in the fact that the wheeler no longer had to carry a rider, it led in the West to a complete revolution in transport. Feats unimaginable by means of the clumsy Western wagons became possible at one blow by means of the coach. Fast and comfortable (by their standards) travel became a commonplace. This new mode of travel made new demands on the Western horse-stock. A demand soon arose for horses that could gallop or trot for long stages, in harness.

The *kocsi*, under various names closely resembling the original Hungarian, was distributed throughout Europe in the space of a few decades in the sixteenth century. But while it facilitated travel it also brought problems in its train, especially on the military side. So long as everyone had been accustomed to travel on horseback, there was no lack of horses "apt for service in the wars", or of horsemen to ride them in battle. But as soon as men took to travelling by coach, both sources began to dry up. Many European Governments intervened directly, among them German principalities, Italian cities, England; all passed laws restricting coach traffic, and inveighing against this new fashion which tended to make men effeminate, and was the cause of senseless luxury. In 1588 the Duke of Brunswick directly reproached his subjects: "young and old, they are turning into idlers and coach-goers". A remount crisis and a dearth of horsemen for military service arose during the reign of Queen Elizabeth of England [at least, this was the official view, though it is doubtful whether her parsimonious regime would possibly have produced the money to pay the number of horsemen who were actually available for service, if all assessable persons had made a true return of horses in their possession and men in their households able to ride. In fact, out of the whole kingdom only 3000 horsemen and suitable horses for them existed *on paper*; this was the ostensible cause for the moving in the House of Lords of a Bill to restrict the use of coaches. Another consideration was the traffic jams which coaches caused in towns still built on the medieval plan (or no plan) with very narrow streets. In fact a true return would probably have shown more than 3000 horses and riders 'apt for service in the wars' north of the Trent alone. *Tr.*] But there were many published works making the same point, such as the oft-cited book by Marx Fugger. He too sees in the rise of coaching the reason for the recession in Western horsemanship: "Yea, these Gotzis serve so much towards idleness, that a man will lead his whole household, even to the cook and the cellar therein." He proposes that in order to preserve the art of horsemanship and maintain military virtues "we should do as in Spain, and forbid the riding of asses under the saddle, or else allow it only under license at a heavy fee"—but the fee is to be for coaches, and in fact many countries now began to introduce the coach licence. He thought that the principle being that those who could afford a saddle could also afford something better than a donkey to put it on, this principle could well be applied to coach-owners, and pointed out that those who formerly bred horses were now giving it up, and "they yearn so for a Gotzi, either to sit in by themselves or with three companions and so journey through a whole province!"

The basis of his argument in favour of half-blood horses is especially interesting; at that time a hundred thalers was being asked and given for Hungarian, Spanish, and Italian horses, though not every horse was suitable for the campaigns against the Turks. "What chance would I have of riding down a Turk on the Hungarian plains, were I mounted on a Frisian or a Dutch stallion, or even on one of our German rouncies, much less if I were loaded on a coach? None, you may be sure."

Marx Fugger was not alone in his strictures. There was a flood of pamphlets and proclamations against the fashion for coaching; many mounted with such fervour that they landed on the far side of the horse. In 1673 an Englishman even went so far as to say that coach-driving was a menace to English trades and harmful to the health.

Incomprehensible as all this is today, it is a significant stage in the evolution. Though more than five centuries had passed since the days of Charles Martel and the Magyar raids, the way of life which they had introduced had not permeated all classes of society. With few exceptions, in the West equitation and the lore of the horse remained the privilege of the knightly class, of the nobility and certain of their specialized servants, and it was among this section of the population that the

78 (above) Scythian Grave from Szentes-Vekerzug,
        Typical Wagon-burial with Horses
79 (left) Magyar Horseman's Grave from the
        Settlement Period
        Excavated at Oroshàza, 1961
80 (below) Ceremonial Wagon from the Ship-grave
        of Oseberg, Norway

81 *St Elizabeth's Journey to Hungary*, 1225
Painted panel in choir of Holy Ghost Hospital, Lübeck

82 Ferdinand of Tyrol dressed as an Eastern Horseman, in the Style adopted by Light
Cavalry in the Sixteenth Century.
National Museum, Budapest

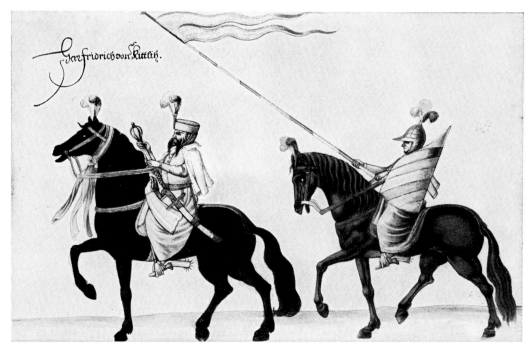

83 Friedrich von Rittlitz in Eastern Horseman's Costume
Sixteenth-century drawing from National Museum, Budapest.

84 Hungarian Hussar
    Engraving by Engelbrecht

85 Prussian Brown Hussar

86 English Officer of XIth Hussars

87 Count Valentine Esterházy, Proprietor of the
    Esterházy Regiment of Hussars in France, 1784

Ein Huſar von des Herrn von Geſchrey Freÿ Compagnie
Wann der Huſar vom Gſchrey auf ſeine Feinde jagt
Und eins noch gegen ſie mit der Piſtohle wagt,
So faßt er den Palaſch ſo eifrig als vermeſſen,
Zum Schröcken in das Maul, als wolt er ſolchen freſſen.

88   Hussar of the Geschrey Free Company in Bavarian Employ.
Engraving by Engelbrecht

89 (left)   Polish Lancer of the 3rd Regiment, 1816–31   90 (right)   Polish Lancer in the Prussian Royal
Service, 1742
National Museum Budapest

91   The Turkoman Stallion Turkmain Atty, 1791–1806

92 Early-seventeenth-century
    Travelling Carriage
    Cabinet of Engravings,
    Berlin

93 The Queen of Spain's
    Berline, with Special
    Suspension for Long
    Journeys
    Mid-eighteenth century.
    Musée de Tourisme et des
    Voitures, Compiègne

94 Swiss Alpine Post-wagon
    for five-in-hand, 1830–40
    Deutsches Museum, Munich

95 Express Mail-coach from Hungary. Lithography by J. Backer. *National Museum, Budapest*

96 The Emperor Franz Josef travelling in Hungary, 1852. *National Museum, Budapest*

new fashion of coaching had made the greatest impact and led to a numerical decline of men accustomed to the saddle.

In Hungary travel on horseback was part of the daily background of rich and poor alike. It is true that a law was passed in 1523 obliging the gentry to take the field either on foot or on horseback, and not in a coach, as many were already doing. But this was only a war emergency measure, and was not intended to maintain the permanent supply of men who could ride. At the time of the Diet of Rakes (1525) there were assembled, according to the Nuncio Burgio, ten thousand horsemen "all equipped as light horse after the Hungarian manner", quite in the tradition of Magyar and Hunnish antiquity.

Horse-breeding

The demand for fast light horses—not so much, as we have shown, for harness work as for light cavalry—led throughout Europe to the inflation of breeding Andalusian and Oriental horses. Chief among the Oriental hot-blooded sires used was the Arab.

To those two chief sources of hot-blood—the Arab and the Andalusian—a third was soon added. During the first half of the eighteenth century, Prussia, once the home of the Borussi, with their Central Asian traditions, saw the beginnings of a breed of light horses of such quality as to afford a landmark in the history of horse-breeding. Not only was it built up on a basis of Oriental horses with *some* Turanian blood, but it used sires which actually came from Turania. In 1732 King Frederick William I founded his famous Trakehnen stud with stock mostly imported from the East. The Turanian line was represented by Persian and Turkoman stallions which reached Prussia by the most varied and devious routes. One of them was the stallion Turkmain Atty who came long after the days of Frederick William I, having been foaled in 1791; a sire of such prepotency that he stamped his quality on the whole breed. He was a present from the Tsarina Catherine II to the Chancellor, Prince Kaunitz. His name is Turkish, and means simply Turkoman Horse, from which we may conclude that he belonged to the Akhal-Tekke breed.

The Trakehnen foundation stock had never before moved outside the confines of the original habitat of the wild horses—the same is also true of all the Hungarian breeds—and hence had not been subjected to the influence of an alien environment, as happened in the case of the Arab and the Barb, and has had an influence on their evolution.

Not only hot-blooded horses but also Oriental breeding techniques were borrowed, as is evident in the method of selecting breeding pairs, so also was castration, the product of which in Continental (but not Scandinavian) languages betrays its Oriental origin. Thus in French there is a verb *hongrer*, to castrate, and two nouns *hongre*, gelding, and *hongreur*, colt-gelder, both derived from *Hongrie*, Hungary. In German the gelding is called *Wallach*, showing that the custom must have been borrowed from the Wallachians (Vlachs) and Transylvanians, no earlier than in the days of the Teutonic Order. But in the extreme west of Europe—the Iberian peninsula—castration is reported by Fugger as being performed in the same manner as Hungary, with a wooden mallet, though not in the intervening countries. The explanation must lie in Arab intermediaries by way of North Africa.

Eighteenth-century tactics necessitated the employment of light cavalry after the Oriental pattern, of which the prime exemplar was the Hungarian hussar; but an equally important one was the Polish lancer. Significantly, the word *Ulan* means 'lancer' in Polish, and *Ölan* means 'nobleman' in the language of the Tartars.

A retrospective view of the development of cavalry warfare over several thousand years enables us to determine a certain continuity; as the people whose livestock husbandry was of the settled-farmstead type, both in prehistoric times and in antiquity, adopted the fighting technique of the mounted pastoralists, the mounted soldier of Oriental type remained a factor in Western armies down to modern times, and long after the bow had yielded to various types of firearm. During the century and a half of conflict with the Turks on Hungarian soil, this 'light-cavalry spirit' was not merely kept alive, it was intensified. In the Middle Ages the commitment of the light horse was initially in skirmishing—but it was more than skirmishing, it was a form of attrition which in later periods could only be achieved by harassing fire or the more intense bombardment of artillery. The light horseman 'ground away'—the very words of an Arab historian quoted above—the resistance of the enemy line-of-battle by long-range arrow-fire, and did not close with him until his stock of arrows was exhausted and the enemy physically weakened and morally shaken. The hussar's forte was a new element—a lightning attack not preceded by any such preliminary 'softening-up'. This became known throughout Europe as the *coup d'hussard*.

Two examples of this gambit may be cited. In the War of the Austrian Succession in 1743, Count Ferenc Nádasdy swam his regiment of hussars across the Rhine without losing a man or a horse, overran a line of field-works regarded by the French as impregnable, and compelled the fortress of Lauterburg to capitulate. (Note 38.) So much for the military axiom that it is useless to employ cavalry against fortifications! Again in 1757, in the Seven Years War, Count Andreas Hadik appeared with 3400 men before Berlin, suddenly, from Elsterwerda in Saxony, overpowering the garrison of the Silesian Gate with his Croatian infantry and Hungarian hussars, and swept away a counter-attack at the Kottbus Gate by a mounted attack ("I ordered the hussars and cavalry to attack with the sabre at a gallop"). With that, the garrison's resistance was broken. He levied a contribution of 700,000 gulden and set off on another forced march in order to escape encirclement by two converging Prussian armies, reaching his original base in three days. (Note 39.)

What opinion was held of hussars in the West we learn from a report by Marshal Villars:

> I feel obliged to state, that there are no troops who will serve with greater courage in the face of greater danger or will stand heavier fire or more severe losses in men and horses. There never were soldiers that fought better than these. I would to God our own cavalry had such spirit.

The pioneers of hussar expansion in the West were the small units which served as mercenaries in various European armies for regular pay in peace-time supplemented by loot on active service. (Note 40.) As every employing state was anxious to keep its hired sabres happy, so their established customs were respected. War as a regular profession was characteristic of, if not peculiar to, the Eastern horseman's way of life. [The obvious parallel in British terms is the companies of Irish and Highland swordsmen in English, French, and other foreign employ, who gained their living in this way without necessarily being political exiles like the famed Wild Geese brigades. *Tr.*] Both their scale of pay and the manner in which they drew it differed from that of the regular troops of the employing Power.

For instance, in France they were compensated for the customary perquisite of ransom for captured enemies by a bounty for every severed enemy head they could produce. [It is said, with or without foundation, that Senegalese troops of the French army were also remunerated for such trophies in this century. *Tr.*] (Note 41.) In the Prussian Army standing regulations laid down: "What the hussar can get by his sword from the enemy he is to keep for himself, without anything being withheld, and no difficulties are to be made." This order forbids, in the case of hussars, the forming of a common pool of loot, as was customary in other units. In 1759 Frederick the Great reactivated an old standing order which brings out the special status of the hussar. "Officers, NCOS and War Office officials are not to wound the pride of the Hungarian hussar; they are to be strict in their behaviour towards him, but must avoid humiliating reprimands and they are never to thrash such a man."

The first Hungarian officer to be seconded together with his troops to a Western service was Colonel George Ráttky, who entered the French service in 1692, and who after the battle of Höchstädt took command of a unit of 300 hussars formerly in the service of the Elector of Bavaria. From 1704 to 1710 Baron Gabriel Bellay-Bellawitz was in Dutch service with 150 hussars, but then went into Danish employ, and after many years returned home by way of Poland. (Note 42.)

After the Peace of Szatmár which brought the rising of Ferenc Rákóczi II to an end in 1711, officers and other ranks of his disbanded force took service with foreign Powers by troops. Thus Ladislaus Bercsényi, son of the Kurutz general Nikolaus of that name, joined Ráttky's regiment in 1713, followed by the two Valentine Esterházys, a son and a grandson of the rebel Anton Esterházy, then living in exile at Rodosto. With their collaboration the first three hussar regiments in the French service, which bore their name, were formed on the Hungarian model. It is significant that the oath of allegiance on attestment was taken in Hungarian down to the French Revolution. But these three regiments survived the Revolution, as the Swiss Guard did not, and still existed down to the end of the First World War.

The first regularly paid hussar unit in Prussia was raised in 1721 by refugee Hungarian officers, and it served the celebrated military maniac, King Frederick William I of Prussia, as a model for his "Black", "Brown", and "Death's Head" hussar regiments among others. In the roll of their commanding officers we find such names as Sigismund Halász of Dabas, Paul Werner of Györ, Michael Székely, Ferenc Carol Köszhegy, and Michael Kovács, the last-named being killed in the American War of Independence. Until 1743 there was a recruiting office in Vienna where officers and men signed on, but in that year it was abolished. No wonder that in 1757 the hussar regiment "Yazyg and Kuman" in the Austrian service called the Prussian hussars opposing them "Black Kuruzes", referring to Rákóczi's rebels. (Note 43.)

The third outlet for East European light horse was in Holland, where in 1743 Count George Frangepani took over the legacy of Colonel Bellay; like Ráttky, he had been in Bavarian service. In the roll of Hungarian officers serving in the Dutch army we find between 1745 and 1752 such names as Michael Zsigray, Gregor Sándor, Michael Ersey, Johann Szakáy, Alexander Jármay, Baron Josef Waha, Samuel Patonay, Ferenc Asztalos, Johann Sándor, and many others. By their aid regular hussar regiments were raised, the new arm being introduced partly by Hungarians, partly by French, Prussian, and Dutch intermediaries, into the establishment of the Russian, Polish, Swedish, Danish, Bavarian, Wuerttemberg, Baden, Saxon, Hanoverian, and British armies, as well as those of minor German states such as Weimar, Kassel, and Hesse-Darmstadt, the episcopal principalities, and Nassau; also Portugal, Spain, Modena, Piedmont, Naples, the Papal territories, Sardinia, some Balkan kingdoms, and—Japan. Besides the uniform, which imposed itself with greater or less completeness on various units, even to the Horse Artillery of the British Army, and (in some respects less suitably) the full-dress uniform of the Royal Air Force, the tactics and sundry customs of the East European light horseman penetrated in the wake of the hussars. In the eighteenth and early nineteenth century the hussar was regarded as the embodiment of the 'modern, progressive' soldier, which of course he was, by contrast with the traditional musketeer fighting in close order and firing by volleys, supported by slow-moving dragoons who were not really cavalry at all. (Note 44.)

Saddlery, Accoutrements, and Riding-Style

Along with the spread of light cavalry the use of the gelding for military purposes went hand in hand, but much more so there grew the use of the Hungarian saddle. The heavy demand for wooden saddles brought an unprecedented revival—indeed, boom—to the Hungarian saddlery industry, and the products of the workshops of Tiszafüred and Igmánd become known throughout Europe, and sought after. J. N. Máttyus, a lieutenant of hussars, wrote in 1828 a cavalry manual dealing comprehensively with this saddle. He wrote in his preface:

> Because of its practical design the Hungarian saddle is the best to fight in, it is the cheapest and the most durable . . . but since, abroad, it has become fashionable to modify and adapt it to locally current fashion, I think it relevant to set forth the essential features of its design, which were probably first introduced into our country by Asiatic peoples, and by us to foreign nations. . . .

By modification, by mass production, by the exaggeration of certain peculiarities which originally had been merely decorative, the foreign-made 'Hungarian' saddle lost much. Count Joseph Gvadányi wrote in 1788 in *Journey of a Village Lawyer to Buda*—a rhyming narrative—

> I think that when they are mounted on their horses, the saddles on their backs will be of Igmánd or Füred make, the bridles hung with fringes in the shape of swallow-tails, the cheek-pieces ornamented with thongs or gold thread with gold or silver agrafes, or decorated with sea-shells—the whole inlaid with coloured strips of leather. This was once the custom of our famous ancestors . . .

The best Western versions of the wooden saddle retained only those features which were of practical use.

Just as the hussar brought new tactics to cavalry warfare, so the Hungarian saddle had its influence on Western riding. We saw above how the Western rider sat with his legs stretched out, and this seat—which now seems so alien to us—was only displaced by the Hungarian style. Now henceforth the European rider began to draw up his knees after the Hungarian manner. Significantly, when Robert Shaw was visiting Yarkand and Kashgar in 1868, having ridden all the way from India, the Turkomans asked how it came about that he rode like a Turk, but his Indian escort in another manner.

When in 1809 the Hungarian pattern of saddle was taken into service by the Austrian army the dragoon saddle was described as: "Hungarian, wooden, the fore-arch (pommel) cut quite short. The stirrup leathers are hung further forward on the bars, and slantwise, so as not to make the man ride too far forward in the saddle." In the second half of the nineteenth century the Hungarian saddle was widely replaced by a modified version of the English saddle, while in Hungary itself the traditional design was still in military use during the Second World War, but by this time some of its originally wooden components were made of steel.

Western Influences and their Historical Effect

Hitherto we have only treated of the Eastern element which went to make up the final European synthesis of horsemanship, but now we will trace the development of some Western traditions which made their way eastward.

The Spread of the Pacing Horse

Armoured cavalry, its characteristic skills at arms, and its tactics, had been gaining ground in Eastern Europe since the thirteenth century, while the Western custom of jousting became the amusement of Eastern courts. The Hungarian Order of the Dragon, founded in 1404, was one result of this; and thereby the principles and customs of chivalry gained a firm footing in what had been hitherto the European stronghold of Eastern practice, in equestrian matters. This relatively late cultural influence had as its corollary the expansion of the palfrey into Hungary.

The pacing gait, as unnatural as riding itself, was still quite unknown to the peoples of Central Asia and those who rode like them in the Middle Ages, and no mention of such a fashion there is to be found either in Oriental or in Western documentary sources. Nevertheless, it is probable that it originated in Western Asia, possibly in imitation of the gait of the riding-camel.

The Romans knew it, and apparently all Mediterranean peoples whose pre-equestrian past included chariot-driving. According to Pliny, it was a speciality of the Celtiberians whose pacing ponies (known in their own language as *thieldones*, and called by the Romans *asturcones* after the province of Asturias) were presumably bred to pace. But they can also be trained to do so, and this was done in Hungary, where the strain of horse genetically *inclined* to pace was less common than in the Celtic west. Training was done before the foal was a year old, by joining fore- to hind-leg on each side with an inflexible link. But since not every horse will perform equally well at this gait, even if successfully trained, efforts were made to breed the right sort, one of the specifications for which was a short body. In Hungary the counties of Doboka and Beszterce Nazód were noted for their pacers. Breeders and trainers bought foundation stock from there. In 1499 King Wladislaw II forbad any more to be sent out of the counties, lest the reservoir of breeding stock should fall below the danger-mark; or else possibly because he did not wish this foreign custom to gain a hold on his country at large. (Note 45.)

The first illustration of an ambling palfrey in Hungary is an illumination in the *Vienna Illustrated Chronicle*, showing the train of the Bohemian King Wenceslaus to Hungary in 1301. The first documentary evidence comes in 1335, in which the pacing palfrey is called "parefridus" and the ambler "dalm"—a word of totally unknown etymology. (Note 46.) It does not seem that the gait became much more widespread until the second half of the fifteenth century. (Note 47.)

Some estimate of the palfrey's popularity is afforded by the price of 100 gulden, asked at a time when other sorts of horse—good ones—were fetching 20 gulden. By the sixteenth century almost all the better-off gentry possessed a palfrey. In 1537 Ferenc Batthyány wrote to his young brother: "When I was your age I would never get on a palfrey, I wanted horses that stepped out more. And such I prefer now. You will be wanting a ride in the Queen's Cage next." By the "Queen's Cage" he meant a litter, borne by two horses, in general use in the West, but especially in mountainous countries such as Spain and Wales, where it survived longest.

It is probable that the pacing/ambling/racking tradition of riding came to Hungary from the south, brought by Yugoslavs displaced by the Turks. Philological evidence, often inconclusive, points if anything to a Slavonic origin for the Hungarian word *poroszka*—palfrey, in the South Slav *pruszati, prusszka*, even though these have been glossed as 'trot' and 'trotter'. The same inference may be drawn from the Hungarian word *paripa* for an ambling horse (*gradarius vulgo parypa* in 1579), derived from the Greek word *parippi* (Note 48), which seems to be a contraction of the Graeco-Latin *paraveredus*. But by contrast with the West the palfrey enjoyed only a short spell of fashion in Hungary. Many deemed it unmanly to ride so, and it is little mentioned towards the end of the sixteenth century, and not at all by 1700. Indeed, the times of the Turkish wars were not at all propitious for the keeping of horses that could not be turned over to military use, and were only suitable for peaceful journeys or for hacking about at home. [The same concentration on *trotting* horses adaptable for light-cavalry use is observable up to about 1600 in Britain, on the marches of Wales and of Scotland, with their endemic state of minor frontier warfare. *Tr.*]

The combination in the West of travel on wheels and the adoption of the 'hussar' style of riding with shorter stirrups also tipped the scale in favour of the trotting horse, though somewhat later. The palfrey decline was steep throughout the eighteenth century, absolute by the nineteenth, by which time it had been stigmatized as 'ugly', and unsuitable for a cavalryman.

The 'five-gaited horse', to use an all-embracing American term, held its own almost everywhere where carriage travel remained difficult. Nineteenth-century travellers describe it as current in the Balkans, the Near East, and in the Far East (pacing was inbred in the now extinct Indian Kathiawari strain), and it may be connected with Arab expansion. From Spain and from Britain it spread to the Americas; in Latin America the *Caballo de paso* and its counterpart the pacing mule still flourish; while the Anglo-Saxon tradition of the palfrey is nowadays confined to such territories as Tennessee and the Carolinas. (Note 49.)

The Spanish School

The other variant of Western horsemanship, the Spanish School, had even less success in Eastern Europe. King Matthias of Hungary (1458–90) not only rejected its method, but refused to accept any Spanish horses "hopping around with their bent hocks". On the other hand, a bare fifty years later most of the higher nobility had Spanish horses in their stables. (Note 50.) Yet the Spanish High School never really caught on east of the Austrian border. The primary reason was that the training method was regarded as a 'purgatory for horses'. Young Ferenc Nádasdy, studying at the University of Vienna, wrote to his mother in 1669, more or less laying this bogy: "I saw how they were trained, and Your Grace may believe me when I say that the Spanish and Italian trainers do not use the horses brutally" and he asks her to engage such a trainer. (Note 51.) We do not know whether the lady did comply with his suggestion; be that as it may, throughout the rule over Hungary of the Habsburgs who were its greatest patrons, the Spanish or Neapolitan High School never took firm root in Hungarian soil.

Driving

What the Hungarians and their neighbours in Eastern Europe thought worth adopting were Western innovations in the harness field. Many technical details were adopted, such as the solid-bar driving bits which automatically "gave the horse a good head-carriage" (Note 52), Western types of hame collar (which are nevertheless ultimately of Turkish origin), French traces and draft-chains—not least horseshoes of modern type which cover, not the whole sole as formerly, but only the rim of the hoof.

Of the Occidental innovations the new-style carriage was unquestionably the most important as a means of locomotion.

While the wagon and the coach, once the most advanced in Europe, had undergone no modification in Hungary since we last noted their appearance—inventories enumerate exactly the same parts under the same names all through the sixteenth and seventeenth centuries (Note 53)—coaches and carriages in the West had developed greatly, if not in the direction of travelling efficiency, at least as far as the comfort of the passengers was concerned. Hungarian light coaches and travelling wagons, the same in 1500 as in 1900, developed in the West into the very heavy caross which had great capacity, and ultimately into such variants as the Victoria, the Berline and Coupé, the Calèche, and the Mail-coach. These and many others have as almost their sole common factor the smaller fore-wheels.

Vehicles designed for comfortable travelling, such as the post-chaise and the 'glass coach' of the nobility, appeared in due course in Hungary, and with them came the more powerful type of carriage horse, often with Andalusian or Neapolitan blood. Whereas the mail-coaches were still harnessed four-in-hand and driven from the saddle by postilions according to old Hungarian usage, the greater landlords drove six horses in three pairs in Western style. Only the leading pair were driven by an outrider on the near horse, the other four being driven by the coachman on the box. This way of driving is not demonstrable in Hungary before the middle of the seventeenth century, but some form of six-in-hand, the exact nature of which is not known at the present day, existed there before that.

The steppe fashion of driving was still evident in the harnessing, of country carts only, in the nineteenth century, using vehicles whose design and the nomenclature of whose parts has remained unchanged from the seventeenth century to the present day. The carrier, driving three horses at the gallop, provided a means of rapid public transport down to the beginnings of the Hungarian railway system. Count Dénes Széchenyi, in his day a great expert on horse transport, mentions in his book (1892) the old Hungarian style of driving, or what was called 'mixed driving', as already outmoded: it consisted of alternate spells of walk, trot, and gallop.

The Battle of Mohács and its Consequences

This chapter, which deals with the expansion of Western practices, would not be complete if it did not point to the historical consequences of such influences. An example, drawn from the Hungarian past, is the calamitous death of King Louis II during a mounted action. We may consider what caused the death of this king on the field of battle, and why he did not succeed in escaping from Mohács in the same way as three hundred years earlier his predecessor King Béla IV had done, under much more adverse circumstances, in getting clear away after a defeat at the hands of the Mongols. Louis II of Hungary (1516–26) was the son of Vladislav II of the Jagellonian dynasty and the French princess Anne de Foix. He was married to Maria of Habsburg, sister of the Emperor Ferdinand I. With this overwhelmingly Western background, appropriate influences prevailed at the Hungarian Court, and the King's death on the field of Mohács can be attributed in some degree to the consequences of adopting Western customs.

This is the sequence of events: on the news that the Turkish host was approaching, the King took the field himself on June 15th, 1526, in order to hasten the concentration of troops from all parts of the kingdom. On his departure from Buda he was riding, according to the Chronicle of Dubravius, a black Frisian horse. The King at the head of his army did not get far on this horse, which according to Istvánffy died under him a mile out of Buda, at the village of Érd. This was regarded by many as an ill omen, nor was the King himself unmoved by it.

On August 29th the two armies were facing each other at Mohács. The battle did not start until three in the afternoon, neither side being fully prepared before then. On the Hungarian side a guard had been detailed for the King, all mounted on fast horses so that if need be the King could escape on one of them, and they had been given the mission, in certain circumstances, of rescuing him from the mêlée and escorting him to a place of safety.

At three o'clock, then, the glitter of lances was observed opposite the Hungarian right wing. The Turkish cavalry was advancing. The Hungarian commander, Archbishop Tomori, at once sent a cavalry unit to oppose them, but this, to the general consternation, was none other than the royal guard. Since at this critical moment no-one wished to commit an apparent infraction of discipline, nobody disputed this ill-considered order; and consequently from the outset of the battle the King was deprived of his escort. At almost the same time the Hungarian vanguard attacked frontally, and with such fury that they almost reached the pavilion of the Sultan. On the heels of this success the King led the main battle to the attack.

A Turkish source continues, with Oriental floweriness: "Recking naught of arrows or bullets, the king put his piebald to a gallop and like a raging evil spirit rushed on to the post of glory." On this attack followed the decisive turn of the battle: the cleverly masked Turkish batteries came into play, opening flanking fire on the attackers, the Hungarian right wing recoiled, bringing the Hungarian centre into

97 Racing at Datchet, near Windsor, 1684

98 Painting by Rosa Bonheur of Stallions fighting, reputed to represent the Duel
between Hobgoblin and the Godolphin Arabian

99 The Thoroughbred Stallion Eclipse, 1764–89   100 The Thoroughbred Mare Kincsem, 1874–87

101   Racing at Epsom

102   Fox-hunting in England.
       The Kill, by Byron Webb, 1851

103   *The Carriage Drive in the Prater, Vienna, 1885.*
Watercolour by G. A. Wilda

104   The Same

disarray, so that though some smaller units fought on, panic engendered by the unexpected Turkish artillery fire decided the issue of the battle.

Subsequent events are recorded in the dispatch by the Papal Nuncio, Burgio, dated from Bratislava and forwarded to the Holy See. He reported that Ulrich Czettricz, Chamberlain and confidant of the King, had told him on his arrival at Bratislava how he, the King, and Stephan Aczél had got free of the mêlée and were getting clear away when they came to the Csele brook, a tributary of the Danube that was normally quite small, but was then swollen by a recent cloudburst. As they were about to cross, the King's horse became refractory and reared up in the water, so that his rider (who was already exhausted) slipped from the saddle and was drowned by the weight of his armour. When Aczél saw the plight of his master he jumped in after him, and was also drowned. (Note 54.)

Czettricz set out at the Queen's behest some two months later, to search for the body. Arrived at the scene of the disaster, he found the dead horse stuck in the bog, and he and his following thought at first that the King's body must be underneath it. But all they found was the weapons. Finally they came on a newly dug grave, and the King's body in it.

Although all the available evidence is that of eye-witnesses, or at least as first-hand as that of Burgie, speculation was rife for centuries because the testimony was so conflicting. The common people simply did not believe that the King could have come by his death through the obstinacy of his horse. The Treasurer Thurzo in a letter to the King of Poland ascribed the accident to the wounding of the King's horse, while Turkish accounts say the King himself was wounded. Istvánffy the historian maintained that the horse came over backward in trying to climb the steep bank. The picture becomes clearer if one takes into account how people rode in those days, especially at the Court of Louis II.

The account books for 1526 show purchases of horses for royal use from Moravia. They are described as "equi armigeri", and, more significantly, they were attended by German grooms (Note 55), thus leaving no room for doubt that they were heavy horses trained in the German manner—in short, destriers intended to carry a man in full armour. But since it is well known that Louis' predecessors Vladislav and Matthias had ridden nothing but Hungarian, Transylvanian, or Turkish horses (Note 56), it therefore follows that these were the first heavy horses to have formed part of the royal establishment.

We noted above that Louis II had set out from Buda, contrary to Hungarian custom, on a Frisian horse, the collapse of which at Érd was probably due to haemo-globinaemia to which heavy horses are subject. It is especially prevalent among highly fed horses that are kept up in stables all the time, and the symptoms appear consequent upon sudden exertion; in acute cases death occurs very quickly.

Plainly, the King took no warning when this first horse collapsed on being galloped straight out of the yard, but once on the battlefield he mounted a fresh heavy horse—a piebald destrier—while at the same time fast light horses were being kept in readiness for him. He was simply following established custom; the Western convention was to ride the destrier only in, or in immediate anticipation of, action, and the other horses afterwards.

This had been the case with the Emperor Otto II, as with all Western knights. And in a like situation Otto had survived. It is always possible that in the confusion Louis was not able to get near the fast reserve horses in order to change on to one of them, so turned to flight on his heavy charger. This is the more likely since his guard had been prematurely committed to action, and since the horse he rode seems to have been wounded. (Note 57.)

The immediate cause, therefore, of the disaster at Mohács, which had portentous consequences both for Hungary and for Europe, may be the death of the King's horse under him, which by its breeding and type was not equal to the task, and probably succumbed to a heart-attack. But the underlying cause was the 'Westernization' of the Court, with its French Queen-Mother and German Queen, both in civil and in military matters. Louis had not the sharp, objective eye of Matthias fifty years earlier, enabling him to see the unsuitability of Western techniques for his purpose. If it were then true that the welfare of the State depended on a horse's back, as the proverb ran, this was a classic example. By the death of the King a successful counter-attack became out of the question and the balance of power in Eastern Europe was permanently upset. The old Magyar dominion was now to be shared by the Turks on the one hand and the Habsburgs on the other, until the defeat of the former a hundred and fifty years later, which would lead inevitably to the formation of a new Great Power, Austria-Hungary. [All through the choice of the wrong stamp of horse. One is reminded, in some respects of the old English proverbial jingle:

> For want of a nail the shoe was lost;
> For want of a shoe the horse was lost;
> For want of a horse the rider was lost;
> For want of a rider the battle was lost;
> And all for the want of a horseshoe-nail. Tr.]

The Thoroughbred

Towards the end of the seventeenth century there began, with the introduction of Arabian and Barb horses into England, a unique stimulus to horsemanship in that country, which also added a new branch to the family tree of the Turanian Horse: this branch is called in most countries—but not in England—the English Thoroughbred (il Purosangue inglese, etc.), and its half-bred derivatives are known as 'Anglo-' whatever—e.g., Anglo-Norman, Anglo-Khabardin, etc., etc. This new kind of hot-blooded horse was a milestone in the history of European horsemanship.

The history of riding in England, as in Western Europe generally, goes back to the days of the Roman occupation and beyond. Riding had become more and more common since the end of the Bronze Age, but for military purposes it only became practicable to the extent that larger horses became available, a process probably accelerated during the Belgic invasions of south-eastern Britain in the last two centuries b.c., and culminating in the introduction of full-scale riding-horses by the Romans, mostly from Iberia.

The medieval or feudal phenomenon of chivalry—that is, a social order which hinges, in military as in civil life, on the armoured mounted lancer with his Great Horse—was only fully developed in England under the Normans, though it had been foreshadowed during the reign of Edward the Confessor (1042–66). There is documentary evidence for the importation of Andalusian stallions in the reign of William the Conqueror, though the most successful use of these as sires was due to the Earl of Shrewsbury, Robert de Belesme, who flourished in the reign of Henry I (1100–35), breeding 'steeds' for knights and 'rouncies' for squires.

King John in the early thirteenth century spent a great deal of money on horses for hunting, and Richard II on 'coursers'—which among other things were race-horses, though we really know nothing about racing as it was in his day (1377–99). The King of Navarre gave him two such horses described as 'Spanish' but more likely belonging to one of the light-horse breeds of South-Western France. The statute books of the Tudors from the reign of Henry VIII to Elizabeth abound in ordinances laying down the minimum height for stallions depastured on common grazings, the object the production of horses "apt for service in the wars"—*i.e.*, capable of carrying a man in half-armour—and the repetition of these enactments over and over again for more than three-quarters of a century shows how ineffective they were. It was in fact impossible to breed potential war-horses except in the traditional manner—in a park, usually attached to a royal castle, kept up in winter and fed with a quantity of protein and an allowance of hay which was quite beyond the resources of ordinary freeholders to provide. More significant, as a foreshadow-ing of the Thoroughbred, are the efforts which Henry VIII made to import horses of Oriental stamp from North Italian sources such as Padua. Royal patronage of racing began seriously with the accession of the first Stuart king, James I, formerly James VI of Scotland, and it may be significant that at the end of the sixteenth century fast horses of native breed were commoner in Southern Scotland than in any part of England. Under James I, importation of Oriental horses from the classical source—Aleppo market—began; declined during the reign of Charles I, who had a penchant for Andalusians; came almost to a standstill during the Civil War of the 1640's; and was resumed on a greater scale under the Commonwealth.

The Ancestors of the Thoroughbred

Oliver Cromwell, Lord Protector, was fond of hunting and racing, although for political reasons he forbade the latter sport during a great part of his years of office, because race-meetings offered too great an opportunity for 'disaffected persons' or 'malignants' to meet together. Place, his Master of the Horse, bought him an Arab known as the White Turk, but unfortunately we do not know by what route it reached England. Its success on the Turf, however, was undoubted. Imports con-tinued on a mounting scale throughout the reign of Charles II.

The first Arabs mentioned in the Stud Book came to England by way of Turkish and Hungarian intermediaries. Thus the Lister Turk was part of the booty taken at the fall of Buda in 1686, and likewise the mare Belgrade Turk at the recapture of Belgrade (1707), presented by General Mercy to the English owner. Of the three stallions who are the corner-stone of the General Stud Book, two came from Turkey; the Byerly Turk imported about 1680, and the Darley Arabian in 1705.

The third was the celebrated Godolphin Arabian (or Barb) who was discovered by a Mr. Coke drawing a water-cart in the streets of Paris. Coke was sorry for the bay stallion, bought him for 75 francs, and brought him to London. As later ap-peared, either the Bey of Tunis or the Sultan of Morocco had sent this stallion to King Louis XV as a present. He gave him to his cook, who sold him to the carter. In England he came into the possession of Lord Godolphin, who used him as a teaser for his stallion Hobgoblin. This was in 1730. In the next year, the mare Roxana was to be served by Hobgoblin, and was first tried by El Sham (the Godolphin Arabian's real name), who tore loose from the stud-groom and attacked Hobgoblin, killing him. He then covered Roxana. The result of this union was a colt named Lath. Among his grandsons was the famous Matchem, from whom many Throughbreds today are descended.

[A certain confusion arises from the fact that in Restoration England the words Turk and Turkey were very loosely used. Thus the Darley Arabian was bought at Aleppo, which was in Turkish territory. But he was actually foaled, in 1700, in the Syrian desert among the Fedan Bedouin. Tr.]

The system on which Thoroughbred breeding in England was organized might accurately be called Egyptian. Records in the private stud books of the eighteenth century, and of the General Stud Book in due course, were made on the principles laid down by El Nasser some centuries earlier, to which we have referred. The only animals admitted to the General Stud Book, from the beginning until today, are those all of whose ancestors are entered in that Book, which records all the Thoroughbreds all over the world. Any horse, one of whose ancestors is of unknown origin, is regarded as half-bred, and so are all its descendants, no matter how brilliantly they may perform.

Although the Arab was a formative factor in the creation of the Thoroughbred, it was only *one* factor. The mares put to the three foundation sires were mostly of unknown origin; primarily the 'Royal Mares' about whose breeding there has been much dispute. Probably they represented the cream of all those horses which had been presented to the Royal Family over many generations, or their descendants, including also those purchased by Henry VIII from the Gonzaga family of Padua. The stud was in fact dispersed by public auction after the execution of Charles I, and it was not possible, after the Restoration, to reassemble more than a certain proportion of these mares and their progeny. But considering the nature of royal gifts and purchases over the preceding hundred years, it is likely that the great majority of these animals were of Oriental origin. Count G. Wrangel, writing in 1888, said: "Charles II, who re-activated the Newmarket races instituted by Charles I, was the first to import [Oriental] mares". This may be true so far as deliberate purchase is concerned, but it takes no account of mares coming into the possession of previous monarchs by way of gift.

He continues:

Unfortunately we lack detailed information about the number and breeding of these Royal Mares. It has however been asserted on the strength of oral tradition, that they came from the Orient, yet there are other circumstances which make it appear more probable that they came from Hungary. What is certain is that the Royal Mares cannot all have come from one source.

Wrangel's assumption is credible in the light of the general picture of European racehorse breeding at that time. If it were justified, then the 'unknown Oriental factor' in the Thoroughbred would be identical with that in such European 'warm-blood' studs as Trakehnen and Czindery; that is to say, descendants of the Bactrian horse which had arrived, not by way of Arabia or even North Africa but by a more northerly route via the Caspian and the Black Sea. That there must be some other factor (and this is most unlikely to be a 'native' element) is proved by the fact that it has not been possible to breed up an animal of Thoroughbred type on a basis of pure Arab foundation stock, either in England or elsewhere.

Erika Schiele, in her book *The Arab Horse in Europe* (London edition, 1970), represents the view (put forward by Carl Raswan, among others) that the genesis of the Thoroughbred was due to the influence of the Muniqi stock of Arabs. The Muniqi, as opposed to the Seglawi and Kehailan types, reached its present form only in the seventeenth century, when the tribes who bred the original Muniqi and Jilfan types migrated to Northern Mesopotamia, where they came in contact with Turkoman nomads, and put some of their mares to the Turkoman stallions. The cross of Muniqi on the other two 'classic' Arabian types is said to produce foals that look more like Thoroughbreds. This theory rests on the same basis as Wrangel's quoted above, pointing to an out-cross of Turanian blood, without which the descendants of the Darley Arabian, Byerly Turk, etc., would without exception have looked like pure-bred Arabians or pure-bred Barbs.

The capabilities of the Thoroughbred on the Turf, in the hunting-field, and in harness are common knowledge nowadays. Nevertheless another proof of their capacity to do everything that a horse can do was given by an experiment which Sir Charles Bunbury made in the last century. He made a bet that his TB mare Eleanor—one of the few females that have won both the Oaks and the Derby—could carry a greater weight than a working horse. Now, this was still in the era when the 'professional' weight-carrying packhorse was an everyday sight in England. A miller's horse, accustomed to carrying great loads of corn and meal, was put up against Eleanor, who walked away quietly under an enormous load, under which the pack-horse could scarcely stand upright, let alone step forward.

The Arab horse which had been pure-bred since the time of El Nasser underwent in England a modification quite apart from the effects of cross-breeding. The biological effect of the changed environment, even taken by itself, would have been very powerful. In terms of climate, of vegetation, of ecology, the English countryside resembled the original habitat of the wild horse much more than the Arabian desert, and those characteristics which the Arab horse had acquired in response to the arid climate of Arabia, with its sparse vegetation and lack of shade, and the very different chemical content of the soil, it would in any case have shed after some generations of life in a more humid climate, with abundant grazing, a different kind of protein (oats instead of barley), more drinking-water with a different mineral content, and a soil containing entirely different trace elements. The only common factor that remained between Arabia and Britain was the close proximity to the human race, the frequent handling from birth, and the amount of time spent 'indoors'—whether in the black tents or in loose-boxes. The average height of the Thoroughbred increased by eight inches in two hundred years; its performance, especially over short distances, improved; and its conformation altered so as to approach nearer to that of Central Asiatic breeds such as the Akhal-Tekke. This combined influence of climate and soil is observable to a greater or less extent in horses of partly Arab descent throughout Europe, as for instance at the Bábolna stud, which has had very frequent refreshments of Arab blood, so that its characteristic Shagya breed is in effect an Arab in all but name. We may well ask ourselves what would happen if a herd of registered Thoroughbred horses were kept in an extensive park without hand-feeding, in a temperate climate, mating being determined by the preference of the mares and the fighting ability or 'pecking-order' of the stallions. Obviously there would be a reversion to the wild type—but what would this wild type be like, if the original components consisted exclusively of

Thoroughbreds? Would it in fact become identical with the 'wild blood-horse' whose existence in the remote past is believed in by some? This would indeed be a costly experiment, but probably not much more costly than those which have gone to the 'breeding-back' of such lost races as the Tarpan and the aurochs. In this age of scientific research it seems that such an investigation might be as rewarding as the two mentioned above, which apart from their objective (pre) historical interest have provided information which is of direct utility in the field of genetics and stock-breeding.

Distribution of the Thoroughbred

The unique English successes soon had their effect on Continental horse-breeding, and a massive importation of Thoroughbreds began in the second half of the eighteenth century. Despite its favourable effect on the balance of trade, British Governments did not welcome this traffic, and a new embargo was imposed. It was so strictly enforced that a ship in which Count Ferdinand Kinsky was personally escorting a stallion and four mares across the Channel was fired on by coastal batteries, in 1760. Restrictions were so far loosened as to permit the export of blood-stock in particular cases, except for certain lines which were deemed too valuable to allow out of the country. With this reservation, it was now possible for blood-stock to reach any country in Europe and any British colony without let or hindrance. Its rapid spread was due to the popularity which horse-racing—English style—soon attained abroad. Another cause was the demand for blood-horses for crossing which arose in many countries, but especially Central Europe, from the remount crises brought about by repeated wars.

But the production of half-blood horses made great strides in Britain and Ireland also. Crossing with the larger 'indigenous' breeds produced the Hunter, the Hackney, and the Coach-horse, especially the Yorkshire Coach-horse which was a cross of the Thoroughbred on the Cleveland Bay, itself a fixed type of uniform colour that was the result of a cross of Barb and (probably) Andalusian horses on the pack-horse mares of North-eastern England, taking shape about 1670.

On the Continent the Electorate of Hanover and Duchy of Brunswick were pioneers in bloodstock breeding. The proximate cause was, as so often, a political event. By the accession of George, Elector of Hanover, to the British throne on the death of Queen Anne in 1714, the thrones of Britain and Hanover were united until 1837. In 1735 the Hanoverian stud of Celle was founded, drawing some foundation sires from England. The Hanoverian half-blood owes its existence to King George II and his son the Duke of Cumberland. It has since become world-famous [and the wheel has come full circle. During the 1960's Hanoverian stallions were standing at stud in England, primarily with the object of getting heavyweight hunters and event horses. Tr.] The story was repeated in East Friesland, once the home of heavy destriers, whose descendants were crossed with Hanoverians to produce a heavy-duty coach-horse. In other North German principalities such as Mecklenburg, Holstein, and Oldenburg, where since the decline of chivalry the emphasis had been on the breeding of Andalusian or Neapolitan chargers, Thoroughbreds were now imported to impart quality to the local stock. From the beginning of the nineteenth century onward German horse-breeders with half-bred stock on either a Thoroughbred or Trakehner basis attained a standard that was not only valuable from a military and transport point of view at home, but became of international importance.

What Prussia was for Germany, what Yorkshire was for England, Hungary for the Habsburg monarchy, Normandy was for France. From the days of the half-Norse Norman Duchy onward, chivalry and horsemanship had been engrained in the Norman people. In the departments of Orne and Manche a heavy horse had been bred time out of mind, and side by side with it a lighter riding type, especially in Merlerault and the Cotentin. A dash of the Thoroughbred here gave rise to the Anglo-Norman, valuable alike as a coach-horse, a hunter, and nowadays as an event horse or show-jumper. Nonius was an Anglo-Norman entire. During the Napoleonic Wars he fell into Austrian hands and gave his name to a whole breed which had its origin in the Imperial stud at Mezöhegyes, where he was sent to stand, so impressed were the authorities by his performance and conformation. This Nonius strain is today a working horse of great substance, which has long proved itself to be of equal merit with the North Star and Furioso strains, likewise bred in Hungary and partly of Thoroughbred ancestry. [North Star was a trotting 'roadster' bred in East Yorkshire. Tr.]

The Thoroughbred appeared in every corner of the world where the military and commercial interests of the British Empire required its presence. The combination of sea-power and horse-power was an essential prerequisite of colonial expansion, just as it had been in the days of the Normans.

When the American colonies united and became independent they soon worked out their own varieties of half-bred horses, a combination of the Thoroughbred with stock mainly of Spanish origin. Here we need mention only the Quarter-Horse, the Morgan, and the American Saddle horse, ridden mostly for pleasure, and the Standard-bred, used for trotting-races. The Standard-bred in its turn has spread to all countries of the world where sulky-racing is carried on. All Standard-breds are descended from the Thoroughbred Messenger, who came to the United States in 1788; his sire, the grey Mambrino, is well known to all admirers of equestrian art through the splendid portrait by Stubbs, which shows him to have been one of the most Arabian-looking racehorses that ever were foaled.

The picture of Thoroughbred breeding would not be complete without some account of the two individuals which are reputed the best horses the world has yet seen. One was bred in England, a great-grandson of the Darley Arabian named Eclipse, foaled at the Duke of Cumberland's stud, in 1764; he lived to the age of twenty-five. The other was the mare Kincsem (1874–87) bred in Hungary by Ernst von Blaskovich. Both were chestnut, both were unbeaten on the Turf throughout a long career. The career of Kincsem in particular is unique. With her 54 wins, some on Hungarian courses but also in Austrian, German, French, and English races, she proved her invincibility against the best horses in the world.

European travel by road, in the saddle or on the box, was pretty much the same in every country, at the time when the Thoroughbred was spreading across the Continent, due to the widespread imitation of English habits which now set in. The admired pattern of a 'horsy' individual, whether riding or driving, was the English Meltonian or Corinthian with his characteristic clothes, mannerisms, saddlery, harness, method of putting the team to, type of carriage driven, rules of sport, and even the custom of rising to the trot which now for the first time became common in Europe. [Both in civil life and in the Army, even though English cavalry, to the present day, differ from civilians in *not* rising to the trot. *Tr.*]

Road traffic made new demands on the horse-breeder throughout Europe as the nineteenth century opened, since the new network of completely metalled roads called for a different pace. The Continental *pavé* was not suitable for galloping stages, either for riders or for drivers, so that the traveller had to trot his horses for long distances. [To what extent the Scottish invention of the Macadam road surface, which was more like the original rammed-gravel surface of Roman roads, made the British Isles an exception to the general rule, is debatable. *Tr.*] Since the once almost universal travelling pace, the 'easy-gaited' lateral amble, had vanished from memory, the 'English trot' called in England 'posting' (because it was originally the habit of postilions) was the only tolerable means of progress. But it presupposes a slightly bent knee and a certain amount of weight placed in the stirrup, so that the rider can clear the saddle at every second pace of the horse; and this particular seat points backward again to the east, and the characteristic seat of the Asiatic mounted archer. Besides racing in harness, the only trotting breeds for travelling in light vehicles which challenged the English Hackney (which was essentially a cross of Arab blood on 'native' Welsh and Norfolk roadsters) were the Russian Orloff and the American Standard-bred mentioned above.

Reaction in the East

Let us now turn back and look eastward across the Leitha River, over those plains which are a continuation into the heart of Europe of the Eurasian steppe.

Count Stephan Széchenyi was, if not the first, the most successful sponsor and patron of imported English Thoroughbreds. By word and deed, and by the organization of various associations, he brought himself to the leading position among Hungarian breeders. Not only did he import bloodstock, he brought over from England hunt servants, gamekeepers, stud grooms, trainers and jockeys and nagsmen, and did all he could to further the spread of English sporting customs.

Outside the closed circle of racing and hunting, the importance of the Thoroughbred in Hungary was most apparent in the production of half-blood horses. What henceforward was to be known throughout Europe as the "Hungarian Horse" was essentially a half-bred horse of outstanding quality, and mostly bred in State studs [which have never existed in England; neither the royal establishments nor the National Stud of today are State Studs in the Continental sense. *Tr.*]

But this did not come to pass without strenuous opposition in Hungarian equestrian circles, which remained faithful to the traditions of Central Asia, and were especially hostile to this manifestation of Anglomania. Extracts from two publications of the nineteenth century will serve by their original phrasing to demonstrate what we mean, quoted verbatim:

An anonymous writer under the pen-name of "Tisza-side Hungarian" issued a broadsheet in 1846, fulminating against the English style of horsemanship as follows: "The English are obsessed by gambling. They put up men to beat each other to death with their fists, just so as to be able to bet on the issue. They train cocks to fight, just in order to bet". [Cockfighting was an Oriental, perhaps originally Indian, custom, introduced into Britain by the Roman army. *Tr.*] "They organize horseraces in order to bet. Therefore why should we Hungarians, who do not like betting,

105 Finish of a Flat Race

106
Trotting Race

107 'The Art of Falconry'
Wood engraving from Weisskunig

108 Lion-hunt, on Sassanid silver plate.
Hermitage, Leningrad

109 Assyrian Wild-horse hunt. Relief from Assurbanipal's palace. Nineveh. 639 B.C.

110 Mounted Archer shooting Hares
Bronze strap-end from Avar grave at Klarafalva.
Szeged Museum, Hungary

111 Deer-hunting, from Roman Tombstone in Pannonia
National Museum, Budapest

race horses? We do it in imitation of the Germans, who thereby copy the French, who copy the English. If anyone thinks these races do the horses any good, he is mightily in error...."

Speaking of the high cost of imported racehorses and the prize money at races, he says:

> Truly we pay a high price for the pleasure of seeing simian-like creatures ride horses that look more like greyhounds. There is no uglier sight in all the world than a jockey sitting in his gaudy colours on a horse fit and ready to run a race. It has come to my ears that owners sometimes ride races themselves. A worthy occupation for a Hungarian gentleman, indeed! But I also hear that they wear jockey's clothes in such cases. The dress of an English groom is a noble costume, most fitting as the apparel of a Magyar landowner. But such noble lords should have a care, lest they inadvertently attend a session of parliament thus arrayed.

Among the papers of John Pálffy, a protagonist of the national rising of 1848, there is much evidence of the distaste of his peers for this aping of English customs. The Transylvanian landowner Josef Daczó was a sworn foe of all foreign customs, but his son Ferenc welcomed them. Pálffy wrote:

> Young Ferenc is a great Anglomaniac, and so he only wanted to ride English-fashion, which consisted, on his part, of tucking his knees under his armpits and whenever the horse trotted beating time on the saddle with a certain portion of his anatomy. This made his father very angry, and he told him repeatedly to learn to ride Hungarian-fashion, as he ought to be able to do by now. But all to no avail. One day when Ferenc went for a ride, the old man lay in wait for him behind the gate. When his son trotted past him, he swung his crutch at him (he was slightly lame) and hit him on the backside just as he was rising to the trot, giving him such a fright that he lost his stirrups and came off. The old gentleman laughed and said "There's English riding for you."

Nevertheless, despite all opposition rising to the trot became universal in quite a short time. In the late 1850s it was introduced into the hussars, first of all by Colonel Baron Edelsheim. The Austro-Hungarian cavalry before that had been accustomed to march at a foot-pace, and preferably by night.

In the nineteenth century two sources of energy were discovered and exploited: steam and oil. This led to a fundamental revolution in travelling. And as once before, in the early days of the exploitation of animal power, these new resources were adapted to military use, so that they ultimately displaced the horse. The epoch that had begun with the domestication of the horse on the plains of Asia, and led to a uniform European horse-borne culture, was now brought irrevocably to an end. The Thoroughbred horse henceforward was to justify its existence only in the field of sport.

Part V Sport and Performance, Past and Present

Equestrian Sports

These have existed in every society in which riding has been part of workaday life, and in which the art has become a passion transcending its utilitarian importance. Its earliest variant was in the furthering of a widespread propensity to hunting (which in itself was originally a means of subsistence), and in the course of time not so much the hunting as the horseman-like skill displayed therein became of greater significance. [This 'hunting to ride' is still, in England, opposed to the creed of devotees of the older craft of venery, who 'ride in order to hunt'. *Tr.*]

An anonymous chronicler of Hungarian affairs in the twelfth century makes a statement that would surprise the present-day reader of any nationality when he says that the Hungarians are the best hunting-men of all, because before they migrated to their Pannonian home they went hunting every day, and so had more practice.

A Hun hunting, second century B.C.
From Chinese brush drawing

We cannot, however, measure this assertion by the standards of today. Taking hunting in the wider meaning it bears in most European languages, as *la chasse*—that is, the pursuit of game by any and every means, each of which has accumulated over the centuries a mass of custom and ritual and expert lore—the modern hunting-man or shooting-man is not a figure comparable with the onetime hunter of the steppes.

In *his* eyes, quite apart from his role as the provider of an alternative meat diet and the controller of predators, as well as of wild herbivores who competed with the domestic herds for grazing, the hunter underwent a daily trial of strength and a warlike exercise, exacting for man and horse alike. The element of danger was not absent, and the chances of the hunter and the quarry were more even than they are now. Dexterity and courage alone availed the hunter, only in a slightly less degree than they did in mounted warfare.

The skilled hunter of the Eastern peoples was therefore also a skilled warrior, who did not shrink from breakneck feats and was in thrall to the oldest of human passions, which became the most aristocratic form of sport. Mounted hunting itself arose in that 'navel of the world' above-mentioned, the Sayan Mountains, where the Uryanchai to this day approach the game on reindeer-back. In all probability it was from this ultimate source also that the Hungarian hunters mentioned by the anonymous chronicler drew their traditional skill, in far-away Hungary. Though the Uryanchai have no dogs, in the course of westward migration the use of hounds to hunt by scent or sight, cheetahs, and various rapacious birds, from the eagle to the kestrel, grew up. No longer was use made of the Stone Age devices of pitfalls, nets, or of archery from ambush; it was now exclusively a matter of hunting *par force*—the pursuit of game on horseback with (occasionally even without) hounds.

This manner of hunting justified, at princely Courts, an establishment of venery that was like an army. Marco Polo says that when the Great Khan went hunting there were several thousand riders in the field, besides the huntsmen and falconers of the royal household. The Khan maintained two Masters of Game, who had under them twenty thousand greyhound leaders alone. Even making allowance for this author, whose well-earned nickname was "Marco Millions", this is still a formidable figure, whose like is only found in medieval Europe in Hungary. The huntsmen, kennelmen, whippers-in, falconers, austringers, and keepers preserving bison, deer, beaver, and hares, maintained by the Hungarian Crown in many counties, were equal to the population of several villages, and remind one of the Oriental establishments. The King himself, devoted to venery by heredity, was the centre of this vast establishment. (Note 58.)

This hunting *en masse* persists today in Mongolia, where every man who can ride, from Cabinet minister to shepherd, takes part in the hunt, which is only now beginning to lose its traditional meaning. Thousands of horsemen surround the game, among the most prized of which is the inedible wolf.

To General Csekonics we owe a detailed description of hunting *par force* in Hungary on the grand scale. The meet was at Mezőhegyes, with a field of six hundred horsemen, and the quarry were wolves, foxes, and hares. No hounds were taken out, and the order of the day was that the game was only to be ridden down or taken with whips.

The hunt lasted two whole days and ended with an extraordinary occurrence. As the last covert of tall thick grass was being surrounded a wolf broke out and through the ring of horsemen. He had already got off to a good start when a man riding a little grey mare set off after him. The grey mare vanished over the horizon, and after five hours came in sight again, the dead wolf hanging over the saddle-bow. This achievement was crowned in the horse-race which followed the hunt, which the little grey mare won. (Note 59.)

In descriptions of these mounted hunts many extraordinary feats are enumerated. Of these it will suffice to mention only one, the most stupendous. In 1613 Bethlen Gábor, Prince of Transylvania, went with his retinue to Torda, to receive the homage of his Turkish and Tartar allies. During the formalities a single hare ran diagonally across the field which was taken as an ill omen. A contemporary witness states: "One of the Tartars, a tall fellow on a white horse, galloped uphill after the hare, caught up with it, leaned down from the saddle and picked it up running in his hand, bringing it to Bethlen Gábor and placing it, still alive, on his saddle-bow." All present were greatly relieved that the ill omen had thus been averted. Anyone who has seen a hunted hare jinking and swerving at high speed will appreciate the standard of horsemanship required. (*Materials for History of Transylvania.*)

Another Eastern technique was falconry. The first written evidence for its practice outside Mongolia is Chinese. A document of the Hsia dynasty, probably of the second millennium B.C., mentions, among gifts distributed by the ruler, trained hunting falcons. Thereafter data is scanty. Ktesias, the Greek physician at the Court of the Persian king in the fourth century B.C., calls falconry a new Indian custom, in his time still little known in Persia. Most histories of the sport say it was brought into Europe by the Huns; the evidence is not very reliable—the falcon standard of Attila is adduced as proof. Charlemagne is said to have been the first Western monarch to keep falcons.

The Hohenstaufen Emperor Frederick II did much to spread knowledge of the art in European Courts with his book *De Arte Venandi Cum Avibus*. This monarch (1212–50), who was himself of Norman descent, being on his mother's side a grandson of the Norman King Roger II of Sicily, wrote the book at Palermo, his capital. He employed Arabian falconers; he had Hungarian connections by marriage (Note 60), and so a threefold influence is perceptible here also—Norman, Arabian, and Hungarian. [If we remember that the Sicilo-Norman house of Tancred de Hauteville was of Scandinavian origin, this takes us even further back into the history of falconry. There is evidence for the domestication of falcons in the Wendel period in Sweden (seventh century), and the sport will have been brought to England and Normandy, among other places, during the Viking invasions. The fact that the falcon is mentioned in *Beowulf* may be due to this late influence, since the poem was first written down after the invasions. On the other hand, it does contain references to Anglo-Saxon customs of an earlier date, such as mound-burial. If falconry existed in pre-Viking England it will have been in East Anglia, a province which then and now abounds in the large aquatic birds that are the falconer's favourite quarry, because the royal house of East Anglia was unique among Anglo-Saxon dynasties in being of Swedish origin, and the royal cenotaph of the Wuffingas at Sutton Hoo contains many heirlooms of Swedish manufacture. It is quite possible that at the time of the last of these burials, in the mid-seventh century, contact still existed between the Swedish and the Suffolk branches of the family. But whether in the ninth or in an earlier century, the falcon, like the stirrup, must have reached England from the steppes by this northern route. Hawking was certainly unknown to the Celts of Britain, and to the Romans also. The Roman *auceps* seems to have been either a fowler with nets or a sharpshooter with bow or sling, and it is significant that the very word for falconer was absent from the Latin vocabulary, so that the Emperor Frederick had to use as the title of his Latin work the clumsy paraphrase "The Art of Hunting with Birds." *Tr.*] (Note 60.)

But Frederick II was not only King of Sicily, he was also German Emperor, and his household in Sicily was often the object of disapproval in Germany. There especial scorn and indignation met the wholesale adoption of foreign customs, and the Emperor was blamed for turning his palace at Palermo into a hunting-lodge, where he was surrounded by baying hounds and screeching hawks.

The Hungarian influence tending to the dissemination of Central Asian hunting techniques in the West was a phenomenon which, as Gy. Laszlo has shown, was repeated in later centuries.

The invention of firearms accurate enough to shoot flying birds dealt a mortal blow to falconry, as in all forms of hunting a principal object was still the provision of a change of diet. The pursuit of deer with hounds also declined, until it became a 'pure' sport, with little thought of the larder in mind. The English, in particular, turned to the pursuit of the inedible fox, and the English foxhunt set the tone for sporting Europe, with its scarlet-coated sportsmen mounted on horses of partly Thoroughbred blood, behind English foxhounds. Nowhere did this fashion meet greater opposition than in Hungary. The 'Tisza-side Hungarian' quoted above in his diatribe against the 'copy-cats' turned his attention from racing to fox-hunting:

Our copy-cats will not let the matter rest there. They must needs hunt after the English fashion. Great Britain is over-populated and game is scarce there. Therefore they have developed the curious habit of pursuing the fox on horse-back, only to catch it and put it in a bag, so as to have something to hunt next time out. This all very well for a rather flat country which abounds in stretches of turf, and roads. But is it not ridiculous to imitate this caricature of hunting in our Carpathian hills, where boar, wolf and bear are to be found in plenty? Our fathers loved hunting as the image of war, making men bold and skilful. They slew the beasts of the forest hand to hand. That made sense, and he must indeed suffer from imitation-mania who would follow the example of the English who themselves would be only too glad if they had our wealth of game to hunt . . .

[This Hungarian from Tisza-side is an easily recognizable type, corresponding exactly, in English terms, to the nineteenth-century encrusted Tory squire, nourished on beefsteak and port, nowadays a stock figure of heavy comedy, with his contempt for Frenchmen (and by extension for all foreigners) as "Frog-eatin' mounseers," and quite incapable of imagining that any other country can afford, or its inhabitants practise, any form of sport equal to, let alone superior to, his own. The kind of officer who 'won' the Crimean War. Tr.] What would he have said if he had witnessed the logical development of the synthetic foxhunt à l'anglaise, the drag which became fashionable throughout Europe, with its line over a prepared course of artificial obstacles following a pack in pursuit of oil of aniseed? For all that, even the drag-hunt had its uses. Like racing, it was a means of selection by performance, and thus a useful ancillary to horse-breeding, as long as horse-breeding itself had a practical aim in view.

Coursing with greyhounds, likewise of Oriental origin, survived the mounted hunt en masse by about a century. It was still practised in Hungary after the Second World War, but when it vanished the Hungarian breed of greyhound went with it. The greyhound is of Oriental origin, and now survives only in the West because it is easier to organize greyhound racing, and the betting that goes with it, than horse-racing. Pig-sticking, introduced in imitation of Anglo-Indian sportsmen who in turn were imitating the aristocracy of the Moghul Empire, also took root briefly in Hungary, where the pig-stickers used a special spear, weighted with a metal knob just above the point, to lend impetus to a downward blow.

Turkoman Gazelle-hunt with Falcon and Salukis
Drawing by Evert van Muyden. After Moser, 1886

There is nothing new under the sun. A relief from Roman Pannonia shows a Roman horseman hunting deer with just such a spear.

The Hungarian horse-herds (Csikós) have a mounted sport peculiar to themselves. It has become well-known through the description of the American sculptor Alexander Finta, who once lived the life of these herdsmen on the *puszta*. Under certain conditions of freezing rain the Great Bustard becomes unable to fly. Flocks of them with their congealed feathers, still able to run very fast, were herded together into circles some fifty yards in diameter, hemmed in by cracking horse-whips. As they ran round in circles, the game was to see which herdsman could pluck the most plumes from the living bird. They entered the circle by turns, each being given five minutes to pluck plumes from the tails of the bustards. The forfeit for dropping hat, whip, etc. was to miss three turns. Success depended on the ability to follow every twist and turn of the fleeing bird while bending down low out of the saddle.

Another kind of simulated hunt is that in which one rider takes over the role of the quarry, as in a paper-chase. Its earliest variety is evidently that practised by the Kirghiz nomads to this day. One of their girls will cry out to a boy "Who can catch the wolf-maiden?" and gallop off on her horse. This is the signal for a mad pursuit uphill and down dale, the boys riding hard after the girl and trying to catch her round the waist, or at least to touch her breast, while she stands them off with blows of her whip. Carl Diem, who recorded many Oriental customs and equestrian sports, thinks this a vestige of marriage by capture. For instance, the bridegroom rides a race with the bride and tries to snatch her veil. This custom persisted in Hungary down to the seventeenth century. [In England, specifically in Cleveland, a similar bridal custom derived from marriage by capture survived into the nineteenth century and involved a horse-race home from church for which the prize was the bride's garter. *Tr.*]

Eye-witness accounts of the wedding of Ferenc Rákóczi to Ilona Zringy outside the fortress of Sboró mention 'the hunting of the basket'. But this game was not played by the high-born couple themselves or their relatives but by some horsemen from their retinue. (Note 61.)

Another of these mounted capture-games is known among the Turks as *baj-rakonju*. In it a horseman holds a pennant in his hand, while two others try to wrest it from him. As soon as one of them succeeds, roles are exchanged, and he becomes 'it', and is pursued in turn. There is a European variety of this game, called in French *jeu de barre*, and played with a ribbon on the shoulder.

But all these entertainments, which might be known collectively in English as gymkhana events, pale beside the great Asiatic mounted sport called by various nomad peoples *baiga* or *kok-buri* in regard to the demands they make on riding skill. It is or was widespread in Central Asia: this is how Franz von Schwarz described the version he saw played among the Turkomans in 1900:

> The patron of the game throws a dead sheep or goat among the players, who are all mounted and armed with the inevitable whip. The object is to pick the carcass up from the ground and give it back to the patron of the game. But this is much harder to do than it sounds, for hardly has the first horseman picked it up at full gallop and laid it across his saddle-bow, than he is surrounded on all sides, by those seeking to snatch his prize from him. Often two men will gallop away side by side, both holding the carcass, tugging and heaving at either end

of it, till they pull it apart and both fall off their horses each holding a part. Every moment in the fearful press and tumult a horse and its rider comes down, and the whole troop ride over them. But I have never seen a serious accident so caused, though I must have watched hundreds of *baigas*; so great is the dexterity of horse and rider. There are no obstacles in this game: if after a long hard struggle one of the players has managed to get hold of the sheep and get clear of the others, then they all set off after him, in full career up hill and down dale, through bush and over briar, over garden walls, ditches, through deep and rapid rivers and down the steepest slopes. Mostly a game lasts several hours, until the most skillful and tireless rider manages to shake off all his opponents and throw the sheep at the feet of his host ... As in Europe, this game was played on such occasions as weddings or to celebrate the birth of an heir. [See p. 146.]

There were various mounted ball games current in Asia, and polo is a development of one of these. It is first mentioned in an epic poem by the Persian Firdausi, celebrating the heroic deeds of the Iranian prince Sijavus (seventh century B.C.), and gives an account of a polo match between Persian and Turanian princes. In the early centuries of our era the game was known from the Pacific to the Bosporus. It has been played in Japan, China, Tibet, Turania, Iran, Asia Minor, India, and the Arab countries. In many of them it is still being played. In the 1870s it was brought to England by the 10th Hussars on their return from India, and this version of the game was reintroduced to Hungary in 1969.

If we follow the development of this game, we see that not only did its progress run parallel with the dissemination of the Turanian horse, but that the rules of the game were modified to conform with the quality of horses in various countries. For instance, in medieval Arabia polo was played in a quite different way from what it was in Persia. The ball was thrown in between the two teams, who started at an equal distance from the half-way line: it was apple-sized and of leather. The object was to drive the ball over the opponents' back-line, instead of aiming at a goal, as today. The stick used was so short that the player had to bend right down out of the saddle to hit the ball. The whole game proceeded at a sharp gallop, with many twists and turns and the constant risk of collision with an opponent, and being trampled underfoot.

The practical importance of mounted games is well expressed in a remark of Nur-ed-Din, the implacable opponent of the Crusaders. He said, when questioned about his passion for the game, which he even played at night by artificial light: "God is my witness, I do this not for pastime only; we have no time to spare. We are waiting, but we are in the presence of the enemy, and we must be ready at any time to take arms and to horse. If we kept our horses hobbled in the lines, they would get fat and soft, unfit to undergo long marches, and they would not be nimble enough for close combat. This game of ball is the best practice for our horses, hardening them and making them not only fit but handy and obedient to the rider."

Not only must the horse be trained and fit; the rider's skill at arms must be improved constantly. In the Orient the racecourses, or maidans, in the environs of every princely palace were used as ranges for the characteristic Asiatic ballistic exercise—archery from the saddle. Such maidans are found from Japan to Turkey. The Turks also used them to practise javelin-throwing from the saddle. Their popular game of 'Atli-Jerid' was played on the At-maidan of Constantinople, which

113   Indians and White Men hunting Bison
Indian Painting on Moose-hide
Museum of the American Indian. Heye Foundation, New York

114
Thirteen-year-old Mongol Girl,
Winner in 1962 of the Annual
Race at Archosta in Mongolia

115
Fantasia by Libyan Bedouin

116   The Rittal Ten-in-hand Coach-team, a *Tour de Force* of Driving

117   Dressage: J. Neckermann with Antoinette

was none other than the Hippodrome of ancient Byzantium. This was a contest between two teams of horsemen armed with wooden unpointed javelins. The individual victor was the one who scored most direct hits. They took turns to ride out between the opposing ranks and throw spears, to which the 'enemy' replied with a volley, and points were counted to each horsemen in turn for the number of 'enemy' spears he caught in the air or parried.

At a time when such games in the Orient could look back on a history of several centuries they began to be diffused through Europe with the Norman expansion. During the Middle Ages there spread from Normandy such sports as riding at the ring or the quintain, wrestling on horseback, and tourneys. Geoffroi, Seigneur de Preully, had codified the laws of the tourney by the end of the eleventh century, and they soon became standard throughout Christendom.

In the beginning there were mass engagements with sword and mace, but not with lances, and the duels with the lance, originally called *jeux de table-ronde* or 'jousts', were a later development. As early as 1252 French chivalry decided that the tourney should take place with the lance only, either with the blunt weapon (*arme courtoise* or *gracieuse*) or *à outrance* with a lance-head consisting of a 'crown' of small diverging points.

The tourney began in England under William I, in Germany under Conrad II (1024–39), but was specially favoured by the Emperor Henry VI (1190–97). In his reign the German knights were organized into four great jousting associations; Rhenish, Bavarian, Swabian, and Franconian, each presided over by a marshal. The rules of combat were very precise, by contrast with the practice obtaining farther east, and the institution of the tourney was supposed to embody the highest ideals of Christian chivalry.

Only those knights might compete in the lists who could show at least four ancestors of equestrian rank, but the sovereign might confer eligibility on others. They were all entered in an index of those entitled to joust. Tournament courts, consisting of marshals, heralds, and arbitrators,were responsible for law and order, the proper conduct of jousts, and the announcement of contests in advance. It was all very German and well organized, with plenty of paper-work and officials with polysyllabic titles. The lists were commonly oval, with raised seats for spectators; with a flourish of trumpets the knights in full armour entered the lists escorted by their squires, where their names were checked against the index, before the tilting began.

The object was to unhorse the opponent, by the weight and impetus of the mighty destrier. The faster the course down the lists, the harder was the impact, aided by the weight of the horse; sometimes both horse and rider were knocked over, sometimes the rider was swept backward out of the saddle, and lances shivered to splinters. In order to avoid outright collision, a barrier was erected all the way down the lists, and in the course of time tilting over this barrier became universal. The jouster took up his station on the left side of it, and kept his horse well in towards this 'pale'.

The object of the tourney was merely display, entertainment, and (decreasingly as time went on) a form of practice for real combat, but before the introduction of the 'pale' many contestants either lost their tempers or found themselves matched by private enemies, so that there were many fatalities to man and horse. Two princes of the House of Babenberg, Leopold I and Leopold the Virtuous, came by

The Game of Baiga
Drawing by Evert van Muyden. After Moser, 1886

their death in the lists. A notorious combat in 1273, known as "The Little War of Châlons", at which Edward I of England and the Count of Châlons met hand to hand, ended in blood and tears, for their retinues became so embroiled that many of them were killed. In a tournament of Darmstadt in 1408 seventeen Franconian and nine Hessian knights were left dead in the lists, and King Henry II of France was killed by Count Montgomery, jousting, in 1559.

At the time of this fatality jousting was still occasionally happening in England, at the very end of an unbroken tradition, but the occasional contests under the Stuarts were a conscious antiquarian revival, just as much so as was the Eglinton Tournament under Queen Victoria (1839). Whereas in the West mounted sports persisted and flourished as much as formerly after the decline of chivalry, in all forms ranging from the staghunt to the gymkhana, decadence in the East set in long before the advent of the machine age. The relics of Asiatic equestrian sport are nowadays more common in the museum than outside it.

The mounted sports of today differ so radically from those of the older tradition that valid comparisons of performance, past and present, can be drawn almost solely in the fields of flat-racing, hurdling, and steeple-chasing.

Carl Diem, looking back in 1960 over the development of equestrian sports, said: "The flowering of Asiatic physical culture came to pass much earlier than that of Europe, and even if it has lost much in the course of time, its seminal ideas in this field have been preserved to the present day".

How much does competitive sport, so universal and so uniform in our day, owe to this tradition of the equestrian peoples? It is not so much a question of the physical similarity between the equestrian exercises of the past and modern sports such as racing, ball games, tests of skill and dexterity, as of the fact that the internationally recognized concept expressed in the English term 'fair play' and embodying the moral essence of chivalry, the sporting ethic as such, together with the very idea of 'rules of the game', were primarily of Oriental origin. We inherit this through the channel of Greek athletics, of which the modern Olympic code is a conscious imitation.

Feats on Horseback

A comparison of equestrian performances, past and present, is not an absolutely feasible task, for it could only be valid on the basis of identical conditions and chances. If it is nevertheless to be attempted, then this is for two reasons: first, to offer an approximate picture of evolution; second, to attempt some sort of comparative scale.

Oriental practice takes into account a factor that is absent from the modern world of sport. It is important, for it serves to divide equestrian performance into two categories which are not fairly comparable, involving a concept embodied in the Hungarian word lóhalál, used to translate various Oriental expressions, all of which imply quite simply that the horse is regarded as expendable. This ultimate ruthlessness was implicit in the speech of English coachmen of the 'great' period when they spoke quite objectively of 'driving to death', and has no exact equivalent in Western tongue, unless it be the Spanish word matacaballos.

This tempo of travel, practised by the peoples of the steppe, was dictated by the degree of urgency which the Palatine Nádasdy had in mind, for example, in his direction to a courier dated 1556 (the equivalent of the vaguer English "Haste, post Haste") "Carry this letter day and night to Kapuvár, though it kills the horse." (Note 62.) The same idea is embodied in the rules of the Turkish game of Jerid, which enjoined the victor to reach the nearest city at top speed, if necessary at the cost of the horse's life, which according to Carl Diem was often the case.

Of course, this does not mean that the horse so ridden or driven must of necessity perish or founder, it simply implies limitless effort, and the condition in which the horse arrived at its destination was a function of its capabilities, its condition at the start, its constitution and state of fitness. A horse could fall dead of effort at the trot, theoretically even at the walk, if more was asked of it than its ultimate capability.

The table contains, even though the available details do not allow an exact match, four sections, each relevant to the Oriental standard of travel, each being a performance at the customary travelling pace, also examples where the horse was ridden to death, and within these examples where there was, and was not, a change of horse.

The first two parts of the table concerned with the speed of travel tell us nothing new. Hourly averages of 7 to 12 km without change of horses and 12 to 15 km with, and a daily journey between 6 and 12 hours are quite customary performances. Rides involving the death of horses, on the other hand, provide results which are worth more detailed consideration. Officers of the German and Austro-Hungarian armies took part in the long-distance rides Berlin–Vienna and Vienna–Berlin over the same route. Sixty-nine out of 97 Austro-Hungarians completed the course, and 76 Germans out of 120. Count Starhemberg, then a lieutenant of hussars, riding a Hungarian half-bred mare, was 1 hour and 40 minutes better than the first rider of the German team, Freiherr von Reizenstein, 73 hours 7 minutes. The winner's horse was one of twenty-five which did not survive the ride.

A ride from Budapest to Vienna organized by the Austro-Hungarian army had 79 entries, of whom 51 completed the course. Of these, seventeen did it in less than twenty hours. The fact that only three horses succumbed points to a fairly moderate speed in relation to the distance, always excepting the remarkably brilliant performance of the winner, a lieutenant of hussars called Bela von Wodianer, riding a Thoroughbred mare.

The long-distance ride from Brussels to Ostend showed results of a quite different order. Hardly half the sixty-one contestants completed the course, though it was comparatively short, with the loss of one-third of the horses. The Dresden–Leipzig ride with 22 entries, six of whom did not finish, and in which seven horses died, showed similar results. But here the performance of the hussar, Lieutenant Zuern of the Royal Saxon Army, on a half-bred mare from Beberbeck is well-nigh incredible.

The similarity of the results leads to the conclusion that results depended in the first instance on the overall length. This is understandable, and most obvious in the case of short journeys. Lieutenant-Colonel Count Otto Hermann Styrum made a bet in 1678 to ride from Vienna to Wiener-Neustadt, and did it in one and three-quarter hours, at an average speed of 28.5 km per hour. Classic races over shorter distances show even better averages: courses of 20 km even show averages like 40 km per hour, and better. Sprints by racehorses often work out at 16–18 metres per second, which is more than 60 km per hour.

Urgency	Performer	Route	Days	km	Riding Hr.	Riding Min.	Rest Hr.	Rest Min.	Total Hr.	Total Min.	Overall speed km per day	Overall speed km per hour	Source
'Normal' travel — using one horse	1244 William of Holland	Venice–Brno	16 days	736							46	not counting rest 7–12 km	Rünger 1925
	1301 Hungarians according to King Wenceslas	6 rasta	1 day	56.4									Austrian Rhyming Chronicle
	9th c. Emperor Constantine	Salonica–Belgrade	8 days	550							56.4		Emperor Constantine *De Administrando Imperio*
	1603 Sir R. Carey	Windsor–Edinburgh	66 hr.	650							65.6		Dent and Goodall 1962
	1629 Transylvanian Embassy	Constantinople–Gyulafehérvár	8 days	620							77.5		Rákóczi, B. 1577
'Normal' travel — with relays	1714 Charles XIII of Sweden	Demotika–Stralsund (driving)	16 days	2400							150	not counting rest 12–15 km	Századok 1869
	1841 Mail Coach	Budapest–Miskolc	1 day	183							183		Timetable 1841
	13th c. Mongol Post	30–40 parasangs	1 day	200							200		Spuler, *Mongols in Iran*
	1241 Subotai's Scouts	Verecke–Pest	3 days	480							160		Diem 1941
	1861 W. Russell	Smith's Creek–Fort Churchill		192	8	10	—	—	8	10	—	23.7	Pony Express Record
"Riding to Death" — using one horse	1892 Count Starhemberg	Vienna–Berlin		580	60	27	11	—	71	27		9.6	Waldbauer 1909
	1908 Von Wodianer	Budapest–Vienna		230	14	48	1	50	16	38		15.5	Waldbauer 1909
"Riding to Death" — with relays	1903 Long-distance ride	Brussels–Ostend		132	6	54	—	—	6	54		18.8	Waldbauer 1909
	1895 Lt. Zuern	Dresden–Leipzig		135	5	57	—	—	5	57		22.5	Waldbauer 1909
	1920 Tzeren, Mongol Courier	Ulias-Sutai–Peking	9 days	2800	158	—	58	—	216	—	311	17.7	Diem 1941
	13th c. Mongol Post	60 Parasangs	1 day	341	18	6	—	—	—	—	341	18.5	Spuler 1937
	19th c. Count Sándor	Buda–Vienna		230	8	10	1	—	9	10	—	26.5	Andrássy 1857
	1830 Osbaldeston	Track		320	8	40	—	—	8	40	—	34	Andrássy 1857

In the next section, showing relays of horses ridden to death, we must remark the performances of Tzeren, Count Sándor, and Osbaldeston, if only because doubt has often been cast on the figures for Sándor. Tzeren, who was a courier in the Mongolian post service, did his ride on post-horses, having the privilege of choosing the best horse at every stage. He was also assisted by people sent in advance, who rode the relay horse alongside him so that he leapt from saddle to saddle at full gallop. In order to stand up to the exertion he was bandaged all over with woollen cloth. He galloped full out for distances of twenty-five or twenty kilometres, and took six or seven hours rest every one of the nine days. This throws some light on the organization of Jenghis Khan's post express service, with its daily stage of 340 km. (Note 63.)

The first to cast doubt on the performance of Count Sándor, "the Devil's Horseman", was Loeffler, and Diem came to share his doubts, because Sándor did the journey from Vienna to Budapest in half Wodianer's time. Their error can be ascribed to the fact that they left out of account Wodianer's single horse, whereas Sándor had many changes of mount.

According to Sándor's diary, an hourly average of 26 km was an exacting test of the rider's powers, although he did do one lap in a carriage. (Note 64.) His achievement is real enough, as is that of Styrum, and not to be reckoned among the fabulous. That Sándor very often rode horses to death is evident from the remark of a contemporary that "he alone used up as many riding-horses as would suffice to mount five regiments of cavalry".

Osbaldeston's ride in England came about owing to a bet that he would ride two hundred miles on a circular track without fences in nine hours. He changed horses every ten furlongs—that is, about 160 times. His friends provided him with the necessary changes of horse. To this, Sándor remarked that on the basis of his own time between Bratislava and Vienna—60 km in 94 minutes with an average of 40 km an hour—he could have ridden Osbaldeston's course in 4 hours 52 minutes. Although results on the racetrack and across country are not to be judged in the same class, nor yet changes of horse every twenty and every two kilometres, we can only accept this remark with reservations, since the average speed kept up by Sándor between Budapest and Vienna is much below that attained by Osbaldeston. (Note 65.)

It further appears from the table that European capabilities in long-distance riding improved in the same measure as Oriental techniques were diffused. Progress is most evident as between the first and third sections. When in Hungary the post organized on the Eastern pattern with relays of horses was introduced in the eleventh century, and by royal decree its horses were classified as able to undertake a stage of one league or only half, even forced marches in the West were scarcely achieving the average speed of the Hungarian post. In 1236 the Emperor Frederick II covered 120 km, on a journey in Italy, in two days and a night, riding say 36 hours; even with 18 hours travelling and 18 hours resting this is still only six or seven kilometres per hour. Even more significant is the race between King Charles VI of France and his son-in-law, the Duke of Touraine, in 1381. (This is the same King Charles VI mentioned in connection with the introduction of the Hungarian slung-wagon.) The chronicler Froissart says:

> The King and the Duke were travelling in the South of France. At Montpellier they made a bet, which of them should get back to Paris first. The two young men, fired by the glances of the fair ladies of Montpellier, were first impelled by

the desire to see their wives again, although the amount of the wager, five thousand francs, did not count for nothing. They each started escorted by a single knight and travelling day and night they repeatedly changed horses. The Duke won the race by taking a boat down the Seine to Melun while the King was having eight hours' sleep at Troyes; the Duke then taking again to horse did the whole journey in 4¼ days, to the King's 4½, taking driving and riding together, over the whole stretch of 150 leagues [about 469 miles]. (Note 66.)

Even if the King's time was no mean achievement, it cannot compare with the 340 km a day that were commonly being ridden at that time in Asia. The difference lay not so much in the riders as in the horses. The royal horses were undoubtedly all stall-fed palfreys and the like, unaccustomed to prolonged galloping, and the harness horses probably even slower; neither could hold a candle to the ordinary run of Mongol or Turk horses. Another disadvantage was that no-one in the West had any conception of how to organize a training programme, with which the Orientals were already familiar. (Note 67.)

A notable feat was performed in France in the eighteenth century, when a certain Count Saillant bet that he would ride from the Porte Saint-Denis at Paris to Chantilly and back (80 km) in 6 hours, changing horses. He did it with 18 minutes to spare, so that his average speed was 27·7 km.p.h., which is by and large the same speed as that of Sándor and Styrum, taking into account the disparity in length of course. Similar speeds and times during that century can be shown among other Western nations.

With the establishment of common standards of horsemanship throughout Europe the test of horse and rider could be measured in terms not only of distance run and time taken but also of obstacles cleared. This is primarily a Western phenomenon, because in the hillier and closer country of the West, often divided by hedges between arable and pasture fields, ability to jump high early became of practicable importance. Such obstacles by and large did not exist either in Western or in Central Asia; it was more important for the horse to be a strong swimmer, and the rider to know how to swim a horse, in order to cross larger rivers without a boat, and the long jump performed by the King of Urartu's horse would have come in useful in crossing a stream without wading. (Note 68.)

It is therefore not possible to cite comparisons in the past for steeple-chasing, for hurdling, or for show-jumping measured against present-day records. (The world record by Captain Alberto Larraguibel Morales of Chile in 1949 on the 16-year-old T. B. Hause—a high jump of 2·47 metres—is still unbroken.) These records were achieved by two factors: systematic training and the use of the Thoroughbred or the half-bred horse of hunter type. The art of riding perfected by hours of practice and training is no longer a monopoly of the East. The spirit in which horsemen of international calibre approach their task with a peculiar devotion is truly international, varying little within Europe, and has its exact counterpart in the American and Australasian continents, of identical historical origin.

In our day the supreme test of horsemanship forms part of the Olympic Games. The Olympic Event, called by the English word Military in most languages but not so called in English, consists of dressage, cross-country, and show-jumping phases, the last over a course comprising fourteen obstacles up to 1·50 metres high. The following table shows the first ten nations with their score in team and individual marks, in which a gold medal counts seven points, a silver five, and a bronze four.

TABLE OF TOTAL POINTS IN OLYMPIC GAMES 1912–68: TOP TEN NATIONS

Nation	Gold	Silver	Bronze	Points
Germany	8	7	8	123
Sweden	10	2	5	100
Italy	4	7	6	87
France	6	5	3	76
U.S.A.	7	7	5	76
Great Britain	3	2	7	59
Holland	5	3	—	50
Mexico	2	1	1	23
Australia	2	1	1	23
Switzerland	1	2	1	21

The performance put up by representatives of various nations is not only a proof of their skill and determination, it is a living testimony to the survival of the spirit of chivalry in our world, in one of the few fields where a limit has been set to the possible technological advance. The breeding and the riding of horses being more of an art than a science, we may regard the combination of man and horse at international level as near the summit of what human and equine endeavour can achieve for all time.

118
Miniature from the
Duc de Berry's *Très
Riches Heures*,
illustrated by the
Limburg brothers
about 1415. The
month of August,
showing a party of
falconers.
*Musée Condé,
Chantilly*

119-120 Tut-Ank-Ahmen hunting Lions, 1358–1349 B.C. From the grave of the king.

121   Persian Miniature showing Game of Polo, Sixteenth Century
Ethnological Museum, Munich.

Epilogue

When we look back over the Equestrian Age we gain a new perspective of the march of historical events. We gain understanding of the rise of humanity from knowledge of prehistoric man's mastering of the problems of transport and communications, and of the historic role of the horse.

Where and when did man find the natural conditions that enabled him to make progress towards civilization? Why did this happen only after the end of the Ice Age, a hundred or a hundred and fifty centuries ago, whereas the remains of recognizably human beings go back hundreds of thousands of years?

These conditions were to be found only in 'the navel of the world'—the Sayan Mountains (52°–55° North and 90°–100° East), the cradle of the pastoral way of life. Only there in the post-glacial world could the flora and fauna of the Ice Age continue to exist south of 60° latitude. At the same time it was the one region that offered mankind optimum climatic conditions for the life of the wandering stock-breeder, and permitted the herding of stock on open range, the riding of reindeer, and subsequently the riding of the horse, which led in the end to the Great Migration of Peoples.

Without this development there would have been no contact within Eurasia between centres of civilization, no exchange of cultural properties, and none of the most fundamental requirements of human progress. The horse ridden by Oriental man must remain the symbol of prehistoric events, contributing decisively to the progress of humanity, east and west.

What of the future? At the end of the Equestrian Age the horse lost all practical significance, and yet its cultural status remained undiminished. It holds its own in the fields of art and literature. A civilization which is founded on millennia of equestrian endeavour still retains its equestrian habits of mind. The popularity of the horse in sport remains undiminished in the Old as in the New World. Thousands of riding clubs and horse shows, equestrian spectacles of all kinds, bear testimony to this.

The breeding of horses of quality is inseparable from the idea of an equestrian civilization. If horse-breeding at the present day has declined and must decline in quantity, it has unquestionably gained in quality, as compared with the past, even the recent past. Still as in the past those countries excel in the production of fine horses which have contributed most to the new unified horsemanship of Europe, and which over the centuries have imposed an indelible national stamp on their light-horse breeding: England, France, Germany, Poland, Hungary. I might mention here also Arabia and Spain, both of which have been the centre of an important national tradition in horsemanship and horse-breeding.

One last thing; now that the Age of the Horse has vanished we see less and less often what we too commonly saw in the past—horses going to rack and ruin through human greed, ignorance, and brutality. It is just and fair that the burden should have been lifted off the horse on to the machine. If the civilization which depended on the horse is gone for ever, it is being replaced now by a civilization which is still enriched by the horse!

A work dealing with such wide aspects of the history of civilization could never have been provided with such abundant historical data unless the author were amply supported on all sides with information and references, whether solicited or not. I wish therefore heartily to thank all those who have so kindly contributed facts and ideas that have gone to the making of this book.

Notes

Part I

1 (*page* 18)   My childhood was spent in the Hungarian countryside and my fantasy-world was innocent of the internal combustion engine. My dreams were filled with colourful visions of horses and horsemen. As to my real boyhood, I cannot remember when I first rode a donkey or a horse. I imperceptibly acquired the daily skills of horse-manship; saddling up, driving, feeding, grooming, and the rest, until at last I was fit to be entrusted with the care of fifteen half-grown colts at pasture. My terms of reference were precise: I was to keep them out of the sown and standing corn. Since grassland was not extensive with us, and surrounded by arable land, this was no easy task, and it was made more difficult by a penchant which the colts had to panic at the slightest sound, and, unaccustomed as they were to grazing in the open, to make off over hill and dale. Nevertheless, I managed to hold down the job of colt-herd for a long time, solely due to the fact that the leader of the herd was a three-year-old. It was simply a question of time before I managed to halter him and break him to ride. Once on his back I could easily lead the herd wherever I wanted it. On our migrations I always rode him in front, and my younger brother on a donkey whipped-in the stragglers. Later, when I became a breeder myself, I kept an old mare among the youngsters. With her help there was never any trouble, even on unfenced pastures.

2 (*page* 18)   Janós Kemény, later Prince of Transylvania, points in his autobiography to this equine instinct by an incident on his journey to Constantinople in 1628. Unknown to him, his horses and those of his suite ran away by night, all but one which was tied up. Awakened by its neighing, the riders set out to look for them in pitch-darkness, and on Kemény's orders tied a long rope to the halter of the one remaining horse, the end of which one of them held in his hand. The horse followed the tracks of the runaways to the place where the previous evening they had been watered by a stream outside the village. And so despite the darkness of the night and the unknown country they soon managed to recover the runaways. (J. Kemény, Autobiography—in Hungarian—Századok 1959.)

3 (*page* 24)   There was migration northward in very early times. The peoples of the late Palaeolithic, who were hunters, followed the reindeer as it migrated from its southern habitat, and according to the 'reindeer-shadowing' theory this led to the de-velopment of the Mesolithic and Kunda cultures. Therefore northward migration meant for reindeer-breeders no more the opening up of unexplored regions than did westward migration to the first horse-breeders.

Part II

4 (*page* 52)   Delbrück describes the Germans as an equestrian people and therefore discounts the evidence of Procopius and Agathius on the points mentioned. In support of his thesis he cites Aurelius (Chapter 21), who described the Alamani as excellent horse-men. Therefore he ascribes to them the victory at the battle of Strasbourg, and in his view the success at the battle of Adrianople was due to Germanic cavalry skill, and not to any failure of generalship on the part of the Romans. In the preceding chapter I have shown the origin of Germanic mounted tactics among those tribes only who were in contact with the Huns, which is in direct opposition to the view put forward by Delbrück in *Geschichte der Kriegskunst im Rahmen der Politischen Geschichte* (II Berlin 3rd ed. 1921, p. 433).

5 (*page 61*)   A writ by Béla IV, King of Hungary, in 1265 shows the mutual esteem in which Hungarian and Polish horsemanship was held. It allows the population of Lipto county, on the Polish border, to trade freely in horses with the Poles. The export embargo was valid only for Bohemia and Germany, not for Poland. (Századok 1908, p. 878.)

6 (*page 62*)   Again and again in medieval documents we find riding described as an upper-class custom. J. Rothe in Luciliburg's *Chronicle* (1434) says of St Elizabeth's journey to Hungary that she travelled in a wagon, but her husband, Margrave Louis of Thuringia, and his suite "came riding after the manner of gentlefolk". (Gombos I. p. 333.)

Part III

7 (*page 72*)   L. S. Ruhl, Curator of the Museum of Electoral Hesse, weighed a complete set of armour, saddlery and accoutrements, with personal weapons of the same period, with the following result:

Steel chamfron for horse	5 lb.
Bridle, bit and headstall	8 lb.
Remainder of horse-armour, steel plate and leather	78 lb.
Saddle, girth and stirrups	24 lb.
Man's complete plate armour	80 lb.
Pair spurs	3 lb. 12 oz.
Sword, mounted pattern	7 lb.
Shield	5 lb. 8 oz.
Lance	10 lb.
Dagger	4 lb. 5 oz.
Man's clothing	10 lb.
Man's surcoat	5 lb.
Housing over horse-armour	10 lb.
Helmet crest and pennant	5 lb.
Total	255 lb. 9 oz.
Rider, say	175 lb.
All-up weight	436 lb. 9 oz.

These weights are in the old Brandenburg (Berlin) pound, which equalled 0·514 kg, and was practically the same as the English pound. The total weight in metric units is therefore 224 kg. It may be compared with the Austro-Hungarian cavalry manual, which gives the average weight of a trooper as 70 kg and the all-up weight to be carried by the troop-horse as 121 to 128 kg; a horse racing under Jockey Club rules was carrying about 8 st. 10 lb. (55·33 kg); or the standard English packhorse load of 2 cwt., which is about half of 224 kg.

8 (*page 73*)   Mention of pugnacious horses employed in battle is rare, but it does occur after the Age of Chivalry. During a lull in the Turkish wars in Hungary Aga Ibrahim of Koppány in 1589 challenged the Constable of Tihany, István Pisky, to a duel, the provocation being a correspondence in which each had abused the other and offered severe insults. (Pisky enclosed with one of his letters a pig's tail, whereupon the Muslim retorted that he must have cut it off his own rump.) The Turkish challenge read "Fight *à outrance*, either with weapons or with teeth".

We do not know whether this combat actually came off, but in that same year another Constable, Mihály Bory, was at odds with the same Turk. Only this time it was agreed to settle the issue in the presence of an equal retinue from both sides. Not until the fight began did it become clear that it was not the principals who were to fight 'tooth and nail', but their horses. The Hungarian was hard pressed, since the Turkish stallion was more vicious than his. The Hungarian retainers were outraged at what they took for a trick, and attacked the Turks.

A massacre ensued from which few of the Turks escaped. The incident was construed both at Vienna and at Constantinople as a breach of the truce, and led to a diplomatic incident. (Széchenyi Provincial Library, MS letter of Aga Ibrahim 16/61. Description of fight in Istvánffy, 1724.)

9 (*page 76*)   The White Huns showed their aptitude for strategic ruses in their campaign against the Persians of A.D. 459 with the following novelty. They set up snares such as hunters use, digging pits on the battlefield, carefully camouflaged. This line could only be crossed in the middle by a passage as wide as six horses abreast. They drew up their array behind the pits, and one of their squadrons made a feint attack. When this body pretended to flee the pursuing armoured Persians were drawn into the pits.

10 (*page 78*)   The Duke of Newcastle in his *Nouvelle Méthode et Invention* described this breed, principally hailing from the Tarbes plain, as follows:

> The best of these are the finest horses in the world, for everything from the tips of their ears to their hind hoofs is fair about them. Neither so light as the Barb nor so heavy as the Andalusian (Neapolitan), for endurance, courage and docility, they excel besides by their action. At a walk, trot or gallop they leave nothing to be desired. I may say there is no horse more worthy to carry a monarch whether on the field of battle or in a triumphal progress.

11 (*page 91*)   The uncommonly high esteem attaching to the wild horses is apparent from the fact that they were bred in game preserves. Thus Tomas Móró writes to the Palatine Nádasdy in 1556: "Your Grace commanded me to release the filly in the game park that is reserved for Your Grace." This was at Sarvar, where bison, elk, red, roe, and fallow deer were also preserved. (Budapest Archives, Hungarian Chamber 185, Nádasdy Family, B 1521, misc. Hirnyk.)

12 (*page 91*)   Ditto Dl. (Eperjes municipal accounts, fol. 363.)

13 (*page 91*)   Ditto Hungarian Chamber. (185, Nádasdy family, B. 1564, fol. 471.)

14 (*page 91*)   Ditto Motesiczky. (fasc. 10, fol. 37.)

15 (*page 93*)   Ditto Lad. Col. III. This document describes the bearings as follows (in Latin): "in the field, proper, the right hand and forearm of a man, holding a mallet upraised as if to strike the member of a horse. . . ."

16 (*page 94*)   From the mass of documents bearing on this the following examples may be cited. In 1280 four horses which were well known throughout the country were priced at 40 marks each. (Budapest Archives, Dl. 38667.) In 1317 a horse lost in battle is described as 'famous'. (Budapest Archives, Dl. 100,0041.) Again in 1557, *equus principalis . . . dignitati conveniens* (Budapest Archives, 185 Nádasdy family, B. 1526, misc. Mágocsi) and in 1579 "a horse fit for any lord." (Budapest Archives, P. 707, Zichy Family, fasc. 10, 186.) Finally, *equus capitalis*, (Ditto. E 185, Nádasdy Family, misc. Rum VI).

17 (*page 96*)   The clerk Adam reported to his employer, the wife of Palatine Nádasdy, on the provenance of the horse known as Harambasha:

> There is an order that the captured captains and their horses are to be sent to the King and his son. As we have to do with the Germans (Habsburgs) things are not easy. Of good horses suitable for a lord (*urnak valo*) there are only two: one of them is with Andras Pethö; we have sent secretly to Kapuvár with orders to tell no-one that it belonged to Harem Pasha, and let no one see it . . . (Budapest Archives E. 185 Nádasdy B1534), td. misc. Adám deak.

18 (*page 96*)   Budapest Archives E 185 Nádasdy Family B 1515 misc. Bebek.

19 (*page 96*)   Traces of direct importation of Arabian horses are to be found even in Hungary. In 1548 the Lady Majláth wrote to her son: "Your beloved father sends you—since you have been so diligent in learning—a Saracen horse from Bethlehem, the City of David, where our Lord was born . . ." (Budapest Archives, 185, Nádasdy Family, B 1528, misc. Majláth.)

20 (*page 97*)   (1) He is to buy me a quiet horse, yet fit for riding: by quiet I mean that it will stand to be mounted. Yet I wish it be a proper riding-horse, swift, with a good gallop and sound legs.
(2) The horse is not to have a hard mouth, for a hard-mouthed horse is a very foe, and if it were the best in the world, what shall that profit, if it have a hard mouth?
(3) It must be sound and not subject to lameness.
(4) It must not be too wide.
(5) It must not be an aged nag, but if possible still young, say between two and seven winters.
(6) . . . not to buy me a weak horse, but as I am a right heavy lad, it must be strong and muscular, fit to carry me.
(7) Let him not take into his head to buy me a horse with devilish tricks, that lashes out or is nappy, nor yet such a one as twirls its tail round, for that kind of horse is not suitable for a gentleman and shameful to ride.
(8) It must be fair and stately, of what colour I care not.
   (Budapest Archives 190, Rákóczi Family, B 1585, fol. 46.)

21 (*page 97*)   Correspondence of the Palatine Tomas Nádasdy shows the wide range of horse exports from Moldavia and Wallachia in the sixteenth century. Writing during 1556 about the repeated purchases made by him on behalf of Archduke Maximilian, he says of one consignment "Three are Walking Horses, three pacers, the former being all Wallachian, one of the pacers is a Turk, grey with some spots; the second is a Szegh (Shagya?) from Moldavia of a striking grey colour, the third a chesnut from beyond the Alps". (Budapest Archives P 1322, Batthyány Family fasc. 112, 123.)

On receipt by the Archduke in Vienna, he "chose three of them, two pacers including the Moldavian Szegh with a white blaze, the chesnut Transalpine horse, and the third the Walking Horse with the hogged mane". (Budapest Archives 185 Nádasdy Family, B 1524, misc. Köver.)

The price of Moldavian horses at that time was equal to that of the Arabs. Adám Perényi paid 120 Talers to Gábor Kende for a Moldavian chesnut broken to ride in a curb in 1669. (Budapest Archives 423 Kende Family, fasc. 7/1669.)

22 (page 97)   There is a hint as to the breeding of the "Ertzel" horses bred in Lad parish, county Somogy, in a Hungarian sporting periodical of 1857. The stud-owner added the following to a description of the horses advertised for sale:

> This stud traces to the stallion and twelve mares which Ignatius von Czindery brought back from Greater Tartary in 1736, and which have been kept pure since then without admission of other blood. The result of this inbreeding is a uniform strain, conformation and performance do not vary as between individuals. The half-bred progeny out of farmer's mares show the prepotency of the Ertzel stallion, as he can get foals of passable quality even out of the commonest mares. (*Lapok a Lovástat es vadaszat köreböl,* 1857.)

The Czindery stock was still important among private studs during the nineteenth century, or at any rate among some of them. It is incomprehensible why the authorities of that day did not further the propagation (together with that of the TB and the pure-bred Arab) of this strain which had been bred on Hungarian soil for more than a century. This principle of Hungarian horse-breeding was still well understood about 1800. Baron Josef Wenkheim, a generally acknowledged specialist in this field, deplores, in the book which he published at Pest in 1815, that the once free trade from Tartary, Caucasia, Bessarabia, Poland, and Moldavia is now blocked and impeded to the detriment of Hungarian horse-breeding. He says:

> The history of our indigenous horse shows . . . that the Hungarian horse is closely allied to the Arab, it comes from the same stock of a warm climate. We must therefore only use as foundation stock horses from such a climate or one similar to our own. But hold aloof from all other strains and try to eliminate them, for they bring us nothing but trouble; they may have a showy exterior, but they beget nothing but bastards. Little by little they will be the ruin of our stock.
>
> Therefore for our purpose the most commendable are the Turk, the Barb, the Persian, Circassian, Caucasian, Turcoman—all the Russian breeds of the South like the purebred Donskoy, specially the Zaporozhie—also the Andalusian and the Neapolitan. . . . But all Northern breeds we should eschew, they have no common ancestry with ours and they degenerate in our climate. . . .

General Csekonics was of the same opinion, saying (Pest 1817) that the Transylvanian horse was "of authentic ancient pure lineage, able to contest the palm in light-horse breeding throughout Europe against all comers, including the English Thoroughbred". This high esteem for the Transylvanian horse runs like a bright thread through the whole tradition of breeding in Hungary. As we have seen, it is evident in the fifteenth-century French traveller Broquière's notes, and occurs again in the histories of Miklós Oláh, who esteemed it even above the Turkish horse. So long as the homeland of the Turanian horse had not been engulfed by Tsarist expansion, even the Russians drew their best horses from Hungary in great measure. This esteem was confirmed by the Russian General Piscsevics, when in 1758 he was ordered by the Tsarina Elisabeth Petrovna to acquire horses from the Transylvanian stud of Count Mikes for the Court of St Petersburg. He was of Yugoslav origin, and had once been in the Austrian service; he noted in his memoirs that they were without fault, and of such quality that he had never in all his life seen better or finer horses. (*Memoirs,* Hungarian trans., Budapest 1904.) His purchase aroused great admiration at St Petersburg.

In the second part of the nineteenth century the same revolution took place in Transylvanian horse-breeding as had happened in Hungary fifty years earlier, but in this case the damage could not be remedied after the extinction of this valuable strain of horses.

23 (*page 99*) "The aforesaid enemy . . . who can cover in one day a distance that we could hardly perform within two days, because they are equipped as light horsemen. . . ." (Budapest Archives, E 245, Rep 3242, fol. 203.)

24 (*page* 100)   Budapest Archives, Dl. 1154 and 2135.

25 (*page* 104)   The proverb "No prophet hath honour in his own country" is also true of the Hussars in Hungary. For decades a lively controversy raged as to whether the hussars were of Hungarian or external origin, and only came to an end—alleviated by the reduced strategic value of cavalry but aggravated by the jealousy of other arms—with the denial of their traditions rooted in the soil of Central Asiatic horsemanship. It is significant that between the World Wars the term Hussar was not used to describe the Hungarian Army (Honved) cavalry. The horse soldiers who in the history of European warfare had won such renown were strangely repudiated in their own country.

There is no hint in contemporary documents, or even a shadow of circumstantial evidence, that the hussar as such was of Balkan origin.

Bonfini, in his account of King Matthias' mercenary troops, mentions three nationalities—Bohemians, Hungarians, and 'Raizes' (Yugoslavs). The King's letter to Gabriel of Verona sets out his order of battle as consisting of heavy cavalry, light hussars, and infantry.

26 (*page* 106)   "Our armoured cavalry are accustomed to stand their ground, though they be all cut down where they stand. But the light troops attack whenever opportunity occurs, and when they are exhausted or menaced by some grave danger they withdraw behind the main body and there re-form, and when their morale and physique is restored they pass again to the offensive."

27 (*page* 106)   Budapest Archives E 254. fasc. 2956. 1574. nov. 8.

28 (*page* 107)   Ditto E 254. fasc. 3188. fol. 582.

29 (*page* 107)   Ditto E 190. Rákóczi Family, B 1584 fol. 146.

30 (*page* 107)   Ditto R 224, 1661, pall. 97.

31 (*page* 108)   Ditto R. 224, 1667, pal. 97.

32 (*page* 108)   Ditto, C 35, Lad. D. no. 18.

33 (*page* 108)   At this time Western stud methods were gaining ground in Hungary. In 1715 the steward of the Zichy estate of Zsámbék wrote to his employer: "The mares will not stay in the herd, but scatter all over the place", and asked him to send them a stallion without delay. (Budapest Archives P 707. Zichy Family, fasc. 126, nb, 17626.) In 1777 the Master of the Horse to the Kárólyis was sent round the neighbourhood "to find out how people manage mares and stallions when covering in hand or running free." (Budapest Archives, 398. Kárólyi Family, misc. Mlinaricz.)

Baron Wenkheim (1815) and General Csekonics (1817) both lay the blame for the decline of quality in breeding which went hand in hand with the cessation of horse-keeping on open range on the fact that mares were no longer covered at their own will. Both stress the importance of mares being served in accordance with their own inclination, that of the stallion, and natural selection. Wenkheim recommends for this purpose four stallions to a herd—Csekonics even more—on the ground that, in any herd, sub-herds tend to form round each stallion, whereby there is more opportunity for insemination according to natural impulse.

Csekonics continues:

As horses have a natural instinct whereby each sire attracts or wins by fighting a given number of mares, according as he feels he is able to serve so many, and thus assert his rights ... Therefore I make so bold as to say, that all breeders should—nay I beseech them, rather—to give up the half-wild husbandry and revert wholly to the totally wild . . .

Now consider all the light cavalry of Europe. Nearly all their remounts are the progeny of wild herds . . . and all civilian horses such as cobs and the like in commercial use, down to cab-horses—you will find that most of them are of wild origin.

Nowadays not only in Hungary, but wherever horses are bred, all is changed. Present experiments, and the practice of artificial insemination, are in complete opposition to all that were once considered fundamental principles. The horses are deprived of their last opportunity to refuse a coupling repugnant to Nature, or to avoid it. I call this a senseless affront offered to Nature, the consequences of which will probably not be realized until the resultant damage is not to be repaired.

34 (*page* 111) There is medieval evidence for branding of horses in Hungary. In 1270 horses from the village of Barcza were marked with *signum in scapula in parte sinistra per modum furce* (fork on near shoulder) and then with *signum in sinistra parte in latere admodum virgule* (twig on near flank), and lastly with *signum in dextro femore 2 ferramenta equorum* (off thigh, 2 horseshoes). (Budapest Archives Dl. 84214 and 84198.)

In 1336 Peter Nagysemjén recognized a horse in the royal camp near Kreisbach which bore the well-known Kállay brand *signum falcastrum luporum* on the near side (a wolf's paw). (Kállay Family archives, 497.) The branding of horses in the Trakehnen and other German studs is a relic of the time when herds were kept on open range, and the practice is still common in the British Isles (*e.g.*, Wales, Exmoor, New Forest) where herds run on common grazing.

34a (*page* 114) "Estland is swythe micel" says the West Saxon king, reporting his informant, the Norwegian merchant skipper Wulfstan (Ulfsteinn):

Estonia is a big country, full of towns, and to every town a king. There is much honey there, and good fishing. The kings and the rich men drink mares' milk, and poor men and serfs drink mead. There is much fighting among them. The Estonians brew no ale, for they have mead enough instead. It is the custom among them, that when a man of any consequence dies he lies in state uncremated in the house of his friends and kinsmen a month and sometimes two, and in the case of kings and nobles as much as half a year. And all the time the body lies in state there are drinking bouts and sports and gambling, till the day of the cremation. And the day they intend to carry him to the pyre, they take all such of his property as is left after the drinking and the gambling, and part it out into five or six lots, or sometimes more, according to how much of it is left. And they put the largest share a mile from the town where the corpse lies, and the other shares in diminishing order between that and the town, so that the smallest lot is nearest the town. There then assemble all those men that have the fastest horses, some five or six miles outside the town. And they all ride at full speed towards the property; and he that has the fastest horse comes first to the outermost share which is also the greatest, and so one after another until it is all taken up. And he that comes fifth or sixth, as it may be, takes the smallest share nearest to the town. Then they all ride on their way with their winnings, for nothing is held back. This is the reason why fast horses are uncommonly dear among them. When all this treasure is dissipated they carry out the corpse and burn it, together with weapons and clothing. [Preface to Orosius' *History. Tr.*]

Part IV

35 (*page* 117) Budapest Archives Dl. 6692/1.

36 (*page* 119) Budapest Archives E 185. Nádasdy Family., B 1514, misc. Arco.

37 (*page* 119) Budapest Archives, Dl. 26171. The six-in-hand slung wagon was in daily use among the more considerable Hungarian landowners in the fifteenth and sixteenth centuries, for travelling. According to a fifteenth-century account book, the Imperial Palatine once progressed through Upper Hungary with five such wagons.

38 (*page* 122) From a deed of grant by Maria Theresa to the Counts Ferenc and Josef Nádasdy of 1744. (Budapest Archives P 507, Nádasdy Family, series 2. no. 46.)

39 (*page* 122) *Leith von Hadik to His Royal Highness concerning the Expedition into the Mark of Brandenburg and the Storming of the Royal Capital and Residence of Berlin.* (Copy of commander's report, made contemporaneously, and in possession of the author.)

40 (*page* 122) The Tschunkenberg case will serve among many examples to demonstrate that the demand for Hussars was not directed exclusively to Hungary, but to Oriental horsemen in general. He was a Turk, his real name Mehmet, and was present at the battles of Kassa, Buda, and Vác; in 1685 he was the last Turkish defender of the fortress of Nógrád. He was very popular among the Hungarians. Fighting bravely, he lost his right arm in battle, and was consequently known as 'Csonkabég'—that is, "the One-Armed Bey". At the storming of Nógrád by the Christians he, his wife, and his son were taken prisoner, and he was brought to interrogation at Wienerneustadt on November 14th, 1686. Ten years later he and his family embraced the Catholic faith. The Emperor himself stood godfather to him, and he was christened Leopold Josef Balthasar Tschunkenberg. An Archduchess stood godmother to his wife.

In the War of the Spanish Succession there were four regiments of hussars, as early as 1702: the Ninth (Czobor), the Eighth (Pál Deák), and the Kollonits and Ebergényi Regiments. In the same year four more regiments were raised; by Simon Forgách, Imre Gombos, Péter János Loósy and Gábor Esterházy, son of the Palatine, the last being commanded by Colonel Tschunkenberg. His new name is of course a Germanization of the old nickname Csonkabég. He became a favourite of Prince Eugène of Savoy, who once freed him after he had been taken prisoner. In December 1704 a second regiment (Lehoczky's) was placed under his command, and this brigade was then attached to the English force fighting on the Moselle. On 16 Feb. 1705 Field-Marshal Groensfeld wrote to Prince Eugène; ". . . poor old Csunkabeck who was commanding the light horse on the Moselle front, was murdered by franc-tireurs, together with Lt. Col. Rudnai of Esterházy's whose son in retaliation burnt six villages to the ground. . . ." to which the Prince replied on Feb 25th: "It is not certain . . .". (Vienna, War Dispatches, 1705.)

Old Csonkabég's son, Ferenc Leopold Tschunkenberg, was made an Austrian baron. No doubt he grew up in Hungary, for like his father he wore Hungarian costume, wrote letters in Magyar, and felt himself a complete Hungarian. He served in Sicily, and in Upper Italy. He died in 1735 at Klausen, in South Tyrol, without male heir extant, and was thus the last of his line. He bequeathed his estate to the founding and endowment of a church at Wienerneustadt. Takáts the historian says that portraits of the Tschunkenbergs, father and son, were to be seen in the Town Hall there.

41 (*page* 123) Moreri: *Dictionnaire*, 1732. When they return from the war the general gives them as many gold pieces as they bring back heads.

42 (*page* 123) Budapest Archives E 169 Bellavitz Family B 1532.

43 (*page* 123) From a contemporary letter in possession of the author. At the time of the Napoleonic Wars we also find hussars serving abroad called 'Kuruzes'. A letter of 1800 mentions the 'Red Kuruzes' in French pay. (Budapest Archives, Jeszenák Family, P 1398, cs. 10. fasc. 12, 1062.)

44 (*page* 124)   The popularity of the Hungarian hussar at that day is expressed in a Rhineland folksong of the eighteenth century:

> Now the Hungarian hussars ride
> From Hungary to the Rhine
> All in red breeches
> And a grass-green cloak about them.
> If a hussar falls, then he rides to Heaven,
> And another loses an arm or a leg;
> What else are chaplains and surgeons for?
> They are well served, body and soul.
> Many a heart these hussars have broken
> Between Hungary and the Rhine
> And many a nut-brown maid asks,
> "Where will my hussar be now?"

From the locally collected and published *Zupfgeigenhansl*.

45 (*page* 125)   Károlyi Family Archives, vol. 3, p. 40.

46 (*page* 126)   Budapest Archives, Dl. 14545.

47 (*page* 126)   The late spread of the pacer to Hungary is evident from the lack of skill in training it, which lasted for a long time. The Master of the Horse at Sárvár, the Nádasdy estate, wrote to his employer in 1557 that he had harnessed three carriage horses in a team with the pacers, and hobbled them near fore to near hind, etc., but had no success, as the mares never did learn to pace, but broke the hobbles. (Budapest Archives, Nádasdy Family. misc. Pálffy János.) The Hungarian proverb "It is hard to make an old horse pace" echoes the English fifteenth-century saying:

> As hors that ever trotted, trewely ich yow telle
> Ful hard were it to teche hym, after, to amble well.

or more succinctly, in the sixteenth century

> Trot sire, trot dam, how shall the foal amble?

and shows the belief then prevalent, that horses could only be bred, not trained, to pace or amble.

48 (*page* 126)   Budapest Archives P 707, Zichy Family, fasc. 10, 186.

49 (*page* 126)   The use of horses of different gaits, in the manner customary in the Age of Chivalry, is now only found, apart from examples in the southern U.S.A. and South Africa, in Iceland, which was settled a thousand years ago by Scandinavian, British, and Irish colonists, with horse-stock drawn from the entire north-west coastal region of Europe. In Iceland, pacing and racking are inbred in some strains of pony.

50 (*page* 127)   It was said of Palatine Nádasdy's horses kept at Sarvar in 1561: "The brown mare has foaled to the King's horse. It is a good colt, like the sire. I have foreborne so far to show him to anyone, for fear of the evil eye" (Budapest Archives E 185, Nádasdy Family, 8, misc. Pálffy János.)

51 (*page* 127)   Ditto E 185 Nádasdy Family B 1528, misc. Nádasdy F.

52 (*page* 127)   Ditto E 185, Nádasdy Family, B 1520, misc. Giczy.

53 (*page* 127)   The component parts of the *kocsi* were mentioned in two documents:
1550: Budapest Archives E 185 Nádasdy Family B 1525 pall. 12 f. 1.
1750: Budapest Archives P 198 Esterházy Family Cseklész Accounts 604. f. 161.

54 (*page* 129)   According to Bartoniek, Aczél rode into the water after the King, whereas Burgio rather implies, with *e intrato*, that he dismounted and waded or dived, which seems inherently more likely. (Bartoniek 1926.)

55 (*page* 129)   Budapest Archives Dl. 24405. *Eodem die Johanni Warkony adulescenti Regie Maiestatis per Maiestatem Suam ad Moraviam pro abducentis equis armigeris misso pro expensis dati sunt in bona moneta per duas flos xxv.*—"The same day were paid His Majesty's esquire John Warkony, for going on His Majesty's errand to Moravia to fetch warhorses twenty-five florins, as his expenses, in good currency."

56 (*page* 129)   The authorities for the content of the royal stables under Matthias and Vladislav II are Csánky, 1883, and Fogel, 1913.
The existence of a French saddle at the Court of Louis II indicates the prevalence of French customs there. The will of Miklós Balinszky, proved in 1515, bequeathed to the royal *dapifer* (cup-bearer) a horse 'together with a saddle made after the French manner' (*una cum sella in more francigerorum facta*). (Budapest Archives Filmtár, C. 267 Bártfa Váre Lt.-a 4563.)

57 (*page* 130)   Burgio's account differs in many particulars from observations made on the spot. If the horse really refused the obstacle and threw the rider it would have been able to climb out on either bank, once loose, just as Aczél's and Czettricz's horses did. At this point the horse was at the exact place where according to the eye-witness Czettricz the weapons were found, and where the King must have lain. In contrast to Burgio's account, it therefore seems more probable that the horse reared up and came over backward, falling on the rider. But this is not part of the refusal behaviour. It is, of course, quite possible that the horse suddenly dropped dead of a wound previously received—but also most unlikely. When its strength fails a wounded horse falls forward. Rearing up and falling backward are the actions of a horse in full possession of its powers, but in a state of panic, mortal fear, and having lost its head. Taking all this into consideration, we must conclude that the horse was overtaxed and exhausted, and immersion in cold water brought on a heart-attack. There is supplementary evidence that a heavy horse was involved. The contemporary Italian chronicle of Marino Sanuto says that the King was drowned in a swamp by 'his fat horse' (*a cavallo grosse s'e impaludo*). Newcastle wrote of the Frisian horse in 1660: ". . . is apt for all exercise, save only for long gallops . . . it is of no use to urge them to gallop long, they have not the wind for it . . ."

Part V

58 (*page* 139)   There are many records from the Arpad period of the hunting and sporting ability of Hungarian rulers. The Hildesheim Annals state that St Imre, only son of St Stephen, was mortally wounded out hunting by a boar. There are numerous accounts of the hunting of Géza I and St Ladislaus. (Gombos, p. 688.) A charter (Budapest Archives Dl. 5625) also mentions King Imre's death in the hunting-field. Endre II also refers in a charter of manumission to one of his youthful experiences while hunting: ". . . the spot where, when I was still a prince, I slew a wild bear and marked a cross on a tree". (Smiciclas.)

59 (*page 139*) General Csekonics comments thus:

> Count Károlyi wanted to buy the mare on account of her great courage, but the owner refused all offers, though respectfully as became a subject of the Count . . . . He declared that great as the honour and favour that would accrue to him might be, if his horse were to enter His Lordship's stables, yet he would take neither money nor goods for it, and would no more think of parting with his grey mare than with his wife.

60 (*page 140*) Frederick II's book, besides its literary value, also affords useful source-material on the history of falconry in Europe. From it we learn that in contemporary England hawking was done on foot, although the Bayeux Tapestry shows the Normans about to invade England, some of them riding with hawk on fist, and that Spain in the thirteenth century was the true home of mounted falconry in the West, due to Moorish influence. Frederick himself brought falconers from the Arab world, chiefly from North Africa. The use of the hawk's hood or *capellum* originated there. But at the same time he employed austringers from other countries (*expertos huius rei tam de Arabia, quam de regionibus undecunque . . . redigere*). The real home of European falconry at that time was Hungary, of which there are many proofs. Hungarian annals often mention the Arpad dynasty hawking, *inter alia* a hawking party of Prince Almos at Szekesfehervar in 1106. (Szentpétery: *Scriptores Rerum Hungaricarum* I.S. 427.)

Frederick II had also personal ties with Hungary. As a boy of ten, under Papal pressure, he was betrothed to the widow of King Imre (who died in 1204), the Aragonese Princess Constance, ten years his senior. The wedding followed many years later, and in the bridal train there came to Palermo a large Hungarian household. Given the nature of Hungarian royal households at that time, and the large suite to which a Queen Dowager would be entitled, there can be no doubt that these will have included huntsmen and falconers.

61 (*page 143*) The encounter took place with much mounted pomp. The men presented a brilliant picture. There were all but a hundred cavaliers in ornate national costume, the bride escorted by the ban of Croatia and a bishop in a triumphal car drawn by six dapple greys with silver-mounted harness inlaid with purple, their manes and tails dyed blue. The Basket Hunt is described thus:

> The basket was hunted near the village of Hesszurét, by five horsemen of the Prince (bridegroom) and one Turk of the Ban's (bride's father). The Prince's man mounted on a Turkish chestnut won the basket (Kelemen Kun), and the second prize, which was a length of scarlet cloth, was won by the Ban's horseman, although his mount collapsed at the winning-post; third came Szoboszlai on a bay horse which had already run in a race at Munkács.

(Budapest Archives R 224, 1666.)

62 (*page 148*) Budapest Archives 185 Nádasdy Family B 1530. Misc. Egerszeghy.

63 (*page 150*) Marco Polo says of the Mongol post system:

> The post-houses are called Djam, and situated each twenty-five leagues apart. Foot couriers are relieved every three leagues, but express post is sent by horsemen. They cover two hundred or two hundred and fifty leagues in a day, horse and rider changing at every post-house, where fresh horses are always in waiting. Every town or village that lies near such a post-house is bound to furnish it with a certain number of horses. It is only in uninhabited places that the Emperor maintains the post-houses at his own charges.

64 (*page 150*) Budapest Archives Dl. 57632.

65 (*page* 150) 1. From Buda to Bia, on a half-blind horse, lame both sides before. 2. From Bia to Bicske, on a Hungarian farm-horse called Sólyom. 3. From Bicske to Bánhida, on a grey. 4. From Bánhida to Kóts, on a brown English half-bred mare. 5. From Kóts to Bábolna on a brown English half-bred mare called Princesse. 6. From Bábolna to Györ, by coach behind four bays from the Kezsthely stud (Count Festetic's) harnessed all abreast in the Russian style. 7. From Györ to Öttéveny on a Hungarian farm-horse called Kedves. 8. From Öttéveny to Mosony, on an English half-bred mare called Julianna. 9. From Mosony to Saida, on a Thoroughbred called Brigliadoro. 10. From Saida to Pahrendorf, on an English half-bred named Coquette. 11. From Parhrendorf to Schwechat, on an English half-bred named Restless. 12. From Schwechat to Vienna, on my own horse Bully. ['English half-bred' here means that the horse was partly Thoroughbred, the other part of its breeding had nothing to do with England. *Tr.*]

66 (*page* 151) "Then rode they four, being young and wilful, night and day, and when they would sleep they took to wagons; and you are to know they changed horses many times."

67 (*page* 151) Giovanni Sforza's ride in 1497 demonstrates the varying capabilities of Eastern and Western strains of horse. When he heard from his wife Lucrezia Borgia of the attack that Cesare Borgia was planning he mounted his Turkish horse in Rome and got to Pesaro 160 miles away in twenty-four hours. But his horse collapsed from exhaustion. This is equal to the average performance in the Budapest-Vienna long-distance ride.

68 (*page* 151) Horse-leaping was known among Orientals in antiquity. An inscription from Urartu of the eighth century B.C. mentions Arcibis, King Menua's horse, that could jump 22 cubits horizontally.

Source of Illustrations

Anglis: 114. E. Bacon: *Digging for History* (A. & C. Black, London, 1960): 22. E. Breuil and H. Obermaier: *La Cueva de Altamira* (Tipographia de Archivos, Madrid, 1935): 15. Bruckmann Bildarchiv: 40. W. Castelli: 81. Duke of Portland: *Memories of Racing and Hunting* (Faber, London, 1935): 86. H. Frankfort: *The Art and Architecture of the Ancient Orient* (Penguin, London, 1954): 19. M. Gábori: 10, 36, 65, 67. Giraudon, Paris: 4, 24, 30, 32, 41, 42. A. Godard, Paris: 31. A. Grote: 45. H. Hell: 14. Hutin, Compiègne: 93. Interfoto-Bilderdienst: 49. Keystone: 116. Kohalmy: 37. L. Ligeti: 12. W. Menzendorf: 99, 100, 106, 117. J. Molnár: 3, 26, 33–35, 39, 44, 50, 51, 69, 70, 72, 73–76, 82–85, 88, 90, 95, 96, 101, 103, 104, 111. W. Pruski: 16, 17, 89, 91. K. Salzle: *Tier und Mensch—Gottheit und Dämon* (BLV 1965): 119, 120. E. Schiele: 46–48, 55–61, 64, 98, 105. Solms-Laubach: *Die schönsten Reiterbilder aus europaischen Sammlungen* (Keysersche Verlagsbuchhandlung, Heidelberg and Munich, 1962): 1, 118, 121. W. Steinkopf: 92. Staatsbibliothek Berlin, Bildarchiv (Handke): 28. Süddeutscher Verlag, Bildarchiv: 52. Szalay: 11. G. Torlichen, Argentina. Chr. Belser Verlag, Stuttgart, 53, 54. E. Trumler: 6. Ullstein-Bilderdienst: 115. R. Viollet, Paris: 25. Zodiaque: 112.

Bibliography

The approximate English equivalents of German, Russian, Polish and Hungarian titles appear in roman after the titles in question. The insertion of an English equivalent title does not necessarily imply that a work has been translated into English.

AJTAI, E.: *A Magyar huszár* (The Hungarian Hussar), Budapest, 1936.
ALISTAI MÁTTYUS, J.: *A nemzeti lovag* (The National Horseman), Pest, 1828.
ALMÁSY, G.: *Vándorutam Ázsia szivében* (Rambles in the Heart of Asia), Budapest, 1903.
ANDRÁSSY, M. GR.: *Hazai vadászatok és sport Magyarországon* (Hunting and Sports in Hungary), Budapest, 1857.
Annales Hildersheimenses.
Anonymi Belae regis notarii: Gesta Hungarorum, ed. Gombos, No. 540.
Anonymi Descriptio Europae Orientalis anno 1308, ed. Gorka, Cracow, 1916.
APOR, P.: *Metamorphosis Transylvaniae.*

BAMM, P.: *Frühe Stätten der Christenheit* (Early Christian Sites), Munich, 1965.
BARTONIEK, E.: *Mohács Magyarországa* (The Hungary of Mohács), Budapest, 1926.
BELÉNYESY, M.: *Az állattartás a XV. században Magyarországon* (Cattle-breeding in Fifteenth-century Hungary), Ethnographic report, 1956.
BERGER, A.: *Die Jagd aller Völker im Wandel der Zeit* (International History of Hunting), Berlin, 1928.
BOESSNECK, J.: *Zur Entwicklung vor- und frühgeschichtlicher Haus- und Wildtiere Bayerns im Rahmen der gleichzeitigen Tierwelt Mitteleuropas. Studien an vor- und frühgeschichtlichen Tierresten Bayerns*, II (History of Prehistoric and Protohistoric Wild and Domestic Animals of Bavaria), Munich, 1958.
BÖKÖNYI, S.: *Die Haustiere in Ungarn im Mittelalter auf Grund der Knochenfunde. Viehzucht und Hirtenleben in Ost-Mitteleuropa* (Medieval Domestic Animals in Hungary from Skeletal Evidence), Budapest, 1961.
BOROSY, A.: *XI–XIV. századi magyar lovasságról* (Hungarian Cavalry of the Eleventh to Fourteenth Centuries), Military History Publications, 1962, II.
BRUNS, U.: *Ponies*, London, 1961.

CALKIN, V. I.: *Drevnyeje zsivotnovodsztvo plemjon vasztocsnoj Jevropu i szregynyej Azii* (Stockbreeding in Antiquity among East European and Central Asian Tribes), Moscow, 1966.
CARRUTHERS, D.: *Unknown Mongolia. A record of travel and exploration in North-West Mongolia and Dzungaria*, London, 1913.
CHLEDOWSKI, C. V.: *Der Hof von Ferrara* (The Court of Ferrara), Berlin, 1913.
Chronicon Budense, ed. Podraczky, J., Buda, 1838.
Chronicon Colmariense, ed. Gombos, No. 1290.
Corpus Juris Hungarici, I. 1000–1526, Budapest, 1899.
CSÁNKY, D.: *I. Mátyás udvara* (The Court of Matthias I), Budapest, 1883.
CSEKONICS, J.: *Praktische Grundsätze, die Pferde betreffend* (Practical Principles regarding the Horse), Pest, 1817.

DADÁNYI, G.: *Csordás voltam Paraguayban* (I was a Paraguayan Cowboy), Budapest, 1943.
DARKÓ, J.: *Turáni hatások a göröh-római hadügy fejlödésében* (Turanian Influence on the Development of Graeco-Roman Tactics), Military History Publications, Budapest, 1934.
DELBRÜCK, H.: *Geschichte der Kriegskunst im Rahmen der politischen Geschichte II.* (History of the Art of War in the Context of Political History), Berlin, 1921.

DENT, A. A. and GOODALL, D. MACHIN: *The Foals of Epona*, London, 1962.

Deutsche Fundgruben der Geschichte Siebenbürgens, I (German Sources for the History of Transylvania).

DIAKONOV: *Epigrafika Vostoka* (Oriental Inscriptions), 1951.

DIEM, C.: *Asiatische Reiterspiele* (Asiatic Mounted Sports), Berlin, 1941.

——: *Weltgeschichte des Sports und der Leibeserziehung* (World History of Sport and Physical Training), Stuttgart, 1960.

DIVÉKY, A.: *Zsigmond lengyel herceg budai, számadásai* (Prince Sigismund of Poland's Account-books at Buda), Hungarian Historical Research, 1914.

DOMANOVSZKY, S.: *Mázsaszekér* (The Wagon), *Fejérpataky Album*, Budapest, 1917.

DUBRAVIUS: *Historia regni Bohemiae*, Budapest, 1917.

EINHARD and NOTKER: *Two Lives of Charlemagne* (trans. Thorpe), Harmondsworth, 1969.

FEJÉR, G.: *Codex diplomaticus* IV/2.

FINTA, A.: *Herdboy of Hungary*, Washington, 1940.

FLADE, J. E.: *Das Araberpferd* (The Arab Horse) Wittenberg, 1962.

FOGEL, J.: II. *Ulászló udvartartása* (The Court of Ladislas II), Budapest, 1913.

FRAKNOI, V.: *Mátyás király levelei* (Letters of King Matthias II), Budapest, 1893–95.

Friderici Romanorum Imperatoris Secundi: De Arte Venandi cum avibus.

FROISSART, J.: *Chronicles.*

FUGGER, M.: *Von der Gestuterey* (Of Stud-farms), Frankfurt a/M 1584.

GÁBORI, M.: *Napfényes Mongolia* (Sunny Mongolia), Budapest, 1961.

GÁRDONYI, A.: *Budapest történeti emlékei* (Historical Memorials of the City of Budapest) Budapest, 1941.

Geneologia Comitum Flandriae, book 3, col. 402 z. von Du Cange.

GOMBOS, A.: *Catalogus fontium Historiae Hungaricae*, III, Budapest, 1938.

GORKA: *Anonymi Descriptio Europae Orientalis anno 1308*, Gracoviae, 1916.

GROUSSET, R.: *L'empire des steppes*, 1939.

GYÖRFFY, GY.: *Magyarok elödeiröl és a honfoglalasról* (Ancestry and Settlements of the Magyars), Budapest, 1958.

HALÁSZ, G.: *Telivérek* (Thoroughbreds), Budapest, 1943.

HANCAR, F.: *Das Pferd in prähistorischer und früher historischer Zeit* (The Horse in Prehistoric and Early Historical Times), Vienna, 1955.

HANKÓ, B.: *Székely lovak* (Székely Horses), Kolozsvár, 1943.

HAVARD, H.: *Dictionaire de l'ameublement et de decoration, depuis le XIII-e siècle jusqu'à nos jours*, Paris.

HEDIN, SVEN: *The Silk Road*, London, 1938.

IBN BATTUTA: *Travels in Asia and Africa 1325–54*, London, 1929.

ISTVÁNFFY, N.: *Regni Hungarici Historia*, ed. Coloniae, 1724.

KAKUK, Z.: *Az orkhoni felirat* (The Orkhon Inscription), *A magyarok elödeiröl, és a honfoglalásról*, Budapest, 1958.

KEMALPASASZADE MOHÁCSNAME: *Török-magyarkori történeti emlékek* (Turco-Hungarian Historical Monuments), Turkish Historical Writings, I.

KEMÉNY JÁNOS: *Önéletrajzleirása* (Autobiography), Századok, 1959.

LAMING, A.: *La Signification de l'Art Rupestre*, Paris, 1959.

LÁSZLÓ, G.: *A koroncói lelet és a honfoglaló magyarok nyerge* (The Koroncó Find and the Saddles of the Hungarian Settlers), Budapest, 1943.

——: *A honfoglaló magyar nép élete* (Life among the Hungarian Settlers), Budapest, 1944.

——: *Kolzsvári Márton és György szobránnak lószerszáma* (Saddlery in the Statue of St George), Transylvanian Scientific Institute Year Book, Kolozsvár, 1943.

László, J.: "Magyar huszárok idegen nemzetek szolgálatában" (Hungarian Hussars in Foreign Service), *The Hungarian Hussar*, Budapest, 1936.

Leo VI imperator dictus Sapiens (Philosophus) *886–912. Tactica.*

Lestyán, S.: *Gróf Sandor Móric, az ördöglovas* (Count M. Sándor, the Devil's Horseman), Budapest, 1942.

Ligeti, L.: *Secret of the Mongols*, London, 1963.

Liliencron, R. v.: *Die historischen Volkslieder der Deutschen vom 13. bis. 16. Jahrhundert* (Historic German Folksongs, 1200–1600), Leipzig, 1865.

Magyar, K.: *Csekonics kapitány emlékirata* (Memorandum by Captain Csekonics), Hungarian Farmers' Union, 1936.

Makkai-Mezey: *Árpádkori és Anjou-kori levelek* (Correspondence of the Arpad and Anjou Periods), Budapest.

Masudi: *Murudzs adz-dzahab*, ed. Czeglédy, K.; *A magyarok elödeiröl és a honfoglaldsról* (Ancestry and Settlements of the Magyars), ed. Györffy, Budapest, 1958.

Miskulin, A.: *Müvelödéstörténeti mozzanatok Giovani és Matteo Villani krónikája alapján* (The Villani Chronicle as Historical Source), Budapest, 1905.

Moser, H.: *Durch Zentralasien* (Through Central Asia), Leipzig, 1888.

Nagy, G.: *A Magyar középkozi fegyverzet* (Weapons in Medieval Hungary), Ért, 1891.

Nestor monachus Kioviensis, *Annales Russorum*, ed. Kniezsa, I., Budapest, 1958.

Newcastle, Duke of: *Nouvelle Methode et Invention*, Antwerp, 1656.

Niederwolfsgruber, F.: *Kaiser Maximilians I. Jagd- und Fischereibücher* (Maximilian I's Books on Hunting and Fishing), Munich, 1965.

Oppyanos: *Kynegetika*, ed. Lehrs, Paris, 1846.

Pálffy János emlékezései, Magyarországi és Erdélyi urak (Memoirs of Hungarian and Transylvanian Noblemen), ed. Szabó T. Attila, Kolozsvár, 1939.

Perjes, G.: *Lóra termette-e a magyar?* (Is the Hungarian born to ride?) Life and Science, 1965.

Pest. Egy Tiszaháti Magyar's öszinte megjegyzései a'hazafiság, utánzási kór és nevelés felett (Honest observations of a Tisza-side Hungarian on Patriotism, Imitation and Training), Leipzig, 1846.

Pettko-Szandtner, T.: *A magyar kocsizás* (Hungarian Coaching), Budapest, 1931.

Pokorny, G.: *Skizzen zur Geschichte des Pferdes* (Sketches on the History of the Horse), Prague, 1878.

Pollay: *Neue Reitkunst, ein Reiterbrevier* (The New Art of Riding), Stuttgart.

Polo, Marco: *Travels.*

Pray, G.: *Annales veteres Hunnorum Avarorum et Hungarorum* II., Vindobonae, 1761.

Pruski, W.: *Dzikie Konie Wschodniej Europy. Roczniki Nauk Rolniczych. 85. Der D.* (Horses of Eastern Europe), Warsaw, 1959.

Razin: *A hadmüvészet története* (History of the Art of War), II. ung. Ub., Budapest, 1961.

Ross, E. J.: *A Chalcolithic Site in Northern Baluchistan*, 1946, INES.

Rudenko, S. I.: *The Frozen Tombs*, London, 1970.

Salet: *Die Nachfolger Alexanders des Grossen in Baktrien und Indien* (Alexander the Great's Successors in Bactria and India), Berlin, 1879.

Sälzle, K.: *Tier und Mensch, Gottheit und Dämon* (Beast and Man, Deity and Devil), Munich 1965.

Schack, Gr., Adolf Friedrich: *Geschichte der Normannen in Sizilien*, X. (History of the Normans in Sicily).

Schadendorf, W.: *Zu Pferd, im Wagen, zu Fuss* (Riding, Driving, and Walking), Munich, 1961.

Schultz, A.: *Deutsches Leben im XIV. und XV. Jahrhundert* (German Life in the Fourteenth and Fifteenth Centuries), Prague; Vienna, Leipzig, 1892.

Schurig, A.: *Die Eroberung von Mexico durch Ferdinand Cortes, mit den eigenhändigen Berichten des Feldherrn an Kaiser Karl, von 1520, und 1522* (The Conquest of Mexico by Hernan Cortés, with Holograph Reports . . .), Leipzig, 1923.

Schwarz, F. v.: *Turkestan, die Wiege der indogermanischen Völker* (Turkestan, Cradle of the Indo-European Peoples), Freiburg i. Br., 1900.

Shaw, H.: *Visits to High Tartary, Yârkand, and Kâshgar*, London, 1871.

Smičiclas, T.: *Codex Diplomaticus Regni Croatiae, Dalmatiae et Slavoniae*, IXX.

Sohns-Laubach, E. Gr. zu: *Die schönsten Reiterbilder aus europäischen Sammlungen* (Selected Equestrian Portraits from European Collections), Heidelberg; Munich, 1962.

Steier, O. or Ottakar von Horneck: *Austrian Rhyming Chronicle*, ed. Gombos.

Szamota, I.: *Travels in Ancient Hungary and the Balkan Peninsula*, Budapest, 1891.

Széchenyi, Gr. D.: *Eszmék a lovaglás és kocsizás köréből* (Thoughts on Riding and Driving), Budapest, 1892.

Szentpétery, I.: *Scriptores rerum Hungaricarum*, Vol. I. Budapest, 1937.

Szilágyi, L.: *Az Anonymus kérdés reviziója* (The 'Anonymus' Question re-opened), Századok, 1937.

Tagán, G.: *A közlekedés módja és eszközei a baskiroknál és kirgizeknél* (Transport among the Bashkirs and Kirghiz), Budapest, 1938.

Takács, S.: *Régi magyar kapitányok* (Constables of Hungarian Castles), Budapest.

——: *Müvelödéstörténeti tanulmányok* (Studies in the History of Civilization), Budapest, 1961.

Teleki, J.: *A Hunyadiak kora Magyarországon* (The Hunyadi Period in Hungary), Pest, 1852.

Tolstov, S. P.: *Az ösi Chorezm* (Ancient Khoresmia), Budapest, 1950.

Tóth, Z.: *A huszárok eredetéröl* (On the Origin of Hussars), Közl, 1934.

Váczy, P.: *A hunok Európában* (The Huns in Europe), Attila és hunjai, ed. Németh, G., Budapest, 1940.

Vámbéri, A.: *A török faj ethnologia és ethnografia tekintetében* (Ethnology and Ethnography of the Turks), Budapest, 1885.

Várady, L.: *Későrómai hadügyek és társadalmi alapjai. A római birodalom utolsó evszázadai* (The Art of War in the Late Roman Period, and its Social Bases), Budapest, 1961.

Villani, G. and M.: *Historie Florentine.*

Vitt, V. O.: *Loshadi Pazirskich Kuvganov* (The Horses in the Pazyryk Barrows), 1952.

Waldbauer, H.-Sárossy, L.: *A messzelovaglás és a Budapest-bécsi distancverseny* (Marathon Rides and the Budapest-Vienna Ride), Pécz, 1909.

Wenczel, G.: *Marino Sanuto világkrónikája* (The Chronicle of Marino Saluto), *Historical Magazine*, 1878.

Wenkheim, J. Fr. v.: *Ideen über eine Wiederherstellung der verfallenen ungarischen Pferdezucht* (Ideas for the Reconstitution of Decadent Hungarian Horse-breeding), Pest, 1815.

Whyte, J. C.: *History of the British Turf*, 1840.

Willemsen, C. A.: *Die Falkenjagd* (Falconry), Leipzig, 1943.

Wrangel, Gr. G.: *Das Buch vom Pferde* (The Book of the Horse), Stuttgart, 1888.

——: *Die Rassen des Pferdes. Ihre Entstehung, Geschichtliche Entwicklung und charakteristische Kennzeichen* (Breeds of Horses, their Characteristics, Ancestry, and Historical Evolution), Stuttgart, 1908–9.

Zeuner, F. E.: *History of Domesticated Animals*, 1962.

Index of Proper Names